Quantitative Financial Economics

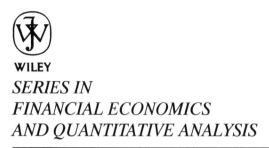

WILEY
SERIES IN
FINANCIAL ECONOMICS
AND QUANTITATIVE ANALYSIS

Series Editor: Stephen Hall, *London Business School, UK*

Editorial Board: Robert F. Engle, *University of California, USA*
John Flemming, *European Bank, UK*
Lawrence R. Klein, *University of Pennsylvania, USA*
Helmut Lütkepohl, *Humboldt University, Germany*

The Economics of Pensions and Variable Retirement Schemes
Oliver Fabel

Applied General Equilibrium Modelling:
Imperfect Competition and European Integration
Dirk Willenbockel

Housing, Financial Markets and the Wider Economy
David Miles

Maximum Entropy Econometrics: Robust Estimation with Limited Data
Amos Golan, George Judge and Douglas Miller

Estimating and Interpreting the Yield Curve
Nicola Anderson, Francis Breedon, Mark Deacon,
Andrew Derry and Gareth Murphy

Further titles in preparation
Proposals will be welcomed by the Series Editor

Quantitative Financial Economics
Stocks, Bonds and Foreign Exchange

Keith Cuthbertson
Newcastle upon Tyne University
and
City University Business School

JOHN WILEY & SONS
Chichester · **New York** · **Brisbane** · **Toronto** · **Singapore**

Published by John Wiley & Sons Ltd,
Baffins Lane, Chichester,
West Sussex PO19 1UD, England

National 01243 779777
International (+44) 1243 779777
e-mail (for orders and customer service enquiries): cs-books@wiley.co.uk
Visit our Home Page on http://www.wiley.co.uk
or http://www.wiley.com

Reprinted December 1996, August 1997

Other Wiley Editorial Offices

John Wiley & Sons, Inc., 605 Third Avenue,
New York, NY 10158-0012, USA

Jacaranda Wiley Ltd, 33 Park Road, Milton,
Queensland 4064, Australia

John Wiley & Sons (Canada) Ltd, 22 Worcester Road,
Rexdale, Ontario M9W 1L1, Canada

John Wiley & Sons (Asia) Pte Ltd, 2 Clementi Loop #02-01,
Jin Xing Distripark, Singapore 129809

Library of Congress Cataloging-in-Publication Data

Cuthbertson, Keith.
Quantitative financial economics : stocks, bonds, and foreign
exchange / Keith Cuthbertson.
p. cm. — (Series in financial economics and quantitative
analysis)
Includes bibliographical references and index.
ISBN 0-471-95359-8 (cloth). — ISBN 0-471-95360-1 (pbk.)
1. Investments — Mathematical models. 2. Capital assets pricing
model. 3. Stocks — Mathematical models. 4. Bonds — Mathematical
models. 5. Foreign exchange — Mathematical models. I. Title.
II. Series.
HG4515.2.C87 1996
332.6 — dc20
95-48355
CIP

British Library Cataloguing in Publication Data

A catalogue record for this book is available from the British Library

ISBN 0-471-95359-8 (Cased)   0-471-95360-1 (Paperback)

Typeset in 10/12pt Times Roman by Laser Words, India
Printed and bound in Great Britain by Bookcraft (Bath) Ltd, Avon
This book is printed on acid-free paper responsibly manufactured from sustainable
forestation, for which at least two trees are planted for each one used for paper production.

Contents

Series Preface   xi

Introduction   xiii

Acknowledgements   xxi

Part 1 Returns and Valuation   **1**

1   Basic Concepts in Finance   3
    1.1   Returns on Stocks, Bonds and Real Assets   3
    1.2   Utility and Indifference Curves   10
    1.3   Physical Investment Decisions and Optimal Consumption   15
    1.4   Summary   20
    Endnotes   21

2   The Capital Asset Pricing Model: CAPM   22
    2.1   An Overview   22
    2.2   Portfolio Diversification, Efficient Frontier and
          the Transformation Line   25
    2.3   Derivation of the CAPM   35
    2.4   Summary   44
    Appendix 2.1 Derivation of the CAPM   45

3   Modelling Equilibrium Returns   47
    3.1   Extensions of the CAPM   47
    3.2   A Simple Mean-Variance Model of Asset Demands   54
    3.3   Performance Measures   57
    3.4   The Arbitrage Pricing Theory (APT)   61
    3.5   Testing the Single Index Model, the CAPM and the APT   67
    3.6   Summary   75

4   Valuation Models   76
    4.1   The Rational Valuation Formula (RVF)   77
    4.2   Summary   88
    Endnotes   89
    Further Reading   89

Part 2 Efficiency, Predictability and Volatility   **91**

5 The Efficient Markets Hypothesis   93
   5.1 Overview   94
   5.2 Implications of the EMH   97
   5.3 Expectations, Martingales and Fair Game   100
   5.4 Testing the EMH   106
   5.5 Summary   113
   Endnotes   114

6 Empirical Evidence on Efficiency in the Stock Market   116
   6.1 Predictability in Stock Returns   122
   6.2 Volatility Tests   134
   6.3 Summary   151
   Endnotes   152
   Appendix 6.1   153

7 Rational Bubbles   156
   7.1 Euler Equation and the Rational Valuation Formula   157
   7.2 Tests of Rational Bubbles   160
   7.3 Intrinsic Bubbles   163
   7.4 Summary   167
   Endnotes   168

8 Anomalies, Noise Traders and Chaos   169
   8.1 The EMH and Anomalies   169
   8.2 Noise Traders   173
   8.3 Chaos   194
   8.4 Summary   201
   Appendix 8.1   202
   Appendix 8.2   204
   Endnote   205
   Further Reading   205

Part 3 The Bond Market   **207**

9 Bond Prices and the Term Structure of Interest Rates   211
   9.1 Prices, Yields and the RVF   211
   9.2 Theories of the Term Structure   218
   9.3 Summary   230
   Endnotes   232

10 Empirical Evidence on the Term Structure   234
    10.1 The Behaviour of Rates of Return   235
    10.2 Pure Discount Bonds   241
    10.3 Coupon Paying Bonds: Bond Prices and the Yield to Maturity   246
    10.4 Summary   249
    Appendix 10.1 Is the Long Rate a Martingale?   249
    Appendix 10.2 Forward Rates   251
    Endnotes   253
    Further Reading   253

Part 4 The Foreign Exchange Market   **255**

11 Basic Arbitrage Relationships in the FOREX Market   259
    11.1   Covered and Uncovered Interest Parity (CIP)   259
    11.2   Purchasing Power Parity (PPP)   261
    11.3   Interrelationships between CIP, UIP and PPP   264
    11.4   Summary   265
    Appendix 11.1 PPP and the Wage–Price Spiral   266

12 Testing CIP, UIP and FRU   268
    12.1   Covered Interest Arbitrage   268
    12.2   Uncovered Interest Parity and Forward Rate Unbiasedness   272
    12.3   Forward Rate: Risk Aversion and Rational Expectations   276
    12.4   Exchange Rates and News   279
    12.5   Peso Problems and Noise Traders   282
    12.6   Summary   288
    Appendix 12.1 Derivation of Fama's Decomposition of the Risk Premium
    in the Forward Market   288

13 The Exchange Rate and Fundamentals   290
    13.1   Flex-Price Monetary Model   291
    13.2   Sticky-Price Monetary Model (SPMM)   292
    13.3   Dornbusch Overshooting Model   293
    13.4   Frankel Real Interest Differential Model (RIDM)   295
    13.5   Testing the Models   298
    13.6   Chaos and Fundamentals   302
    13.7   Summary   306
    Further Reading   308

Part 5 Tests of the EMH using the VAR Methodology   **309**

14 The Term Structure and the Bond Market   315
    14.1   Cross-equation Restrictions and Informational Efficiency   315
    14.2   The VAR Approach   320
    14.3   Empirical Evidence   326
    14.4   Summary   332
    Endnotes   332

15 The FOREX Market   334
    15.1   Efficiency in the FOREX Market   334
    15.2   Recent Empirical Results   339
    15.3   Summary   342
    Endnotes   343

16 Stock Price Volatility   344
    16.1   Theoretical Issues   345
    16.2   Stock Price Volatility and the VAR Methodology   348
    16.3   Empirical Results   353
    16.4   Persistence and Volatility   361
    Appendix 16.1 Returns, Variance Decomposition and Persistence   368

Endnotes   373
Further Reading   374

Part 6 Time Varying Risk Premia   **375**

17   Risk Premia: The Stock Market   377
     17.1   What Influences Stock Market Volatility?   378
     17.2   The Impact of Risk on Stock Returns   380
     17.3   Summary   389

18   The Mean-Variance Model and the CAPM   391
     18.1   The Mean-Variance Model   391
     18.2   Tests of the CAPM Using Asset Shares   395
     18.3   Summary   401

19   Risk Premia and the Bond Market   402
     19.1   Time Varying Risk: Pure Discount Bonds   402
     19.2   Time Varying Risk: Long-Term Bonds   406
     19.3   Interaction Between Stock and Bond Markets   411
     19.4   Summary   413
     Endnotes   414
     Further Reading   414

Part 7 Econometric Issues in Testing Asset Pricing Models   **415**

20   Economic and Statistical Models   417
     20.1   Univariate Time Series   417
     20.2   Multivariate Time Series Models   427
     20.3   Simple ARCH and GARCH Models   438
     20.4   Rational Expectations: Estimation Issues   442
     Further Reading   452

References   453

Index   466

Series Preface

This series aims to publish books which give authoritative accounts of major new topics in financial economics and general quantitative analysis. The coverage of the series includes both macro and micro economics and its aim is to be of interest to practitioners and policy-makers as well as the wider academic community.

The development of new techniques and ideas in econometrics has been rapid in recent years and these developments are now being applied to a wide range of areas and markets. Our hope is that this series will provide a rapid and effective means of communicating these ideas to a wide international audience and that in turn this will contribute to the growth of knowledge, the exchange of scientific information and techniques and the development of cooperation in the field of economics.

Stephen Hall
Imperial College, London, UK

Introduction

This book has its genesis in a final year undergraduate course in Financial Markets, although parts of it have also been used on postgraduate courses in quantitative aspects of the behaviour of financial markets. Participants in these courses usually have somewhat heterogeneous backgrounds: some have a strong basis in standard undergraduate economics, some in applied finance while some are professionals working in financial institutions. The mathematical and statistical knowledge of the participants in these courses is also very mixed. My aim in writing the book is to provide a self-contained, modern introduction to some of the theories and empirical methods used by financial economists in the analysis of speculative assets prices in the stock, bond and foreign exchange markets. It could be viewed as a selective introduction to some of the recent journal literature in this area, with the emphasis on applied work. The content should enable the student to grasp that although much of this literature is undoubtedly very innovative, it is often grounded in some fairly basic intuitive ideas. It is my hope that after reading the book, students and others will feel confident in tackling the original sources.

The book analyses a number of competing models of asset pricing and the methods used to test these. The baseline paradigm throughout the book is the efficient market hypothesis EMH. If stock prices always fully reflect the expected discounted present value of future dividends (i.e. fundamental value) then the market will allocate funds among competing firms, optimally. Of course, even in an efficient market, stock prices may be highly volatile but such volatility does not (generally) warrant government intervention since prices are the outcome of informed optimising traders. Volatility may increase risk (of bankruptcy) for some financial institutions who hold speculative assets, yet this can be mitigated via portfolio diversification and associated capital adequacy requirements.

Part 1 begins with some basic definitions and concepts used in the financial economics literature and demonstrates the 'separation principle' in the certainty case. The (one-period) Capital Asset Pricing Model (CAPM) and (to a much lesser extent) the Arbitrage Pricing Theory (APT) provide the baseline models of equilibrium asset returns. These two models, presented in Chapters 2 and 3, provide a rich enough menu to illustrate many of the empirical issues that arise in testing the EMH. It is of course repeatedly made clear that any test of the EMH is a joint test of an equilibrium returns model and rational expectations (RE). Also in Part 1, the theoretical basis of the CAPM (and its variants, including the consumption CAPM), the APT and some early empirical tests of these models are discussed, and it is concluded with an examination, in Chapter 4, of the relationship between returns and prices. It is demonstrated that any model of expected returns, together with the assumption of rational expectations, implies the rational valuation formula (i.e. asset prices equal the expected discounted present value of future payments). This link between 'returns' and 'prices' and tests based on these two variables is a recurring theme throughout the book.

In Part 2, Chapter 5, the basic assumptions and mathematical formulation of the RE–EMH approach are outlined. One view of the EMH is that equilibrium excess returns are unpredictable, another slightly different interpretation is that one cannot make persistent abnormal profits after taking account of transactions costs and adjustment for risk. In Chapter 6, an examination is made of a variety of statistical tests which seek to establish whether stock returns (over different holding periods) are predictable and if so whether one can exploit this predictability to earn 'abnormal' profits. This is followed by a discussion of the behaviour of stock *prices* and whether these are determined solely by fundamentals or are excessively volatile. When discussing 'volatility tests' it is possible to highlight some issues associated with inference in small samples and problems encountered in the presence of non-stationary data. The usefulness of Monte Carlo methods in illuminating some of these problems is also examined. The empirical evidence in Part 2 provides the reader with an overview of the difficulties faced in establishing firm conclusions about competing hypotheses. However, at a minimum, a prima facie case is established that when using fairly simple models, the EMH may not adequately capture the behaviour of stock prices and returns.

It is well known that stock returns may contain a (rational) bubble which is unpredictable, yet this can lead to a discrepancy between the stock price and fundamental value. Such bubbles are a 'self-fulfilling prophecy' which may be generated exogenously or may depend on fundamentals such as dividends (i.e. intrinsic bubbles). The intrinsic bubble is 'anchored' to dividends and if dividends are fairly stable then the actual stock price might not differ too much from its fundamental value. However, the dividend process may be subject to 'regime changes' which can act as a catalyst in generating a change in an intrinsic bubble. Periodically collapsing bubbles are also possible: when the bubble is positive, stock prices and fundamentals diverge, but after the 'collapse' they are again brought into equality. These issues are addressed in Chapter 7 which also assesses whether the empirical evidence supports the presence of rational bubbles.

Stock market 'anomalies' and models of noise trader behaviour are discussed in Chapter 8, the final chapter in Part 2. The evidence on 'anomalies' in the stock market is voluminous and students love providing a 'list' of them in examination answers. While they are invaluable pieces of evidence, which may be viewed as being complementary to the statistical/regression-based approaches, I have chosen to 'list' only a few of the major ones, since the analytic content of these studies is usually not difficult for the student to follow, in the original sources. Such anomalies highlight the potential importance of noise traders, who follow 'fads and fashions' when investing in speculative assets. Here, asset prices are seen to be the outcome of the interaction between 'smart money' traders and 'noise traders'. The relative importance of these two groups in particular markets and at particular times may vary and hence prices may sometimes reflect fundamental value and at other times may predominantly reflect fads and fashions.

There are several approaches to modelling noise trader behaviour. For example, some are based on maximising an explicit objective function, while others involve non-linear responses to market signals. As soon as one enters the domain of non-linear models the possibility of chaotic behaviour arises. It is possible for a purely (non-linear) deterministic process to produce an apparently random time series which may closely resemble the patterns found in actual speculative prices. The presence of noise traders may also give rise to 'short-termism'. The latter is a rather imprecise term but broadly speaking it implies that market participants place too much weight on expected events (e.g. higher dividends) in the near future, relative to those in the more distant future, when pricing stocks. Stocks are therefore mispriced and physical investment projects with returns over a short horizon are erroneously preferred to those with long horizon returns, even though the latter have a higher expected net present value. Illustrative models which embody the above ideas are presented in Chapter 8, along with some empirical tests.

Overall, the impression imparted by the theoretical models and empirical results presented in Part 2 is that for the stock market, the EMH under the assumption of a time invariant risk premium may not hold, particularly for the post-1950s period. However, the reader is made aware that such a conclusion is by no means clear cut and that more sophisticated tests are to be presented in Parts 5 and 6 of the book. Throughout Part 2, it is deliberately shown how an initial hypothesis and tests of the theory often lead to the unearthing of further puzzles, which in turn stimulates the search for either better theoretical models or improved data and test procedures. Hence, by the end of Part 2, the reader should be well versed in the basic theoretical constructs used in analysing asset prices and in testing hypotheses using a variety of statistical techniques.

Part 3 examines the EMH in the context of the bond market. Chapter 9 outlines the various hypotheses of the term structure of interest rates applied to spot yields, holding period yields and the yield to maturity and demonstrates how these are interrelated. The dominant paradigms here are the expectations hypothesis and the liquidity preference hypothesis, both of which assume a time invariant term premium. Chapter 10 examines empirical tests of the competing hypotheses, for the short and long ends of the maturity spectrum. In addition, cointegration techniques are used to examine the complete maturity spectrum. On balance, the results for the bond market (under a time invariant term premium) are found to be in greater conformity with the EMH than are the results for the stock market (as reported in Part 2). These differing results for these two speculative asset markets are re-examined later in the book.

Part 4 examines the FOREX market and in particular the behaviour of spot and forward exchange rates. Chapter 11 begins with a brief overview of the relationship between covered and uncovered interest parity, purchasing power parity and real interest rate parity. Chapter 12 is mainly devoted to testing covered and uncovered interest parity and forward rate unbiasedness. The degree to which the apparent failure of forward rate unbiasedness may be due to a failure either of rational expectations or of risk neutrality is examined. The difficulty in assessing 'efficiency' in the presence of the so-called Peso problem and the potential importance of noise traders (or chartists) are both discussed, in the light of the illustrative empirical results presented. In the final section of Part 4, in Chapter 13, various theories of the behaviour of the spot exchange rate based on 'fundamentals', including flex-price and sticky-price monetary models, are outlined. These monetary models are not pursued at great length since it soon becomes clear from empirical work that (other than for periods of hyperinflation) these models, based on economic fundamentals, are seriously deficient. The final chapter of Part 4 therefore also examines whether the 'stylised facts' of the behaviour of the spot rate may be explained by the interaction of noise traders and smart money and, in one such model, chaotic behaviour is possible. The overall conclusion is that the behaviour of spot and forward exchange rates is little understood.

It appears that a freely floating spot rate is not firmly 'anchored' by fundamentals such as the money supply. Also, changes in the spot rate in the presence of sticky goods prices can have a major impact on the real economy. This has led some governments in Western industrialised nations to adopt currency bands to 'guide' the exchange rate expectations of market participants (although space constraints prevent a discussion of target zone models).

In Part 5 the EMH using the VAR methodology is tested. Chapter 14 begins with the term structure of interest rates and demonstrates how the VAR equations can be used to provide a time series for the forecast of (a weighted average of) future changes in short-term rates of interest, which can then be compared with movements in the long–short spread, using a variety of metrics. Under the null of the expectations hypothesis the VAR yields a set of cross-equation parameter restrictions. These restrictions are shown to have an intuitive interpretation, namely, that forecast errors are independent of information used in generating the forecast and that no abnormal profits can be made. Having established the basic principles behind the VAR methodology it is then possible succinctly to deal with its application to the FOREX (Chapter 15) and stock market (Chapter 16). There are two further interesting aspects to the VAR methodology applied to the stock market. First, the VAR methodology is useful in establishing links between early empirical work that looked at the predictably of *one-period* returns and *multi-period returns* and those that examined volatility tests on stock *prices*. Second, the link between the *persistence* of one-period returns and the volatility of stock prices is easily examined within the VAR framework. Broadly speaking the empirical results based on the VAR approach suggest that the stock and FOREX markets (under a time invariant risk premium) do not conform to the EMH, while for the bond market the results are more in conformity — although some puzzles still remain.

Part 6 examines the potential impact of time varying risk premia in the stock and bond markets. If returns depend on a time varying risk premium which is persistent, then sharp movements in stock prices may ensue as a result of shocks to such premia: hence, observed price movements may not be 'excessively' volatile. An analysis is made of the usefulness of the CAPM with time varying variances and covariances which are modelled by ARCH and GARCH processes. This framework is applied to both the (international) stock and bond markets. There appears to be more support for a time varying (GARCH type) risk premium influencing expected returns in the stock market than in the bond market. Some unresolved issues are whether such effects are stable over time and are robust to the inclusion of other variables that represent trading conditions (e.g. turnover in the market).

As the book progresses, the reader should become aware that to establish whether a particular speculative market is efficient, in the sense that either no excess (abnormal) profits can be earned or that market price reflects economic fundamentals, is far from straightforward. It often requires the use of sophisticated statistical tests many of which have only recently appeared in the literature. Data on asset prices often exhibit 'trends' and such 'non-stationary' data require analysis using concepts from the literature on unit roots and cointegration — otherwise grossly misleading inferences may ensue. Some readers will also be aware that, although the existence of time varying risk premia has always been acknowledged in the theoretical finance literature, it is only recently that empirical work has been able to make advances in this area using ARCH and GARCH models. The assumption of rational expectations has also played a major role in the analysis of asset prices and this too involves special econometric procedures.

I believe that the above statistical techniques, which are extensively used in the analysis of speculative asset prices, are complex enough to warrant specific treatment in the book. However, I did not want these issues to dominate the book and 'crowd-out' the economic and behavioural insights. I therefore decided that the best way forward, given the heterogeneous background of the potential readership of the book, was to provide an overview of the purely statistical aspects in a self-contained section (Part 7) at the end of the book. This has allowed me to limit my comments on the statistical nuances to a minimum, in the main body of the text. A pre-requisite for understanding Part 7 would be a final year undergraduate course or a specialist option on an MBA in applied time series econometrics.

Naturally, space constraints imply that there are some interesting areas that had to be omitted. To have included general equilibrium and other 'factor models' of equilibrium returns based on continuous time mathematics (and associated econometric procedures) would have added considerably to the mathematical complexity and length of the book. While continuous time equilibrium models of the term structure would have provided a useful comparison to the discrete time approach adopted, I nevertheless felt it necessary to exclude this material. This also applies to some material I initially wrote on options and futures — I could not do justice to these topics without making the book inordinately long and there are already some very good specialist, academically oriented texts in this area. I also do not cover the recent burgeoning theoretical and applied literature on 'market micro-structure' and applications of neural networks to financial markets.

Readership

In order to make the book as self-contained as possible and noting the often short half-life of even some central concepts in the minds of some students, I have included some key basic theoretical material at the beginning of the book (e.g. the CAPM and its variants, the APT and valuation models). As noted above, I have also relegated detailed statistical issues to a separate chapter. Throughout, I have kept the algebra as simple as possible and usually I provide a simple exposition and then build up to the more general case. This I hope will allow the reader to interpret the algebra in terms of the economic intuition which lies behind it. Any technically difficult issues or tedious (yet important) derivations I relegate to footnotes and appendices. The empirical results presented in the book are merely illustrative of particular techniques and are not therefore meant to be exhaustive. In some cases they may not even be representative of 'seminal contributions', if the latter are thought to be too technically advanced for the intended readership. As the reader will already have gathered, the empirics is almost exclusively biased towards time series analysis using discrete time data.

This book has been organised so that the 'average student' can move from simple to more complex topics as he/she progresses through the book. Theoretical ideas and constructs are developed to a particular level and then tests of these ideas are presented. By switching between theory and evidence using progressively more difficult material, the reader becomes aware of the limitations of particular approaches and can see how this leads to the further development of the theories and test procedures. Hence, for the less adventuresome student one could end the course after Part 4. On the other hand, the advanced student would probably omit the more basic material in Part 1 but would cover the rest of the book including the somewhat more challenging issues of the VAR methodology (Part 5), modelling time varying risk premia (Part 6) and the details of the econometric methodology (Part 7).

Had I been writing a survey article, I would not of course have adopted the above approach. In a survey article, one often presents a general framework from which most other models may be viewed as special cases. This has the merit of great elegance but it can often be difficult for the average student to follow, since it requires an immediate understanding of the general model. My alternative approach, I believe, is to be preferred on pedagogic grounds but it does have some drawbacks. Most notably, not all of the possible theoretical approaches and empirical evidence for a particular market, be it for stocks, bonds or foreign exchange, appear in one single chapter. However, this is deliberate and I can only hope my ordering of the material does not obscure the underlying common approaches that may be applied to all speculative markets.

The book should appeal to the rising undergraduate final year, core financial markets area and to postgraduate courses in financial economics, including electives on specialist MBA finance courses. It should also provide useful material for those working in the research departments of large financial institutions (e.g. investment banks, pension funds and central and commercial banks). The book covers a number of important recent advances in the financial markets area, both theoretical and econometric/empirical. Recent innovative areas that are covered include chaos, rational and intrinsic bubbles, the inter-action of noise traders and smart money, short-termism, anomalies, predictability, the VAR methodology and time varying risk premia. On the econometrics side problems of non-stationarity, cointegration, rational expectations, ARCH and GARCH models are examined. These issues are discussed with empirical examples taken from the stock, bond and FOREX markets.

Professional traders, portfolio managers and policy-makers will, I hope, find the book of interest because it provides an overview of some of the theoretical models used in explaining the determination of asset prices and returns, together with the techniques used to assess their empirical validity. The performance of such models provides the basic input to key policy issues such as capital adequacy proposals (e.g. for securities dealers), the analysis of mergers and takeovers and other aspects of trading arrangements such as margin requirements and the use of trading halts in stock markets. Also, to the extent that monetary policy works via changes in interest rates across the maturity spectrum and changes in the exchange rate, the analysis of the bond and FOREX markets is of direct relevance. At a minimum the book highlights some alternative ways of examining the behaviour of asset prices and demonstrates possible pitfalls in the empirical analysis of these markets.

I remember, from reading books dealing with the development of quantum mechanics, that for several years, even decades, there would coexist a number of competing theories of the behaviour of elementary particles. Great debates would ensue, where often more 'heat than light' would be generated — although both could be construed as manifestations of (intellectual) energy. What becomes clear, to the layman at least, is that as one tries to get closer to the 'micro-behaviour' of the atom, the more difficult it becomes to understand the underlying physical processes at work. These controversies in natural science made me a little more sanguine about disputes that persist in economics. We know (or at least I think we know) that in a risky and uncertain world our 'simple' economic models often do not work terribly well. Even more problematic is our lack of data and inability to replicate results via controlled experiments. Also, we have the additional problem that individuals learn and adapt and that 'group behaviour' may be different from the aggregate of each individual's behaviour. However, given the resources devoted to economics as compared to natural science, I hold the view that substantial progress has and is being made in the analysis of speculative asset prices and I hope this is reflected in the material in the book.

It has been said that some write so that other colleagues can better understand, while others write so that colleagues know that only they understand. I hope this book will achieve the former aim and will convey some of the recent advances in the analysis of speculative asset prices. In short, I hope it ameliorates the learning process of some, stimulates others to go further and earns me a modicum of 'holiday money'. Of course, if the textbook market were (instantaneously) efficient, there would be no need for this book — it would already be available from a variety of publishers. My expectations of success are therefore based on a view that the market for this type of book is not 'efficient' and is currently subject to favourable fads.

Acknowledgements

I have had useful discussions and received helpful comments on various chapters from many people including: David Barr, George Bulkley, Charles Goodhart, David Gaspatto, Eric Girardin, Louis Gallindo, Stephen Hall, Simon Hayes, David Miles, Michael Moore, Dirk Nitzsche, Barham Pesaran, Bob Shiller, Mark Taylor, Dylan Thomas, Ian Tonks and Mike Wickens. My thanks to them and naturally any errors and omissions are down to me. I also owe a great debt to Brenda Munoz who expertly typed the various drafts, and to my colleagues at the University of Newcastle and City University Business School, who provided a conducive working environment.

PART 1
Returns and Valuation

1

Basic Concepts in Finance

The aim in this chapter is to quickly run through some of the basic tools of analysis used in the finance literature. The topics covered are not exhaustive and they are discussed at a fairly intuitive level. The topics covered include

- Compounding, discounted present value DPV, the rate of return on pure discount bonds, coupon paying bonds and stocks.
- Utility functions, indifference curves, measures of risk aversion, and intertemporal utility.
- The use of DPV in determining the optimal level of physical investment and the optimal consumption stream for a two-period horizon problem.

1.1 RETURNS ON STOCKS, BONDS AND REAL ASSETS

Much of the theoretical work in finance is conducted in terms of compound rates of return or interest rates even though rates of interest quoted in the market use 'simple interest'. For example, an interest rate of 5 percent payable every six months will be quoted as a simple interest rate of 10 percent per annum in the market. However, if an investor rolled over two six-month bills and the interest rate remained constant, he could actually earn a 'compound' or 'true' or 'effective' annual rate of $(1.05)^2 = 1.1025$ or 10.25 percent. The effective annual rate of return exceeds the simple rate because in the former case the investor earns 'interest-on-interest'.

We now examine how to calculate the terminal value of an investment when the frequency with which interest rates are compounded alters. Clearly, a quoted interest rate of 10 percent per annum when interest is calculated monthly will amount to more at the end of the year than if interest accrues only at the end of the year.

Consider an amount $\$x$ invested for n years at a rate of R per annum (where R is expressed as a decimal). If compounding takes place only at the end of the year the future value after n years is FV_n where

$$FV_n = \$x(1+R)^n \tag{1.1}$$

However, if interest is paid m times per annum then the terminal value at the end of the n years is:

$$FV_n^m = \$x \left(1 + \frac{R}{m}\right)^{mn} \tag{1.2}$$

R/m is often referred to as the *periodic interest rate*. As m, the frequency of compounding, increases the rate becomes *continuously compounded* and it may be shown that the investment accrues to

$$FV_n^c = \lim_{m \to \infty} \$x \left(1 + \frac{R}{m}\right)^{mn} = \$x[\exp(Rn)] \tag{1.3}$$

where $\exp = 2.71828$. For example, using (1.2) and (1.3) if the quoted (simple) interest rate is 10 percent per annum then the value of $100 at the end of one year ($n = 1$) for different values of m is given in Table 1.1. For practical purposes daily compounding gives a result very close to continuous compounding (see the last two entries in Table 1.1).

We now consider how we can switch between simple interest rates, periodic rates, effective annual rates and continuously compounded rates. Suppose an investment pays a periodic interest rate of 2 percent each quarter. This will usually be quoted in the market as 8 percent per annum, that is, as a *simple annual rate*. The effective annual rate R_f exceeds the simple rate because of the payment of interest-on-interest. At the end of the year $\$x = \$100$ accrues to

$$\$x \left[1 + \frac{R}{m}\right]^m = 100\left[1 + \frac{0.08}{4}\right]^4 = \$108.24 \tag{1.4}$$

The effective annual rate R_f is clearly 8.24 percent since

$$\$100(1 + R_f) = 108.24 \tag{1.5}$$

The relationship between the quoted simple rate R with payments m times per year and the *effective annual rate* R_f is

$$[1 + R_f] = \left[1 + \frac{R}{m}\right]^m \tag{1.6}$$

We can use equation (1.6) to move from periodic interest rates to effective rates and vice versa. For example, an interest rate with quarterly payments that would produce an effective annual rate of 12 percent is given by

$$1.12 = \left[1 + \frac{R}{4}\right]^4$$

$$R = \left[(1.12)^{1/4} - 1\right]4 = 0.0287 \times 4 = (11.48 \text{ percent}) \tag{1.7}$$

Table 1.1 Compounding Frequency

Compounding Frequency	Value of $100 at End of Year ($R = 10\%$ p.a.)
Annually ($m = 1$)	110.00
Quarterly ($m = 4$)	110.38
Weekly ($m = 52$)	110.51
Daily ($m = 365$)	110.52
Continuous ($n = 1$)	110.517

Thus 2.87 percent compounded quarterly would be quoted as a simple interest rate of 11.48 percent per annum and is equivalent to a 12 percent effective rate.

We can use a similar procedure to switch between a rate R per annum which applies to compounding which takes place over m periods and an equivalent continuously compounded rate, R_c. One reason for doing this calculation is that much of the advanced theory of bond pricing (and the pricing of futures and options) uses continuously compounded rates.

Suppose we wish to calculate a value for R_c when we know the m-period rate R. Since the terminal value after n years of an investment of $\$A$ must be equal when using either interest rate we have

$$A \exp(R_c \cdot n) = A \left[1 + \frac{R}{m}\right]^{mn} \tag{1.8}$$

and

$$R_c = m \ln \left[1 + \frac{R}{m}\right] \tag{1.9}$$

Also, if we are given the continuously compounded rate R_c we can use the above equation to calculate the simple rate R which applies when interest is calculated m times per year:

$$R = m[\exp(R_c/m) - 1] \tag{1.10}$$

We can perhaps best summarise the above array of alternative interest rates by using one final illustrative example. Suppose an investment pays a periodic interest rate of 5 percent every six months ($m = 2$, $R/2 = 0.05$). In the market, this would be quoted as 10 percent per annum and clearly the 10 percent represents a simple annual rate. An investment of $\$100$ would yield $100(1 + (0.1/2))^2 = \$110.25$ after one year (using (1.2)). Clearly the effective annual rate is 10.25 percent per annum. Suppose we wish to convert the simple annual rate of $R = 0.10$ to an equivalent continuously compounded rate. Using (1.9) with $m = 2$ we see that this is given by $R_c = 2 \cdot \ln(1 + 0.10/2) = 0.09758$ (9.758 percent per annum). Of course, if interest is continuously compounded at an annual rate of 9.758 percent then $\$100$ invested today would accrue to $\exp(R_c n) = \$110.25$ in $n = 1$ years' time.

Discounted Present Value (DPV)

Let the annual rate of interest on a completely safe investment over n years be denoted $rs^{(n)}$. The future value of $\$x$ in n years' time with interest calculated annually is

$$FV_n = \$x(1 + rs^{(n)})^n \tag{1.11}$$

It follows that if you were given the opportunity to receive with certainty $\$FV_n$ in n years time then you would be willing to give up $\$x$ today. The value *today* of a certain payment of FV_n in n years time is $\$x$. In more technical language the *discounted present value* (DPV) of FV_n is

$$DPV = \frac{FV_n}{(1 + rs^{(n)})^n} \tag{1.12}$$

We now make the assumption that the safe interest rate applicable to $1, 2, 3, \ldots n$ year horizons is *constant* and equal to r. We are assuming that the term structure of interest rates is flat. The DPV of a *stream* of receipts $FV_i (i = 1$ to $n)$ which carry no default risk is then given by

$$DPV = \sum_{i=1}^{n} \frac{FV_i}{(1+r)^i} \tag{1.13}$$

Physical Investment Project

Consider a physical investment project such as building a new factory which has a set of prospective net receipts (profits) of FV_i. Suppose the capital cost of the project which we assume all accrues today (i.e. at time $t = 0$) is $\$KC$. Then the entrepreneur should invest in the project if

$$DPV \geqslant KC \tag{1.14}$$

or equivalently if the net present value (NPV) satisfies

$$NPV = DPV - KC \geqslant 0 \tag{1.15}$$

If NPV $= 0$ it can be shown that the net receipts (profits) from the investment project are just sufficient to pay back both the principal ($\$KC$) and the interest on the loan, which was taken out to finance the project. If NPV > 0 then there are surplus funds available even after these loan repayments.

As the cost of funds r increases then the NPV falls for any given stream of profits FV_i from the project (Figure 1.1). There is a value of r ($= 10$ percent in Figure 1.1) for which the NPV $= 0$. This value of r is known as the *internal* rate of return (IRR) of the investment. Given a stream of net receipts FV_i and the capital cost KC for a project, one can always calculate a project's IRR. It is that *constant* value of y for which

$$KC = \sum_{i=1}^{n} \frac{FV_i}{(1+y)^i} \tag{1.16}$$

An equivalent investment rule to the NPV condition (1.15) is then to invest in the project if[1]

$$IRR(= y) \geqslant \text{cost of borrowing} \ (= r) \tag{1.17}$$

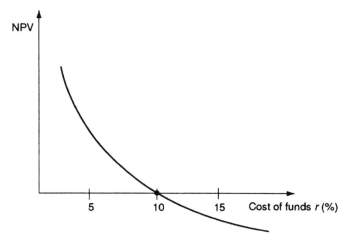

Figure 1.1 NPV and the Discount Rate.

We will use these investment rules throughout the book beginning in this chapter with the derivation of the yield on bills and bonds and the optimal scale of physical investment projects for the economy. Note that in the above calculation of the DPV we assumed that the interest rate used for discounting the future receipts FV_i was constant for all horizons. Suppose, however, that 'one-year money' carries an interest rate of $rs^{(1)}$, two-year money costs $rs^{(2)}$, etc. Then the DPV is given by

$$\text{DPV} = \frac{FV_1}{(1 + rs^{(1)})} + \frac{FV_2}{(1 + rs^{(2)})^2} + \frac{FV_3}{(1 + rs^{(3)})^3} + \cdots \frac{FV_n}{(1 + rs^{(n)})^n}$$

$$= \sum_{i=1}^{n} \delta_i FV_i \tag{1.18}$$

where $\delta_i = (1 + rs^{(i)})^{-i}$. The $rs^{(i)}$ are known as *spot rates* of interest since they are the rates that apply to money lent over the periods $rs^{(1)} = 0$ to 1 year, $rs^{(2)} = 0$ to 2 years, etc. (expressed at annual compound rates). The relationship between the spot rates, $rs^{(i)}$, on default free assets is the subject of the *term structure of interest rates*. For example, if $rs^{(1)} < rs^{(2)} < rs^{(3)} \ldots$ then the yield curve is said to be upward sloping. The DPV formula can also be expressed in real terms. In this case, future receipts FV_i are deflated by the aggregate goods price index and the discount factors are then real rates of interest.

In general, physical investment projects are not riskless since the future receipts are uncertain. There are a number of alternative methods of dealing with uncertainty in the DPV calculation. Perhaps the simplest method and the one we shall adopt has the discount rate δ_i consisting of the risk-free spot rate $rs^{(i)}$ plus a risk premium rp_i:

$$\delta_i = (1 + rs^{(i)} + rp^{(i)})^{-i} \tag{1.19}$$

Equation (1.19) is an identity and is not operational until we have a model of the risk premium (e.g. rp_i is constant for all i). We examine some alternative models for rp in Chapter 3.

Pure Discount Bonds and Spot Yields

Instead of a physical investment project consider investing in a pure discount bond (zero coupon bond). At short maturities, these are usually referred to as bills (e.g. Treasury bills). A pure discount bond has a fixed redemption price M_1, a known maturity period and pays no coupons. The yield on the bill if held to maturity is determined by the fact that it is purchased at a market price P_t below its redemption price M_1. For a *one-year* bill it seems sensible to calculate the yield or interest rate as:

$$rs_t^{(1)} = \frac{M_1 - P_{1t}}{P_{1t}} \tag{1.20}$$

where $rs_t^{(1)}$ is measured as a proportion. However, viewing the problem in terms of DPV we see that the one-year bill promises a future payment of M_1 at the end of the year in exchange for a capital cost paid out today of P_{1t}. Hence the IRR, y_{1t} of the bill can be calculated from

$$P_{1t} = \frac{M_1}{(1 + y_{1t})} \tag{1.20a}$$

But on rearrangement we have:

$$y_{1t} = \frac{M_1 - P_{1t}}{P_{1t}} \tag{1.21}$$

and hence the one-year spot yield $rs_t^{(1)}$ is simply the IRR of the bill. Applying the above principal to a two-year bill with redemption price M_2, the annual (compound) interest rate $rs_t^{(2)}$ on the bill is the solution to

$$P_{2t} = \frac{M_2}{(1 + rs_t^{(2)})^2} \tag{1.22}$$

which implies

$$rs_t^{(2)} = [M_2/P_{2t}]^{1/2} - 1 \tag{1.23}$$

We now see how we can, in principle, calculate a set of (compound) spot rates for different maturities from the market prices of pure discount bonds (bills). One further practical issue the reader should note is that, in fact, dealers do not quote the compound rates $rs_t^{(i)}(i = 1, 2, 3, 4 \ldots)$ but the equivalent simple interest rates. For example, if the periodic interest rate on a six-month bill using (1.20) is 5 percent, then the quoted rate will be 10 percent. However, we can always convert the periodic interest rate to an equivalent compound annual rate of 10.25 percent or, indeed, into a continuously compounded rate of 9.758, as outlined above.

Coupon Paying Bonds

A *level coupon* (non-callable) bond pays a fixed coupon C at known fixed intervals (which we take to be every year) and has a fixed redemption price M_n payable when the bond matures in year n. For a bond with n years left to maturity let the current market price be $P_t^{(n)}$. The question is how do we measure the return on the bond if it is held to maturity? The bond is analogous to our physical investment project with the capital outlay today being $P_t^{(n)}$ and the future receipts being C each year (plus the redemption price). The internal rate of return on the bond, which is called the *yield to maturity*, R_t^y, can be calculated from

$$P_t^{(n)} = \frac{C}{(1 + R_t^y)} + \frac{C}{(1 + R_t^y)^2} + \cdots \frac{C + M_n}{(1 + R_t^y)^n} \tag{1.24}$$

The yield to maturity is that *constant* rate of discount which at a point in time equates the DPV of future payments with the current market price. Since $P_t^{(n)}$, M_n and C are the known values in the market, equation (1.24) has to be solved to give the quoted screen rate for the yield to maturity R_t^y. There is a subscript 't' on R^y because as the market price falls, the yield to maturity rises (and vice versa) as a matter of actuarial arithmetic in equation (1.24). Although widely used in the market and in the financial press there are some theoretical/conceptual problems in using the yield to maturity as an unambiguous measure of the return on a bond even when it is held to maturity. We deal with some of these issues in Part 3.

In the market, coupon payments C are usually paid every six months and the interest rate from (1.24) is then the periodic six-month rate. If this periodic yield to maturity is calculated as say 6 percent, then in the market the quoted yield to maturity will be the simple annual rate of 12 percent per annum (known as the *bond-equivalent yield* in the USA).

The *flat yield* or *interest yield* or *running yield* is calculated as $(C/P_t^{(n)})100$ and is quoted in the financial press but it is not a particularly useful concept in analysing the pricing and return on bonds.

A *perpetuity* is a level coupon bond that is never redeemed by the primary issuer (i.e. $n \to \infty$). If the coupon is C per annum and the current market price of the bond is $P_t^{(\infty)}$ then a simple measure of the return $R_t^{(\infty)}$ is the flat yield:

$$R_t^{(\infty)} = C/P_t^{(\infty)} \tag{1.25}$$

This simple measure is in fact also the yield to maturity for a perpetuity, since as $n \to \infty$ in (1.24) then it reduces to (1.25). It is immediately obvious from (1.25) that for small changes, the percentage change in the price of a perpetuity equals the percentage change in the yield to maturity.

Holding Period Return

Much empirical work on stocks deals with the one-period holding period return, H_{t+1}, which is defined as

$$H_{t+1} = \left[\frac{P_{t+1} - P_t}{P_t}\right] + \frac{D_{t+1}}{P_t} \tag{1.26}$$

The first term is the proportionate capital gain or loss (over one period) and the second term is the (proportionate) dividend yield. H_{t+1} can be calculated *ex post* but, of course, viewed from time t, P_{t+1} and (perhaps) D_{t+1} are uncertain and investors can only try and forecast these elements. It also follows that

$$1 + H_{t+i+1} = \left[\frac{P_{t+i+1} + D_{t+i+1}}{P_{t+i}}\right] \tag{1.27}$$

where H_{t+i} is the one period return between $t+i$ and $t+i+1$. Hence, *ex post* if A is invested in the stock (and all dividend payments are reinvested in the stock) then the Y payout after n periods is

$$Y = A[1 + H_{t+1}][1 + H_{t+2}]\ldots[1 + H_{t+n}] \tag{1.28}$$

Beginning with Chapter 4 and throughout the book we will demonstrate how expected one-period returns H_{t+1} can be directly related to the DPV formula. Much of the early empirical work on whether the stock market is efficient centres on trying to establish whether one-period returns H_{t+1} are predictable. Later empirical work concentrated on whether the stock price equalled the DPV of future dividends and the most recent empirical work brings together these two strands in the empirical literature.

With slight modifications the one-period holding period return can be defined for any asset. For a coupon paying bond with initial maturity of n periods and coupon payment of C we have

$$H_{t+1}^{(n)} = \frac{P_{t+1}^{(n-1)} - P_t^{(n)}}{P_t^{(n)}} + \frac{C}{P_t^{(n)}} \tag{1.29}$$

and is referred to as the (one-period) holding period yield (HPY). The first term is the capital gain on the bond and the second is the coupon (or running) yield. Broadly speaking we can often apply the same type of economic ideas to explain movements in holding period returns for both stock and bonds (and other speculative assets) and we begin this analysis with the CAPM in the next chapter.

Stocks

The difficulty with direct application of the DPV concept to stocks is that future payments, namely the dividends, are uncertain. Also because the future dividend payments are uncertain these assets are risky and one therefore might not wish to discount all future receipts at some *constant* risk-free interest rate. It can be shown (see Chapter 4) that if the expected *one-period* holding period return $E_t H_{t+1}$ equals q_t then the *fundamental value* of the stock can be viewed as the DPV of *expected* future dividends $E_t D_{t+j}$ deflated by the appropriate discount factors (which are likely to embody a risk premium). The fundamental value V_t is therefore:

$$V_t = E_t \left[\frac{D_{t+1}}{(1 + q_1)} + \frac{D_{t+2}}{(1 + q_1)(1 + q_2)} + \cdots \right] \tag{1.30}$$

In (1.30) q_i is the *one-period* return between time period $t + i - 1$ and $t + i^{(2)}$.

If there are no systematic profitable opportunities to be made from buying and selling shares between well-informed rational traders, then the actual market price of the stock P_t must equal fundamental value V_t, that is, the DPV of expected future dividends. For example, if $P_t < V_t$ then investors should purchase the undervalued stock and hence make a capital gain as P_t rises towards V_t. In an efficient market such profitable opportunities should be immediately eliminated.

Clearly one cannot directly calculate V_t to see if it does equal P_t because expected dividends (and discount rates) are unobservable. However, in Chapters 6 and 16 we discuss methods of overcoming this problem and examine whether the stock market is efficient in the sense that $P_t = V_t$. Also if we add some simplifying assumptions to the DPV formula (e.g. future dividends are expected to be constant) then it can be used in a relatively crude manner to calculate V_t and assess whether shares are under- or over-valued in relation to their current market price. Such models are usually referred to as dividend valuation models (see Elton and Gruber (1987)) and are dealt with in Chapter 4.

1.2 UTILITY AND INDIFFERENCE CURVES

In this section we briefly discuss the concept of utility but only to a level such that the reader can follow the subsequent material on portfolio choice.

Economists frequently set up portfolio models where the individual chooses a set of assets in order to maximise either some monetary amount such as profits or one-period returns on the portfolio or the utility (satisfaction) that such assets yield. For example, a certain level of wealth will imply a certain level of satisfaction for the individual as he contemplates the goods and services he could purchase with the wealth. If his wealth is doubled his level of satisfaction may not be. Also, for example, if the individual consumes one bottle of wine per night the *additional* satisfaction from consuming an *extra* bottle may not be as great as from the first. This is the assumption of diminishing marginal utility. Utility theory can also be applied to decisions involving uncertain outcomes. In fact we can classify investors as 'risk averters', 'risk lovers' or 'risk neutral' in terms of the shape of their utility function. Finally, we can also examine how individuals might evaluate 'utility' which arises at different points in time, that is the concept of discounted utility, in a multiperiod or intertemporal framework.

Expected Utility

Suppose W represents the possible outcomes of a football game, namely, win, lose or draw. Suppose an individual attaches probabilities $p(W)$ to these outcomes, that is $p(W) = N(W)/T$ where $N(W)$ equals the number of wins, losses or draws in the season and $T = $ total number of games played. Finally, suppose the individual attaches subjective levels of satisfaction or utility U to win ($= 4$ units), lose ($= 0$ units) and draw ($= 1$ unit) so that $U(\text{win}) = 4$, etc. Then his *expected* utility from the season's forthcoming games is:

$$EU(W) = \sum_W p(W)U(W) \qquad (1.31)$$

Uncertainty and Risk

The first restriction placed on utility functions is that more is always preferred to less so that $U'(W) > 0$ where $U'(W) = \partial U(W)/\partial W$. Now, consider a simple gamble of receiving $2 for a 'head' on the toss of a coin and $0 for tails. Given a fair coin the expected *monetary* value of the risky outcome is $1:

$$(1/2)2 + (1/2)0 = \$1 \qquad (1.32)$$

Suppose it costs the investor $1 to 'invest' in the game. The outcome from not playing the game (i.e. not investing) is the $1 which is kept. Risk aversion means the investor will reject a fair gamble; $1 for certain is preferred to an equal chance of $2 or $0. Risk aversion implies that the second derivative of the utility function is negative $U''(W) < 0$. To see this, note that the utility from not investing $U(1)$ must exceed the expected utility from investing

$$U(1) > (1/2)U(2) + (1/2)U(0)$$

or

$$U(1) - U(0) > U(2) - U(1) \qquad (1.33)$$

so that the utility function has the concave shape given in Figure 1.2 marked 'risk averter'.

It is easy to deduce that for a risk lover the utility function is convex while for a risk neutral investor who is just indifferent to the gamble or the certain outcome, the utility function is linear (i.e. the equality sign applies to equation (1.33)). Hence we have:

$$U''(W) < 0 \quad \text{risk averse}$$

$$U''(W) = 0 \quad \text{risk neutral}$$

$$U''(W) > 0 \quad \text{risk lover}$$

A risk averse investor is also said to have diminishing marginal utility of wealth: each *additional* unit of wealth adds less to utility the higher the initial level of wealth (i.e. $U''(W) < 0$). The degree of risk aversion is given by the concavity of the utility function in Figure 1.2 and equivalently by the absolute size of $U''(W)$. Two measures of the degree

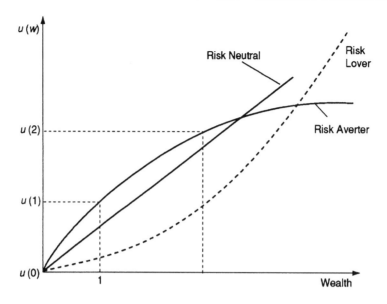

Figure 1.2 Utility Functions.

of risk aversion are commonly used:

$$R_A(W) = -U''(W)/U'(W) \qquad (1.34)$$

$$R_R(W) = R_A(W) \cdot W \qquad (1.35)$$

$R_A(W)$ is the Arrow–Pratt measure of absolute risk aversion, the larger is $R_A(W)$ the greater the degree of risk aversion. $R_R(W)$ is the coefficient of relative risk aversion. R_A and R_R are a measure of how the investor's risk preferences change with a change in wealth. For example, assume an investor with $10 000 happens to hold $5000 in risky assets. If his wealth were to increase by $10 000 and he then put more than $5000 in sum into risky assets, he is said to exhibit *decreasing* absolute risk aversion. (The definitions of increasing and constant absolute risk aversion are obvious.)

The natural assumption to make as to whether relative risk aversion is decreasing, increasing or constant is less clear cut. Suppose you have 50 percent of your wealth (of $100 000) in risky assets. If, when your wealth doubles, you increase the *proportion* held in risky assets then you are said to exhibit decreasing relative risk aversion. (Similar definitions apply for constant and increasing relative risk aversion.) Different mathematical functions give rise to different implications for the form of risk aversion. For example the function

$$U(W) = \ln W \qquad (1.36)$$

exhibits diminishing *absolute* risk aversion and constant *relative* risk aversion.

Certain utility functions allow one to reduce the problem of maximising expected utility to a problem involving only the maximisation of a function of expected return Π^e and the risk of the return (measured by the variance) σ_Π^2. For example, maximising the constant absolute risk aversion utility function

$$E[U(W)] = E[a - b\exp(-cW)] \qquad (1.37)$$

is equivalent to maximising

$$\Pi^e - \frac{c}{2}\sigma_\Pi^2 \tag{1.38}$$

given normally distributed asset returns and where $c =$ the constant coefficient of absolute risk aversion. Apart from the unobservable 'c' the maximand (1.38) is in terms of the mean and variance of the return on the portfolio: hence the term mean-variance criterion. However, the reader should note that in general maximising $EU(W)$ *cannot* be reduced to a maximisation problem in terms of Π^e and σ_Π^2 only and often portfolio models *assume* at the outset that investors are concerned with the mean-variance maximand and they discard any direct link with a specific utility function[3].

Indifference Curves

Although it is only the case under somewhat restrictive circumstances, let us assume that the utility function in Figure 1.2 for the risk averter can be represented solely in terms of the expected return and the variance of the return on the portfolio. The link between end of period wealth W and investment in a portfolio of assets yielding an expected return Π is $W = (1 + \Pi)W_0$ where W_0 equals initial wealth. However, we assume the utility function can be represented as

$$U = U(\Pi^e, \sigma_\Pi^2) \quad U_1 > 0, U_2 < 0, U_{11}, U_{22} < 0 \tag{1.39}$$

The sign of the first-order partial derivatives (U_1, U_2) imply that expected return adds to utility while more 'risk' reduces utility. The second-order partial derivatives indicate *diminishing* marginal utility to additional expected 'returns' and increasing marginal disutility with respect to additional risk. The indifference curves for the above utility function are shown in Figure 1.3.

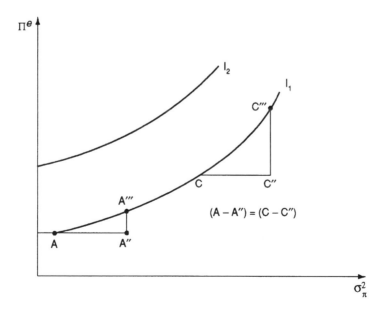

Figure 1.3   Indifference Curves.

At a point such as A on difference curve I_1 the individual requires a higher expected return (A'' to A''') as compensation for a higher level of risk (A to A''), if he is to maintain the level of satisfaction (utility) pertaining at A: the indifference curves have a positive slope in risk-return space. The indifference curves are convex to the 'risk axis' indicating that at higher levels of risk, say at C, the individual requires a higher expected return (C'' to $C''' > A''$ to A''') for each additional increment to risk he undertakes, than he did at A: the individual is 'risk averse'.

The indifference curves in risk-return space will be used when analysing portfolio choice in the one-period CAPM in the next chapter and in a simple mean-variance model in Chapter 3.

Intertemporal Utility

A number of economic models of individual behaviour assume that investors obtain utility solely from consumption goods. At any point in time, utility depends positively on consumption and exhibits diminishing marginal utility

$$U = U(C_t) \quad U'(C_t) > 0, U''(C_t) < 0$$

The utility function therefore has the same slope as the 'risk averter' in Figure 1.2 (with C replacing W). The only other issue is how we deal with consumption which accrues at different points in time. The most general form of such an *intertemporal lifetime utility* function is

$$U_N = U(C_t, C_{t+1}, C_{t+2} \ldots C_{t+N}) \tag{1.40}$$

However, to make the mathematics tractable some restrictions are usually placed on the form of U, the most common being additive separability with a constant subjective rate of discount $0 < \delta < 1$:

$$U_N = U(C_t) + \delta U(C_{t+1}) + \delta U(C_{t+2}) + \cdots \delta^N U(C_{t+N}) \tag{1.41}$$

It is usually the case that the functional form of $U(C_t)$, $U(C_{t+1})$, etc. are taken to be the same and a specific form often used is

$$U(C_t) = aC_t^{(1-d)}$$

$$U'(C_t) = a(1-d)C_t^{-d} > 0$$

$$U''(C_t) = -a(1-d)dC_t^{-d-1} < 0 \tag{1.42}$$

where $d < 1$. The lifetime utility function can be truncated at a finite value for N or if $N \to \infty$ then the model is said to be an overlapping generations model since an individual's consumption stream is bequeathed to future generations.

The discount rate used in (1.41) depends on the 'tastes' of the individual between present and future consumption. If we define $\delta = 1/(1+d)$ then d is known as the subjective rate of time preference. It is the rate at which the individual will swap utility at time $t + j$ for utility at time $t + j + 1$ and still keep lifetime utility constant. The additive separability in (1.41) implies that the extra utility from say an extra consumption bundle in 10 years' time is independent of the extra utility obtained from an identical consumption bundle in any other year (suitably discounted).

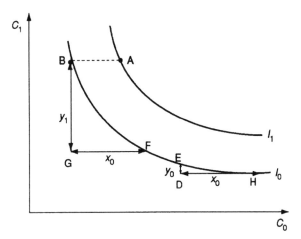

Figure 1.4 Intertemporal Consumption: Indifference Curves.

For the two-period case we can draw the indifference curves that follow from a simple utility function of the form $U = C_0^{\alpha_1} C_1^{\alpha_2} (0 < \alpha_1, \alpha_2 < 1)$ and these are given in Figure 1.4. Point A is on a higher indifference curve than point B since at A the individual has the same level of consumption in period 1, C_1 as at B, but at A, he has more of consumption in period zero, C_0. At point H if you reduce C_0 by x_0 units then for the individual to maintain a constant level of lifetime utility he must be compensated by y_0 extra units of consumption in period 1, so he is then indifferent between points H and E. Diminishing marginal utility arises because at F if you take away x_0 units of C_0 then he requires $y_1 (> y_0)$ extra units of C_1 to compensate him. This is because at F he starts off with a lower initial level of C_0 than at H, so each unit of C_0 he gives up is *relatively* more valuable and requires more compensation in terms of extra C_1.

The intertemporal indifference curves in Figure 1.4 will be used in discussing investment decisions under certainty in the next section and again when discussing the consumption CAPM model of portfolio choice and equilibrium asset returns under uncertainty.

1.3 PHYSICAL INVESTMENT DECISIONS AND OPTIMAL CONSUMPTION

Under conditions of certainty about future receipts the investment decision rules in section 1.1 indicate that managers should rank physical investment projects according either to their net present value (NPV), or internal rate of return (IRR). Investment projects should be undertaken until the NPV of the last project undertaken equals zero or equivalently until IRR $= r$, the risk-free rate of interest. Under these circumstances the marginal (last) investment project undertaken earns just enough net returns (profits) to cover the loan interest and repayment of principal. For the economy as a whole, undertaking real investment requires a sacrifice in terms of lost current consumption output. Higher real investment implies that labour skills, man-hours and machines are, at $t = 0$, devoted to producing new machines or increased labour skills, which will add to output and consumption but only in future periods. The consumption profile (i.e. fewer consumption goods today, and more in the future) which results from the decisions of producers may not coincide with the consumption profile desired by individual consumers. For example, a high level of physical investment will drastically reduce resources available for current consumption and this may be viewed as undesirable by consumers who prefer, at-the-margin, consumption today rather than tomorrow. How can financial markets through facilitating borrowing and lending ensure that entrepreneurs produce the optimal level of physical investment (i.e. which yields high levels of future consumption goods) and also allows individuals to spread their consumption over time according to their preferences? Do the entrepreneurs have to know the preferences of individual consumers in order to choose the optimum level of physical investment? How can the consumers acting as shareholders ensure that the managers of firms undertake the 'correct' physical investment decisions and can we assume that financial markets (e.g. stock markets) ensure funds are channelled to the most efficient investment projects? These questions of the interaction between 'finance' and real investment decisions lie at the heart of the market system. The full answer to these questions involves complex issues. However, we can gain some useful insights if we consider a simple two period model of the investment decision where all outcomes are certain (i.e. riskless) in real terms (i.e. we assume zero price inflation). We shall see that under these assumptions a *separation principle* applies. If managers ignore the preferences of individuals and simply invest in projects until the NPV = 0 or IRR = r, that is, maximise the value of the firm, then this policy will, given a capital market, allow *each* consumer to choose his desired consumption profile, namely, that which maximises his individual welfare. There is therefore a two-stage process or separation of decisions, yet this still allows consumers to maximise their welfare by distributing their consumption over time according to their preferences. In step one, entrepreneurs decide the optimal level of physical investment, disregarding the preferences of consumers. In step two, consumers borrow or lend in the capital market to rearrange the time profile of their consumption to suit their individual preferences. In explaining this separation principle we first deal with the production decision and then the consumers' decision before combining these two into the complete model.

All output is either consumed or used for physical investment. The entrepreneur has an initial endowment W_0 at time $t = 0$. He ranks projects in order of decreasing NPV using the risk-free interest rate r as the discount factor. By foregoing consumption $C_0^{(1)}$ he obtains resources for his first investment project $I_0 = W_0 - C_0^{(1)}$. The physical investment in that project which has the highest NPV (or IRR) yields consumption output at $t = 1$ of $C_1^{(1)}$ (where $C_1^{(1)} > C_0^{(1)}$, see Figure 1.5). The IRR of this project (in terms of consumption goods) is:

$$1 + \text{IRR}^{(1)} = C_1^{(1)}/C_0^{(1)} \tag{1.43}$$

As he devotes more of his initial endowment W_0 to other investment projects with lower NPVs then the internal rate of return (C_1/C_0) falls, which gives rise to the *production opportunity curve* with the shape given in Figure 1.5 (compare the slope at A and B).

The first and most productive investment project has a NPV of

$$\text{NPV}^{(1)} = \frac{C_1^{(1)}}{(1+r)} - I_0 > 0$$

and

$$\text{IRR}^{(1)} = C_1^{(1)}/C_0^{(1)} > r \tag{1.44}$$

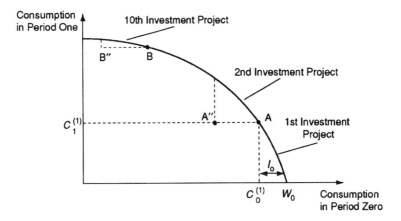

Figure 1.5 Production Possibility Curve. Note $(A–A'' = B–B'')$.

Let us now turn to the financing problem. In the capital market, *any two* consumption streams C_0 and C_1 have a present value (PV) given by:

$$PV = C_0 + C_1/(1+r)$$

hence

$$C_1 = PV(1+r) - (1+r)C_0 \qquad (1.45)$$

For a given value of PV, this gives a straight line in Figure 1.6 with a slope equal to $-(1+r)$. Equation (1.45) is referred to as the *money market line* since it represents the rate of return on lending and borrowing money in the *financial* market place. If you lend an amount C_0 today you will receive $C_1 = (1+r)C_0$ tomorrow.

Our entrepreneur, with an initial endowment of W_0, will continue to invest in physical assets until the IRR on the nth project just equals the risk-free market interest rate

$$IRR^{(n)} = r \qquad (1.46)$$

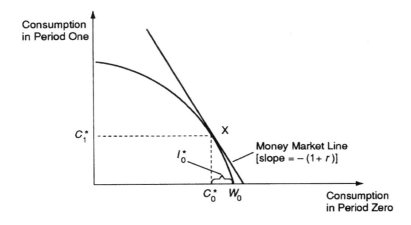

Figure 1.6 Money Market Line.

which occurs at point (C_0^*, C_1^*). Hence the investment strategy that maximises the (net present) value of the firm involves an investment of

$$I_0^* = W_0 - C_0^* \tag{1.47}$$

current consumption of C_0^* and consumption at $t = 1$ of C_1^* (Figure 1.6). At any point to the right of X the slope of the investment opportunity curve ($= $ IRR) exceeds the market interest rate ($= r$) and at points to the left of X, the opposite applies.

However, the optimal levels of consumption (C_0^*, C_1^*) from the production decision may not conform to those preferred by individual consumers. We now leave the production decision and turn exclusively to the consumer's decision.

Suppose the consumer has income accruing in both periods and this income stream has present value of PV. The consumption possibilities which fully exhaust this income (after two periods) are represented by:

$$PV = C_0 + \frac{C_1}{(1+r)} \tag{1.48}$$

We now assume that lifetime utility (satisfaction) of the consumer depends on C_0 and C_1

$$U = U(C_0, C_1)$$

and there is diminishing marginal utility in both C_0 and C_1 (i.e. $\partial U/\partial C_i > 0$, $\partial^2 U/\partial C_i^2 < 0$, for $i = 0, 1$). The indifference curves are shown in Figure 1.7. To give up one unit of C_0 the consumer must be compensated with additional units of C_1, if he is to maintain his initial level of utility. The consumer wishes to choose C_0 and C_1 to maximise lifetime utility subject to his budget constraint (1.48). Given his endowment PV, his optimal consumption in the two periods is (C_0^{**}, C_1^{**}). In general, the optimal production or physical investment plan which yields consumption (C_0^*, C_1^*) will not equal the consumer's optimal consumption profile (C_0^{**}, C_1^{**}). However, the existence of a capital market ensures that the consumer's optimal point can be attained. To see this consider Figure 1.8.

The entrepreneur has produced a consumption profile (C_0^*, C_1^*) which maximises the value of the firm. We can envisage this consumption profile as being paid out to the

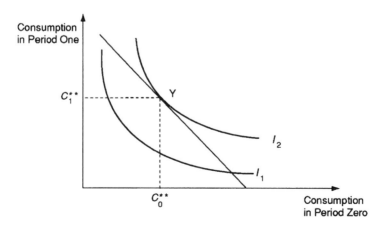

Figure 1.7 Consumers' Maximisation Problem.

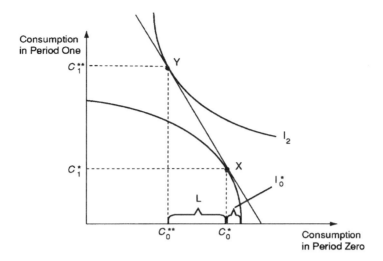

Figure 1.8 Investing I_0 and Lending 'L' in the Capital Market.

owners of the firm in the form of (dividend) income. The present value of this 'cash flow' is PV^* where

$$PV^* = C_0^* + C_1^*/(1+r)$$

This is, of course, the 'income' given to our individual consumer as owner of the firm. But, under conditions of certainty, the consumer can 'swap' this amount PV^* for *any* combination of consumption that satisfies

$$PV^* = C_0 + \frac{C_1}{(1+r)}$$

Given PV^* and his indifference curves (i.e. tastes or preferences) in Figure 1.8 he can then borrow or lend in the capital market at the riskless rate r to achieve that combination C_0^{**}, C_1^{**} which maximises his own utility function.

Thus, there is a separation of investment and financing (borrowing and lending) decisions. Optimal borrowing and lending takes place independently of the physical investment decision. If the entrepreneur and consumer are the same person(s), the separation principle still applies. The investor (as we now call him) first decides how much of his own initial endowment W_0 to invest in physical assets and this decision is independent of his own (subjective) preferences and tastes. This first stage decision is an objective calculation based on comparing the internal rate of return of his investment projects with the risk-free interest rate. His second stage decision involves how much to borrow or lend in the capital market to 'smooth out' his desired consumption pattern over time. The latter decision *is* based on his preferences or tastes, at the margin, for consumption today versus (more) consumption tomorrow.

Much of the rest of this book is concerned with how financing decisions are taken when we have a risky environment. The issue of how shareholders ensure that managers act in the best interest of the shareholders, by maximising the value of the firm, comes under the heading of corporate control mechanisms (e.g. mergers, takeovers). The analysis of corporate control is not directly covered in this book. Consideration is given only to whether market prices provide correct signals for resource allocation (i.e. physical investment) and not to issues involving the incentive structure within the firm based on these market signals: this is the principal–agent problem in corporate finance. We can draw a parallel between the above results under certainty with those we shall be developing under a risky environment.

(i) In a risky environment a somewhat different separation principle applies. This is that each investor when choosing his portfolio of risky marketable assets (e.g. shares, bonds) will hold risky assets in the same proportion as all other investors, regardless of his preferences of risk versus return. Having undertaken this first stage decision, each investor then decides how much to borrow or lend in the money market, at the risk-free interest rate. This separation principle is the basis of optimal portfolio choice and of the capital asset pricing model (CAPM) which provides a model of equilibrium asset returns.

(ii) The optimal amount of borrowing and lending in the money market in the riskless case occurs where the individual's subjective marginal rate of substitution of future for current consumption (i.e. $(dC_1/dC_0)_u$) equals $-(1 + r)$, where $r =$ price or opportunity cost of money. Under uncertainty a parallel condition applies, namely, that the individual's subjective trade-off between expected return and risk is equal to the market price of risk.

(iii) Under certainty, the slope of the money market (or present value) line measures the price (interest rate) of money, or equivalently the increase in value of $1 invested today in the money market. Under risky investment opportunities the slope of the so-called capital market line (CML) along which investors can borrow and lend, provides a measure of the market price of risk.

1.4 SUMMARY

In this chapter we have developed some basic tools for analysing in financial markets. There are many nuances on the topics discussed which have not been elaborated in detail and in future chapters these omissions will be rectified.

The main conclusions to emerge are:

- Market participants generally quote 'simple' annual interest rates but these can always be converted to effective annual (compound) rates or to continuously compounded rates.

- The concepts of DPV and IRR can be used to analyse physical investment projects and provide measures of the return on bills and bonds.

- Theoretical models often have either returns *and* risk or utility as their maximands. Utility functions and their associated indifference curves can be used to represent risk averters, risk lovers and risk neutral investors.

- Under certainty, a type of separation principle applies. Managers can choose investment projects to maximise the value of the firm and disregard investor preferences. Then investors are able to borrow and lend to allocate consumption between 'today' and 'tomorrow' in order to maximise their satisfaction (utility).

ENDNOTES

1. There are cases where the NPV and IRR investment rules are not equivalent but we ignore these.

2. There are two points worth noting at this point. First, the expectations operation E_t is applied to the whole of the RHS expression in (1.30). If q_i and D_{t+i} are both random variables then, for example, $E_t[D_{t+1}/(1 + q_1)]$ does not equal $E_t D_{t+1}/E_t(1 + q_1)$. Second, equation (1.30) is expressed in terms of *one-period* rates q_i. If $r_t^{(2)}$ is the (annual) rate applicable between $t = 0$ and $t = 2$ on a *risky asset*, then we can always *define* $(1 + r^{(2)})^2 = (1 + q_1)(1 + q_2)$. Then (1.30) is of a similar form to (1.18), if we ignore the expectations operator. These rather subtle distinctions need not delay the reader at this point and they will become clear later in the text.

3. Note that the function $U = U(\mu_N, \sigma_N^2)$ is very different from either $EU(\mu_N, \sigma_N^2)$ or from $E[U(W)]$ where W is end of period wealth.

2
The Capital Asset
Pricing Model: CAPM

This chapter presents a detailed derivation of the (basic) one-period capital asset pricing model (CAPM). This model, interpreted as a model of equilibrium asset returns, is widely used in the finance literature and the concepts which underlie its derivation, such as portfolio diversification, measures of risk and return, and the concept of the market portfolio are also fundamental to the analysis of all asset prices. Throughout this chapter we will consider that the only risky assets are equities (stocks) although strictly the model applies to choices among *all* risky assets (i.e. stocks, bonds, real estate, etc.).

The CAPM attempts to answer what at first sight appears to be a rather complex set of interrelated questions, namely:

- Why it is beneficial for agents to hold a diversified portfolio consisting of a number of risky assets rather than say one single risky asset or a small subset of all the available risky assets?
- What determines the expected equilibrium return on each *individual* risky asset in the market, so that all the risky assets are willingly held by investors?
- What determines an individual investor's choice between his holdings of the risk-free asset and the 'bundle' of risky assets?

As will be seen in the next chapter, there are a number of models of equilibrium asset *returns* and there are a number of variants on the 'basic' CAPM. The concepts used in the derivation of the CAPM are quite numerous and somewhat complex, hence it is useful at the outset to sketch out the main elements of its derivation and draw out some basic implications. Section 2.2 carefully sets out the principles that underlie portfolio diversification and the efficient set of portfolios. Section 2.3 derives the optimal portfolio and the equilibrium returns that this implies.

2.1 AN OVERVIEW

Our world is restricted to one in which agents can choose a set of risky assets (stocks) and a risk-free asset (e.g. fixed-term bank deposit or a three-month Treasury bill). Agents can borrow and lend as much as they like at the risk-free rate. We assume agents like higher expected returns but dislike risk (i.e. they are risk averse). The return on an *individual* security is denoted ER_i and we assume that the risk on an *individual* security 'i' can be measured by the variance of its return, σ_i^2. All individuals have homogeneous expectations about expected returns and the variances and covariances (correlation) between the various returns. Transactions costs and taxes are assumed to be zero.

Consider the reason for holding a *diversified portfolio* consisting of a *set* of risky assets. Assume for the moment that the funds allocated to the safe asset have already been fixed. Putting all your wealth in asset 1, you incur an expected return ER_1 and a risk element σ_1^2, the variance of the returns on this one asset. Similarly holding just asset 2 you expect to earn ER_2 and incur risk σ_2^2. Let us assume a two-asset world where there is a negative covariance of returns $\sigma_{12} < 0$. Hence when the return on asset 1 rises that on asset 2 tends to fall. (This also implies a negative correlation coefficient $\rho_{12} = \sigma_{12}/\sigma_1\sigma_2$.) Hence if you diversify and hold both assets, this would seem to reduce the variance of the *overall* portfolio (i.e. of asset 1 plus asset 2). To simplify even further suppose that $ER_1 = ER_2$ and $\sigma_1^2 = \sigma_2^2$. In addition assume that when the return on asset 1 increases by 1 percent, that on asset 2 falls by 1 percent (i.e. returns are perfectly negatively correlated, $\rho = -1$). Under these conditions when you hold half your initial wealth in each of the risky assets the expected return on the overall portfolio is $ER_1 = ER_2$. However, diversification has reduced the risk on the portfolio to zero: an above average return on asset 1 is always matched by an equal below average return on asset 2 (since $\rho = -1$). Our example is, of course, a special case but in general, even if the covariance of returns is zero or positive (but not perfectly positively correlated) it still pays to diversify and hold a combination of both assets.

The above simple example also points to the reason why *each* individual investor might at least hold *some* of each of *all* the available stocks in the market, if we allow him to borrow (or lend) unlimited funds at the risk-free rate r. To demonstrate this point we set up a counter example. If *one* stock were initially not desired by any of the investors then its current price would fall as investors sold it. However, a fall in the current price implies that the *expected return* over the coming period is higher, *ceteris paribus* (assuming one expected it to pay some dividends in the future). One might therefore see the current price fall until the expected return increases so that the stock is sufficiently attractive to hold.

The reader may now be summising that the individual investor's tastes or preferences must come into the analysis at some point and he would be correct. However, there is a quite remarkable result, known as the *two-fund separation theorem*. The investment decision can be broken down into two separate decisions. The first decision concerns the choice of the *optimal proportions* x_i^* of risky assets held and this is *independent of the individual's preferences* concerning his subjective trade-off between risk and return. This choice depends only on the individual's views about the objective market variables, namely, expected returns, variances and covariances. Expectations about these variables are assumed to be homogeneous across investors. All individuals therefore hold the same proportions of the risky assets (e.g. all investors hold 1/20 of 'α shares', 1/80 of 'β shares', etc.) irrespective of their preferences. Hence aggregating, all individuals will hold these risky assets in the same proportions as in the (*aggregate*) market portfolio (e.g. if the share of ICI in the total stock market index is 1/20 by value, then all investors hold 1/20 of their own risky asset portfolio, in ICI shares).

It is only after mimicking the market portfolio that the individual's preferences enter the calculation. In the second stage of the decision process the individual decides how much to borrow (lend) in order to augment (reduce the amount of) his own initial wealth invested in the (fixed proportions in the) market portfolio of risky assets. It is at this point that the individual's preferences enter the decision process. If the individual is *very* risk averse, he will use most of his own wealth to invest in the risk-free asset (which pays r) and only invest a small amount of his own wealth in the risky assets in the fixed proportions x_i^*. The converse applies to a less risk averse person who will *borrow* at the risk-free rate and use these proceeds (as well as his own initial wealth) to invest in the fixed bundle of risky assets in the optimal proportions x_i^*. Note, however, this second stage, which involves the individual's preferences, does not impinge on the *relative demands* for the risky assets (i.e. the proportions x_i^*). Hence the *equilibrium expected returns* on the set of risky assets are independent of individuals' preferences and depend only on market variables such as the variances and covariances in the market.

Throughout this and subsequent chapters the following equivalent ways of expressing expected returns, variances and covariances will be used:

Expected return $= \mu_i = ER_i$

Variance of returns $= \sigma_i^2 = \text{var}(R_i)$

Covariance of returns $= \sigma_{ij} = \text{cov}(R_i, R_j)$

Let us turn now to some specific results about equilibrium returns which arise from the CAPM. The CAPM provides an elegant model of the determinants of the equilibrium expected return ER_i on any *individual* risky asset in the market. It predicts that the expected excess return on an individual risky asset $(ER_i - r)$ is directly related to the expected excess return on the market portfolio $(ER^m - r)$, with the constant of proportionality given by the *beta* of the individual risky asset:

$$(ER_i - r) = \beta_i(ER^m - r) \tag{2.1}$$

or

$$ER_i = r + \beta_i(ER^m - r) \tag{2.2}$$

where

$$\beta_i = \text{cov}(R_i, R^m)/\text{var}(R^m) \tag{2.3}$$

ER^m is the expected return on the market portfolio that is the 'average' expected return from holding *all* assets in the optimal proportions x_i^*. Since actual returns on the market portfolio differ from expected returns, the variance $\text{var}(R^m)$ on the market portfolio is non-zero. The definition of firm i's *beta*, namely β_i indicates that it depends on

(i) the covariance between the return on security i and the market portfolio $\text{cov}(R_i, R^m)$ and

(ii) is inversely related to the variance of the market portfolio, $\text{var}(R^m)$.

Loosely speaking, if the *ex-post* (or actual) returns when averaged approximate the *ex-ante* expected return ER_i, then we can think of the CAPM as explaining the average return (over say a number of months) on security i.

What does the CAPM tell us about equilibrium returns on individual securities in the stock market? First note that $(ER^m - r) > 0$, otherwise no risk averse agent would hold the market portfolio of risky assets when he could earn more, *for certain*, by investing all his wealth in the risk-free asset.

Returns on individual stocks tend to move in the same direction and hence, in general, $\text{cov}(R_i, R^m) \geqslant 0$ and $\beta_i \geqslant 0$. The CAPM predicts that for those stocks which have a zero covariance with the market portfolio, they will be willingly held as long as they have an expected return equal to the risk-free rate (put $\beta_i = 0$ in (2.1)). Securities that have a large positive covariance with the market return ($\beta_i > 0$) will have to earn a relatively high expected return: this is because the addition of such a security to the portfolio does little to reduce *overall portfolio* variance. Conversely any security for which $\text{cov}(R_i, R^m) < 0$ and hence $\beta_i < 0$ will be willingly held even though its expected return is *below* the risk-free rate (equation (2.1) with $\beta_i < 0$) because it tends to reduce overall portfolio variance.

The CAPM also allows one to assess the relative volatility of the expected returns on individual stocks on the basis of their β_i values (which we assume are accurately measured). Stocks for which $\beta_i = 1$ have a return that is expected to move one-for-one with the market portfolio (i.e. $ER_i = ER^m$) and are termed 'neutral stocks'. If $\beta_i > 1$ the stock is said to be an aggressive stock since it moves *more* than changes in the expected market return (either up or down) and conversely defensive stocks have $\beta_i < 1$. Therefore investors can use betas to rank the relative safety of various securities. However, the latter should not detract from one of the CAPM's key predictions, namely that *all* investors should hold stocks in the same optimal proportions x_i^*. Hence the 'market portfolio' held by all investors will include neutral, aggressive and defensive stocks held in the *optimal proportions* x_i^* predicted by the CAPM. Of course, an investor who wishes to 'take a position' in particular stocks may use betas to rank the stocks to include in his portfolio (i.e. he doesn't obey the assumptions of the CAPM and therefore doesn't attempt to mimic the market portfolio).

The basic concepts of the CAPM can be used to assess the performance of portfolio managers. The CAPM can be applied to *any portfolio p* of stocks composed of a *subset* of the assets of the market portfolio. For such a portfolio we can see that $PI = [(ER_p - r)/\sigma_p]$ is a measure of the excess return (over the risk-free rate) per unit of risk (σ_p) and may loosely be referred to as a 'Performance Index' (PI). The higher the PI the higher is the expected return corrected for risk (σ_p). Thus for two investment managers, the one whose portfolio has the higher value for PI may be deemed the more successful. These ideas are developed further in Chapter 5.

2.2 PORTFOLIO DIVERSIFICATION, EFFICIENT FRONTIER AND THE TRANSFORMATION LINE

Before we analyse the key features of the CAPM we discuss the mean-variance criterion, the concept of an efficient portfolio and the gains from diversification in minimising portfolio risk. We then consider the relationship between the expected return μ_p on a diversified portfolio and the risk of the portfolio, σ_p. If agents are interested in minimising risk for any given level of return, then such efficient portfolios lie along the *efficient frontier* which is non-linear in (μ_p, σ_p) space. We then examine the return-risk relationship for a specific two-asset portfolio where one asset consists of the amount of borrowing or lending in the safe asset and the other asset is a single portfolio of risky assets. This gives rise to the *transformation line* which gives a *linear* relationship between expected return and portfolio risk for any two-asset portfolio comprising a risk-free asset and risky portfolio. Armed with the concepts of the efficient frontier and the transformation line we are then in a position to explore the CAPM.

2.2.1 Mean-Variance Criterion (MVC)

It is assumed that the investor would prefer a higher expected return (ER) rather than a lower expected return, but he dislikes risk (i.e. is risk averse). We choose to measure risk by the variance of the returns var(R) on the portfolio of risky assets. Thus, if the agent is presented with a portfolio 'A' (of n securities) and a portfolio 'B' (of a different set of n securities), then according to the MVC, portfolio A is preferred to portfolio B if

(i) $E_A(R) \geqslant E_B(R)$ and

(ii) $\text{var}_A(R) \leqslant \text{var}_B(R)$ or $SD_A(R) \leqslant SD_B(R)$

where SD = standard deviation. Of course if, for example, $E_A(R) > E_B(R)$ but var$_A(R) >$ var$_B(R)$ then we cannot say what portfolio the investor prefers using the MVC.

Portfolios that satisfy the MVC are known as the set of *efficient portfolios*. A portfolio A that has a lower expected return *and* a higher variance than another portfolio B is said to be 'inefficient' and an individual would (in principle) never hold a portfolio such as A if portfolio B is available.

2.2.2 Portfolio Diversification

To demonstrate in a simple fashion the gains to be made from holding a diversified portfolio of assets, the simple two-(risky) asset model will be used.

Suppose the actual return (over one period) on each of the two assets is R_1 and R_2 with *expected* returns $\mu_1 = ER_1$ and $\mu_2 = ER_2$. The variance of the returns on each security is measured by $\sigma_i^2 (i = 1, 2)$ which is defined as

$$\sigma_i^2 = E(R_i - \mu_i)^2$$

In addition assume that the *correlation coefficient* between movements in the returns on the two assets is ρ, $(-1 \leqslant \rho \leqslant 1)$ where ρ is defined as

$$\rho = \sigma_{12}/\sigma_1\sigma_2 \tag{2.4}$$

and

$$\sigma_{12} = E[(R_1 - \mu_1)(R_2 - \mu_2)] \tag{2.5}$$

Hence $\sigma_{12} = \text{cov}(R_1, R_2)$ is the covariance between the two returns. If $\rho = +1$ the two asset returns are perfectly positively (linearly) related and the asset returns *always* move in the same direction. For $\rho = -1$ the converse applies and for $\rho = 0$ the asset returns are not (linearly) related. As we see below, the 'riskiness' of the portfolio consisting of both asset 1 and asset 2 depends crucially on the sign and size of ρ. If $\rho = -1$, risk may be completely eliminated by holding a specific proportion of initial wealth in *both* assets. Even if ρ is positive (but less than $+1$) the riskiness of the overall portfolio is reduced (although not to zero) by diversification.

Suppose for the moment that the investor chooses the proportion of his total wealth to invest in each asset in order to *minimise portfolio risk*. He is not, at this stage, allowed to borrow or lend or place any of his wealth in a *risk-free* asset. Should the investor put 'all his eggs in one basket' and place *all* of his wealth either in asset 1 or asset 2 and incur risk of either σ_1^2 or σ_2^2, or should he hold some of his wealth in each asset and if so how much of each? We begin with an algebraic exposition but then demonstrate the points made using a simple numerical example. Suppose the investor chooses to hold a proportion x_1 of his wealth in asset 1 and a proportion $x_2 = (1 - x_1)$ in asset 2. The *actual return* on this diversified portfolio (which will not be revealed until one period later) is:

$$R_p = x_1 R_1 + x_2 R_2 \tag{2.6}$$

The *expected return* on the portfolio (formed at the beginning of the period) is defined as:

$$ER_p = \mu_p = (x_1 ER_1 + x_2 ER_2) = x_1 \mu_1 + x_2 \mu_2 \tag{2.7}$$

The *variance of the portfolio* is given by:

$$\begin{aligned}
\sigma_p^2 &= E(R_p - ER_p)^2 = E[x_1(R_1 - \mu_1) + x_2(R_2 - \mu_2)]^2 \\
&= x_1^2 E(R_1 - \mu_1)^2 + x_2^2 E(R_2 - \mu_2)^2 + 2x_1 x_2 [E(R_1 - \mu_1)(R_2 - \mu_2)] \\
&= x_1^2 \sigma_1^2 + x_2^2 \sigma_2^2 + 2x_1 x_2 \sigma_{12} \\
&= x_1^2 \sigma_1^2 + x_2^2 \sigma_2^2 + 2x_1 x_2 \rho \sigma_1 \sigma_2 \\
&= x_1^2 \sigma_1^2 + (1 - x_1)^2 \sigma_2^2 + 2x_1(1 - x_1)\rho \sigma_1 \sigma_2 \tag{2.8}
\end{aligned}$$

For the moment we assume the investor is not concerned about expected return (or equivalently that both assets have the same expected return, so only the variance of returns matters to him). Knowing σ_1^2, σ_2^2 and ρ (or σ_{12}) the individual has to choose that value of x_1 (and hence $x_2 = 1 - x_1$) to minimise the total portfolio risk, σ_p^2. Differentiating (2.8) gives

$$\frac{\partial(\sigma_p^2)}{\partial x_1} = 2x_1 \sigma_1^2 - 2(1 - x_1)\sigma_2^2 + 2(1 - 2x_1)\rho \sigma_1 \sigma_2 = 0 \tag{2.9}$$

Solving (2.9) for x_1 gives

$$x_1 = (\sigma_2^2 - \rho \sigma_1 \sigma_2)/(\sigma_1^2 + \sigma_2^2 - 2\rho \sigma_1 \sigma_2) \tag{2.10}$$

or

$$x_1 = (\sigma_2^2 - \sigma_{12})/(\sigma_1^2 + \sigma_2^2 - 2\sigma_{12}) \tag{2.11}$$

Note that from (2.10) 'the total variance' will be smallest when $\rho = -1$ and largest when $\rho = +1$.

For illustrative purposes assume $\sigma_1^2 = (0.4)^2$, $\sigma_2^2 = (0.5)^2$, $\rho = 0.25$ (i.e. positive correlation). Then the value of x_1 for minimum variance using (2.10) is:

$$x_1 = \frac{(0.5)^2 - 0.25(0.4)(0.5)}{(0.4)^2 + (0.5)^2 - 2(0.25)(0.4)(0.5)} = \frac{20}{31} \tag{2.12}$$

and substituting this value of x_1 in (2.8) gives

$$\sigma_p^2 = 12.1 \text{ percent}$$

which is smaller than the variance if all his wealth had been put in asset 1, $\sigma_1^2 = (0.4)^2 = 16$ percent or all in asset 2, $\sigma_2^2 = (0.5)^2 = 25$ percent.

If the correlation coefficient is $\rho = -1$, then using (2.10) we obtain $x_1 = 5/9$ and substituting this value in (2.8) we obtain $\sigma_p^2 = 0$. Thus all risk can be diversified when the two assets returns are perfectly negatively correlated. It follows from this analysis that an individual asset may be highly risky *taken in isolation* (i.e. has a high variance, σ^2) but if it has a negative covariance with assets already held in the portfolio, then agents will be willing to add it to their existing portfolio even if its expected return is relatively low since such an asset tends to reduce *overall* portfolio risk (σ_p^2). This basic intuitive notion lies behind the explanation of determination of equilibrium asset returns in the CAPM.

Even in the case where asset returns are totally uncorrelated then portfolio variance can be reduced by adding more assets to the portfolio. To see this, note that for n assets (all of which have $\rho_{ij} = 0$) the portfolio variance is:

$$\sigma_p^2 = (x_1^2\sigma_1^2 + x_2^2\sigma_2^2 + \cdots + x_n^2\sigma_n^2) \tag{2.13}$$

Simplifying further, if all the variances are equal ($\sigma_i^2 = \sigma^2$) and all the assets are held in equal proportions $(1/n)$ we have

$$\sigma_p^2 = \frac{1}{n^2}(n\sigma^2) = \frac{1}{n}\sigma^2 \tag{2.14}$$

Hence as $n \to \infty$ the variance of the portfolio approaches zero. Thus, if uncorrelated risks are pooled, total risk is diversified away. The risk attached to each security (σ_i^2) which is known as *idiosyncratic risk* can be completely diversified away. Intuitively, one is inclined to suggest that such idiosyncratic risk should not require any additional return over the risk-free rate. As we shall see this intuition carries through to the CAPM.

Portfolio Expected Return and Portfolio Variance as ρ Varies

In the above example we neglected the expected return on the portfolio. Clearly individuals are interested in expected portfolio return μ_p as well as the risk of the portfolio σ_p. The question now is how μ_p and σ_p vary, relative to each other, as the agent *alters the proportion of wealth held in each of the risky assets*. Remember that $\mu_1, \mu_2, \sigma_1, \sigma_2$ and σ_{12} (or ρ) are fixed and known. As the agent alters x_1 (and $x_2 = 1 - x_1$) then equations (2.7) and (2.8) allow us to calculate the combinations of μ_p and σ_p that ensue for each of the values of x_1 (and x_2) that we have arbitrarily chosen. (Note that there is no maximisation/minimisation problem here, it is a purely *arithmetic* calculation given the definitions of μ_p and σ_p). A numerical example is given in Table 2.1 for

$$\mu_1 = 10 \quad \mu_2 = 20 \quad \rho = -0.5$$
$$\sigma_1 = 100 \quad \sigma_2 = 900$$

and is plotted in Figure 2.1.

The above calculations could be repeated using different values for ρ (between $+1$ and -1). In general as ρ approaches -1 the (μ_p, σ_p) locus moves closer to the vertical axis as in Figure 2.2, indicating that a greater reduction in portfolio risk is possible for any given expected return. (Compare portfolios A and B corresponding to $\rho = 0.5$ and $\rho = -0.5$.) For $\rho = -1$ the curve hits the vertical axis indicating there is some value for

Table 2.1 Calculation of Mean and Variance of a Portfolio for $\rho = -0.5$

Proportions x_1 Invested in Asset 1	Expected Return μ_p	Variance of the Portfolio $\sigma_p^2(\sigma_p)$
0	20	900 (30.0)
1/5	18	532 (23.1)
2/5	16	268 (16.4)
3/5	14	108 (10.4)
4/5	12	52 (7.2)
1	10	100 (10.0)

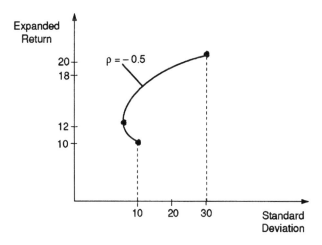

Figure 2.1 Expected Return on Standard Deviation.

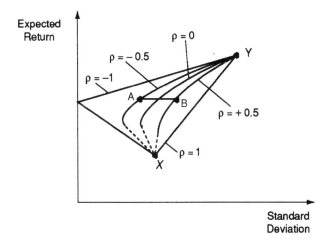

Figure 2.2 Efficient Frontier and Correlation.

the proportion x_i held in the two assets that reduces risk to zero. For $\rho = 1$ the risk-return locus is a straight line between the (μ_i, σ_i) points for each individual security.

In the above example we have *arbitrarily chosen* a specific set of x_i values and there is no maximisation problem involved. Also in the real world there is only one value of ρ (at any point in time) and hence only one risk-return locus and corresponding x_i values. This risk-return combination is part of the *feasible set* or *opportunity set* for every investor.

More than Two Securities

If we allow the investor to distribute his wealth between any *two* securities A and B or B and C or A and C we obtain (μ_p, σ_p) combinations given by curves I, II, III respectively in Figure 2.3. If we now allow the agent to invest *in all three* securities, that is we vary the proportions x_1, x_2, x_3 (with $\sum_1^3 x_i = 1$) then the (μ_p, σ_p) locus is a curve like IV. This demonstrates that holding more securities reduces portfolio risk for *any given level of expected return* (i.e. the three-security portfolio at Y is preferred to portfolio at point Z (securities B and C only) in Figure 2.3 and X also *dominates* Y and Z). It follows that any agent adopting the mean-variance criterion will wish to move from points like Y and Z to points at X.

The slope of IV is a measure of how the agent can trade-off expected return against risk by altering the proportions x_i held in the three assets. By altering the composition of his portfolio from M to Q he can obtain an increase in expected return $(\mu_2 - \mu_1)$ by taking on an amount of additional risk $(\sigma_2 - \sigma_1)$.

Note that the dashed portion of the curve IV indicates a mean-variance *inefficient* portfolio. An investor would never choose portfolio L rather than M because L has a lower expected return for a given level of portfolio risk than does portfolio M. Portfolio M is said to *dominate* portfolio L on the mean-variance criterion.

Limited Investment and Portfolio Variance

In general the agent may reduce σ_p for any given μ_p by including additional stocks in his portfolio (particularly those that have negative covariances with the existing stocks already held). In fact portfolio variance (σ_p^2) falls very quickly as one increases the

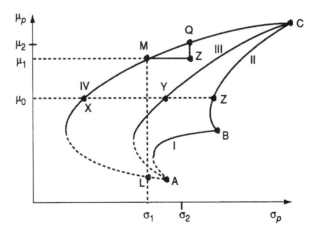

Figure 2.3   Efficient Frontier.

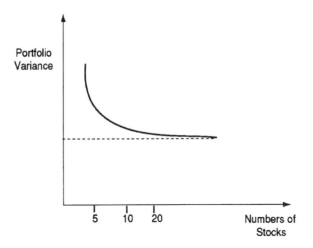

Figure 2.4 Portfolio Combinations.

number of stocks held from 1 to 10, and thereafter the reduction in portfolio variance is quite small (Figure 2.4). This, coupled with the brokerage fees and information costs of monitoring a large number of stocks, may explain why individuals tend to invest in only a relatively small number of stocks. Individuals may also obtain the benefits of diversification by investing in mutual funds (unit trusts) and pension funds since these institutions use funds from a large number of individuals to invest in a very wide range of financial assets and each individual then owns a proportion of this 'large portfolio'.

2.2.3 The Efficient Frontier

Consider now the case of N assets. When we vary the proportions x_i $(i = 1, 2, \ldots N)$ to form portfolios it is obvious that there is potentially a large number of such portfolios. We can form $2, 3, \ldots$ to N asset portfolios. We can also form portfolios consisting of the same number of assets but in different proportions. The set of every possible portfolio is given by the convex 'egg' of Figure 2.5.

If we apply the mean-variance dominance criterion then all of the points in the interior of the *portfolio opportunity set* (e.g. P_1, P_2, Figure 2.5) are dominated by those on the curve AB since the latter has a lower variance for a given expected return. Points on the curve AB also dominate those on BC, so the curve AB represents the proportions x_i in the *efficient set* of portfolios and is referred to as the *efficient frontier*.

We now turn to the problem of how the investor *calculates* the x_i values that make up the efficient frontier. The investor faces a *known* set of n expected returns μ_i and variances σ_i^2 and $n(n-1)/2$ covariances σ_{ij} (or correlation coefficients ρ_{ij}) and the formulae for the expected return and variance of the portfolio are:

$$\mu_p = \sum_{i=1}^{n} x_i \mu_i \tag{2.15}$$

$$\sigma_p^2 = \sum x_i^2 \sigma_i^2 + \sum_{\substack{i=1 \\ i \neq j}}^{n} \sum_{j=1}^{n} x_i x_j \sigma_{ij} \tag{2.16}$$

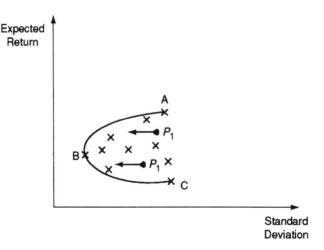

Figure 2.5

or

$$\sigma_p^2 = \sum x_i^2 \sigma_i^2 + \sum_{i=1}^{n} \sum_{\substack{j=1 \\ i \neq j}}^{n} x_i x_j \rho_{ij} \sigma_i \sigma_j \tag{2.17}$$

We assume our investor wishes to *choose* the proportions invested in each asset x_i but he is concerned about expected return and risk. Risk is measured by the standard deviation of returns on the portfolio (σ_p). The *efficient frontier* shows all the combinations of (μ_p, σ_p) which *minimises* risk σ_p for a *given level* of μ_p.

The investor's budget constraint is $\Sigma x_i = 1$, that is all his wealth is placed in the set of risky assets. (For the moment he is not allowed to borrow or lend money in a riskless asset.) Short sales $x_i < 0$ are permitted.

A stylised way of representing how the agent seeks to map out the efficient frontier is as follows:

1. Choose an arbitrary 'target' return on the portfolio μ_p^* (e.g. $\mu_p = 10$ percent).

2. Arbitrarily choose the proportions of wealth to invest in each asset $(x_i)_1$ $(i = 1, 2, \ldots n)$ such that μ_p is achieved (using equation (2.15)).

3. Work out the variance or standard deviation of this portfolio $(\sigma_p)_1$ with these values of $(x_i)_1$ using equation (2.17).

4. Repeat (2) and (3) with a new set of $(x_i)_2$ if $(\sigma_p)_2 < (\sigma_p)_1$ then discard the set $(x_i)_1$ in favour of $(x_i)_2$ (and vice versa).

5. Repeat (2)–(4) until you obtain that set of asset proportions x_i^* (with $\Sigma x_i^* = 1$) which meets the target rate of return μ_p^* and yields the *minimum portfolio variance* denoted $(\sigma_p)^*$. The assets held in the proportions x_i^* is an *efficient portfolio* and gives *one point* in (μ_p, σ_p) space — point A in Figure 2.6.

6. Choose another arbitrary 'target' rate of return μ_p^{**} ($= 9$ percent say) and repeat the above to obtain the new efficient portfolio with proportions x_i^{**} and *minimum* variance $(\sigma_p)^{**}$ — point B.

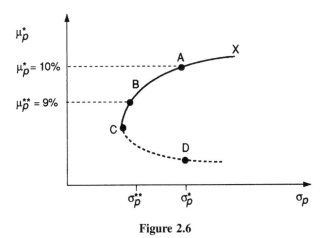

Figure 2.6

We could repeat this exercise for a wide range of values for alternative expected target rates μ_p and hence trace out the curve XABCD. However, only the upper portion of the curve, that is XABC, yields the *set* of efficient portfolios and this is the *efficient frontier*.

It is worth noting at this stage that the general solution to the above problem could (and usually does) involve some x_i^* being negative as well as positive. A positive x_i^* indicates stocks that have been purchased and included in the portfolio (i.e. stocks held 'long'). Negative x_i^* represent stocks held 'short', that is stocks that are owned by someone else (e.g. a broker) that the investor borrows and then sells in the market. He therefore has a negative proportion held in these stocks (i.e. he must return the shares to the broker at some point *in the future*). He uses the proceeds from these *short sales* to augment his holding of other stocks.

Interim Summary

1. Our investor, given expected returns μ_i and the variances σ_i and covariances σ_{ij} (or ρ_{ij}) on all assets, has constructed the efficient frontier. There is only *one* efficient frontier for a given set of $\mu_i, \sigma_i, \sigma_{ij}, (\rho_{ij})$.

2. He has therefore chosen the optimal proportions x_i^* which satisfy the budget constraint $\Sigma x_i^* = 1$ and minimise the risk of the portfolio σ_p for any *given level* of expected return on the portfolio μ_p.

3. He has repeated this procedure and calculated the minimum value of σ_p for each level of expected return μ_p and hence mapped out the (μ_p, σ_p) points which constitute the efficient frontier.

4. Each *point* on the efficient frontier corresponds to a different set of *optimal* proportions $x_1^*, x_2^*, x_3^*, \ldots$ in which the stocks are held.

Points 1–4 constitute the first 'decision' the investor makes in applying the two-fund separation theorem — we now turn to the second part of the decision process.

2.2.4 Borrowing and Lending: The Transformation Line

Our agent can now be allowed to borrow or lend an asset which has the same maturity as the holding period and yields a 'certain' and hence risk-free rate of interest, r. Because

r is fixed over the holding period the variance on the risk-free asset is zero as is its covariance with the set of n risky assets. Thus, the agent can

(i)   invest all of his wealth in risky assets and undertake no lending or borrowing,

(ii) invest less than his total wealth in the risky assets and use the remainder to lend at the risk-free rate,

(iii) invest more than his total wealth in the risky assets by borrowing the additional funds at the risk-free rate. In this case he is said to hold a *levered portfolio*.

The *transformation line* is a relationship between expected return and risk on a specific portfolio. This specific portfolio consists of (i) a riskless asset and (ii) a portfolio of risky assets.

The *transformation line* holds for *any* portfolio consisting of these two assets and it turns out that the relationship between expected return and risk (measured by the standard deviation of the 'new' portfolio) is linear. Suppose we construct a portfolio (call it K) consisting of *one* risky asset with expected return ER_1 and variance σ_1^2 and the riskless asset. Then we can show that the relationship between the return on this new portfolio K and its standard deviation is

$$\mu_k = a + b\sigma_k$$

where 'a' and 'b' are constants and μ_k = expected return on the new portfolio, σ_k = standard deviation on the new portfolio. Similarly we can create another new portfolio 'N' consisting of (i) a set of q risky assets held in proportions x_i ($i = 1, 2, \ldots q$) which together constitute our one risky portfolio and (ii) the risk-free asset. Again we have:

$$\mu_N = \delta_0 + \delta_1 \sigma_N \tag{2.18}$$

To derive the equation of the transformation line let us assume the individual has somehow already chosen a particular combination of *proportions* (i.e. the x_i) of q risky assets (stocks) with actual return R, expected return μ_R and variance σ_R^2. Note that the x_i need not be optimal proportions but can take any values. Now he is considering what proportion of his wealth to put in this one portfolio of q assets and how much to borrow or lend at the riskless rate. He is therefore considering a 'new' portfolio, namely combinations of the risk-free asset and his 'bundle' of risky assets. If he invests a proportion y of his own wealth in the risk-free asset, then he invests $(1 - y)$ in the risky 'bundle'. Denote the actual return and expected return on his new portfolio as R_N and μ_N, respectively.

$$R_N = yr + (1 - y)R \tag{2.19}$$

$$\mu_N = yr + (1 - y)\mu_R \tag{2.20}$$

where (R, μ_R) is the (actual, expected) return on the risky 'bundle' of his portfolio held in stocks. When $y = 1$ all wealth is invested in the risk-free asset and $\mu_N = r$ and when $y = 0$ all wealth is invested in stocks and $\mu_N = \mu_R$. For $y < 0$ the agent borrows money at the risk-free rate r to invest in the risky portfolio. For example, when $y = -0.5$ and initial wealth = \$100, the individual borrows \$50 (at an interest rate r) but invests \$150 in stocks (i.e. a levered position).

Since r is known and fixed over the holding period then the standard deviation of this 'new' portfolio depends only on the standard deviation of the risky portfolio of stocks σ_R. From (2.19) and (2.20) we have

$$\sigma_N^2 = E(R_N - \mu_N)^2 = (1 - y)^2 E(R - \mu_R)^2 \tag{2.21}$$

Hence

$$\sigma_N = (1 - y)\sigma_R \tag{2.22}$$

where σ_R is the standard deviation of the return on the set of risky assets. Equations (2.20) and (2.22) are both definitional but it is useful to rearrange them into a single equation in terms of mean and standard deviation (μ_N, σ_N) of the 'new' portfolio. From (2.22)

$$(1 - y) = \sigma_N/\sigma_R \tag{2.23}$$

$$y = 1 - (\sigma_N/\sigma_R) \tag{2.24}$$

Substituting for y and $(1 - y)$ from (2.23) and (2.24) in (2.20) gives the identity:

$$\mu_N = r + \left[\frac{\mu_R - r}{\sigma_R}\right] \sigma_N = \delta_0 + \delta_1\sigma_N \tag{2.25}$$

where $\delta_0 = r$ and $\delta_1 = (\mu_R - r)/\sigma_R$. Thus for *any* portfolio consisting of two assets, one of which is a risky asset (portfolio) and the other is a risk-free asset, the relationship between the expected return on this new portfolio μ_N and its standard error σ_N *is linear* with slope given by δ_1 and intercept $= r$. Equation (2.25) is, of course, an identity, there is no behaviour involved. $(\mu_R - r)$ is always positive since otherwise no one would hold the set of risky assets.

When a portfolio consists only of *n risky* assets, then as we have seen the efficient opportunity set in return-standard deviation space is curved (see Figure 2.6). However, the opportunity set for a two-asset portfolio consisting of a risk-free asset and *any* single risky portfolio is a positive straight line. This should not be unduly confusing since the portfolios considered in the two cases are different and in the case of the 'efficient set' the curve is derived under an optimising condition and is not just a rearrangement of (two) identities.

Equation (2.25) says that μ_N increases with (σ_N/σ_R). This arises because from (2.23) an increase in σ_N/σ_R simply implies an increase in the proportion of wealth held in the risky asset (i.e. $1 - y$) and since ER $> r$ this raises the expected return on the new portfolio μ_N. Similarly for a given $(\sigma_N/\sigma_R) = (1 - y)$ (see equation (2.23)), an increase in the expected excess return on the risky asset $(\mu_R - r)$ increases the overall portfolio return μ_N. This is simply because here, the investor holds a fixed proportion $(1 - y)$ in the risky asset but the excess return on the latter is higher.

We can see from (2.25) that when all wealth is held in the set of risky assets $y = 0$ and hence $\sigma_N = \sigma_R$ and this is designated the 100 percent equity portfolio (point X, Figure 2.7). When all wealth is invested in the risk-free asset $y = 1$ and $\mu_N = r$ (since $\sigma_N/\sigma_R = 0$ from (2.33)). At points between r and X, the individual holds some of his initial wealth in the risk-free asset and some in the equity portfolio. At points like Z the individual holds a levered portfolio (i.e. he borrows some funds at a rate r and also uses all his own wealth to invest in equities).

2.3   DERIVATION OF THE CAPM

2.3.1   The Optimal Portfolio

The transformation line gives us the risk-return relationship for *any* portfolio consisting of a combination of investment in the risk-free asset and any 'bundle' of stocks. There

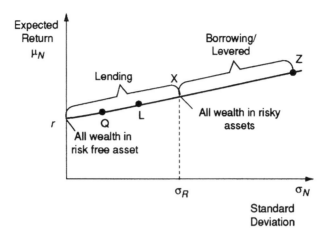

Figure 2.7 The Transformation Line.

is no behavioural or optimisation by agents behind the derivation of the transformation line: it is an identity. At each point on a given transformation line the agent holds the risky assets in the *same* fixed proportions x_i. Suppose point X (Figure 2.7) represents a combination of $x_i = 20$ percent, 25 percent and 55 percent in the three risky securities of firms 'alpha', 'beta' and 'gamma'. Then points Q, L and Z also represent the same proportions of the risky assets. The only 'quantity' that varies along the transformation line is the proportion held in the *one* risky bundle of assets relative to that held in the risk-free asset.

The investor can borrow or lend and be anywhere along the transformation line rZ. (Exactly where he ends up along rZ depends on his preferences for risk versus return but as we shall see this consideration does not enter the analysis until much later.) For example, point Q in Figure (2.8) might represent 40 percent in the riskless asset and 60 percent in the bundle of risky securities. Hence an investor with \$100 would at point Q hold \$40

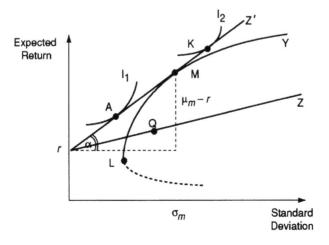

Figure 2.8 Portfolio Choice.

in the risk-free asset and $60 in the risky assets made up of $0.2 \times \$60 = \$12$ in alpha, $0.25 \times \$60 = \$15$ in beta and $0.55 \times \$60 = \$33$ in the gamma securities.

Although an investor (see Figure 2.8) can attain any point along rZ, *any* investor (regardless of his preferences) would prefer to be on the transformation line rZ'. This is because at any point on rZ' the investor has a greater expected return for any given level of risk compared with points on rZ. In fact because rZ' is tangent to the efficient frontier it provides the investor with the best possible set of opportunities. Point M represents a 'bundle' of stocks held in certain *fixed* proportions. As M is on the efficient frontier the proportions x_i held in risky assets are optimal (i.e. the x_i^* referred to earlier). An investor can be anywhere along rZ', but M is always a fixed bundle of stocks (or rather fixed proportions of stocks) held by *all* investors. Hence point M is known as the *market portfolio* and rZ' is known as the *capital market line* (CML). The CML is therefore that transformation line which is tangential to the efficient frontier.

Investor's preferences only determine at which point along the CML, rZ', each *individual* investor ends up. For example, an investor with little or no risk aversion would end up at a point like K where he borrows money (at r) to augment his own wealth and he then invests all of these funds in the bundle of securities represented by M (but he still holds *all* his risky stocks in the fixed proportions x_i^*).

Separation Principle

Thus the investor makes two separate decisions

(i) He uses his knowledge of expected returns, variances and covariances to calculate the efficient set of stocks represented by the efficient frontier YML (Figure 2.8). He then determines point M as the *point of tangency* of the line from r to the efficient frontier. All this is accomplished without any recourse to the individual's preferences. *All* investors, regardless of preferences (but with the same view about expected returns, etc.) will 'home in' on the portfolio proportions (x_i^*) of the risky securities represented by M. All investors hold the *market portfolio* or more correctly all investors hold their risky assets in the same proportions as their relative value in the market. Thus if the value of ICI shares constitutes 10 percent of total stock market valuation then each investor holds 10 percent of his own risky portfolio in ICI shares.

(ii) The investor now determines how he will combine the market portfolio of risky assets with the riskless asset. This decision does depend on his subjective risk-return preferences. At a point to the left of M the *individual* investor is reasonably risk averse and holds a percentage of his wealth in the market portfolio (in the fixed optimal proportions x_i^*) and a percentage in the risk-free asset. If the *individual* investor is less risk averse then he ends up to the right of M such as K with a levered portfolio (i.e. he borrows to increase his holdings of the market portfolio in excess of his own initial wealth). At M the individual puts all his own wealth into the market portfolio and neither borrows nor lends at the risk-free rate.

The CML, rZ', which is tangential at M, the market portfolio, must have the form given by (2.25), that is:

$$\mu_N = r + \left[\frac{\mu_m - r}{\sigma_m} \right] \sigma_N \tag{2.26}$$

The Market Price of Risk

The amounts of the riskless asset and the bundle of risky assets held by any individual investor depends on his tastes or preferences. An investor who is relatively risk averse, with indifference curve I_1, will put some of his wealth in the risk-free asset and some in the market portfolio (point A, Figure 2.8). A less risk averse investor will end up borrowing in order to invest more in the risky assets than allowed by his initial wealth (point K, Figure 2.8). However, one thing all investors have in common is that the optimal portfolio of risky assets for all investors lies on the CML and for each investor

$$\text{slope of CML} = (\mu_m - r)/\sigma_m$$

$$= \text{slope of the indifference curve} \qquad (2.27)$$

The slope of the CML is often referred to as the 'market price of risk'. The slope of the indifference curve is referred to as the marginal rate of substitution, MRS, since it is the rate at which the individual will 'trade off' more return for more risk.

All investors portfolios lie on the CML and therefore they all face the same market price of risk. From (2.27) and Figure (2.8) it is clear that for *both* investors at A and K the market price of risk equals the MRS. The latter measures the individual's *subjective* trade off or 'taste' between risk and return. Hence *in equilibrium, all* individual's have the same trade-off between risk and return.

The derivation of the efficient frontier and the market portfolio have been conducted in terms of the standard deviation being used as a measure of risk. When risk is measured in terms of the variance of the portfolio then

$$\lambda_m = (\mu_m - r)/\sigma_m^2 \qquad (2.28)$$

is also frequently referred to as 'the market price of risk'. Since σ_m and σ_m^2 are conceptually very similar, this need not cause undue confusion. (See Roll (1977) for a discussion of the differences in the representation of the CAPM when risk is measured in these two different ways.)

Market Equilibrium

In order that the efficient frontier be the same for *all* investors they must have *homogeneous expectations* about the underlying market variables $\mu_i = ER_i$, σ_i^2 and σ_{ij}. (Of course, this does *not* mean that they have the same degree of risk aversion.) Hence with homogeneous expectations *all* investors hold *all* the risky assets in the proportions given by point M, the market portfolio. The assumption of homogeneous expectations is crucial in producing a *market equilibrium* where all risky assets are willingly held in the optimal proportions x_i^* given by M or in other words, in producing *market clearing*. For example, if the price of shares of 'alpha' is temporarily low and those of delta shares temporarily high, then all investors will wish to hold more alpha shares and less delta shares. The price of the former rises and the latter falls as investors with homogeneous expectations buy alpha and sell delta shares.

In What Proportions are the Assets Held?

When we allow borrowing and lending we know that the individual will hold the set of risky assets in the optimal proportions represented by the point M. He holds a portfolio (the x_i^*s) on the efficient frontier since he wishes to minimise portfolio variance for any given expected return. All investors choose the *proportions* in risky assets represented by M because by borrowing or lending at r this enables them to reach the *highest* transformation line given the efficient set or 'bundles' of risky assets. (This will ultimately allow *each* individual to be on his *own* highest indifference curve.)

But a problem remains. How can we calculate the risky asset proportions x_i^* represented by point M? So far we have only shown how to calculate each set of x_i^* for each point on the efficient frontier. We have not demonstrated how the proportions x_i^* for the particular point M are derived. This can, in fact, be quite a technically complicated process. To illustrate, note from Figure 2.8 that for *any* transformation line:

$$\tan \alpha = \left[\frac{ER_p - r}{\sigma_p} \right] \tag{2.29}$$

where 'p' represents *any* risky portfolio, and as we have seen ER_p and σ_p depend on x_i (as well as the known values of μ_i and σ_{ij} for the risky assets). Hence to achieve point M equation (2.29) can be maximised with respect to x_i, subject to the budget constraint $\Sigma x_i = 1$ and this yields the optimum proportions x_i^*. Some of the x_i^* may be less than zero, indicating short selling of assets. If short sales are not allowed then the additional constraint, $x_i^* \geqslant 0$ for all i, is required and to find the optimal x_i^* requires a solution using quadratic programming techniques.

2.3.2   Determining Equilibrium Returns

Let us now use the ideas developed above to derive the CAPM equation representing the equilibrium return on each security. We do so using a mixture of graphical analysis (Figure 2.9) and simple algebra (see Appendix 2.1 for a more formal derivation). The slope of the CML is constant and represents the market price of risk which is the same for all investors.

$$\text{slope of CML} = \frac{\mu_m - r}{\sigma_m} \tag{2.30}$$

We now undertake a thought experiment whereby we 'move' from M (which contains *all* assets in fixed proportions) and create an artificial portfolio by investing some of the funds

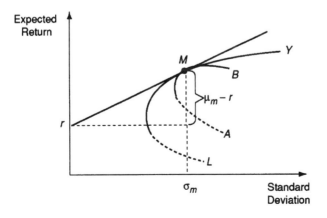

Figure 2.9   The Market Portfolio.

at present in the assets represented by M, in any risky security i. This artificial portfolio (call it 'p') consists of two *risky* portfolios of proportions x_i in asset i and $(1 - x_i)$ in the portfolio at M. This portfolio 'p' has expected return μ_p and standard deviation σ_p given by:

$$\mu_p = x_i \mu_i + (1 - x_i)\mu_m \tag{2.31}$$

$$\sigma_p = \left[x^2 \sigma_i^2 + (1 - x_i)^2 \sigma_m^2 + 2x_i(1 - x_i)\sigma_{im}\right]^{1/2} \tag{2.32}$$

The portfolio 'p' lies along the curve AMB and is tangent at M. It doesn't cross the efficient frontier since the latter by definition is the *minimum* variance portfolio for any given level of expected return. Note also that at M there is no borrowing or lending. Altering x_i and moving along MA we are 'shorting' security i and investing more than 100 percent of the funds in portfolio M.

The key element in this derivation is to note that at point M the curves LMY and AMB coincide and since M is the market portfolio $x_i = 0$. To find the slope of the efficient frontier at M, we require

$$\left[\frac{\partial \mu_p}{\partial \sigma_p}\right]_{x_i=0} = \left[\frac{\partial \mu_p}{\partial x_i}\right]\left[\frac{\partial \sigma_p}{\partial x_i}\right]^{-1} \tag{2.33}$$

where all the derivatives are evaluated at $x_i = 0$. From (2.31) and (2.32):

$$\left[\frac{\partial \mu_p}{\partial x_i}\right]_{x_i=0} = \mu_i - \mu_m \tag{2.34}$$

$$\left[\frac{\partial \sigma_p}{\partial x_i}\right] = \frac{1}{2\sigma_p}[2x_i\sigma_i^2 - 2(1 - x_i)\sigma_m^2 + 2\sigma_{im} - 4x_i\sigma_{im}] \tag{2.35}$$

At $x_i = 0$ (point M) we know $\sigma_p = \sigma_m$ and hence

$$\left[\frac{\partial \sigma_p}{\partial x_i}\right]_{x_i=0} = [\sigma_{im} - \sigma_m^2]/\sigma_m \tag{2.36}$$

Substituting in (2.34) and (2.36) in (2.33):

$$\left[\frac{\partial \mu_p}{\partial \sigma_p}\right]_{x_i=0} = \frac{(\mu_i - \mu_m)\sigma_m}{\sigma_{im} - \sigma_m^2} \tag{2.37}$$

But at M the slope of the efficient frontier (equation (2.37)) equals the slope of the CML (equation (2.30)):

$$\frac{(\mu_i - \mu_m)\sigma_m}{(\sigma_{im}^2 - \sigma_m^2)} = \frac{\mu_m - r}{\sigma_m} \tag{2.38}$$

From (2.38) we obtain the CAPM relationship:

$$\mu_i = r + (\sigma_{im}/\sigma_m^2)(\mu_m - r) \tag{2.39}$$

Using alternative symbols:

$$ER_i = r + \left[\frac{\text{cov}(R_i, R^m)}{\text{var}(R^m)}\right](ER^m - r) \tag{2.40}$$

Hence when borrowing and lending in the risk-free asset is allowed then in order for asset i to be willingly held, it must command an *expected or required return* in the market given by the CAPM relationship (2.40). We now *define* the *beta* for asset i as

$$\beta_i = \frac{\text{cov}(R_i, R^m)}{\text{var}(R^m)} \tag{2.41}$$

and the CAPM relationship is:

$$ER_i = r + \beta_i(ER^m - r) \tag{2.42}$$

There is one further rearrangement of (2.42) to consider. Substituting for $(ER^m - r)$ from (2.28) in (2.24)

$$ER_i = r + \lambda_m \text{cov}(R_i, R^m) \tag{2.43}$$

The CAPM therefore gives three equivalent ways represented by (2.40), (2.42) and (2.43) of expressing the equilibrium required return on any single asset or subset of assets in the market portfolio.

2.3.3 Beta and Systematic Risk

If we define the extra return on asset i over and above the risk-free rate as a *risk premium*:

$$ER_i \equiv r + rp_i \tag{2.44}$$

then the CAPM gives an explicit form for the risk premium

$$rp_i = \beta_i(ER^m - r) \tag{2.45}$$

or equivalently:

$$rp_i = \lambda_m \text{cov}(R_i, R^m) \tag{2.46}$$

The CAPM predicts that only the covariance of returns between asset i and the market portfolio influences the excess return on asset i. No additional variables such as the dividend price ratio, the size of the firm or the earnings price ratio should influence expected excess returns. All changes in the portfolio risk of asset i are summed up in changes in $\text{cov}(R_i, R^m)$. The expected excess return on asset i relative to asset j is given by β_i/β_j since

$$\frac{(ER_i - r)}{(ER_j - r)} = \frac{\beta_i}{\beta_j} \tag{2.47}$$

Given the definition of β_i in (2.41) we see that the market portfolio has a beta of 1. For any *individual* security that has a $\beta_i = 1$, then its expected excess return moves one-for-one with the market excess return $(ER^m - r)$ and could be described as a neutral stock. For $\beta_i > 1$, the stock's expected return moves more than the market return and could be described as an aggressive stock, while for $\beta_i < 1$ we have a defensive stock. The CAPM only explains the excess rate of return relative to the excess rate of return on the market portfolio (equation (2.42)): it is not a model of the absolute price level of individual stocks.

The *systematic risk* of a portfolio is defined as risk which cannot be diversified away by adding extra securities to the portfolio (this is why it is also known as 'non-diversifiable', 'portfolio' or 'market risk'). There is always some non-zero risk even in a well-diversified portfolio and this is because of the covariance terms. To see this note that

$$\sigma_p^2 = \sum_{i=1}^{n} x_i^2 \sigma_i^2 + \sum_{i}^{n} \sum_{j}^{n} x_i x_j \sigma_{ij} \tag{2.48}$$

With n assets there are n variance terms and $n(n-1)/2$ covariance terms that contribute to the variance of the portfolio. The number of covariance terms rises much faster than the number of assets in the portfolio and the number of variance terms (both of the latter increase at the same rate, n). To illustrate this dependence on the covariance term consider a simplified portfolio where all assets are held in the same proportion ($x_i = 1/n$) and where all variances and covariances are constant (i.e. $\sigma_i^2 = $ var and $\sigma_{ij} = $ cov, where 'var' and 'cov' are constant). Then (2.48) becomes

$$\sigma_p^2 = n \left[\frac{1}{n^2} \text{var} \right] + n(n-1) \cdot \left[\frac{1}{n^2} \text{cov} \right] = \frac{1}{n} \text{var} + \left[1 - \frac{1}{n} \right] \text{cov} \tag{2.49}$$

It follows that as $n \to \infty$ the influence of the variance term approaches zero and the variance of the portfolio equals the (constant) covariance (cov) of the assets. Thus the variance of the individual securities is diversified away. However, the covariance terms cannot be diversified away and the latter (in a loose sense) give rise to systematic risk, which is represented by the beta of the security.

We can rearrange the definition of the variance of a portfolio as follows:

$$\begin{aligned} \sigma_m^2 = {} & x_1(x_1\sigma_{11} + x_2\sigma_{12} + x_3\sigma_{13} + \cdots + x_n\sigma_{1n}) \\ & + x_2(x_1\sigma_{21} + x_2\sigma_{22} + x_3\sigma_{23} + \cdots + x_n\sigma_{2n}) \\ & + x_3(x_1\sigma_{31} + x_2\sigma_{32} + x_3\sigma_{33} + \cdots + x_n\sigma_{3n}) \\ & + x_n(x_1\sigma_{n1} + x_2\sigma_{n2} + \cdots + x_n\sigma_{nn}) \end{aligned} \tag{2.50}$$

where we have rewritten σ_i^2 as σ_{ii}. If the x_i are those for the market portfolio then in equilibrium we can denote the variance as σ_m^2.

The contribution of security 2 to the portfolio variance may be interpreted as the bracketed term in the second line of (2.50) which is then 'weighted' by the proportion x_2 of security 2 held in the portfolio. The bracketed term contains the covariance between security 2 with all other securities including itself (i.e. the term $x_2\sigma_{22}$) and each covariance is weighted by the proportion of each asset in the market portfolio. It is easy to show that the term in brackets in the second line of (2.50) is the covariance of security 2 with the return on the market portfolio R^m:

$$\begin{aligned} \text{cov}(R_2, R^m) &= E(R^m - \mu_m)(R_2 - \mu_2) \\ &= E \left[\sum_{i=1}^{n} x_i (R_i - \mu_i)(R_2 - \mu_2) \right] \\ &= x_1\sigma_{21} + x_2\sigma_{22} + x_3\sigma_{23} + \cdots + x_n\sigma_{n2} \end{aligned} \tag{2.51}$$

It is also easy to show that the contribution of security 2 to the risk of the portfolio is given by the above expression since $\partial \sigma_m^2 / \partial x_2 = 2\,\text{cov}(R_2, R^m)$. Similarly, we can replace the third bracketed term in (2.50) by $\text{cov}(R_3, R^m)$ and so on, so that the variance of the market portfolio may be written:

$$\sigma_m^2 = x_1 \text{cov}(R_1, R^m) + x_2 \text{cov}(R_2, R^m) + \cdots + x_n \text{cov}(R_n, R^m) \qquad (2.52)$$

Now, rearranging the expression for the definition of β_i:

$$\text{cov}(R_i, R^m) = \beta_i \sigma_m^2 \qquad (2.53)$$

and substituting (2.53) in (2.52) gives:

$$\sum_{i=1}^{n} x_i \beta_i = 1 \qquad (2.54)$$

The β_i of a security therefore measures the *relative* impact of security i on the risk of the portfolio of stocks, as a proportion of the total variance of the portfolio. A security with $\beta_i = 0$ when added to the portfolio has zero *additional* proportionate influence on total variance, whereas $\beta_i < 0$ reduces the variance of the portfolio. Of course, the greater the amount of security i held (i.e. the larger is the absolute value of x_i) the more the impact of β_i on total portfolio variance, *ceteris paribus*. Since an asset with a small value of β_i considerably reduces the overall variance of a risky portfolio, it will be willingly held even though the security has a relatively low expected return. All investors are trading off risk, which they dislike, against expected return, which they like. Assets which reduce overall portfolio risk therefore command relatively low returns but are nevertheless willingly held in equilibrium.

2.3.4 The Predictability of Equilibrium Returns

This section outlines how our equilibrium model of returns, namely the CAPM, is consistent with returns being both variable and predictable. The CAPM applied to the *market portfolio* implies that equilibrium expected (excess) returns are given by:

$$E_t R_{t+1}^m - r_t = \lambda E_t [\sigma_{mt+1}^2] \qquad (2.55)$$

where subscripts 't' have been added to highlight the fact that these variables will change over time. From (2.55) we see that equilibrium excess returns will vary over time provided the conditional variance of the forecast error of returns is not constant. From a theoretical standpoint the CAPM is silent on whether the conditional variance is time varying. For the sake of argument suppose it is an *empirical fact* that periods of turbulence or great uncertainty in the stock market are generally followed by further periods of turbulence. Similarly, assume that periods of tranquillity are generally followed by further periods of tranquillity. A simple mathematical way of demonstrating such *persistence* in volatility is to assume volatility follows an autoregressive AR(1) process. When volatility (i.e. the second moment of the distribution) is autoregressive this process is referred to as autoregressive conditional heteroscedasticity or ARCH for short:

$$\sigma_{t+1}^2 = \alpha \sigma_t^2 + v_t \qquad (2.56)$$

where v_t is a zero mean (white noise) error process independent of σ_t^2. The best forecast of σ_{t+1}^2 at time t is:

$$E_t \sigma_{t+1}^2 = \alpha \sigma_t^2 \qquad (2.57)$$

The CAPM plus ARCH gives:

$$E_t R_{t+1}^m - r_t = \lambda \alpha \sigma_t^2 \tag{2.58}$$

and equilibrium expected returns are:

(i) non-constant
(ii) depend on information available at time t, namely σ_t^2.

Hence we have an equilibrium model in which expected returns vary and depend on information at time t, namely σ_t^2. The reason expected returns vary with σ_t^2 is quite straightforward. The conditional variance $\alpha \sigma_t^2$ is the investor's best guess of next periods' systematic risk in the market $E_t \sigma_{t+1}^2$. In equilibrium such risks are rewarded with a higher expected return.

The above model may be contrasted with a much simpler hypothesis, namely that equilibrium expected returns are *constant*. Rejection of the latter model, for example, by finding that actual returns depend on information Ω_t at time t, or earlier (e.g. dividend price ratio), may be because the variables in Ω_t are correlated with the omitted variable σ_t^2 which occurs in the 'true' model of expected returns (i.e. CAPM + ARCH).

The above argument about the predictability of returns can be repeated for the equilibrium excess return on an *individual* asset

$$E_t R_{it+1} - r_t = \lambda \operatorname{cov}(R_{it+1}, R_{t+1}^m) \tag{2.59}$$

If the covariance term is, in part, predictable from information at time t then equilibrium returns on asset i will be non-constant and predictable. Hence the empirical finding that returns are predictable need not necessarily imply that investors are irrational or are ignoring potentially profitable opportunities in the market. It is important to bear this in mind when discussing certain empirical tests of the so-called efficient markets hypothesis (EMH) in Chapter 5.

2.4 SUMMARY

The basic one-period CAPM seeks to establish the optimal proportions in which risky assets are held. Since the risky assets are all willingly held, the CAPM can also be used to establish the determinants of equilibrium returns on all of the individual assets in the portfolio. The key results from the one-period CAPM are:

- All investors hold their risky assets in the same proportions (x_i^*) regardless of their preferences for risk versus return. These optimal proportions constitute the market portfolio.

- Investors' preferences enter in the second stage of the decision process, namely the choice between the fixed bundle of risky securities and the risk-free asset. The more risk averse is the individual the smaller the proportion of his wealth he will place in the bundle of risky assets.

- The CAPM implies that in equilibrium the expected excess return on any *single* risky asset $ER_i - r$ is proportional to the excess return on the market portfolio, $ER^m - r$. The constant of proportionality is the asset's beta, where $\beta_i = \operatorname{cov}(R_i, R_m)/\sigma_m^2$.

- The CAPM does not necessarily imply that equilibrium returns are constant. If the covariance, $cov(R_i, R_m)$, varies over time then so will equilibrium returns. In addition, equilibrium returns may be predictable from information available at time t. This will arise if the variances and covariances, which measure 'risk' in the CAPM model, are themselves predictable.

APPENDIX 2.1   DERIVATION OF THE CAPM

The expected return and standard deviation for any portfolio 'p' consisting of n risky assets and a risk-free asset are:

$$ER_p = \sum_1^n x_i ER_i + \left[1 - \sum_1^n x_i\right] r \tag{1}$$

$$\sigma_p = \sqrt{\sum_{i=1}^n x_i^2 \sigma_i^2 + 2 \sum_{i=1}^n \sum_{\substack{j=1 \\ i \neq j}}^n x_i x_j \, cov(x_i, x_j)} \tag{2}$$

where x_i = proportion of wealth held in asset i. The CAPM is the solution to the problem of minimising σ_p subject to a given level of expected return ER_p. The Lagrangian is:

$$C = \sigma_p + \Psi \left[ER_p - \sum x_i ER_i + \left(1 - \sum x_i\right) r\right] \tag{3}$$

Choosing x_i ($i = 1, 2, \ldots n$) to minimise C gives a set of first-order conditions (FOC) of the form:

$$\partial C / \partial x_1 = \tfrac{1}{2}(\sigma_p^2)^{-1/2} \left[2x_1 \sigma_1^2 + 2 \sum_{j=2}^n x_j \, cov(R_1, R_j)\right] - \Psi(ER_1 - r) = 0$$

$$\partial C / \partial x_2 = \tfrac{1}{2}(\sigma_p^2)^{-1/2} \left[2x_2 \sigma_2^2 + 2 \sum_{\substack{j=1 \\ j \neq 2}}^n x_j \, cov(R_2, R_j)\right] - \Psi(ER_2 - r) = 0$$

$$\partial C / \partial x_n = \tfrac{1}{2}(\sigma_p^2)^{-1/2} \left[2x_n \sigma_n^2 + 2 \sum_{\substack{j=1 \\ j \neq n}}^n x_j \, cov(R_n, R_j)\right] - \Psi(ER_n - r) = 0 \tag{4}$$

Differentiation with respect to Ψ gives:

$$\partial C / \partial \Psi = ER_p - \sum_{i=1}^n x_i ER_i - \left(1 - \sum_{i=1}^n x_i\right) r = 0 \tag{5}$$

Multiplying the first equation in (4) by x_1, the second by x_2, etc. and summing over all equations gives:

$$\sigma_p = \Psi \left[\sum_{i=1}^n x_i ER_i - \sum_{i=1}^n x_i r\right] = \Psi \left[\sum_{i=1}^n x_i ER_i + \left(1 - \sum_{i=1}^n x_i\right) r - r\right] \tag{6}$$

At the point where $\sum_{i=1}^n x_i = 1$ gives:

$$\sigma_m = \Psi(ER_m - r) \tag{7}$$

$$1/\Psi = (ER_m - r)/\sigma_m \tag{8}$$

where $ER_m = (\Sigma x_i ER_i)$ and m denotes the market portfolio. From (8) we see that the term $1/\Psi$ is the slope of the capital market line (CML). The term $1/\Psi$ measures the price of a unit of risk, which is the same for all investors. (In the above the fact that $\Sigma x_i = 1$ doesn't restrict the results since the slope of the capital market line is identical at all points.)

Since the FOC in (4) hold for all investors independent of their 'tastes' we can use this to derive the CAPM expression for equilibrium returns on each individual share in the portfolio. The ith equation in (4) at the point $\sum_{i=1}^{n} x_i = 1$ is:

$$ER_i = r + \frac{1}{\Psi \sigma_m} \left[x_i \sigma_i^2 + \sum_{\substack{j=1 \\ i \neq j}}^{n} x_j \operatorname{cov}(R_i, R_j) \right] \tag{9}$$

Substitute for $(1/\Psi)$ from (8) in (9):

$$ER_i = r + \frac{ER_m - r}{\sigma_m^2} \left[x_i \sigma_i^2 + \sum_{\substack{j=1 \\ i \neq j}}^{n} x_j \operatorname{cov}(R_i, R_j) \right] \tag{10}$$

Note that:

$$\operatorname{cov}(R_i, R_m) = \operatorname{cov}[R_i, (x_1 R_1 + x_2 R_2 + \cdots + x_n R_n)] = x_i \sigma_i^2 + \sum_{\substack{j=1 \\ i \neq j}}^{n} x_j \operatorname{cov}(R_i, R_j) \tag{11}$$

and substituting (11) in (10) we obtain the CAPM expression for the equilibrium expected return on asset i:

$$ER_i = r + (ER_m - r)\beta_i \tag{12}$$

where $\beta_i = \operatorname{cov}(R_i, R_m)/\sigma_m^2$.

3
Modelling Equilibrium Returns

The last chapter dealt at some length with the principles behind the simple one-period CAPM. In this chapter this model is placed in the wider context of alternative models that seek to explain equilibrium asset returns. The mean-variance analysis that underlies the CAPM also allows one to determine the optimal asset proportions (the x_i^*) for the risky and risk-free asset. This chapter highlights the close relationship between the mean-variance analysis of Chapter 2 and a strand of the monetary economics literature that deals with the determination of asset demands for a risk averse investor. This mean-variance model of asset demands is elaborated and used in later chapters. In this chapter we therefore look at the following interrelated set of ideas.

- Some of the restrictive assumptions of the basic CAPM model are relaxed though the general principles of the model still largely apply. Expected returns on asset i still depend on the asset's beta and on the excess return on market portfolio.

- The mean-variance criterion is used to derive a risk aversion model of asset demands and this model is then compared with the CAPM.

- We examine how the CAPM can be used to provide alternative performance indicators to assess the abilities of portfolio managers.

- The arbitrage pricing theory APT provides an alternative model of equilibrium returns to the CAPM and we assess its strengths and weaknesses.

- We examine the single index model and early empirical tests of the CAPM.

3.1 EXTENSIONS OF THE CAPM

The standard one-period CAPM is derived under somewhat restrictive assumptions. It is possible to relax some of these assumptions and yet still retain the basic conceptual framework of the CAPM together with its predictions for the determinants of equilibrium returns. In any economic model there is often a trade-off between 'simplicity' in terms of the theory and 'fruitfulness' in terms of a good statistical model. The popularity of the standard CAPM arises in part because it is relatively tractable when it comes to testing the model (and it does have some empirical validity). Inevitably when some of its restrictive assumptions are relaxed, the resulting models become more complex, less tractable and for some, less mathematically elegant. In interpreting the empirical results from the standard CAPM it is important to be aware of the less restrictive variants of the

CAPM as these provide insights into why the standard CAPM may not always perform well in statistical tests. Each of the variants is dealt with in turn.

3.1.1 Zero-Beta CAPM: No Riskless Asset

Although investors can lend as much as they like at the riskless rate (e.g. by purchasing government bills and bonds), usually they cannot borrow unlimited amounts. In addition, if the future course of price inflation is uncertain then there is no riskless borrowing in real terms (riskless lending is still possible in this case, if government issues index-linked government bonds).

This section reworks the CAPM under the assumption that there is no riskless borrowing or lending (although short sales are still allowed). This gives rise to the so-called *zero-beta* CAPM where the equilibrium expected return on any asset (or portfolio i) is given by:

$$ER_i = ER^z + (ER^m - ER^z)\beta_i \tag{3.1}$$

where ER^z is the expected return on the so-called zero-beta portfolio (see below).

To get some idea of this rather peculiar entity called the zero-beta portfolio, consider the *security market line* (SML) of Figure 3.1. The SML is a graph of the expected return on a set of securities against their beta values. From the standard CAPM we know that $(ER_i - r)/\beta_i$ is the same for all securities (and equals $ER^m - r$). Hence if the CAPM is correct all assets should, in equilibrium, lie along the SML.

$$ER_i = r + \beta_i(ER^m - r)$$

If a security C existed it would be preferred to security B because it offers a higher expected return but has the same systematic risk (i.e. value of β_i). Investors would short security B and buy security C thus raising the current price of C until its expected return (from t to $t + 1$) equalled that on security B.

In general the equation of the SML is that of a straight line:

$$ER_i = a + b\beta_i \tag{3.2}$$

and we can use this heuristically to derive a variant of the CAPM and the SML when there is no risk-free asset. A convenient point to focus on is where the SML cuts the vertical axis (i.e. at the point where $\beta_i = 0$). The intercept in equation (3.2) occurs at a

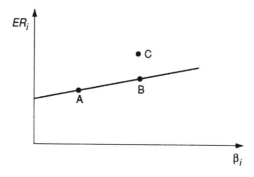

Figure 3.1 Security Market Line.

point where $\beta_i = 0$. If we denote the expected rate of return at the point $\beta_i = 0$ as ER^z then from (3.2) we have

$$ER^z = a \tag{3.3}$$

The SML holds for the return on the market portfolio ER^m and noting that, for the market portfolio $\beta_i = 1$, we have

$$ER^m = ER^z + b(1) \quad \text{or} \quad b = ER^m - ER^z \tag{3.4}$$

Hence the expected return on *any* security (on the SML) may be written

$$ER_i = ER^z + (ER^m - ER^z)\beta_i \tag{3.5}$$

where ER^z is the rate of return on *any* portfolio that has a zero-beta coefficient (with respect to any other portfolio that is mean-variance efficient).

A more rigorous proof (see Levy-Sarnat, 1984) derives the above equilibrium returns equation in a similar fashion to that of the standard CAPM. The only difference is that with no borrowing and lending, investors choose the x_i^* to minimise portfolio variance σ_p^2 subject to:

$$\sum_{i=1}^{n} x_i = 1 \qquad \text{(budget constraint: no borrowing/lending)}$$

$$\overline{ER}^p = \Sigma x_i ER_i \quad \text{(a given level of expected return)}$$

whereas in the standard CAPM the budget constraint and the definition of the expected return are slightly different (see Appendix 2.1) because of the presence of a risk-free asset.

We can represent our zero-beta portfolio in terms of our usual graphical analysis using the efficient frontier (Figure 3.2). Portfolio Z is constructed by drawing a tangent to the efficient frontier at M, and where it cuts the horizontal axis at ER^z we construct a horizontal line to Z. All risky portfolios on the SML obey equation (3.5), including portfolio Z. At point X, $ER_i = ER^z$ by construction, hence from (3.5) it follows that the β for portfolio Z must be zero (given that $ER^m \neq ER^z$ by construction). Hence:

$$\beta_z = \frac{\text{cov}(R^z, R^m)}{\text{var}(R^m)} = 0 \tag{3.6}$$

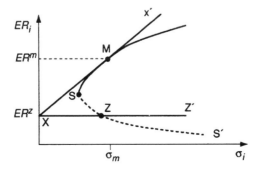

Figure 3.2 Zero-beta CAPM.

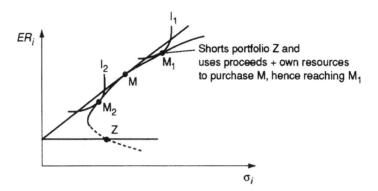

Figure 3.3 Asset Choice: No Risk Free Asset.

By construction, a zero-beta portfolio has zero covariance with the market portfolio. Since we can measure $cov(R^z, R^m)$ from a sample of data this allows us to 'choose' a zero-beta portfolio. We simply find any portfolio whose return is not correlated with the market portfolio. Note that all portfolios along ZZ' are zero-beta portfolios but Z is also that portfolio which has minimum variance (within this particular set of portfolios). It can also be shown that Z is always an inefficient portfolio (i.e. lies on the segment SS' of the efficient frontier).

Since we chose the portfolio M on the efficient frontier quite arbitrarily then it is possible to construct an infinite number of combinations of various Ms with their corresponding zero-beta counterparts. Hence we lose a key property found in the standard CAPM, namely that *all* investors choose the same *mix* of risky assets, regardless of their preferences. This is a more realistic outcome since we know that individuals do hold different mixes of the risky assets. The equilibrium return on asset i could equally well be represented by (3.5) or by an alternative combination of portfolios M* and Z* with:

$$ER_i = ER^{z^*} + (ER^{m^*} - ER^{z^*})\beta_i^* \tag{3.7}$$

Of course, both equations (3.5) and (3.6) must yield the same expected return for asset i. This result is in contrast to the standard CAPM where the combination (r,M) implies a unique opportunity set. In addition, in the zero-beta CAPM the line XX' does *not* represent the opportunity set available to investors.

Given any two mutual funds M and their corresponding orthogonal risky portfolio Z then all investors can (without borrowing or lending) reach their optimum portfolio by combining these two mutual fund portfolios.

Thus a *separation property* also applies for the zero-beta CAPM. Investors first choose the efficient portfolio M and its inefficient counterpart Z, then in the second step each investor mixes the two portfolios in proportions determined by his *individual* preferences. For example, the investor with indifference curve I_1, will short portfolio Z and invest the proceeds and his own resources in portfolio M thus reaching point M_1. The investor with indifference curve I_2 reaches point M_2 by taking a long position in both portfolios M and Z.

The zero-beta CAPM provides an alternative model of equilibrium returns to the standard CAPM and we investigate its empirical validity in later chapters. The main features of the zero-beta model are as follows:

- With no borrowing or lending at the riskless rate an individual investor can reach his own optimal portfolio (given his preferences) by combining *any* mean-variance efficient portfolio (M) with its corresponding zero-beta portfolio Z.

- A zero-beta portfolio is one which combines risky assets in certain proportions x_i such that the return on this portfolio $ER^z = \Sigma x_i ER_i$ is
  (i)   uncorrelated with the risky portfolio M,
  (ii) the minimum variance portfolio (in the set of portfolios given by (i)).

- The combination of portfolios M and Z is not unique. Nevertheless the equilibrium return on any asset i (or portfolio of assets) is a linear function of ER^z and ER^m and is given by equation (3.5).

3.1.2   Different Lending and Borrowing Rates

Next, consider what is in fact a rather realistic case for many individual investors, namely that the risk-free borrowing rate r_B exceeds the risk-free lending rate r_L. The implications for the CAPM of this assumption are similar to the no-borrowing case, in that all investors no longer hold the same portfolio of risky assets in equilibrium.

In Figure 3.4, if an individual investor is a lender, his optimal portfolio may be anywhere along the straight line segment $r_L L$. If he is a borrower, then the relevant segment is BC. LL' and $r_B B$ are not feasible. Finally, if he neither borrows nor lends, his optimum portfolio lies at any point along the curved section LMB. The market portfolio is (by definition) a weighted average of the portfolios at L, B and *all* the portfolios along the curved segment LMB, held by the set of investors. In Figure 3.4 M represents the market portfolio. We can always construct a zero-beta portfolio for those who neither borrow nor lend and for such an unlevered portfolio the equilibrium return on asset i is given by:

$$ER_i = ER^z + (ER^m - ER^z)\beta_i \tag{3.8}$$

For portfolios held by lenders we have

$$ER_q = r_L + (ER^m - r_L)\beta_{qL} \tag{3.9}$$

where β_{qL} is the beta of the portfolio or security q relative to the lender's optimum unlevered portfolio at L:

$$\beta_{qL} = \text{cov}(R_q, R_L)/\sigma_L^2 \tag{3.10}$$

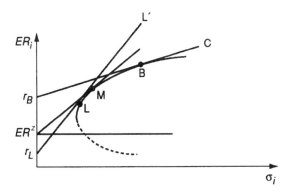

Figure 3.4   Different Borrowing and Lending Rates.

A similar equation to (3.8) holds for borrower portfolios

$$ER_k = r_B + (ER^m - r_B)\beta_{kB} \tag{3.11}$$

Note that *all* lenders hold the *same* risky portfolio of assets at L. Unlevered portfolios, however, differ among individuals depending on the point where their indifference curves are tangent along LMB. Similarly all borrowers hold risky assets in the same proportions as at B but the levered portfolio of any *individual* can be anywhere along B–C.

For large institutional investors it may be the case that the lending rate is not much different from the borrowing rate and that changes in both are dominated by changes in the return on market portfolio (or in the β_i over time, see Part 6). In this case the standard CAPM may provide a reasonable approximation for institutional investors who may also be large players in the market.

3.1.3 Non-Marketable Assets

Some risky assets are not easily marketable yet the standard CAPM, in principle, applies only to the choice between the complete set of *all* risky assets. For example, human capital, namely an individual's future lifetime income, cannot be sold because slavery is illegal. Some assets such as one's house may not for psychological reasons or inertia be considered marketable. When some assets are not marketable the CAPM can be reworked and results in the equilibrium return on asset i being determined by

$$ER_i = r + \beta_i^*(ER^m - r) \tag{3.12}$$

where

$$\beta_i^* = \frac{\text{cov}(R_i, R^m) + (V_N/V_m)\,\text{cov}(R_i, R^N)}{\sigma_m^2 + (V_N/V_m)\,\text{cov}(R^m, R^N)} \tag{3.13}$$

and V_N = value of all non-marketable assets, V_m = value of marketable assets and R^N = one-period rate of return on non-marketable assets.

Our 'new' beta, denoted β_i^*, consists in part of the 'standard-beta' (i.e. $\beta_i = \text{cov}(R_i, R^m)/\sigma_m^2$) but also incorporates a covariance term between the return on the (observed) marketable assets and that on the (unobserved) non-marketable assets, $\text{cov}(R_i, R^N)$.

In empirical work one has to make a somewhat arbitrary choice as to what constitutes the portfolio of marketable assets (e.g. an all-items stock or bond index). Empirical anomalies arising from the standard CAPM may be due to time variation in $\text{cov}(R_i, R^N)$. In Part 6 we make an attempt at modelling the time variation in the covariance of the 'omitted assets' and hence attempt to improve the empirical performance of the CAPM.

3.1.4 Taxes and Transactions Costs

Investors pay tax on dividends received and may also be subject to capital gains taxes when securities are sold. Hence investors who face different tax rates will have different *post-tax* efficient frontiers. Under such circumstances the standard CAPM has to be modified so that the equilibrium return on asset i (or portfolio i) is given by an equation of the form (see Litzenberger and Ramaswamy (1979))

$$ER_i = r + (ER^m - r)\beta_i + f(\delta_i, \delta_m, \tau) \tag{3.14}$$

where δ_i = dividend yield of the ith stock, δ_m = dividend yield of the market portfolio and τ = weighted average of various tax rates.

Hence the standard CAPM is augmented by the function $f(\cdot)$ which depends in part on tax parameters. Equation (3.14) also predicts that equilibrium expected returns depend on the dividend yield — a result often found in empirical work, as shown in Chapter 6.

Because of transactions costs in buying and selling stocks, individuals might limit the number of stocks in their portfolio. Most small investors (usually individuals) own only a few stocks, say five or less. If the number of stocks held is limited by transactions costs then there is no simple relationship for equilibrium returns (Levy, 1978). However, individuals can avoid very high transactions costs by purchasing one or more mutual funds and so the 'high transactions cost' variant of the CAPM may not be particularly realistic.

3.1.5 Heterogeneous Expectations

Investors may have different *subjective* expectations of expected returns, variances and covariances. This could not be the case under rational expectations where all investors are *assumed* to know the true probability distribution (model) of the stochastic returns, at all points in time. Hence the assumption of heterogeneous expectations is a violation of the assumption that all investors have rational expectations. Under heterogeneous expectations each investor will have his own *subjective* efficient frontier and hence each investor holds a different proportion of risky assets (x_i) in his optimal unlevered portfolio: the *separation theorem* no longer holds. In order to guarantee that the market clears there must be the same amount of 'buy' and 'sell' orders and some investors may be selling stock i short while others with different expectations are holding stock i. For *each* investor the problem is the standard CAPM one of minimising σ_p subject to his budget constraint and a given level of expected return (see section 2.3 and Appendix 2.1). This gives an optimum portfolio of the riskless asset and the bundle of risky assets x_i^k (for $i = 1, 2, \ldots n$ assets) where the x_i^k differ for different investors.

In general, when we aggregate over all investors $(k = 1, 2, \ldots P)$ so that the market for each asset clears, we obtain a complex expression for the expected return on any asset i which is a complex weighted average of investors' subjective preferences (of risk against return) and the σ_{ij}^k. In general the marginal rate of substitution depends on the level of wealth of the individual. Hence in general, equilibrium returns and asset prices depend on wealth, which itself depends on prices, so there is no 'closed form' or explicit solution in the heterogeneous expectations case.

We can obtain a solution in the heterogeneous expectations case if we restrict the utility function so that the marginal rate of substitution between expected return and risk (variance) is *not* a function of wealth. Lintner (1971) assumed a negative exponential utility function in wealth which implies a constant absolute risk aversion parameter, c^k. Even in this case equilibrium returns, although independent of wealth, still depend on a complex weighted average of individuals' subjective expectations of σ_{ij}^k and individuals' risk aversion parameters, c^k.

In general, the heterogeneous expectations version of the CAPM is largely untestable. However, as will be seen later, one can introduce different expectations in a more tractable fashion. In Chapter 8, we assume that rational traders (or 'smart money') obey the standard CAPM while there are some other traders who have different expectations and indeed a different model of returns, based on the view that stock prices are influenced by 'fads and fashions'. This group of 'noise traders' then react with the smart money and both types of agent may influence equilibrium returns.

3.1.6 Inflation

If investors are concerned about the real return on their portfolio (i.e. the nominal returns adjusted for inflation) then there is no safe asset (unless there are sufficient index-linked assets available such as index-linked gilts). The *zero-beta* CAPM then applies with all returns measured in real terms:

$$ER_i^* = ER^{z^*} + (ER^m - ER^{z^*})\beta_i^*$$

Under certain restrictive assumptions, the above equation can be transposed into an equation involving only nominal returns (Friend et al (1976)).

$$ER_i - r = \sigma_{i\pi} + \frac{(ER^m - r - \sigma_{m\pi})}{\sigma_m^2 - \sigma_{m\pi}/\alpha} \left[\sigma_{im} - \frac{\sigma_{i\pi}}{\alpha}\right] \tag{3.15}$$

where α = ratio of nominal risky assets to total nominal value of all assets (i.e. risky + non-risky), $\sigma_{i\pi}$ = covariance of R_i with inflation (π) and $\sigma_{m\pi}$ = covariance of R^m with inflation (π).

If inflation is uncorrelated with the returns on the market portfolio or on asset i then $\sigma_{i\pi} = \sigma_{m\pi} = 0$ and (3.15) reduces to the standard CAPM. However, in general one can see from equation (3.15) that the equilibrium return on asset i is far more complex than in the standard one-period CAPM of Chapter 2.

The main conclusions to emerge from relaxing some of the restrictive assumptions of the standard CAPM are as follows.

- Assuming that no riskless borrowing or lending opportunities are possible does not seriously undermine the basic results of the standard CAPM. The equilibrium expected return on asset i depends linearly on a weighted average of the returns on two risky portfolios. One is an arbitrary efficient portfolio M_1 (say), and the other is another risky portfolio that has a zero covariance with M_1, and is known as the zero-beta portfolio. A form of the separation theorem still holds.

- Introducing taxes or inflation uncertainty yields an equilibrium returns relationship which is reasonably tractable. However, assuming either heterogeneous expectations by rational mean-variance investors or assuming agents hold only a limited number of stocks, produces acute problems which results in complex and non-tractable equations for equilibrium returns.

- The variants on the standard CAPM may well appeal to some on grounds of 'increased realism'. However, this is of limited use if the resulting equations are so complex as to be virtually inestimable, for whatever reason. Ultimately, the criteria must be simplicity versus fruitfulness. Nevertheless, examining a variety of models or variants does alert one to possible deficiencies and hence may provide some insight into any empirical failures of the standard CAPM that may occur.

3.2   A SIMPLE MEAN-VARIANCE MODEL OF ASSET DEMANDS

In this section we derive a simple model of asset demands based on the mean-variance criterion, which often goes under the name of Tobin's risk aversion model, and briefly discuss the relationship between the mean-variance (MV) model and the CAPM and return to this issue in Chapter 17 when discussing the so-called international CAPM model of returns.

It was noted in section 1.2 that it is *sometimes* possible to reduce the problem of maximising the expected utility from end of period wealth $EU(W)$ to an objective function involving only the expected return μ_N and the variance of the portfolio σ_N^2. However, we do not wish to delve into the complexities of this link (see Cuthbertson (1991), Jones and Roley (1983) and Courakis (1989)) and sidestep the issue somewhat by asserting that the individual wishes to maximise a function depending only on μ_N and σ_N^2:

$$U = U(\mu_N, \sigma_N^2) \quad U_1 > 0, U_2 > 0, (U_{11}, U_{22}) < 0 \tag{3.16}$$

and in particular that the explicit maximand can be approximated by:

$$\mu_N - \frac{c}{2}\sigma_N^2 \tag{3.17}$$

where c is a constant representing the degree of risk aversion. In the simplest version of the MV model the individual is faced with a choice between a *single* riskless asset and a *bundle* of risky assets which we can consider as a *single* risky asset. There are therefore only two assets. The riskless asset carries a known certain return, r, and the risky asset has an actual return R, expected return μ_R and variance σ^2. This set-up is exactly that discussed under the heading of the 'transformation line' in section 2.2.4. However, what we want to do here is to concentrate on how this problem can yield an equation to determine the optimal amount of the riskless and risky asset held as a function of the relative rates of return and the riskiness of the portfolio. We shall find that the proportion held in the risky asset x_i^* is given by:

$$x_i^* = \frac{(\mu_R - r)}{c\sigma_R^2} \tag{3.18}$$

Equation (3.18) is Tobin's (1958) mean-variance model of asset demands. It holds for any risky portfolio and not necessarily for just the market portfolio.

Derivation of Asset Demands

Repeating the algebra in the derivation of the transformation line gives the expected return and standard deviation for the two-asset portfolio:

$$\mu_N = yr + (1 - y)\mu_R \tag{3.19}$$

$$\sigma_N = (1 - y)\sigma_R \tag{3.20}$$

where $y =$ proportion of wealth held in the safe asset. The transformation line is a re-arrangement of (3.19) and (3.20):

$$\mu_N = r + \left[\frac{\mu_R - r}{\sigma_R}\right]\sigma_N \tag{3.21}$$

which is a straight line in (μ_N, σ_N) space with intercept r and slope $(\mu_R - r)/\sigma_R$ (Figure 3.5).

As we see below equation (3.20) is reinterpreted as the budget constraint for the individual. By superimposing the indifference curves I_1 and I_2 in Figure 3.4 the individual, in attempting to maximize utility, will attempt to reach the highest indifference curve.

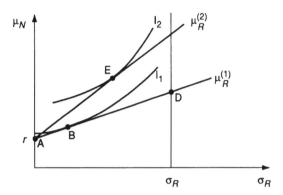

Figure 3.5 Simple Mean-Variance Model.

However, his choices are limited by his budget constraint. If all wealth is held in the risk-free asset then $(1 - y) = 0$ and from (3.20), $\sigma_N = 0$ and hence $\mu_N = r$, using (3.21). Hence we are at point A. If *all* wealth is held in risky assets $y = 0$ and from (3.20) $\sigma_N = \sigma_R$ which when substituted in (3.21) gives $\mu_N = \mu_R$. At point D the individual incurs maximum risk σ_R and a maximum expected return on the whole portfolio μ_R. A combination of the risk-free and risky assets is represented by points on the line AD, and hence AD can be interpreted as the budget constraint. Given expected return $\mu_R^{(1)}$ and hence the budget constraint AD, the individual attains the highest indifference curve at point B which involves a diversified portfolio of the risky and risk-free asset. This, in a nutshell, is the basis of mean-variance models of asset choice and in Tobin's (1958) article the risk-free asset was taken to be money and the risky assets, bonds.

If the expected return on the risky assets μ_R increases or its perceived riskiness σ_R falls, then the budget line pivots about point A and moves upwards (e.g. line $r-\mu_R^{(2)}$). In Figure 3.5 this results in a new equilibrium at E where the individual holds more of the risky asset in his portfolio. This geometric result is consistent with the asset demand function in (3.18).

The asset demand function can be derived algebraically in a few steps. Using (3.17), (3.19) and (3.20), maximising utility is equivalent to choosing y in order to maximise

$$\Psi = yr + (1 - y)\mu_R - (c/2)(1 - y)^2\sigma_R^2 \tag{3.22}$$

$$\partial\Psi/\partial y = (\mu_R - r) + c(1 - y)\sigma_R^2 = 0 \tag{3.23}$$

Therefore the optimal proportion of the holding of the risky asset $x_i^* = (1 - y)$ is

$$x_i^* = \frac{(\mu_R - r)}{c\sigma_R^2} \tag{3.24}$$

Hence the demand for the risky asset increases with the expected excess return $(\mu_R - r)$ and is inversely related to the degree of riskiness σ_R^2. Equation (3.24) is often used in models of asset demands and will be used in Chapter 8 on noise trader models.

In a rather simplistic way the MV model can be turned into a model of equilibrium returns. If the supply of the risky assets x_t is exogenous then using $x_t^s = x_t^*$ and inverting (3.24) we obtain

$$(\mu_R - r) = c\sigma_R^2 x_t^s \tag{3.25}$$

Hence the expected excess return depends on the variance of returns, the coefficient of risk aversion and x_i^s. This is broadly similar to the CAPM result for the market portfolio.

The derivation of the mean-variance model above assumes a fixed bundle of risky assets x_i which may be considered as one asset. However, the MV model can be generalised to the choice between a *set* of risky assets and the risk-free asset: this is discussed in Chapter 18. The observant reader might also note that in this general mean-variance framework the decision problem appears to be identical to that for the CAPM, namely choosing the optimum proportions of the risky assets and the riskless asset to hold. This is in fact correct, except that the mean-variance *asset demand* approach uses a representative individual who has subjective preferences for the rate at which he will substitute additional risk for additional return. This is encapsulated in a specific functional form for the utility function and the associated indifference curves. The CAPM avoids this problem by splitting the decision process into two independent decisions (the separation theorem). In the CAPM it is only in the second stage of the decision process that the preferences of the individual influence his choices. This is because in the first stage decision we assume *all* investors wish to minimise the risk of the portfolio (and not the *utility* from risk), for any given level of expected return. The correspondence between the CAPM and the mean-variance model of asset demands is discussed further in Chapter 18.

3.3 PERFORMANCE MEASURES

The CAPM predicts that the excess return on any stock adjusted for the risk on that stock β_i, should be the same for all stocks (and all portfolios). Algebraically this may be expressed as:

$$(ER_i - r)/\beta_i = (ER_j - r)/\beta_j = \ldots \tag{3.26}$$

Equation (3.26) applies, of course, under the somewhat restrictive assumptions of the standard CAPM which include

- all agents have homogeneous expectations
- agents maximise expected return relative to the standard deviation of the portfolio
- agents can borrow or lend unlimited amounts at the riskless rate
- the market is in equilibrium at all times

In the real world, however, it is possible that over short periods the market is not in equilibrium and profitable opportunities arise. This is more likely to be the case either if agents have divergent expectations, or if they take time to learn about a new environment which affects the returns on stocks of a particular company, or if there are some agents who base their investment decisions on what they perceive are 'trends' in the market. Future chapters will show that, if there is a large enough group of agents who 'follow trends' then the rational agents (smart money) will have to take account of the movements in stock prices produced by these 'trend followers' or noise traders (as they are often called in the academic literature).

It would be useful if we could assess actual investment performance against some overall index of performance. Such an index would have to measure the actual returns of traders relative to some equilibrium risk-return relationship. A trader who consistently turns in a higher return than all other traders is not necessarily 'the best' trader, since his portfolio might carry a higher level of risk than that borne by other traders. Hence any performance index has to consider the return *relative to* the risk of the portfolio and then rank alternative portfolios accordingly.

One area where a performance index would be useful is in ranking the performance of specific mutual funds. A mutual fund allows the managers of that fund to invest in a wide portfolio of securities. For the moment, put to one side the difference in transactions costs of the individual versus the mutual fund manager (who buys and sells in large quantities and may reap economies of scale). What one might wish to know is whether the mutual fund manager provides a 'better return' than is provided by a random selection of stocks by the individual. It may also be the case that whatever performance index is chosen, it may itself be useful in predicting the *future performance* of a particular mutual fund.

Any chief executive or group manager of a mutual fund will wish to know whether his subordinates are investing wisely. Again, a performance index ought to be able to tell us whether some investment fund managers are either doing better than other managers or better than a policy of mere random selection of stocks. The indices we will look at are known as the Sharpe, Treynor and Jensen performance indices.

3.3.1 Sharpe's Performance Index (S)

The index suggested by Sharpe is a *reward to variability ratio* and is defined for portfolio i as:

$$S_i = \frac{ER_i - r}{\sigma_i} \tag{3.27}$$

where ER_i = expected return on portfolio i, σ_i = variance of portfolio i and r = risk-free rate.

Sharpe's index measures the slope of the transformation line and can be calculated for any portfolio using historic data. Over a run of (say) quarterly periods we can work out the average *ex-post* return and the standard deviation on the portfolio, held by the mutual fund manager. We can also do the same for a portfolio of stocks which has been randomly selected. The mutual fund manager will be outperforming the random selection strategy provided his value of S_i is greater than that given by the randomly selected portfolio. The reason for this is that the mutual fund portfolio will then have a transformation line with a higher slope than that given by the randomly selected portfolio. It follows that any investor could end up with a higher level of expected utility if he mixed the portfolio of the mutual fund manager with the riskless asset.

Underlying the use of Sharpe's performance index are the following assumptions:

(i) Investors hold only one risky portfolio (either the mutual fund or a randomly selected portfolio) together with the risk-free asset.

(ii) Investors are risk averse and rates of return are normally distributed (the latter assumption is required if we are to use the mean-variance framework).

3.3.2 Treynor's Performance Index (T)

When discussing Sharpe's performance index it was assumed that individual investors hold only the riskless asset and a single portfolio of risky assets. Treynor's performance index assumes that the individual investor has a choice between the mutual fund or another portfolio of risky assets. Treynor's index is given by

$$T_i = \frac{ER_i - r}{\beta_i} \tag{3.28}$$

It is therefore a measure of excess return per unit of risk but this time the risk is measured by the beta of the portfolio. The Treynor index comes directly from the CAPM which may be written as

$$\left[\frac{ER_i - r}{\beta_i} \right] = ER^m - r \tag{3.29}$$

Under the CAPM the value of T_i should be the same for all portfolios of securities when the market is in equilibrium. It follows that if the mutual fund manager invests in a portfolio where the value of T_i exceeds the excess return on the market portfolio he will be earning an abnormal return relative to that given by the CAPM.

We can calculate the sample value of the excess return on the market portfolio given by the right-hand side of equation (3.29). We can also estimate the β_i for any given portfolio, using a time series regression of $(R_i - r)_t$ on $(R^m - r)_t$. Given the fund manager's average excess return $(ER_i - r)$ we can compute all the elements of (3.29). The fund manager outperforms the market if his particular portfolio (denoted i) has a value of T_i which exceeds the expected excess return on the market portfolio. Values of T_i can be used to rank individual investment manager's portfolios. There are difficulties in interpreting the Treynor index if $\beta_i < 0$, but this is uncommon in practice.

3.3.3 Jensen's Performance Index (J)

Jensen's performance index also assumes that investors can hold either the mutual fund denoted i or a well-diversified portfolio such as the market portfolio. Jensen's index is given by the intercept J_i in the following regression:

$$[E_t R_{it+1} - r_t] = J_i + \beta_i [E_t R_{t+1}^m - r_t] \tag{3.30}$$

To run the regression we need time series data on the expected excess return on the market portfolio and the expected excess return on the portfolio i adopted by the mutual fund manager to obtain estimates for J_i and β_i. In practice, one replaces the expected return variables by the actual return (by invoking the rational expectations assumption (see Chapter 5)). It is immediately apparent from equation (3.30) that if $J_i = 0$ then we have the standard CAPM. Hence the mutual fund denoted i earns a return in excess of that given by the CAPM if J_i is greater than zero. For J_i less than zero, the mutual fund manager has underperformed relative to the risk adjusted rate of return given by the CAPM. Hence Jensen's index actually measures the *abnormal return* on the portfolio of the mutual fund manager (i.e. a return in excess of that given by the CAPM).

Comparing Treynor's and Jensen's Performance Measures
We can rearrange equation (3.30) as follows:

$$\frac{(E_t R_{it+1} - r_t)}{\beta_i} = \frac{J_i}{\beta_i} + [E_t R_{t+1}^m - r_t] \tag{3.31}$$

The left-hand side of equation (3.31) is simply the Treynor index T_i. If beta is positive (which it is for most portfolios) then it is easy to see that when $T_i > E_t R_{t+1}^m - r_t$ then J_i is greater than zero. Hence 'success' using the Treynor index also implies 'success' on Jensen's index.

It may be shown, however, that when ranking two mutual funds, say X and Y, by these indices they can give different inferences. That is to say a higher value of T_i for fund Y over fund X may be consistent with a value of J_i for fund Y which is less than that for fund X. Hence the relative performance of two mutual funds depends on the index chosen.

In section 6.1 the above indices will be used to rank alternative portfolios based on a particular 'passive' and a particular 'active' investment strategy. This allows us to ascertain whether the active strategy outperforms a buy-and-hold strategy.

Roll's Critique and Performance Measures

Roll's critique, which concerns the estimation of the CAPM using a *sample of data*, indicates that in any dataset the following relationship will always hold

$$\overline{R}_i = \overline{r} + [\overline{R}^m - \overline{r}]\hat{\beta}_i \qquad (3.32)$$

where $\overline{R}_i$ = sample mean of the return on portfolio i and
$\overline{R}^m$ = sample mean of the return on the market portfolio.

There is an exact linear relationship in *any* sample of data between the mean return on portfolio i and that portfolio's beta, *if* the market portfolio is correctly measured. Hence if the CAPM were a correct description of investor behaviour then Treynor's index would *always* be equal to the sample excess return on the market portfolio and Jensen's index would always be zero. It follows that if the measured Treynor or Jensen indices are other than suggested by Roll then that simply means that we have incorrectly measured the market portfolio.

Faced with Roll's critique we can therefore only recommend the use of these performance indices on the basis of a fairly *ad-hoc* argument. Because of transactions costs and information costs, investors may not fully diversify their portfolio and hold all the risky assets in the market portfolio. On the other hand, most investors do not confine their holdings to a single security: they hold a diversified, but not the fully diversified, portfolio given by the market portfolio of the CAPM. Thus the appropriate measure of risk for them is neither the (correctly measured) β_i of the portfolio nor the own variance σ_i^2 on their own individual portfolio.

It may well be the case that something like the S&P index is a good approximation to the portfolio held by the representative investor. Then the Treynor, Sharpe and Jensen indices may well provide a useful summary statistic of the relative performance of a mutual fund against the S&P index (which one must admit may not be mean-variance efficient).

3.3.4 Performance of Mutual Funds

There have been a large number of studies of mutual fund performance using the above three indices. Most studies have found that fund managers are unable systematically to beat the market and hence they do not outperform an unmanaged (yet diversified) portfolio, such as the S&P index. Shawky (1982) examines the performance of 255 mutual funds covering the period 1973–1977. First, he finds that the same ranking is obtained for all three indices. This is because there is a very strong correlation between the σ_i and β_i for each portfolio.

On calculating Jensen's performance index. Shawky found that it was significantly different from zero in only 25 out of the 255 mutual funds studied and, of these, 16 had negative values of J_i and only nine had positive values. Thus, out of more than 250 mutual funds only nine outperformed an unmanaged diversified portfolio such as the S&P index. Using Sharpe's index, between 15 and 20 percent of mutual funds outperformed an unmanaged portfolio, while for Treynor's index the figure was slightly higher with around 33 percent outperforming the unmanaged portfolio. Hence, although there are some mutual funds which outperform an unmanaged portfolio these are not particularly large in number.

Given the above evidence, there seems to be something of a paradox in that mutual funds are highly popular, and their growth in Western developed nations throughout the 1970–1990 period has been substantial. While it is true that mutual funds on average do not outperform the unmanaged S&P index, nevertheless, they do outperform almost any unmanaged portfolio consisting of only a small number of shares. Relatively high transaction costs for small investors often imply that investing in the S&P index is not a viable alternative and hence they purchase mutual funds. The key results to emerge from this section are:

- Sharpe's reward-to-variability index is an appropriate performance measure when the investor holds mutual fund shares plus a riskless asset.

- Treynor's and Jensen's performance indices are appropriate when the investor is assumed to diversify his portfolio and holds both mutual fund shares, together with many other risky assets and the riskless asset.

3.4   THE ARBITRAGE PRICING THEORY (APT)

An alternative to the CAPM in determining the expected rate of return on individual stocks and on portfolios of stocks is the arbitrage pricing theory (APT). Broadly speaking, the APT implies that the return on a security can be broken down into an expected return and an unexpected or surprise component. For any individual stock this surprise or news component can be further broken down into 'general news' that affects all stocks and specific 'news' which affects only this particular stock. For example, news which affects all stocks might be an unexpected announcement of an increase in interest rates by the government. News that affects the stocks of a specific industrial sector, for example, might be the invention of a new radar system which might be thought to influence the aerospace industry but not other industries like chemicals and service industries. The APT predicts that 'general news' will affect the rate of return on *all* stocks but by different amounts. For example, a 1 percent unexpected rise in interest rates might affect the return on stocks of a company that was highly geared, more than that for a company that was less geared. The APT, in one sense, is more general than the CAPM in that it allows a large number of factors to affect the rate of return on a particular security. In the CAPM there is really only one factor that influences expected return, namely the covariance between the return on the security and the return on the market portfolio.

The APT may be represented as:

$$R_{it} = R_{it}^e + u_{it} \tag{3.33}$$

where R_{it} = actual rate of return on the ith stock, R_{it}^e = the expected return on the ith stock and u_{it} = the unexpected, surprise or news element.

We can further subdivide the surprise or news element u_{it} into *systematic or market risk* m_t, that is risk that affects a large number of stocks each to a greater or lesser degree and *unsystematic (idiosyncratic or specific) risk* ε_{it}, which specifically affects a single firm or a small group of firms:

$$u_{it} = m_t + \varepsilon_{it} \tag{3.34}$$

As in the case of the CAPM, the systematic risk cannot be diversified away because this element of news or new information affects *all* companies. However, as seen below unsystematic or specific risk may be diversified away.

In order to make the APT operational we need some idea of what causes systematic risk. News about economy-wide variables are, for example, a government announcement that GDP is higher than expected or a sudden increase in interest rates by the Central Bank. These economy-wide factors F (indexed by j), may have different effects on different securities and this is reflected in the different values for the coefficients b_{ij} or 'betas' given below:

$$m_t = \sum_j b_{ij}(F_j - EF_j)_t = b_{i1}(F_{1t} - EF_{1t}) + b_{i2}(F_{2t} - EF_{2t}) + \cdots \tag{3.35}$$

where the expectations operator E applies to information at time $t - 1$ or earlier. For example, if for a particular firm the beta attached to the surprise in interest rates is equal to 0.5 then for every 1 percent that the interest rate rises above its expected level, this would increase the return on security i by half a percent (above its expected value). Note that the 'betas' here are *not* the same as the CAPM betas and hence are denoted b rather than β. (Later it will be shown that the betas of the APT may be reconciled with the betas of the CAPM under certain restrictive assumptions.)

A crucial assumption of the APT is that the idiosyncratic or specific risk ε_i is uncorrelated across different securities:

$$\text{cov}(\varepsilon_i, \varepsilon_j) = 0 \tag{3.36}$$

In fact, as we shall see below, specific risk can be diversified away by holding a large number of securities.

Return on the Portfolio

For simplicity, suppose there is only one systematic risk factor, F_t, and three securities in the portfolio. The return on a portfolio R_t^p of three securities held in proportions x_i is, by definition

$$R_t^p = \sum_{i=1}^3 x_i R_{it} = \sum_{i=1}^3 x_i (R_{it}^e + b_i F_t + \varepsilon_i)$$

$$= \sum_{i=1}^3 x_i R_{it}^e + \left(\sum_{i=1}^3 b_i x_i \right) F_t + \sum_{i=1}^3 x_i \varepsilon_i \tag{3.37}$$

Thus the return on the portfolio is a weighted average of the expected return *plus* the weighted average of the beta for each security (multiplied by the factor F) *plus* a weighted average of the specific risk terms ε_i. If the specific risk is uncorrelated across securities then some of the ε_i will be positive and some negative but their weighted sum is likely to be close to zero. In fact, as the number of securities increases the last term on the right-hand side of (3.37) will approach zero and the specific risk will have been diversified away. Hence the return on the portfolio is made up of the expected returns on the individual securities and the systematic risk as represented by the single economy-wide news term F_t.

A More Formal Approach

The beauty of the APT is that it does not require any assumptions about utility theory or that the mean and variance of a portfolio are the only two elements in the investor's objective function. The model is really a mechanism (an algorithm almost) that allows one to derive an expression for the expected return on a security (or a portfolio of securities) based on the idea that *riskless* arbitrage opportunities will be instantaneously eliminated. Not surprisingly, the APT does, however, require *some* (arbitrary) assumptions. First, assume that agents have homogeneous expectations and that the return R_{it} on *any* stock is *linearly* related to a set of k factors F_{jt}:

$$R_{it} = a_i + \sum_{j=1}^{k} b_{ij} F_{jt} + \varepsilon_{it} \tag{3.38}$$

where the b_{ij} are known as *factor weights*. Taking expectations of (3.38) and assuming $E\varepsilon_{it} = 0$, and subtracting it from itself:

$$R_{it} = ER_{it} + \sum_{j}^{k} b_{ij}(F_{jt} - EF_{jt}) + \varepsilon_{it} \tag{3.39}$$

Equation (3.39) shows that although each security is affected by all the factors, the impact of any particular F_k depends on the value of b_{ik} and this is different for each security. This is the source of the covariance between returns R_{it} on different securities.

Assume that we can continue adding factors to (3.39) until the unexplained part of the return ε_i is such that

$$E(\varepsilon_i \varepsilon_j) = 0 \quad \text{for all } i \neq j \text{ and all time periods} \tag{3.40}$$

$$E[\varepsilon_i(F_j - EF_j)] = 0 \quad \text{for all stocks and factors (and all } t) \tag{3.41}$$

Respectively, (3.40) and (3.41) state that the *unsystematic* (or specific) risk is uncorrelated across securities and is independent of the factors F, that is of *systematic risk*. Note that the factors F are common across *all* securities. Now we perform an 'experiment' where investors form a *zero-beta portfolio* with *zero net investment*. The zero-beta portfolio must satisfy

$$\sum_{i=1}^{n} x_i b_{ij} = 0 \quad \text{for all } j = 1, 2, \ldots k. \tag{3.42}$$

and the assumption of zero investment implies

$$\sum_{i=1}^{n} x_i = 0 \tag{3.43}$$

It follows from (3.43) that some x_i are less than zero, that is some stocks are held short and the proceeds invested in other securities.

The next part of the argument introduces the arbitrage element. If investors put up no funds and the zero-beta portfolio earns a non-zero expected return then a risk-free profit can be earned by arbitrage. This arbitrage condition places a restriction on the expected return of the portfolio, so using (3.34) we have:

$$R_t^p = \sum_{i=1}^{n} x_i R_{it} = \sum_{i=1}^{n} x_i \left(ER_{it} + \sum_{j=1}^{k} b_{ij} F_{jt} + \varepsilon_{it} \right)$$

$$= \sum_{i=1}^{n} x_i ER_{it} + \left(\sum_{i=1}^{n} x_i b_{i1} \right) (F_{1t} - EF_{1t}) + \left(\sum_{i=1}^{n} x_i b_{i2} \right) (F_{2t} - EF_{2t}) + \cdots + \sum_{i=1}^{n} x_i \varepsilon_{it}$$

(3.44)

Using (3.42) and the assumption that for a large well-diversified portfolio the last term on the RHS approaches zero gives:

$$R_t^p = \sum_{i=1}^{n} x_i ER_{it} = ER_t^p$$

(3.45)

where the second equality holds *by definition*. Since this artificially constructed portfolio has an *actual* rate of return R_t^p equal to the expected return ER_t^p, there is a zero *variability* in its return and it is therefore riskless. Arbitrage arguments then suggest that this riskless return must be zero:

$$ER_t^p = \sum_{i=1}^{n} x_i ER_{it} = 0$$

(3.46)

We now have to invoke a proof based on linear algebra. Given the conditions (3.41), (3.42), (3.43) and (3.46) which are known as orthogonality conditions then it may be shown that the expected return on any security i may be written as a linear combination of the factor weightings b_{ij}. For example, for a *two-factor model*:

$$ER_i = \lambda_0 + \lambda_1 b_{i1} + \lambda_2 b_{i2}$$

(3.47)

It was noted above that b_{i1} and b_{i2} in (3.39) are specific to security i. The expected return on security i weights these security-specific betas by a weight λ_j that is *the same for all securities*. Hence λ_j may be interpreted as the *extra* expected return required because of a securities sensitivity to the jth attribute (e.g. GNP or interest rates) of the security.

Interpretation of the λ_j

Assume for the moment that the values of b_{i1} and b_{i2} are known. We can interpret the λ_j as follows. Consider a zero-beta portfolio (i.e. b_{i1} *and* $b_{i2} = 0$) which has an expected return ER^z. If riskless borrowing and lending exist then $ER^z = r$, the risk-free rate. Setting $b_{i1} = b_{i2} = 0$ in (3.47) gives

$$\lambda_0 = ER^z \quad \text{(or } r) $$

(3.48)

Next consider a portfolio having $b_{i1} = 1$ and $b_{i2} = 0$ with an expected return ER_1. Substituting in (3.47) we obtain

$$\lambda_1 = ER_1 - \lambda_0 = E(R_1 - R^z)$$

(3.49)

Similarly,

$$\lambda_2 = E(R_2 - R^z) \tag{3.50}$$

Hence an alternative to (3.47) is

$$ER_i = ER^z + b_{i1}E(R_1 - R^z) + b_{i2}E(R_2 - R^z) \tag{3.51}$$

Thus one interpretation of the APT is that the expected return on a security i depends on the sensitivity of the actual return to the factor loadings (i.e. the b_{ij}). In addition, each factor loading (e.g. b_{i1}) is 'weighted' by the expected excess return $E(R_1 - R^z)$, that is the (excess) return on a portfolio whose beta with respect to the first factor is one and with respect to all other factors is zero. This portfolio with a 'beta of 1' therefore mimics the unexpected movements in the factor F_1.

3.4.1 Implementation of the APT

The APT may be summed up in two equations:

$$R_{it} = a_i + \sum_{j=1}^{k} b_{ij} F_{jt} + \varepsilon_{it} \tag{3.52}$$

$$ER_{it} = \lambda_0 + \sum_{j=1}^{k} b_{ij} \lambda_j \tag{3.53}$$

where $\lambda_0 = r_t$ or ER^z. The APT may be implemented in the following (stylised) way. A 'first-pass' time series regression of R_{it} on a set of factors F_{jt} (e.g. inflation, GDP growth, interest rates) will yield estimates of a_i and the b_{i1}, b_{i2}, etc. This can be repeated for $i = 1, 2, \ldots m$ securities so that we have m values for *each* of the betas, one for each of the different securities. In the 'second-pass' regression the b_i vary over the m securities and are therefore the RHS *variables* in (3.53). Hence in equation (3.53) the b_{ij} are the variables which are different across the m securities. The λ_j are the same for *all* securities and hence these can be estimated from the cross-section regression (3.53) of R_i on the b_{ij} (for $i = 1, 2, \ldots m$). The risk-free rate is constant across securities and hence is the constant term in the cross-section regression.

The above estimation is a two-step procedure. There exists a superior procedure (in principle at least) whereby both equations (3.52) and (3.53) are estimated simultaneously. This is known as *factor analysis*. Factor analysis chooses a subset of all the factors F_j so that the covariance between each equation's residuals is (close to) zero (i.e. $E(\varepsilon_i \varepsilon_j) = 0$) which is consistent with the theoretical assumption that the portfolio is fully diversified. One stops adding factors F_j when the next factor adds 'little' additional explanation. Thus we simultaneously estimate the appropriate number of F_js and their corresponding b_{ij}s. The λ_j are then estimated from the cross-section regression (3.53).

There are, however, problems in interpreting the results from factor analysis. First, the signs on the b_{ij} and λ_js are arbitrary and could be reversed (e.g. a positive b_{ij} and negative λ_j is statistically undistinguishable from a negative b_{ij} and positive λ_j). Second, there is a scaling problem in that the results still hold if the β_{ij} are doubled and the λ_j halved. Finally, if the regressions are repeated on different samples of data there is no guarantee that the same factors will appear in the same order of importance. Thus, the only *a priori* constraints in the APT model are that some λ_j and b_{ij} are (statistically) non-zero: there is not a great deal of economic intuition one can impart to this result.

The reason we have spent a little time at this point in discussing the testing of the APT is that although the structure of the model is very general (based as it is on arbitrage arguments plus a few other minimal restrictive assumptions) nevertheless it is difficult to implement and make operational. As well as the problems of interpretation of the b_{ij} and λ_j which we cannot 'sign' *a priori* (i.e. either could be positive or negative), we might also have problems in that the b_{ij} or λ_j may not be constant over time. In general terms, applied work has concentrated on regressions of equation (3.52) in an effort to isolate a few factors that explain actual returns.

3.4.2 The CAPM and the APT

It must by now be clear to the reader that these two models of equilibrium expected returns are based on rather different (behavioural) assumptions. The APT is often referred to as a *multi-factor* (or *multi-index*) model. The standard CAPM in this terminology may be shown to be a very special case of the APT, namely a single-factor version of the APT, where the single factor is the expected return on the market portfolio ER_t^m. If the return generating equation for security i is hypothesised to depend on only one factor *and* this factor is taken to be the return on the market portfolio, then the APT gives:

$$R_{it} = a_i + b_i R_t^m + \varepsilon_{it} \tag{3.54}$$

This single index APT equation (3.54) can be shown to imply that the expected return is given by:

$$ER_{it} = r_t + b_i(ER_t^m - r_t) \tag{3.55}$$

which conforms with the equilibrium return equation for the CAPM.

The standard CAPM may also be shown to be consistent with a multi-index APT. To see this consider the two-factor APT:

$$R_i = a_i + b_{i1}F_1 + b_{i2}F_2 \tag{3.56}$$

and

$$ER_i = r + b_{i1}\lambda_1 + b_{i2}\lambda_2 \tag{3.57}$$

Now λ_j (as we have seen) is the excess return on a portfolio with a b_{ij} of unity on one factor and zero on all other factors. Since λ_j is an excess return, then *if the CAPM is true*:

$$\lambda_1 = \beta_1(ER^m - r) \tag{3.58}$$

$$\lambda_2 = \beta_2(ER^m - r) \tag{3.59}$$

where the β_i are the CAPM betas. (Hence $\beta_i = \text{cov}(R_i, R^m)/\text{var}(R^m)$ — note that the β_i are *not* the same as the b_{ij} in (3.56).) Substituting for λ_j from (3.58) and (3.59) in (3.57) and rearranging

$$ER_i = r + \beta_i^*(ER^m - r) \tag{3.60}$$

where $\beta_i^* = b_{i1}\beta_1 + b_{i2}\beta_2$. Thus the two-factor APT model with the factors (λ_j) determined by the *betas of the CAPM* yields an equation for the expected return on asset i which is of the form given by the standard CAPM itself. Hence, in testing the APT, if one finds that more than one factor λ_j is statistically significant in (3.57) then this *may* or *may not* reject the CAPM. If the estimate of λ_j is such that this just equals $\beta_j(ER^m - r)$, where β_j is the CAPM beta, then the APT is consistent with the CAPM. If the latter restriction on λ_j does not hold then, of course, the APT and CAPM are not consistent with each other. (The argument is easily generalised to the k factor case.)

The APT model involves some rather subtle arguments and it is not easily interpreted at an intuitive level. The main elements of the APT model are:

- It provides a structure for determining equilibrium returns based on constructing a portfolio that has zero risk (i.e. zero-beta portfolio) and requires no cash investment. Arbitrage arguments imply that such a riskless portfolio has an actual and expected return of zero.

- The above conditions, plus the assumptions of linear factor weightings and a large enough number of securities to give an infinitely small (zero) specific risk, allow orthogonality restrictions to be placed on the parameters of the expected returns equation. These restrictions give rise to an expected returns equation that depends on the factor loadings (b_{ij}) and the indices of risk $(\lambda_j s)$.

- The APT does not rely on any assumptions about utility functions or that agents consider only the mean and variance of prospective portfolios. The APT does, however, require homogeneous expectations.

- The CAPM is not necessarily inconsistent with even a multi-index APT but *in general* it may not be consistent with the APT.

- The APT contains arbitrary elements when its empirical implementation is considered (e.g. what are the appropriate factors F_j? Are the b_{ij} constant over time?) and may be difficult to interpret (e.g. there are no *a priori* restrictions on the signs of the b_{ij} and λ_j).

- The CAPM is more restrictive than the APT but it has a more immediate intuitive appeal and is somewhat easier to test in that the 'factor' is more easily 'pinned down' (e.g. in the standard CAPM it is the excess return on the market portfolio).

3.5 TESTING THE SINGLE INDEX MODEL, THE CAPM AND THE APT

This section discusses some early tests of the CAPM and APT models and a particularly simple (yet theoretically naive) model known as the single index model. We shall return to the question of the appropriate methods to use in testing models of equilibrium returns in future chapters.

3.5.1 The Single Index Model SIM

This is not really a 'model' in the sense that it embodies any behavioural hypotheses but it is merely a *statistical assumption* that the return on *any* security R_{it} may be adequately represented as a linear function of a single (economic) variable I_t (e.g. GNP)

$$R_{it} = \theta_i + \delta_i I_t + \varepsilon_{it} \tag{3.61}$$

where ε_{it} is white noise and (3.61) holds for $i = 1, 2, \ldots m$ securities and for all time periods. If the unexplained element of the return ε_{it} for any security i is independent of that for any other security j we have:

$$\text{cov}(\varepsilon_{it}, \varepsilon_{jt}) = E(\varepsilon_{it} \cdot \varepsilon_{jt}) = 0 \quad i \neq j \tag{3.62}$$

and if I_t is independent of ε_{it}

$$\text{cov}(I_t, \varepsilon_{it}) = 0 \quad \text{for all } i \text{ and } t \tag{3.63}$$

Under the above assumptions, unbiased estimates of (θ_i, δ_i) for each security (or each portfolio of securities) can be obtained by an OLS regression using (3.61) on time series data for R_{it} and I_t.

The popularity of the SIM arises from the fact that it considerably reduces the number of parameters (or inputs) in order to calculate the mean and variance of a portfolio of n securities and hence to calculate the efficient portfolio. Given our assumptions, it is easy to show that

$$ER_i = \theta_i + \delta_i EI_t$$

$$\sigma_i^2 = \delta_i^2 \sigma_I^2 + \sigma_{\varepsilon_i}^2$$

$$\sigma_{ij} = \delta_i \delta_j \sigma_I^2 \tag{3.64}$$

For a portfolio of n securities we have

$$ER^p = \sum_{i=1}^{n} x_i ER_i$$

$$\sigma_p^2 = \sum_{i=1}^{n} x_i^2 \sigma_i^2 + \sum_{i=1}^{n} \sum_{j=1}^{n} x_i x_j \sigma_{ij} \tag{3.65}$$

To calculate the optimal proportions x_i^*, *in general* requires

$$n - \text{expected returns } ER_i$$

$$n - \text{variances } \sigma_i^2$$

$$n(n-1)/2 - \text{covariances}$$

as 'inputs'. However, if the SIM is a good statistical description of asset returns we require as 'inputs' n values of $(\theta_i, \delta_i, \sigma_{\varepsilon_i}^2)$ and values for EI_t and σ_I^2 in order to calculate ER^p and σ_p^2 using (3.64). However, to calculate *all* the covariance terms σ_{ij} no *additional* information is required (see equation 3.64) and compared with the general case (3.65) we 'save' on $n(n-1)/2$ calculations: if n is large this is a considerable advantage of the SIM. When the SIM is used in this way the 'single index' I_t is often taken to be the actual (*ex-post*) return on the *market* portfolio R_t^m with variance σ_m^2 (replacing σ_I^2 above). The *expected value* of the market return ER_t^m and σ_m^2 might then be based on (historic) sample averages over a recent data period. However, as we see below, the SIM is a poor representation of expected returns and in particular the independence assumption, $E(\varepsilon_i \varepsilon_j) = 0$, rarely holds in practice. The reason for this is that if R_i for two (or more) securities depends on more than one index then ε_i and ε_j will not be uncorrelated. (This is a case of omitted variables bias with a common omitted variable in each equation.) Put another way, it is unlikely that shocks or news which influence shares in portfolio A do not also influence the returns on portfolio B.

3.5.2 Simple Tests of the CAPM

The standard CAPM and the zero-beta CAPM predict that the expected excess return on a security over time is determined by

$$ER_{it} - r_t = \beta_i(ER_t^m - r_t) \quad \text{(standard CAPM)} \tag{3.66}$$

$$E(R_{it} - R_t^z) = \beta_i E(R_t^m - R_t^z) \quad \text{(zero-beta CAPM)} \tag{3.67}$$

where we assume in both models that β_i is constant *over time*. If we now assume rational expectations (see Chapter 5) so that the difference between the out-turn and the forecast is random then:

$$R_{it} = ER_{it} + \varepsilon_{it}$$

$$R_t^m = ER_t^m + w_t$$

where ε_{it} and w_t are white noise (random) errors. Equations (3.66) and (3.67) become

$$(R_{it} - r_t) = \beta_i(R_t^m - r_t) + \varepsilon_{it}^* \quad \text{(standard CAPM)} \tag{3.68}$$

$$(R_{it} - R_t^z) = \beta_i(R_t^m - R_t^z) + \varepsilon_{it}^* \quad \text{(zero-beta CAPM)} \tag{3.69}$$

where $\varepsilon_{it}^* = \varepsilon_{it} - \beta_i w_t$. Rearranging equations (3.68) and (3.69):

$$R_{it} = r_t(1 - \beta_i) + \beta_i R_t^m + \varepsilon_{it}^* \quad \text{(standard CAPM)} \tag{3.70}$$

$$R_{it} = R^z(1 - \beta_i) + \beta_i R_t^m + \varepsilon_{it}^* \quad \text{(zero-beta CAPM)} \tag{3.71}$$

Comparing either the standard CAPM or the zero-beta CAPM with the SIM of equation (3.61) with $I_t = ER_t^m$ then it is easy to see why the SIM is deficient. If the standard CAPM is true then

$$\delta_i = r_t(1 - \beta_i) \tag{3.72}$$

and for the zero-beta CAPM:

$$\delta_i = R_t^z(1 - \beta_i) \tag{3.73}$$

Thus, even if β_i is constant over time we would not expect δ_i in the SIM to be constant since r_t or R_t^z vary over time. Also since ε_{it}^* and ε_{jt}^* depend on w_t, the error in forecasting the return on the market portfolio, then ε_{it}^* and ε_{jt}^* in the SIM will be correlated, if the CAPM is the true model. This violates a key assumption of the SIM. Finally note that if the CAPM is true and r_t is correlated with R_t^m then the SIM has an 'omitted variable' and by standard econometric theory the OLS estimate of δ_i is biased and if the correlation $\rho(r, R^m) < 0$ then δ_i is biased *downward* and cannot be taken as a 'good' estimate of the true β_i given by the CAPM. (In these circumstances the intercept θ_i in the SIM is biased upwards.) Hence results from the SIM certainly throw no light on the validity of the CAPM or, put another way, if the CAPM is 'true' and given that r_t (or R^z) vary over time then the SIM model is invalid.

Direct Tests of the CAPM

These often take the form of a two-stage procedure. Under the assumption that β_i is constant over time, a *first-pass time series regression* of $(R_{it} - r_t)$ on $(R_t^m - r_t)$ and a constant term gives:

$$(R_{it} - r_t) = \alpha_i + \beta_i(R_t^m - r_t) + \varepsilon_{it}^* \tag{3.74}$$

where we expect $\alpha_i = 0$ for each security $(i = 1, 2, \ldots k)$ or for a portfolio of securities. The estimates β_i *for each security* may then be used in a *second-pass cross-section* regression. Here the *sample average* returns $\overline{R}_i$ on all k securities are regressed on the $\hat{\beta}_i$s from the first-pass regression:

$$\overline{R}_i = \Psi_0 + \Psi_1 \hat{\beta}_i + v_i \tag{3.75}$$

Comparing (3.75) with the standard CAPM relation

$$R_i = r_t + \beta_i (R_t^m - r_t) + \varepsilon_{it}^* \tag{3.76}$$

we expect

$$\Psi_0 = \overline{r}, \quad \Psi_1 = \overline{R}^m - \overline{r}_t$$

where a bar indicates the sample mean values. An even stronger test of the CAPM in the second-pass regression is to note that if there is an unbiased estimate of the β_i $(i = 1$ to $k)$ then *only* β_i should influence R_i. Under the null that the CAPM is true, then in the following second-pass cross-section regression:

$$\overline{R}_i = \Psi_0 + \Psi_1 \beta_i + \Psi_2 \beta_i^2 + \Psi_3 \sigma_{\varepsilon_i}^2 + \eta_i \tag{3.77}$$

we expect

$$H_0 : \Psi_2 = \Psi_3 = 0$$

where $\sigma_{\varepsilon_i}^2$ is an unbiased estimate of the (own) variance of security i from the first-pass regression (3.76). If $\Psi_2 \neq 0$ then there are said to be non-linearities in the security market line. If $\Psi_3 \neq 0$ then diversifiable risk affects the expected return on a security: both are violations of the CAPM.

We can repeat the above tests for the zero-beta CAPM by replacing r_t with R_t^z. In particular, if the zero-beta CAPM is the true model

$$R_{it} = R_t^z (1 - \beta_i) + \beta_i R_t^m \tag{3.78}$$

The first-pass time series regression (3.74) rearranged is:

$$R_{it} = \alpha_i + r_t (1 - \beta_i) + \beta_i R_t^m \tag{3.79}$$

Comparing (3.78) and (3.79)

$$\alpha_i = (R^z - r)(1 - \beta_i) \tag{3.80}$$

Hence if the zero-beta CAPM is true rather than the standard CAPM then in the first-pass regression (3.79) we expect $\alpha_i > 0$ when $\beta_i < 1$ and vice versa, since we know from our theoretical discussion in section 3.1 that $R^z - r > 0$.

There are yet further econometric problems with the two-step approach. First, the CAPM doesn't rule out the possibility that the error terms may be heteroscedastic (i.e. the variances of the error terms are not constant). In this case the OLS standard errors are incorrect and other estimation techniques need to be used (e.g. Hansen's GMM estimator or some other form of GLS estimator). The CAPM does rule out the error terms ε_{it}^* being serially correlated over time unless the data frequency is finer than the investment horizon for R_{it} (e.g. weekly data and monthly expected returns). In the latter case a GMM estimator is required (see Chapter 19).

Another econometric problem is that in the first-pass time series regression the estimate $\hat{\beta}_i$ may be unbiased but it is measured with error. Hence in the second-pass regression (3.75) there is a classic 'errors in variables' problem which means that the OLS coefficient of Ψ_1 is downward biased (and Ψ_0 is upward biased). Also if the true β_i is positively correlated with a securities' error variance $\sigma^2_{\varepsilon_i}$, then the latter serves as a proxy for the true β_i and hence if $\hat{\beta}_i$ is measured with error, then $\sigma^2_{\varepsilon_i}$ may be significant in the second-pass regression. Finally, note that if the error distribution of ε_{it} is non-normal (e.g. positively skewed) then any estimation technique based on normality will produce biased estimates. In particular positive skewness in the residuals of the cross-section regressions will show up as an association between residual risk and return even though in the true model there is no association.

The reader can see that there are acute econometric problems in trying successfully to estimate the true betas from the first-pass regression and to obtain correct and meaningful results in the second-pass regressions. These problems have been listed rather than explained or proved for those who are familiar with the econometric methodology.

As an illustration of these early studies consider that of Black et al (1972) using monthly rates of return 1926–1966 in the first-pass time series regressions. They minimised the heteroscedasticity problem and the error in estimating the betas by grouping all stocks into a set of ten portfolios based on the size of the betas for *individual* securities (i.e. the time series estimates of β_i for individual securities over a rolling five-year estimation period are used to assemble the portfolios). For the ten 'size portfolios' the monthly return R^p_{it} is regressed on R^m_t over a period of 35 years

$$R^p_{it} = \hat{\alpha}_i + \hat{\beta}_i R^m_t \tag{3.81}$$

and the results are given in Table 3.1. In the second-pass regressions they obtain

$$\overline{R}^p_i - r = 0.00359 + 0.0108\beta_i$$

with the R squared, for the regression = 0.98. The non-zero intercept is not consistent with the standard CAPM but is consistent with the zero-beta CAPM. (At least for the *portfolio* of stocks used here rather than for *individual* stocks.) Note that when $\beta > 1$

Table 3.1 Estimates of β for Ten Portfolios

Portfolio	β_i	Excess Return[a]	α_i
1	1.56	2.13	−0.08
2	1.38	1.77	−0.19
3	1.25	1.71	−0.06
4	1.16	1.63	−0.02
5	1.05	1.45	−0.05
6	0.92	1.37	−0.05
7	0.85	1.26	0.05
8	0.75	1.15	0.08
9	0.63	1.10	0.19
10	0.49	0.91	0.20
Market	1.0	1.42	–

(a) Percent per month.
Source: Black et al (1972)

then usually $\alpha < 0$ (and vice versa) in the results in Table 3.1: this is what we expect if the zero-beta CAPM is the true model.

Fama and MacBeth (1974) extended the above second-pass cross-section regression by including β_i^2 and $\sigma_{\varepsilon i}^2$ (from the first-pass regression)

$$\overline{R}_i^p = \Psi_0 + \Psi_1 \beta_i + \Psi_2 \beta_i^2 + \Psi_3 \sigma_{\varepsilon i}^2 + \eta_i \qquad (3.82)$$

where the data consist of 20 portfolios. The second-pass regression is repeated for *each month* over 1935–68 to see how the Ψs vary over time. They find that the average of the Ψ_2 and Ψ_3 estimates are *not* significantly different from zero and hence support the standard CAPM. They also find that η_i is not serially correlated over the 35-year time period for the monthly residuals, again weak support for the CAPM.

Our final illustrative second-pass regression uses a *sample estimate* of the variance of the return on individual securities $\sigma_i^2[= \sum_t (R_{it} - \overline{R}_t)/(n-1)]$ and *not* the residual variance from the first-pass regression. A representative result from Levy (1978) is

$$\overline{R}_i = 0.117 + 0.008\hat{b}_i + 0.197\hat{\sigma}_i^2 \qquad (3.83)$$
$$\quad\;\; (14.2) \quad\;\; (0.9) \quad\;\;\; (5.2)$$

$$R^2 = 0.38, \, (\,\cdot\,) = t \text{ statistic}$$

and hence $\hat{b}_i$ provides no additional explanation of the expected return over and above that provided by the own variance σ_i^2. This directly contradicts the CAPM. However, note that recent econometric research (see Pagan and Ullah (1988)) has shown that using an estimate of the sample variance as a measure of the true (conditional) variance leads to biased estimates, so Levy's early results are open to question. A more sophisticated method of estimating variances and covariances is examined in Chapter 17.

The Post-Tax Standard CAPM

If individuals face different tax rates on dividend income and capital gains then even with homogeneous expectations about pre-tax rates of return, each investor will face a different after-tax efficient frontier. However, in this extension of the CAPM, a general equilibrium 'returns equation' for all assets and all portfolios exists and is given by:

$$ER_i = r + \beta_i[(ER^m - r) - \tau(\delta_m - r)] + \tau(\delta_i - r) \qquad (3.84)$$

where $\delta_m =$ dividend yield of the market portfolio, $\delta_i =$ dividend yield for stock i and $\tau =$ tax rate parameter depending on a weighted average of the tax rates for all investors and their wealth.

From (3.84) any cross-section second-pass regression β_i and the dividend yield δ_i will affect expected returns. (The security market line (SML) is now a plane in three-dimensional (R_i, β_i, δ_i) space rather than a straight line.) When dividends are taxed at a higher *effective* rate than capital gains (which is the case in the US and UK since capital gains tax is largely avoidable) then $\tau > 0$ and hence expected return increases with dividend yield. In this extended CAPM model, all investors hold a widely diversified portfolio, but those investors with high income tax rates will hold more low-dividend paying stocks in their portfolio (relative to the market portfolio holdings of an individual who faces average tax rates).

There are empirical studies that find no effect from δ_i (e.g. Black and Scholes (1974)) in the second-pass regression:

$$R_i = \alpha_0 + \alpha_1\beta_i + \alpha_2\delta_i + \eta_i \qquad (3.85)$$

However, the study by Litzenberger and Ramaswamy (1979) uses 'superior' maximum likelihood methods and carefully considers the exact monthly timing of dividend payments. They find that over the period 1936–77 on monthly time series data:

$$R_{it} - \tau = 0.0063 + 0.0421\beta_{it} + 0.23(\delta_{it} - r_t) \qquad (3.86)$$
$$[2.6] \qquad [1.9] \qquad [8.6]$$

$$[\cdot] = t \text{ statistic}$$

The model (3.85) suggests that in (3.86) we expect $\alpha_2 = \tau$. When $t_g = 0$ (i.e. zero effective capital gains tax) then the tax parameter τ is equal to the average income tax rate. In their study Litzenberger and Ramaswamy run equation (3.86) over several different time periods and they find $0.24 < \alpha_2 < 0.38$. The true income tax rate is within this band and their results support the post-tax CAPM. In addition Litzenberger and Ramaswamy find that over six subperiods during the 1936–77 time span the coefficient on δ_{it} is always positive and is statistically significant in five of these subperiods. Unfortunately, the coefficient on β_{it} is statistically significant in only two of the subperiods and is somewhat temporally unstable as it changes sign over different periods. It appears that the dividend yield is a better predictor of expected returns than is beta. Hence overall the model does not provide support for the CAPM. We shall encounter the importance of the dividend yield in determining expected returns in more advanced studies in later chapters.

This schematic overview of the conflicting results yielded by early tests of the CAPM can be summarised by noting

- difficulties in using actual data to formulate the model correctly, particularly in measuring variances correctly

- the assumption of constant betas (over time) may not be correct

- econometric techniques have advanced so that these early studies may give misleading results

- on balance the results (after consulting the original sources) suggest to this author that the CAPM (particularly the zero-beta version) certainly has *some* empirical validity

Roll's Critique

Again, it is worth mentioning Roll's (1977) powerful critique of tests of the zero-beta CAPM based on the security market line (SML). He demonstrated that for *any* portfolio that is efficient *ex post* (call it q) then in a *sample* of data there is an exact linear relationship between the mean return and beta. It follows that there is really only one testable implication of the zero-beta CAPM, namely that the market portfolio is mean-variance efficient. If the market portfolio is mean-variance efficient then the SML *must* hold in the sample. Hence violations of the SML in empirical work may be indicative that the portfolio chosen by the researcher is not the true 'market portfolio'. Unless the researcher is confident he has the true market portfolio (which may include land, commodities, human capital, as well as stocks and bonds) then tests based on the SML are largely superfluous and provide no *additional* confirmation of the zero-beta CAPM. Despite this critique researchers have continued to explore the empirical validity of the CAPM even though their proxy for the market portfolio could be incorrect. This is because it is still of interest to see how far a particular empirical model, even an imperfect one, can explain equilibrium returns. Also once one recognises that the betas may be time varying (see Chapter 17) this considerably weakens the force of Roll's argument which is directed at the second-pass regressions on the SML.

3.5.3 Tests of the APT

Roll and Ross (1984) applied factor analysis to 42 groups of 30 stocks using daily data between 1962 and 1972. In their first-pass regressions they find that for most groups about five 'factors' provide a sufficiently good statistical explanation of R_{it}. In the second-pass regression they find that three factors are sufficient. However, Dhrymes et al (1984) show that one problem in interpreting results from factor analysis is that the number of statistically significant factors appears to increase as more securities are included in the analysis.

The second-pass regressions of Fama and MacBeth (1973) and Litzenberger and Ramaswamy (1979) reported above may be interpreted as second-pass regression tests of the APT since they are of the form

$$R_i = \lambda_0 + \lambda_1 b_{i1} + \lambda_2 b_{i2} \tag{3.87}$$

where b_{i2} equals β_i^2, $\sigma_{\varepsilon i}^2$ or δ_i. These results are conflicting on whether the CAPM beta is a sufficient statistic for R_i or whether additional 'factors' are required as implied by the APT.

Sharpe (1982), Chen (1983), Roll and Ross (1984), and Chen et al (1986) specify a wide variety of factors F_t that might influence expected return in the first-pass time series regression. Such factors include the dividend yield, a long–short yield spread on government bonds and changes in industrial production. The estimated b_{ij} from the first-pass regressions are then used as cross-section variables in the second-pass regression (3.87) for each month. Several of the λ_j are statistically significant thus supporting a multi-factor APT model. In Sharpe's results the securities' CAPM beta was significant whereas for Chen et al (1986) the CAPM beta when *added* to the factors already included in the APT returns equation contributed no additional explanatory power to the second-pass regression. However, the second-pass regressions have a maximum R^2 of around 0.1 on monthly data so there is obviously a great deal of 'noise' in asset returns and this makes it difficult to make firm inferences.

Overall this early empirical work on the APT is suggestive that more than one factor is important in determining assets returns. This is confirmed by more recent studies on US data (e.g. Shanken (1992) and Shanken and Weinstein (1990)) and UK data (Clare and Thomas (1994) and Poon and Taylor (1991), which use improved variants of the two-stage regression tests.

Yet another approach to testing the APT uses the two basic equations:

$$R_{it} = E(R_{it}) + \sum_{j=1}^{k} b_{ij} F_{jt} + \varepsilon_{it}$$

$$E(R_{it}) = \lambda_0 + \lambda_1 b_{i1} + \cdots + \lambda_k b_{ik}$$

to give:

$$R_{it} = \lambda_0 + \sum_{j=1}^{k} b_{ij}\lambda_j + \sum_{j=1}^{k} b_{ij}F_{jt} + \varepsilon_{it} \tag{3.88}$$

Comparing (3.88) with regressions with unrestricted constant terms α_i (and setting $\lambda_0 = r$):

$$(R_{it} - r_t) = \alpha_i + \Sigma b_{ij}F_{jt} + \varepsilon_{it} \tag{3.89}$$

Comparing (3.88) and (3.89) we see that there are non-linear restrictions,

$$\alpha_i = \sum_{j=1}^{k} b_{ij}\lambda_j$$

in (3.89), if the APT is the correct model. In the combined time series cross-section regressions we can apply non-linear least squares to (3.88) and test these restrictions. The λs and b_{ij}s are jointly estimated in (3.88) and results on US portfolios (McElroy et al (1985)) suggest that the restrictions do not hold.

The key issues in testing and finding an acceptable empirical APT model are:

- how to measure the 'news' factors, F_{jt}. Should one use first differences of the variables, or residuals from single equation regressions or VAR models, and should one allow the coefficients in such models to vary, in order to mimic learning by agents (e.g. recursive least squares, time varying parameter models)?

- are the set of factors F_{jt} and the resulting values of λ_j constant over different sample periods and across different portfolios (e.g. by size or by industry)? If the λ_j are different in different sample periods then the price of risk for factor j is time varying (contrary to the theory) and the returns equation for R_i is non-unique

Although there has been considerable progress in estimating and testing the APT, the empirical evidence on the above issues is far from definitive.

3.6 SUMMARY

This chapter has extended our analysis of the CAPM and analysed an alternative model of equilibrium returns, the APT. It explained how the concepts behind the CAPM can be used to construct alternative performance indicators and briefly looked at some early empirical tests of the CAPM and tests of the APT. In addition, it showed how the mean-variance approach can be used to derive an individual's asset demand function and briefly compared this approach to the CAPM.

4
Valuation Models

In this chapter we look at models that seek to determine how investors in the market decide what is the *correct, fundamental* or *fair* value V_t for a particular stock. Having decided on what is the fair value for the stock, market participants (in an efficient market) should set the actual price P_t equal to the fundamental value. If $P_t \neq V_t$ then unexploited profit opportunities exist in the market. For example, if $P_t < V_t$ then risk neutral investors would buy the share since they anticipate they will make a capital gain as P_t rises towards its 'correct value' in the future. As investors purchase the share with $P_t < V_t$ then this would tend to lead to a rise in the current price as demand increases, so that it quickly moves towards its fundamental value. The above, of course, assumes that investors at the margin have homogeneous expectations or more precisely that their subjective view of the probability distribution of the fundamental value reflects the 'true' underlying distribution.

A key proposition running through this chapter is that stock *returns* and stock *prices* are closely linked. Indeed, alternative models of expected returns give rise to different expressions for the determination of fundamental value and hence stock prices. The main themes covered in the chapter are as follows:

- We begin with a simple model where equilibrium expected stock returns are assumed to be constant and this implies that stock prices equal the discounted present value (DPV) of future dividends, with a constant discount rate. This expression can be further simplified if one also assumes either a constant level of dividends or a constant dividend growth rate.

- We explore the implications for the determination of stock prices when equilibrium expected returns are assumed to vary over time and then show how the risk premium of the CAPM helps to determine a (possibly time varying) discount rate in the DPV formula for stock prices.

- We discuss a somewhat more general CAPM than that discussed in Chapters 2 and 3 which is known as the consumption CAPM (or C-CAPM). This model is intertemporal, in that investors are assumed to maximise expected utility of current and future consumption. Financial assets allow the consumer to smooth his consumption pattern over time, selling assets to finance consumption in 'bad' times and saving in 'good' times. Assets whose returns have a high negative covariance with consumption will be willingly held even though they have low expected returns. This is because they can be 'cashed in' at a time when they are most needed, namely when consumption is low and therefore extra consumption yields high marginal utility. This model associates an assets systematic risk with the state of the real economy (i.e. consumption).

4.1 THE RATIONAL VALUATION FORMULA (RVF)

Expected Returns are Constant

One of the simplest assumptions one can make is that expected returns are constant. The expected return is defined as

$$E_t R_{t+1} = \frac{E_t V_{t+1} - V_t + D_{t+1}^e}{V_t} \tag{4.1}$$

where V_t is the value of the stock at the end of time t and D_{t+1} are dividends paid between t and $t+1$. E_t is the expectations operator based on information at time t or earlier, Ω_t. The superscript 'e' is equivalent to E_t; it helps to simplify the notation and is used when no ambiguity is likely to arise, that is:

$$D_{t+1}^e \equiv E(D_{t+1}|\Omega_t) \equiv E_t D_{t+1}$$

Assume investors are willing to hold the stock as long as it is expected to earn a constant return $(= k)$. We can think of this 'required return' k as that rate of return that is just sufficient to compensate investors for the inherent riskiness of the stock:

$$E_t R_{t+1} = k \quad k > 0 \tag{4.2}$$

The form of (4.2) is known as the *fair game* property of excess returns (see Chapter 5). The stochastic behaviour of $R_{t+1} - k$ is such that no abnormal returns are made, *on average*: the expected (conditional) excess return on the stock is zero:

$$E_t(R_{t+1} - k|\Omega_t) = 0 \tag{4.3}$$

Using (4.1) and (4.2) we obtain a differential (Euler) equation which determines the movement in 'value' over time:

$$V_t = \delta E_t(V_{t+1} + D_{t+1}) \tag{4.4}$$

where δ = discount factor $= 1/(1+k)$ with $0 < \delta < 1$. Leading (4.4) one period:

$$V_{t+1} = \delta E_{t+1}(V_{t+2} + D_{t+1}) \tag{4.5}$$

Now take expectations of (4.5) assuming information is only available up to time t:

$$E_t V_{t+1} = \delta E_t(V_{t+2} + D_{t+2}) \tag{4.6}$$

In deriving (4.6) we have used the *law of iterated expectations*:

$$E_t(E_{t+1} V_{t+2}) = E_t V_{t+2} \tag{4.7}$$

The expectation formed today (t) of what one's expectation will be tomorrow $(t+1)$ of the value at $t+2$ is the LHS of (4.7). This simply equals one's expectation today of V_{t+2} (i.e. the RHS of (4.7)) since one cannot know *how* one will alter one's expectations in the future. Strictly (4.7) is an assumption that agents use *rational expectations* (see Chapter 5). Equation (4.6) holds for all periods so that

$$E_t V_{t+2} = \delta E_t (V_{t+3} + D_{t+3}), \text{ etc.} \tag{4.8}$$

The next part of the solution requires substitution of (4.8) in (4.6):

$$V_t = \delta[\delta E_t(V_{t+2} + D_{t+2})] + \delta(E_t D_{t+1})$$

By successive substitution

$$V_t = \delta D_{t+1}^e + \delta^2 D_{t+2}^e + \delta^3 D_{t+3}^e + \cdots + \delta^N (D_{t+N}^e + V_{t+N}^e) \tag{4.9}$$

Now let $N \to \infty$ and hence $\delta^N \to 0$. If the expected growth in D is not explosive so that D_{t+N}^e is finite and if V_{t+N}^e is also finite then:

$$\lim_{n \to \infty} E_t[\delta^N D_{t+N} + V_{t+N}] \to 0 \tag{4.10}$$

Equation (4.10) is known as a terminal condition or *transversality condition* and it rules out rational speculative bubbles (see Chapter 7). Equation (4.9) then becomes:

$$V_t = \sum_{i=1}^{\infty} \delta^i D_{t+i}^e \tag{4.11}$$

Where $\delta = 1/(1+k)$ we have derived (4.11) under the assumptions:

- expected returns are constant
- the law of iterated expectations (i.e. *RE*) holds for all investors
- dividend growth is not explosive and the terminal condition holds
- all investors have the same view (model) of the determinants of returns and have homogeneous expectations

Hence the correct or fundamental value V_t of a share is the DPV of expected future dividends. If we add the assumption that

- investors instantaneously set the actual market price P_t equal to fundamental value V_t then we obtain the *rational valuation formula* (RVF) for stock prices with a constant discount rate:

$$P_t = E_t \left[\sum_{i=1}^{\infty} \delta^i D_{t+i} \right] \tag{4.12}$$

If investors ensure (4.12) holds at all times then the Euler equation (4.6) and the DPV formula can be expressed in terms of P_t, the actual price (rather than V_t), and as this simplifies the notation, we use this whenever possible.

In the above analysis we did not distinguish between real and nominal variables and indeed the mathematics goes through for either case: hence (4.12) is true whether all variables are nominal or are all deflated by an aggregate goods price index. Nevertheless intuitive reasoning and causal empiricism suggest that expected *real* returns are more likely to be constant than expected nominal returns (not least because of goods price inflation). Hence this particular version of the RVF is usually expressed in terms of real variables.

Finite or Infinite Horizon

If investors have a finite horizon, that is they are concerned with the price they can obtain in the near future, does this alter our view of the determination of fundamental value? Consider the simple case of an investor with a one-period horizon:

$$P_t = \delta D^e_{t+1} + \delta^2 P^e_{t+1}$$

The price today depends on the expected price at $t+1$. But how is this investor to determine the value P^e_{t+1} at which he can sell at $t+1$? If he is consistent (rational), he should determine this in exactly the same way that he does for P_t. That is

$$P^e_{t+1} = \delta D^e_{t+2} + \delta^2 P^e_{t+2}$$

But by repeated forward induction each investor with a one-period horizon will believe that P_{t+j} is determined by the above Euler equation and hence today's price will equal the DPV of dividends in *all future periods*.

Thus even if some agents have a finite investment horizon they will still collectively determine the fundamental value in such a way that it is equal to that of an investor who has an infinite horizon. This is the usual counterargument to the view that if investors have short horizons then price cannot reflect fundamental value (i.e. short-termism). This counterargument assumes, of course, that investors are homogeneous, that they all consider the underlying equilibrium model of returns given by (4.2) is the true model and they 'push' price immediately to its equilibrium value. Later in this section the assumption that equilibrium returns are constant is relaxed and we find the RVF still holds. In contrast, Chapter 8 allows non-rational agents or noise traders to influence returns and in such a model price may not equal fundamental value.

Expected Dividends are Constant

Let us simplify the RVF further by assuming a time series model for (real) dividends which has the property that the best forecast of *all* future (real) dividends is equal to the current level of dividends, that is the random walk model:

$$D_{t+1} = D_t + w_{t+1}$$

where w_{t+1} is white noise. Under *RE* we have $E_t(w_{t+j}|\Omega_t) = 0$ $(j \geqslant 1)$ and $E_t D_{t+j} = D_t$ and hence the growth in dividends is expected to be zero. The RVF (4.12) then reduces to:

$$P_t = \delta(1 + \delta + \delta^2 + \cdots)D_t = \delta/(1 - \delta)D_t = (1/k)D_t \qquad (4.13)$$

Equation (4.13) predicts that the dividend price (D/P) ratio or *dividend yield* is a constant equal to the required (real) return, k. (Note that the ratio D/P is the same whether the variables are measured in real or nominal terms.) If the required (real) return $k = 0.08$ (8 percent per annum) then the zero dividend growth model predicts a *constant* dividend price ratio which also equals 8 percent. The model (4.13) also predicts that the percentage change in stock prices P_t equals the percentage change in current dividends. Price changes only occur when *new* information about dividends becomes available: the model predicts that *volatility* in stock prices depends on the volatility (uncertainty) in dividends. Although an investor's best *forecast* of dividends for all future periods is D_t, the random element w_{t+1} (i.e. news or uncertainty) may cause actual D_{t+1} to differ from the investor's best forecast. Prices therefore only change because of 'news' about fundamentals (i.e. dividends). The conditional variance of prices therefore depends on the variance in news about these fundamentals:

$$P_{t+1} - P_t = (1/k)(D_{t+1} - D_t) = (1/k)w_{t+1} \tag{4.14}$$

and

$$\text{var}(P_{t+1} - P_t | \Omega_t) = (\sigma_w/k)^2 \tag{4.15}$$

Much later in the book, Chapter 16 examines the more general case where the volatility in prices depends not only on the volatility in dividends but also the volatility in the discount rate. In fact, an attempt is made to ascertain whether the volatility in stock prices is mainly due to the volatility in dividends, or the discount factor.

Expected Dividend Growth is Constant

A time series model in which (real) dividends grow at a constant rate g is the AR(1) model:

$$D_{t+1} = (1+g)D_t + w_{t+1} \tag{4.16}$$

where w_t is white noise and $E(w_{t+1}|\Omega_t) = 0$. *Expected* dividend growth from (4.16) is easily seen to be equal to g.

$$E_t D_{t+1} = (1+g)D_t$$

$$(E_t D_{t+1} - D_t)/D_t = g \tag{4.17}$$

Note that if the *logarithm* of dividends follows a random walk with drift parameter $= g$, then this also gives a constant expected growth rate for dividends (i.e. $\ln D_{t+1} = g + \ln D_t + w_t$). The optimal forecasts of future dividends may be found by leading (4.16) one period

$$D_{t+2} = (1+g)D_{t+1} + w_{t+2}$$

and using

$$E_t D_{t+2} = (1+g)E_t D_{t+1} = (1+g)^2 D_t$$

Hence by repeated substitution:

$$E_t D_{t+j} = (1+g)^j D_t \tag{4.18}$$

Substituting the forecast of future dividends from (4.18) in the rational valuation formula gives:

$$P_t = \sum_{i=1}^{\infty} \delta^i (1+g)^i D_t \tag{4.19}$$

which after some simple algebra yields

$$P_t = \frac{(1+g)}{(k-g)} D_t \quad \text{with } (k-g) > 0 \tag{4.20}$$

Thus the stock price depends on current dividends D_t, the required rate of return k and the expected growth rate of dividends g. (Again, (4.20) holds whether all the variables are measured in real or nominal terms.) Equation (4.20) represents a particular valuation model which involves the assumptions listed earlier *plus* the hypothesis that the time series properties of dividend payouts is such that it is reasonable (rational) for investors to expect that dividends grow at a constant rate. Equation (4.20) 'collapses' to (4.13) when $g = 0$.

Time Varying Expected Returns

Suppose investors require a different expected return in each future period in order that they will willingly hold a particular stock. (Why this may be the case is investigated later.) Our model is therefore:

$$E_t R_{t+1} = k_{t+1} \tag{4.21}$$

where we have a time subscript on k to indicate it is time varying. Repeating the previous steps, involving forward substitution, gives:

$$P_t = \delta_{t+1} D_{t+1}^e + \delta_{t+1} \delta_{t+2} D_{t+2}^e + \delta_{t+1} \delta_{t+2} \delta_{t+3} D_{t+3}^e + \cdots + \delta_{t+N} E_t (D_{t+N} + P_{t+N}^N) \tag{4.22}$$

which can be written in more compact form (assuming the transversality condition holds):

$$P_t = E_t \left[\sum_{j=1}^{\infty} \left[\prod_{i=1}^{j} \delta_{t+i} \right] D_{t+j} \right] \tag{4.23}$$

where $\delta_{t+i} = 1/(1 + k_{t+i})$. The current stock price therefore depends on all future expectations of the discount rate δ_{t+j} and all future expected dividends. Note that $0 < \delta_{t+j} < 1$ for all periods and hence expected dividends $-for-$ have less influence on the current stock price the further they accrue in the future. However, it is possible (but perhaps unlikely) that an event *announced* today (e.g. a merger with another company) could be expected to have a *substantial* $ impact on dividends starting in say five years' time. In this case the announcement could have a large effect on the current stock price even though it is relatively heavily discounted. Note that in a well-informed ('efficient') market one expects the stock price to respond immediately and completely to the announcement even though no dividends will actually be paid for five years. In contrast, if the market is inefficient (e.g. noise traders are present) then the price might rise not only in the current period but also in subsequent periods. Tests of the stock price response to announcements are known as *event studies*.

At the moment (4.23) is 'non-operational' since it involves unobservable expectations terms. We cannot calculate fundamental value (i.e. the RHS of (4.23)) and hence cannot see if it corresponds to the observable current price P_t. We need some ancillary tractable hypotheses about investors' forecasts of dividends and the discount rate. It is relatively straightforward to develop forecasting equations for dividends (and hence provide numerical values for $E_t D_{t+j}$ ($j = 1, 2, \ldots$). For example on annual data an AR(1) or AR(2) model for dividends fits the data quite well. The difficulty arises with the equilibrium rate of return $k_t (\delta_t = 1/(1 + k_t))$ which is required for investors willingly to hold the stock. There are numerous competing models of equilibrium returns and next it will be shown how the CAPM can be combined with the rational valuation formula so that the stock *price* is determined by a time varying discount rate.

4.1.1 The CAPM and the RVF

Market Portfolio

The one-period CAPM predicts that in equilibrium all investors will hold the market portfolio (i.e. all risky assets will be held in the same proportions in each individual's portfolio). Merton (1973) developed this idea in an intertemporal framework and showed that the (nominal) *excess return* over the risk-free rate, on the market portfolio, is proportional to the expected variance of returns on the market portfolio

$$ER_{t+1}^m - r_t = \lambda(E_t\sigma_{mt+1}^2) \tag{4.24}$$

The expected return can be defined as comprising a risk-free return plus a risk premium rp_t:

$$ER_t^m = r_t + rp_t \tag{4.25}$$

where $rp_t = \lambda E_t\sigma_{mt+1}^2$. Comparing (4.21) and (4.25) we see that according to the CAPM, the required rate of return on the market portfolio is given by:

$$k_t = r_t + \lambda(E_t\sigma_{mt+1}^2) \tag{4.26}$$

The equilibrium required return depends positively on the risk-free interest rate r_t and on the (non-diversifiable) risk of the market portfolio, as measured by its conditional variance $E_t\sigma_{mt+1}^2$. If either:

- agents do not perceive the market as risky (i.e. $E_t\sigma_{mt+1}^2 = 0$), or
- agents are risk neutral (i.e. $\lambda = 0$)

then the appropriate discount factor used by investors is the risk-free rate, r_t. Note that to determine price using the RVF, investors in general must determine k_t and hence forecast future values of the risk-free rate and the risk premium.

Individual Securities

Consider now the price of an individual security or a portfolio of assets which is a subset of the market portfolio (e.g. shares of either all industrial companies or all banking firms). The CAPM implies that to be willingly held as part of a diversified portfolio the expected (nominal) return on portfolio i is given by:

$$E_tR_{it+1} = r_t + \beta_{it}(E_tR_{t+1}^m - r_t) \tag{4.27}$$

where

$$\beta_{it} = E_t(\sigma_{im}/\sigma_m^2)_{t+1} \tag{4.28}$$

Substituting from (4.24) for $E_t\sigma_{mt+1}^2$ we have[1]:

$$E_tR_{it+1} = r_t + \lambda E_t(\sigma_{im})_{t+1} \tag{4.29}$$

where σ_{im} is the covariance between returns on asset i and the market portfolio. Again comparing (4.21) and (4.29) the equilibrium required rate of return on asset i is:

$$k_{t+1} = r_t + \lambda E_t(\sigma_{im})_{t+1} \tag{4.30}$$

The covariance term may be time varying and hence so might the future discount factors δ_{t+j} in the RVF for an individual security (or portfolio of securities).

Risk Premium

We can now give a firm definition of the risk premium on an individual stock (or group of stocks) that is consistent with the CAPM. The market only rewards investors for non-diversifiable (systematic) risk. The required (nominal) rate of return k_t to willingly hold an individual stock as part of a wider portfolio is equal to the risk-free rate *plus* a reward for risk or *risk premium* rp_t

$$k_{it} = r_t + rp_{it} = r_t + E_t(\sigma_{im})_{t+1} \qquad (4.31)$$

Summary: The RVF

- From the definition of the expected return on a stock it is possible via the Euler equation and rational expectations to derive the rational valuation formula (RVF) for stock prices.

- Stock prices in an efficient and well-informed market are determined by the DPV of expected future dividends and expected future discount rates.

- If equilibrium expected returns are constant then the discount rate in the RVF is constant.

- If equilibrium (nominal) expected returns are given by the CAPM then the discount factor in the RVF may be time varying and depends on the (nominal) risk-free rate and a variance/covariance term.

4.1.2 The Consumption CAPM

In the one-period CAPM the individual investor's objective function is assumed to be fully determined by the standard deviation and return on the portfolio. The investor tries to earn the highest expected return for any given level of portfolio risk.

An alternative view of the determination of equilibrium returns in a well-diversified portfolio is provided by the intertemporal consumption CAPM (denoted C-CAPM). Here, the investor maximises expected utility which depends only on current and future consumption (see Lucas (1978) and Mankiw and Shapiro (1986)). Financial assets play a role in this model in that they help to smooth consumption over time. Securities are held to transfer purchasing power from one period to another. If an agent had no assets and was not allowed to accumulate assets then his consumption would be determined by his current income. If he holds assets, he can sell some of these to finance consumption when his current income is low. An individual asset is therefore more 'desirable' if its return is expected to be high when consumption is expected to be low. Thus the systematic risk of the asset is determined by the covariance of the assets return with respect to consumption (rather than its covariance with respect to the return on the market portfolio as in the 'basic' CAPM). The C-CAPM is an intertemporal model unlike the basic one-period CAPM. In the C-CAPM, dividends and prices are all denominated in consumption units and hence all analysis is in terms of real variables. In the C-CAPM the individual investor maximises

$$E_t \left[\sum_{j=0}^{\infty} \theta^j U(C_{t+j}) \right] \qquad 0 < \theta < 1 \qquad (4.32)$$

where $U(C)$ is the utility function and $\theta_t = (1 + t_p)^{-1}$ where t_p is the individual's subjective rate of time preference for consumption today versus consumption tomorrow (and is assumed to be constant). The budget constraint is of the form:

$$C_t = D_t X_{t-1} + P_t(X_{t-1} - X_t) \tag{4.33}$$

where D_t = dividends received (e.g. see Sheffrin, 1983), X_t = holdings of securities at time t which will yield dividend payments at $t + 1$. The first term on the RHS of (4.33) is dividend income and the second term represents receipts from the sale of the risky assets (shares). The individual must choose the amount of consumption today and thereby simultaneously choose the quantity of risky assets to be carried forward into the next period.

First-Order Condition

The first-order condition for maximising expected utility has the agent equating the utility loss from a reduction in *current* consumption, with the additional gain in (discounted) consumption *next period*. Lower consumption expenditure at time t allows investment in an asset which has an expected positive return and therefore yields extra resources for future consumption. More formally, a \$1 reduction in (real) consumption today reduces utility by $U'(C_t)$ but results in an expected payout of \$$(1 + E_t R_{it+1})$ next period. When spent on next period's consumption, the extra utility per (real) \$ next period, discounted at a (real) rate θ_t is $\theta_t U'(C_{t+1})$. Hence the *total extra* utility expected next period is $E_t[(1 + R_{it+1})\theta_t U'(C_{t+1})]$. In equilibrium we have

$$U'(C_t) = E_t[(1 + R_{it+1})\theta_t U'(C_{t+1})] \tag{4.34}$$

or

$$E_t(1 + R_{it+1})S_{t+1} = 1 \tag{4.35}$$

where

$$S_{t+1} = \theta_t U'(C_{t+1})/U'(C_t)$$

is the marginal rate of substitution of current for future (discounted) consumption. Apart from the discount rate θ_t, the MRS depends on the *ratio* of the marginal utility from consumption at $t + 1$ to that at time t. The MRS therefore depends on agents' preferences ('tastes') between consumption today versus consumption tomorrow and hence ought to be constant or vary only slowly over time (as tastes change).

We can now use equation (4.34) to

- calculate the implied rational valuation formula (or DPV) for stock *prices*
- obtain a relationship for the expected *return* in terms of the covariance between consumption and asset returns, that is the C-CAPM

Consumption and the Rational Valuation Formula

The RVF for stock prices can be calculated by using (4.35) in the Euler equation which is then solved by forward substitution as in our earlier examples. The expected return is defined as

$$1 + E_t R_{it+1} \equiv E_t \frac{(V_{t+1} + D_{t+1})}{V_t} \tag{4.36}$$

where V_t = the (fundamental) value of the asset at time t. Substituting for $1 + ER_{it+1}$ from (4.35) in (4.36) and rearranging we obtain an Euler equation in V_t:

$$V_t = E_t[S_{t+1}[V_{t+1} + D_{t+1}]]$$

Forward substitution yields (given a suitable terminal condition and restrictions on the sequence $S_{t+1}, S_{t+2} \ldots$):

$$V_t = E_t[S_{t+1}D_{t+1} + S_{t+1}S_{t+2}D_{t+2} + S_{t+1}S_{t+2}S_{t+3}D_{t+3} + \cdots$$

$$= E_t \sum_{j=1}^{\infty} \left[\prod_{i=1}^{j} S_{t+i} \right] D_{t+j} \tag{4.37}$$

and it is easily seen that the marginal rate of substitution S_{t+i} plays the role of a time varying discount factor. Further simplification assuming θ is constant yields:

$$V_t = \sum_{j=1}^{\infty} \theta^i E_t \left[\left[\frac{U'(C_{t+j})}{U'(C_t)} \right] \right] D_{t+j} \tag{4.38}$$

Thus the discount factor for dividends in the C-CAPM depends on θ and the marginal rate of substitution of consumption at $t + j$ for consumption today. However, as $0 < \theta < 1$ the weight attached to the marginal utility of future consumption (relative to today's marginal utility) declines, the further into the future the consumption is expected to accrue. It is worth noting that (4.38) reduces to the 'constant discount rate' case if agents are risk neutral. Under risk neutrality the utility function is linear and $U'(C) = $ constant.

Consumption and the CAPM

To obtain the 'usual' covariance term, note that for *any* two random variables:

$$E(x \cdot y) = \text{cov}(x, y) + (Ex)(Ey)$$

Hence substituting for $E(R_{it+1} \cdot S_{t+1})$ in (4.34) and rearranging we have

$$E_t[1 + R_{it+1}] = [1 - \text{cov}(R_{it+1}, S_{t+1})]/E_t S_{t+1} \tag{4.39}$$

The C-CAPM therefore predicts that the expected return on *any* asset i depends

- negatively on the covariance of the return on asset i with the MRS of consumption and
- varies inversely with the expected marginal rate of substitution of consumption

The intuitive interpretation behind equations (4.35) and (4.39) is as follows. If it is believed that tomorrow will bring 'good times' and a high level of consumption, then with *diminishing* marginal utility of consumption the additional utility value of this consumption will be low, next period. Hence S_{t+1} will be relatively low. According to (4.35) the expected return on security i will then have to be higher than average, to persuade an individual to defer consumption today, hold the asset and carry the consumption opportunity forward to tomorrow, when its contribution to additional utility will be low. For example, the equilibrium expected return on securities during the Great Depression when consumption was low must have been relatively high. Unless investors in the 1930s expected a high return on their portfolio of stocks they would have sold their shares and used the funds to finance current consumption which at the margin would have added a great deal to their utility, as they were starting from a very low level of consumption.

We can interpret equation (4.39) in a similar fashion. Assets whose returns have a high negative covariance with S are very 'risky' and will be willingly held only if they have a high expected return. This is because they would be sold to finance 'high utility' *current* consumption unless the investor is compensated by the high expected return.

Thus, the C-CAPM explains why different assets earn different equilibrium returns. It also allows equilibrium returns to vary over time as agents' marginal rate of substitution varies over the business cycle. The C-CAPM therefore links asset returns with the real economy (i.e. economic fundamentals).

In order to make the C-CAPM operational, we need to calibrate the terms on the RHS of (4.39). To investigate this it is assumed that the intertemporal utility function to be maximised by the investor is additively separable over time (and with respect to leisure) and that the utility from future consumption $U(C_{t+j})$ is discounted each period at a *constant rate* θ $(0 < \theta < 1)$. The specific form for the utility function in each period t exhibits diminishing marginal utility (and has a constant Arrow–Pratt measure of relative risk aversion, α):

$$U(C_t) = \frac{C_t^{1-\alpha}}{1-\alpha} \qquad 0 < \alpha < 1 \qquad (4.40)$$

It may be shown that with utility function (4.40) the unobservable covariance term in (4.39) may be approximated as

$$\text{cov}(R_{it+1}, S_{t+1}) = -\alpha\theta[\text{cov}(R_{it+1}, g_{t+1}^c)] \qquad (4.41)$$

where $g_{t+1}^c = C_{t+1}/C_t$, the growth in consumption. The 'unobservable' covariance is now proportional to the observable covariance between the return on asset i and the growth in consumption. Finally, substituting (4.41) in (4.39) we obtain an expression that is similar in form to that for the basic CAPM:

$$E_t(R_{it+1}) = \gamma_{0t} + \gamma_{1t}[\text{cov}(R_{it+1}, g_{t+1}^c)] \qquad (4.42)$$

where

$$\gamma_{0t} = (1 - ES_t)/ES_t \qquad (4.43)$$

$$\gamma_{1t} = \alpha\theta/ES_t \qquad (4.44)$$

The terms γ_{0t} and γ_{1t} depend on the MRS of present for future consumption and if this is assumed to be constant then (4.42) provides a straightforward interpretation of the C-CAPM. If the return on asset i has a 'low' covariance with consumption growth then it will be willingly held, even if its expected return is relatively low. This is because the asset on average has a high return when consumption is low and hence can be sold to finance current consumption which has a high marginal utility.

Equation (4.35) suggests a way in which we can test the C-CAPM model of equilibrium returns. If we assume a constant relative risk aversion utility function, then (4.35) for two assets i and j becomes (see Scott, (1991)):

$$[(1 + R_{it+1})\theta(g_{t+1}^c)^{-\alpha} - 1] = \varepsilon_{it+1}$$

$$[(1 + R_{jt+1})\theta(g_{t+1}^c)^{-\alpha} - 1] = \varepsilon_{jt+1} \qquad (4.45)$$

where we have assumed rational expectations $(R_{it+1} = ER_{it+1} + \varepsilon_{it+1})$ and 'replaced' ER_{it+1} by its outturn value R_{it+1}. The two (illustrative) equations imply that expected returns on all assets are proportional. More formally, the two non-linear equations (4.46) have the restriction that the same parameters (θ, α) appear in each equation. Hence if we estimate these equations jointly, using time series data, these cross-equation restrictions provide a strong test of the C-CAPM. We do this in Chapter 6.

C-CAPM and the Discount Rate

The C-CAPM implies that in the equation underlying the derivation of the rational valuation formula, namely:

$$E_t R_{t+1} = k_{t+1} \tag{4.46}$$

the required equilibrium (real) rate of return is given by

$$k_{t+1} = \gamma_{0t} + \gamma_{1t} \cdot E_t \operatorname{cov}(R_{it+1}, g_{t+1}^c) \tag{4.47}$$

Hence the required (real) rate of return in the RVF would only be constant if the covariance term is expected to be constant in the future, which in general one would not expect to be the case.

Of course if one assumes risk neutrality (i.e. a linear utility function), then the risk aversion parameter $\alpha = 0$, the MRS is constant and then (4.39) reduces to $E_t R_{t+1} =$ 'constant'. Hence the RVF becomes the simple expression $P_t = \sum_{i=1}^{\infty} \delta^i D_{t+i}^e$, where the (real) discount factor δ depends on the *constant* MRS.

Appraisal of C-CAPM

For economic theorists the C-CAPM model has the advantage that it is firmly grounded in an intertemporal maximisation problem and is based on views about agents' tastes that are reasonably uncontroversial (at least among economists), such as diminishing marginal utility from consumption. The theory (Grossman and Shiller, 1981) holds for *any* asset or portfolio of assets. It holds for *any* individual consumer who has the *option* of investing in stocks even though he may not actually invest in stocks. It incorporates any aspects of uncertainty as long as these are reflected in consumption decisions. It also holds for any time horizon of returns (e.g. month, year). It is therefore a very general theory of equilibrium asset returns. However, sceptics would question some of the assumptions of the C-CAPM, for example:

(i) a constant discount rate (θ) for future consumption and that utility only depends on the level of consumption in each future period. Critics might suggest that the rate at which investors discount future utility may vary over time due to waves of optimism or pessimism about the future. More importantly perhaps, utility is also likely to be influenced by the uncertainty attached to future consumption (i.e. we need to introduce second moments, namely the variance of consumption into the mathematical model).

(ii) Critics might argue that insurance companies and pension funds are not interested in maximising intertemporal consumption of policyholders but in maximising short-term profits or the size of the firm. As these agents are 'big players' in the stock market the C-CAPM may be an incomplete model of valuation.

(iii)   Because individuals who hold stocks are concentrated among the wealthy, then *aggregate* consumption might not accurately reflect the consumption opportunities of this group.

(iv)   The usual criticisms of such models can also be raised such as the assumption of rational expectations, homogeneous expectations by agents, etc.

When we discuss tests of the C-CAPM in Chapter 6, the above potential limitations of the model should aid our interpretation of the empirical results.

Wealth in the Utility Function

A more general version of the CAPM than the C-CAPM may be obtained by assuming investors maximise the DPV of expected future *real* wealth W (see Scott (1991)). The marginal utility of consumption is then replaced with the marginal utility of real wealth $U'(W_t)$. If the intertemporal utility function is separable over time then $U'(W) = U'(C)$ and the model collapses to the C-CAPM. However, where this is not the case, it is the MRS of current for future real wealth which determines the discount factor in the RVF. In general, models based on intertemporal maximisation of consumption or wealth result in equations for fundamental value V_t of the form:

$$V_t = \sum_{j=1}^{\infty} \theta^j E_t \left[\frac{U'(Z_{t+j})}{U'(Z_t)} \cdot D_{t+j} \right] \tag{4.48}$$

with a constant real discount rate θ (in the intertemporal utility function) and $Z =$ real consumption or real wealth. The first term in the square brackets is the MRS (between $t + j$ and t). Since these models are based on utility functions involving real 'quantities', all the variables are also in real terms. However, with a small modification they yield a similar relationship for *nominal* fundamental value which then depends on *nominal* dividends and the MRS between \$1 at time $t + j$ and \$1 at time t.

4.2   SUMMARY

In this chapter we have concentrated on two main themes. The first is to demonstrate the relationship between any model of equilibrium expected *returns* and the RVF formula for stock *prices*. The second is the development of a CAPM based on utility theory. The main conclusions to emerge are:

- Assuming $E_t R_{t+1} = k_{t+1}$ where k_{t+1} represents some equilibrium model of expected returns we can then invoke the (rational expectations) chain rule of forecasting to obtain the RVF for stock prices. In general, stock prices depend on the DPV of expected future dividends and expected future discount rates. Any changes in these fundamental variables will cause a change in stock prices.

- Models such as the CAPM and C-CAPM, which give rise to equilibrium returns that are (potentially at least) time varying, also imply time varying discount rates in the RVF of stock prices.

- The C-CAPM is based on utility theory and is a very general intertemporal model of equilibrium asset returns. It implies that assets whose returns have a high negative correlation with consumption will be willingly held even though they have a low expected return. This is because such assets can be sold when consumption is low and therefore the *marginal* utility from extra consumption is high.

ENDNOTE

1. There is a sleight of hand here, since for two random variables x and y, $E(x/y) \neq Ex/Ey$.

FURTHER READING

An entertaining and informative history of the origin of modern finance is provided by Bernstein (1992). There are many very good basic text books in finance dealing with the issues in Part 1. A clear and simple exposition is Kolb (1995), with Levy and Sarnat (1984) and Elton and Gruber (1993) covering similar ground at a more advanced level. Blake (1990) provides an intermediate approach bridging the gap between theory and the techniques used by practitioners. Applications of the basic concepts in finance to practical issues can also be found in issues of the *Bank of England Quarterly Bulletin*, publications of the US Federal Reserve Banks (many of which are provided free on request) and professional journals such as the *Journal of Portfolio Management*, *Journal of Fixed Income*, *Financial Analysts Journal* and *Risk*.

PART 2
Efficiency, Predictability and Volatility

5
The Efficient Markets Hypothesis

The efficient markets hypothesis (EMH) may be expressed in a number of alternative ways (not all of which are equivalent) and the differences between these alternative representations can easily become rather esoteric, technical and subtle (e.g. see LeRoy (1989)). In this introductory section these technical issues will be avoided as far as possible and general terms will be used about the ideas which lie behind the concept of an efficient market — the more technical aspects will be 'filled in' later, in this and other chapters.

When economists speak of capital markets as being *efficient* they usually mean that they view asset prices and returns as being determined as the outcome of supply and demand in a competitive market, peopled by rational traders. These rational traders rapidly assimilate any information that is relevant to the determination of asset prices or returns (e.g. future dividend prospects) and adjust prices accordingly. Hence, individuals do not have different comparative advantages in the acquisition of information. It follows that in such a world there should be no opportunities for making a return on a stock that is in excess of a fair payment for the riskiness of that stock. In short, abnormal profits from trading should be zero. Thus, agents process information efficiently and immediately incorporate this information into stock prices. If current and past information is immediately incorporated into current prices then only new information or 'news' should cause changes in prices. Since news is by definition unforecastable, then price changes (or returns) should be unforecastable: no information at time t or earlier should help to improve the forecast of returns (or equivalently to reduce the forecast error made by the individual). This independence of forecast errors from previous information is known as the orthogonality property and it is a widely used concept in testing the efficient markets hypothesis.

The above are the basic ideas behind the EMH, but financial economists, being good academics, need to put these ideas into a testable form and this requires some mathematical notation and terminology. In order to guide the reader through the maze that is the EMH the procedure will be as follows:

- In order to introduce readers to the concepts involved an overview is provided of the basic ideas using fairly simple mathematics.
- To motivate our subsequent technical analysis of the EMH an overview is given of the implications of the EMH (and violations of it). Consideration will be given to the role of investment analysts, public policy issues concerning mergers and takeovers, capital adequacy, the cost of capital, the excess volatility of stock prices and calls for trading halts and margin requirements on stock transactions. In general, violations of

the EMH provide a prima facie case for government intervention in the workings of the financial system. (But note that we do not deal with the public policy implications which arise from the assumption of asymmetric information and adverse selection in financial markets).

- It will be shown how general common sense ideas of 'efficiency' can be put into mathematical form. For example, if investors use all available relevant information to forecast stock returns thus eliminating abnormal profits this can be shown to involve concepts such as a fair game, a martingale and a random walk.

- Empirical tests of the EMH can be based either on survey data on expectations or on a specific model of equilibrium expected returns (such as those discussed in earlier chapters) and a fairly simple overview is given of such tests which are examined in detail in later chapters.

The basic concepts of the EMH using the stock market as an example are discussed, but the same general ideas are applicable to other financial instruments (e.g. bonds, futures, options).

5.1 OVERVIEW

Under the EMH the stock *price* P_t already incorporates all relevant information and the only reason for prices to change between time t and time $t + 1$ is the arrival of 'news' or unanticipated events. Forecast errors, that is, $\varepsilon_{t+1} = P_{t+1} - E_t P_{t+1}$ should therefore be zero on average and should be uncorrelated with any information Ω_t that was available at the time the forecast was made. The latter is often referred to as the *rational expectations* (RE) element of the EMH and may be represented:

$$P_{t+1} = E_t P_{t+1} + \varepsilon_{t+1} \tag{5.1}$$

The forecast error is expected to be zero on average because prices only change on the arrival of 'news' which itself is a random variable, sometimes 'good' sometimes 'bad'. The expected value of the forecast error is zero

$$E_t \varepsilon_{t+1} \equiv E_t(P_{t+1} - E_t P_{t+1}) \equiv E_t P_{t+1} - E_t P_{t+1} \equiv 0 \tag{5.1a}$$

An implication of $E_t \varepsilon_{t+1} = 0$ is that the forecast of P_{t+1} is unbiased (i.e. on *average*, actual price equals expected price). Note that ε_{t+1} could also be (loosely) described as the *unexpected* profit (or loss) on holding the stock between t and $t + 1$. Under the EMH, unexpected profits must be zero on average and this is represented by (5.1a).

The statement that 'the forecast error must be independent of any information Ω_t available at time t (or earlier)' is known as the *orthogonality property*. It may be shown that if ε_t is serially correlated then the orthogonality property is violated. An example of a serially correlated error term is the first-order autoregressive process, AR(1).

$$\varepsilon_{t+1} = \rho \varepsilon_t + v_t \tag{5.2}$$

where v_t is a (white noise) random element (and by assumption is independent of information at time t, Ω_t). The forecast error $\varepsilon_t = P_t - E_{t-1} P_t$ is known at time t and hence forms part of Ω_t. Equation (5.2) says that this period's forecast error ε_t has a *predictable effect* on next period's forecast error ε_{t+1} but the latter according to (5.1) would be useful in forecasting future prices. This violates the EMH since information known at time t, namely the forecast error ε_t, helps forecast future prices.

We can see more directly why serial correlation in ε_t implies that information at time t helps to forecast P_{t+1} as follows. Lag equation (5.1) one period and multiply it by ρ giving

$$\rho P_t = \rho(E_{t-1} P_t) + \rho \varepsilon_t \tag{5.3}$$

subtracting (5.1) from (5.3), rearranging and using $v_t = \varepsilon_{t+1} - \rho \varepsilon_t$ from (5.2), we have

$$P_{t+1} = \rho P_t + (E_t P_{t+1} - \rho E_{t-1} P_t) + v_t \tag{5.4}$$

We can see from (5.4) that when ε is serially correlated, tomorrow's price depends upon today's price and is therefore (partly) forecastable from the information available today. (Note that the term in brackets being a *change* in expectations is not forecastable.) Therefore, the assumption of 'no serial correlation' in ε is really subsumed under the EMH assumption that information available today should be of no use in forecasting tomorrow's stock price (i.e. the orthogonality property).

Note that the EMH/RE assumption places no restrictions on the form of the second and higher moments of the distribution of ε_t. For example, the variance of ε_{t+1} (denoted σ^2_{t+1}) may be related to its past value, σ^2_t, without violating RE. (This is an ARCH process, see Chapter 17.) RE places restrictions only on the behaviour of the first moment (i.e. expected value) of ε_t.

The efficient markets hypothesis is often applied to the *return* on stocks, R_t, and implies that one cannot earn supernormal profits by buying and selling stocks. Thus an equation similar to (5.1) applies to stock returns. Actual returns R_{t+1} will sometimes be above and sometimes below expected returns $E_t R_{t+1}$ but *on average, unexpected* returns denoted ε_{t+1} are zero:

$$\varepsilon_{t+1} = R_{t+1} - E_t R_{t+1} \tag{5.5}$$

$$E_t \varepsilon_{t+1} = E_t R_{t+1} - E_t R_{t+1} = 0 \tag{5.6}$$

The variable ε_{t+1} could also be described as the 'forecast error' of returns. To test the EMH we need a model of how investors form a view about *expected* returns. This model should be based on rational behaviour (somehow defined). For the moment assume a very simple model where

(i)   stocks pay no dividends, so that the expected return is the expected capital gain due to price changes

(ii) investors are willing to hold stocks as long as expected or required returns are constant, hence:

$$E_t R_{t+1} = k \tag{5.7}$$

Substituting in (5.5) in (5.3):

$$R_{t+1} = k + \varepsilon_{t+1} \tag{5.8}$$

where ε_{t+1} is white noise and independent of Ω_t. We may think of the required rate of return k on the risky asset as consisting of a risk-free rate r and a risk premium rp (i.e. $k = r + rp$) and (5.7) assumes both of these are constant over time. Since for a non-dividend paying stock, $R_{t+1} = (P_{t+1} - P_t)/P_t \approx \ln(P_{t+1}/P_t)$ equation (5.8) implies that *ex post* the *proportionate change* in the stock price will equal a constant plus a random error, or equivalently:

$$\ln P_{t+1} = k + \ln P_t + \varepsilon_{t+1} \tag{5.9}$$

Equation (5.9) is a random walk in the logarithm of P with drift term k. Note that (the logarithm of) stock prices will only follow a random walk under the EMH if the risk-free rate r and the risk premium rp are constant and dividends are zero. Often in empirical work the 'price' at $t + 1$ is adjusted to include dividends paid between t and $t + 1$ and when it is stated that 'stock prices follow a random walk', this usually applies to 'prices inclusive of dividends'. In some empirical work researchers may take the view that the stock return is dominated by capital gains (and losses) and hence will use quoted prices excluding dividends.

For *daily changes* in stock prices over a period of relative tranquillity (e.g. excluding the crash of October 1987) it may appear a reasonable assumption that the risk premium is a constant. However, when daily changes in stock prices are examined it is usually found that the error term is serially correlated and that the return varies on different days of the week. In particular, price changes between Friday and Monday are smaller than on other days of the week. This is known as the *weekend effect*. It has also been found for some stocks that daily price changes in the month of January are different from those in other months. 'Weekends' and 'January' are clearly predictable events! Therefore returns on stocks depend in a predictable way upon information readily available (i.e. what day of the week it is). This is a violation of the EMH under the assumption of a constant risk premium since returns are in part predictable. However, in the 'real world' it may *not* be the case that this predictability implies that investors can earn supernormal profits since transactions costs need to be taken into account.

It should be clear from the above discussion that in order to test the EMH we require some view of how prices or rates of return are determined in the market. That is we require an economic model of the determination of equilibrium returns and asset prices. Our test of whether agents use information efficiently is conditional on our having chosen the *correct* model to explain either stock prices or the rate of return on such stocks. Failure or rejection of the efficient markets hypothesis may be either because we have the wrong equilibrium 'pricing model' or because agents genuinely do not use information efficiently.

As noted above, another way of describing the EMH is to say that in an efficient market it is impossible for investors to make supernormal profits. Under the EMH investors make a return on each security which covers the riskiness of that security (and they can make sufficient profits just to cover their costs in order to stay in the industry, that is in the business of buying and selling shares). However, there must not be opportunities available to make abnormal profits by dealing in stocks. The latter is often referred to as the 'fair game' property.

One particular equilibrium valuation model is the CAPM. The CAPM predicts that in equilibrium the expected excess return on asset i should depend only on its beta and the expected excess return on the market.

$$(E_t R_{i,t+1} - r_t) = \beta_i (E_t R_{t+1}^m - r_t) \tag{5.10}$$

Since the excess return on the *market* portfolio is constant at a particular point in time then two assets will have different expected excess returns only if their respective betas differ. Put another way, if we plot the *expected* return on a set of assets against their beta values we expect *all* securities to lie on the Security Market Line (SML) (and for *actual* returns to be distributed randomly around the line). If a security *persistently* had an excess return above the SML, then this security is earning a 'supernormal return' given its risk class and this would be a violation of the EMH. However, note that it would be a violation of the EMH under the assumption that the CAPM is the *true model* of equilibrium asset pricing. This again emphasises the fact that tests of the EMH usually involve the joint hypotheses (i) that agents use information rationally, (ii) that they all use the same equilibrium model for asset pricing which happens to be the 'true model'.

5.2 IMPLICATIONS OF THE EMH

The view that the return on shares is determined by the actions of rational agents in a competitive market and that equilibrium returns reflect all available public information, is probably quite a widely held view among financial economists. The slightly stronger assertion, namely that stock prices also reflect their fundamental value (i.e. the DPV of future dividends) is also widely held. What then are the implications of the EMH applied to the stock market?

As far as a risk averse investor is concerned the EMH means that he should adopt a 'buy and hold' policy. He should spread his risks and hold the market portfolio (or the 20 or so shares that mimic the market portfolio). Andrew Carnegie's advice to 'put all your eggs in one basket and watch the basket' should be avoided. The role for investment analysts, if the EMH is correct, is very limited and would, for example, include:

(i)   advising on the choice of the 20 or so shares that mimic the market portfolio,

(ii)   altering the *proportion* of wealth held in each asset to reflect the market share portfolio weights (the x_i^* of the CAPM) which will alter over time. The latter alters both as expected returns change and as the riskiness of each security relative to the market changes (i.e. covariances of returns),

(iii) altering the portfolio as taxes change (e.g. if dividends are more highly taxed than capital gains then for high rate income tax payers it is optimal, at the margin, to move to shares which have low dividends and high expected capital gains),

(iv) 'shopping around' in order to minimise transactions costs of buying and selling.

Under EMH the current share price incorporates all relevant publicly available information, hence the investment analyst cannot pick winners by reanalysing publicly available information or by using trading rules (e.g. buy 'low', wait for a price rise and sell 'high'). Thus the EMH implies that a major part of the current activities of investment managers is wasteful. We can go even further. The individual investor can buy a *proportion* of an *index fund* (e.g. mutual fund or unit trusts). The latter contains enough securities to closely mimic the market portfolio and transactions costs for individual investors are extremely low (say less than 2 percent of the value of the portfolio). Practitioners such as investment managers do not take kindly to the assertion that their skills are largely redundant. However, somewhat paradoxically they often support the view that the market is 'efficient'. But their use of 'efficient' is usually the assertion that the stock market has low transactions costs and should be free of government intervention (e.g. zero stamp duty, minimal regulations on trading positions and capital adequacy).

It is worth noting that most individuals and institutions do not hold anything like the 'market portfolio' of all marketable assets. Except for residents of the USA this would require most investors to hold predominantly *foreign securities* (i.e. most corporations would be owned by foreigners). Also most mutual funds and unit trusts *specialise* and sell funds in particular sectors (e.g. chemicals or services) or specific geographical areas (e.g. Japanese stocks). There is a marketing reason for this. If finance houses operate a number of such funds, then *they* effectively hold the market portfolio, while the individual can speculate on individual 'packages' of mutual funds. Also with this strategy the finance house will usually have at least one fund that it can boast has 'beaten the market'.

Takeovers, Conglomerates and Financial Institutions

Let us turn now to some public policy issues. The stock market is supposed to provide the 'correct' signals for the allocation of real resources (i.e. fixed investment). Only a small proportion of corporate investment is financed from new issues (e.g. about 4 percent on a gross basis in the UK); nevertheless, the rate of return of a quoted company on the stock market provides a measure of the opportunity cost of funds corrected for risk. The latter can be used in discounting future expected profits from a physical investment project (i.e. in investment appraisal). Other things equal, if profits from a firm's new investment project are expected to be high the existing share price will be 'high' and the firm can obtain its funds by issuing fewer shares. However, if the share price does not reflect *fundamentals* but is influenced by whim or fads of 'irrational' investors then this link is broken. An abnormally low share price which reflects ill-informed extraneous factors (e.g. irrational market prejudice) will then inhibit a firm from embarking on what (on a rational calculation) is a viable investment project.

The above analysis also applies to takeovers. If the stock market is myopic, that is only considers profits and dividends that accrue in the *near* future, then managers fearful of a takeover may distribute more in current dividends rather than using the retained profits to undertake profitable real investment say on R&D expenditure. This strategy will boost the share price if the market is myopic. This is generally known as 'short-termism'. A possible response by government to such short-termism might be to forbid hostile takeovers (e.g. as in Japan). The impact of short-termism on share prices might also be exacerbated by an incentive system whereby part of a manager's remuneration is in the form of share options. See Chapter 8 for a discussion on the theoretical and empirical issues that are relevant to the debate on short-termism.

The opposite view to the above, namely that hostile takeovers are welfare enhancing (i.e. in terms of the output and profits of the firm) requires the assumption that markets are efficient and that takeovers enable 'bad' incumbent managers to be replaced. In this scenario, the hostile bidder recognises that the incumbent 'bad' management has led shareholders to mark down the firm's share price. The hostile bidder pays a price in excess of the existing share price. After replacing the 'bad' managers and reorganising the firm, the ensuing higher future profits are just sufficient to compensate for the higher price he paid for the shares.

In the 1960s and 1970s there was a wave of conglomerate formation followed in the 1980s by leveraged buyouts and conglomerate breakups (i.e. 'asset stripping'). Conglomerate mergers were sometimes justified on the grounds that the acquisition of unrelated firms by 'firm A' reduced risk to the shareholder who held A's shares since the 'conglomerate' constituted a diversified portfolio of firms. The latter is an analogous argument to that developed in Chapter 2 when discussing portfolio diversification by individuals across a range of companies. Since diversification is easily accomplished by individuals altering *their* portfolio of stocks, then the above reason for the formation of conglomerates is invalid. (Of course, it carries more weight if, for some reason, risk averse individuals do not diversify their share holdings.)

Note that if share prices do reflect fundamentals but 'news' occurs frequently and is expected to make a substantial impact on a firm's future performance, then one would still expect to observe *highly volatile* share prices, even if the market is efficient. However, if on occasions such volatility had adverse implications for parts of the real economy (i.e. an 'externality') — for example, that a stock market crash led to insolvencies in financial institutions, a 'credit crunch' and less physical investment — this would at least provide a prima facie argument for governments to try and limit share price movements (e.g. by closing markets for a 'cooling-off period'). Also, where systemic risk is involved (e.g. a 'run' on one bank causes a run on other banks) one might be prepared to prohibit certain institutions from holding 'highly volatile' assets such as shares (e.g. banks in the USA).

By definition, 'news' is random around zero. Hence 'news' will not influence the level of share prices over a long horizon. Therefore except in exceptional circumstances 'news' would be unlikely to cause panics leading to a 'run' on banks or financial institutions by their depositors. However, if the market is inefficient and prices are subject to longer-term 'irrational swings' then stock price volatility may be greater than that predicted from the efficient markets hypothesis. Here, a prima facie case for financial institutions to have enough resources (reserves) to weather such storms seems stronger. This is one argument for general capital adequacy rules applied to financial institutions. If there are systematic risks (i.e. a form of externality) then, in principle, government action is required to ensure that the level of capital reflects the marginal social costs of the systematic risk, rather than the marginal private costs (for any individual financial institution).

What are the implications of market efficiency in stock and bond markets for issues in corporate finance? If the market is efficient then there is no point in delaying a physical investment project in the hope that 'financing conditions will improve' (i.e. that the share price will be higher): under the EMH the current price is the correct price and reflects expected future earnings from the project. Also under the EMH the firm's cost of capital cannot be lowered by a given *mix* of securities (e.g. by altering the proportions of debt and equity). The Modigliani–Miller theorem (in the absence of taxes and bankruptcy) suggests that the cost of capital is independent of the capital mix (i.e. debt-equity ratio) in an efficient market. The issue of capital mix can also be applied to the maturity (term) structure of debt. Since rates on long and short corporate bonds fully reflect available information the proportion of long debt to short-dated debt will also not alter the cost of capital to the firm. For example, under the expectations hypothesis, low long rates and *high current* short rates simply reflect an expectation of lower *future* short rates, so there is no advantage *ex ante* to financing an investment project by issuing long bonds rather than 'rolling over' a series of short bonds. (This is discussed in Chapter 9 on the term structure.)

It follows from the above arguments that the role of the corporate treasurer as an 'active manager' either as regards the choice over the appropriate 'mix' of sources of finance or in analysing the optimum time to float new stock or bond issues is futile, under the EMH. Of course, if the market is not efficient the corporate treasurer may attempt to 'beat the market' and he can also alter the stock market valuation of the firm by his chosen dividend policy or by share repurchase schemes, etc.

As one might imagine, the issue economists find hard to evaluate is what are the precise implications for public policy and the behaviour of firms if markets are *not* fully efficient (i.e. a so-called 'second best' policy). If markets are efficient there is a presumption that government intervention is not required. If markets are inefficient there is a prima facie case for government intervention. However, given uncertainty about the impact of any government policies on the behaviour of economic agents, the government should only intervene if, on balance, it feels the expected return from its policies outweigh the risks attached to such policies. Any model of market *in*efficiency needs to ascertain how far from efficiency the market is on average and what implications this has for public policy decisions and economic welfare in general. This is a rather difficult task given present knowledge, as subsequent chapters will show.

5.3 EXPECTATIONS, MARTINGALES AND FAIR GAME

As previously mentioned, the EMH can be formally stated in a number of different ways. We do not wish to get unduly embroiled in the finer points of these alternatives, since our main concern is to see how the hypothesis may be tested and used in understanding the behaviour of asset prices and rates of return. However, some formal definitions of the EMH are required. To this end, let us begin with some properties of conditional *mathematical* expectations; we can then state the basic axioms of rational expectations such as unbiasedness, orthogonality and the chain rule of forecasting. Next we introduce the concepts of a martingale and a fair game. We then have the basic tools to examine alternative representations and tests of the 'efficient markets hypothesis'.

Mathematical Expectations

If X is a random variable (e.g. heights of males in the UK) which can take discrete values $X_1, X_2, X_3 \ldots$ with probabilities π_i then the expected value of X, denoted EX, is *defined as*

$$EX = \sum_{i=1}^{\infty} \pi_i X_i \tag{5.11}$$

If X is a continuous random variable $(-\infty < X < \infty)$ with a continuous probability distribution $f(X)$ (e.g. normal distribution) then

$$E(X) = \int_{-\infty}^{\infty} X f(X) \, dX \tag{5.12}$$

Conditional probability distributions or conditional density functions are used extensively in the RE literature. For example, a fair die has a probability of (1/6)th of landing on any number from 1 to 6. However, suppose a friend lets you know that the die to be used is biased and lands on the number 6 for half the time and on the other numbers equally for the remaining throws. Conditional on the information from your friend you would then alter your probabilities to (1/2) for a 6 and (1/10) for the remaining five numbers. Your conditional expected value would therefore be different from the expected value from an unbiased die, since the associated probabilities (or probability density function) are different. The *conditional expectation* based on the information set (denoted) Ω_t is defined as

$$E(X_t|\Omega_t) = \int_{-\infty}^{\infty} X_t f(X_t|\Omega_t) \, dX_t \tag{5.13}$$

where $f(X_t|\Omega_t)$ is the *conditional* density function. A conditional expectation may be viewed as an optimal forecast of the random variable X_t, based on all relevant information Ω_t. The conditional forecast error is defined as ε_{t+1} where

$$\varepsilon_{t+1} = X_{t+1} - E(X_{t+1}|\Omega_t) \tag{5.14}$$

This (mathematical) conditional forecast error can be shown (always) to be zero on average:

$$E(\varepsilon_{t+1}|\Omega_t) = E(X_{t+1}|\Omega_t) - E(X_{t+1}|\Omega_t) = 0 \tag{5.15}$$

We can rearrange (5.14) as:

$$X_{t+1} = E(X_{t+1}|\Omega_t) + \varepsilon_{t+1} \tag{5.16}$$

and hence reinterpret (5.16) as stating that the conditional expectations are an unbiased forecast of the outturn value.

The second property of conditional mathematical expectations is that the forecast error is uncorrelated with all information at time t or earlier which, stated mathematically:

$$E(\varepsilon_{t+1}' \Omega_t | \Omega_t) = 0 \tag{5.17}$$

This is known as the *orthogonality property* of conditional expectations. The intuitive reason why (5.17) holds is that if Ω_t could be used to reduce the forecast error ε_{t+1}, then it could be used to improve the forecast: hence all relevant information could not have been used in forecasting X_{t+1}. It also follows that an optimal conditional forecast is one where subsequent forecast errors are unpredictable.

Note that an optimal forecast need not necessarily predict X_{t+1} accurately. Each ε_{t+j} can be large and the conditional expectation $E_t X_{t+j}$ may only explain a small part of the variation in actual X_{t+j}. What is important is that the optimal forecast cannot be improved upon (in the sense of using Ω_t to reduce the forecast errors ε_{t+j}). It is also worth noting that it is only the behaviour of the *mean* of the forecast error that has been restricted in (5.17). The variance of the conditional forecast error denoted $E(\sigma_t^2|\Omega_t)$ need not be constant and indeed may in part be predictable. The latter is of importance when discussing the implications for market volatility within the framework of the EMH.

Consider for a moment making a forecast in January (at time t) as to what the forecast you will make in February ($t+1$) will be, about the outcome of the variable X in March (i.e. X_{t+2}). Mathematically this may be represented as

$$E_t[E_{t+1}(X_{t+2}|\Omega_{t+1})] \tag{5.18}$$

If information Ω_t at time t is used efficiently then you cannot predict today *how you will change* your forecast in the future, hence

$$E_t[E_{t+1}(X_{t+2})] = E_t(X_{t+1}) \tag{5.19}$$

where $E_t(X_{t+1})$ is equivalent to $E(X_{t+1}|\Omega_t)$. This is the rule of *iterated expectations* which may be succinctly represented as:

$$E_t E_{t+1} E_{t+2} \ldots = E_t \tag{5.20}$$

The above three properties, unbiasedness, orthogonality and iterated expectations, all hold for conditional mathematical expectations (as a matter of mathematical 'logic'). What rational expectations does is to assume that individual agent's *subjective expectations* equal the conditional mathematical expectations, based on the *true* probability distribution of outcomes. Economic agents are therefore assumed to behave *as if* they formed their subjective expectations as the mathematical expectations of the true model of the economy. This is generally referred to as 'Muth-RE' (Muth, 1961).

To get a feel for what this entails consider a simple supply and demand model for, say, wheat. The supply and demand curves are subject to random shocks (e.g. changes in the weather on the supply side and changes in 'tastes' on the demand side for wheat-based products such as cookies). The actual equilibrium price depends in part on the actual value of such 'shocks' which will only be revealed after the market has cleared. Conceptually the individual RE farmer has to determine his supply of wheat, at each price and the expected supplies of wheat of all other farmers (based on known factors such as technology, prices of inputs, etc.). He makes a similar calculation of the known factors influencing demand such as income, x_t^d. He then solves for the *expected* equilibrium price by setting the demand and supply shocks to their expected values of zero. Thus the farmers behave *as if* they use a competitive stochastic model of supply and demand. The difference between the equilibrium or expected price and the outturn price is a random unforecastable 'error' due to the random shocks to the supply and demand functions. No additional information available to the farmer can reduce such errors any further (i.e. the RE orthogonality property holds). The stochastic reduced form is

$$P_{t+1} = P_{t+1}^e + \varepsilon_{t+1} = f(x_t^d, x_t^s) + \varepsilon_{t+1} \qquad (5.21)$$

where $P_{t+1}^e = f(x_t^d, x_t^s)$ is the equilibrium price based on the known factors x_t^i which influence supply and demand. The forecast error is the random variable ε_{t+1}. Hence under Muth-RE the uncertainty or randomness in the economy (e.g. the weather or new product innovations) gives rise to agents' forecast errors for the actual equilibrium price.

To test whether agents' actual *subjective* expectations obey the axioms of mathematical conditional expectations we either need an accurate measure of individual agent's subjective expectations or we need to know the form of the true model of the economy used by all agents. Survey data on expectations can provide a 'noisy' proxy variable for each agent's subjective expectations. If we are to test that actual forecast errors have the properties of conditional mathematical expectations via the second method (i.e. using the true model of the economy) the researcher has to choose a particular model from among the many available on the 'economist's shelf' (e.g. Keynesian, monetarist, real business cycle, etc.). Clearly, a failure of the forecast errors from such a model to obey the RE axioms could be due to the researcher choosing the wrong model from the 'shelf'. (That is, agents in the real world actually use another model.) The latter can provide a convenient alibi for a supporter of RE, since he can always claim that failure to conform to the axioms is not due to agents being non-rational but because the 'wrong' economic model was used.

Martingale and Fair Game Properties

Suppose we have a stochastic variable X_t which has the property:

$$E(X_{t+1}|\Omega_t) = X_t \qquad (5.22)$$

then X_t is said to be a martingale. Given (5.22) the best forecast of all future values of $X_{t+j}(j \geq 1)$ is the current value X_t. No other information in Ω_t helps to improve the forecast once the agent knows X_t. A stochastic process y_t is a *fair game* if:

$$E(y_{t+1}|\Omega_t) = 0 \qquad (5.23)$$

Thus a fair game has the property that the expected 'return' is zero given Ω_t. It follows trivially that if X_t is a martingale $y_{t+1} = X_{t+1} - X_t$ is a fair game. A fair game is therefore sometimes referred to as a martingale difference. A fair game is such that the expected return is zero. For example, tossing an (unbiased) coin with a payout of \$1 for a head and minus \$1 for a tail is a fair game. The fair game property implies that the 'return' to the random variable y_t is zero on average even though the agent uses all available information Ω_t in making his forecast.

One definition of the EMH is that it embodies the fair game property for *unexpected stock returns* $y_{t+1} = R_{t+1} - R_{t+1}^*$, where R_{t+1}^* is the *equilibrium return* given by some economic model of the supply and demand for risky assets (e.g. CAPM). The excess (or abnormal) return is the profit from holding the risky asset. The fair game property implies that *on average* the abnormal return is zero[1]. Thus an investor may experience large gains and losses (relative to the equilibrium return R_{t+1}^*) in specific periods but these average out to zero over a series of 'bets'.

Stock Prices and Martingales

Let us assume a simple model of returns, namely that the equilibrium or required return is a constant $= k$. The fair game property implies that the conditional expected excess return is zero:

$$E[(R_{t+1} - k)|\Omega_t] = 0 \qquad (5.24)$$

Given the definition of R_{t+1} we have

$$E_t[\ln(P_{t+1}/P_t) + D_{t+1}/P_t] = k \qquad (5.25)$$

where we have used the logarithmic approximation for the proportionate price change (i.e. $\ln(P_{t+1}/P_t) = \ln[1 + (P_{t+1} - P_t)/P_t] \approx \Delta P_{t+1}/P_t$). Since, in general, the dividend price ratio is non-zero and varies over time then, in general, the (log of the) *price level* cannot be a martingale in this class of model. In fact any increase in the expected capital gain must be exactly offset by a lower expected dividend yield. Hence in the efficient markets literature when it is said that stock prices follow a martingale, it should be understood that this refers to stock prices *including dividends*. In fact we could define a new stock price variable q_t such that

$$\ln(q_{t+1}/q_t) = R_{t+1}$$

Then the logarithm of q_t is a martingale (under the assumption that expected returns are constant).

Fair Game and the Rational Valuation Formula

If we let equilibrium or required returns by investors $= k_t$ then the fair game property implies

$$E\left[(R_{t+1} - k_{t+1})|\Omega_t\right] = 0 \qquad (5.26)$$

The fair game property also applies for abnormal returns in future periods R_{t+j} so that these are also expected to be zero. Equation (5.26) is the equilibrium model analysed in section 4.1 and as we saw it gives rise to the rational valuation formula (with either a time varying or, if $k_{t+1} = k$, a constant discount rate). Hence, the fair game property for returns also implies that the price of a stock equals the DPV of future dividends. (Note, however, that in the presence of rational bubbles — discussed in Chapter 7 — the fair game property holds but the RVF does not). The apparent paradox that abnormal returns can be unforecastable (i.e. a fair game), yet prices are determined by economic fundamentals, is resolved.

A straightforward test of whether returns violate the fair game property under the assumption of constant equilibrium returns is to see if returns can be predicted from past data, Ω_t. Assuming a linear regression:

$$R_{t+1} = \alpha + \beta' \Omega_t + \varepsilon_{t+1} \tag{5.27}$$

then if $\beta' \neq 0$ (or ε_{t+1} is serially correlated), the fair game property is violated. Here the test of the fair game property is equivalent to the orthogonality test for RE.

Economic Models and the Fair Game Property

Samuelson (1965) points out that the fair game model with constant required returns, that is $E_t(R_{t+1} - k) = 0$, can be derived under (restrictive) assumptions about investor preferences. All investors would have to have a common and constant time preference rate, have homogeneous expectations and be risk neutral. Investors then prefer to hold whichever asset has the highest expected return, regardless of risk. All returns would therefore be equalised and the required (real) rate of return equals the real interest rate which in turn equals the *constant* rate of time preference.

Martingales and Random Walks

A stochastic variable X_t is said to follow a random walk with drift parameter δ, if

$$X_{t+1} = \delta + X_t + \varepsilon_{t+1} \tag{5.28}$$

where ε_{t+1} is an identically and independently distributed random variable with:

$$E_t \varepsilon_{t+1} = 0, \quad E_t(\varepsilon_m \cdot \varepsilon_s | X_t) = \begin{bmatrix} \sigma^2 \\ 0 \end{bmatrix} \begin{matrix} m = s \\ m \neq s \end{matrix} \tag{5.29}$$

As the ε_t are *independent* random variables then the joint density function $f(\varepsilon_m, \varepsilon_s) = f(\varepsilon_m) f(\varepsilon_s)$ for $m \neq s$ and this rules out *any* dependence between ε_s and ε_m whether linear or non-linear. The first way in which the martingale model is less restrictive than the random walk is that for a martingale ε_s and ε_t need only be uncorrelated (i.e. not *linearly* related).

A random walk without drift has $\delta = 0$. Clearly X_{t+1} is a martingale and $\Delta X_{t+1} = X_{t+1} - X_t$ is a fair game (for $\delta = 0$). However, the random walk is more restrictive than a martingale since a martingale does not restrict the higher conditional moments (e.g. σ^2) to be statistically independent. For example, if the price of a stock (including any dividend payments) is a martingale then successive price changes are unpredictable but it allows the conditional variance of the price changes $E(\varepsilon_{t+1}^2 | X_t)$ to be predictable from past variances (e.g. $\sigma_{t+1}^2 = \theta\sigma_t^2$). However, time varying conditional variances are not allowable if prices follow a random walk.

A Formal Definition of the EMH

Suppose that at any point in time all *relevant* (current and past) information for predicting the return on an asset is denoted Ω_t while market participants, p, have an information set Ω_t^p which is assumed to be available without cost. In an efficient market, agents are assumed to know all relevant information (i.e. $\Omega_t^p = \Omega_t$) and they know the complete (true) probability density function of the possible outcomes for returns

$$f^p(R_{t+n}|\Omega_t^p) = f(R_{t+n}|\Omega_t) \tag{5.30}$$

Hence in an efficient market, investors *know* the true (stochastic) economic model that generates future returns and use all relevant information to form their 'best' forecast of the expected return. This is the *rational expectations* element of the EMH.

Ex post, agents will see that they have made forecast errors and this will involve *ex-post* profits or losses

$$\eta_{t+1}^p = R_{t+1} - E^p(R_{t+1}|\Omega_t^p) \tag{5.31}$$

where the superscript 'p' indicates that the expectations and forecast errors are conditional on the equilibrium model of returns used by investors[2]. The expected or equilibrium return will include an element to compensate for any (systematic) risk in the market and to enable investors to earn normal profits. (Exactly what determines this risk premium depends on the valuation model assumed.) The EMH assumes that excess returns (or forecast errors) only change in response to news so that η_{t+1}^p are innovations with respect to the information available (i.e. the orthogonality property of RE holds).

For empirical testing a definition is needed of what constitutes 'relevant information' and three broad types have been distinguished.

- *Weak Form*: the current price (return) is considered to incorporate all the information in past prices (returns).
- *Semi-strong Form*: the current price (return) incorporates all *publicly available* information (including past prices or returns).
- *Strong Form*: prices reflect *all* information that can possibly be known, including 'insider information' (e.g. such as an impending announcement of a takeover or merger).

In empirical testing and general usage, tests of the EMH are usually considered to be tests of the semi-strong form. We can now sum up the basic ideas that constitute the EMH[1].

(i) All agents act as if they have an equilibrium (valuation) model of returns (or price determination).

(ii) Agents process all relevant information in the same way, in order to determine equilibrium returns (or fundamental value). Forecast errors and hence excess returns are unpredictable from information available at the time the forecast is made.

(iii) Agents cannot repeatedly make excess profits.

Conditional on the researcher having the true economic model used by agents then tests in (ii) reduce to tests of the axioms of rational expectations (e.g. unbiasedness, orthogonality) and are generally referred to as tests of *informational efficiency*. Tests based on (iii) are slightly different. Excess returns may be predictable but whether one can make abnormal profits depends on correctly adjusting returns, for risk and transactions costs. Perhaps (iii) is best expressed by Jensen (1978):

> a market is efficient with respect to an information set Ω_t if it is impossible to make economic profits by trading on the basis of Ω_t. By economic profits we mean the risk adjusted rate of return, net of all costs.

5.4 TESTING THE EMH

This section provides an overview of some of the test procedures used in assessing the EMH. It is useful to break these down into the following types:

(i) Tests of whether excess (abnormal) returns $\eta_{t+1}^p = R_{it+1} - E_t^p R_{it+1}$ are independent of information Ω_t available at time t or earlier. To test this proposition consider:

$$R_{it+1} = E_t^p R_{it+1} + \gamma' \Omega_t + \eta_{t+1}^p \tag{5.32}$$

where $E_t^p R_{it+1} =$ equilibrium returns. If information Ω_t adds any *additional* explanatory power then $R_{it+1} - E_t^p R_{it+1}$ is forecastable. This type of test is referred to as a test of *informational efficiency* and it requires an explicit representation of the equilibrium asset pricing model used by agents. These tests are discussed in the next chapter.

(ii) Tests of whether actual 'trading rules' (e.g. buy low, sell high) can earn supernormal or above average profits after taking account of transaction costs and an amount to cover the general (systematic) riskiness of the assets in question. These tests usually involve 'experiments' which mimic possible investor behaviour and they are discussed in Chapter 8.

(iii) Tests of whether market prices are always equal to fundamental value. These tests use past data and try and calculate fundamental value (or the variance of fundamental value) using some form of DPV calculation. They then test to see whether actual prices equal the fundamental value or more precisely whether the variation in actual prices is consistent with that dictated by the variability in fundamentals. These volatility tests are discussed in the next chapter.

In principle the above tests are not mutually exclusive but in practice it is possible that results from the different type of tests can conflict and hence give different inferences concerning the validity of the EMH. In fact in one particular case, namely that of rational bubbles (see Chapter 7), tests of type (i) even if supportive of the EMH can nevertheless (as a matter of principle) be contradicted by those of type (iii). This is because if rational bubbles are present in the market, expectations are formed rationally and forecast errors are independent of Ω_t but price *does not equal* fundamental value.

5.4.1 Tests of the RE Axioms using Survey Data

In the course of this book a large number of tests of increasing complexity will be presented. The EMH consists of the joint hypothesis of a particular equilibrium model of returns (or price determination) together with the assumption of rational expectations. However, suppose we have accurate survey data which provide a time series of an individual's subjective expectations. We can then, without having to choose a particular equilibrium model, see if these forecasts obey the axioms of rational expectations. Therefore our joint hypothesis is reduced to a test only of the informational efficiency assumptions. Our results will be valid regardless of the equilibrium model used by agents. Although tests using survey data appear to avoid a key problem area in testing the EMH (i.e. which equilibrium model to use) nevertheless such tests have their own in-built difficulties.

Survey data are sometimes available on individual agents' expectations of economic variables (e.g. of future inflation, exchange rates or interest rates). This may be in the form of *quantitative* information collected on an individual's expectations, for example; he may reply that 'interest rates will be 10 percent this time next year'. This information for each individual i provides a time series of his expectations Z^e_{it+j}. Using past data we can directly calculate the forecast error $\varepsilon_{it+1} = Z_{it+j} - Z^e_{it+j}$ for each individual, over all time periods. We do not need to know the precise model the individual uses to forecast Z_{it+j} yet we can test for informational efficiency by running the regression:

$$Z_{it+j} = \beta_0 + \beta_1 Z^e_{it+j} + \beta'_2 \Lambda_t + \varepsilon_{it+j} \tag{5.33}$$

and testing the null H_0: $\beta_0 = \beta_2 = 0$ and $\beta_1 = 1$. If H_0 is not rejected then from (5.33) the forecast error is zero on average

$$E_t(Z_{it+j} - Z^e_{it+j})|\Omega_t) = E_t(\varepsilon_{it+j}|\Omega_t) = 0 \tag{5.34}$$

and is independent of *any* information Λ_t available at time t. The limited information set $\Lambda_t(\subset \Omega_t)$ consists of any variables known at time t or earlier (e.g. past interest rates, stock prices, exchange rates). For the forecast error ε_{it+1} to be independent of information at time t, we also require ε_{it+1} to be serially uncorrelated. Standard test statistics are available to test the latter proposition (e.g. Box–Pierce Q statistic, Lagrange multiplier statistic).

Frequently, survey data on expectations are only available 'in aggregate', that is for a sample of individuals (i.e. the figures are for the average forecast for any period $t + j$ for *all* participants in the survey) and clearly this makes the interpretation of the results more problematic. For example, if only *one* person in a small sample of individuals exhibits behaviour that violates the information efficiency assumptions, this might result in a rejection of the RE axioms. However, under the latter circumstances most people would argue that the information efficiency was largely upheld. Indeed, even when there are survey data on *individual's* expectations it is always possible that individuals do not reveal their 'true' expectations, that is the forecasts they would have made in an actual real world situation (e.g. by backing their hunch with a large $ investment). In other words our survey data might reject the information efficiency assumption of RE because participants in the survey had little *incentive* to reveal their true forecasts, since they lose nothing if such forecasts are erroneous. Another problem is that participants in a survey may not be typical of those in the market who are actually doing the trades and 'making the market' (i.e. those who are 'on the margin' rather than intramarginal). Finally, although there are econometric techniques available (such as instrumental variables estimation) to correct for random errors of measurement in the survey data, such methods cannot deal with mismeasurement based on an individual's systematic inaccurate reporting of their true expectations.

Even more problems arise in these kind of tests when the survey data is *qualitative* or categorical. In this case participants respond to questions like 'Will interest rates in one year's time be (a) higher, (b) lower, (c) the same as they are at present?' Such responses have to be 'transformed' into quantitative data and all the methods currently available require one to impose some restrictive assumptions, which may invalidate the tests under consideration.

The applied work in this area is voluminous and the results are not really central to the subject matter of this book (see Pesaran (1987) for an excellent survey). However, it is worth briefly illustrating the basic methodology. For example, Taylor (1988) converts *monthly* categorical data from UK investment managers into quantitative expectations series for expected annual price inflation $_t p^e_{t+12}$, annual wage inflation $_t w^e_{t+12}$, the annual percentage change in the FTA all share index $_t f_{t+12}$ and the US Standard & Poor's composite share index $_t s_{t+12}$. The axioms of RE imply that the forecast errors are independent of the information set used in making the forecast. Consider the regression

$$(x_{t+12} - _t x^e_{t+12}) = \beta' \Lambda_t + \varepsilon_t$$

for $x = p, w, f, s$ and where Λ_t is a subset of the complete information set. If the informational efficiency (orthogonality) property of RE holds, we expect $\beta = 0$. If we assume no measurement error in x^e_{t+12} then ε_t is a moving average error of order 11 at most. OLS yield consistent estimates of β because Λ_t and ε_t are uncorrelated asymptotically but the usual formula for the covariance matrix of β is incorrect. However, the OLS residuals can be used to construct a consistent estimate of the variance–covariance matrix (White, 1980) along the lines outlined in Chapter 20 (i.e. the GMM–Hansen–Hodrick adjustment).

The results of this procedure are given in Table 5.1 for the information set $\Lambda_t = (x_{t-1}, x_{t-2})$. For the price inflation, wage inflation and the FT share index, the standard errors on the own lagged variables indicate that all of these variables taken individually are not significantly different from zero. This is confirmed by the Wald test $W(2)$ which indicates that the two RHS variables in each of the first three equations are jointly not significantly different from zero. For the S&P index the lagged values are significantly

Table 5.1 Orthogonality Regressions with Small Information Sets 1981(7)–1985(7), Ordinary Least Squares with Adjusted Covariance Matrix[a]

Estimated Equation	R^2	SEE	$W(2)$
$p_{t+12} - _t p^e_{t+12} = -0.155 - 0.310 p_{t-1} + 0.214 p_{t-2}$ $\quad\quad\quad (0.695)\quad (0.255)\quad\quad (0.245)$	0.06	1.131	2.96 (0.23)
$w_{t+12} - _t w^e_{t+12} = 2.596 - 0.492 w_{t-1} + 0.109 w_{t-2}$ $\quad\quad\quad (1.918)\quad (0.282)\quad\quad (0.204)$	0.20	1.891	4.25 (0.12)
$f_{t+12} - _t f^e_{t+12} = 9.842 - 0.262 f_{t-1} - 0.2227 f_{t-2}$ $\quad\quad\quad (3.075)\quad (0.179)\quad\quad (0.226)$	0.07	11.519	6.33 (0.04)
$s_{t+12} - _t s^e_{t+12} = 15.747 - 0.933 s_{t-1} + 0.463 s_{t-2}$ $\quad\quad\quad (9.597)\quad (0.233)\quad\quad (0.336)$	0.21	24.17	19.99 (0.00)

(a) R^2 is the coefficient of determination, SEE the standard error of the equation; $W(2)$ is a Wald test statistic for the coefficients of the two lagged regressors to be zero and is asymptotically central chi square under the null of orthogonality, with two degrees of freedom: figures in parentheses denote estimated standard errors or for $W(2)$ marginal significance levels.

Source: Taylor (1988), Table 1. Reproduced by permission of Blackwell Publishers

Table 5.2 Orthogonality Regressions with Small Information Sets 1981(7)–1985(7), Generalised Method of Moments[a]

Estimated Equation	R^2	SEE	$H(3)$	$W(2)$
$p_{t+12} = 0.550_t p^e_{t+12} + 1.315 - 0.399 p_{t-1} + 0.488 p_{t-2}$ $\quad(0.202)\quad\quad(1.122)\quad(0.286)\quad\quad(0.270)$	0.97	1.000	0.04 (0.99)	6.17 (0.05)
$w_{t+12} = 0.021_t w^e_{t+12} + 6.151 + 0.006 w_{t-1} + 0.185 w_{t-2}$ $\quad(0.144)\quad\quad(1.712)\quad(0.075)\quad\quad(0.122)$	0.97	1.436	0.05 (0.99)	3.85 (0.15)
$f_{t+12} = 0.473_t f^e_{t+12} + 20.066 + 0.199 f_{t-1} + 0.124 f_{t-2}$ $\quad(0.340)\quad\quad(6.925)\quad(0.125)\quad\quad(0.175)$	0.89	8.004	0.06 (0.99)	46.49 (0.00)
$s_{t+12} = -0.725_t s^e_{t+12} + 62.658 - 0.614 s_{t-1} - 0.154 s_{t-2}$ $\quad(0.468)\quad\quad(16.716)\quad(0.179)\quad\quad(0.260)$	0.66	19.761	0.04 (0.99)	18.86 (0.00)

(a) Instruments used for the expectations variable were p_t, w_t, f_t and s_t; H(3) is Hansen's (1982) test statistic for the instruments, and is asymptotically central chi square with three degrees of freedom for three valid overidentifying instruments. See note to Table 5.1 for other definitions.

Source: Taylor (1988), Table 2. Reproduced by permission of Blackwell Publishers

different from zero thus rejecting the RE orthogonality axiom. If there are measurement errors in the expectations series then in the regression:

$$x_{t+12} = \lambda_0 + \lambda_1 {}_t\tilde{x}^e_{t+12} + \beta'_2 \Lambda_t + \varepsilon_t$$

we do not expect the coefficient on ${}_t\tilde{x}^e_{t+12}$ to be unity. There is also a non-zero correlation between ${}_t\tilde{x}^e_{t+12}$ and the error term and hence an instrumental variable estimator is required. Taylor uses p_t, f_t, w_t, s_t as instruments for the expectations variables ${}_t\tilde{x}^e_{t+12}$. Taylor's results using the IV estimator are given in Table 5.2. The results are similar to those in Table 5.1, except for the FT share price index f_{t+12}. Here the GMM estimator indicates that the forecast error for the FT share price index is not independent of the information set (W(2) = 46.9). This demonstrates that when testing the axioms of RE, correct inference may require careful choice of the appropriate estimation technique. Taylor repeats the above exercise using a larger information set $\Lambda^* = (p_{t-j}, w_{t-j}, f_{t-j}, s_{t-j})$; $j = 1, 2$. With this extended information set the GMM estimator indicates that the orthogonality condition is decisively rejected for *all* four variables.

Surveys of empirical work on direct tests of the RE assumptions of unbiasedness and informational efficiency using survey data, for example those by Pesaran (1988) and Sheffrin (1983) tend frequently to reject the RE axioms (for recent results see *inter alios* Batchelor and Dua (1987), Cavaglia et al (1993), Ito (1990) and Frankel and Froot (1988). At this point the reader may feel that it is not worth proceeding with the RE assumption. If expectations are not rational why go on to discuss models of asset prices that assume rationality? One answer to this question is to note that tests based on survey data are not definitive and have their limitations as outlined above. Indirect tests of RE based on data on returns or prices that are actually generated by 'real world' trades in the market might therefore provide useful complementary information to direct tests based on survey data.

5.4.2 Orthogonality and Cross-Equation Restrictions

The use of survey data means that the researcher does not have to postulate an *explicit* model to explain *expected* returns. If survey data are not available, the null hypothesis of efficiency may still be tested but only under the additional assumption that the equilibrium pricing model (e.g. the CAPM) chosen by the researcher is the one actually used by *market participants* and is therefore the 'true' model. To illustrate orthogonality and tests using cross-equation restrictions in the simplest possible way let us assume that an equilibrium pricing model for Z_{t+1} may be represented as:

$$E^p_t Z_{t+1} = \gamma_0 + \gamma' x_t \tag{5.35}$$

where x_t is a set of variables suggested by the equilibrium pricing model. A test of informational efficiency (or orthogonality), conditional on the chosen equilibrium model, involves a regression

$$Z_{t+1} = \gamma_0 + \gamma' x_t + \beta'_2 \Lambda_t + \varepsilon_{t+1} \tag{5.36}$$

The orthogonality test is H_0: $\beta_2 = 0$. One can also test any restrictions on γ_0 and γ suggested by the pricing model chosen. The test for $\beta_2 = 0$ is a test that the determinants of the equilibrium pricing model (i.e. x_t) fully explain the behaviour of Z_{t+1} (except for the RE (random error) or innovation ε_{t+1}). Of course, informational efficiency may be tested using different equilibrium pricing models.

Note that in all of the tests discussed above, ε_{t+1} must be serially uncorrelated (since $\varepsilon_t \subset \Omega_t$ the full information set). However, ε_{t+1} need not be *homoscedastic* and the *variance* of ε_{t+1} may vary over time or may depend on other economic variables, without violating informational efficiency. This is because informational efficiency depends only on the first moment of the distribution, namely the expected value of ε_{t+1}. However, if ε_{t+1} is *not* homoscedastic, additional econometric problems arise in testing H_0 and some of these are discussed in Chapter 19.

Cross-Equation Restrictions

There are stronger tests of 'informational efficiency' which involve cross-equation restrictions. A simple example will suffice at this point and will serve as a useful introduction to the more complex cross-equation restrictions which arise in the vector autoregressive (VAR) models of Part 5. To keep the algebraic manipulations to a minimum, consider a one-period stock which simply pays an uncertain dividend at the end of period $t+1$ (this could also include a known redemption value for the stock at $t+1$). The rational valuation formula determines the current equilibrium price:

$$P_t = \delta E_t D_{t+1} = \delta D_{t+1}^e \tag{5.37}$$

where δ is the constant discount factor. Assume now an *expectations generating equation* for dividends based on the limited information set $\Lambda_t = (D_t, D_{t-1})$:

$$D_{t+1} = \gamma_1 D_t + \gamma_2 D_{t-1} + v_{t+1} \tag{5.38}$$

with $E(v_{t+1}|\Lambda_t) = 0$, under RE. It can now be demonstrated that the equilibrium pricing model (5.37) *plus* the assumed explicit expectations generating equation (5.38) *plus* the assumption of RE; in short the EMH implies certain restrictions between the parameters of the complete model. To see this, note that from (5.38) under RE

$$D_{t+1}^e = \gamma_1 D_t + \gamma_2 D_{t-1} \tag{5.39}$$

and substituting in (5.37):

$$P_t = \delta \gamma_1 D_t + \delta \gamma_2 D_{t-1} \tag{5.40}$$

We can rewrite (5.40) as a regression equation[3]:

$$P_t = \pi_1 D_t + \pi_2 D_{t-1} \tag{5.41}$$

where $\pi_1 = \delta \gamma_1$, $\pi_2 = \delta \gamma_2$. A regression of P_t on (D_t, D_{t-1}) will yield coefficient estimates π_1 and π_2. Similarly, the regression equation (5.38) will yield estimates π_3 and π_4:

$$D_{t+1} = \pi_3 D_t + \pi_4 D_{t-1} + v_{t+1} \tag{5.42}$$

where $\pi_3 = \gamma_1$ and $\pi_4 = \gamma_2$. However, if (5.38) and (5.40) are true then we know that

$$\pi_1/\pi_3 = \pi_2/\pi_4 = \delta \tag{5.43}$$

The values of (γ_1, γ_2) can be directly obtained from the estimated values of π_3 and π_4, while from (5.43) δ can be obtained either from π_1/π_3 or π_2/π_4. Hence in general we obtain two different values for δ (i.e. the system is 'overidentified').

We have four estimated coefficients (i.e. π_1 to π_4) and only three underlying parameters in the model ($\delta_1, \gamma_1, \gamma_2$). There is therefore *one* restriction (relationship) among the π's given in (5.43) which involves a relationship between *estimated* parameters in two distinct equations, namely (5.41) and (5.43). Hence (5.43) constitutes a non-linear *cross-equation* restriction and is an implication of the pricing model plus RE. (Note that when we impose this restriction we only obtain one value for δ.)

An intuitive interpretation of the cross-equation restrictions is possible. It is shown below that these restrictions do nothing more than ensure that no supernormal profits are earned *on average* and that errors in forecasting dividends are independent of information at time t or earlier. First, consider the profits that can be earned by using our *estimated* equations (5.41) and (5.42). The best forecast of the DPV of future dividends V is given by $V = \delta D_{t+1}^e$ and using (5.42)

$$V = \delta(\pi_3 D_t + \pi_2 D_{t-1}) \tag{5.44}$$

Usually, the realised price will be different from the fundamental value given by (5.44) because the researcher has less information than the agent operating in the market (i.e. $\Lambda_t \subset \Omega_t$). The price is given by (5.41) and hence excess returns or profits are given by:

$$P_t - V_t = (\pi_1 D_t + \pi_2 D_{t-1}) - \delta(\pi_3 D_t + \pi_4 D_{t-1})$$

$$= (\pi_1 - \delta\pi_3)D_t + (\pi_2 - \delta\pi_4)D_{t-1} \tag{5.45}$$

For all values of (D_t, D_{t-1}), profit will be zero only if:

$$\delta = \pi_1/\pi_3 = \pi_2/\pi_4$$

but this is exactly the value of δ which is imposed in the cross-equation restrictions (5.43). Now consider the error in forecasting dividends:

$$D_{t+1} - D_{t+1}^e = [\pi_3 D_t + \pi_4 D_{t-1} + v_{t+1}] - (1/\delta)P_t \tag{5.46}$$

where we have used (5.42) and the equilibrium model (5.37). Substituting for P_t from (5.41) gives:

$$D_{t+1} - D_{t+1}^e = (\pi_3 - \pi_1/\delta)D_t + (\pi_4 - \pi_2/\delta)D_{t-1} + v_{t+1} \tag{5.47}$$

Hence the forecast error can only be independent of information at time t (i.e. D_t and D_{t-1}) if $\delta = \pi_1/\pi_3 = \pi_2/\pi_4$.

By estimating (5.41) plus (5.42) without the restrictions imposed and then re-estimating with the restrictions (5.43) imposed, a suitable test statistic can be used to test the validity of EMH for the given equilibrium model, under the *specific* expectations generating equation (5.37). These tests of cross-equation restrictions are very prevalent in the EMH/RE literature and are frequently much more complex algebraically than the simple example above, as we shall see in Part 5. However, no matter how complex, such restrictions merely ensure that no abnormal profits are earned on average and that forecast errors are orthogonal to the information set assumed.

One additional problem with the above test procedure is that it is conditional on the *specific* expectations-generating equation chosen for D_{t+1}. If this is an incorrect representation of how agents form expectations then the parameters γ_1 and $\gamma_2(\pi_3, \pi_4)$ are likely to be biased estimates of the true parameters and the cross-equation restrictions based on the *estimated* parameters may not hold. This concludes our overview of the types of tests used to assess the EMH and it remains to mention briefly some conceptual limitations of the EMH.

Interpretation of Tests of Market Efficiency

The EMH assumes information is available at zero cost or that the movement in market prices is determined *as if* this were the case. The assumption that the acquisition and processing of information, as well as the time involved in acting on such information is costless, is a very strong one. If prices 'always reflect all available relevant information' which is also costless to acquire, then why would anyone invest resources in acquiring information? Anyone who did so would clearly earn a lower return than those who costlessly observed current prices, which under the EMH contain all relevant information. As Grossman and Stiglitz (1980) point out, if information is costly, prices *cannot* perfectly reflect the information available. They also make the point that speculative markets cannot be completely efficient at all points in time. The profits derived from speculation are the result of being faster in the acquisition and correct interpretation of existing and new information. Thus one might expect the market to move towards efficiency as the 'well informed' make profits relative to the less well informed. In so doing the smart money sells when actual price is above fundamental value and this moves the price closer to its fundamental value. However, this process may take some time, particularly if agents are unsure of the true model generating fundamentals (e.g. dividends) which may alter through time. If, in addition, agents have different endowments of wealth and hence different market power in influencing price changes, they may not form the same expectations of a particular variable. Also irrational traders or noise traders might be present and then the rational traders have to take account of the behaviour of the noise traders. It is therefore possible that prices might deviate from fundamental value for substantial periods and these issues are discussed further in Chapter 8. Recently, much research has been done on the nature of sequential trading, the acquisition of costly information and the behaviour of noise traders. These models imply that regression tests of the orthogonality and the unbiasedness properties of RE are tests of a rather circumscribed hypothesis, namely one where the true model is assumed known at zero cost and where expectations are based on predictions from this true model.

5.5 SUMMARY

Consideration has been given to the basic ideas that underlie the EMH in both intuitive and mathematical terms and the main conclusions are:

- The outcome of tests of the EMH are important in assessing public policy issues such as the desirability of mergers and takeovers, short-termism and regulation of financial institutions.

- The EMH assumes investors process information efficiently so that persistent abnormal profits cannot be made by trading in financial assets. The return on a portfolio comprises a 'payment' to compensate for the (systematic) risk of the portfolio but information available in the market cannot be used to increase this return.

- The EMH can be represented in technical language by stating that returns are a martingale process.

- Tests of the informational efficiency (RE) element of the EMH can be undertaken using survey data on expectations. In general, however, tests of the EMH require an explicit equilibrium model of expected returns. Tests often involve an analysis of whether returns are predictable and in certain cases stronger tests involving cross-equation restrictions are possible.

In general, failure of the EMH in empirical tests may be due either to a failure of informational efficiency (RE) or an inappropriate choice of the model for equilibrium returns or simply that the EMH does not hold in the 'real world'.

ENDNOTES

1. LeRoy (1989) favours a definition of the EMH as constituting the proposition that returns follow the fair game property and that agents have rational expectations. For practical purposes, his definition is not that different from the one adopted here.
2. Equation (5.32), which uses the superscript 'p' to represent the forecast error for market participants η^p_{t+1}, makes it clear that these forecast errors only obey the properties of conditional mathematical expectations if agents actually do use the true model of the economy (i.e. then $E^p_t R_{t+1} = E_t R_{t+1}$).
3. There are some rather subtle issues in developing these cross-equation restrictions and a simplified account has been presented in the text. A more complete derivation of the issues in this section is given below. The researcher is unlikely to have the full information set that is available to market participants, $\Lambda_t \subset \Omega_t$. This implies that equation (5.40) has an error term which reflects the difference in the informational sets available, that is $\omega_{t+1} = [E(D_{t+1}|\Omega_t) - E(D_{t+1}|\Lambda_t)]$. To see this, note that the stock price is determined by the full information set available to agents:

$$P_t = \delta E(D_{t+1}|\Omega_t) \qquad (1)$$

The econometrician uses a subset $\Lambda_t = (D_t, D_{t-1})$ of the full information set to forecast dividends:

$$D_{t+1} = \pi_3 D_t + \pi_4 D_{t-1} + v_{t+1} \qquad (2)$$

where $\pi_3 = \gamma_1$, $\pi_4 = \gamma_2$. Then employing the identity:

$$E(D_{t+1}|\Omega_t) = E(D_{t+1}|\Lambda_t) + \{E(D_{t+1}|\Omega_t) - E(D_{t+1}|\Lambda_t)\}$$

$$= E(D_{t+1}|\Lambda_t) + \omega_{t+1} \qquad (3)$$

where

$$\omega_{t+1} = [(D_{t+1} - E(D_{t+1}|\Lambda_t)] - [D_{t+1} - E(D_{t+1}|\Omega_t)]$$

$$= v_{t+1} - \eta_{t+1} \qquad (4)$$

and η_{t+1} is the true RE forecast error made by agents when using the full information set, Ω_t. Note that $E(\omega_{t+1}|\Lambda_t) = 0$. To derive the correct expression for (5.41) we use (1), (2) and (3):

$$P_t = \delta E_t(D_{t+1}|\Omega_t) = \delta E(D_{t+1}|\Lambda_t) + \delta \omega_{t+1}$$

$$= \delta \gamma_1 D_t + \delta \gamma_2 D_{t-1} + \varepsilon_{t+1}$$

$$= \pi_1 D_t + \pi_2 D_{t-1} + \varepsilon_{t+1} \qquad (5)$$

where $\varepsilon_{t+1} = \delta \omega_{t+1}$.

The complete derivation of the 'no-profit' condition (5.45) has agents using the full information set to determine $V_t = \delta E(D_{t+1}|\Omega_t) = \delta E(D_{t+1}|\Lambda_t) + \delta \omega_{t+1}$ and hence using (5):

$$P_t - V_t = (\pi_1 D_t + \pi_2 D_{t-1} + \delta \omega_{t+1}) - \delta(\pi_3 D_t + \pi_4 D_{t-1} + \omega_{t+1})$$

$$= (\pi_1 - \delta \pi_3)D_t + (\pi_2 - \delta \pi_4)D_{t-1} \qquad (6)$$

which is equation (5.45) in the text.

The forecast for dividends is based on the full information set available to agents (although not to the econometrician) and using (2) and (1) is given by:

$$D_{t+1} - E(D_{t+1}|\Omega_t) = (\pi_3 D_t + \pi_4 D_{t-1} + v_{t+1}) - (1/\delta)P_t \qquad (7)$$

However, substituting for P_t from (5) and noting that $\omega_{t+1} = v_{t+1} - \eta_{t+1}$ gives:

$$D_{t+1} - E(D_{t+1}|\Omega_t) = (\pi_3 - \pi_1/\delta)D_t + (\pi_4 - \pi_2/\delta)D_{t-1} + \eta_{t+1} \qquad (8)$$

Hence equation (8) above, rather than equation (5.47), is the correct expression. However, derivation of (5.47) in the text is less complex and provides the intuition required at this point.

6
Empirical Evidence on Efficiency in the Stock Market

In Chapter 4 it was noted that any specific model of expected returns implies a specific model for stock prices. The RVF provides a general expression for stock prices which depend on the DPV of expected future dividends and discount rates. The EMH implies that expected equilibrium returns corrected for risk are unforecastable and via the RVF this implies that stock prices are unforecastable. Hence tests of the EMH are based on examining the behaviour of both returns and stock prices. In principle, both types of test (rational bubbles are ignored here) should give the same inferences but, in practice, this is not always the case. This chapter aims to:

- Provide a set of alternative tests to ascertain whether stock *returns* are forecastable. Tests are conducted for returns measured over different horizons and results are based on an examination of the correlogram (autocorrelations) of returns, from regression tests using a variety of alternative information sets and a variance ratio test. In addition, the profitability of 'active' trading strategies based on forecasts from regression equations will be examined.

- Next stock *prices* and the empirical validity of the EMH as represented by the RVF formula are examined. Shiller (1979, 1981) and LeRoy and Porter (1981) pioneered a set of *variance bounds tests*. They show that if stock prices are determined by fundamentals (i.e. RVF), this puts a limit on the variability of prices which can then be tested empirically, even though expected future dividends are unobservable.

To make the above tests of the EMH operational we require an equilibrium model of asset prices. We can think of the equilibrium or expected return on a risky asset as consisting of a risk-free rate r_t (e.g. on Treasury bills) and a risk premium, rp_t

$$E_t R_{t+1} = r_t + rp_t \tag{6.1}$$

At present, there is no sharp distinction between nominal and real variables and equation (6.1) could be expressed in either form. Equation (6.1) is a non-operational identity. An economic model of the risk premium is required. Many (early) empirical tests of the EMH either assume rp_t and r_t are constant or sometimes they assume only rp_t is constant and examine data on excess returns, $(R_{t+1} - r_t)$. If we assume expected equilibrium returns are constant and RE holds (i.e. $R_{t+1} = E_t R_{t+1} + \varepsilon_{t+1}$) then:

$$R_{t+1} = k + \varepsilon_{t+1}$$

Consider the regression:

$$R_{t+1} = k + \gamma' \Omega_t + \varepsilon_{t+1} \tag{6.2}$$

where Ω_t = information available at time t. A test of $\gamma' = 0$ provides evidence on the 'informational efficiency' element of the EMH. These regression tests vary, depending on the information assumed which is usually of the following type:

(i)   data on past returns $R_{t-j} (j = 0, 1, 2, \ldots m)$ — that is, weak form efficiency,

(ii) data on scale variables such as the dividend price ratio, the earnings price ratio or interest rates at time t or earlier,

(iii) data on past forecast errors $\varepsilon_{t-j} (j = 0, 1, \ldots m)$.

When (i) and (iii) are examined together this gives rise to ARMA models, for example the ARMA(1,1) model:

$$R_{t+1} = k + \gamma_1 R_t + \varepsilon_{t+1} - \gamma_2 \varepsilon_t \tag{6.3}$$

If one is only concerned with weak form efficiency then the autocorrelation coefficients between R_{t+1} and $R_{t-j} (j = 0, 1, \ldots m)$ can be examined to see if they are non-zero. It is also possible to test weak form efficiency using a variance ratio test on returns, over different horizons. All of these alternative tests of weak form efficiency should, of course, give the same inferences (ignoring small sample problems). The EMH gives no indication of the horizon over which the returns should be calculated. The above tests can therefore be done for alternative holding periods of a day, week, month or even over many years. We may find violations of the EMH at some horizons but not at others.

Suppose the above tests show that informational efficiency does not hold. Hence information at time t can be used to help predict future returns. Nevertheless, it may be highly risky for an investor to bet on the outcomes predicted by a regression equation which has a high standard error or low $\bar{R}^2$. It is therefore worth investigating whether such predictability really does allow one to make abnormal profits in actual trading, after taking account of transactions costs and possible borrowing constraints, etc. Thus there are two somewhat distinct aspects to the EMH as applied to data on returns: one is informational efficiency and the other is the ability to make supernormal profits.

Volatility tests directly examine the RVF for stock prices. Under the assumption of RE and that expected one-period returns are a known constant, the RVF gives

$$P_t = \sum_{i=1}^{\infty} \delta^i E_t D_{t+i} \tag{6.4}$$

If we had a reliable measure of *expected* dividends then we could calculate the RHS of (6.4). A test of this model of stock prices would then be to see if $\text{var}(\Sigma \delta^i E_t D_{t+i})$ equalled $\text{var}(P_t)$. Shiller (1982), in a seminal article, obviated the need for data on expected dividends. He noted that under RE, actual and expected dividends only differ by a random (forecast) error and therefore so do the actual price P_t and the perfect foresight price P_t^*, defined as $P_t^* = \Sigma \delta^i D_{t+i}$. (Note that P_t^* uses *actual* dividends). Shiller demonstrated that $\mathrm{var}(P_t) \leqslant \mathrm{var}(P_t^*)$ if the RVF + RE is true. At the same time as Shiller, two other economists LeRoy and Porter (1981) provided similar tests. However, whereas Shiller found that for US stock prices the variance inequality was grossly violated, LeRoy and Porter found that the inequality was only marginally rejected (in a statistical sense). These two papers led to plethora of contributions using variants of this basic methodology. Early commentaries emphasised the small sample biases that might be present, whereas later work examined the robustness of the volatility tests, under the assumption that dividends are a non-stationary process. It is impossible to describe all the nuances in this debate, which provides an excellent illustration of the incremental improvements obtained by the scientific approach, applied to a specific, yet important, economic issue. The second part of this chapter concentrates on the difficulties in implementing and interpreting results of these direct tests of the RVF based on variance bounds. Chapter 16 returns to the question of excess volatility and the issue of non-stationary data is dealt with in an improved analytic framework.

In this chapter illustrative examples are provided of tests of the EMH for stock *returns* and there is a discussion of volatility tests based on stock *prices*. It is by no means a straightforward matter to interpret the results from the wide variety of tests available, as to whether investor behaviour in the stock market is consistent with the EMH. As well as presenting illustrative empirical results there is an indication of how the various types of test are interrelated.

Smart Money and Noise Traders

Before discussing the details of the various empirical tests enumerated above it is worth briefly discussing the implications for stock returns and prices of there being some non-rational or noise traders in the market. This enables us to introduce the concepts of mean reversion and excess volatility in a fairly simple way. Assume that the market contains a particular type of noise trader, namely a *positive feedback trader* whose demand for the stock increases after there has been a price rise. To simplify matters assume that the rational traders or smart money believe that (one plus) the expected or equilibrium return is constant

$$1 + E_t R_{t+1} = k^*$$

or equivalently

$$E_t[(P_{t+1} + D_{t+1})/P_t] = k^* \qquad (6.5)$$

Hence the expected proportionate change in price (including any dividend payments) is a constant which we assume equals 8 percent. If only the smart money is present in the market then the price only responds to new information or news and therefore the path of prices and the return per period are unpredictable. An example where only a few items of news hit the market is shown in Figures 6.1 and 6.2, respectively. For example, the price change from A to B could be due to 'good news' about dividends. Price changes are random. The price level follows a random walk (with drift), that is it tends to move away from its starting point in a random fashion and rarely crosses its starting point. The return on the stock is unpredictable and past returns cannot be used to predict future returns. Indeed any information available is of no use in predicting returns.

Now consider introducing positive feedback traders into the market. After the good news about dividends revealed at A, the positive feedback traders purchase the stock,

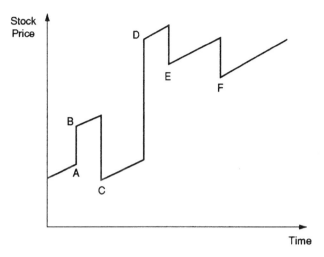

Figure 6.1   Random Walk for Stock Price.

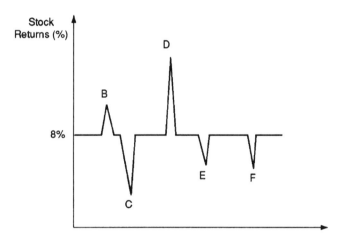

Figure 6.2   Stock Returns.

initially increasing its price still further. The price reaches a peak at Y (Figure 6.3). Then, if there is some 'bad' news at Y, the positive feedback traders sell (or short sell) and the price moves back towards fundamental value. Prices are said to be mean reverting.

Two things are immediately obvious. First, prices have *overreacted* to fundamentals (i.e. news about dividends). Second, prices are more volatile than would be predicted by the change in fundamentals. It follows that prices are *excessively volatile* compared to what they would be under the EMH. Volatility tests based on the early work of Shiller and LeRoy and Porter attempt to measure this excess volatility in a precise way.

The per period return on the stock is shown in Figure 6.4. Over short horizons returns are positively serially correlated: positive returns are followed by further positive returns (points P,Q,R) and negative returns by further negative returns (points R,S,T). Over long horizons, returns are negatively serially correlated. An increase in returns between P and R is followed by a fall in returns between R and T (or Y). Thus, in the presence of feedback

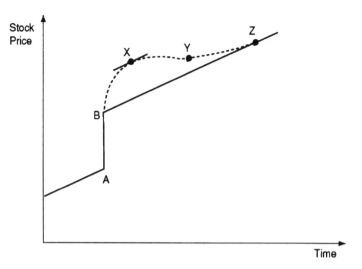

Figure 6.3   Positive Feedback Traders: Stock Prices.

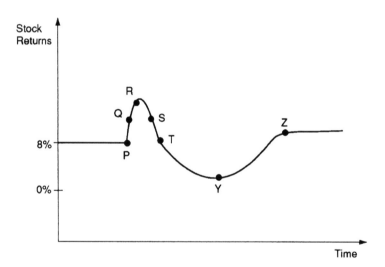

Figure 6.4   Positive Feedback Traders: Stock Returns.

traders, returns are serially correlated and hence predictable. Also, returns are likely to be correlated with changes in dividends. Hence regressions which look at whether returns are predictable have been interpreted as evidence for the presence of noise traders in the market.

From Figure (6.5) one can also see why feedback traders can cause changes in the variance of prices *over different return horizons*. In an efficient market, suppose that prices will either rise or fall by 15 percent per annum. After two years the variability in prices might be 30 percent higher or 30 percent lower. The variance in returns over $N = 2$ years equals twice the variance over one year and in general

$$\text{var}(R^N) = N \, \text{var}(R^1)$$

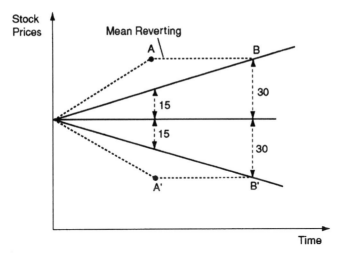

Figure 6.5 Mean Reversion and Volatility. *Source*: Engel and Morris (1991).

or

$$\frac{\text{var}(R^N)}{N \, \text{var}(R^1)} = 1 \tag{6.6}$$

However, with mean reversion the variance of the returns over $N(= 2)$ years will be less than N times the variance over one year. This is because prices overshoot their fundamental value in the short run but not in the long run. (Compare points A–A′ and B,B′ in Figure 6.5.) This is the basis of the Poterba–Summer tests of volatility over different horizons discussed below. (For a useful summary of these tests see Engel and Morris (1991).)

So far we have assumed that the smart money believes that equilibrium expected returns are constant. Let us examine how the above regression (or serial correlation) tests may be interpreted when expected returns are not constant. Expected equilibrium returns might vary either because subjective attitudes to risk versus return (i.e. preferences) change or because of changes in the risk-free rate of interest or because shares are viewed as inherently more risky at certain periods (i.e. the variance of the market portfolio changes over time). Let us take the simple example whereby the risk-free (real) interest rate r_t varies and that in equilibrium the (real) return is given by:

$$E_t R_{t+1} = r_t$$

In determining stock prices, agents will forecast future interest rates in order to calculate the discount factor for future dividends. If there is an unexpected fall in the interest rate, then the stock price will show an unexpected rise (A to B in Figure 6.6).

If the lower interest rate is expected *to persist* then the rate of growth of prices (i.e. stock returns) will be low in all future periods. Thus even though we are in an efficient market, the response of the smart money may cause prices to follow the path ABCD which is rather similar to the time path when noise traders are present (i.e. ABXYZ in Figure 6.3). In short, if equilibrium real interest rates are mean reverting then equilibrium and actual returns will also be mean reverting in an efficient market. We take up this

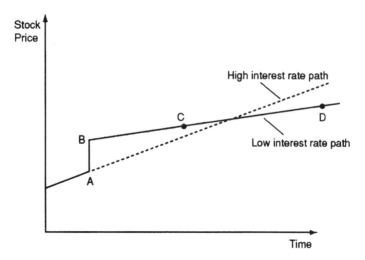

Figure 6.6 Stock Prices and Interest Rates. *Source*: Engel and Morris (1991).

issue in a more formal way later in this chapter when discussing tests of the consumption CAPM based on both returns and stock price data.

The above intuitive argument demonstrates that it may be difficult to infer whether a given observed path for returns is consistent with market efficiency or with the presence of noise traders. This problem arises because tests of the EMH are based on a *specific* model of equilibrium returns and if the latter is incorrect then this *version* of the EMH will be rejected by the data. However, another model of equilibrium returns might conceivably support the EMH. Nevertheless, an indication of a possible test is to note that in Figure 6.6 where only the smart money operates, a large positive return is immediately followed by smaller positive returns. When noise traders are present (Figure 6.3) large positive returns are immediately followed by further large positive returns (i.e. in the short run), which is a slightly different autocorrelation pattern. However, it is clear that unless we posit very clear and well-defined models for the behaviour of both the smart money and the noise traders it may well be difficult to sort out exactly who is dominant in the market and who exerts the predominant influence on prices. Formal models which incorporate noise trader behaviour and tests of these models are only just appearing in the literature and these will be discussed further in Chapters 8 and 17.

6.1 PREDICTABILITY IN STOCK RETURNS

6.1.1 Daily Stock Returns

Over short horizons such as a day, one would not expect equilibrium returns to be highly variable. Hence daily changes in stock prices probably provide a good approximation to daily abnormal returns on stocks. Fortune (1991) provides an interesting illustrative statistical analysis of the random walk hypothesis of stock prices using over 2700 *daily observations* on the S&P 500 share index (closing prices, 2 January 1980–21 September 1990). Stock returns are measured as the proportionate daily change in (closing) stock prices $R_t = \Delta \ln P_t$. A typical regression is

$$R_t = 0.0007 + 0.054\varepsilon_{t-1} - 0.037\varepsilon_{t-2} - 0.019\varepsilon_{t-3} - 0.054\varepsilon_{t-4} + 0.051\varepsilon_{t-5}$$
$$\quad (2.8) \qquad (2.8) \qquad\quad (1.9) \qquad\quad (1.0) \qquad\quad (2.8) \qquad\quad (2.7)$$

$$\quad - 0.0017 \text{ WE} + 0.0006 \text{ HOL} + 0.0006 \text{ JAN} + \varepsilon_t \qquad\qquad (6.7)$$
$$\qquad (3.2) \qquad\qquad (0.2) \qquad\qquad\quad (0.82)$$

$\overline{R}^2 = 0.0119$, SEE $= 0.0108$, $(\cdot) = t$ statistic.

The variable WE $= 1$ if the trading day is a Monday and zero otherwise, HOL $= 1$ if the current trading day is preceded by a one-day holiday (zero otherwise) and JAN $= 1$ for trading days in January (zero otherwise). The only statistically significant dummy variable (for this data spanning the 1980s) is for the 'weekend effect' which implies that price changes over the weekend are less on average than those on other trading days. The January effect is not statistically significant in the above regression for the 'aggregate' S&P 500 index (but it could still be important for stocks of small companies). The error term in the equation is serially correlated and follows a moving average of order 5, although only the MA(1), MA(4) and MA(5) terms are statistically significant. Since previous periods' forecast errors ε are known (at time t) this is a violation of informational efficiency, under the null of constant equilibrium returns. If there is a positive forecast error in one period then this will be followed by a further increase in the return R next period, a slight decline in the next three periods, followed finally by a rise in period $t + 5$. The MA pattern might not be picked up by longer-term weekly or monthly data which might therefore have white noise errors and hence be supportive of the EMH.

However, the above data might not indicate a failure of the EMH where the latter is defined as the inability to *persistently* make supernormal profits. Only about 1 percent ($\overline{R}^2 = 0.01$) of the variability in daily stock returns is explained by the regression: hence potential profitable arbitrage possibilities are likely to involve substantial risk. If prices fell unexpectedly on Tuesday then a strategy to beat the market based on (6.7) would involve buying the portfolio at close of trading on Wednesday and then selling the portfolio after a further two days. Alternatively, because of the weekend effect, short selling on Friday and purchasing the portfolio on a Monday yields a predictable return *on average* of 0.17 percent. In these two cases, as the portfolio in principle consists of all the stocks in the S&P 500 index, this would involve very high transactions costs which might well outweigh any profits from these strategies.

The difficulty in assessing regression tests of the above kind (particularly on a stock index) are that they may reject the strict RE/EMH element of 'unpredictability', but not necessarily the view of the EMH which emphasises the impossibility of making supernormal profits. Since the coefficients in equation (6.7) are in a sense averages over the sample data, one would have to be pretty confident that these 'average effects' were to persist in the future. To make money using (6.7) one would have to undertake repeated investments sequentially (e.g. each weekend based on the WE coefficient). By selling on Friday, the investor would find he had 'won' on *some* Mondays and could buy back the shares on Monday at a lower price. On other Mondays he would have lost money because the arrival of good news between Friday and Monday (i.e. the current period error $\varepsilon_t > 0.0017$WE would increase prices). Of course if *in the future* the coefficient on WE remains negative his *repeated strategy* will earn profits (ignoring transactions costs). But at a minimum one would wish to test the temporal stability of coefficients such as that on WE before embarking on such a set of repeated gambles. In addition, one would probably need a substantial amount of financial resources as the investor may be unlucky in the first few weeks of this strategy and may initially lose a considerable amount of money. Whether the latter is a problem for 'big players' such as pension fund managers depends on how often their performance is evaluated. To test adequately the 'supernormal profits' view of the EMH one needs to examine 'real world' trading strategies in individual stocks within the portfolio, taking account of all transactions costs, bid–ask spreads and managerial and dealers' time and effort. (The latter should be measured by the opportunity cost of the manpower involved compared with other investment strategies which may also earn substantial profits, e.g. analysis of mergers). In short, if the predictability indicated by regression tests cannot yield supernormal profits in the real world, one may legitimately treat the statistically significant 'information' in the regression equation as *not economically* relevant.

6.1.2 Long Horizon Returns

Are stock returns mean reverting, that is higher than average returns are followed by lower returns in the future? Fama and French (1988a) and Poterba and Summers (1988) find evidence of mean reversion in stock returns *over long* horizons (i.e. in excess of 18 months). Fama and French estimate an autoregression where the return over the interval $t - N$ to t, call this $R_{t-N,t}$ is correlated with $R_{t,t+N}$ (LeRoy, 1989):

$$R_{t,t+N} = \alpha + \beta R_{t-N,t} + \varepsilon_t \tag{6.8}$$

Fama and French consider return horizons N from one to ten years. They found little or no autocorrelation, except for holding periods of between $N = 2$ and $N = 7$ years for which β is less than zero. There was a peak at $N = 5$ years when $\beta \approx -0.5$, indicating that a 10 percent negative return over five years is, on average, followed by a 5 percent positive return over the next five years. The $\overline{R}^2$ in the regressions for the three to five-year horizons are about 0.35. Such mean reversion ($\beta < 0$) is consistent with that from the 'anomalies literature' where a 'buy low, sell high' trading rule earns persistent positive profits (see Chapter 8). However, the Fama–French results appear to be mainly due to inclusion of the 1930s sample period (Fama and French, 1988a).

Poterba and Summers (1988) investigate mean reversion by looking at *variances* of holding period returns *over different horizons*. If stock returns are random then variances of holding period returns should increase in proportion to the length of the holding period. To see this, assume the one-period expected return $E_t R_{t+1}$ can be approximated by $E_t \ln P_{t+1} - \ln P_t$. If the expected return is assumed to be constant $(= \mu)$ and we assume RE, this implies the random walk model of stock prices (including cumulated dividends).

$$\ln P_{t+1} = \mu + \ln P_t + \varepsilon_{t+1} \tag{6.9}$$

The average return over N periods is approximately

$$R_{t+1}^N = (\ln P_{t+N} - \ln P_t) = N\mu + (\varepsilon_{t+1} + \varepsilon_{t+2} \ldots + \varepsilon_{t+N}) \tag{6.10}$$

Under RE the forecast errors ε_t are independent, with zero mean, hence the *expected* return over N periods is:

$$E_t R_{t+1}^N = N\mu \tag{6.11}$$

If we assume the variance of ε_t is constant $(= \sigma^2)$ then

$$\text{var}[R_{t+1}^N] = N\sigma^2 \tag{6.12}$$

The variance ratio (VR) used by Poterba and Summers uses returns at different horizons and is defined as:

$$\text{VR}(N) = \frac{\text{var}(R_t^N)}{N} \bigg/ \frac{\text{var}(R_t^{12})}{12} \tag{6.13}$$

where

$$R_t^N = \sum_{i=0}^{N-1} R_{t-i}$$

and R_t is the return over one month. Poterba and Summers show that the variance ratio is closely related to tests based on the sequence of sample autocorrelation coefficients, ρ_N (for various values of N). If the ρ_N are statistically significant at various lags this should in principle show up in a value for VR which is less than unity. Not surprisingly, statistically significant values for the regression coefficient β in the Fama–French regressions also imply VR $\neq$ 1. However, the statistical properties of these three statistics VR, ρ and β *in small samples* are not equivalent and this is reported below.

Poterba and Summers (1988) find that the variance of returns increases at a rate which is less than in proportion to N, which implies that returns are mean reverting (for $8 > N > 3$ years). This conclusion is generally upheld when using a number of alternative stock price indexes, although the power of the tests is low when detecting persistent yet transitory returns. However, note that these results from the Poterba–Summers test may also be due to restrictive ancillary assumptions being incorrect, for example constant expected (real) returns or constant variance (σ^2). In fact portfolio theory suggests that neither of the latter assumptions is likely to be correct particularly over long horizons and therefore the Fama and French and Poterba and Summers results could equally well be explained in terms of investors having time varying expected returns or time varying variances and not as a violation of the EMH. Again it is the problem of inference when testing the joint hypothesis of market efficiency and an explicit (and maybe incorrect) returns model (i.e. random walk).

Power of Tests

It is always possible that in a sample of data, a particular test statistic fails to reject the null hypothesis of randomness in returns, even when the true model has returns which really are non-random (i.e. predictable). The 'power of a test' is the probability of rejecting a false null. To evaluate the power properties of the statistics ρ_N, VR and β_N, Poterba and Summers set up a true model of stock prices which has a persistent (i.e. non-random) transitory component. The logarithm of actual prices p_t is assumed to comprise a permanent component p_t^* and a transitory component u_t. The permanent component follows a random walk.

$$p_t = p_t^* + u_t \tag{6.14}$$

$$p_t^* = p_{t-1}^* + \varepsilon_t \tag{6.15}$$

However, the transitory (zero mean) component u_t is persistent, that is positive values of u tend to be followed by further positive values. In the AR(1) model:

$$u_t = \rho_1 u_{t-1} + v_t \qquad (6.16)$$

(where ε_t and v_t are independent) the degree of persistence is determined by how close ρ_1 is to unity. Poterba and Summers set ρ_1 to 0.98 implying that innovations in the transitory price component have a half-life of 2.9 years (if the basic time interval is considered to be monthly). From the above three equations we obtain:

$$\Delta p_t = \rho_1 \Delta p_{t-1} + [(\varepsilon_t - \rho_1 \varepsilon_{t-1}) + (v_t - v_{t-1})] \qquad (6.17)$$

and therefore the model implies that the change in (the logarithm of) prices follows an ARMA(1,1) process. Poterba and Summers then generate data on p_t taking random drawings from independent distributions of ε_t and v_t with the relative share of the variance of Δp_t determined by the relative size of σ_ε^2 and σ_v^2. They then calculate the statistics ρ_N, VR and β from a *sample* of the generated data of 720 observations (i.e. the same 'length' as that for which they have historic data on returns). They repeat the calculations 25 000 times to obtain the frequency distributions of the statistics ρ_N, VR and β. They find that all three test statistics have little power to distinguish the random walk model from the above alternative of a highly persistent yet transitory price component.

Autoregressive Moving Average (ARMA) Representations

If weak form efficiency doesn't hold then actual returns R_{t+1} might not only depend upon past returns but could also depend on past forecast errors

$$\varepsilon_{t-1} = R_t - E_{t-1} R_t$$

The simplest representation is the ARMA(1,1) model:

$$R_{t+1} = k + \gamma_1 R_t + \theta \varepsilon_t + \varepsilon_{t+1} = k + \gamma_1 R_t + u_t \qquad (6.18)$$

The autoregressive element is the independent variable R_t and the 'total' error term (denoted u_t) consists of a linear combination of white noise errors:

$$u_t = \varepsilon_{t+1} + \theta \varepsilon_t$$

The error term u_t is a moving average error (of order 1) and u_t is serially correlated. To see the latter, note that

$$\text{cov}(u_t, u_{t-1}) = E(\varepsilon_{t+1} + \theta \varepsilon_t)(\varepsilon_t + \theta \varepsilon_{t-1}) = \theta \sigma^2$$

since $E(\varepsilon_{t-s} \varepsilon_{t-m}) = 0$ for $m \neq s$. Hence $\text{cov}(u_t, u_{t-1}) \neq 0$ and u_t is serially correlated (of order 1). Past forecast errors are in the agents' information set and hence even if $\gamma_1 = 0$, weak form efficiency is still violated if $\theta \neq 0$. By including p lags of R_t and q lags of ε_t one can estimate a general ARMA(p, q) model for returns which may be represented:

$$R_{t+1} = k + \gamma(L) R_t + \theta(L) \varepsilon_{t+1}$$

where $\gamma(L)$ is a polynomial in the lag operator such that

$$\gamma(L) = 1 + \gamma_1 L + \gamma_2 L^2 + \gamma_3 L^3 + \ldots + \gamma_p L^p$$

and $L^n R_t = R_{t-n}$. In a similar fashion we define

$$\theta(L) = 1 + \theta_1 L + \theta_2 L^2 + \ldots + \theta_q L^q$$

Under the EMH we expect all parameters in $\gamma(L)$ and $\theta(L)$ to be zero. ARMA(p, q) models provide fairly general and flexible representations of the behaviour of any time series variable and tests are available to choose the 'best' values of p and q given the available data on R (although this usually involves judgement as well as formal statistical tests).

Regressions based on ARMA models are often used to test the informational efficiency assumption of the EMH. In fact Poterba and Summers attempt to fit an ARMA(1,1) model to their *generated* data on stock returns which, of course, should fit this data by construction. However, in their estimated model (equation 6.18) they find $\gamma_1 = 0.98$ and $\theta = 1$ and because γ_1 and θ are 'close to' each other, the estimation package often could not 'separate out' (identify) and successfully estimate statistically distinct values for γ_1 and θ. When Poterba and Summers do succeed in obtaining estimates of γ_1 and θ then less than 10 percent of the regressions have parameters that are close to the (known) true values. This is another example of an estimated model failing to mimic the true model in a finite sample.

Poterba and Summers are aware that their results on mean reversion are subject to the problems of inference in small samples and that any element of predictability can only be taken as evidence against the EMH, if the chosen equilibrium returns model is the true model. Cecchetti et al (1990) take up the last point and question whether the results of Poterba and Summers (1988) and Fama and French (1988a) that stock prices are mean reverting should be interpreted in terms of the presence of noise traders. They note that serial correlation of returns does not in itself imply a violation of efficiency. For example, in the consumption CAPM if agents smooth their consumption, then stock returns are mean reverting. Cecchetti et al go on to demonstrate that empirical findings on mean reversion are consistent with data that could have been generated by an equilibrium model. They take a specific parameterisation of the consumption CAPM as their representative equilibrium model and use Monte Carlo methods to generate artificial data sets. They then subject the artificial data sets to the variance ratio tests of Poterba and Summers and the long horizon return regressions of Fama and French. They find that measures of mean reversion in stock prices calculated from historic returns data nearly always lie within a 60 percent confidence interval of the median of the Monte Carlo distributions implied by the equilibrium consumption CAPM.

Like all Monte Carlo studies the results are specific to the parameters chosen for the equilibrium model. Cecchetti et al note that in the Lucas (1978) equilibrium model, consumption equals output which equals dividends, and their Monte Carlo study investigates all three alternative 'fundamental variables'. Taking dividends as an example, the Monte Carlo simulations assume

$$\ln D_t = \ln D_{t-1} + (\alpha_0 + \alpha_1 S_{t-1}) + \varepsilon_t$$

The term S_t is a Markov switching variable which has transition probabilities

$$Pr(S_t = 1 | S_{t-1}) = p, \quad Pr(S_t = 0 | S_{t-1} = 1) = 1 - p,$$

$$Pr(S_t = 0 | S_{t-1} = 0) = q, \quad Pr(S_t = 1 | S_{t-1} = 0) = 1 - q$$

Since α_1 is restricted to be negative then $S_t = 0$ is a 'high growth' state $E_t \Delta \ln D_{t+1} = \alpha_0$ and $S_t = 1$ is a low growth state $E_t \Delta \ln D_{t+1} = \alpha_0 + \alpha_1$ (with $\alpha_1 < 0$). Therefore $\ln D_t$

is a random walk with *stochastic* drift $(\alpha_0 + \alpha_1 S_{t-1})$. The parameters of the dividend process are estimated by maximum likelihood (Hamilton, 1994) and then used to generate the artificial series for dividends. The Euler equation for the consumption CAPM (with dividends replacing consumption) is

$$P_t U'(D_t) = \delta E_t[U'(D_{t+1})(P_{t+1} + D_{t+1})]$$

With preferences given by a constant coefficient of relative risk aversion $(= \gamma)$ form of utility function $U(D) = (1 + \gamma)^{-1} D^{(1-\gamma)}$ with $-\infty < \gamma \leqslant 0$, the solution to the Euler equation is:

$$P_t = D_t^{-\gamma} \sum_{i=1}^{\infty} \delta^i E_t D_{t+i}^{(1+\gamma)}$$

Simplifying somewhat the artificial series for dividends when used in the above equation (with representative values for δ and γ) gives the generated series for prices, which obey the parameterised consumption CAPM general equilibrium model. Generated data on returns $R_{t+1} = [(P_{t+1} + D_{t+1})/D_t] - 1$ are then used to calculate the Monte Carlo distributions for the Poterba–Summers variance ratio statistic and the Fama–French long horizon return regressions.

Essentially, the Cecchetti et al results demonstrate that with the available 116 annual observations of historic data on US stock returns, one cannot have great faith in empirical results based on say returns over a 10-year horizon, since there are only about 10-non-overlapping observations. The historic data is therefore too short to make a choice between an equilibrium model and a 'fads' model, based purely on an empirical analysis of historic *returns* data. Note, however, that the Cecchetti et al analysis does not preclude the possibility that variance bounds tests (see below) or other direct tests of the RVF (see Chapter 16) *may* provide greater discriminatory power between alternative models. Of course, there are also a number of ancillary assumptions in the Cecchetti et al parameterisation of the consumption CAPM model which some may contest — an issue which applies to all Monte Carlo studies. However, the Cecchetti et al results do make one far more circumspect in interpreting weak-form tests of efficiency (which use only data on lagged returns), as signalling the presence of noise traders.

6.1.3 Multivariate Tests

The Fama and French and Poterba and Summers results are univariate tests. However, a number of variables other than past returns have also been found to help predict current returns. For example, Keim and Stambaugh (1986) using *monthly* excess returns on US common stocks (over the Treasury bill rate) for the period from about 1930 to 1978 find that for a number of portfolios (based on size) the following (somewhat arbitrary) variables are usually statistically significant:

  (i)   the difference in the yield between low-grade corporate bonds and the yield on one-month Treasury bills,

 (ii)   the deviation of last periods (real) S&P index from its average over the past 45 years,

(iii)   the level of the stock price index based only on 'small stocks'.

They also find a 'pure' January effect and that the impact of (i)–(iii) are different in January from other months. (They also find that the above variables influence the monthly rates of return on other assets such as government long-term bonds and high-grade long-term corporate bonds.) However, it should be noted that for *monthly* return data on *stocks*, the regressions only explain about 0.6–2.0 percent of the actual excess return. (These results are broadly similar to those found by Chen et al (1986), see section 3.5 on testing the APT.)

Fama and French (1988b) extend their earlier univariate study on the predictability of expected returns over different horizons and examine the relationship between (nominal and real) returns and the dividend yield D/P.

$$R_{t+N}^N = \alpha + \beta(D/P)_t + \varepsilon_t \qquad (6.19)$$

The equation is run for monthly and quarterly returns and for annual returns of one to four years on the NYSE index. They also test the robustness of the equation by running it over various subperiods. For monthly and quarterly data the dividend yield is often statistically significant (and $\beta > 0$) but only explains about 5 percent of the variability in monthly and quarterly actual returns. For longer horizons the explanatory power increases. For example, for nominal returns over the 1941–1986 period the explanatory power for 1-, 2-, 3-, 4-year return horizons are 12, 17, 29 and 49 percent. The longer return horizon regressions are also useful in forecasting 'out-of-sample'.

The difficulty in assessing these results is that they are usually based on the simplest model possible for equilibrium returns, namely that expected real returns are constant. The EMH implies that *abnormal* returns are unpredictable, not that *actual* returns are unpredictable. These studies reject the latter but as they do not incorporate a reasonably sophisticated model of equilibrium returns we do not know if the EMH would be rejected in a more general model. For example, the finding that $\beta > 0$ in (6.19) implies that when current prices increase relative to dividends (i.e. $(D/P)_t$ falls) then returns and hence the future price tends to fall. This is an example of mean reversion in *prices* but it can be viewed as a mere statistical correlation where (D/P) may be a proxy for changes in equilibrium returns.

To take another example if, as in Keim and Stambaugh, an increase in the yield on low-grade bonds reflects an increase in investors' general perception of 'riskiness' then we would under the CAPM or APT expect a change in *equilibrium* and *actual* returns. Here *predictability* could conceivably be consistent with the EMH since there are no *abnormal* returns. Nevertheless the empirical regularities found by many authors do provide us with some useful stylised facts about variables which might influence returns in a statistical sense.

When looking at regression equations that attempt to explain returns, an econometrician would be interested in general diagnostic tests (e.g. are the residuals normal, serially uncorrelated, non-heteroscedastic and the RHS variables weakly exogenous), the outside sample forecasting performance of the equations and the temporal stability of the parameters. In many of the above studies this useful statistical information is not always fully presented so it becomes difficult to ascertain whether the results are as 'robust' as they seem. However, Pesaran and Timmermann (1992) provide a study of stock returns which attempts to meet the above criticisms of earlier work. First, as in previous studies, they run regressions of the excess return on variables known at time t or earlier. They are, however, very careful about the dating of the information set. For example, in explaining annual returns from end January to end January (i.e. last trading day) they use interest rates (or a term structure variable) up to the last trading day but industrial output only up to December of the previous year (since it is published with a lag).

They looked at excess returns on the S&P 500 index and the Dow Jones index measured over one year, one quarter and one month for the period 1954–1971 and subperiods. For annual excess returns a small set of independent variables including the dividend yield, annual inflation, the change in the three-month interest rate and the term premium, explain about 60 percent of the variability in the excess return. For quarterly and monthly data, broadly similar variables explain about 20 percent and 10 percent of excess returns, respectively. Interestingly, for monthly and quarterly regressions they find a non-linear effect of *previous* excess returns on current returns. For example, *squared* previous excess returns are often statistically significant while past positive returns have a different impact than past negative returns, on future returns. The authors also provide diagnostic tests for serial correlation, heteroscedasticity, normality and 'correct' functional form and these test statistics indicate no misspecification in the equations.

To test the predictive power of these equations they use recursive estimation (OLS) and *predict* the sign of next periods excess return (i.e. at $t + 1$) based on *estimated coefficients* which only use data up to period t. For annual returns, 70–80 percent of the predicted returns have the correct sign, while for quarterly excess returns the regressions still yield a (healthy) 65 percent correct prediction of the sign of returns (see Figures 6.7 and 6.8). Thus Pesaran and Timmermann (1994) reinforce the earlier results that excess returns are predictable and can be explained quite well by a relatively small number of independent variables.

Profitable Trading Strategies

Transactions costs in stock and bond trades arise from the bid–ask spread (i.e. dealers buy stock at a low price and sell to the investor at a high price) and the commission charged on a particular 'buy' or 'sell' order given to the broker. Pesaran and Timmermann use 'closing prices' which may be either 'bid' or 'ask' prices. They therefore assume that all

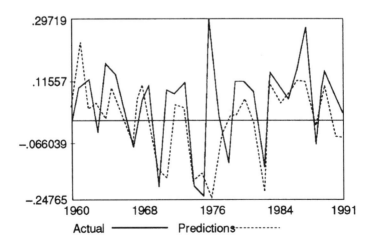

Figure 6.7 Actual and Recursive Predictions of Annual Excess Returns (SP 500). *Source*: Pesaran and Timmermann (1994). Reproduced by permission of John Wiley and Sons Ltd

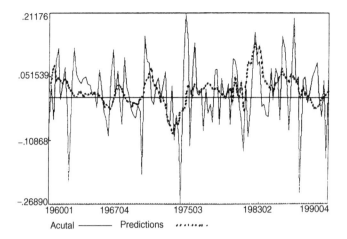

Figure 6.8 Actual and Recursive Predictions of Quarterly Excess Returns (SP 500). *Source*: Pesaran and Timmermann (1994). Reproduced by permission of John Wiley and Sons Ltd

trading costs are adequately represented by a fixed transactions cost per $ of sales. They assume costs are higher for stocks c_s than for bonds c_b. They consider a simple trading rule, namely:

> If the predicted excess return (from the recursive regression) is positive then hold the market portfolio of stocks, otherwise hold government bonds with a maturity equal to the length of the trading horizon (i.e. annual, quarterly, monthly).

The above 'switching strategy' has no problems of potential bankruptcy since assets are not sold short and there is no gearing (borrowing). The passive *benchmark strategy* is one of holding the market portfolio at all times. They assess the profitability of the switching strategy over the passive strategy for transactions costs that are 'low', 'medium' or 'high'. (The values of c_s are 0, 0.5 and 1.0 percent for stocks and for bonds c_b equals 0.0 and 0.1 percent.)

In general terms they find that the returns from the switching strategy are higher than those for the passive strategy for annual returns (i.e. switching once per year in January) even when transactions costs are 'high' (see Table 6.1). However, it pays to trade at quarterly or monthly intervals only if transactions costs are less than 1/2 percent for stocks. In addition they find that the standard deviation of returns for the switching portfolio for annual (see Table 6.1) and quarterly but not monthly returns is below that for the passive portfolio (even under high transactions cost scenario). Hence the 'annual' switching portfolio dominates the passive portfolio on the mean-variance criterion (for the whole data period 1960–1990).

The above results are found to be robust with respect to different sets of regressors in the excess return equations and over subperiods 1960–1970, 1970–1980 and 1980–1990. In Table 6.1 are reported the Sharpe, Treynor and Jensen indices of mean-variance efficiency for the switching and passive portfolios for the one-year horizon. For any portfolio 'p' these are given by:

$$S = (ER^p - r)/\sigma_p$$

$$T = (ER^p - r)/\beta_p$$

$$(R^p - r)_t = J + S(R^m - r)_t$$

Table 6.1 Performance Measures of the S&P 500 Switching Portfolio Relative to the Market Portfolio and Treasury Bills[a],[b] (Annual Returns 1960–1990)

	Portfolios							
	Market			Switching			Treasury Bills	
Transaction Cost (%)								
Stocks	0.0	0.5	1.0	0.0	0.5	1.0	–	–
Treasury Bills	–	–	–	0.0	0.1	0.1	0.0	0.1
Arithmetic Mean								
Return (%)	10.78	10.72	10.67	12.70	12.43	12.21	6.75	6.64
SD of Return (%)	13.09	13.09	13.09	7.24	7.20	7.16	2.82	2.82
Sharpe's Index	0.31	0.30	0.30	0.82	0.79	0.76	–	–
Treynor's Index	0.040	0.040	0.039	0.089	0.085	0.081	–	–
Jensen's Index	–	–	–	0.045	0.043	0.041	–	–
	–	–	–	(4.63)	(4.42)	(4.25)	–	–
Wealth at End of Period*	1913	1884	1855	3833	3559	3346	749	726

(a) The switching portfolio is based on recursive regressions of excess returns on the change in the three-month interest rate, the term premium, the inflation rate, and the dividend yield. The switching rule assumes that portfolio selection takes place once per year on the last trading day of January.
(b) For a description and the rationale behind the various performance measures used in this table see Chapter 3. The 'market' portfolio denotes a buy and hold strategy in the S&P 500 index. 'Treasury bills' denotes a roll-over strategy in 12-month Treasury bills.
* Starting from $100 in January 1960.
Source: Pesaran and Timmermann (1994). Reproduced by permission of John Wiley and Sons Ltd

One can calculate S and T for the switching and market portfolios. The Jensen index is the intercept J in the above regression. In general, except for the monthly trading strategy under the high cost scenario they find that these performance indices imply that the switching portfolio has the higher risk adjusted return.

Our final example of predictability based on regression equations is due to Clare et al (1993) who provide a relatively simple model based on the gilt–equity yield ratio (GEYR). The GEYR is widely used by market analysts to predict capital gains (e.g. Hoare Govett 1991). The $\text{GEYR}_t = (C/B_t)/(D/P_t)$, where C = coupon on a consol/perpetuity, B_t = bond price, D = dividends, P_t = stock price (of the FT All Share index). It is argued that UK pension funds, which are big players in the market, are concerned about income flows rather than capital gains, in the short run. Hence, when (D/P) is low relative to (C/B) they sell equity (and buy bonds). Hence a high GEYR implies a fall in stock prices, next period. Broadly speaking the rule of thumb used by market analysts is that, if GEYR > 2.4, then sell some equity holdings, while for GEYR < 2, buy more equity and if $2.0 \leqslant \text{GEYR} \leqslant 2.4$ then 'hold' an unchanged position.

A simple model which encapsulates the above is:

$$\Delta \ln P_t = \alpha_0 + \beta\, \text{GEYR}_{t-1} + \sum_{i=1}^{3} \alpha_i \Delta\, \text{GEYR}_{t-i} + \varepsilon_t$$

In static equilibrium the long-run GEYR is $-\alpha_0/\beta$ and Clare et al (using quarterly data) find this to be equal to 2.4. For every 0.1 that the GEYR exceeds 2.4, then the estimated equation predicts that the FT All Share index will fall 5 percent:

$$\Delta \ln P_t = 122.1 - 50.1 \, \text{GEYR}_{t-1} + 48.1\Delta \, \text{GEYR}_{t-1} + 6.5\Delta \, \text{GEYR}_{t-2}$$
$$\quad\quad (3.7) \quad\ (3.4) \quad\quad\quad\quad (2.4) \quad\quad\quad\quad\quad (3.4)$$

$$+ \, 32.6\Delta \, \text{GEYR} + [\text{dummy variables } 73(3), \, 73(4), \, 75(1), \, 87(4)]$$
$$\quad (2.8)$$

$$1969(1)\text{--}1992(2) \quad \overline{R}^2 = 0.47$$

They use recursive estimates of the above equation to forecast over 1990(1)–1993(3) and assume investors' trading rule is to hold equity if the forecast capital gain exceeds the three-month Treasury bill rate (otherwise hold Treasury bills). This strategy, using the above estimated equation, gives a higher *ex-post* capital gain = 12.3 percent per annum and lower standard deviation ($\sigma = 23.3$) than the simpler analysts' 'rule of thumb' noted above (where the return is 0.4 percent per annum and $\sigma = 39.9$). The study thus provides some prima facie evidence against weak-form efficiency. Although, note that capital gains rather than returns are used in the analysis and transactions costs are not considered. However, it seems unlikely that these two factors would undermine their conclusions.

Returns and the Consumption CAPM

The C-CAPM model of equilibrium returns discussed in Chapter 4 can be tested either using cross-section or time series data. A cross-section test of the C-CAPM is based on the following rearrangement of 4.42 (see Chapter 4) which constitutes the SML for this model.

$$ER_i = a_0 + a_1\beta_{ci} \tag{6.20}$$

$$a_0 = (1 - ES)/ES$$

$$a_1 = \alpha\theta \, \text{cov}(R^m, g^c)/ES$$

$$\beta_{ci} = \text{cov}(R_i, g^c)/\text{cov}(R^m, g^c)$$

where we have assumed that the expected value of the marginal rate of substitution ES and $\text{cov}(R^m, g^c)$ are constant (over time). Since a_1 depends only on the market return R^m and consumption growth g^c it should be the same for all stocks i. We can calculate the sample mean value $\overline{R}_i$ as a proxy for ER_i and use the sample covariance for β_{ci}, for each stock i. The above cross-section regression should then yield a statistically significant value for a_1 (and a_0). In Chapter 3 we noted that the basic CAPM can be similarly tested using the cross-section SML, where β_{ci} is 'replaced' by $\beta_{mi} = \text{cov}(R_i, R^m)/\text{var}(R_m)$. Mankiw and Shapiro (1986) test these two versions of the CAPM using cross-section data on 464 companies (listed on the NYSE) and sample values (e.g. for $\overline{R}_i$, $\text{cov}(R^m, g^c)$) calculated from quarterly data over the period 1959–1982. They find that the basic CAPM clearly outperforms the C-CAPM, since when $\overline{R}_i$ is regressed on both β_{mi} and β_{ci} the former is statistically significant while the latter is not.

A test of the C-CAPM based on time series data uses (4.45) (see Chapter 4), that is:

$$[(1 + R_{it+1})\theta(g_{t+1}^c)^{-\alpha} - 1] = \varepsilon_{it+1} \tag{6.21}$$

Since (6.21) holds for all assets (or portfolios i), then it implies a set of cross-equation restrictions, since the parameters (θ, α) appear in all equations. Again this particular model does not appear to perform well for a wide range of alternative assets included in the portfolio (e.g. portfolios comprising just US equities or US equities plus US bonds, or portfolios consisting of equities and bonds in different countries, see *inter alios*, Hodrick (1987), Cumby (1990) and Smith (1993). In Smith's (1993) study which uses an 'international' basket of assets, the coefficient restrictions in (4.46) are often found to hold but these parameters are not constant over time. Hence the model or some of its ancillary assumptions appear to be invalid.

We can also apply equation (6.21) to the aggregate stock market return and noting that (6.21) applies for any return horizon $t + j$, we have, for $j = 1, 2, \ldots$:

$$[(1 + R^m_{t+j})\theta(g^c_{t+j})^{-\alpha} - 1] = \varepsilon_{t+j} \tag{6.22}$$

Equation (6.22) can be estimated on time series data and because it holds for horizons, $j = 1, 2, \ldots$, etc. we again have a system of equations with 'common' parameters (θ, α). Equation (6.22) for $j = 1, 2, \ldots$ are similar to the Fama and French (1988a) regressions using returns over different horizons, except here we implicitly incorporate a time varying expected return. Flood et al (1986) find that the C-CAPM represented by (6.22) performs worse, in statistical terms, as the time horizon is extended. Hence they find against (this version of) the C-CAPM and their results are consistent with those of Fama and French. Overall, the C-CAPM does not appear to perform well in empirical tests.

6.2 VOLATILITY TESTS

A number of commentators often express the view that stock markets are excessively volatile: prices alter from day to day or week to week by large amounts which do not appear to reflect changes in fundamentals. If true, this constitutes a rejection of the EMH. Of course, to say that stock prices are excessively volatile requires one to have a model based on rational behaviour which provides a 'yardstick' against which one can compare volatilities.

Whether or not the stock market is excessively volatile is of course closely connected with whether, if left to itself, the stock market is an efficient device for allocating financial resources between alternative real investment projects (or firms). If stock prices do not reflect economic fundamentals then resources will be misallocated. For example, an unexpectedly low price for a share of a particular company may result in a takeover by another company. However, if the price is not giving a correct signal about the economic efficiency of that company then the takeover may be inappropriate and will involve a misallocation of resources.

Commonsense tells us, of course, that we expect stock prices to exhibit some volatility. This is because of the arrival of 'news' or new information about companies. For example, if the announced dividend payout of a company were unexpectedly high then its stock price is likely to rise sharply, to reflect this. Also if a company engaged in research and development or mineral exploration suddenly discovers a profitable new invention or mineral deposits, then this will effect future profits and hence future dividends and the stock price. We would again expect a sudden jump in stock prices. However, the question we wish to address here is not whether stock prices are volatile but whether they are excessively volatile.

Before embarking on a formal presentation of volatility tests it is worth mentioning two relatively simple yet informative 'tests' of the RVF which assume agents have to learn about the future growth rate of dividends. The first study by Barsky and De Long (1993) uses the simple Gordon (1962) growth model, where (real) stock prices $P_t = D_t/(k - g_t)$, where k is the (known) required real rate of return and g_t is the expected growth rate of dividends based on information up to time t. Barsky and De Long (1993) use this model to calculate fundamental value $V_t = D_t/(k - g_t)$ assuming that agents have to continually update their estimate of the future growth in dividends. They then compare V_t with the actual S&P stock price in the US over the period 1880–1988. Even for the simple case of a constant value of $(k - g)^{-1} = 20$ and $V_t = 20D_t$ the broad movements in V_t over a long horizon of ten years are as high as 67 percent of the variability in P_t (see their Table III, page 302) with the pre-Second World War movements in the two data series being even closer. They then propose that agents estimate g_t, at any point in time, as a long distributed lag of past dividend growth rates

$$g_t = (1 - \theta) \sum_{i=0}^{t} \theta^i \Delta g_{t-i} + \theta^t g_0$$

For $\theta = 1$ the level of log dividends follows a random walk but for $\theta = 0.97$ past dividend growth has some influence on g_t. When g_t is updated in this manner then the volatility of one-year changes in V_t are as high as 76 percent of the volatility in P_t. However, it should be noted that although long swings in P_t are in part explained by this model, changes over shorter horizons such as one year or even five years are not well explained and movements in the (more stationary) price dividend ratio are also not well explained. The above evidence is broadly consistent with the view that real dividends and real prices move together in the long run (and hence are likely to be cointegrated) but price and fundamental value can diverge quite substantially for a number of years.

Bulkley and Tonks (1989) exploit the fact that $P_t \neq V_t$ to generate profitable trades based on an aggregate UK stock price index (annual 1918–1985). The prediction equation for real dividends is $\ln D_t = \hat{a}_s + \hat{g}_s t$, where a_s and g_s are estimated recursively. They then assume that the growth rate of dividends $\hat{g}_s$ is used in the RVF and they estimate fundamental value from recursive estimates using the regression $\hat{P}_t = \hat{c}_s + \hat{g}_s t$ where $\hat{g}_s$ is constrained to be the same as in the dividend equation (but $\hat{c}_s$ varies period by period). They then investigate the profitability of a 'switching' trading rule whereby if actual price P_t exceeds the predicted price $\hat{P}_t$ from the regression by more than K_t percent, sell the index and hold (risk-free) bonds. The investor then holds bonds until P_t is K_t percent below $\hat{V}_t$ and then buys back the index. (At any date t, the value of K_t is chosen which would have maximised profits over the period $(0, t - 1)$.) The passive strategy is to buy and hold the index. They find that (over 1930–1985) the switching strategy earns pre-tax annual excess return of 1.61 percent over the buy and hold strategy. Also, the degree of risk for the switching strategy is no higher than in the buy and hold strategy. As the switching strategy only involves trades on seven separate occasions, transactions costs would have to be the order of 12.5 percent to outweigh net profits from the switching strategy.

Thus the above models, where an elementary learning process is introduced, show that broad movements in price and fundamentals (i.e. dividends) are linked over long horizons. However, they also indicate that for long periods prices may deviate from fundamentals and profitable trades are possible. We now examine more formal tests of the RVF based on variance bounds. Broadly speaking, variance bounds tests examine whether the variance of stock prices is consistent with the variability in fundamentals (i.e. dividends and discount rates) given by the RVF. These tests can be classified into two broad types: 'model-free' tests and 'model-based' tests. In the former we do not have to assume a particular *statistical* model for the fundamental variables[1]. However, as we shall see, this implies that we merely obtain a point estimate of the relevant test statistic but we cannot derive confidence limits on this measure. Formal hypothesis testing is therefore not possible. All one can do is to try and ensure that the estimator (based on sample data) of the desired statistic is an unbiased estimate of its population value[2]. Critics of the early variance ratio tests highlighted the problem of bias in finite samples (Flavin, 1983).

A 'model-based test' assumes a particular stochastic process for dividends and hence an associated statistical distribution. This provides a test statistic with appropriate confidence limits and enables one to examine small sample properties using Monto Carlo analysis. However, with model-based tests, rejection of the null that the RVF is correct is conditional on having the correct statistical model for dividends. We therefore have the problem of a joint null hypothesis.

A further key factor in interpreting the various tests on stock prices is whether the dividend process is assumed to be stationary or non-stationary. Under non-stationary the usual distributional assumptions do not apply and interpretation of the results from variance bounds tests is problematic. Much recent work has been directed towards test procedures that take account of non-stationarity in the data. This issue is discussed for variance bounds tests in this chapter and is taken up again in Chapter 16.

6.2.1 Shiller Volatility Tests

Shiller takes the *rational valuation formula* as his model of the determination of stock prices. Hence stock prices are determined by economic fundamentals, V_t, namely the discounted present value (DPV) of expected future dividends.

$$P_t = V_t = \sum_{i=1}^{n-1} \delta^i E_t D_{t+i} + \delta^n E_t P_{t+n} \tag{6.23}$$

where P_{t+n} is the expected 'terminal price' at time $t + n$. It is assumed that *all* investors take the same view of the future. Hence all investors form the same expectation of future dividends and it is also assumed for the moment that the *discount factor* $\delta(0 < \delta < 1)$ is a constant in all future periods. δ is defined as $1/(1 + k)$ where k is the *required* rate of return (see Chapter 4). Clearly the assumption of a constant *nominal* required rate of return is rather unrealistic and hence tests of the model invariably assume a constant *real* discount rate and therefore stock prices are also measured in real terms.

To set the ball rolling, it is instructive to note that if, for each time period t, we had data on *expected* future dividends, the *expected* terminal price and the constant δ then we could work out the right-hand side of equation (6.23) and compare it with the actual stock price P_t. Of course, at time t, we do not know what investors' forecasts of expected future dividends would have been. However, Shiller (1981) proposed a simple yet very ingenious way of getting round this problem.

Data are available on *actual* dividends in the past, say from 1900 onwards, and we have the actual price P_{t+n} today, say in 1996. It is assumed δ is a known value, say

0.95 for annual data. Then, using the DPV formula we can calculate what the stock price in 1900 *would have been* if investors had forecast dividends exactly, in all years from 1900 onwards. We call this the *perfect foresight stock price* P_t^*, in 1900. By moving one year forward and repeating the above, we can obtain a data series for P_t^* for all years from 1900 onwards. As described above, the data series P_t^* has been computed using the following formula:

$$P_t^* = \sum_{i=1}^{n-1} \delta^i D_{t+i} + \delta^n P_{t+n} \tag{6.24}$$

When calculating P_t^* for 1900 the influence of the terminal price P_{t+n} is fairly minimal since n is large and δ^n is relatively small. As we approach the end-point of 1996 the term $\delta^n P_{t+n}$ carries more weight in our calculation of P^*. One option is therefore to truncate our sample, say ten years prior to the present, in order to apply the DPV formula. Alternatively, we can assume that the actual price at the terminal date is 'close to' its expected value $E_t P_{t+n}^*$ and the latter is usually done in empirical work.

Comparing P_t and P_t^* we see that they differ by the *sum* of the forecast errors of dividends ω_{t+i}, weighted by the discount factors δ^i where

$$\omega_{t+i} = (D_{t+i} - E_t D_{t+i}) \tag{6.25}$$

If agents do not make systematic forecast errors then we would expect these forecast errors in a long sample of data to be positive about as many times as they are negative (and on average for them to be close to zero). This is the unbiasedness assumption of RE cropping up again. Hence we might expect the (weighted) sum of ω_{t+i} to be relatively small and the *broad movements* in P_t^* should then be correlated with those for P_t. Shiller (1981) provides a graph of (detrended) P_t and P_t^* (in real terms) for the period 1871–1979 (Figure 6.9).

One can immediately see that the correlation between P_t and P_t^* is low thus implying rejection of the view that stock prices are determined by fundamentals in an efficient

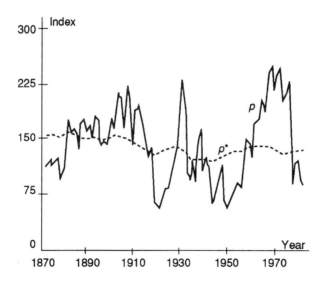

Figure 6.9 *Source*: Shiller (1981). Reproduced by permission of the American Economic Association

market. However, we can do better than just 'eyeball' the two series and Shiller examines the relationship between the variances of P_t and P_t^* where for $x_t = P_t$ or P_t^* the *sample variance* is given by

$$\text{var}(x) = \sum_{t=1}^{n}(x_t - \bar{x})^2/(n - 1) \tag{6.26}$$

where $\bar{x}$ = sample mean and n = number of observations. In 1900 investors did not know what future dividends were going to be and therefore the actual stock price will differ from the perfect foresight stock price. Hindsight has shown that investors made forecast errors, η_t, which may be represented as

$$\eta_t = P_t^* - P_t \quad \text{or} \quad P_t^* = P_t + \eta_t \tag{6.27}$$

(where η_t is a weighted average of the forecast errors for dividends ω_{t+i} at $t + 1$, $t + 2$, etc.). If investors are *rational* then η_t will be independent of all information at time t when investors made their forecast. In particular, η_t will be independent of the stock price at time t. From (6.27) we obtain:

$$\text{var}(P_t^*) = \text{var}(P_t) + \text{var}(\eta_t) + 2\,\text{cov}(\eta_t, P_t) \tag{6.28}$$

Informational efficiency (orthogonality) implies $\text{cov}(P_t, \eta_t)$ is zero and (6.28) then gives:

$$\text{var}(P_t^*) = \text{var}(P_t) + \text{var}(\eta_t) \tag{6.29}$$

Since the variance of the forecast error is positive then:

$$\text{var}(P_t^*) > \text{var}(P_t) \tag{6.30}$$

or

$$\text{VR} = \text{var}(P_t^*)/\text{var}(P_t) > 1$$

or

$$\text{SDR} = \sigma(P_t^*)/\sigma(P_t) > 1 \tag{6.31}$$

Hence if the market sets stock prices according to the rational valuation formula and ('identical') agents are rational in processing information and the discount factor is constant, we would expect the variance inequality in equation (6.31) to hold and the variance ratio (VR) (or standard deviation ratio (SDR)) to exceed unity.

For expositional reasons it is assumed that P_t^* is calculated as in (6.24) using the DPV formula. However, in much of the empirical work an equivalent method is used. The DPV formula (6.24) is consistent with the Euler equation:

$$P_t^* = \delta(P_{t+1}^* + D_{t+1}) \quad t = 1, 2, \ldots n \tag{6.32}$$

Hence if we assume a terminal value for P_{t+n}^* we can use (6.32) to calculate P_t^*, etc. by backward recursion. This, in fact, is the method used in Shiller (1981). However, whatever method is used to calculate an *observable version* of P_t^*, a terminal condition is required. One criticism of Shiller (1981) is that he uses the *sample mean* of prices for the terminal value, i.e.

$$P_{t+n}^* = n^{-1}\sum_{i=1}^{n}P_t$$

Marsh and Merton (1986) point out that this yields a biased estimate of P_t^*. However, Grossman and Shiller (1981) and Shiller's (1989) later work uses the *actual* stock price at P_{t+n} for the unobservable P_{t+n}^*. The observable series, denoted $P_{t|n}^*$, then uses (6.32) with P_{t+n} in place of P_{t+n}^*. This preserves the logical structure of the model since $P_{t|n}^* = E(P_t^*|\Omega_t)$.

6.2.2 First Generation Volatility Tests

Empirical tests of the RVF often use 'real variables', that is nominal variables such as the stock price and dividends are deflated by some general price index of goods (e.g. consumer price index (CPI)). In this case the discount rate δ must also be in real terms. Early work on volatility tests assumes a constant real discount rate and Shiller (1981) found that US stock prices are excessively volatile, that is to say, inequality (6.31) is grossly violated (i.e. SDR = 5.59). However, LeRoy and Porter (1981) using a slightly different formulation (see Appendix 6.1) found that although the variance bound is violated, the rejection was of borderline statistical significance.

Time Varying Real Interest Rates

So far, in our analysis, we have assumed that the real discount factor δ is constant. However, we could rework the perfect foresight price, assuming the real required return k_t and hence $\delta_t = (1 + k_t)^{-1}$ varies over time. For example, we could set k_t to equal the *actual* real interest rate which existed in all future years r_t, plus a constant risk premium, $(k_t = r_t + rp)$. Hence k_t varies in each year and P_t^* is calculated as:

$$P_t^* = \frac{D_{t+1}}{(1 + k_{t+1})} + \frac{D_{t+2}}{(1 + k_{t+1})(1 + k_{t+2})} + \cdots \tag{6.33}$$

with a terminal value equal to the end of sample actual price. However, when the variance bounds test is repeated using this new measure of P_t^* it is still violated (e.g. Mankiw et al (1989) and Scott (1990)).

We can turn the above calculation on its head. Knowing what the variability in the actual stock price was, we can calculate the *variability* in real returns k_t that would be necessary to equate var(P_t^*) with var(P_t). Shiller (1981) performs this calculation under the assumption that P_t and D_t have deterministic trends. Using the detrended series, he finds that the standard deviation of real returns needs to be greater than 4 percent per annum for the variance in the perfect foresight price to be brought into equality with the variance of actual prices. However, the actual historic variability in real interest rates is much smaller than that required to 'save' the variance bounds test. Hence the explanation for the violation of the excess volatility relationship does not appear to lie with a time varying *ex-post* real interest rate.

Consumption CAPM

Another line of attack, in order to 'rescue' the violation of the variance bound, is to assume that the actual or *ex-post* real interest rate (as used above) may not be a particularly good proxy for the *ex-ante* real interest rate. The consumption CAPM, where the individual maximises the discounted present value of the utility from future consumption subject to a lifetime budget constraint, can give one a handle on what the *ex-ante* real interest rate may be (see section 4.1.2). This method is also not without its difficulties, since the researcher has to assume an explicit form for the utility function and has to choose an estimate of the average rate of time preference of individuals. If one assumes a constant relative risk aversion utility function then it may be shown that the *ex-ante* required real rate of return by investors (i.e. the discount rate) depends upon the rate of growth of consumption and the constant rate of time preference.

For simplicity, assume for the moment that dividends have a growth rate g_d so that $D_t = D_0(g_d)^t$ and the perfect foresight price is:

$$P_t^{c^*} = D_0(g_d)^t \left[C_t^\alpha \sum_{s=0}^{\infty} (\theta g_d)^s C_{t+s}^{-\alpha} \right]$$

Hence $P_t^{c^*}$ varies over time (Grossman and Shiller, 1981) depending on the current level of consumption relative to a weighted harmonic average of future consumption, $C_{t+s}^{-\alpha}$. Clearly, this introduces much greater variability in $P_t^{c^*}$ than does the constant discount rate assumption (i.e. where the coefficient of relative risk aversion, $\alpha = 0$). Replacing the constant growth rate of dividends by actual *ex-post* dividends while retaining the C-CAPM formulation, Shiller (1987) recalculates the variance bounds tests for the US for the period 1889–1985 using $\alpha = 4$. The pictorial evidence (Figure 6.10) suggests that up to about 1950 the variance bounds test is not violated.

However, the relationship between the variability of actual prices and perfect foresight prices is certainly not close, in the years after 1950. Over the whole period Shiller finds that the variance ratio is not violated under the assumption that $\alpha = 4$, which some might view as an implausibly high value of the risk aversion parameter. Thus, on balance, it does not appear as if the assumption of a time varying discount rate based on the consumption CAPM can wholly explain movements in stock prices.

Small Sample Problems

Flavin (1983) and Kleidon (1986) point out that there are biases in small samples in measuring $\text{var}(P_t)$ and $\text{var}(P_t^*)$ which might invalidate some of the 'first generation'

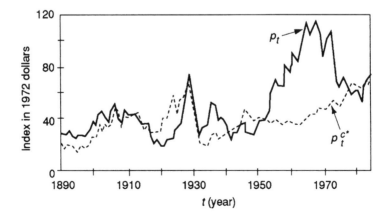

Figure 6.10 Consumption-based Time-Varying Interest Rates. *Source*: Grossman and Shiller (1981). Reproduced by permission of the American Economic Association

variance bounds tests. Flavin (1983) analysed these tests under the constant discount rate assumption and made two key points.

(i) Both $\text{var}(P_t^*)$ and $\text{var}(P_t)$ are estimated with a downward bias in small samples, the degree of bias depending on the degree of serial correlation in P_t^* and P_t. Since P_t^* is more strongly autocorrelated than P_t then $\text{var}(P_t^*)$ is estimated with greater downward bias than $\text{var}(P_t)$. Hence it is possible that the sample values yield $\text{var}(P_t^*) < \text{var}(P_t)$ in a finite sample, even when the null of the RVF is true[3].

(ii) Shiller's use of the sample average of prices as a proxy for terminal value of P^* at $t + n$ also induces a bias towards rejection.

There is a further issue surrounding the terminal price, noted by Gilles and LeRoy (1991). The correct value of the perfect foresight price is

$$P_t^* = \sum_{i=1}^{\infty} \delta^i D_{t+i}$$

which is unobservable. The observable series $P_{t|n}^*$ should be constructed using the actual price P_{t+n} at the end of the sample, since this ensures $P_{t|n}^* = E(P_t^*|\Omega_t)$. However, there is still a problem since the *sample variance* of $P_{t|n}^*$ understates the true (but unobservable) variance of P_t^*. Intuitively this is because $P_{t|n}^*$ is 'anchored' on P_{t+n} and hence does take account of innovations in dividends which occur after the end of the sample ($P_{t|n}^*$ implicitly sets these to zero but P_t^* includes these, since the summation is to infinity). Clearly this problem is minimal if the sample is very large (infinite) but may be important in finite samples.

Flavin's (1983) criticisms of these 'first generation tests' assumed, as did the authors of these tests, stationarity of the series being used. Later work tackled the issue of the validity of variance bounds tests when the price and dividend series are non-stationary (i.e. have a stochastic trend). The problem posed by non-stationary series is that the population variances are functions of time and hence the sample variances (which are constant) are not correct measures of their population values. However, it is not obvious how to 'remove' these stochastic trends from the data, in order meaningfully to apply the variance bounds tests. It is to this issue that we now turn.

6.2.3 Volatility Tests and Stationarity

Shiller's volatility inequality is a consequence purely of the assumption that the actual stock price is an unbiased and optimal predictor of the perfect foresight price P_t^*

$$P_t^* = P_t + u_t \tag{6.34}$$

where u_t is a random error term, with $E(u_t|\Omega_t) = 0$. Put another way, P_t is a sufficient statistic to forecast P_t^*. No information other than P_t can improve ones forecast of P_t^*: in this sense P_t is 'optimal'. The latter implies that the conditional forecast error $E[(P_t^* - P)_t|\Omega_t]$ is independent of all information available at time t or earlier. Hence u_t is independent and therefore uncorrelated with Ω_t. Since $P_t \subset \Omega_t$ then P_t is independent of u_t (i.e. $\text{cov}(P_t, u_t) = 0$). The latter is the 'informational efficiency' or *RE* orthogonality assumption. Using the definition of covariance for a *stationary series*, it follows directly from (6.34):

$$\text{cov}(P_t^*, P_t) = \text{cov}(P_t + u_t, P_t)$$

$$= \text{cov}(P_t, P_t) + \text{cov}(P_t, u_t) = \sigma^2(P_t) \tag{6.35}$$

where we have used $\text{cov}(P_t, u_t) = 0$. The definition of the correlation coefficient between P_t and P_t^* is

$$\rho(P_t P_t^*) = \frac{\text{cov}(P_t, P_t^*)}{\sigma(P_t) \cdot \sigma(P_t^*)} \tag{6.36}$$

Substituting for 'cov' from (6.36) in (6.35) we obtain a *variance equality*

$$\sigma(P_t) = \rho(P_t, P_t^*)\sigma(P_t^*) \tag{6.37}$$

Since the maximum value of $\rho = 1$ then (6.37) implies the familiar *variance inequality*

$$\sigma(P_t) \leqslant \sigma(P_t^*) \tag{6.38}$$

Under the assumption of informational efficiency and that P_t is determined solely by fundamentals, then (6.38) must hold in the population for any stationary series P_t, P_t^*. Stationary series have a time invariant and constant *population* mean variance (standard deviation) and covariance. The difficulty in applying (6.38) to a *sample* of data is knowing whether the sample is drawn from an underlying stationary series in the population.

It is also worth noting that the standard deviations in (6.38) are simple *unconditional* measures. If a time series plot is such that it changes direction often and hence crosses its mean value frequently (i.e. is 'jagged') then in a short sample of data we may obtain a 'good' estimate of the population value of $\sigma(P)$ from its sample value. However, if the time series wanders substantially from its (constant) mean value in long slow swings then one will need a long sample of data to obtain a good estimate of the 'true' population variance (i.e. a representative series of 'cycles' in the data set is required, not just say one-quarter or one-half a cycle). In fact, stock *prices* appear to move in quite long swings or cycles (see Figure 6.9) and hence a long data set is required to measure accurately the true standard deviation (or variance).

If a series is non-stationary then it has a time varying population mean or variance and hence (6.38) is undefined[4]. We then need to devise an alternative variance inequality in terms of a transformation of the variables P_t and P_t^* into 'new' variables that are stationary. The latter has led to alternative forms of the variance inequality condition. The problem is that it is often difficult to ascertain whether a particular series is stationary or not, from statistical tests based on any *finite* data set. For example, the series generated as $x_t = x_{t-1} + \varepsilon_t$ is non-stationary while $x_t = 0.98x_{t-1} + \varepsilon_t$ is stationary. However, in any finite data set (on stock prices) it is often difficult statistically to discriminate between the two, since in a regression $x_t = a + bx_{t-1} + \varepsilon_t$, the estimate of '$b$' is subject to sampling error and often one could take it as being either 1 or 0.98. (Also the distribution of the test statistic that $b = 1$ is 'non-standard'.)

The fact that P_t is an optimal forecast of P_t^* does not necessarily imply that it is an accurate forecast but only that one cannot improve upon the forecast based on P_t *alone*. For example, if dividends are accurately described by $D_t = \alpha + \omega_t$ where ω_t is white noise, then using the DPV formula, P_t will be constant. However, the variability in P_t^* will depend on a weighted average of the variance of ω_t and is certainly greater than zero.

Since P_t^* varies and P_t is constant then P_t^* and P_t are uncorrelated, and $\rho(P_t, P_t^*) = 0$. However, the variance inequality still holds since $\sigma(P_t) = 0$ which is less than $\sigma(P_t^*) > 0$. Consider now the converse case. It is possible (although extremely unlikely) that agents forecast future dividends exactly, in which case $\omega_t = 0$ and $P_t = P_t^*$ for all t so that $\rho(P_t, P_t^*) = 1$. Then the equality in (6.37) holds and $\sigma(P_t) = \sigma(P_t^*)$. The intermediate position is most likely to occur in practice as agents make imperfect forecasts of P_t^* and hence $0 < \rho(P_t, P_t^*) < 1$.

Let us return now to the issue of whether (real) dividends and (therefore for a constant δ) P_t^* and P_t are non-stationary. How much difference does non-stationarity make in practice when estimating the sample values of $\sigma(P_t)$ and $\sigma(P_t^*)$ from a finite data set? One can generate artificial data for these variables (i.e. the population) under the assumption of non-stationarity and see if in *the generated sample* of data the variance inequality (6.38) is met (i.e. Monte Carlo studies). For example, in his early work Shiller (1981) 'detrended' the variables P_t and P_t^* by dividing by a simple deterministic trend $\lambda_t = e^{bt}$ where b is estimated from the regression $\ln P_t = a + bt$ over the whole sample period. If P_t follows a stochastic trend then 'detrending' by assuming a deterministic trend is statistically invalid. Use of λ_t will not 'correctly' detrend the series. The question then arises as to whether the violation of the variance bounds found in Shiller's (1981) study is due to this inappropriate detrending of the data.

Kleidon (1986)[5] and LeRoy and Parke (1992) examine this question using Monte Carlo methods. For example, Kleidon (1986) assumes that expected dividend growth is a constant ($= \theta$) so actual dividends are generated by a (geometric) random walk with drift:

$$\ln D_t = \theta + \ln D_{t-1} + \varepsilon_t \tag{6.39}$$

where ε_t is white noise. This yields a non-stationary stochastic trend for D_t. Given a generated series for D_t for m observations using (6.39) one can use the DPV formula to generate a time series of length 'm' for P_t^* and for P_t. One can then establish whether $\text{var}(P_t) > \text{var}(P_t^*)$ in the *artificial sample* of data of length m. One can repeat this 'experiment' n times (each time generating m observations) and see how many times $\text{var}(P_t) > \text{var}(P_t^*)$. Since the EMH/fundamentals model is 'true' by construction, one would not expect the variance bound to be violated in a large number of cases in the n repeated experiments. (Some violations will be due to chance or 'statistical outliers'.) In fact Kleidon (1986) finds that when using the generated data and detrending by using λ_t the variance bound is frequently violated even though the EMH/fundamentals model is true. The frequency of violations is 90 percent (when using Shiller's method of detrending) while the frequency of 'gross violations' (i.e. $VR > 5$) varied considerably depending on the rate of interest (discount rate) assumed in the simulations. (For example, for $r = 7.5$ percent the frequency of gross violations is only about 5 percent, but for $r = 5.0$ percent, the figure rises dramatically to about 40 percent.)

Shiller (1988) refined Kleidon's procedure by noting that Kleidon's combined assumptions for the growth rate of dividends ($= \theta$) and the level of interest rates implied an implausible value for the dividend price ratio. Shiller allows θ to vary with r so that in the artificially generated data, the dividend price ratio equals its average historic level. Under the null of the RVF he finds that the gross violations of the variance ratio are substantially less than those found by Kleidon.

Further, Shiller (1989, page 85) notes that in none of the above Monte Carlo studies is the violation of the variance inequality as large as that actually found by Shiller (1981) when using the 'real world' sample data. Shiller also points out that the 'special case' used by Kleidon (and others), namely that (the log of real) dividends follow a random walk with drift, may not be a correct statistical representation of the true path of dividends. Actual regressions on real world data suggest that current dividends may depend on many past values of dividends (i.e. an $AR(q)$ process where q is large) and may not have a unit root (i.e. the sum of the coefficients on lagged dividends is less than unity).

This debate highlights the problem of trying to discredit results which use 'real data' by using 'specific special cases' (e.g. random walk) in a Monte Carlo analysis. These Monte Carlo studies provide a highly specific 'sensitivity test' of empirical results, but such experiments may not provide an *accurate* description of real world data. Again, the problem is that in a finite 'real world' data set one often does not know what is the 'most realistic' statistical representation of the data. Often, data are equally well represented by a stationary or non-stationary univariate or multivariate series. However, one must agree with Shiller (1989) that on *a priori economic grounds* it is hard to accept that investors believe that when faced with an unexpected increase in *current* dividends, of z percent, they *expect* that dividends will be higher by z percent, *in all future periods*. However, the latter is implied by the (geometric) random walk model of dividends (equation (6.39)) used by Kleidon and others. Shiller (1989) prefers the view that firms attempt to smooth *nominal* dividends (and hardly ever cut dividends). In this case *real* dividends (as used in the above studies) may appear to be 'close to' a unit root series but the 'true' series is stationary.

The outcome of all of the above arguments is that not only may the small sample properties of the variance bounds tests be unreliable but if there is non-stationarity then even tests based on large samples may be suspect. Clearly, all one can do in practice (while awaiting new time series data as 'time' moves on!) is to assess the robustness of the volatility results under different methods of detrending. For example, Shiller (1989) reworks some of his earlier variance inequality results using P_t/E_t^{30} and P_t^*/E_t^{30} where the real price series are 'detrended' using a (backward) 30-year moving average of real earnings E_t^{30}. He also uses P_t/D_{t-1} and P_t^*/D_{t-1} where D_{t-1} is real dividends in the previous year. To counter the criticism that detrending using a deterministic trend (Shiller, 1981) estimated *over the whole sample period* uses information not known at time t, Shiller (1989) in his later work detrends P_t and P_t^* using a time trend estimated only with data up to time t (that is $\lambda_t = \exp[b_t]t$ where the estimated b_t changes as more data is included — that is, recursive least squares).

The results using these various transformations of P_t and P_t^* to try and ensure a stationary series are given in Table 6.2. The variance inequality (6.38) is always violated but the violation is not as great as in Shiller's original (1981) study using a (fixed) deterministic trend. However, the variance equality (6.37) is strongly violated in all of the variants[6].

To ascertain the robustness of the above results Shiller (1989) repeats Kleidon's Monte Carlo study using the geometric random walk model for dividends. He detrends the artificially generated data on $\tilde{P}_t$ and $\tilde{P}_t^*$ by a generated real earnings series $\tilde{E}_t$ (generated earnings are assumed to be proportional to generated dividends) and assumes a constant real discount rate of 8.32 percent (equal to the sample average annual real return on stocks). In 1000 runs he finds that in 75.8 percent of cases $\sigma(P_t/E_t^{30})$ exceeds $\sigma(P_t^*/E_t^{30})$. Hence when dividends are non-stationary there is a tendency for spurious violation of the variance bounds when the series are detrended by E_t^{30}. However, some comfort can be

Table 6.2 Variance Bounds Tests[a]

Method of Detrending	ρ	$\sigma(P_t^*)$	$\rho\sigma(P_t^*)$	$\sigma(P_t)$	VR
1. Time Varying Deterministic	n.a	n.a	n.a	n.a	2.12
2. Using D_{t-1}	0.133	4.703	0.54	6.03	1.28
	(0.06)	(7.779)	(0.23)	(6.03)	(1.29)
3. Using E_t^{30}	0.296	1.611	0.47	6.706	3.77
	(0.048)	(4.65)	(0.22)	(6.706)	(1.44)

(a) The figures are for a constant real discount rate while those in parentheses are for a time varying real discount rate.

Source: Shiller 1989.

gained from the fact that for the generated data the mean value of $VR = 1.447$ which, although in excess of the 'true' value of 1.00, is substantially less than the 4.16 observed in the real world data. (And in only one of the 1000 'runs' did the 'generated' variance ratio exceed 4.16.)

Clearly since E_t^{30} and P_t^* are long moving averages, they both make long, smooth swings and one may only pick up part of the potential variability in P_t^*/E_t^{30} in small samples (i.e. we observe only a part of its full cycle). The *sample* variance may therefore be biased downwards. Since P_t is not smoothed (P_t/E_t^{30}) may well show more variability than P_t^*/E_t^{30} even though in a *much longer* sample the converse could apply. Again this boils down to the fact that statistical tests on such data can only be definitive if one has a long data set. The Monte Carlo evidence and the results in Table 6.2 do, however, place the balance of evidence against the EMH when applied to stock prices.

Mankiw et al (1991), in an update of their earlier 1985 paper, tackle the non-stationarity problem by considering the variability in P and P^* relative to a naive forecast P^0. For the naive forecast they assume dividends follow a random walk and hence $E_t D_{t+j} = D_t$ for all j. Hence using the rational valuation formula the naive forecast is

$$P_t^0 = [\delta/(1-\delta)]D_t$$

where $\delta = 1/(1+k)$ and k is the equilibrium required return on the stock. Now consider the identity

$$P_t^* - P_t^0 = (P_t^* - P_t) + (P_t - P_t^0) \tag{6.40}$$

The RE forecast error is $P_t^* - P_t$ and hence is independent of information at time t and hence of $P_t - P_t^0$. Dividing (6.40) by P_t and squaring gives

$$q_t = E\left[\frac{P_t^* - P_t^0}{P_t}\right]^2 - \left[E\left[\frac{P_t^* - P_t}{P_t}\right]^2 + E\left[\frac{P_t - P_t^0}{P_t}\right]^2\right] \tag{6.41}$$

and the inequalities are therefore

$$E\left[\frac{P_t^* - P_t^0}{P_t}\right]^2 \geqslant E\left[\frac{P_t^* - P_t}{P_t}\right]^2 \tag{6.42}$$

$$E\left[\frac{P_t^* - P_t^0}{P_t}\right]^2 \geqslant E\left[\frac{P_t - P_t^0}{P_t}\right]^2 \tag{6.43}$$

The beauty of the above relationships is that each element of the expressions is likely to be stationary, and deflating by P_t is likely to minimise problems of heteroscedasticity. Equation (6.42) states that the market price is a better forecast of the *ex-post* 'rational price', P_t^*, than is the naive forecast and the former should have a lower mean squared error. Equation (6.43) states that the *ex-post* rational price P_t^* is more volatile around the naive forecast P_t^0 than is the market price and is analogous to Shiller's volatility inequality. An alternative test of the EMH is that $\Psi = 0$ in:

$$q_t = \Psi + \varepsilon_t \tag{6.44}$$

and the benefit of using this formulation is that we can construct a (asymptotically) valid standard error for Ψ (after using a GMM correction for any serial correlation or heteroscedasticity, see Part 7). Using annual data 1871–1988 in an aggregate stock price index Mankiw et al find that equation (6.41) is rejected at only about the 5 percent level for constant required real returns of $k = 6$ or 7 (although the model is strongly rejected when the required return is assumed to be 5 percent). When they allow the required equilibrium nominal return to equal the (nominal) risk-free rate plus a constant risk premium (i.e. $k_t = r_t + rp$) then the EMH using (6.41) is rejected more strongly than for the constant real returns case.

The paper by Mankiw et al (1991) also tackles another problem that has caused difficulties in the interpretation of variance bounds tests, namely the importance of the terminal price P_{t+N} in calculating the perfect foresight price. Merton (1987) points out that the end of sample price P_{t+N} picks up the effect of out-of-sample events on the (within sample) stock price, since it reflects all future (unobserved) dividends. Hence volatility tests that use a fixed end point value for *actual* price may be subject to a form of measurement error if P_{t+N} is a very poor proxy for $E_t P_{t+N}^*$. Mankiw et al (and Shiller (1989)) point out that Merton's criticism is of less importance if actual dividends paid out 'in sample' are sufficiently high so that the importance of out-of-sample events (measured by P_{t+N}) is circumscribed. Empirically, the latter case applies to the data used by Mankiw et al since they have a long representative sample of data. However, Mankiw et al provide another ingenious yet simple counterweight to this argument (see also Shea (1989)). The perfect foresight stock price (6.24) can be calculated for different horizons ($n = 1, 2, \ldots N$) and so can q_t used in (6.44). Hence, several values of q_t^n (for $n = 1, 2, \ldots N$) can be calculated in which many end-of-holding-period prices are observed in a sample. Therefore, they do not have to worry about a *single* end-of-sample price dominating their results. In general they find that the EMH has greater support at short horizons (i.e. $n = 1$–5 years) rather than long horizons (i.e. $n > 10$ years).

In a recent paper, Gilles and LeRoy (1991) present some further evidence of the difficulties of correct inference when using variance bounds tests in the presence of non-stationarity data. They derive a variance bound test that is valid if dividends follow a geometric random walk and stock prices are non-stationary (but cointegrated, see Chapter 20). They therefore assume the dividend price ratio is stationary and their variance inequality is $\sigma^2(P_t|D_t) \leqslant \sigma^2(P_t^*|D_t)$. The sample estimates of the variances (1871–1988 US aggregate index as used in Shiller (1981)) indicate excess volatility since $\sigma^2(P_t|D_t) = 26.4$ and $\sigma^2(P_t^*|D_t) = 19.4$. However, they note that the *sample* variance of $\sigma(P_t^*|D_t)$ is biased downwards for two reasons. First, because $(P_t^*|D_t)$ is positively serially correlated (Flavin, 1983) and second because at the terminal date the unobservable $E_t P_{t+n}^*$ is assumed to equal the actual (terminal) price P_{t+n}. (Hence dividend innovations after the end of the sample are assumed to be zero, Merton (1986).) Using Monte Carlo experiments they find that the first source of bias is the most important and is very severe. The Monte Carlo experiment assumes a geometric random walk for dividends, $\ln D_{t+1} = \ln D_t + \varepsilon_{t+1}$, with $E\varepsilon_{t+1} = \mu$, $\text{var}(\varepsilon_{t+1}) = \sigma^2$. The value of $\sigma^2(P_t^*|D_t)$ in the Monte Carlo runs is 89.3 compared with 19.4 using actual sample data. On the other hand, the sample value of $\sigma^2(P_t|D_t)$ is found to be a fairly accurate measure of the population variance. Hence Gilles and LeRoy conclude that the Shiller-type variance bounds test 'is indecisive' (Gilles and LeRoy (1991), page 986). However, all is not lost. Gilles and LeRoy develop a test based on the *orthogonality* of P_t and P_t^* (West, 1988) which is more robust. This 'orthogonality test' uses the geometric random walk assumption for dividends and involves a test statistic with much less bias and less sample variability than the Shiller-type test. The orthogonality test rejects the present value model quite decisively (although note that there are some nuances involved in this procedure which we do not document here). Thus a reasonable summary of the Gilles–LeRoy study would be that the RVF is rejected, provided one accepts the geometric random walk model of dividends.

Scott (1990) follows a slightly different procedure and compares the behaviour of P_t and P_t^* using a simple regression rather than a variance bounds test. If the DPV formula holds for stocks then $P_t^* = P_t + \varepsilon_t$ and in the regression

$$P_t^* = a + bP_t + \varepsilon_t \tag{6.45}$$

the EMH implies $a = 0$, $b = 1$. Scott deflates P_t^* and P_t by dividends in the previous year so that the variables are stationary and he adjusts for serial correlation in the regression residuals. He finds that the above restrictions are violated for US stock price data so that P_t is not an unbiased predictor of P_t^*. The $\overline{R}^2$ of the regression is very low, so that there is little (positive) correlation between P_t and P_t^* and P_t provides a very poor forecast of the *ex-post* perfect foresight price, P_t^*. (Note, however, that it is the unbiasedness proposition that is important for the refutation of the efficient markets model, not the low $\overline{R}^2$ which in itself is not inconsistent with the EMH.)

The EMH, however, does imply that any information Ω_t included in (6.45) should not be statistically significant. Scott (1990) regresses $(P_t^* - P_t)$ on the dividend price ratio (i.e. dividend yield) and finds it is statistically significant, thus rejecting informational efficiency. Note that since $P_t^* - P_t$ may be viewed as a long horizon return Scott's result is not inconsistent with those studies that find long horizon returns are predictable (e.g. Fama and French (1988b)).

Shiller (1989, page 91) deflated P_t and P_t^* using a 30-year backward looking earnings series E_t^{30} and in the regression (corrected for serial correlation):

$$(P^*/E_t^{30}) = a + b(P_t/E_t 30) + \varepsilon_t$$

finds that $\hat{b} \ll 1$. Although Shiller finds that $\hat{b}$ based on Monte Carlo evidence is downward biased, such bias is not sufficient to account for the *strong* rejection (i.e. $\hat{b} \ll 1$) found in the above regression on the real world data.

6.2.4 Peso Problems and Variance Bounds Tests

It should now be obvious that there are some complex statistical issues involved in assessing the EMH. We now return to a theoretical issue which also can cause similar problems — the so-called 'Peso problem'. In the presence of a Peso problem the variance bound in a *sample of data* may be violated even though agents use RE and set price equal to fundamental value.

The Peso problem arises in the following way. Suppose we have a *sample* of data in which investors attach a small probability to the possibility of a large rise in dividends in the future. However, suppose this rise in dividends never occurs and actual dividends remain constant. An investor's expectation of dividends over this sample of data is a weighted average of the higher level of dividends and the 'normal' constant dividends. But the outturn for dividends is constant and is lower than investors' true expectations (i.e. $D < E_t D_{t+1}$). Investors have therefore made a systematic forecast error *within this sample period*. If the sample period is extended then we would also observe periods when investors expect lower dividends (which never occur), hence $D > E_t D_{t+1}$, and hence over the *extended* 'full' sample, forecast errors average zero. The Peso problem arises because we only 'observe' the first sample of data. To illustrate the Peso problem more fully the maths will be simplified, and this issue examined by considering an asset which pays out a *stream* of expected dividend payments $E_t D_{t+1}$ all of which are discounted at the constant rate δ. We can think of period '$t+1$' as constituting m data points. The stock price is set equal to fundamental value:

$$P_t = \delta E_t D_{t+1} \tag{6.46}$$

where $\delta =$ constant discount factor. Suppose there is a *small* probability π_2 of being in regime 2 so that the true expectation of investors is:

$$E_t D_{t+1} = \pi_2 D_{t+1}^{(2)} + (1 - \pi_2) D_{t+1}^{(1)} \tag{6.47}$$

To simplify even further suppose that in regime 1, future dividends are expected to be constant and *ex-post* are equal to D so that $D_{t+1}^{(1)} = D$. Regime 2 can be thought of as a rumour of a takeover bid which, if it occurs, will increase dividends so that $D_{t+1}^{(2)} > D$. Call regime 2 'the rumour'. The key to the Peso problem is that the researcher only has data for the periods over which 'the rumour' does not materialise. Although influencing investor's 'true' expectations and hence the stock price, 'the takeover' doesn't in fact occur and dividends actually remain at their constant value D.

Since 'the rumour' exists then rational investors set the price of the share equal to its fundamental value:

$$P_t = \delta[\pi_2 D_{t+1}^{(2)} + (1 - \pi_2) D_{t+1}^{(1)}] = \delta \pi_2 [D_{t+1}^{(2)} - D] + \delta D \tag{6.48}$$

where $D_{t+1}^{(1)} = D$, a constant. Variability in the actual price given by (6.48) will take place either because of changing views about π_2 (the probability of a takeover) or because of changing views about future dividends, should the takeover actually take place, $D_{t+1}^{(2)}$. If the takeover never takes place, then the constant level of dividends D will be paid out and the researcher will measure the *ex-post* perfect foresight price over our m data points, as the *constant* value $P_t^* = \delta D$ and hence var$(P_t^*) = 0$. However, the actual price may vary as π_2 and $D_{t+1}^{(2)}$ change and hence var$(P_t) > 0$. Thus we have a violation of the variance bound, that is var$(P_t) >$ var(P_t^*), even though prices always equal fundamental value as given by (6.48). This is a consequence of a sample of data which may not be representative of the (whole) population of data. If we had a longer data set then the expected event might actually happen and hence P_t^* would vary along with the actual price.

Consider now the implications of the Peso problem for regression tests of P_t^* on P_t:

$$P_t^* = \alpha + \beta P_t + w_t \tag{6.49}$$

when the true model for P_t is based on fundamental value. Assume that dividends in regime 1, $D_{t+1}^{(1)}$, vary over time. Since the takeover never actually occurs, the perfect foresight price measured by the researcher is $P_t^* = \delta D_{t+1}^{(1)}$. However, the actual price is determined by fundamentals and is given by:

$$P_t = \delta(\pi_2 D_{t+1}^{(2)} + (1 - \pi_2) D_{t+1}^{(1)}) = \delta\pi_2(D_{t+1}^{(2)} - D_{t+2}^{(1)}) + P_t^* \tag{6.50}$$

where we have substituted $P_t^* = \delta D_{t+1}^{(1)}$. Rearranging (6.50) gives

$$P_t^* = -\delta\pi_2[D_{t+1}^{(2)} - D_{t+1}^{(1)}] + P_t \tag{6.51}$$

Comparing (6.51) and (6.49) we expect $\alpha \neq 0$ and for α to be time varying if π_2 and $(D_{t+1}^{(2)} - D_{t+1}^{(1)})$ are time varying. If the first term in (6.51) is time varying then (6.49) is misspecified since it has an 'omitted variable'. The OLS estimate of β from the sample of data will be biased because of the correlation between P_t and dividends in (6.51). A weak test of the absence of a Peso problem is to check on the temporal stability of α and β. Only if (α, β) are stable can one proceed to test H_0: $\alpha = 0$, $\beta = 1$. However, empirical studies often do not test the constancy of α and β before proceeding with the usual test of H_0. Of course, if α and β are temporally unstable this could be due to a host of other factors as well as Peso problems (e.g. use of a constant discount rate in forming P_t^* when the true discount rate is time varying). But non-constancy of α and β would still invalidate any tests based on the assumption that these regression parameters are constant. Of course, for $\pi_2 = 0$ equation (6.51) 'collapses' to the unbiasedness case.

The Peso problem arises because of one-off 'special events' which *could* take place within the sample period but in actual fact do not. It considerably complicates tests of hypotheses which are based on rational expectations such as the EMH which assume outturn data differ from expectations by a (zero mean) random error.

6.2.5 Volatility Tests and Regression Tests: A Comparison

Volatility tests are a joint test of informational efficiency and that price equals fundamental value. Regression tests on the relationship between actual price P_t and the perfect foresight price P_t^* also test these two elements of the EMH. Regression tests such as those of Fama and French (1988b) on *returns* are tests of informational efficiency under the assumption that expected (real) returns are constant. But as we have seen in Chapter 4 the joint hypothesis that $ER_{t+1} = k$ and that rational expectations holds, yields the rational valuation formula and so in principle results from both types of test should yield similar inferences. However, results from such tests might differ because of statistical issues (e.g. stationarity of the data, power of the tests).

The easiest way of seeing the relationship between the volatility tests and regression tests is to note that in the regression

$$P_t^* = a + bP_t + \varepsilon_t \tag{6.52}$$

the coefficient b is given by

$$b = \frac{\text{cov}(P_t, P_t^*)}{\sigma^2(P_t)} = \frac{\rho(P_t, P_t^*)\sigma(P_t^*)}{\sigma(P_t)} \tag{6.53}$$

Substituting for ρ from the variance equality (6.37) in (6.53) we obtain

$$b = 1$$

Hence if the variance equality holds then we expect $b = 1$ in the regression (6.52).
   Consider the regression tests involving P_t and P_t^* of the form

$$P_t^* = a + bP_t + c\Omega_t + \eta_t \tag{6.54}$$

Under the orthogonality assumption of the EMH we expect

$$H_0 : a = c = 0, \quad b = 1 \tag{6.55}$$

If this proves to be the case then (6.54) reduces to

$$P_t^* = P_t + \eta_t \tag{6.56}$$

and hence the variance bounds test must also hold. The two tests are therefore equivalent
under the null hypothesis.
   As a slight variant consider the case where $c = 0$ but $b < 1$ (as is found in much recent
empirical work described above). Then (6.54) reduces to

$$\text{var}(P_t^*) = b^2 \, \text{var}(P_t) + \text{var}(\eta_t) \tag{6.57}$$

$$\text{var}(P_t^*) - \text{var}(P_t) = (b^2 - 1)\,\text{var}(P_t) + \text{var}(\eta_t) \tag{6.58}$$

where informational efficiency implies $\text{cov}(P_t, \eta_t) = 0$. (An OLS regression would also
impose this restriction in the sample of data.) Since $b^2 < 1$ then the first term on the
RHS of (6.58) is negative and it is possible that the whole of the RHS of (6.58) is also
negative. Hence if $b < 1$ this may also imply a violation of the variance bounds test.
   Next, consider the long-horizon regressions of Fama and French:

$$R_t^N = a + bR_{t-N}^N + \eta_t \tag{6.59}$$

$$\ln P_{t+N} = a + (b+1)\ln P_{t-N} - b\ln P_t + \eta_t \tag{6.60}$$

where we have used $R_t^N = \ln P_{t+N} - \ln P_t$. Under the null hypothesis that expected returns
are constant $(a \neq 0)$ and independent of information at time t or earlier then we expect
$H_0: b = 0$. If H_0 is true then from (6.60)

$$\ln P_{t+N} = a + \ln P_t + \eta_t \tag{6.61}$$

Hence under the null, $H_0: b = 0$, the Fama–French regressions are broadly consistent
with the random walk model of stock prices. Finally note that the Scott (1990) regression
under the null is

$$\ln P_t^* = a + \ln P_t + \eta_t \tag{6.62}$$

and hence it is similar to the Fama–French regression (6.60) under the null, $b = 0$, but with
the perfect foresight price $\ln P_t^*$ replacing the *ex-post* future price $\ln P_{t+N}$. However, $\ln P_t^*$

may be interpreted as a long-horizon view of future prices since it depends on dividends in all future periods so it is not 'unlike' $\ln P_{t+N}$, for large N. In fact the major difference is that in calculating $\ln P_t^*$ the actual price at the *terminal date* is used and therefore the holding period in (6.62) is the end of the sample whereas Fama and French have a holding period of fixed length (see also Shiller (1989), page 91). In fact one can calculate P_t^* at a fixed distance from t and then the correspondence between the two regressions (6.60) and (6.62) is even closer (e.g. Joerding (1988) and Mankiw et al (1989)).

In the wide-ranging study of Mankiw et al (1991) referred to above they also consider the type of regression tests used by Fama and French. More specifically consider the following autoregression of (pseudo) returns:

$$\left[\frac{P_t^{*^n} - P_t}{P_t}\right] = \alpha + \beta \left[\frac{P_t - P_t^0}{P_t}\right] + e_t \tag{6.63}$$

where $P_t^{*^n}$ is the perfect foresight price calculated using a specific horizon ($n = 1, 2, \ldots$). Mankiw et al use a Monte Carlo study to demonstrate that under plausible conditions that hold in real world data, estimates of β and its standard error can be subject to very severe small sample biases. These biases increase as the horizon n is increased. However, when using their annual data set, under the constant real returns case (of 5, 6 or 7 percent per annum) it is still the case that $H_0: \beta = 0$ is rejected at the 1–5 percent level, for most horizons between one and ten years (see Mankiw et al Table 5, page 470). When P_t^* is constructed under the assumption that equilibrium returns depend on the nominal interest rate plus a constant risk premium then $H_0: \beta = 0$ is only rejected at around the 5–10 percent significance levels for horizons greater than five years (see their Table 6, page 471). Overall, these results suggest that the evidence that long-horizon returns (i.e. $n > 5$ years) are forecastable as found by Fama and French are not necessarily clear cut when the small sample properties of the test statistics are carefully examined.

It has been shown that under the null of market efficiency, regression tests using P_t and P_t^* should be consistent with variance bounds inequalities and with regressions based on autoregressive models for stock returns. However, the small sample properties of these tests need careful consideration and although the balance of the evidence is probably against the EMH, this evidence is far from conclusive.

6.3 SUMMARY

There have been innumerable tests of the EMH applied to stock prices and returns. We have discussed a number of these tests and the interrelationships between them. All tests of the EMH are conditional on a particular equilibrium model for returns (or prices). The main conclusions are:

- In principle, autocorrelation coefficients of returns data, regression-based tests (including ARMA models) of stock returns and variance bounds tests for stock prices should all provide similar inferences about the validity of the EMH. Usually they do not. This is in part because tests on returns are sometimes based on a slightly different equilibrium model to those based on stock prices. Also the small sample properties of the test statistics differ.

- Tests based on stock returns indicate that (*ex-post*) real returns and excess returns are predictable but this is a violation of the EMH only if one accepts that either *equilibrium* real or equilibrium excess returns represents the 'true' expected returns model. In view of the analysis of models of equilibrium returns in Chapters 2 and 3, these rather simple assumptions seem unlikely to hold.

- Not only are stock returns predictable from regression equations but there is considerable evidence that actual trading strategies based on the predictions from these equations can result in profits, net of dealing costs. The key question for the validity or otherwise of the EMH is whether these profits when corrected for *ex-ante* risk are positive. There is certainly evidence that this might well be the case although it can always be argued that methods used to correct for the risk of the portfolio (e.g. use of sample variance of returns) are inadequate.

- Shiller's (1981) original seminal work using variance bounds inequalities appeared decisively to reject the RVF. Subsequent work in the 1980s pointed out deficiencies in Shiller's original approach (e.g. Kleidon (1986) and Flavin (1983)) but Shiller's (1987) later work rather successfully answered his critics. However, very recent work (e.g. Mankiw et al (1991) and Gilles and LeRoy (1991)) has certainly demonstrated that violations of the RVF are statistically far from clear cut and considerable judgment is required in reaching a balanced view on this matter.

- Thus where the balance of the evidence for the EMH lies is very difficult to ascertain given the plethora of somewhat conflicting results and the acute problems of statistical inference involved. To this author it appears that the evidence cited in this chapter, particularly that based on stock prices, is on balance marginally against the EMH.

The intuitive appeal of Shiller's volatility inequality and the simple elegance of the basic insight behind this approach have become somewhat overshadowed by the practical (statistical) issues surrounding the actual test procedures used. As we shall see in Parts 5 and 6 some recent advances in econometric methodology have allowed a more satisfactory treatment of problems of non-stationarity and the modelling of time varying risk premia.

ENDNOTES

1. Note, however, that the term 'model free' is used here in a statistical sense (see Gilles and LeRoy (1991)). A model of stock prices always requires some assumptions about behaviour and to derive the RVF we need a 'model' of expected returns and the assumption of RE (see Chapter 4). Hence the RVF is not 'model free' if the latter is interpreted to mean free of a specific *economic* hypothesis.

2. A formal hypothesis testing procedure requires one to specify a test statistic *and* a rejection region such that if the null (e.g. RVF) is true, then it will be rejected with a pre-assigned probability 'α'. A test is biased towards rejection if the probability of rejection exceeds 'α'. Hence in the variance bounds literature 'bias' has the highly restrictive definition given in the text.

3. If a series $(x_1, x_2, \ldots x_n)$ is drawn from a common distribution and the variance is estimated using:

$$\hat{\sigma}^2 = \sum_{i=1}^{n} (x_i - \bar{x})^2 / (n-1)$$

where $\bar{x}$ = sample mean, then $\hat{\sigma}^2$ is an unbiased estimator of σ^2 only if the x_i are mutually uncorrelated.

4. Strictly speaking (6.38) holds *for each t*, for a non-stationary series. The problem is that the variances are non-constant and hence the usual sample estimators of the variances are incorrect.

5. Kleidon (1986) also makes the point that the variance bounds inequality applies to a cross-section of data and not to a time series. He argues that evidence from a single time series of data is uninformative about the violation of the correctly interpreted variance bound. This aspect of Kleidon's work is not discussed here and the interested reader should consult the original article and the clear exposition of this argument in Gilles and LeRoy (1991).

6. It is worth nothing that LeRoy and Porter (1981) were aware of the problem of non-stationarity in P_t and they also adjusted the raw data series to try and achieve stationary variables. However, it appears as if they were not wholly successful in removing these trends (see Gilles and LeRoy (1991), footnotes 3 and 4).

APPENDIX 6.1

The LeRoy–Porter and West Tests

The above tests do not fit neatly into the main body of this chapter but are important landmarks in the literature in this area. We therefore discuss these tests and their relationship to each other and to other material in the text.

The LeRoy and Porter (1981) variance bounds test is based on the mathematical property that the conditional expectation of any random variable is less volatile than the variable itself. Their analysis begins with a forecast of future dividends based on a limited information set $\Lambda_t = (D_t, D_{t-1}, \ldots)$. The forecast of future dividends based on Λ_t is defined as

$$\hat{P}_t = E(P_t^*|\Lambda_t) = \sum_{i=1}^{\infty} \delta^i E(D_{t+i}|\Lambda_t) \tag{1}$$

The actual stock price P_t is determined by forecasts based on the full information set Ω_t:

$$P_t = E(P_t^*|\Omega_t) \tag{2}$$

Applying the law of iterated expectations to (2) gives

$$E(P_t|\Lambda_t) = E[E(P_t^*|\Omega_t)|\Lambda_t] = E(P_t^*|\Lambda_t) \tag{3}$$

Using (1) and (3):

$$\hat{P}_t = E(P_t|\Lambda_t) \tag{4}$$

Since $\hat{P}_t$ is the conditional expectation of P_t, then from (4) the LeRoy–Porter variance inequality is:

$$\text{var}(\hat{P}_t) \leqslant \text{var}(P_t) \tag{5}$$

Assuming stationarity, the sample variances of $\hat{P}_t$ and P_t provide consistent estimates of their population values given in (5). Given an ARMA model for D_t and a known value of δ the series $\hat{P}_t$ can be constructed using (1).

As in Shiller (1981), the procedure adopted by LeRoy and Porter yields a variance inequality. However, the LeRoy–Porter analysis also gives rise to a form of 'orthogonality test'. To see this, define the one-period forecast error of the $ return as

$$e_{t+1} \equiv (D_{t+1} + P_{t+1}) - E(D_{t+1} + P_{t+1}|\Omega_t) \tag{6}$$

The Euler equation is

$$P_t = \delta E(P_{t+1} + D_{t+1}|\Omega_t) \tag{7}$$

Substituting (6) in (7), iterating forward and applying the usual transversality condition:

$$P_t^* = P_t + \sum_{i=1}^{\infty} \delta^i e_{t+i} \tag{8}$$

where $P_t^* = \Sigma \delta^i D_{t+i}$. If e_{t+i} is stationary:

$$\text{var}(P_t^*) = \text{var}(P_t) + 2\,\text{cov}(P_t, \Sigma \delta^i e_{t+i}) + [\delta^2/(1 - \delta^2)]\,\text{var}(e_t) \tag{9}$$

where the e_{t+i} are mutually uncorrelated under RE. Also, under RE the covariance term is zero, that is P_t and e_{t+i} are *orthogonal*, hence

$$\text{var}(P_t^*) = \text{var}(P_t) + [\delta^2/(1 - \delta^2)]\,\text{var}(e_t) \tag{10}$$

Equation (10) is both a variance equality and an orthogonality test of the RVF.

It is perhaps worth noting at this juncture that equation (9) is consistent with Shiller's inequality. If in the data we find a violation of Shiller's inequality, that is $\text{var}(P_t) > \text{var}(P_t^*)$, then from (9) this implies $\text{cov}(P_t, \Sigma \delta^i e_{t+i}) < 0$. Hence a weighted average of one-period \$ forecast errors is correlated with information at time t, namely P_t. Thus violation of Shiller's variance bound implies that (a weighted average of) one-period \$ returns are forecastable. A link has therefore been provided between Shiller's variance bounds test and the predictability of one-period \$ returns. However, the returns here are \$ returns not *percentage* returns and therefore violation of Shiller's variance bound cannot be *directly* compared with those studies that find one-period returns are forecastable (e.g. Fama and French 1988b). In Chapter 19 we pursue this analysis further and a log-linearisation of the RVF allows us to directly link a failure of the RVF with the predictability of one-period and multiperiod *percentage* returns.

The West (1988) test is important because it is valid even if dividends are non-stationary (but cointegrated with the stock price) and it does not require a proxy for the unobservable P_t^*. Like the LeRoy–Porter variance inequality, the West test is based on a property of mathematical expectations. Specifically, it is that the variance of the forecast error with a limited information set Λ_t must be greater than that based on the full information set Ω_t.

The West inequality can be shown to be a direct implication of the LeRoy–Porter inequality. We begin with equation (1) and note that

$$\delta(\hat{P}_{t+1} + D_{t+1}) = \delta D_{t+1} + \delta E(\delta D_{t+2} + \delta^2 D_{t+3} + \dots |\Lambda_{t+1}) \tag{11}$$

Applying the law of iterated expectations $E[E(\cdot|\Lambda_{t+1})|\Lambda_t] = E(\cdot|\Lambda_t)$ to (11)

$$\delta E(\hat{P}_{t+1} + D_{t+1}|\Lambda_t) = \sum_{i=1}^{\infty} \delta^i E(D_{t+i}|\Lambda_t) \tag{12}$$

Substituting for the LHS of (12) from (1)

$$E(\hat{P}_{t+1} + D_{t+1})|\Lambda_t = \delta^{-1}\hat{P}_t \tag{13}$$

Now define the forecast error of the \$ return, based on information Λ_t, as

$$\hat{e}_{t+1} \equiv P_{t+1} + D_{t+1} - E(\hat{P}_{t+1} + D_{t+1}|\Lambda_t) \tag{14}$$

Substituting from (13) in (14):

$$\hat{e}_{t+1} = P_{t+1} + D_{t+1} - \delta^{-1}\hat{P}_t \tag{15}$$

Equation (15) is the forecast error based on Λ_t while (6) is the forecast error based on Ω_t (with $\Lambda_t \subset \Omega_t$) hence by the law of conditional mathematical expectations

$$\text{var}(\hat{e}_{t+1}) > \text{var}(e_{t+1}) \tag{16}$$

Equation (16) is the West inequality and using US data West (1988) finds (16) is violated. Even if the *level* of dividends is non-stationary the population variances in (16) are constant (stationary) and the sample variances provide consistent estimators. However, unfortunately the latter is only true if the *level* of dividends is non-stationary (e.g. $D_{t+1} = D_{t+1} + \omega_{t+1}$). LeRoy and Parke (1992) investigate the properties of the West test if dividends follow a *geometric* random walk (i.e. $\ln D_{t+1} = \ln D_t + \varepsilon_{t+1}$) and the reader should consult the original paper for further information.

The LeRoy–Porter and West inequalities are both derived by considering variances under a limited information set and under the complete information set. Hence one might guess that these inequalities provide similar inferences on the validity of the RVF. This is indeed the case, as can now be demonstrated. The LeRoy–Porter equality (10) holds for any information set and therefore it holds for Λ_t which implies

$$\text{var}(P_t^*) = \text{var}(\hat{P}_t) + [\delta^2/(1 - \delta^2)]\,\text{var}(\hat{e}_t) \tag{17}$$

The LeRoy–Porter inequality (5) is

$$\text{var}(\hat{P}_t) \leqslant \text{var}(P_t) \tag{18}$$

Substituting for $\text{var}(\hat{P}_t)$ from (17) and for $\text{var}(P_t)$ from (10) we obtain the West inequality.

7
Rational Bubbles

The idea of self-fulfilling 'bubbles' or 'sunspots' in asset prices has been discussed almost since organised markets began. Famous documented 'first' bubbles (Garber, 1990) include the South Sea share price bubble of the 1720s and the Tulipmania bubble. In the latter case, the price of tulip bulbs rocketted between November 1636 and January 1637 only to collapse suddenly in February 1637 and by 1739 the price had fallen to around 1/200th of 1 percent of its peak value. The increase in stock prices in the 1920s and subsequent 'crash' in 1929, the stock market crash of 1987 and the rise of the dollar between 1982 and 1985 and its subsequent fall, have also been interpreted in terms of a self-fulfilling bubble. Keynes (1936), of course, is noted for his observation that stock prices may not be governed by an objective view of 'fundamentals' but by what 'average opinion expects average opinion to be'. His analogy for the forecasting of stock prices was that of trying to forecast the winner of a beauty contest. Objective beauty is not necessarily the issue; what is important is how one thinks the other judges' perceptions of beauty will be reflected in their voting patterns.

Rational bubbles arise because of the indeterminate aspect of solutions to rational expectations models, which for stocks is implicitly reflected in the Euler equation for stock prices. The price you are prepared to pay today for a stock depends on the price you think you can obtain at some point in the future. But the latter depends on the expected price even further in the future. The Euler equation determines a sequence of prices but does not 'pin down' a unique price level unless somewhat arbitrarily we impose a terminal condition (i.e. transversality condition) to obtain the unique solution that price equals fundamental value (see Chapter 4). However, in general the Euler equation does not rule out the possibility that the price may contain an explosive bubble. (There are some subtle qualifications to the last statement and in particular in the representative agent model of Tirole (1985) he demonstrates uniqueness for an economy with a finite number of rational, infinitely lived traders and he also demonstrates that bubbles are only possible when the rate of growth of the economy is higher than the steady state return on capital.)

While one can certainly try and explain prolonged rises or falls in stock prices as due to some kind of irrational behaviour such as 'herding', or 'market psychology', nevertheless recent work emphasises that such sharp movements or 'bubbles' may be consistent with the assumption of rational behaviour. Even if traders are perfectly rational, the actual stock price may contain a 'bubble element' and therefore there can be a divergence between the stock price and its fundamental value. This chapter investigates the phenomenon of rational bubbles and demonstrates:

- how explosive rational bubbles and periodically collapsing bubbles arise as solutions to the Euler equation, and how one tests for the presence of these 'exogenous' bubbles

- how bubbles may also depend on fundamentals such as dividends, and how one might test for the presence of these 'intrinsic bubbles'

7.1 EULER EQUATION AND THE RATIONAL VALUATION FORMULA

We wish to investigate how the market price of stocks may deviate, possibly substantially, from their fundamental value even when agents are homogeneous, rational and the market is informationally efficient. To do so it is shown that the market price may equal its fundamental value *plus* a 'bubble term' and yet the stock will still be willingly held by rational agents and no supernormal profits can be made. The exposition is simplified by assuming (i) agents are risk neutral and have rational expectations and (ii) investors require a constant (real) rate of return on the asset $E_t R_t = k$. The Euler equation is:

$$P_t = \delta(E_t P_{t+1} + E_t D_{t+1}) \tag{7.1}$$

where $\delta = 1/(1 + k)$. We saw in Chapter 4 that this may be solved under RE by repeated forward substitution to yield the rational valuation formula for the stock price:

$$P_t = P_t^f = \sum_{i=1}^{\infty} \delta^i E_t D_{t+i} \tag{7.2}$$

if we assume the transversality condition holds (i.e. $\lim(\delta^n E_t D_{t+n}) = 0$, as $n \to \infty$). The transversality condition ensures a unique price given by (7.2). The RHS of (7.2) denotes the fundamental value P_t^f. The basic idea behind a rational bubble is that there is another mathematical expression for P_t that satisfies the Euler equation, namely:

$$P_t = \sum_{i=1}^{\infty} \delta^i E_t D_{t+i} + B_t = P_t^f + B_t \tag{7.3}$$

and the term B_t is described as a 'rational bubble'. Thus the actual market price P_t deviates from its fundamental value P_t^f by the amount of the rational bubble B_t. So far there is no indication of any properties of B_t: clearly if B_t is large relative to fundamental value then *actual* prices can deviate substantially from their fundamental value.

In order that (7.3) should satisfy (7.1) some restrictions have to be placed on the dynamic behaviour of B_t and these restrictions are determined by establishing a potential contradiction. This is done by assuming (7.3) is a valid solution to (7.1) and this then restricts the dynamics of B_t. Start by leading (7.3) by one period and taking expectations at time t:

$$E_t P_{t+1} = E_t[\delta E_{t+1} D_{t+2} + \delta^2 E_{t+1} D_{t+3} + \cdots + B_{t+1}]$$
$$= [\delta E_t D_{t+2} + \delta^2 E_t D_{t+3} + \cdots + E_t B_{t+1}] \tag{7.4}$$

where use has been made of the law of iterated expectations $E_t(E_{t+1} D_{t+j}) = E_t D_{t+j}$. The RHS of the Euler equation (7.1) contains the term $\delta(E_t P_{t+1} + E_t D_{t+1})$ and using (7.4) we can see that this is given by:

$$\delta[E_t D_{t+1} + E_t P_{t+1}] = \delta E_t D_{t+1} + [\delta^2 E_t D_{t+2} + \delta^3 E_t D_{t+3} + \cdots + \delta E_t B_{t+1}] \tag{7.5}$$

Substituting the *definition* of P_t^f from (7.2) in the RHS of (7.5) we have:

$$\delta[E_t D_{t+1} + E_t P_{t+1}] = P_t^f + \delta E_t B_{t+1} \tag{7.6}$$

Substituting from (7.6) into (7.1)

$$P_t = P_t^f + \delta E_t B_{t+1} \tag{7.7}$$

But we now seem to have a contradiction since (7.3) and (7.7) cannot *in general* both be solutions to (7.1). Put another way, if (7.3) is assumed to be a solution to the Euler equation (7.1) then we also obtain the relationship (7.7) as a valid solution to (7.1). We can make these two solutions (7.3) and (7.7) equivalent if:

$$E_t B_{t+1} = B_t/\delta = (1+k)B_t \tag{7.8}$$

Then (7.3) and (7.7) collapse to the same expression and satisfy (7.1). More generally, (7.8) implies

$$E_t B_{t+m} = B_t/\delta^m \tag{7.9}$$

Hence (apart from the (known) discount factor) B_t must behave as a martingale: the best forecast of all future values of the bubble depend only on its current value. While the bubble solution satisfies the Euler equation, it violates the transversality condition (for $B_t \neq 0$) and because B_t is arbitrary, the stock price in (7.3) is non-unique.

What kind of bubble is this mathematical entity? Note that the bubble is a valid solution provided the bubble is expected to grow at the rate of return required for investors willingly to hold the stock (from (7.8) we have $E(B_{t+1}/B_t) - 1 = k$). Investors do not care if they are paying for the bubble (rather than fundamental value) because the bubble element of the actual market price pays the *required* rate of return, k. Market participants, however, do not know how much the bubble contributes to the actual price: the bubble is unobservable and is a self-fulfilling expectation.

Consider a simple case where expected dividends are constant and the value of the bubble at time t, $B_t = b(> 0)$, a constant. The bubble is deterministic and grows at the rate k, so that $E_t B_{t+m} = (1+k)^m b$. Thus once the bubble exists, the actual stock price at $t + m$ even *if dividends are constant* is from (7.3)

$$P_{t+m} = \frac{\delta D}{(1-\delta)} + b(1+k)^m \tag{7.10}$$

Even though fundamentals (i.e. dividends) indicate that the actual price should be constant, the presence of the bubble means that the actual price can rise continuously, since $(1+k) > 1$.

In the above example, the bubble becomes an increasing proportion of the actual price since the bubble grows but the fundamental value is constant. In fact even when dividends are not constant the stock price always grows at a rate which is less than the rate of growth of the bubble $(= k)$ because of the payment of dividends:

$$(E_t P_{t+1}/P_t) - 1 = k - E_t D_{t+1}/P_t \tag{7.11}$$

In the presence of a bubble the investor still uses all available information to forecast prices and rates of return. Hence we still expect forecast errors to be independent of information at time $t(\Omega_t)$ and that excess returns are unforecastable. Tests of informational efficiency are therefore useless in detecting bubbles. However, the bubble does not allow one to make (supernormal) profits since all information on the future course of dividends and the bubble is incorporated in the current price: the bubble satisfies the fair game property.

The above model of rational bubbles can be extended (Blanchard, 1979) to include the case where the bubble collapses with probability $(1 - \pi)$ and continues with probability π; mathematically:

$$B_{t+1} = B_t(\delta\pi)^{-1} \quad \text{with probability } \pi \tag{7.12a}$$

$$= 0 \quad \text{with probability } 1 - \pi \tag{7.12b}$$

This structure also satisfies the martingale property. These models of rational bubbles, it should be noted, tell us nothing about how bubbles start or end, they merely tell us about the time series properties of the bubble once it is underway. The bubble is 'exogenous' to the fundamentals model of expected returns.

As noted above, investors cannot distinguish between a price rise that is due solely to fundamentals from one that is due to fundamentals plus the bubble. Individuals do not mind paying a price over the fundamental price as long as the bubble element yields them the required rate of return next period *and is expected to persist*. One implication of rational bubbles is that they cannot be negative (i.e. $B_t < 0$). This is because the bubble element falls at a faster rate than the stock price. Hence a negative rational bubble ultimately ends in a zero price (say at time $t + N$). Rational agents realise this and they therefore know that the bubble will eventually burst. But by backward induction the bubble must burst immediately since no one will pay the 'bubble premium' in the earlier periods. Thus if actual price P_t is below fundamental value P_t^f, it cannot be because of a rational bubble. If negative bubbles are not possible, then if a bubble is ever zero it cannot restart. This arises because the innovation $(B_{t+1} - E_t B_{t+1})$ in a rational bubble must have a zero mean. If the bubble started again, the innovation could not be mean zero since the bubble would have to go in one direction only, that is increase, in order to start up again.

In principle, a positive bubble is possible since there is no upper limit on stock prices. However, in this case, we have the rather implausible state of affairs where the bubble element B_t becomes an increasing proportion of the actual price and the fundamentals P_t^f of the price become relatively small. One might conjecture that this implies that individuals will feel that at some time in the future the bubble must burst. Again, if investors think that the bubble must burst at some time in the future (for whatever reason), then it will burst. To see this suppose individuals think the bubble will burst in the year 2020. They must realise that the market price in the year 2019 will reflect only the fundamental value because the bubble is expected to burst over the coming year. But if the price in 2019 reflects only the fundamental value then by backward induction this must be true of the price in all earlier years. Therefore the price *now* will reflect only fundamentals. Thus it seems that in the real world, rational bubbles can really only exist if the market's horizon is shorter than the time period when the bubble is expected to burst. The idea here is that one would pay a price above the fundamental value because one believes that someone else will pay an even greater price in the future. Here investors are myopic and the price at some future time $t + N$ depends on what they think other investors think the price will be.

Bubbles and Volatility Tests

It is relatively easy to demonstrate that violation of Shiller's variance bound inequality cannot be taken to imply the presence of rational bubbles. Intuitively this is because the terminal price P_N used in the test will contain any bubble element. More formally, note that in calculating the perfect foresight price an approximation to the infinite horizon discounting in the RVF is used and the *calculated* perfect foresight price is P_t^*:

$$P_t^* = \sum_{i=1}^{N} \delta^i D_{t+i} + \delta^N P_{t+N} \tag{7.13}$$

and P_{t+N} is the *actual* market price at the end of the data set. The variance bound under the null of constant (real) required returns is $\mathrm{var}(P_t) \leqslant \mathrm{var}(P_t^*)$. However, a bubble is incorporated in this null hypothesis. To see this, note that with a rational bubble:

$$P_t = P_t^f + B_t \tag{7.14}$$

and $E_t(B_{t+N}) = (1+k)^N B_t = \delta^{-N} B_t$. If we now replace P_{t+N} in (7.13) by a term containing the bubble $P_{t+N} = P_{t+N}^f + B_{t+N}$ then:

$$E_t P_t^* = P_t^f + \delta^N E_t B_{t+N} = P_t^f + B_t \tag{7.15}$$

and hence even in the presence of a bubble we have from (7.14) and (7.15) that $P_t = E(P_t^*)$.

7.2 TESTS OF RATIONAL BUBBLES

An early test for bubbles (Flood and Garber, 1980) assumed a non-stochastic bubble, that is $P_t = P_t^f + (B_0/\delta)^t$ where B_0 is the value of the bubble at the beginning of the sample period. Hence in a regression context there is an additional term of the form $(B_0/\delta)^t$. Knowing δ, a test for the presence of a bubble is then $H_0 : B_0 \neq 0$. Unfortunately, because $(1/\delta) > 1$, the regressor $(1/\delta)^t$ is exploding and this implies that tests on B_0 depend on non-standard distributions and correct inferences are therefore problematic. (For further details see Flood, Garber and Scott (1984)).

An ingenious test for bubbles is provided by West (1987). The test involves calculating a particular parameter by two alternative methods. Under the assumption of no bubbles, the two parameter estimates should be equal within the limits of statistical accuracy, while in the presence of rational bubbles the two estimates should differ. A strength of this approach (in contrast to Flood and Garber (1980) is that it does not require a specific parameterisation of the bubble process: *any* bubble that is correlated with dividends can in principle be detected.

To illustrate the approach, note first that δ can be estimated from (instrumental variables) estimation of the 'observable' Euler equation:

$$P_t = \delta(P_{t+1} + D_{t+1}) + u_{t+1} \tag{7.16}$$

where invoking RE, $u_{t+1} = -\delta[(P_{t+1} + D_{t+1}) - E_t(P_{t+1} - D_{t+1})]$. Now assume an AR(1) process for dividends

$$D_t = \alpha D_{t-1} + v_t \qquad |\alpha| < 1 \tag{7.17}$$

Under the no-bubbles hypothesis the RVF and (7.17) give

$$P_t = \Psi D_t + \varepsilon_{t+1} \tag{7.18}$$

where $\Psi = \delta\alpha/(1 - \delta\alpha)$ and ε_{t+1} arises because the econometrician has a subset Λ_t of the true information set (but $E_t(\varepsilon_{t+1}|\Lambda_t) = 0$). An *indirect* estimate of Ψ, denoted $\hat{\Psi}$, can be obtained from the regression estimates of δ from (7.16) and α from (7.17). However, a *direct* estimate of Ψ denoted $\hat{\Psi}^*$ can be obtained from the regression of P_t on D_t in (7.18). Under the null of no bubbles, the indirect and direct estimates of Ψ should be equal.

Consider the case where bubbles are present and hence $P_t = P_t^f + B_t = \Psi D_t + B_t$. The regression of P_t on D_t now contains an omitted variable, namely the bubble and the estimate of Ψ denoted $\hat{\Psi}^\dagger$ will be inconsistent:

$$\text{plim } \hat{\Psi}^\dagger = \Psi + \text{plim}(T^{-1}\Sigma D_t^2)^{-1}\,\text{plim}(T^{-1}\Sigma D_t B_t) \tag{7.19}$$

If the bubble B_t is correlated with dividends then $\hat{\Psi}^\dagger$ will be biased (upwards if $\text{cov}(D_t, B_t) > 0$) and inconsistent. But the Euler equation and the dividend forecasting equations still provide consistent estimators of the parameters and hence of $\hat{\Psi}$. Therefore in the presence of bubbles, $\hat{\Psi} \neq \hat{\Psi}^\dagger$ (and a Hausman (1978) test can be used to detect any possible change in the coefficients).[1]

The above test procedure is used by West (1987) whose data consists of the Shiller (1981) S&P index 1871–1980 (and the Dow Jones index 1928–1978). West finds a substantive difference between the two sets of estimates thus rejecting the null of no bubbles. However, this result could be due to an incorrect model of equilibrium returns or dividend behaviour. Indeed West recognises this and finds the results are reasonably robust to alternative ARMA processes for dividends but in contrast, under time varying discount rates, there is no evidence against the null of no bubbles. Flood et al (1986) point out that if one iterates the Euler equation for a second period, the estimated ('two period') Euler equation is not well specified and estimates of δ may therefore be biased. Since the derivation of RVF requires an infinite number of iterations of the Euler equation, this casts some doubt on the estimate of δ and hence on West's (1987) results.

West (1988a) develops a further test for bubbles which again involves comparing the difference between two estimators, based on two different information sets. One limited information set Λ_t consists of current and past dividends and the other information set is the optimal predictor of future dividends, namely the market price P_t. Under the null of no bubbles, forecasting with the limited information set Λ_t ought to yield a larger forecast error (strictly, innovation variance) but West finds the opposite. This evidence refutes the no-bubbles hypothesis but of course it is also not necessarily inconsistent with the presence of fads.

Some tests for the presence of rational bubbles are based on investigating the stationarity properties of the price and dividend data series in the RVF. An exogenous bubble introduces an explosive element into prices which is not (necessarily) present in the fundamentals (i.e. dividends or discount rates). Hence if the stock price and dividends 'grow' at the same rate, this is indicative that bubbles are not present. If P_t 'grows' faster than D_t then this could be due to the presence of a bubble term B_t. These intuitive notions can be expressed in terms of the literature on unit roots and cointegration. Using the RVF (under the assumption of a constant discount rate) it can be shown that if the change in dividends ΔD_t is a stationary (ARMA) process and there are no bubbles, then ΔP_t is also a stationary series and P_t and D_t are cointegrated.

The concept of cointegration (see Chapter 20) can be illustrated by assuming dividends follow a random walk $D_{t+1} = D_t + \varepsilon_{t+1}$ so that $\Delta D_{t+1} = \varepsilon_{t+1}$ is stationary. Dividends are then said to be integrated of order one I(1) because taking the *first* difference of dividends yields a stationary I(0) series. The optimal forecast of all future dividends equals current dividends and the RVF (without bubbles) gives $P_t = [\delta/(1 - \delta)]D_t$. Since D_t follows a random walk then P_t must also follow a random walk and therefore ΔP_t is stationary. In addition, the (stochastic) trend in P_t must 'track' the stochastic trend in D_t so that the 'gap'

$$z_t = P_t - \delta/(1 - \delta)D_t$$

is not explosive. In other words the RVF plus the random walk assumption for dividends implies that z_t must be a stationary I(0) variable. If z_t is stationary then P_t and D_t are said to be cointegrated with a cointegrating parameter equal to $\delta/(1 - \delta)$. Testing for bubbles (Diba and Grossman, 1988b) then involves the following:

(i) Demonstrate that P_t and D_t contain a unit root and are non-stationary I(1) series. Next, demonstrate that ΔP_t and ΔD_t are both stationary I(0) series. This is then adduced as evidence against the presence of an explosive bubble in P_t.

(ii) The next step is to test for cointegration between P_t and D_t. Heuristically, this test involves a regression of $P_t = \hat{c}_0 + \hat{c}_1 D_t$ and then testing to see if the constructed series $z_t = (P_t - \hat{c}_0 - \hat{c}_1 D_t)$ is stationary. If there are no bubbles, we expect z_t to be stationary I(0), but z_t is non-stationary if explosive bubbles are present.

Using aggregate stock price and dividend indexes Diba and Grossman (1988b) perform the above tests and on balance they find that ΔP_t and ΔD_t are stationary and P_t and D_t are cointegrated, thus rejecting the presence of explosive bubbles of the type represented by equation (7.8).

Unfortunately, the interpretation of the above tests has been shown to be potentially misleading in the presence of what Evans (1991) calls 'periodically collapsing bubbles'. The type of rational bubble that Evans examines is one that is always positive but can 'erupt' and grow at a fast rate before collapsing to a positive mean value, when the process begins again. The path of the periodically collapsing bubble (see Figure 7.1) can be seen to be different from a bubble that grows continuously.

Intuitively one can see why testing to see if P_t is a non-stationarity I(1) series might not detect a bubble component like that in Figure 7.1. The (Dickey–Fuller) test for stationarity essentially tries to measure whether a series has a strong upward trend or an unconditional variance that is non-constant. Clearly, there is no strong upward trend in Figure 7.1 and although the variance alters over time, this may be difficult to detect particularly if the bubbles have a high probability of collapsing (within any given time period). If the bubbles have a very low probability of collapsing, then we are close to the case of 'explosive bubbles' (i.e. $E_t B_{t+1} = B_t/\delta$) examined by Diba and Grossman and here one might expect standard tests for stationarity to be more conclusive.

Heuristically (and simplifying somewhat), Evans proceeds by artificially generating a series for a periodically collapsing bubble. Adding the bubble to the fundamentals P_t^f (e.g. under the assumption that D_t is a random walk with drift) gives the generated stock price series. The generated stock price series containing the bubble is then subject to standard tests for the presence of unit roots. The experiment is then repeated a number of times. Evans finds that the results of his unit root tests depend crucially on π, the probability

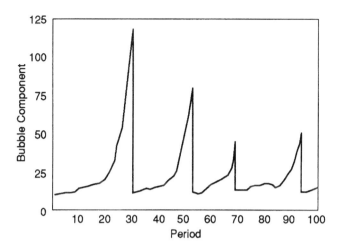

Figure 7.1 Bubble Component. *Source*: Evans (1991). Reproduced by permission of the American Economic Association

(per period) that the bubble does not collapse. For values of $\pi < 0.75$, more than 90 percent of the simulations erroneously indicate that ΔP_t is stationary. Also, P_t and D_t are erroneously found to be cointegrated. Hence using Monte Carlo simulations Evans demonstrates that a particular class of rational bubbles, namely 'periodically collapsing bubbles', are often not detectable using standard unit root tests. (The reason for this is that 'standard tests' assume a *linear* autoregressive process whereas Evan's simulations involve a complex non-linear bubble process). Thus the failure of Diba and Grossman to detect continuously explosive bubbles in stock prices does not necessarily rule out other types of rational bubble. Clearly, more sophisticated statistical tests of non-stationarity are required to detect periodically collapsing bubbles (see, for example, Hamilton (1994)).

7.3 INTRINSIC BUBBLES

One of the problems with the type of bubble discussed so far is that the bubble is a *deus ex-machina* and is exogenous to fundamentals such as dividends. The bubble term arises as an alternative solution (strictly the homogeneous part of the solution) to the Euler equation for stock prices. Froot and Obstfeld suggest a different type of bubble phenomenon which they term an intrinsic bubble. 'Intrinsic' is used because the bubble depends (in a non-linear deterministic way) on fundamentals, namely the level of (real) dividends. The bubble element therefore remains constant if 'fundamentals' remain constant but increases (decreases) along with the level of dividends. For this form of intrinsic bubble, if dividends are persistent then so is the bubble term and stock prices will exhibit persistent deviations from fundamental value. In addition, the intrinsic bubble can cause stock prices to overreact to changes in dividends (fundamentals) which is consistent with empirical evidence.

To analyse this form of intrinsic bubble assume a constant real required rate of return r (in continuous time). The Euler equation is

$$P_t = e^{-r}E_t(D_{t+1} + P_{t+1}) \tag{7.20}$$

which implies a fundamentals price P_t^f (assuming the transversality condition holds) given by

$$P_t^f = \sum_{S=t}^{\infty} e^{-r(s-t+1)} E_t(D_S) \tag{7.21}$$

However, $P_t = P_t^f + B_t$ is also a solution to the Euler equation, if B_t is a martingale, that is $B_t = e^{-r}[E_t B_{t+1}]$. The 'intrinsic bubble' is constructed by finding a non-linear function of dividends such that B_t is a martingale and hence satisfies the Euler equation. Froot and Obstfeld show that a non-linear function, denoted $B(D_t)$, of the form:

$$B(D_t) = cD_t^\lambda \qquad c > 0, \lambda > 1 \tag{7.22}$$

satisfies these conditions. If log dividends follow a random walk with drift parameter μ and conditional variance σ^2, that is $\ln(D_{t+1}) = \mu + \ln(D_t) + \varepsilon_{t+1}$, then the bubble solution $\hat{P}_t$ is:

$$\hat{P}_t = P_t^f + B(D_t) = \alpha D_t + cD_t^\lambda \tag{7.23}$$

where[2], $\alpha = (e^r - e^{\mu+\sigma^2/2})^{-1}$. The fundamentals solution $P_t^f = \alpha D_t$ is a stochastic version of Gordon's (1962) growth model which gives $P_t^f = (e^r - e^\mu)^{-1} D_t$ under certainty. It is clear from (7.23) that stock prices overreact to current dividends compared to the 'fundamentals only' solution (i.e. $\partial P_t^f/\partial D_t = \alpha$) because of the bubble term (i.e. $dP_t/dD_t = \alpha + c\lambda D_t^{\lambda-1}, c > 0$). Froot and Obstfeld simulate the intrinsic bubble in (7.22) assuming reasonable values for (r, μ, σ^2), estimated values of α, c and λ (see below) and with ε_{t+i} drawn from an independent normal distribution. They compare the pure fundamentals path P_t^f, the intrinsic stochastic bubble path $\hat{P}_t$ given by (7.23) and, in addition, an intrinsic bubble that depends on time as well as dividends, which gives rise to a path for prices denoted $\tilde{P}_t$:

$$\tilde{P}_t = \alpha D_t + bD_t e^{(r-\mu-\sigma^2/2)t} \tag{7.24}$$

The intrinsic bubble which depends on time (7.24) allows a comparison with parametric bubble tests, which often invoke a deterministic exponential time trend (Flood and Garber, 1980, Blanchard and Watson, 1982 and Flood and Garber, 1994, page 1192). The simulated values of these three price series are shown in Figure 7.2 and it is clear that the intrinsic bubble can produce a plausible looking path for stock prices $\hat{P}_t$ and one that is persistently above the fundamentals path P_t^f. (Although in other simulations the intrinsic bubble $\hat{P}_t$ can be above the fundamentals path P_t^f and then 'collapse' towards P_t^f.) From Figure 7.2, we see that in a *finite* sample the intrinsic bubble may not look explosive and hence it would be difficult to detect in statistical tests that use a finite data set. (The time dependent intrinsic bubble $\tilde{P}_t$ on the other hand yields a path which looks explosive and this is more likely to be revealed by statistical tests.) In other simulations, the intrinsic bubble series $\hat{P}_t$ may end up (after 200 periods of the simulation) substantially above the fundamentals price P_t^f.

Froot and Obstfeld test for the presence of intrinsic bubbles using a simple transformation of (7.23).

$$P_t/D_t = c_0 + cD_t^{\lambda-1} + \eta_t \tag{7.25}$$

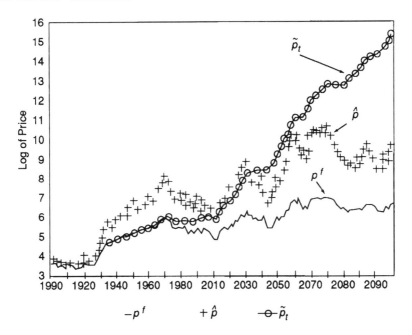

Figure 7.2 Simulated Stock Price Paths. *Source*: Froot and Obstfeld (1991). Reproduced by permission of the American Economic Association

where the null of no bubble implies $H_0 : c_0 = \alpha$ and $c = 0$ (where $\alpha = e^r - e^{\mu+\sigma^2/2}$). Using representative values of $e^r = 1.09$ per annum for the real S&P index and for the real dividend process, $\mu = 0.011$, $\sigma = 0.122$ and therefore the sample average value for α equals 14. Hence under the null of no bubbles P_t and D_t should be cointegrated with cointegration parameter $c_0 = \alpha$, of about 14. In a simple OLS cointegrating regression of P_t on D_t, Froot and Obstfeld find that $P_t = \Psi + 37D_t$ and hence P_t overreacts to dividends. In addition, $P_t - 14D_t$ is not stationary and therefore P_t and D_t are not cointegrated (with a cointegration parameter equal to 14). The 'fundamentals only' solution $P^f = \alpha D_t$ also implies that $\ln P_t$ and $\ln D_t$ are cointegrated with a cointegration parameter of unity. However, estimates reveal this parameter to be in the range 1.6–1.8 and that $(\ln P_t - \ln D_t)$ may not be stationary. Hence taken at face value, these tests tend to reject the (no-bubble) fundamentals model. However, Froot and Obstfeld note that the OLS cointegrating parameter could be heavily biased (Banerjee et al, 1993), and that the power and size of these tests are problematic.

Froot and Obstfeld then consider a direct test for the presence of intrinsic bubbles based on estimation of (7.25). A representative result is:

$$(P/D)_t = 14.6 + 0.04D_t^{1.6(1.1)} \tag{7.26}$$
$$(2.28) \quad (0.12)$$

Annual: 1900–1988, $R^2 = 0.57$, $(\cdot)$ = Newy–West standard errors.

Although there are some subtle econometric issues involved in testing for $c = 0$ and $\lambda - 1 = 0$ in (7.25) in a finite sample, the evidence above is in part supportive of the intrinsic bubble. The joint null, that c and $\lambda - 1$ equal zero is strongly rejected. However, the empirical evidence is not decisive since we do not reject the null that $c = 0$. One can

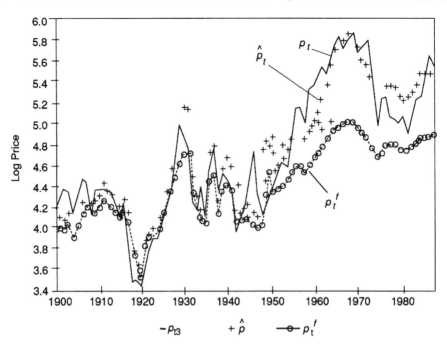

Figure 7.3 Actual and Predicted Stock Prices. *Source*: Froot and Obstfeld (1991). Reproduced by permission of the American Economic Review

simulate values for the fundamentals price $P_t^f = 14.6D_t$, and the price with an intrinsic bubble $\hat{P}_t$ given by (7.23) and compare these two series with the actual price P_t. The path of the intrinsic bubble (Figure 7.3) is much closer to the actual path of stock prices than is P^f. The size of the bubble can also be very large as in the post-Second World War period. Indeed, at the end of the period, the bubble element of the S&P stock price index appears to be large.

Finally, Froot and Obstfeld assess the sensitivity of their results to different dividend models (using Monte Carlo methods) and to the addition of various additional functions of D_t or other deterministic time trends in the regression (7.22). The estimates of the basic intrinsic bubble formulation in (7.23) are quite robust.

Driffill and Sola (1994) repeat the Froot–Obstfeld model assuming dividend growth undergoes regime shifts, in particular that the (conditional) variance of dividend growth varies over the sample. A graph of (real) dividend growth for the US shows relatively low variance between 1900 and 1920, followed by periods of fairly rapid 'switches' in variance over 1920–1950 and then relatively low and constant variance post-1950. Driffill and Sola use the two-state Markov switching model of Hamilton (1989) (see Chapter 6) to model dividend growth and this confirms the results given by 'eyeballing' the graph. They then have two equations of the form (7.23) corresponding to each of the two states, of 'high' and 'low' variance. However, their graph of the price with an intrinsic bubble is very similar to that of Froot and Obstfeld (see $\hat{P}_t$, Figure 7.3) so this particular variant does not appear to make a major difference.

There are a number of statistical assumptions required for valid inference in the approach of Froot and Obstfeld (some of which we have mentioned). For this reason they are content to state that 'the results above merely show that there is a coherent case to be made for bubbles'. They would probably agree that current evidence could also be consistent with other hypotheses, for example a time varying required rate of return or the presence of slowly mean reverting fads.

Econometric Issues

There are severe econometric problems in testing for rational bubbles and the interpretation of the results is also problematic. Econometric problems that arise include the analysis of potentially non-stationary series using finite data sets, the behaviour of test statistics in the presence of explosive regressors as well as the standard problems of obtaining precise estimates of non-linear parameters (as in the case of intrinsic bubbles) and of corrections for heteroscedasticity and moving average errors. Some of these issues are examined further in Chapter 20. Tests for rational bubbles are often contingent on having the correct equilibrium model of expected returns: we are therefore testing a joint hypothesis. Rejection of the no-bubbles hypothesis may simply be a manifestation of an incorrect model based on fundamentals.

Another difficulty in interpreting results from tests of rational bubbles arises from the Peso problem which is really a form of omitted variables problem. Suppose investors in the market had information, within the sample period studied by the researcher, that dividends would increase in the future, but the researcher did not (or could not) include this 'variable' in his model of fundamentals used to forecast dividends. In the sample of data, the stock price would rise but there would be no increase in dividends forecast by the researcher. Stock prices would look as if they have overreacted to (current) dividends and more importantly such a rise in price might be erroneously interpreted as a bubble. This problem of interpretation is probably most acute when there are severe price changes since one cannot rule out that the econometrician has omitted some factor (in say an ARMA model for dividends or discount rates) which might have a large impact on expected dividends (or discount rates) but is expected to occur with a small probability. Turning to the issue of periodically collapsing bubbles, it appears unlikely that standard tests will detect such phenomena.

7.4 SUMMARY

Mathematically, rational bubbles arise because, in the absence of an (arbitrary) transversality condition, the Euler equation yields a solution for stock prices that equals fundamental value plus a 'bubble term', where the latter follows as a martingale process. The key results in this chapter are as follows:

- In the presence of a bubble, stock returns are unpredictable and therefore orthogonality tests cannot be used to detect rational bubbles.
- In the early literature bubbles were exogenous to fundamentals (e.g. dividends). The 'origin' of the bubble cannot be explained and only the time path of the bubble is given by these models.
- Standard unit root and cointegration tests may be able to detect continuously exploding bubbles but are unlikely to detect periodically collapsing bubbles.
- Intrinsic bubbles depend, in a non-linear deterministic way, on economic fundamentals (e.g. dividends) yet still satisfy the Euler equation. The evidence for intrinsic bubbles

is based in part on direct estimation of bubble solutions, where price depends on a specific non-linear parametric function of dividends. Evidence for or against intrinsic bubbles is inconclusive.

In the next chapter we examine a model of contagion which yields a form of intrinsic bubble which is subject to 'eruptions' and subsequent collapse. However, this model involves information being passed between a heterogeneous set of agents with different beliefs, so it does not fit neatly into the type of intrinsic bubble in this chapter which assumed a homogeneous set of rational agents.

ENDNOTES

1. Strictly speaking, for the Hausman test to be valid we do not require dividends (or discount rates) and the bubble to be correlated. This is because bias may arise in the constant term of the regression of P_t on D_t (and lagged values of D) or because the excluded bubble has an exploding variance.

2. This solution arises because $D_{t+1} = D_t \exp(\varepsilon_{t+1})$ and hence $E(D_{t+1}|D_t) = D_t E[\exp(\varepsilon_{t+1})]$. The log-normal distribution has the property that $E[\exp(\varepsilon_{t+1})] = \exp(\mu + \sigma^2/2)$ where ε_{t+1} is distributed as independent normal with mean μ and variance σ^2.

8
Anomalies, Noise Traders and Chaos

8.1 THE EMH AND ANOMALIES

In an 'efficient market' all 'players' have access to the same information, they process the information in the same 'rational way' and all have equal opportunities for borrowing and lending. In the real world these conditions are unlikely to be met. For example, different investors may form different probability assessments about future outcomes or use different economic models in determining expected returns. They may also face differences in transactions costs (e.g. insurance companies versus individuals when purchasing shares), or face different tax rates, and of course they will each devote a different amount of resources (i.e. time and money) in collecting and processing information. Of course, if these heterogeneous elements play a rather minor role then asset prices and rates of return will be determined mainly by economic fundamentals and rational behaviour. But if not, prices may deviate substantially and persistently from their fundamental values. As we see below it is often the assumption of *heterogeneity* in behaviour which allows us to analyse why markets may not be efficient. In this chapter we examine the EMH from a slightly different angle to the technical statistical research outlined in Chapter 6, in particular:

- By observing actual behaviour in the stock market one can seek to isolate profitable trading opportunities which persist for some time. If these 'profitable trades' do not reflect a payment for risk and are persistent, then this refutes the EMH. This evidence is referred to as stock market anomalies.

- Theoretical models are examined in which irrational 'noise traders' in the market interact with rational 'smart money' traders. This helps to explain why stock prices might deviate from fundamental value for substantial periods and why stock prices might be excessively volatile.

- Continuing the above theme of the interaction of noise traders and smart money it is shown how a non-linear *deterministic* system can yield seemly random behaviour in the time domain: this provides an applied example of chaos theory.

8.1.1 Weekend and January Effects

The weekend effect refers to the fact that there appears to be a systematic fall in the daily rate of return on (some) stocks between the Friday closing and Monday opening.

One explanation of the weekend effect is that firms and governments release 'good news' between Monday and Friday but wait until the weekend to release bad news. The bad news is then reflected in 'low' stock prices on Monday. However, in an efficient market some agents should recognise this and should (short) sell on Friday (price is 'high') and buy on Monday (price is 'low') assuming that the expected profit more than covers transactions costs and a payment for risk. This should then lead to a 'removal' of the anomaly since this should result in prices falling on Friday and rising on Monday.

The so-called January effect is a similar phenomenon to the weekend effect. The daily rate of return on common stocks appears to be unusually high during the early days of the month of January. For the USA one explanation is due to year-end selling of stock in order to generate some capital losses which can be set against capital gains in order to reduce tax liability. (This is known as 'bed and breakfasting' in the UK.) In January investors wish to return to their equilibrium portfolios and therefore move into the market to purchase stock. Again if the EMH holds, this predictable pattern of price changes should lead to purchases by non-tax payers (e.g. pension funds) in December when the price is low and selling in January when the price is high, thus eliminating the profitable arbitrage opportunity. The January effect seems to take place in the first five trading days of January (Keane, 1983) and also appears to be concentrated in the stocks of small firms (Reinganum, 1983).

8.1.2 The Small Firm Effect

Between 1960 and the middle of the 1980s all small-capitalized companies earned on average a higher rate of return than the overall stock market index. Of course, according to the CAPM this could be due to the higher risks attached to these small firms which should be reflected in their higher beta values. However, Reinganum (1983) suggests that the rate of return, even after adjustment for risk, is higher on stocks of small-capitalised firms. Hence Reinganum has found that stocks of small firms *do not* lie on the security market line.

8.1.3 Closed End Funds

Closed end funds issue a fixed number of shares at the outset and trading in those shares then takes place between investors. Shares which comprise the 'basket' in the closed end mutual fund are generally also traded openly on the stock market. The value of the fund ought therefore to equal the market value of the individual shares in the fund. But it is often the case that closed end mutual funds trade at a discount on their market value. This violates the EMH, for investors could buy the closed end fund's shares at the discount price and at the same time sell short a portfolio of stocks which are identical to that held by the fund. The investor would thereby ensure he earned a riskless profit equal to the discount. Figure 8.1 shows that the discount on such funds can often be substantial (see Fortune (1991)) and appears to vary inversely with the return on the stock market itself. For example, the bull markets of 1968–1970 and 1982–1986 are associated with declining discount where the bear markets of the 1970s and 1987 are associated with large discounts.

Several reasons have been offered for such closed end fund discounts. First, closed end fund members face a tax liability (in the form of capital gains tax), if the fund should sell securities after they have appreciated. This potential tax liability justifies paying a lower

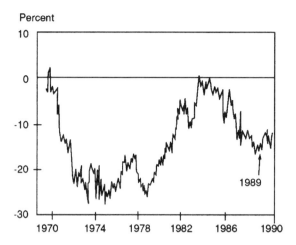

Figure 8.1 Average Premium (+) or Discount (−) on Seven Closed-End Funds. *Source*: Fortune (1991), Fig. 3, p. 23. Reproduced by permission of The Federal Reserve Bank of Boston

price than the market value of the underlying securities. Second, some of the assets in the closed end funds are less marketable (i.e. have 'thin' markets). Third, agency costs in the form of management fees might also explain the discounts. However, Malkiel (1977) found that the discounts were substantially in excess of what could be explained by the above reasons, while Lee et al (1990) find that the discounts on closed end funds are primarily determined by the behaviour of stocks of small firms.

There is a further anomaly. This occurs because at the initial public offering of the closed end fund shares, they incur underwriting costs and the shares in the fund are therefore priced at a premium over their true market value. The value of the closed end fund then generally moves to a discount within six months. The anomaly is, then, why any investors purchase the initial public offering and thereby pay the underwriting costs via the future capital loss. Why don't investors just wait six months before purchasing the mutual fund at the lower price?

8.1.4 The Value Line Enigma

The Value Line Investment Survey (VLIS) produces reports on public traded firms and ranks these stocks in terms of their 'timeliness', by which it means the desirability of purchasing them. In Figure 8.2 is shown the excess return of 'rank 1' stocks over 'rank 3' stocks and of 'rank 5' stocks over 'rank 3' stocks. 'Rank 3' stocks are designated as those that are expected to increase in line with the market, while rank 1 stocks are a 'good buy' and rank 5 stocks a 'bad buy', in terms of their expected future returns. Clearly rank 1 stocks earn a higher return than rank 3 stocks. This could be due to the fact that rank 1 stocks have higher risk (reflected in higher betas) than do rank 3 stocks. Also in order for a trading strategy to be profitable account must be taken of transactions costs. Holloway (1981) found that even after adjustments for risk and transactions costs, a passive strategy of purchasing rank 1 stocks at the beginning of the year and selling them at the end of the year outperformed the passive strategy using rank 3 stocks. The Value Line Ranking System therefore does provide profitable information for a buy and hold strategy and this is inconsistent with the EMH.

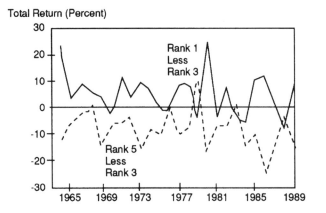

Figure 8.2 Annual Excess Return on Stocks, Classified by Value Link Rank, 1965 to 1989. *Source*: Fortune (1991), Fig. 4, p. 24. Reproduced by permission of The Federal Reserve Bank of Boston

8.1.5 Winner's Curse

There exists a strong negative serial correlation for stock *returns* for those stocks that have experienced extreme price movements (particularly those which experience a price fall *followed by* a price rise). Thus for some stocks (or portfolios of stocks) there is *mean reversion* in stock price behaviour. Put another way there is some predictability in stock returns. The issue for the EMH is then whether such predictability can lead to supernormal profits net of transactions costs and risk.

De Bondt and Thaler (1985) take 35 of the most extreme 'winners' and 35 of the extreme 'losers' over the five years from January 1928 to December 1932 (based on monthly return data from the NYSE) and form two distinct portfolios of these companies' shares. They follow these companies for the next five years (= 'test period'). They repeat the exercise 46 times by advancing the start date by one year each time. Finally, they calculate the average 'test period' performance (in excess of the return on the *whole* NYSE index) giving equal weight (rather than value weights) to each of the 35 companies. They find (Figure 8.3):

(i)   The five-year price reversals for the 'loser portfolio' (at about plus 30 percent) are more pronounced than for the 'winner portfolio' (at minus 10 percent).

(ii) The excess returns on the 'loser portfolio' occur in January (i.e. 'January effect').

(iii) The returns on the portfolios are mean reverting (i.e. a price fall is followed by a price rise and vice versa).

It is worth emphasising that the so-called 'loser portfolio' (i.e. one where prices have fallen dramatically *in the past*) is in fact the one that makes high returns *in the future*: a somewhat paradoxical definition of 'loser'. An arbitrage strategy of selling the 'winner portfolio' short and buying the 'loser portfolio' earns profits at an annual rate of around 5–8 percent (see De Bondt and Thaler (1989)).

Bremer and Sweeney (1988) find that the above results also hold for very short time periods. For example, for a 'loser portfolio' comprising stocks where the *one-day* price fall has been greater than 10 percent, the subsequent returns are 3.95 percent *after five days*. They use stocks of *large firms only*. Therefore they have no problem that the bid–ask

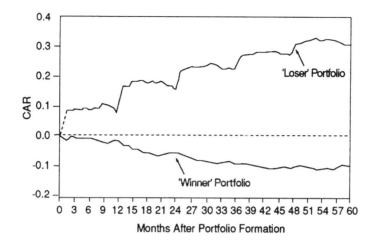

Figure 8.3 Cumulative Excess Returns for 'Winner' and 'Loser' Portfolios. *Source*: De Bondt and Thaler (1989). Reproduced by permission of the American Economic Association

spread is a large percentage of the price (which could distort the results). Also they avoid problems with 'the small firm effect' (i.e. smaller firms are more 'risky' and hence require a greater than average equilibrium excess return). Hence Bremer and Sweeney also seem to find evidence of supernormal profits and a violation of the EMH.

One explanation of the above results is that 'perceived risk' and actual risk may diverge. That is the perceived risk of the 'loser portfolio' is judged to be 'high' hence requiring a high excess return in the future, if one is to hold them. Evidence from psychological studies suggests that misperceptions of risk do occur. For example, people rank the probability of dying from homicide greater than the risk of death from diabetes but probabilistically they are wrong.

The above evidence certainly casts doubt on the EMH in that it may be possible to make supernormal profits because of some predictability in stock prices. However, it must be noted that many of the above anomalies are most prominent among small firms (e.g. January effect and winner's curse of De Bondt and Thaler (1985) and discounts on Closed End Funds (Lee et al, 1990). If the 'big players' (e.g. pension funds) do not trade in small-firm stocks then it is possible that the markets are too thin and information gathering is costly, so the EMH doesn't apply. The EMH may therefore be a better paradigm for the stocks of large firms. These will be actively traded by the 'big players' who can be expected to have the resources to process quickly all relevant information and have access to cash and credit to execute trades so that prices (of such stocks) always equal fundamental value. Of course, without independent confirmation this is mere conjecture.

8.2 NOISE TRADERS

The EMH does not require that *all* participants in the market are 'efficient' and well informed. There can be a set of irrational or 'noise' traders in the market who do not quote prices equal to fundamental value. All the EMH requires is that there is sufficient 'smart money' around who recognise that P_t will eventually equal fundamental value V_t. So, if some irrational traders quote $P_t < V_t$, the smart money will quickly move in and purchase stocks from the irrational traders, thus pushing P_t quickly towards V_t. However, if irrational traders, who are perhaps new to the game, are continually entering the market (e.g. after Big Bang in the UK in 1986) it may be possible for prices at least on occasions to diverge from fundamental value. Also it has recently been shown that irrational investors are able to survive in the market (De Long et al, 1990).

If investors have finite horizons then they will be concerned about the price at some future time N. However, if they base their expectations of the value of $E_t P_{t+N}$ on expected future dividends from $t + N$ onwards, then we are back to the infinite horizon assumption of the rational investor (see Chapter 4). However, if we allow heterogeneous agents in our model then if agents believe the world is not dominated by rational investors, the price at $t + N$ will depend in part on what the rational investor feels the irrational investors view of P_{t+N} will be (i.e. Keynes' beauty contest). This general argument also applies if rational investors know that other rational investors use different models of equilibrium asset returns. Here we are rejecting the EMH assumption that all investors instantaneously know the true model, or equivalently that learning by market participants about the changing structure of the economy (e.g. 'shipbuilding in decline, chemicals to grow') is instantaneous. In these cases, rational investors may take the view that the actual price is a weighted average of the rational valuation (or alternative rational valuations) and effect on price of the irrational traders (e.g. chartists). Hence price does not always equal fundamental value at $t + N$. The rational traders might be prevented by risk factors from buying or selling until the market price equals what perhaps *only they* believe is the fundamental value. Bonus payments to market traders based on profits over a fixed time period (e.g. monthly) might reinforce such behaviour. The challenge is to devise testable models that mimic such noise-trader behaviour.

A great deal of the analysis of financial markets relies on the principle of arbitrage (e.g. see Shleifer and Summers (1990)). *Arbitrageurs* or *smart money* or *rational speculators* continually watch the market and quickly eliminate any divergence between actual price and fundamental value and hence immediately eliminate any profitable opportunities. If a security has a perfect substitute then arbitrage is riskless. For example, a (very simple) mutual fund where one unit of the fund consists of '1 alpha + 2 beta' shares should sell at the same price that one can purchase this bundle of *individual* shares in the open market. If the mutual fund is 'underpriced' then a rational trader should purchase the fund and simultaneously sell (or short sell) the securities which constitute the fund, on the stock market, thus ensuring a riskless profit (i.e. buy 'low', sell 'high'). If the smart money has unlimited funds and recognises and acts on this profit opportunity then this should quickly lead to a rise in price of the mutual fund (as demand increases) and a fall in price of the securities on the stock exchange (due to increased sales). Riskless arbitrage ensures that *relative* prices are equalised. However, if there are no close substitutes and hence if arbitrage is risky then arbitrage may not pin down the *absolute* price levels of stocks (or bonds) as a whole.

The smart money may consider short selling a share that appears to be overpriced relative to fundamentals. They do so in the expectation that they can purchase it later when the actual price falls to the price dictated by fundamentals. If enough of the smart money acts on this premise then their actions will ensure that the price does fall as they all start short selling. The risks faced by the smart money are twofold. First, dividends may turn out to be 'better than expected' and hence the actual price of the share rises even further: this we can call *fundamentals risk*. Second, if arbitrageurs know that there are non-rational traders or *noise traders* in the market, who can, by their collective herding instincts or 'fads', push prices even higher than they are at present, then the arbitrageurs can again lose money: this is *noise-trader risk*.

The risk in taking an arbitrage position only occurs if the smart money has a finite horizon. The smart money may believe that prices will *ultimately* fall to their fundamental value and hence in the long term, profits will be made. However, if arbitrageurs have either to borrow cash or securities (for short sales) to implement their trades and hence pay *per period fees* or report their profit position on their 'book' to their superiors at frequent intervals (e.g. monthly, quarterly) then an infinite horizon certainly cannot apply to all or even most trades undertaken by the smart money.

It may be that there are enough arbitrageurs, with sufficient funds in the aggregate, so that even over a finite horizon, risky profitable opportunities are arbitraged away. The force of the latter argument is weakened, however, if we recognise that any single arbitrageur is unlikely to know either the fundamental value of a security, or to realise when observed price changes are due to deviations from the fundamental price. Arbitrageurs as a group are also likely to disagree among themselves about fundamental value (i.e. they have heterogeneous expectations) hence increasing the general uncertainty they perceive about profitable opportunities, even in the long term. Hence the smart money has difficulty in *identifying* any mispricing in the market and if funds are limited (i.e. a less than perfectly elastic demand for the underpriced securities by arbitrageurs) or horizons are finite, it is possible that profitable *risky* arbitrage opportunities can persist in the market for some time.

If one recognises that 'information costs' (e.g. man-hours, machines, buildings) may be substantial and that marginal costs rise with the breadth and quantity of trading then this also provides some limit on arbitrage activity in some areas of the market. For example, to take an extreme case, if information costs are so high that dealers either concentrate solely on bonds or solely on stocks (i.e. complete market segmentation) then differences in expected returns between bonds and stocks (corrected for risk) will not be arbitraged away.

Noise Traders and Herding

It was explained above why risky arbitrage may be limited and insufficient to keep actual prices of stocks in line with their fundamental value. We can now discuss why a market might contain *a substantial number* of noise traders who follow simple 'rules of thumb' or 'trends' or waves of investor sentiment (herding behaviour) rather than act on the basis of fundamentals. In order that noise traders as a group are capable of influencing market prices their demand shifts must broadly move in unison (i.e. be correlated across noise traders).

General information on these issues can be had from psychological experiments (see Shleifer and Summers (1990) and Shiller (1989) for a summary) which tend to show that *individuals* make systematic (i.e. non-random) mistakes. Subjects are found to over-react to new information (news) and they tend to extrapolate past price trends. They are overconfident, which makes them take on excessive risk.

As the stock market involves groups of traders it is useful to consider some experiments on *group behaviour* (Shiller, 1989). In Sherif's (1937) 'autokinetic experiment' individuals in total darkness were asked to predict the movement of a pencil of light. In the experiment with individuals there was no consensus about the degree of movement (which in fact was zero). When a group of individuals performed the same experiment but this time each individual could hear the views of the others then a consensus emerged (which differed across groups) about the degree of movement. In an experiment by Asch (1952) individuals acting alone compare lengths of line segments. The experiment is then repeated with a group where all other members of the group are primed to give the *same wrong answers*. The individual when alone usually gave correct answers but when faced with group pressure the 'individual' frequently gave wrong answers. After the experiment it was ascertained that the individual usually knew the correct answer but was afraid to contradict the group. If there is no generally accepted view of what is the correct or fundamental price of a given stock then investors may face uncertainty rather than risk. This is likely to make them more susceptible to investor sentiment.

Models of the *diffusion of opinions* are often rather imprecise. There is evidence that ideas can remain dormant for long periods and then be triggered by some seemingly trivial event. The news media obviously play a role here, but research on persuasion often finds that informal face-to-face communication among family, friends and co-workers is of greater importance in the diffusion of views than is the media.

There are mathematical theories of the diffusion of information based on models of epidemics. In such models there are 'carriers' who meet 'susceptibles' and create 'new carriers'. Carriers die off at a 'removal rate'. The epidemic can give rise to a humped shape pattern if the infection 'takes off'. If the infection doesn't take off (i.e. because of either a low infection rate or a low number of susceptibles or a high removal rate) then the number of new carriers declines monotonically. The difficulty in applying such a model to investor sentiment is that one cannot accurately quantify the behavioural determinants of the various variables (e.g. the infection rate) in the model, which are likely to differ from case to case.

Shiller (1989) uses the above ideas to suggest that the bull market of the 1950s and 1960s may have something to do with the speed with which general information about how to invest in stocks and shares (e.g. investment clubs) spreads among individuals. He also notes the growth in institutional demand (e.g. pension funds) for stocks over this period, which could not be offset by individuals selling their own holdings to keep their *total* savings constant. This was because individuals' holdings of stocks were not large or evenly distributed (most being held by wealthy individuals): some people in occupational pension funds simply had no shares to sell.

Herding behaviour or 'following the trend' has frequently been observed in the housing market, in the stock market crash of 1987 (see Shiller (1990)) and in the foreign exchange market (Frankel and Froot, 1986 and Allen and Taylor, 1989b). Summers (1986) (Shleifer and Summers, 1990) also shows that a time series for share prices that is *artificially generated* from a model in which price deviates from fundamentals in a *persistent way*, does produce a time series that mimics actual price behaviour (i.e. close to a random walk) so that some kind of persistent noise-trader behaviour is broadly consistent with the observed data.

Survival of Noise Traders

If we envisage a market in which there are smart speculators who tend to set prices equal to fundamental value and noise traders who operate on rules of thumb, then a question arises as to how the noise traders can survive in this market. If noise traders hold stocks when the price is above the fundamental value, then the smart money should sell these assets to the noise traders thus pushing down the price. As the price falls towards its fundamental value the noise traders lose money and tend towards bankruptcy while the smart money can if they wish buy back the stocks at the lower price. On the other hand, if the noise traders hold assets whose price is below fundamental value, then the smart money should purchase such assets from the noise traders and they will then make a profit as the price rises towards the fundamental value. Hence the net effect is that the noise traders lose money and therefore should disappear from the market leaving only the smart money. When this happens prices should then reflect fundamentals.

Of course, if there were an army of noise traders who *continually entered* the market (and continually went bankrupt) it would be possible for prices to diverge from fundamental value for some significant time. One might argue that it is hardly likely that noise traders would enter a market where previous noise traders have gone bankrupt in large numbers. However, entrepreneurs often believe they can succeed where others have failed. To put the reverse argument, some noise traders will be successful over a finite horizon and this may encourage others to attempt to imitate them and enter the market, ignoring the fact that the successful noise traders had in fact taken on more risk and just happened to get lucky.

Can it be explained why an *existing cohort* of noise traders can still make profits in a market which contains smart money? The answer really has to do with the potential for herding behaviour. No individual smart money trader can know that all other smart money traders will force the market price towards its fundamental value in the period of time for which he is contemplating holding the stock. Thus any strategy that the sophisticated traders adopt given the presence of noise traders in the market is certainly not riskless. There is always the possibility that the noise traders will push the price even further away from fundamental value and this may result in a loss for the smart money. Thus risk averse smart money may not fully arbitrage away the influence of the noise traders. If there are enough noise traders who follow *common* fads then noise-trader risk will be pervasive (systematic). It cannot be diversified away and must therefore earn a reward or risk premium, in equilibrium. Noise trading is therefore consistent with an average return which is greater than that given by the pure CAPM. If noise traders hold a large share of assets subject to noise-trader risk they *may* earn above average returns and survive in the market. If there are some variables at time t which influence the 'mechanical' behaviour of noise traders and noise-trader behaviour is persistent then such variables may influence expected returns in the market. This may explain why additional variables, when added to the CAPM, prove to be statistically significant.

Shiller (1989) presents a simple yet compelling argument to suggest that as far as *non-institutional* investors are concerned, the smart money may not dominate the market. He notes that if the smart money investor accumulates wealth at a rate 'n' (percent per annum) greater than the ordinary individual investor (e.g. noise trader) then given a bequest at age 50, he can expect to accumulate *additional* terminal wealth of $(1 + n)^{15}$. If $n = 5$ percent then the smart investor ends up with 2.1 times as much wealth as the ordinary (noise-trader) investor. Thus if the percentage of smart investors in the market is 'moderate' then they are unlikely to take over the market completely. Also if the smart money investor wishes only to preserve the real value of the 'family wealth', then he will not accumulate *any* additional wealth, he will spend it. However, given that institutional investors play an important role in the market it must be explained why noise traders influence institutional decisions on portfolio allocation.

Volatility and Anomalies

It should be fairly obvious that the existence of noise traders can explain some of the anomalies and empirical results cited above. For example, if stock prices are not determined purely by fundamental value then it is possible that stock prices will be more volatile than indicated by the volatility in future dividends and discount rates. Hence Shiller's variance bounds inequalities might not hold in a world which includes noise traders. To see this, note that the stock price is now determined by its fundamental value $V_t = E_t(\Sigma \delta^i D_{t+i})$ (i.e. the DPV of future dividends) formed by rational traders and the influence of the noise traders denoted N_t:

$$P_t = V_t + N_t \tag{8.1}$$

For simplicity assume $\text{cov}(V_t, N_t) = 0$ and hence from (8.1) $\text{cov}(P_t, N_t) = \text{var}(N_t)$. As before the perfect foresight price P_t^* differs from the fundamental value by a random forecast error (due entirely to rational traders):

$$P_t^* = V_t + \eta_t \tag{8.2}$$

From (8.1) and (8.2)

$$P_t^* = P_t + \eta_t - N_t$$

$$\text{var}(P_t^*) = \text{var}(P_t) + \text{var}(\eta_t) + \text{var}(N_t) - 2\,\text{cov}(P_t, N_t)$$

$$= \text{var}(P_t) + \text{var}(\eta_t) - \text{var}(N_t) \tag{8.3}$$

where it has been assumed $\text{cov}(P_t, \eta_t) = 0$ by RE and for simplicity we set $\text{cov}(N_t, \eta_t) = 0$. From (8.3) we see that if $\text{var}(N_t)$ is large enough then we expect the variance of P_t^* to be less than the variance of P_t. Hence, the variance bound, $\text{var}(P_t^*) - \text{var}(P_t) > 0$ may not hold in the presence of noise traders. The intuition behind this result is simple. Noise traders directly influence the variance of actual prices (via (8.1)) but do not influence the variance of future dividends and hence the perfect foresight price. Also note that if noise trader behaviour N_t is mean reverting at long horizons then price changes will also be mean reverting and this is consistent with the empirical evidence on mean reversion in stock *returns*.

If noise traders are more active in dealing in shares of small firms than for large firms this may explain why small firms earn an above average return corrected for the normal CAPM risk. Again, this is because the noise-trader risk is greater for small-firm stocks than for large-firm stocks, and as this risk is systematic it is reflected in the higher return on small-firm stocks.

The impact of noise traders on prices may well be greater when most investors follow the advice given in finance text books and *passively* hold the market portfolio. If noise traders move into a particular group of shares based on 'hunch', the holders of the market portfolio will do nothing (unless the movement is so great as to require a change in the 'market value' proportions held in each asset). The actions of the noise traders need to be countered by a set of genuine arbitrageurs who are active in the market. In the extreme, if *all* investors hold the market portfolio but *one* noise trader enters the market wishing to purchase shares of a particular firm then its price will be driven to infinity.

Arbitrageurs may not only predict fundamentals but may also divert their energies to anticipating changes in demand by the noise traders. If noise traders are optimistic about particular securities it will pay arbitrageurs to create more of them (e.g. junk bonds,

Japanese mutual funds, oil stocks) via, for example, the expansion of the activities of the securities business of investment banks. Suppose a conglomerate has interests in the oil market and noise traders are temporally attracted by 'oil', then it may pay 'asset strippers' to take over the conglomerate, split off the oil division and sell off the separate parts of the business. The arbitrageurs (e.g. an investment bank) can then earn a share of profits from the 'abnormally high priced' issues of new oil shares which are currently in vogue with noise traders.

Arbitrageurs will also behave like noise traders in that they attempt to *pick stocks* that noise-trader sentiment is likely to favour: the arbitrageurs do not necessarily counter shifts in demand by noise traders. Just as entrepreneurs invest in casinos to exploit gamblers, it pays the smart money to spend considerable resources in gathering information on possible future noise-trader demand shifts (e.g. by studying chartists' forecasts). Hence arbitrageurs have an incentive to behave like noise traders. For example, if noise traders are perceived by arbitrageurs to be positive feedback traders then as prices are pushed above fundamental value, arbitrageurs get in on the bandwagon themselves in the hope that they can sell out 'near the top'. They therefore 'amplify the fad'. Arbitrageurs may expect prices in the longer term to return to fundamentals (perhaps aided by arbitrage sales), but in the short term, arbitrageurs will 'follow the trend'. This evidence is consistent with findings of positive autocorrelation in returns at short horizons (e.g. weeks or months) as arbitrageurs follow the short-term trend, and negative correlation at longer horizons (e.g. over two or more years) as some arbitrageurs take a long horizon view and sell overpriced shares. Also if 'news' triggers off noise-trader demand, then this is consistent with prices overreacting to 'news'.

So far we have been discussing the implications of the presence of noise traders in fairly general terms. It is now time to examine more formal models of noise-trader behaviour. As one might imagine it is by no means easy to introduce noise-trader behaviour in any fully optimising framework since almost by definition noise traders are irrational — they misperceive the true state of the world. Noise-trader models therefore contain somewhat arbitrary (non-maximising) assumptions about behaviour. Nevertheless, the outcome of the *interaction* between smart money traders (who do maximise a well-defined objective function) and the (ad-hoc) noise traders is of interest since we can then ascertain whether such models confirm the general conjectures made above. Generally speaking, as we shall see, these more formal models do not contradict our 'armchair speculations' as outlined above.

8.2.1 Noise Traders and the Rational Valuation Formula

Shiller (1989) provides a simple piece of analysis in which noise-trader demand as well as smart money influence the price of stocks. It follows that the smart money then has to predict the noise-trader demand for stocks, if it is to predict price correctly and hence attempt to eliminate profitable opportunities. The proportionate demand for shares by the smart money is Q_t. The demand function for the smart money is based (loosely) on the mean-variance model and is given by:

$$Q_t = (E_t R_{t+1} - \rho)/\theta \tag{8.4}$$

If $E_t R_{t+1} = \rho$ then demand by the smart money equals zero. If $Q_t = 1$ then the smart money holds all the outstanding stock and this requires an expected return $E_t R_{t+1} = \rho + \theta$. Hence θ is a kind of risk premium payment to induce the smart money to hold all the stock.

Now let (Y_t/P_t) equal the *proportion of* stock held by noise traders. For equilibrium, the proportions held by the smart money and the noise traders must sum to unity:

$$Q_t + (Y_t/P_t) = 1 \tag{8.5}$$

substituting (8.4) in (8.5):

$$E_t R_{t+1} = \theta[1 - (Y/P)_t] + \rho \tag{8.6}$$

Hence the expected return as perceived by the smart money depends on how they perceive current and future demand by noise traders: the higher is noise-trader demand, the higher are current prices and the lower is the expected return perceived by the smart money. Using (8.6) and the definition

$$E_t R_{t+1} = E_t[(P_{t+1} + D_{t+1})/P_t - 1]$$

we obtain

$$P_t = \delta E_t(P_{t+1} + D_{t+1} + \theta Y_t) \tag{8.7}$$

where $\delta = 1/(1 + \rho + \theta)$. Hence by repeated forward substitution:

$$P_t = \sum_{1}^{\infty} \delta^i (E_t D_{t+i} + \theta E_t Y_{t+i-1}) \tag{8.8}$$

Thus if the smart money is *rational* and recognises the existence of a demand by noise traders then the smart money will calculate that the market clearing price is a weighted average of fundamentals (i.e. $E_t D_{t+i}$) and of future noise-trader demand, $E_t Y_{t+i}$. The weakness of this 'illustrative model' is that noise-trader demand is completely exogenous. However, as we see below, we can still draw some useful insights.

If $E_t Y_{t+i}$ and hence aggregate noise-trader demand is random around zero, then the moving average of $E_t Y_{t+i}$ (for all future i) in (8.8) will have little influence on P_t, which will be governed primarily by fundamentals. Price will deviate from fundamentals but only randomly. On the other hand, if demand by noise traders is expected to be persistent (i.e. 'large' values of Y_t are expected to be followed by further large values) then small changes in current noise-trader demand can have a powerful effect on current price and price can deviate substantially from fundamentals over a considerable period of time.

Shiller (1989) uses the above model to illustrate how tests of market efficiency based on regressions of *returns* on information variables known at time t (Ω_t), have low power to reject the EMH when it is false. Suppose dividends (and the discount rate) are constant for all time periods and hence the EMH (without noise traders) predicts that the stock price is constant. Now suppose that the market is actually driven *entirely* by noise traders and fads. Let noise trader demand be characterised by

$$Y_t = u_{t-1} + u_{t-2} + u_{t-3} + \cdots + u_{t-n} \tag{8.9}$$

and hence:

$$Y_{t+1} = u_t + u_{t-1} + u_{t-2} + \cdots + u_{t-n-1}$$

$$Y_{t+2} = u_{t+1} + u_t + u_{t-1} + \cdots + u_{t-n-2}$$

$$Y_{t+3} = u_{t+2} + u_{t+1} + u_t + \cdots + u_{t-n-3} \tag{8.10}$$

where u_t is white noise. Equation (8.9) has the property that a unit increases in u_t at time t and generates changes in Y in future periods that follow a 'square hump' which dies away after n periods[1]. Using (8.8) price *changes* $(P_{t+1} - P_t)$ only arise because of *revisions* to expectations about future noise-trader demand which are weighted by δ, δ^2, δ^3, etc. Because $0 < \delta < 1$, price changes are heavily dominated by u_t (rather than by past u_{t-j}). However as u_t is random, price changes in this model, which by construction are dominated by noise traders, are nevertheless largely unforecastable.

Shiller *generates* a ΔP_{t+1} series using (8.8) for various values of the persistence in Y_t (given by the lag length n) and for alternative values of ρ and θ. He then regresses the generated data for ΔP_{t+1} on the information set consisting only of P_t. Under the EMH we expect the R-squared of this regression to be zero. For $\rho = 0$, $\theta = 0.2$ and $n = 20$ he finds $R^2 = 0.015$. The low R-squared supports the EMH, but it results from a model where price changes are *wholly determined* by noise traders. In addition, the price *level* can deviate substantially from fundamentals even though price *changes* are hardly forecastable. He also calculates that if the generated data includes a constant dividend price ratio of 4 percent then the 'theoretical R-squared' of a regression of the return R_{t+1} on the dividend price ratio (D_t/P_t) is only 0.079 even though the noise-trader model is the 'true model'. Hence empirical evidence that returns are only very weakly related to information at time t (e.g. D_t/P_t) are not necessarily inconsistent with prices being determined by noise traders and not by fundamentals.

Overall, Shiller makes an important point about empirical evidence. The evidence using real world data is not that stock returns are unpredictable (as suggested by the EMH) but that stock returns are not *very* predictable. However, the latter evidence is also not inconsistent with possible models in which noise traders play a part.

If the behaviour of Y_t is exogenous (i.e. independent of dividends) but is stationary and mean reverting then we might expect *returns* to be predictable. An above average level of Y will eventually be followed by a fall in Y (to its mean long-run level). Hence prices are mean reverting and current returns are predictable from previous periods' returns.

In addition our noise-trader model can explain the positive association between the dividend price ratio and next periods' return on stocks. If dividends vary very little over time, a price rise caused by an increase in EY_{t+j} will produce a fall in the dividend price ratio. If Y_t is mean reverting then prices will fall *in the future*, so returns R_{t+1} also fall. Hence one might expect a fall in the dividend price ratio at time t to be followed by a fall in returns. Hence $(D/P)_t$ is *positively* related to returns R_{t+1}, as found in empirical studies.

Shiller also notes that if noise trader demand Y_{t+j} is influenced either by past returns (i.e. bandwagon effect) or past dividends then the share price might overreact to current dividends compared to that given by the first term in (8.8), that is the fundamentals part of the price response.

8.2.2 An Optimising Model of Noise-Trader Behaviour

In the model of De Long et al (1990), both smart money and noise traders maximise expected lifetime utility. Both noise traders and smart money are risk averse. There is a finite horizon in the model so that arbitrage is risky. The (basic) model is constructed so that there is no fundamental risk (i.e. dividends are known with certainty) but only noise-trader risk. The noise traders create risk for themselves and the smart money by generating fads in demand for the risky asset. The smart money forms optimal forecasts of the future price based on the correct distribution of price changes but noise traders develop biased forecasts. The degree of *price misperception* of noise traders ρ_t represents the *difference* between the noise-trader forecasts and optimal forecasts. In the DeLong et al model ρ_t is a random variable, normally distributed with mean ρ^* and variance σ^2.

$$\rho_t \sim N(\rho^*, \sigma^2) \tag{8.11}$$

If $\rho^* = 0$, noise traders agree on their forecasts with the smart money (on average). If noise traders are on average pessimistic (e.g. in a bear market) then $\rho^* < 0$, and the stock price will be below fundamental value. If noise traders are optimistic $\rho^* > 0$, the converse applies. As well as having this long-run view $(= \rho^*)$ of the divergence of their forecasts from the optimal forecasts, 'news' also arises so there can be *abnormal but temporary* variations in optimism and pessimism (given by a term, $\rho - \rho^*$). The specification of ρ_t is ad hoc but does have an intuitive appeal based on introspection and evidence from behavioural/group experiments.

In the DeLong et al model the *fundamental value* of the stock is a constant and is arbitrarily set at unity. The market consists of two types of asset: a risky asset and a safe asset. Both noise traders and smart money are risk averse so their demand for the risky asset depends positively on expected return and inversely on the noise-trader risk. The noise trader demand also depends on an additional element of return depending on whether they feel bullish or bearish about stock prices (i.e. the variable ρ_t). The risky asset is in fixed supply (set equal to unity) and the market clears to give an equilibrium price P_t. The equation which determines P_t looks rather complicated but we can break it down into its component parts and give some intuitive feel for what is going on. The DeLong et al equation for P_t is given by

$$P_t = 1 + \left[\frac{\mu}{r}\right]\rho^* + \frac{\mu}{(1+r)}[\rho_t - \rho^*] - \frac{2\gamma\mu^2\sigma^2}{r(1+r)^2} \tag{8.12}$$

where μ = the proportion of investors who are noise traders, r = the riskless real rate of interest, γ = the degree of (absolute) risk aversion and σ^2 = variance of noise-trader misperceptions.

If there are no noise traders $\mu = 0$ and (8.12) predicts that the market price equals its fundamental value (of unity) as set by the smart money. Now let us suppose that at a particular point in time, noise traders have the same long-run view of the stock price as does the smart money (i.e. $\rho^* = 0$) and that there are no 'surprises' (i.e. no abnormal bullishness or bearishness), so that $(\rho_t - \rho^*) = 0$. We now have a position where the noise traders have the same view about future prices as do the smart money. However, the equilibrium market price still *does not solely reflect fundamentals* and in fact the market price will be less than the fundamental price by the amount given by the last term on the RHS of equation (8.12). This is because the mere presence of noise traders introduces an additional element of uncertainty since their potential actions may influence future prices. The price is below fundamental value so that the smart money (and noise traders) may obtain a positive expected return (i.e. capital gain) because of this additional noise-trader risk. Both types of investor therefore obtain a reward for risk and risk is generated entirely by fads and not by uncertainty about fundamentals. This mispricing is probably the key result of the model and involves a *permanent* deviation of price from fundamentals. The effect of the third term is referred to in (8.12) as the amount of 'basic mispricing'.

Turning now to the second term in equation (8.12) we see, for example, that the noise traders will push the price above fundamental value if they take a *long-term view* that the market is bullish ($\rho^* > 0$). The third term reflects abnormal short-term bullishness or bearishness, that is at any point in time, noise traders might feel that the stock market will perform even better than average. These terms imply that at particular time periods price may be above or below fundamentals.

The *duration* of the deviation of the actual stock price from its fundamental value ($= 1$) depends upon how *persistent* the effects on the RHS of equation (8.12) are. If only ρ_t varies so that $\rho_t - \rho^*$ is random around zero then the actual price would deviate randomly around its 'basic mispricing' level. In this case the model would give a movement of stock prices which was 'excessively volatile' (relative to fundamentals). From (8.12) we see that the variance of prices is:

$$E_t(P_t - E_t P_t)^2 = \frac{\mu^2 \cdot \text{var}(\rho_t - \rho^*)}{(1 + r)^2} = \frac{\mu^2 \sigma^2}{(1 + r)^2} \tag{8.13}$$

Hence excess volatility is more severe, the greater is the variability in the misperceptions of noise traders σ^2, the more noise traders there are in the market μ and the lower is the cost of borrowing funds r.

The above mechanism does not cause stock prices to move away from its basic mispricing level *for long periods of time* and to exhibit volatility which is persistent over time (i.e. periods of tranquillity and turbulence). To enable the model to reproduce *persistence* in price movements and hence the broad bull and bear movements in stock prices, we need to introduce 'fads' and 'fashions'. Broadly speaking this implies, for example, that periods of bullishness are followed by further periods of bullishness. Statistically this can be represented by a random walk in ρ_t^*:

$$\rho_t^* = \rho_{t-1}^* + \omega_t \tag{8.14}$$

where $\omega_t \sim N(0, \sigma_\omega^2)$. (Note that σ_ω^2 is different from σ^2, above.)

At any point in time the investors' best guess (optimal forecast) of ρ^* is its current value. However, as 'news' (ω_t) arrives noise traders alter their views about ρ_t^* and this 'change in perceptions' persists over future periods. It should be clear from the second term in (8.12) that a random walk in ρ^* can generate a sequence of values for P_t that also follow a random walk and therefore mimic a stochastic cyclical path (i.e. movements over time which are *not* smooth and not of equal amplitude and wavelength). This results in 'bull and bear' patterns in P_t.

Fortune (1991) assumes for illustrative purposes independent normal distributions for ω_t and $(\rho_t - \rho_t^*)$ and uses representative values for r, μ, γ in (8.12). He then generates values for ω_t and $(\rho - \rho_t^*)$ using a random number generator and obtains a time series for P_t shown in Figure 8.4. The graph indicates that on this *one* simulation, price falls to 85 percent of fundamental value (which itself may be rising) with some dramatic rises and falls in the short run.

An additional source of *persistence* in prices could be introduced into the model by assuming that σ^2 is also autoregressive. The latter, of course, embodies the hypothesis that variances can be time varying and this may, for example, be modelled using ARCH and GARCH models (see Part 7). It is also not unreasonable to assume that the 'conversion rate' from being a smart money trader to being a noise trader may well take time and

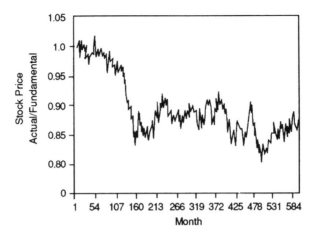

Figure 8.4 Simulated 50-Year Stock Price History. *Source*: Fortune (1991), Fig. 6, p. 34. Reproduced by permission of The Federal Reserve Bank of Boston

move in cycles. This will make μ (i.e. the proportion of noise traders) exhibit persistence and hence so might P_t. It follows that price may differ from fundamentals for substantial periods of time in this type of model. Mispricing can therefore be severe and prolonged because arbitrage is incomplete.

Mean Reversion and Predictability of Returns

Waves of optimism and pessimism in noise-trader behaviour could also imply some persistence in $\rho_t - \rho^*$. The behaviour of $(\rho_t - \rho^*)$ could be mean reverting so that when $(\rho_t - \rho^*)$ is positive it will fall back towards its mean, some time in the future. This would imply that prices are mean reverting and that *returns* on the stock market are partly predictable from past returns or from variables such as the dividend price ratio. Note that to introduce mean reversion in prices an ad-hoc assumption has been made that fads are mean reverting: this latter assumption has not been derived from within the formal optimising model.

Can Noise Traders Survive?

DeLong et al show that where the proportion of noise traders is fixed in each period (i.e. μ is constant) it is possible (although not guaranteed) that noise traders do survive even though they tend to buy high and sell low (and vice versa). This is because they are over-optimistic and underestimate the true riskiness of their portfolio. As a consequence they tend to 'hold more' of the assets subject to bullish sentiment. In addition, if noise-trader risk σ^2 is large, the smart money will not step in with great vigour, to buy underpriced assets because of the risk involved.

The idea of imitation can be included in the model by assuming that the conversion rate from smart money to noise trader depends on the excess returns earned by noise traders over the smart money $(R^n - R^s)$ in the previous period:

$$\mu_{t+1} = \mu_t + \Psi(R^n - R^s)_t \tag{8.15}$$

where μ is bounded between 0 and 1. De Long et al also introduce fundamental risk into the model. The per period return on risky assets becomes a random variable $r + \varepsilon_t$

where $\varepsilon_t \sim N(0, \sigma_\varepsilon^2)$. In this version of the model the probability of noise-trader survival is always greater than zero. This is because of what they call the 'create space' effect, whereby risk is increased to such an extent that it further inhibits risk averse smart money from arbitraging any potential gains. (The latter result requires that Ψ is 'small' since otherwise the newly converted noise traders may influence price and this has to be forecast by the 'old' noise traders who retire.)

Closed End Fund Anomalies

We have noted that closed end funds often tend to sell at a discount and this discount varies over time, usually across *all* funds. Sometimes such funds sell at a premium. Using our noise-trader model we can get a handle on reasons for these empirical anomalies. Let the risky asset be the closed end fund itself and the safe asset the actual underlying stocks. The smart money will try and arbitrage between the fund and the underlying stocks (e.g. buy the fund and sell the stocks short, if the fund is at a discount). However, even if $\rho_t = \rho^* = 0$, the fund (risky asset) will sell at a discount (see equation (8.12)) because of inherent noise-trader risk. Changes in noise-trader sentiment (i.e. in ρ^* and $\rho_t - \rho^*$) will cause the discounts to vary over time and as noise-trader risk is systematic, discounts on most funds are expected to move together.

In the noise-trader model a number of closed end funds should also tend to be started at the same time, namely when noise-trader sentiment for closed end funds is high (i.e. $\rho^* > 0$, $\rho_t - \rho^* > 0$). When existing closed end funds are at a premium it pays the smart money to purchase shares (at a relatively low price), bundle them together into a closed end fund and sell them at a premium to optimistic noise traders.

Again the key feature of the De Long et al model is to demonstrate the possibility of underpricing in *equilibrium*. The other effects mentioned above depend on one's adherence to the possibility of *changes* in noise-trader sentiment, which are persistent. However, 'persistence' is not the outcome of an optimising process in the model although it is an intuitively appealing one.

Changes in Bond Prices

In empirical work on bonds we shall see (Chapter 14) that when the long–short spread $(R-r)$ on bonds is positive, then long rates tend to fall, and hence the *prices* of long bonds tend to rise. This is the opposite to what one would expect from the pure expectations hypothesis of the term structure, which incorporates the behaviour of rational risk neutral agents only. The stylised facts of this anomaly are consistent with our noise-trader model with the long bond being the risky asset (and the short bond the safe asset). When $R_t > r_t$ then the price of long bonds as viewed by noise traders could be said to be abnormally low. If noise-trader fads are mean reverting they will expect bond prices to rise in the future and hence long rates R to fall. This is observed in the empirical work on the term structure. Of course, even though the noise-trader model explains the stylised facts this still leaves us a long way from a formal test of the noise-trader model in the bond market.

Short-Termism

In a world of only smart money, the fact that some of these investors take a 'short-term' view of returns should not lead to a deviation of price from fundamentals. The argument is based on the implicit forward recursion of the rational valuation formula. If you buy today at time t, in order to sell tomorrow, your return depends (in part) on the expected capital gain and hence on the price you can get tomorrow. But the latter depends on what the person you sell to at $t + 1$ thinks the price will be at $t + 2$, etc. Hence a linked chain of short-term 'rational fundamental' investors performs the same calculation as an investor with an infinite horizon.

With a finite investment horizon and the presence of noise traders the above argument doesn't hold. True, the longer the horizon of the smart money the more willing he may be to undertake risky arbitrage based on divergences between price and fundamental value. The reason being that in the meantime he receives the insurance of dividend payments each period and he has a number of periods over which he can wait for the price to rise to fundamental value. However, even with a 'long' but finite horizon there is some price resale risk. The share in the total return from dividend payments over a 'long' holding period is large but there is still some risk present from uncertainty about price in the 'final period'.

We note from the noise-trader model that if a firm can make its equity appear less subject to noise-trader sentiment (i.e. to reduce σ^2) then its underpricing will be less severe and its price will rise. This reduction in uncertainty might be accomplished by

(i)   raising current dividends (rather than investing profits in an uncertain long-term investment project, for example R&D expenditures)

(ii) substitutes debt for equity,

(iii) share buybacks.

Empirical work by Jensen (1986) has shown that items (i)–(iii) do tend to lead to an increase in the firm's share price and this is consistent with our interpretation of the influence of noise traders described above. It follows that in the presence of noise traders one might expect changes in capital structure to affect the value of the firm (contrary to the Modigliani–Miller hypothesis).

Mispricing and Short-Termism: Shleifer–Vishny Model

The underpricing of an *individual* firm's stock is not a direct result of the formal noise-trader model of De Long et al since the formal model requires noise-trader behaviour to be systematic across all stocks. However, the impact of high borrowing costs on the *degree* of mispricing in individual shares has been examined in a formal model by Shleifer and Vishny (1990). They find that current mispricing is most severe for those stocks where mispricing is *revealed* at a date in the distant future (rather than next period, say). Suppose physical investment projects with uncertain long horizon payoffs are financed with shares whose true value is only revealed to the market at long horizons. In the Shleifer–Vishny model these shares will be severely underpriced. It follows that the firm might be less willing to undertake such long horizon yet profitable projects. Short-termism on the part of the firm's managers might ensue, that is they choose less profitable short-term physical investment projects rather than long-term projects since this involves less current undervaluation of the share price and less risk of them losing their jobs from a hostile takeover or management reorganisation by the board of directors. This is a misallocation of real resources. We begin our description of this model considering the infinite horizon case where the smart money is indifferent as to when the actual price moves to its fundamental value.

Timing of Arbitrage Profits in a Perfect Capital Market

If the smart money (arbitrageur) has access to a perfect capital market where he can borrow and lend unlimited amounts then he does not care how long it takes a mispriced security to move to fundamental value. Table 8.1 considers a simple case of underpricing where the cost of borrowing r, and the fundamentals return on the security (i.e. dividend return q), are identical at 10 percent. If the mispriced security moves from $5 to its fundamental value of $6 after only one period, the price including the dividend payout is $6 $(1 + q) = \$6.6$ in period 1. At the end of period 1 the arbitrageur has to pay back the loan plus interest, that is $5(1 + r) = \$5.5$. If the price only achieves its fundamental value in period 2 the arbitrageur receives $6(1 + q)^2 = \$7.26$ at $t + 2$ but has to pay out additional interest charges between $t + 1$ and $t + 2$. However, in *present value terms* the arbitrageur has an equal gain of $1 regardless of when the mispricing is irradicated. Also, with a perfect capital market he can take advantage of any further arbitrage possibilities that arise since he can always borrow more money at any time.

Finite Horizon

In the case of a finite horizon, fundamentals and noise-trader risk can lead to losses from arbitrage. If suppliers of funds (e.g. banks) find it difficult to assess the ability of arbitrageurs to pick genuinely underpriced stocks, they may limit the amount of funds to the arbitrageur. Also, they may charge a higher interest rate to the arbitrageur because they have less information on his true performance than he himself has (i.e. the interest charge under asymmetric information is higher than that which would occur under symmetric information).

If $r = 12$ percent in the above example, while the fundamentals return on the stock remains at 10 percent then the arbitrageur gains more if the mispricing is eliminated *sooner* rather than *later*. If a strict credit limit is imposed then there is an additional cost to the arbitrageur, namely that if his money is tied up in a long-horizon arbitrage position then he cannot take advantage of other potentially profitable arbitrage opportunities.

An arbitrageur earns more potential $ profits the more he borrows and takes a position in undervalued stocks. He is therefore likely to try and convince (signal to) the suppliers of

Table 8.1 Arbitrage Returns: Perfect Capital Market

Assumptions:

Fundamental Value	= $6
Current Price	= $5
Interest Rate, r	= 10% per period
Return on Risky Asset, q	= 10% per period (on fundamental value)

Smart Money Borrows $5 at 10% and Purchases Stock at $t = 0$.

	Selling Price (including dividends)	Repayment of Loan	Net Gain	DPV of Gain (at $r = 10\%$)
Period 1	$6(1 + q) = \$6.60$	$5(1 + r) = \$5.5$	$1.10	$1
Period 2	$6(1 + q)^2 = \$7.26$	$5(1 + r)^2 = \$6.05$	$1.21	$1

funds that he really is 'smart', by engaging in repeated short-term arbitrage opportunities since long-horizon positions are expensive and risky. Hence smart money may have an incentive to invest with a short horizon rather than eliminating long-horizon arbitrage possibilities.

The formal model of Shleifer and Vishny (1990) has both noise traders and smart money (see Appendix 8.2). Both the short and long assets have a payout at the *same time* in the future but the *true value* of the short asset is *revealed* earlier than that for the 'long' asset. They show that in equilibrium, arbitrageurs' rational behaviour results in greater *current* mispricing of 'long assets' when the mispricing is revealed at long horizons. The terms 'long' and 'short' therefore refer to the date at which the mispricing is revealed (and not to the actual cash payout of the two assets). Both types of asset are mispriced but the long-term asset suffers from *greater mispricing* than the short asset.

In essence the model relies on the cost of funds to the arbitrageur being greater than the fundamentals return on the mispriced securities. Hence the longer the arbitrageur has to *wait* before he can liquidate his position (i.e. sell the underpriced security) the more it costs him. The sooner he can realise his capital gain and pay off his 'expensive' debts the better. Hence it is the 'carrying cost' or per period costs of borrowed funds that is important in the model. The demand for the long-term mispriced asset is lower than that for the short-term mispriced asset and hence the current price of the long-term mispriced asset is lower than that for the short-term asset.

To the extent that investment *projects* by a firm have uncertain payoffs (profits) which accrue in the distant future then such projects may be funded with assets whose true fundamental value will not be revealed until the distant future (e.g. the Channel Tunnel between England and France, where passenger revenues begin to accrue many years after the finance for the project has been raised). In this model these assets will be (relatively) strongly undervalued.

The second element of the Shleifer and Vishny (1990) argument which yields adverse outcomes from short-termism concerns the behaviour of the managers of the firm. They conjecture that managers of a firm have an asymmetric weighting of mispricing. *Underpricing* is perceived as being relatively worse than an equal amount of overpricing. This is because underpricing either encourages the board of directors to change its managers or that managers could be removed after a hostile takeover based on the underpricing. *Overpricing* on the other hand gives little benefit to managers who usually don't hold large amounts of stock or whose earnings are not strongly linked to the stock price. Hence incumbent managers might underinvest in long-term physical investment projects.

A hostile acquirer can abandon the long-term investment project and hence improve short-term cash flow and current dividends, all of which reduce uncertainty and the likely duration of mispricing. He can then sell the acquired firm at a higher price, since the degree of underpricing is reduced because in essence the acquirer reduces the duration of the firm's assets. The above scenario implies that some profitable (in DPV terms) long-term investment projects are sacrificed because of (the rational) short-termism of arbitrageurs who face 'high' borrowing costs or outright borrowing constraints. This is contrary to the view that hostile takeovers involve the replacement of inefficient (i.e. non-value maximising) managers by more efficient acquirers. Thus, if smart money cannot wait for long-term arbitrage possibilities to unfold they will support hostile takeovers which reduce the mispricing and allow them to close out their arbitrage position more quickly.

Short-Termism: Some Empirics

The variance bounds tests of Chapter 6 tell us little about short-termism, that is the persistent *undervaluation* of *individual* shares relative to fundamentals. This is because volatility tests are concerned with testing positive and negative departures from fundamental value and they use aggregative stock price indices. Following Miles (1993) we can examine an explicit model of short-termism by considering variants on the RVF. Using a five-year horizon the RVF for the price of equity of the jth company at time t is:

$$P_{jt} = \sum_{i=1}^{5} d_{jt+i} E_t D_{jt+i} + d_{jt+5} E_t P_{t+5} \tag{8.16}$$

where $d_{jt+i} = 1/(1 + r_{t,t+i} + rp_j)^i$ and $r_{t,t+i}$ is the risk-free rate at horizon t+i and rp_j is the risk premium for company j which is assumed to be constant for each horizon. Short-termism could involve a discount factor that is 'too high' or cash flows that are too low (relative to a rational forecast). Hence we would have either:

$$d_{jt+i} = 1/(1 + r_{t,t+i} + rp_j)^{bi} \quad \text{with } b > 1 \tag{8.17}$$

or $x^i E_t D_{t+i}$ replacing $E_t D_{t+i}$ in (8.16). In the above examples, 'short-termism' applies in each time period $t + i$. Another form of short-termism is when the correct (rational) DPV calculation is undertaken for periods $t + 1$ to $t + 5$, but either all future cash flows or all discount factors for $t + 6$, $t + 7$, etc. are not weighted correctly, hence the last term in (8.16) becomes either

$$E_t P_{jt+5}/(1 + r_{t,t+5} + rp_j)^{\alpha 5} \tag{8.18}$$

or

$$\lambda E_t P_{jt+5}/(1 + r_{t,t+5} + rp_j)^5 \tag{8.19}$$

Short-termism implies either $\alpha > 1$ or $\lambda < 1$, respectively. In order to make the above relationships operational we need a model of the risk premium for each company. Miles assumes rp_j depends on that firm's beta, β_j, and the firm's level of gearing, G_j:

$$rp_j = a_1 \beta_j + a_2 G_j \tag{8.20}$$

Miles uses a cross-section of 477 UK non-financial companies, with P_{jt} set for $t = 1984$. He then invokes RE and 'replaces' the expectations terms in dividends and the terminal price by their known outturn values in 1985–1989 (and uses instrumental variables in estimation). The $r_{t,t+j}$ are measured by the yield to maturity on UK government bonds for maturities 1–5 years. Substituting for rp_j from (8.20) in any of the variants (8.17), (8.18) or (8.19) which are then substituted in (8.16), we have a cross-section regression which is non-linear in the unknown parameters a_1 and a_2 (which appear in all the models) and in the unknown short-termism parameters, i.e. either b, x, α or λ.

Miles also adjusts the RVF formulae for the taxation of dividends. Some of his results can be found in Table 8.2 (for the 'central' tax case). All the measures (see column 2, Table 8.2) used indicate that short-termism leads to substantial undervaluation of equity prices relative to that given by a rational forecast of either dividends or discount rates. For example, the estimate of $b = 1.65$ implies that cash flows five years hence are discounted as if they did not accrue for more than eight years. The value of $x = 0.93$ implies that cash

Table 8.2 Tests of Short-Termism

Model		Beta Coefficient (a_1)	Gearing Coefficient (a_2)	R^2
1. All discount factors are high	$b = 1.67$ (5.6)	−0.4 (2.9)	8.7 (3.5)	0.54
2. All cash flows pessimistic	$x = 0.93$ (30.6)	−0.07 (2.1)	14.9 (5.3)	0.54
3. 'Year $t + 5$' discount rates high	$\alpha = 2.0$ (6.3)	−0.05 (4.7)	7.4 (3.8)	0.58
4. 'Year $t + 5$' cash flows pessimistic	$\lambda = 0.52$ (6.1)	−0.10 (3.7)	13.2 (5.2)	0.59

Source: Miles (1993).
$(\cdot)$ = t statistic.

flows five years hence are 'undervalued' by 30 percent (i.e. $1 - x^5$) and hence projects with more than five years to maturity need to be 30 percent more profitable than is optimal.

If we take the value of the gearing coefficient as $a_2 \approx 7$–10 then this implies that a company with average gearing $\overline{G} = 57$ percent (in the sample) will have a risk premium about 5.7 percent higher than a company with zero debt. There is one peculiar outcome, namely the *negative* beta coefficient a_1 (which also varies over different specifications). Under the basic CAPM, a_1 should equal the mean of R_{jt} — which should be positive. However, Miles demonstrates that in the presence of inflation the CAPM has to be modified as in section 3.16 and it is possible (but not certain) that the coefficient on β_i may be negative. However, when a_1 is set to zero the results still indicate short-termism. Thus, although the robustness of these results requires further investigation there is prima facie evidence of short-termism.

8.2.4 Noise Traders and Contagion

We now discuss a noise trader model based on Kirman (1993). Kirman's model is very different to that of DeLong et al in that it explicitly deals with the interaction between individuals, the rate at which individuals' opinions are altered by recruitment and hence the phenomena of 'herding' and 'epidemics'. The basic phenomenon of 'herding' was noted by entomologists. It was noted that ants, when 'placed' equidistant from two identical food sources which were constantly replenished, were observed to distribute themselves between each source in an asymmetric fashion. After a time, 80 percent of the ants ate from one source and 20 percent from the other. Sometimes a 'flip' occurred which resulted in the opposite concentrations at the two food sources. The experiment was repeated with one food source and two symmetric bridges leading to the food. Again, initially 80 percent of the ants used one bridge and only 20 percent used the other, whereas intuitively one might have expected that the ants would be split 50–50 between the bridges. One type of recruitment process in an ant colony is 'tandem recruiting' whereby the ant that finds the food returns to the nest and recruits by contact or chemical secretion. Kirman notes that Becker (1991) documents similar herding behaviour when people are faced with very similar restaurants in terms of price, food, service, etc. on either side of the road. A large majority choose one restaurant rather than the other even though they have to 'wait in line' (queue). Note that there may be externalities in being 'part of the crowd' at work here which it is assumed do not apply to ants. However, one still needs to explain any 'flip' from one restaurant to another.

It has already been noted that stock prices may deviate for long periods from fundamental value and in Part 7 it will be shown that the spot exchange rate appears to be only loosely tied to 'fundamentals'. The parallel with the behaviour of the ants is obvious. A model that explains 'recruitment', and results in a concentration at one source for a considerable time period and then a possibility of a 'flip', clearly has relevance to the observed behaviour of speculative asset prices. Kirman makes the point that although economists (unlike entomologists) tend to prefer models based on optimising behaviour, optimisation is not necessary for survival (e.g. plants survive because they have evolved a system whereby their leaves follow the sun, but they might have done much better to develop feet which would have enabled them to walk into the sunlight).

Kirman's stochastic model of recruitment has the following assumptions:

(i)   There are two views of the world, 'black' and 'white', and each agent holds one (and only one) of them at any one time.

(ii) There are a total of N agents and the system is defined by the number $(= k)$ of agents holding the 'black' view of the world.

(iii) The evolution of the system is determined by individuals who meet at random and there is a probability $(1 - \delta)$ that a person is converted (δ = probability not converted) from black to white or vice versa. There is also a small probability ε that an agent changes his 'colour' independently before meeting anyone (e.g. due to exogenous 'news' or the replacement of an existing trader by a new trader with a different view).

(iv) The above probabilities evolve according to a statistical process known as a Markov chain and the probabilities of a conversion from k to $k + 1$, $k - 1$ or no change given by:

$$k \nearrow \begin{array}{l} k + 1 \text{ with probability } p_1 = p(k, k + 1) \\ \longrightarrow \text{ no change with probability } = 1 - p_1 - p_2 \\ \searrow \ k - 1 \text{ with probability } p_2 = p(k, k - 1) \end{array}$$

where

$$p_1 = \left[1 - \frac{k}{N}\right]\left[\varepsilon + \frac{(1 - \delta)k}{N - 1}\right]$$

$$p_2 = \frac{k}{N}\left[\varepsilon + \frac{(1 - \delta)(N - k)}{N - 1}\right] \tag{8.21}$$

In the special case $\varepsilon = \delta = 0$ the first person always gets recruited to the second person's viewpoint and the dynamic process is a martingale with a final position at $k = 0$ or $k = N$. Also when the probability of being converted $(1 - \delta)$ is relatively low and the probability of self-conversion ε is high then a 50–50 split between the two ensues (see Figure 8.5).

Kirman works out what proportion *of time* the system will spend in each state (i.e. the equilibrium distribution). The result is that the smaller the probability of spontaneous conversion ε relative to the probability of not being converted δ, the more time the system spends at the extremes, that is 100 percent of people believing the system is in one or other of the two states. (The required condition is that $\varepsilon < (1 - \delta)/(N - 1)$, see Figure 8.6.)

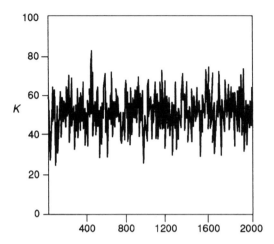

Figure 8.5 100 000 Meetings Every Fiftieth Plotted: $\varepsilon = 0.15$, $\delta = 0.8$. *Source*: A. Kirman (1993). *The Quarterly Journal of Economics*. © 1993 by the President and Fellows of Harvard College and the Massachusetts Institute of Technology. Reproduced by permission

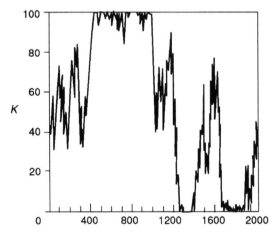

Figure 8.6 100 000 Meetings Every Fiftieth Plotted: $\varepsilon = 0.002$, $\delta = 0.8$. *Source*: A. Kirman (1993). *The Quarterly Journal of Economics*. © 1993 by the President and Fellows of Harvard College and the Massachusetts Institute of Technology. Reproduced by permission

The *absolute* level of δ, that is how 'persuasive' individuals are, is not important here, only that ε is small *relative to* $1 - \delta$. Although persuasiveness is independent of the number in each group, a majority once established will tend to persist. Hence individuals are more likely to be converted to the *majority* opinion of their colleagues in the market and the latter is the major force in the evolution of the system (i.e. the probability that any single meeting will result in an increase in the majority view is higher than that for the minority view).

Kirman (1991) uses this type of model to examine the possible behaviour of an asset price such as the exchange rate which is determined by a *weighted average* of fundamentalists and noise traders' views. The proportion of each type of trader w_t depends on the above evolutionary process of conversion via the Markov chain process. He simulates the

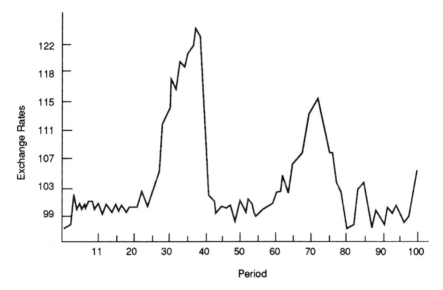

Figure 8.7 Simulated Exchange Rate for 100 Periods with $S = 100$. *Source*: Kirman (1991) in Taylor, M.P. (ed) *Money and Financial Markets* Figure 17.3, p. 364. Reproduced by permission of Blackwell Publishers

model and finds that the asset price (exchange rate) may exhibit periods of tranquillity followed by bubbles and crashes as in Figure 8.7.

In a later paper Kirman (1993) assumes the fundamental's price, P_t^f, is determined by some fundamentals, $\overline{P}_t$, while the chartists' forecast by simple extrapolation, hence the change in the market view, is

$$\Delta p_{t+1}^m = \omega_t \Delta p_{t+1}^f + (1 - \omega_t) \Delta p_{t+1}^c$$

where $\Delta p_{t+1}^f = \nu(\overline{p}_t - p_t)$, $\Delta p_{t+1}^c = p_t - p_{t-1}$ and the weights ω_t depend on the parameters governing the rate of conversion of market participants. The weights are endogenous and incorporate Keynes' beauty queen idea. Individuals meet each other and are either converted or not. They then try and assess which opinion is in the majority and base their forecasts on who they think is in the majority, fundamentalists or chartists. Thus the agent does not base his forecast on his own beliefs but on what he perceives is the majority view. This is rational since it is the latter that determines the market price, not the individual's minority view. The model is then simulated and exhibits a pattern that resembles a periodically collapsing bubble. When the chartists totally dominate P_t is constant and when the fundamentalists totally dominate P_t follows a random walk. Standard tests for unit roots are then applied (e.g. Dickey and Fuller (1979) and Phillips and Perron (1988)) and cointegration tests between P_t and $\overline{P}_t$ tend (erroneously) to suggest there are no bubbles present. A modification of the test by Hamilton (1989) which is designed to detect points at which the system switches from one process to another was only moderately successful. Thus as in the cases studied by Evans (1991, see Chapter 7) when a periodically collapsing bubble is present, it is very difficult to detect.

There is very little hard evidence on the behaviour of noise traders and the diffusion of opinions in financial markets. Allen and Taylor (1989) use survey techniques to investigate the behaviour of chartists in the FOREX market. These 'players' base their views about the future course of the spot exchange rate as extrapolations from graphs of the past behaviour of the exchange rate and they believe they can exploit recurring patterns in the graphs (e.g. 'head and shoulders'). Allen and Taylor find that chart analysis is mainly used for short horizons (intra-day to 1–3 months) and then 'fundamentals' become more important. Also there is a tendency for chartists to underpredict the spot rate in a rising market and vice versa. Hence the elasticity of expectations is less than one (i.e. a rise in the actual rate does not lead to expectations of a bigger rise next period). They argue that the heterogeneity in chartists' forecasts (i.e. some forecast 'up' when others are forecasting 'down') means that they probably do not as a group influence the market over-strongly and hence are not destabilising. The evidence from this study is discussed in more detail in Chapter 12.

8.3 CHAOS

Before commencing our analysis of chaotic systems it is useful briefly to review the nature of the solutions we have obtained so far, to explain returns on stocks and the stock price. In earlier chapters we noted that *stochastic* linear systems, even as simple as the random walk with drift, can generate quite complex time series patterns. In contrast, consider a dynamic linear *deterministic* system such as

$$y_t = a + b y_{t-1} + c y_{t-2} \tag{8.22}$$

Equation (8.22) is a second-order difference equation. Given starting values y_0, y_1, and the parameters (a, b, c) we can determine all future values of y_t to any degree of accuracy by repeated substitution in (8.22). The time path of y_t can converge on a stable equilibrium value $\bar{y} = a/(1 - b - c)$ or for certain parameter values may either have an oscillatory path or a monotonic path. For some parameter values the path may either be oscillatory and explosive (i.e. cycles of ever increasing amplitude) or monotonic and explosive. The problem in basing models on deterministic differential equations like (8.22) is that in the 'real world' we do not appear to observe deterministic paths for economic variables. Hence equations like (8.22) require an additional additive (linear) stochastic element ε_t:

$$y_t = a + b y_{t-1} + c y_{t-2} + \varepsilon_t \tag{8.23}$$

or

$$y_t = (1 - bL - cL^2)^{-1}(a + \varepsilon_t) = f(\varepsilon_t, \varepsilon_{t-1}, \varepsilon_{t-2}) \tag{8.24}$$

If we assume ε_t is white noise then we can see that y_t is generated by a infinite moving average of the random disturbances ε_t. The latter can produce a time series that appears to have cyclical elements (see Part 6) on which are superimposed random shocks. However, these cycles are not of fixed periodicity (unlike the deterministic case). The random walk with drift is a special case of (8.24) with $a \neq 0$, $b = 1$, $c = 0$.

In our 'first look' at empirical results on stock prices and stock returns we have noted the apparent randomness in the behaviour of these series. Indeed the EMH suggests that stock prices and (excess) returns should only change on the arrival of new information or news (about future fundamentals such as dividends). Hence the randomness we observe in the data is given an explicit theoretical basis and is represented by linear stochastic models such as the random walk.

Next, consider an exogenous rational bubble (Chapter 7) where the RVF for stock prices is augmented by the bubble term B_t:

$$P_t = P_t^f + B_t$$

The course of the bubble is unpredictable, so unpredictability of stock returns still holds. *Intrinsic* bubbles again yield a solution for stock prices which consists of two parts

$$P_t = P_t^f + f(D_t) \tag{8.25}$$

where $f(D_t)$ is a *non-linear* function of dividends. An arbitrary linear stochastic process for dividends (e.g. random walk with drift) then completes the model and working via (8.25) yields a stochastic process for P_t. Because the function $f(D_t)$ is non-linear then the linear stochastic process for D_t is 'transformed' by (8.25) to yield a non-linear stochastic process for P_t.

So far, therefore, our models to explain the random nature of stock price (returns) data have involved introducing explicit stochastic processes somewhere into the model; for example, the equilibrium model in which expected returns are assumed to be constant, plus the assumption of RE yields the random walk model. The latter equilibrium returns model via the RVF implies that stock prices only move in response to news about dividends, that is the *random* forecast errors in the stochastic dividend process. In contrast to the above, in *chaotic models*, apparent random patterns observed in real world data can be generated by a *non-linear* system that is purely *deterministic*.

There is no commonly agreed definition of chaos but loosely speaking chaotic systems are deterministic yet they exhibit seemingly random and irregular time series patterns. The time series produced by chaotic systems are highly sensitive to the initial conditions (i.e. the starting point y_0 of the system) and to slight changes in the parameter values. However, this sensitivity to initial conditions and parameter values does not rule out the possibility of producing reasonably accurate forecasts *over short* horizons. This is because the time series from a chaotic system will be broadly repetitive in the early part of the time series, even if the initial conditions differ slightly.

The 'sensitivity' of chaotic systems is such that if the same chaotic system is simulated on two 'identical' computers (which estimate each data point to a precision of 10^{-8} say) then after a certain time, the path of the two series will differ substantially because of the minute rounding errors reacting with the highly non-linear system. This kind of result is the source of the observation that if the weather can be represented as a chaotic system then a butterfly flapping its wings in China can substantially influence weather patterns and hence may result in a hurricane in Florida.

Although chaotic systems produce apparent random patterns in the time domain they nevertheless have a discernible structure (e.g. a specific frequency distribution) which can be used to provide statistical tests for the presence of chaos. Space constraints mean we shall not analyse these tests (but see De Grauwe et al 1993). As one might imagine, it can be very difficult to ascertain whether a particular 'random looking' time series has been generated from a deterministic chaotic system or from a genuinely stochastic system. The latter becomes even more difficult if the chaotic system is *occasionally* hit by 'small' random shocks: this is known as 'noisy chaos'. Tests for chaotic systems require a large amount of data, if inferences are to be reliable (e.g. in excess of 20 000 data points) and hence with the 'length' of most economic data this becomes an acute problem.

Most people would agree that human behaviour is not wholly deterministic and therefore the analysis of chaotic models only provides a starting point in explaining economic phenomena. In essence, chaos theory suggests that economists take greater note of the possibility of non-linearities in relationships. Having obtained a model that is non-linear in the variables one can always 'add on' stochastic elements to represent the randomness in human behaviour. Hence as a first step we need to examine the dynamics produced by non-linear systems. If asset prices appear random and returns are largely unpredictable we must at least entertain the possibility that these results might be generated in chaotic systems.

We have so far spoken in rather general terms about chaos. We now briefly discuss an explicit chaotic system and outline how an economic model based on noise traders and smart money is capable of generating a chaotic system.

The Logistic Equation

About the simplest representation of a system capable of chaotic behaviour is the (non-linear) logistic equation:

$$Y_{t+1} = \lambda Y_t (1 - Y_t) \tag{8.26}$$

The steady state Y^* is given when $Y_{t+1} = Y_t = Y_{t-1} \ldots$

$$Y^* = \lambda Y^* (1 - Y^*)$$

and the two solutions are:

$$Y^* = 0 \quad Y^* = 1 - 1/\lambda \tag{8.27}$$

Not all non-linear systems give rise to chaotic behaviour: it depends on the parameter values and initial conditions. For some values of λ the system is globally stable and given *any* starting value Y_0, the system will converge to one of the steady state solutions Y^*. For other values of λ the solution is a *limit cycle* whereby the time series eventually oscillates (for ever) between *two* values Y_1^* and Y_2^* (where $Y_i^* \neq Y^*$, $i = 1, 2$): this is known as a two-cycle (Figure 8.8). The 'solution' to the system is therefore a differential equation and is known as a *bifurcation*. Again for different values of λ the series can alter from a two-cycle to a 4, 8, 16 cyclic pattern. Finally, for a range of values of λ the time series of Y_t appears random and chaotic behaviour occurs (Figure 8.9). In this case if the starting value is altered from $Y_0 = 0.3$ to 0.30001, the 'random' time path differs after about 20 time periods, demonstrating the sensitivity to very slight parameter changes.

The dynamics of the non-linear logistic system in the single variable Y_t has to be solved by simulation rather than analytically. The latter usually applies *a fortiori* to more complex single variable non-linear equations and to a system of non-linear equations where variables X, Y, Z, say, interact with each other. A wide variety of very diverse patterns which are seemingly random or irregular can arise in such models.

Noise Traders and Smart Money

It is not difficult to set up ad-hoc models of the interaction of noise traders (NT) and smart money (SM) that are non-linear in the variables and hence that may exhibit chaos. When we say ad hoc we imply that the NT and SM need not necessarily maximise some well-defined function (e.g. utility of end of period wealth). De Grauwe et al (1993) provide an

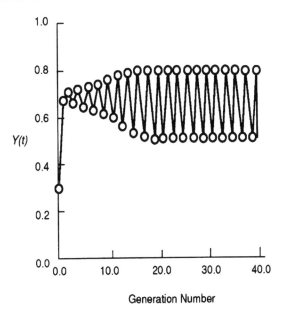

Figure 8.8 Period 2: Limit Cycle. *Source*: De Grauwe (1993). Reproduced by permission of Blackwell Publishers

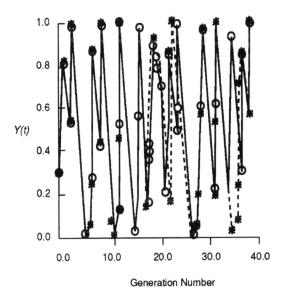

Figure 8.9 Chaotic Regime. Start Value $Y_0 = 0.3$ (Solid Line), Start Value $Y_0 = 0.30001$ (Dashed Line). *Source*: De Grauwe (1993). Reproduced by permission of Blackwell Publishers

interesting model of this interaction where NT exhibit extrapolative behaviour (positive feedback) and the SM have negative feedback, since they sell when the price is above fundamentals. The model they develop is for the exchange rate S_t, although the reader can replace this by the price of any speculative asset, without loss of generality. A key aspect of the model is the heterogeneity of expectations of different traders. The market price S_t is therefore a weighted average of the expectations of NT and the SM with a weight m_t given to NT (which is time varying). Hence:

$$E_t[S_{t+1}/S_{t-1}] = E_t^N[S_{t+1}/S_{t-1}]^{m_t} \cdot E_t^s[S_{t+1}/S_{t-1}]^{(1-m_t)} \tag{8.28}$$

where $E_t S_{t+1}$ is the *market expectation* at time t. The dating of the variables in (8.28) needs some comment. The time period of the model is short. Agents are assumed to have information for time $t-1$ and they take positions in the market at time t, based on their forecasts for period $t+1$. This is required because S_t is the *market* solution of the model and is not observable by the NT and SM when they take their positions in the market. The expectations of NT are extrapolative so that

$$E_t^N[S_{t+1}/S_{t-1}] = f[S_{t-1}, S_{t-2}, \ldots S_{t-N}] \tag{8.29}$$

where f is a non-linear function. A simple form of extrapolative predictor used by De Grauwe et al is based on chartists' behaviour, who predict that the price will rise in the future if the short moving average SMA crosses the long moving average LMA from below. (Hence at point A in Figure 8.10, chartists buy the asset since they expect a price rise.) A simplified representation of this NT extrapolative behaviour is:

$$E_t^N[S_{t+1}/S_t] = (\text{SMA}/\text{LMA})^{2\gamma} = [[S_{t-1}/S_{t-2}]/[S_{t-1}/S_{t-2}]^{1/2} \, [S_{t-2}/S_{t-3}]^{1/2}]^{2\gamma}$$

$$= [S_{t-1}/S_{t-2}]^{\gamma}[S_{t-3}/S_{t-2}]^{\gamma} \tag{8.30}$$

In contrast, the SM have regressive expectations, relative to the long-run equilibrium value S_{t-1}^* given by fundamentals:

$$E_t^s[S_{t+1}/S_{t-1}] = [S_{t-1}^*/S_{t-1}]^{\alpha} \tag{8.31}$$

and adjust their expectations at the rate given by the parameter α. Note that the SM do not have RE since they do not take into account the behaviour of the NT and the effect

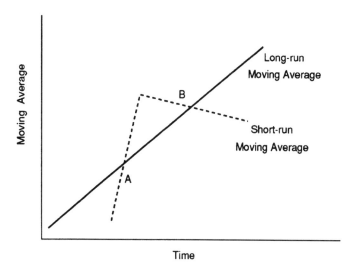

Figure 8.10 Moving Average Chart. A, Chartists Buy Foreign Exchange; B, Chartists Sell Foreign Exchange. *Source*: De Grauwe (1993). Reproduced by permission of Blackwell Publishers

they might have on the price: they do not have or do not use all available information when forming their expectations.

In Kirman's (1993) model the interaction between NT and SM was one of 'random conversion' and this gave rise to the randomness in the asset price. In the model of De Long et al (1990) the relative weight given to NT depends on the profits made by NT relative to those of the SM. The model of De Grauwe et al is rather akin to that of De Long et al in that the relative weight of NT and SM varies over time depending on economic conditions and it provides the key non-linearity in the model. The weight of NT in the market m_t is given by:

$$m_t = 1/[1 + \beta[S_{t-1} - S_{t-1}^*]^2] \qquad \beta > 0 \qquad (8.32)$$

The SM are assumed to have different views about the equilibrium value S_t^* but these views are normally distributed around S_t^*. Hence if the actual market price S_{t-1} equals the true equilibrium rate then 50 percent of the SM think the equilibrium rate is too low and 50 percent think it is too high. If we assume all the SM have the same degree of risk aversion and initial wealth then they will exert equal and opposite pressure on the market rate. Hence when $S_{t-1} = S_{t-1}^*$ the SM as a whole do not influence the market price and the latter is entirely determined by the NT, that is m_t in (8.32) equals unity and the weight of the SM $= (1 - m_t)$ is zero (Figure 8.11). On the other hand, if S_{t-1} falls below the *true* market rate then more of the SM will believe that in *their view*, the equilibrium market rate is above the actual rate and as a group they begin to influence the market rate, hence m_t in (8.32) falls and the weight of the SM $= 1 - m_t$ increases.

Finally, note that β measures the degree of confidence about the true equilibrium market rate held by the SM as a whole. As β increases then $m_t \to 0$ and $(1 - m_t) \to 1$. Hence the larger is β the greater the degree of homogeneity in the SMs' view of where the true equilibrium rate lies. In this case a small deviation of S_{t-1} from S_{t-1}^* will lead to a strong influence of SM in the market. Conversely if β is small there is a greater dispersion of views of the SM about where the true equilibrium market rate lies and the weight of the SM in the market $(1 - m_t)$ increases relatively slowly (Figure 8.11).

To close the model we need an equation to link the markets' non-linear expectations formation equation:

$$E_t[S_{t+1}/S_{t-1}] = f^N[S_{t-1}, S_{t-2}]^{m_t}[S_{t-1}^*/S_{t-1}]^{\alpha(1-m_t)} \qquad (8.33)$$

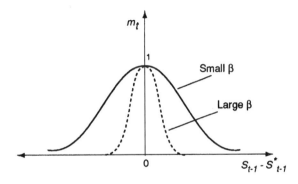

Figure 8.11 The Weighting Function of Chartists. *Source*: De Grauwe et al (1993). Reproduced by permission of Blackwell Publishers

(with m_t given by (8.32)) to the actual market rate S_t. For the stock price P_t (rather than S_t) we could use the Euler equation:

$$P_t = \delta E_t P_{t+1} + \delta E_t D_{t+1} \tag{8.34}$$

If for simplicity we assume $E_t D_{t+1} = $ constant and substitute for $E_t P_{t+1}$ (i.e. equivalently, $E_t S_{t+1}$) from (8.33) we have a non-linear difference equation in P_t. However, returning to our exchange rate example, we see in Chapter 13 that the Euler equation linking S_t to $E_t(S_{t+1})$ is of the form:

$$S_t = X_t[E_t S_{t+1}]^b \tag{8.35}$$

where $X_t = $ fundamentals, for example relative money supplies, that influence the exchange rate (and De Grauwe et al set $b = 0.95$ and $X_t = 1$, initially). De Grauwe et al simulate the model for particular parameter values and find that when the extrapolative parameter γ is sufficiently high, chaotic behaviour ensues. This can be clearly seen in Figure 8.12(a) where the equilibrium exchange S_t^* rate is normalised to unity. When the initial condition is changed by 1 percent the time series is similar for about the first 100 periods but then the two patterns deviate quite substantially (e.g. compare the patterns in Figures 8.12(a) and 8.12(b) for periods 200–400).

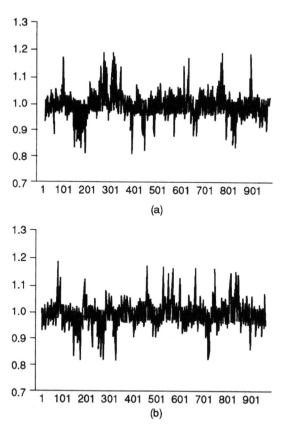

(a)

(b)

Figure 8.12 Sensitivity to Initial Conditions Generated by a Difference in the Initial Exchange Rate. (a) Base Run; (b) A 1 Percent Change in the Initial Exchange Rate Compared to the Base Run. *Source*: De Grauwe et al (1993). Reproduced by permission of Blackwell Publishers

Thus even in this relatively simple model, involving heterogeneous traders we can obtain time series that begin to approximate those found in actual high frequency data (e.g. daily) for speculative prices such as the exchange rate. The similarity of the first 100 data points in Figures 8.12(a) and 8.12(b) make clear that if we know (or can approximate closely enough) the form of the chaotic system, it may be possible to undertake short-term forecasting. Note also that there has been no random events or 'news' that have been required to produce the graphs in Figures 8.12(a) and 8.12(b), which are the result of a pure deterministic non-linear system. Hence the RE hypothesis is not required in order to yield apparent random behaviour in asset prices and asset returns. Finally it is worth recalling that 'fundamentals' X_t have been held constant in the above simulations and it is the inherent dynamics of the system that yield the random time path. Hence if the real world does contain chaotic dynamics, then agents may discard fundamentals (i.e. the path of X_t) when trying to predict future asset prices and instead concentrate on more ad-hoc methods, as used, for example, by chartists and other NTs.

Clearly, the above analysis is a long way from providing a coherent theory of asset price movements but it does alert one to alternative possibilities to the RE paradigm where all agents have homogeneous expectations, know the true model of the economy (instantly) and use all available useful information, when forecasting. The above points will be developed further in Chapter 13 when we look in more detail at models of the exchange rate and discuss tests which attempt to distinguish between systems that are predominantly deterministic yet yield chaotic solutions and those that are genuinely stochastic.

8.4 SUMMARY

It is now time to summarise this rather diverse set of results on market inefficiency. It would appear that some of the anomalies in the stock market are merely manifestations of a small firm effect. Thus the January effect appears to be concentrated primarily among small firms as are the profits to be made from closed end mutual funds, where the discount available is highly correlated with the presence of small firms in the portfolio of stocks. Thus it may be the case that there is some market segmentation taking place whereby the smart money only deals in large tranches of frequently traded stocks of large companies. The market for small firms' stocks may be rather 'thin' allowing these anomalies to persist. The latter is, strictly speaking, a violation of the efficient markets hypothesis. However, once we recognise the real world problems of transactions costs, information costs, and costs of acquiring information in particular markets, it may be that the smart money, at the margin, does not find it profitable to deal in the shares of small firms and eliminate these arbitrage opportunities. Nevertheless, where the market consists of large frequent trades undertaken primarily by institutions, then violation of variance bounds tests, and the existence of very sharp changes in stock prices in the absence of 'news', still need to be explained.

The idea of noise traders coexisting with smart money is a recent and important theoretical innovation. Here price can diverge from fundamentals simply because of the extra uncertainty introduced by the noise traders. Also the noise traders coexist alongside the smart money and they do not necessarily go bankrupt. Though this theory can in principle explain sharp movements in stock prices (i.e. bull and bear markets) and indeed the high volatility experienced in the stock market, nevertheless it has to embrace some ad-hoc assumptions about behaviour. We have seen that one way to obtain the above results is to assume that 'opinion' or 'fads' are persistent. However, this is a purely arbitrary assumption and merely says that a part of the stock market may be subject to quite violent changes of 'mood', unrelated to fundamentals. Thus, 'changes of mood' are not based on any rational behaviour, we do not know what economic variables might cause such changes and indeed whether such changes go through tranquil or turbulent periods. The noise-trader model also allows stock prices to undergo persistent swings if we make the assumption that there is persistence in agents' perceptions of volatility. Such persistence in volatility is often found in empirical research (e.g. ARCH models, Chapter 17). Again, however, this is merely an empirical regularity and there is no rational optimising model of why this should be the case. It all boils down to the mass psychology and herding behaviour of participants in the market.

Chaos theory demonstrates how a non-linear deterministic system can generate apparently random behaviour. This applies *a fortiori* to noisy chaotic systems. What is perhaps most important about this strand of the literature is that it alerts us to the possibility of non-linearities in economic behavioural equations (e.g. see Pesaran and Potter (1993)). However, at present it is very much a 'technique in search of a good economic theory' although it has been outlined how it can be used to develop a plausible economic model of asset price movements. Another major difficulty in trying to analyse economic systems in terms of chaotic models is the very large amount of data required to detect a chaotic (as opposed to a stochastic) process. A reasonable conjecture might be that chaotic dynamics (and its allied companion, neural networks) could become important statistical tools in short-term forecasting of asset prices, but unless they are allied to economic theory models their usefulness in general policy analysis will be very limited.

Of course none of the models discussed in this chapter are able to explain what is a crucial fact, as far as public policy implications are concerned. That is to say, they do not tell us how far away from the fundamental price a portfolio of particular stocks might be. For example, if the deviation from fundamental value is only 5 percent for a portfolio of stocks, then even though this persists for some time it may not represent a substantial misallocation of investment funds, given other uncertainties that abound in the economy. Noise-trader behaviour may provide an *a priori* case for public policy in the form of trading halts, during specific periods of turbulence or of insisting on higher margin requirements. The presence of noise traders also suggests that hostile takeovers may not always be beneficial for the predators since the actual price they pay for the stock of the target firm may be substantially above its fundamental value. However, establishing a prima facie argument for intervention is a long way short of saying that specific government action in the market is beneficial.

APPENDIX 8.1

The De Long et al Model of Noise Traders

The basic model of De Long et al (1990) is a two-period overlapping generations model. There are no first-period consumption or labour supply decisions: the resources agents have to invest are therefore exogenous. The only decision is to choose a portfolio in the first-period (i.e. when young) to maximise the expected utility of end of period wealth. The 'old' then sell their risky assets to the 'new young' cohort and use the receipts from the safe asset to purchase the consumption good. The safe asset s is in perfectly elastic supply. The supply of the uncertain/risky asset u is fixed and normalised at unity. Both assets pay a known real dividend r (riskless rate) so there is no fundamental risk. One unit of the safe asset buys one unit of the consumption good and hence the real price of the safe asset is unity.

The proportion of noise traders (NT) is μ, with $(1 - \mu)$ smart money (SM) operators in the market. The SM correctly perceive the distribution of returns on the risky asset for $t + 1$. NT can be 'bullish' or 'bearish' and misperceive the true price distribution. The NT average misperception of the expected price is denoted ρ^* and at any point in time the actual misperception ρ_t behaves according to:

$$\rho_t \sim N(\rho^*, \sigma^2) \tag{1}$$

Each agent maximises a constant absolute risk aversion utility function in end of period wealth, w:

$$U = -\exp(-2\gamma w) \tag{2}$$

If returns on the risky asset are normally distributed then maximising (2) is equivalent to maximising

$$\bar{w} - \gamma \sigma_w^2 \tag{3}$$

where $\bar{w}$ = expected final wealth, γ = coefficient of absolute risk aversion. The SM therefore choose the amount of the risky asset to hold, λ_t^s by maximising

$$E(U) = c_o + \lambda_t^s[r + {}_tP_{t+1}^e - P_t(1 + r)] - \gamma(\lambda_t^s)^2 {}_t\sigma_{p_{t+1}}^2 \tag{4}$$

where c_o is a constant (i.e. period zero income) and ${}_t\sigma_{p_{t+1}}^2$ is the one-period ahead conditional expected variance of price:

$$\sigma_{p_{t+1}}^2 = E_t[P_{t+1} - E_tP_{t+1}]^2 \tag{5}$$

The NT has the same objective function as the SM except his expected return has an additional term $+ \lambda_t^n \rho_t$ (and of course λ^n replaces λ_t^s in (4)). These objective functions are of the same form as those found in the simple two-asset, mean-variance model (where one asset is a safe asset) as discussed in Chapter 3.

Setting $\partial E(U)/\partial \lambda_t = 0$ in (4) then the objective function gives the familar mean-variance asset demand functions for the risky asset for the SM and the NTs

$$\lambda_t^s = \frac{R_t^e}{2\gamma \left[{}_t\sigma_{p+1}^2\right]} \tag{6}$$

$$\lambda_t^n = \frac{R_{t+1}^e}{2\gamma \left[{}_t\sigma_{pt+1}^2\right]} + \frac{\rho_t}{2\gamma \left[{}_t\sigma_{pt+1}^2\right]} \tag{7}$$

where $R_{t+1}^e = r_t + {}_tP_{t+1} - (1 + r)P_t$. The demand by NTs depends in part on their abnormal view of expected returns as reflected in ρ_t. Since the 'old' sell their risky assets to the young and the fixed supply of risky assets is 1, we have:

$$(1 - \mu)\lambda_t^s + \mu\lambda_t^n = 1 \tag{8}$$

Hence using (6) and (7), the equilibrium pricing equation is:

$$P_t = \frac{1}{(1 + r)}[r + {}_tP_{t+1} - 2\gamma {}_t\sigma_{p_{t+1}}^2 + \mu\rho_t] \tag{9}$$

The equilibrium in the model is a steady state where the *un*conditional distribution of P_{t+1} equals that for P_t. Hence solving (9) recursively:

$$P_t = 1 + \mu \frac{(\rho_t - \rho^*)}{(1 + r)} + \frac{\mu\rho^*}{r} - \left[\frac{2\gamma}{r}\right] {}_t\sigma_{p_{t+1}} \tag{10}$$

Only ρ_t is a variable in (10) hence:

$${}_t\sigma_{p_{t+1}}^2 = \sigma_{p_{t+1}}^2 = \frac{\mu^2\sigma^2}{(1 + r)^2} \tag{11}$$

where from (1), $\rho_t - \rho^* = N(0, \sigma^2)$. Substituting (11) in (10) we obtain the equation for the price level given in the text:

$$P_t = 1 + \mu \frac{(\rho_t - \rho^*)}{(1 + r)} + \frac{\mu \rho^*}{r} - \frac{2 \gamma \mu^2 \sigma^2}{r(1 + r)^2} \tag{12}$$

APPENDIX 8.2

The Shleifer–Vishny Model of Short-Termism

This appendix formally sets out the Shleifer–Vishny (1990) model whereby long-term assets are subject to greater mispricing than short-term assets even though arbitrageurs/smart money (SM) act rationally. As explained in the text this may then lead to managers of firms pursuing investment projects with short-horizon cash flows to avoid severe mispricing and the risk of a takeover. The model may be developed as follows.

There are three periods, 0, 1, 2, and firms can invest either in a 'short-term' investment project with a \$ payout of V_s in period 2 or a 'long-term' project also with payout only in period 2 of V_g. The key distinction between the projects is that the *true value* of the short-term project becomes *known* in period 1, but the true value of the long-term project doesn't become known until period 2. Thus arbitrageurs are concerned not with the timing of the cash flows from the project but with the timing of the mispricing and in particular the point at which such mispricing is revealed and hence disappears. The market riskless interest rate = 0. All investors are risk neutral.

There are two types of trader, noise traders (NT) and smart money (SM) (arbitrageurs). Noise traders can either be pessimistic ($S_i > 0$) or optimistic at time $t = 0$ about the payoffs V_i from both types of project ($i = s$ or g). Hence *both* projects suffer from systematic optimism or pessimism. We deal only with the pessimistic case (i.e. 'bearish' or pessimistic views by NTs). The demand for the equity of firm engaged in project $i(= s$ or $g)$ by noise traders is:

$$q(\text{NT}, i) = (V_i - S_i)/P_i \tag{1}$$

For the bullishness case q would equal $(V_i + S_i)/P_i$. Smart money (arbitrageurs) face a borrowing constraint of \$b at an interest rate $R > 1$ (i.e. greater than one plus the riskless rate). The SM traders are risk neutral so they are indifferent between investing all \$b in either of the assets i. Their demand curve is:

$$q(\text{SM}, i) = n_i b/P_i \tag{2}$$

where n_i = number of SM traders who invest in asset i ($= s$ or g). There is a unit supply of each asset i so equilibrium is given by:

$$1 = q(\text{SM}, i) + q(\text{NT}, i) \tag{3}$$

and hence using (1) and (2) the equilibrium price for each asset is given by:

$$P_i^e = V_i - S_i + n_i b \tag{4}$$

It is assumed that $n_i b < S_i$ so that both assets are mispriced at time $t = 0$. If SM invests \$b, at $t = 0$, he can obtain b/P_s^e shares of the short-term asset. At $t \neq 1$ the payoff per share of the short-term asset V_s is revealed. There is a total \$ payoff in period 1 of $V_s(b/P_s^e)$. The net return NR_s in period 1 over the borrowing cost of bR is:

$$\text{NR}_s = \frac{V_s b}{P_s^e} - bR = \frac{b V_s}{(V_s - S_s + n_s b)} - bR \tag{5}$$

(where we have used equation 4). Investing at $t = 0$ in the long-term asset the SM purchases b/P_g^e shares. In period $t = 1$, he does nothing. In period $t = 2$, the true value V_g per share is revealed which discounted to $t + 1$ at the rate R implies a \$ payoff of $bV_g/P_g R$. The amount owed at $t = 2$

is bR^2 which when discounted to $t + 1$ is bR. Hence the net return in period 1 NR_t is:

$$NR_g = \frac{bV_g}{P_g R} - bR = \frac{1}{R} \frac{bV_g}{(V_g - S_g + n_g b)} - bR \qquad (6)$$

The only difference between (5) and (6) is that in (6) the return to holding the (mispriced) long-term share is discounted back to $t = 1$, since its true value is not revealed until $t = 2$.

In equilibrium the returns to arbitrage over one period, on the long and short assets, must be equal ($NR_g = NR_s$) and hence from (5) and (6):

$$\frac{(V_g/R)}{P_g^e} = \frac{V_s}{P_s^e} \qquad (7)$$

Since $R > 1$, then in equilibrium the long-term asset is *more* underpriced (in percentage terms) than the short-term asset (when the noise traders are pessimistic, $S_i > 0$). The differential in the mispricing occurs because payoff uncertainty is resolved for the short-term asset in period 1 but for the long-term asset this does not occur until period 2. Price moves to fundamental value (V_s) for the short asset in period 1 but for the long asset not until period 2. Hence the long-term fundamental value V_g has to be discounted back to period 1 and this 'cost of borrowing' reduces the return to holding the long asset.

ENDNOTE

1. To see this, note that $E_t Y_{t+1} = u_t$, and $E_t Y_{t+2} = u_t$ but after n periods u_t disappears from $E_t Y_{t+n+1}$ which then equals zero. So if Y_t starts at zero, a single positive shock u_t results in a higher expected value for EY_{t+k} for a further n periods only.

FURTHER READING

There is a vast and ever expanding journal literature on the topics covered in Part 2. We will concentrate on accessible overviews of the literature excluding those found in basic finance texts.

On predictability and efficiency, in order of increasing difficulty, we have Fortune (1991), Scott (1991) and LeRoy (1989). A useful practitioner's viewpoint with excellent references to the applied literature is Lofthouse (1994). Shiller (1989), particularly Section II: 'The Stock Market', is excellent on volatility tests. On 'bubbles' the special section in the *Journal of Economic Perspectives* (1990 Vol. 4, No. 2) is a useful starting point with the collection of papers by Flood and Garber (1994) providing a more technical overview.

At a general level Thaler's (1994) book provides a good overview of 'anomalies' while Thaler (1987) and De Bondt and Thaler (1989) provide examples of anomalies in the finance area. Finally, Shiller (1989) in parts I: 'Basic Issues' and VI: 'Popular Models and Investor Behaviour' are informative and entertaining. Gleick (1987) provides a general non-mathematical introduction to chaos, Baumol and Benhabib (1989) cover the basics of non-linear models while Barnett et al (1989) provide a more technical viewpoint with economic examples. Peters (1991) provides a clear introduction to chaos, applied to financial markets while De Grauwe et al (1993) is a very accessible account using the exchange rate as an example. The use of neural networks in finance is clearly explained in Azoff (1994).

PART 3
The Bond Market

Most governments at some time or another attempt to influence short-term interest rates as a lever on the real economy or in an attempt to influence the rate of inflation. This is usually accomplished by the monetary authority either engaging in open market operations (i.e. buying or selling bills) or threatening to do so. Changes in short rates (with unchanged inflationary expectations) may influence real inventory holdings and consumers' expenditure, particularly on durable goods. Short-term interest rates may have an effect on *the level* of long-term interest rates on government (and corporate) bonds: this is the yield curve relationship. Corporate bond rates may affect real investment in plant and machinery. Hence the government's monetary policy can influence real economic activity. Closely allied to this is the idea that governments may be able to 'twist' the yield curve, that is, to raise short-term interest rates (to encourage personal saving) while simultaneously lowering long-term rates to encourage fixed investment. However, if the so-called expectations hypothesis of the yield curve holds then the authorities *cannot* alter the *relationship* between short-term and long-term rates and must accept the 'free market' consequences for long rates of any change in short rates they might engineer. The authorities can try and influence future short rates through various mechanisms, such as a declared anti-inflation policy. Also its open market operations at short maturities may have a direct impact on short rates and hence, via the expectations hypothesis, on long rates. Changes in domestic short rates may influence capital flows, the exchange rate and hence price competitiveness, the volume of net trade (exports minus imports) and the level of output and employment. Part 4 deals with the link between short rates and the exchange rate.

Another reason for governments being interested in the determinants of movements in bond prices is that bonds constitute a substantial proportion of the portfolio of a number of financial institutions (e.g. life insurance and pension funds). Variations in bond prices influence the balance sheets of financial institutions, while Central Banks, when they have a statutory role as the regulatory authority, will wish to know whether this is likely to put the financial viability of such institutions at risk. If the bond market can be shown to be excessively volatile, that is the degree of volatility exceeds that which would result from the behaviour of agents who use RE, then there is an added reason for government intervention in such markets over and above any supervisory role (e.g. introducing 'circuit breakers' or 'cooling-off' procedures whereby the market is temporarily closed if price changes exceed a certain specified limit in a downward direction).

Financial economists are interested in the behaviour of bond prices and interest rates as a test-bed for various behavioural hypotheses about market participants and market efficiency. Bond prices may shed light on the validity of the EMH, the results of which may be compared with tests based on stock returns and stock prices (as discussed in earlier chapters).

Before we plunge into the details of models of the behaviour of bond prices and returns it is worth giving a brief overview of what lies ahead. Bonds and stocks have several features in common and, as we shall see, many of the tests used to assess 'efficiency' in stock prices and returns can be applied to bonds. For stocks we investigated whether (one-period holding period) returns are predictable. Bonds have a flexible market price just like stocks. Unlike stocks they pay a *known fixed* 'dividend' in nominal terms, which is the coupon on the bond. The 'dividend' on a stock is not known with certainty, whereas the stream of nominal coupon payments is. The one-period holding period yield (HPY) on a bond is defined analogously to the 'return' on stocks, namely as the price change (capital gain) plus the coupon payment, denoted $H_{t+1}^{(n)}$ for a bond with term to maturity of n periods. Hence we can apply the same type of regression tests as we did for stocks, to see if the excess HPY on bonds is predictable from information at time t or earlier.

The nominal stock price under the EMH is equal to the DPV of expected dividend payments. Similarly, the nominal price of a bond may be viewed as the DPV of future nominal coupon payments. However, since the nominal coupon payments are known with certainty the only source of variability in bond prices under rational expectations is news about future one-period interest rates (i.e. the discount factors). We can construct a perfect foresight bond price P_t^* using the DPV formula for bonds with *actual (ex-post)* interest rates (rather than expected interest rates) as the discount factors, in the same way as we did for stocks. By comparing P_t and P_t^* for bonds, we can then perform Shiller variance bounds tests, and also examine whether $P_t - P_t^*$ is independent of information at time t, using regression tests. A similar analysis can be applied to the yield on a bond, to give either the perfect foresight yield R_t^* or the perfect foresight yield spread S_t^*. The time series behaviour of the *ex-post* variables R_t^* and S_t^* can then be compared with their actual values R_t and S_t, respectively.

Chapter 9 discusses various theories of the determination of bond prices, one-period returns and 'yields', while Chapter 10 discusses empirical tests of these theories. There is a plethora of technical terms used in analysing the bond market and therefore we begin by defining such concepts as pure discount bonds, coupon paying bonds, the holding period yield (HPY), spot yields, the yield to maturity and the term premium. We then examine the various theories of the determination of one-period HPYs on bonds of different maturities (e.g. expectations hypothesis (EH), liquidity preference, market segmentation and preferred habitat hypotheses).

Models of the term structure are usually applied to spot yields and it will be demonstrated how the various hypotheses about the determination of the spot yield on an n period bond $R_t^{(n)}$ can be derived from a model of the one-period HPYs on zero coupon bonds. Under the pure expectations hypothesis (PEH), it will be shown how the spread between the long rate and a short rate is the optimal predictor of both the *expected change* in *long* rates and the *expected change* in (a weighted average) of future *short* rates. These relationships provide testable predictions of the expectations hypothesis, under rational expectations. Strictly speaking the expectations hypothesis only applies to spot yields but we briefly examine how an approximate term structure relationship can be formulated using yields to maturity.

Chapter 10 examines the variance bounds and regression tests that have been applied to HPYs, spot rates and yields to maturity. More complex tests of the EH (under a constant term premium) are deferred to Chapter 14 and tests involving time varying term premia to Chapter 19.

9

Bond Prices and the Term Structure of Interest Rates

The main aim in this chapter is to present a set of tests which may be applied to assess the validity of the EMH in the bond market. However, several preliminaries need to be set out before we are in a position to formulate these hypotheses. The procedure is as follows:

- We analyse zero coupon and coupon paying bonds, spot yields, continuously compounded spot yields, the holding period and the yield to maturity
- We see how the rational valuation formula may be applied to the determination of bond prices
- It will be demonstrated how a model of the one-period HPY on pure discount bonds can lead to the term structure relationship, namely that the yield on an n-period bond is equal to a weighted average of expected future short rates plus a term premium
- Various hypotheses of the term structure applied to holding period yields, spot yields and the yield to maturity are examined. Theories include the expectations hypothesis, the liquidity preference hypothesis, the market segmentation hypothesis and the CAPM (applied to HPYs)

9.1 PRICES, YIELDS AND THE RVF

The investment opportunities on bonds can be summarised not only by the holding period yield but also by spot yields and the yield to maturity. Hence, the 'return' on a bond can be defined in a number of different ways and this section clarifies the relationships between these alternative measures. We then look at various hypotheses about the behaviour of participants in the bond market based on the EMH, under alternative assumptions about expected 'returns'.

Bonds and stocks have a number of basic features in common. Holders of a stock expect to receive a stream of future dividends and may make a capital gain over any given holding period. Coupon paying bonds provide a stream of income called coupon payments C_{t+i}, which are known (in nominal terms) for all future periods, at the time the bond is purchased. In most cases C_{t+i} is constant for all time periods but it is sometimes useful to retain the subscript for expositional purposes. Most bonds, unlike stocks, are redeemable at a fixed date in the future $(= t + n)$ for a known price, namely the *par value*, *redemption price* or *maturity value*, M_n. There are some bonds which, although they pay coupons, are never redeemed and these are known as *perpetuities* (e.g. $2\frac{1}{2}$ percent Consols, issued by the UK government).

A bill (e.g. Treasury bill) has no coupon payments but its redemption price is fixed and known at the time of issue. The return on the bill is therefore the difference between its issue price (or market price when purchased) and its redemption price (expressed as a percentage). A bill is always issued at a *discount* (i.e. the issue price is less than the redemption price) so that a positive return is earned over the life of the bill. Bills are therefore often referred to as *pure discount bonds* or *zero coupon bonds*. Most bills that are traded in the market are for short maturities (i.e. they have a maturity at issue of three months, six months or a year). Coupon paying bonds, on the other hand, are usually for maturities in excess of one year with very active markets in the 5–15 year band.

This book is concerned only with (non-callable) government bonds and bills and it is assumed that these carry no risk of default. Corporate bonds are more risky than government bonds since firms that issue them may go into liquidation, hence considerations of the risk of default then enter the analysis.

Because coupon paying bonds and stocks are similar in a number of respects, many of the analytical ideas, theories and formulae derived for the stock market can be applied to the bond market. As we shall see below, because the 'return' or 'yield' on a bond can be measured in several different ways, the terminology (although often *not* the underlying ideas) in the bond market differs somewhat from that in the stock market.

Spot Yields/Rates

The spot yield (or spot rate) is that rate of return which applies to funds which are borrowed or lent at a known (usually risk-free) interest rate *over a given horizon*. For example, suppose you can lend funds (to a bank, say) at a rate of interest $rs^{(1)}$ which applies to a one-year loan. For an investment of $\$A$ the bank will pay out $M_1 = \$A(1 + rs^{(1)})$ after one year. Suppose the bank's rate of interest on 'two-year money' is $rs^{(2)}$ expressed at a proportionate *annual* compound rate. Then $\$A$ invested will accrue to $M_2 = A(1 + rs^{(2)})^2$ after two years. The spot rate (or spot yield) therefore assumes that the initial investment is 'locked in' for a fixed term of either one or two years.

An equivalent way of viewing spot yields is to note that they can be used to provide a discount rate applicable to money accruing at *specific* future dates. If you are offered $\$M_2$ payable in two years then the DPY of this sum is $M_2/(1 + rs^{(2)})^2$ where $rs^{(2)}$ is the two-year spot rate.

In principle, a sequence of spot rates can be calculated from the observed market price of pure discount bonds (i.e. bills) of different maturities. Since these assets offer a fixed one-off payment (i.e. the maturity value M) in 'n' years' time, their yields (expressed at an annual compound rate, rather than as a quoted simple interest rate) are a sequence of spot rates $rs_t^{(1)}, rs_t^{(2)} \ldots$, etc. For example, suppose the redemption price on *all* discount bonds is $\$M$ and the observed market price of bonds of maturity $n = 1, 2, \ldots$ are $P_t^{(1)}, P_t^{(2)} \ldots$, etc. Then each spot yield can be derived from $P_t^{(1)} = M/(1 + rs_t^{(1)})$, $P_t^{(2)} = M/(1 + rs_t^{(2)})^2$, etc.

For a n-period pure discount bond $P_t = M/(1 + rs_t)^n$ where rs (here without the superscript) is the n-period spot rate, hence:

$$\ln P_t = \ln M - n \ln(1 + rs_t) \tag{9.1}$$

We can also express the price in terms of a continuously compounded rate (see Chapter 1) which is defined as $rc_t = \ln(1 + rs_t)$ hence:

$$\ln P_t = \ln M - n[rc_t]$$

or

$$P_t = M \exp(-rc_t \cdot n) \qquad (9.2)$$

In practice (discount) bills or pure discount bonds often do not exist at the long end of the maturity spectrum (e.g. over one year). However, spot yields at longer maturities can be *approximated* using data on coupon paying bonds (although the details need not concern us here, see McCulloch (1971) and (1990)).

If we have an n-period coupon paying bond and market determined spot rates exist for all maturities, then the market price of the bond is determined as:

$$P_t^{(n)} = \frac{C_{t+1}}{(1 + rs_t^{(1)})} + \frac{C_{t+2}}{(1 + rs_t^{(2)})^2} + \cdots + \frac{C_{t+n} + M_{t+n}}{(1 + rs_t^{(n)})^n} = \sum_{i=1}^{n} V_i \qquad (9.3)$$

where M = maturity (redemption) value and $V_i = C_{t+i}/(1 + rs_t^{(i)})^i$ for $i = 1, 2, \ldots n - 1$ and $V_n = (C_{t+n} + M_n)/(1 + rs_{t+n}^{(n)})^n$. The market price is the DPV of future coupons (and maturity value) where the discount rates are spot yields. If the above formula does not hold then riskless arbitrage profits can be made by 'coupon stripping'. To illustrate this point consider a two-period bond and assume its market price $P_t^{(2)}$ is less than $V_1 + V_2$. The current market price of two, *zero coupon* bonds with payouts of C_{t+1} and $(C_{t+2} + M_{t+2})$ will be V_1 and V_2, respectively. The coupon paying bond can be viewed as a set of zero coupon bonds. If $P_t^{(2)} < V_1 + V_2$ then one could purchase the two-year coupon bond and sell a claim on the 'coupon payments' in years 1 and 2, that is C_{t+1} and $(C_{t+2} + M_{t+2})$ to other market participants. If zero coupon bonds are correctly priced then these claims could be sold *today* for V_1 and V_2, respectively. Hence an instantaneous riskless profit of $(V_1 + V_2 - P_t^{(2)})$ can be made. In an efficient market, the increased demand for the two-year coupon paying bond would raise $P_t^{(2)}$, while sales of the coupons would depress prices of one and two-year zero coupon bonds. Hence this riskless arbitrage would lead to the restoration of the equality in (9.3).

Holding Period Yield (HPY) and the Rational Valuation Formula (RVF)

As with a stock, if one holds a coupon paying bond between t and $t + 1$ the return is made up of the capital gain plus any coupon payment. For bonds this measure of 'return' is known as the (one-period) *holding period yield* (HPY).

$$H_{t+1}^{(n)} = \frac{P_{t+1}^{(n-1)} - P_t^{(n)} + C_t}{P_t} \qquad (9.4)$$

Note that in the above formula the n-period bond becomes an $(n - 1)$ period bond after one period. (In empirical work on long-term bonds (e.g. with $n > 10$ years) researchers often use $P_{t+1}^{(n)}$ in place of $P_{t+1}^{(n-1)}$ since for data collected weekly, monthly or quarterly they are approximately the same.)

At any point in time there are bonds being traded which have different time periods to maturity or 'term to maturity'. For example, a bond which *when issued* had an original maturity of 20 years will after five years have a term to maturity of $n = 15$ years. The term to maturity of the bond is indicated by the superscript 'n' on the variables such as P and H only when this is required to avoid ambiguity. The definition of H_{t+1} in (9.17) is the *ex-post* (or actual) HPY. As investors at time t do not know P_{t+1} they will have to form *expectations* of P_{t+1} and hence of the expected HPY. (Note that future coupon payments are known and fixed at time t for all future time periods and are usually constant so that $C_t = C$).

Rational Valuation Formula (RVF) for Bonds

In our most general model for determining stock prices in Chapter 4 it was assumed the expected one-period return required by investors to willingly hold the stock might vary over time. The *required one-period* return (or HPY) on an n-period bond we denote k_t and hence for bonds we have:

$$E_t \left[\frac{P_{t+1}^{(n-1)} - P_t^{(n)} + C_{t+1}}{P_t^{(n)}} \right] = k_t \qquad (9.5)$$

This equation can be solved forward (as demonstrated in Chapter 4) to give the *current bond price* as the DPV of future known coupon payments discounted at the expected *one-period* spot returns k_{t+i}. For an n-period bond:

$$P_t^{(n)} = E_t \left[\sum_{j=1}^{n} \frac{C_{t+j}}{\prod_{i=0}^{j-1}(1 + k_{t+i})} + \frac{M}{\prod_{i=0}^{n-1}(1 + k_{t+i})} \right] \qquad (9.6)$$

where M = the redemption price and it is usually assumed that $C_{t+j} = C$ (a constant)[1]. Note that the only variable the investor has to form expectations about is his required one-period return k_{t+i} in (all) future periods. Also no transversality condition needs to be imposed since after iterating forward for n periods the expected price is equal to the known redemption value, M.

As with our analysis of stocks we can 'split' the per period required return k_t into a one-period risk-free (interest) rate r_t and a risk premium. However, when talking about the government bond market the risk premium on an n-period bond is frequently referred to as the *term premium*, $T_t^{(n)}$ Hence[2]:

$$k_{t+i} \equiv r_{t+i} + T_{t+i}^{(n)} \quad (i > 1) \qquad (9.7)$$

where r_{t+i} is the *one-period* rate applicable between $t + i$ and $t + i + 1$. Because government bonds carry little or no risk of default, the only 'risk' attached to such bonds in the eyes of the investor arises because they have different *terms* to maturity; hence the use of 'term premium'. One aspect of risk arises if the investor wishes to liquidate his holdings before the maturity date of the bond; the investor faces 'price uncertainty'. Alternatively, if the investor holds the bond to maturity there is no (nominal) price uncertainty but the rate at which future coupon payments can be reinvested is uncertain; this is referred to as 'reinvestment risk'. Note that (9.7) is an identity which is used to define the term premium and there is as yet no behavioural content in (9.7).

If a specific model for k_t is assumed then (9.6) can form the basis of a variance bounds test (similar to that derived for stock prices in Chapter 4). For example, if $k_{t+i} = r_{t+i} + \alpha$ (where α is some known constant) then we can calculate the perfect foresight price

$$P_t^* = \sum_{j=1}^n \left[C_{t+j} \bigg/ \prod_{i=0}^{j-1} (1 + k_{t+i}) \right] + M \bigg/ \prod_{i=0}^{n-1} (1 + k_{t+i}) \tag{9.8}$$

The variance bounds test is then $\text{var}(P_t) \leqslant \text{var}(P_t^*)$. We can also test the EMH (under this explicit assumption for k_{t+i}) by running the regression

$$(P_t - P_t^*) = a + bP_t + c\Omega_t + \varepsilon_t \tag{9.9}$$

where Ω_t is any information available at time t. Under the null of the EMH we have $a = b = c = 0$.

Strictly speaking one cannot have both (9.3) and (9.6) determining the price of the bond since there is only one quoted market price. Rather, equation (9.3) determines the price of the bond via riskless arbitrage. Equation (9.6) may then be viewed as determining a set of expected one-period returns that yield the same bond price given by (9.3). Investor preferences working via the supply and demand for bonds of different maturities will establish a set of equilibrium one-period rates k_{t+i}. Of course, when there does *not* exist a set of market determined spot rates for all maturities n then equation (9.6) may conceptually be viewed as determining bond prices. Since for $n > 2$ years, zero coupon bonds are usually not available, equation (9.6) can be used legitimately to examine the pricing of long-term bonds. The reason equations (9.3) and (9.6) give different expressions for the price of the bond is that they are based on different behavioural assumptions. In the derivation of (9.6) agents are only concerned with the sequence of one-period expected returns k_{t+i} whereas the bond pricing equation (9.3) involving spot rates rs_t is derived under the assumption of (instantaneous) riskless arbitrage[3].

Yield to Maturity/Redemption Yield

For coupon paying bonds the rate which is quoted in the market is the yield to maturity (YTM). Investors know the current market price of the bond P_t, the stream of (annual) coupon payments C, the redemption value of the bond ($= M$) and its maturity date n. Now *assume* that the coupon payments at different horizons are discounted using a *constant* discount rate $1/(1 + R_t^y)$. Note that R_t^y has a subscript t because it may vary over time (but it does not vary in each period in the DPV formula). If we now equate the DPV of the coupon payments with the current market price we have

$$P_t = \frac{C}{(1 + R_t^y)} + \frac{C}{(1 + R_t^y)^2} + \cdots + \frac{C + M}{(1 + R_t^y)^n} \tag{9.10}$$

The bond may be viewed as an investment for which a capital sum P_t is paid out today and the investment pays the known stream of dollar receipts (C and M) in the future. The *constant* value of R_t^y which *equates* the LHS and RHS of (9.10) is the 'internal rate of return' on this investment and when the investment is a bond R_t^y it is referred to as the *yield to maturity* or *redemption yield* on the (n-period) bond. Clearly one has to calculate R_t^y each time the market price changes and this is done in the financial press which generally report bond prices, coupons and yields to maturity. It is worth noting that the yield to maturity is *derived from* the market variables (P_t, C, M, n) and it does not *determine* the price in any economic sense. In fact, equation (9.3) using spot rates rs_{t+i} determines the bond price and the latter is then used by the financial community to calculate R_t^y using (9.9). The reason for quoting the YTM in the market is that it provides a 'single number' for each bond (whereas (9.3) involves a *sequence* of spot rates). The yield to maturity on an n-period bond and another bond with q periods to maturity will generally be different at any point in time, since each bond may have different coupon payments C and of course the latter will be discounted over different time periods (i.e. n and q). It is easy to see from (9.10) that bond prices and redemption yields move in opposite directions and that for any given change in the redemption yield R_t^y the percentage change in price of a long bond is greater than that for a short bond. Also, the yield to maturity formula (9.10) reduces to $P_t = C/R_t^y$ for a *perpetuity* (i.e. as $n \to \infty$).

Although redemption yields are widely quoted in the financial press they are a somewhat ambiguous measure of the 'return' on a bond. For example, two bonds that are identical except for their maturity dates will generally have different yields to maturity. Next, note that in the calculation of the yield to maturity, it is implicitly assumed that agents are able to reinvest the coupon payments at the *constant rate* R_t^y in all future periods over the life of the bond. To see this consider the yield to maturity for a two-period bond given by (9.10) rearranged to give:

$$(1 + R_t^y)^2 P_t = C(1 + R_t^y) + (C + M) \tag{9.11}$$

The LHS is the terminal value (in two years' time) of $\$P_t$ invested at the constant annualised rate R_t^y. The RHS consists of the amount $(C + M)$ paid at $t + 2$ and an amount $C(1 + R_t^y)$ which accrues at $t + 2$ after the first year's coupon payments have been reinvested at the rate R_t^y. Since (9.10) and (9.11) are equivalent, the DPV formula assumes that the first coupon payment is reinvested in year 2 at a rate R_t^y. However, there is little reason to argue that investors always believe that they will be able to reinvest *all* future coupon payments at the constant rate R_t^y. Note that the issue here is not that investors have to form a view of future reinvestment rates for their coupon payments but that they choose to assume, for example, that the reinvestment rate applicable on a 20-year bond, between years 9 and 10 say, will equal the *current* yield to maturity R_t^y on the 20-year bond.

There is another inconsistency in using the yield to maturity as a measure of the return on a coupon paying bond. Consider two bonds with different coupon payment streams $C_{t+i}^{(1)}, C_{t+i}^{(2)}$ but the same price, maturity date and maturity value. Using (9.10) this will imply two different yields to maturity R_{1t}^y and R_{2t}^y. If an investor holds both of these bonds in his portfolio and he believes equation (9.10) then he must be implicitly assuming that he can reinvest coupon payments for bond 1 between time $t + j$ and $t + j + 1$ at the rate R_{1t}^y and at the *different* rate R_{2t}^y for bond 2. But in reality the reinvestment rate between $t + j$ and $t + j + 1$ will be the same for both bonds and will equal the one-period spot rate applicable between these years.

In general, because of the above defects in the concept of the yield to maturity, *yield curves* based on this measure are usually difficult to interpret in an unambiguous fashion (see Schaefer (1977)). However, later in this chapter we see how the yield to maturity may be legitimately used in tests of the term structure relationship.

Duration

Despite its drawbacks, the yield to maturity is widely used in *duration matching* or *portfolio immunisation*. A financial institution can immunise its bond portfolio against changes in interest rates such that the change in the value of its assets equals the change in value of its liabilities. It is easiest to examine the concept of duration using the continuously compounded YTM, which we denote as y. Duration is a measure of the average time one has to wait to receive coupon payments. For a zero coupon bond that matures in n years the duration is also n years. However, a coupon paying bond maturing in n years has a duration less than n since some of the cash payments are received prior to n. Let us determine the price response of a coupon paying bond to a small change in the YTM. The price of the bond with coupons C_i (where C_n also includes the redemption price) is:

$$P = \sum_{i=1}^{n} C_i \exp(-yt_i) = \sum_{i=1}^{n} PV_i$$

where $PV_i = C_i \exp(-yt_i)$ is the present value of cash flows C_i. Differentiating with respect to y and dividing both sides by P:

$$\frac{dP}{P} = -\sum_{i=1}^{n} t_i \left[\frac{C_i \exp(-yt_i)}{P} \right] dy = -\Sigma t_i \left[\frac{PV_i}{P} \right] dy$$

If we now define duration D as:

$$D = \sum_{i=1}^{n} t_i [PV_i/P]$$

then $dP/P = -D\, dy$. From the definition of D we see that it is a time weighted average of the present value of payments (as a proportion of the price). If we know the duration of a bond then we can calculate the capital gain or loss consequent on a small change in the yield. The simplest case of immunisation is when one has a single *liability* of duration D_L. Here immunisation is most easily achieved by purchasing a single bond which also has a duration equal to D_L. However, one can also immunise against a single liability with duration D_L by purchasing two bonds with maturity D_1 and D_2 such that

$$\sum_{i=1}^{2} w_i D_i = D_L$$

and w_i are the proportions of total assets held in the two bonds

$$\left(\text{and } \sum_{i=1}^{2} w_i = 1 \right).$$

Clearly this principle may be generalised to bond portfolios of any size. There are limitations when using duration to immunise a portfolio of liabilities, the key ones being that the calculations only hold for small changes in yields and for parallel shifts in the (spot) yield curve. Also since D alters as the remaining 'life' of the bond(s) alters, the immunised portfolio must be continually rebalanced, so that the duration of assets and liabilities remains equal (for further details see Fabozzi (1993) and Schaefer (1977)).

Nominal Versus Real Values

So far we have discussed the RVF in terms of nominal variables. If the variables P and C are expressed in nominal terms then the required rate of return k_t depends on the *nominal* risk-free rate (e.g. rate of interest on Treasury bills).

The RVF can also be written in terms of real variables. In this case, the nominal bond price P_t and nominal coupon payments are deflated by a (nominal) goods price index so they are then measured in real terms. The required *real* rate of return which we denote k_t^* is determined by the real rate of interest (i.e. the nominal one-period rate less the expected one-period rate of inflation $E_t\pi_{t+1}$) and the term premium:

$$k_t^* = (r_t - E_t\pi_{t+1}) + T_t = E_t(rr_t) + T_t \tag{9.12}$$

where rr_t = real rate of interest (and is assumed to be independent of the rate of inflation). It should be fairly obvious that the nominal price of the bond is influenced to a large degree by forecasts of future inflation. Coupon payments are (usually) fixed in nominal terms, so if higher expected inflation is reflected in higher nominal discount rates, then the nominal price will fall (see equation (9.6)). More formally, this can be seen most easily by taking a typical term in (9.6), for example the term at $t + 2$ where we substitute $(1 + k_{t+i}) = (1 + k_{t+i}^*)(1 + \pi_{t+i})$

$$P_t = \cdots + E_t \left[\frac{C_{t+2}}{(1 + k_t^*)(1 + k_{t+1}^*)(1 + \pi_{t+1})(1 + \pi_{t+2})} \right] + \cdots \tag{9.13}$$

where k_t^* is the real rate of return (discount factor). Equation (9.13) can be rewritten:

$$P_t = \cdots + E_t \left[\frac{C/(1 + \pi_{t+1})(1 + \pi_{t+2})}{(1 + k_t^*)(1 + k_{t+1}^*)} \right] + \cdots \tag{9.14}$$

Hence for constant real discount factors k_{t+i}^* the nominal bond price depends negatively on the expected future one-period rates of inflation over the remaining life of the bond.

Let us now demonstrate that the *real* bond price is independent of the rate of inflation, as one might expect. If we define the real coupon payment at $t + 2$ as $C_{t+2}^* = C_{t+2}/I_{t+2}$ where I_{t+2} is the goods price index at $t + 2$, and note that $I_{t+2} = (1 + \pi_{t+1})(1 + \pi_{t+2})I_t$, then from (9.14) the *real* bond price has a typical term:

$$P_t/I_t = \cdots + E_t \left[\frac{C_{t+2}^*}{(1 + k_t^*)(1 + k_{t+1}^*)} \right] + \cdots \tag{9.15}$$

Hence as one would expect, the real bond price depends only on real variables. Note that if the variables are all measured in real terms or all in nominal terms, the term premium is invariant to this transformation of the data.

9.2 THEORIES OF THE TERM STRUCTURE

We now examine various theories of the term structure based on different assumptions made about the required rate of return k_t. These are summarised in Table 9.1. We begin with theories of the term structure based on the one-period HPY as a measure of the return on the bond. In subsequent sections we then consider how these same theories can be implemented using spot yields and the yield to maturity[4]. Our aim is to formulate

Table 9.1 Theories of the Term Structure: A Summary

---

1. Pure Expectations Hypothesis (PEH)
    (i) Expected excess return is zero
or (ii) The term premium is zero for all maturities

$$E_t H_{t+1}^{(n)} - r_t = 0 \qquad R_t^{(n)} - E_t(r_{t+j}'s) = 0$$

2. Expectations Hypothesis or Constant Term Premium
    (i) Expected excess return equals a constant which is the same for all maturities
or (ii) The term premium 'T' is a constant and the same for all maturities

$$E_t H_{t+1}^{(n)} - r_t = T \qquad R_t^{(n)} - E_t(r_{t+j}'s) = T$$

3. Liquidity Preference Hypothesis
    (i) Expected excess return on a bond of maturity n is a constant but the value of the constant is larger the longer the period to maturity
or (ii) The term premium increases with n, the time period to maturity

$$E_t H_{t+1}^{(n)} - r_t = T^{(n)} \qquad R_t^{(n)} - E_t(r_{t+j}'s) = T^{(n)}$$

where $T^{(n)} > T^{(n-1)} \ldots$, etc.

4. Time Varying Risk
    (i) Expected excess return on a bond of maturity n varies both with n and over time
    (ii) The term premium depends on the maturity n and varies over time

$$E_t H_{t+1}^{(n)} - r_t = T(n, z_t) \qquad R_t^{(n)} - E_t(r_{t+j}'s) = T(n, z_t)$$

where $T(\cdot)$ is some function of n and a set of variables z_t.

5. Market Segmentation Hypothesis
    (i) Excess returns are influenced at least in part by the outstanding stock of assets of different maturities
    (ii) The term premium depends in part on the outstanding stock of assets of different maturities

$$E_t H_{t+1}^{(n)} - r_t = T(z_t^{(n)}) \qquad R_t^{(n)} - E_t(r_{t+j}'s) = T(z_t^{(n)})$$

where $z_t^{(n)}$ is some measure of the *relative* holdings of assets of maturity 'n' as a proportion of total assets held.

6. Preferred Habitat Theory
    (i) Bonds which mature at dates which are close together should be reasonably close substitutes and hence have similar term premia

---

clearly the tests implied by the various hypotheses: actual empirical results are discussed in the next chapter and more advanced tests in Chapter 14.

Using the HPY

The theories based on the HPY include the expectations hypothesis, the liquidity preference hypothesis, market segmentation and the preferred habitat hypothesis. They differ only in their treatment of the term premium. Each will be dealt with in turn.

The Expectations Hypothesis

If all agents are risk neutral and concerned only with expected return then the expected one-period HPY (over say one month, or one quarter) on all bonds, no matter what their maturity, would be equalised and would be equal to the known (safe) return r_t on a one-period asset (e.g. one-month Treasury bill).

$$E_t H_{t+1}^{(n)} = r_t \quad \text{(for all } n) \tag{9.16}$$

This is the pure expectations hypothesis (PEH). The term premium T is zero for all maturities and the discount factor in the RVF (9.6) is simply $k_{t+i} = r_{t+i}$, the sequence of one-period risk-free rates. All agents at the margin are 'plungers'. For example, suppose a bond with three years to maturity has a HPY in excess of that on a bond with two years' maturity. Agents would sell the two-year bond and purchase the three-year bond thus pushing up the *current* price of the three-year bond and reducing its one-period HPY. The opposite would occur for the two-period bond and hence all holding period returns would be equalised. To (9.16) we now add the assumption of rational expectations; $H_{t+1}^{(n)} = E_t H_{t+1}^{(n)} + \eta_{t+1}^{(n)}$, where $E_t(\eta_{t+1}^{(n)}|\Omega_t) = 0$ and $\eta_{t+1}^{(n)}$ is the (one-period) rational expectations forecast error:

$$H_{t+1}^{(n)} - r_t = \eta_{t+1}^{(n)} \quad \text{(for all n)} \tag{9.17}$$

Hence a test of the PEH + RE is that the *ex-post excess* holding period yield should have a zero mean, be independent of all information at time $t(\Omega_t)$ and should be serially uncorrelated.

It seems reasonable to assert that because the return on holding a long bond (for one period) is uncertain (because its price at the end of the period is uncertain), that the excess holding period yield ought to depend on some form of 'reward for risk' or term premium $T_t^{(n)}$.

$$E_t H_{t+1}^{(n)} = r_t + T_t^{(n)} \tag{9.18}$$

Without a model of the term premium, equation (9.18) is a tautology. The simplest (non-trivial) assumption to make about the term premium is that it is (i) constant over time and (ii) that it is also independent of the term to maturity of the bond (i.e. $T_t^n = T$). This constitutes the *expectations hypothesis* (EH) (Table 9.1). Obviously this yields similar predictions as the PEH, namely no serial correlation in excess yields and that the latter should be independent of Ω_t. Note that the excess yield is now equal to the constant term premium T and the discount factor in the RVF is $k_t = r_t + T$.

Under RE and a *time invariant* term premium we obtain (see (9.18) with $T_t^{(n)} = T^{(n)}$) the following variance inequality.

$$\text{var}[H_{t+1}^{(n)}] \geqslant \text{var}(r_t) \tag{9.19}$$

Thus the variance of the HPY on an n period bond should be greater than or equal to the variance of the one-period safe rate such as the interest rate on Treasury bills.

Liquidity Preference Hypothesis (LPH)

Here, the assumption is that the term premium does not vary over time but it does depend on the term to maturity of the bond (i.e. $T_t^{(n)} = T^{(n)}$). For example, bonds with longer periods to maturity may be viewed as being more 'risky' than those with a short period to maturity, even though we are considering a fixed holding period for both bonds. This might arise because the price change is larger for any given change in the yield, for bonds with longer maturities. Consider the case where the one-month HPY on 20-year bonds is more *volatile* than that on 10-year bonds. Here one might require a higher expected return on the 20-year bond in order that it is willingly held in the portfolio, alongside the 10-year bond. If this difference in volatility depends only on the difference in the term to maturity then this could give rise to a liquidity premium which depends only on n.

The liquidity preference hypothesis asserts that the excess yield is a constant for any given maturity but for those bonds which have a longer period to maturity, the term premium will increase. That is to say the expected excess HPY on a 10-year bond would exceed the expected excess HPY on a 5-year bond but this gap would remain constant over time. Thus, for example, 10-year bonds might have *expected* excess returns 1 percent above those on 5-year bonds, for all time periods. Of course, in the data, *actual* 10-year excess returns will vary randomly around their expected HPY because of (zero mean) forecast errors in each time period. Under the liquidity preference hypothesis we have $k_t = r_t + T^{(n)}$ as the discount factor in the RVF and expected excess HPYs are given by:

$$E_t H_{t+1}^{(n)} - r_t = T^{(n)} \qquad T^{(n)} > T^{(n-1)} > \ldots \qquad (9.20)$$

Under rational expectations, the liquidity preference hypothesis predicts that excess HPYs are serially uncorrelated and independent of information at time t. Thus, apart from a fairly innocuous constant term, the main testable implications using regressions analysis of the PEH, EH and the LPH are identical. For the PEH we have a zero constant term for the EH, we have $T = $ constant and for the LPH we have a different constant for each bond of maturity n, as in (9.20).

Time Varying Risk

If the risk or term premium varies over time and varies differently for bonds of different maturities then

$$k_t = r_t + T(n, z_t) \qquad (9.21)$$

where z_t is a set of variables that influences investors' perceptions of risk. This is our most general model so far, but unless one specifies an explicit form of the function T, our model of expected excess HPYs is non-operational. Below is an illustration of how the CAPM provides a model of the term premium, and Chapter 19 examines the behaviour of HPYs on bonds when the term premium is assumed to depend on *time varying* variances and covariances.

CAPM and HPY

An obvious theoretical approach to explain the excess HPY on bonds and to provide an explicit form for the risk premium are the CAPM-type models which we have already discussed when examining stock returns. Thus, for those who are familiar with portfolio theory, it should not come as a surprise that the term premium may vary both for different maturities and over time. The CAPM predicts that the expected holding period return on *any* asset, which of course includes an n period bond, is given by

$$E_t H_{t+1}^{(n)} = r_t + \beta_t^{(n)} [E_t R_{t+1}^m - r_t] \qquad (9.22a)$$

where

$$\beta_t^{(n)} = \text{cov}[H_{t+1}^{(n)}, R_{t+1}^m]/\sigma_{mt+1}^2 \qquad (9.22b)$$

and $E_t R^m_{t+1}$ is the expected return on the market portfolio. Comparing equations (9.18) and (9.22) we see that the CAPM would predict that the term premium is given by the second term in equation (9.22a). There is absolutely no reason to believe that either the excess return on the market portfolio or the beta for a bond of maturity 'n' will remain constant over time and in general one might therefore expect time variation in the term premium.

According to Merton's (1973) model, the excess return on the *market* portfolio is proportional to the conditional variance of the forecast errors on the market portfolio

$$E_t R^m_{t+1} - r_t = \lambda(E_t \sigma^2_{mt+1}) \tag{9.23}$$

Combining equations (9.22) and (9.23):

$$E_t H^{(n)}_{t+1} - r_t = \lambda E_t \, \text{cov}(H^{(n)}_{t+1}, R^m_{t+1}) \tag{9.24}$$

Hence the excess HPY depends upon the *covariance* between the holding period return on the bond and the return on the market portfolio. It is possible that this covariance is time varying and that it may be serially correlated, implying serial correlation in the excess HPY. Notice that the CAPM version of the determination of term premia does not imply that expected holding period returns on 10-year bonds should necessarily be higher than those on 5-year bonds. To take an extreme (non-general equilibrium) example, suppose 10-year bonds have a negative covariance with the market portfolio, while 5-year bonds have a zero or positive covariance, then the CAPM implies that expected excess HPYs on 10-year bonds should be below those on 5-year bonds.

The standard one-period CAPM model assumes the existence of a risk-free asset. Black (1972) developed the zero-beta CAPM to cover the case where there is no risk-free asset and this results in the following equation:

$$E_t H^{(n)}_{t+1} = [1 - \beta^{(n)}]E_t R^z_{t+1} + \beta^{(n)} ER^m_{t+1} \tag{9.25}$$

Here the expected HPY on the n period bond equals a weighted average of the expected return on the market portfolio and the so-called 'zero-beta portfolio'. A zero-beta portfolio is one which has zero covariance with the market portfolio. The next chapter examines empirical results from the CAPM applied to bonds under the assumption of a constant beta, but empirical results from CAPM models which incorporate time variation in the betas of bonds of different maturities are not discussed until Chapter 17.

The above taxonomy of models might at first sight seem rather bewildering but in the main all we are doing is repeating the analysis of valuation models that we applied to stocks in Chapters 4 and 6. We have gradually relaxed the restrictive assumptions on the return required by investors to hold bonds (i.e. k_t) and naturally as we do so the models become more general (see Table 9.1) but also more difficult to implement empirically. Indeed, Table 9.1 contains two further hypotheses which will be dealt with briefly.

Market Segmentation Hypothesis

The market segmentation hypothesis may be viewed as a reduced form or market equilibrium solution of a set of standard asset demand equations. To simplify, suppose we have only two risky assets (i.e. bonds B_1 and B_2) and the proportion of wealth held in B_1 and B_2 is given by their respective demand functions

$$(B_1/W)^d = f_1(H^e_1 - r, H^e_2 - r) \tag{9.26a}$$

$$(B_2/W)^d = f_2(H_1^e - r, H_2^e - r) \tag{9.26b}$$

where r = the safe return on Treasury bills and H_i^e are the expected holding period yields on bonds. The demand function for TB is given as a residual from the budget constraint

$$(TB/W) = 1 - (B_1 + B_2)/W \tag{9.27}$$

and need not concern us. If we now assume that the supply of B_1 and B_2 is exogenous then market equilibrium rates of return, given by solving (9.26), result in equations of the form

$$H_1^e - r = G_1[B_1/W, B_2/W] \tag{9.28a}$$

$$H_2^e - r = G_2[B_1/W, B_2/W] \tag{9.28b}$$

Hence the expected excess HPYs on the two bonds of different maturities depend on the proportion of wealth held in each of these assets. This is the basis of the market segmentation hypothesis of the determination of excess HPYs.

Tests of the market segmentation hypothesis based on (9.28) are often a gross oversimplification of the rather complex asset demand functions usually found in the empirical literature in this area. In general, the demand functions (9.26) contain many more independent variables than holding period yields; for example, the variance of returns, real wealth, price inflation and their lagged values and lags of the dependent variable often appear as independent variables (see Cuthbertson (1991)). Hence the reduced form equilibrium equations (9.28) should also include these variables. However, tests of market segmentation hypothesis usually only include the proportion of debt held in bonds of maturity 'n' in the equation to explain excess holding period yields.

Preferred Habitat Hypothesis

The preferred habitat theory is, in effect, agnostic about the determinants of the term premium. It suggests that we should only compare 'returns' on government bonds of similar maturities and one might then expect excess holding period yields to move closely together.

9.2.1 Theories Using Spot Yields

The term structure of interest rates deals with the relationship between the yields on bonds of different maturities. The yields in question are *spot yields* and therefore conceptually, the analysis applies to pure discount bonds or zero coupon bonds. Pure discount government bonds for long maturities do not exist, nevertheless as we noted earlier, spot yields can be derived from a set of coupon paying bonds (McCulloch, 1990). Another measure of the return on a bond is the *yield to maturity* and our analysis of the term structure in terms of spot yields can be applied with minor modification (and an element of approximation) to yields to maturity.

For the moment we proceed as follows. First, we examine how the term structure relationship can be derived from a model of expected one-period HPYs and this 'mirrors' our derivation of the RVF for stock prices in Chapter 4, since it involves a forward difference equation in one-period rates. This derivation requires the use of continuously compounded rates. We then examine the economic behaviour behind the term structure before demonstrating how it may be rewritten in a number of equivalent ways.

The relationship between the (continuously compounded) rate for maturity n, $R_t^{(n)}$ and a sequence of one-period (continuously compounded) rates r_{t+i} can be derived by considering a model[5] where the (continuously compounded) expected HPY equals the risk-free one-period rate plus a risk premium.

$$E_t h_{t+1}^{(n)} \equiv E_t[\ln P_{t+1}^{(n-1)} - \ln P_t^{(n)}] = r_t + T_t^{(n)} \tag{9.29}$$

Equation (9.29), although based on the HPY, leads to a term structure relationship in terms of spot yields. For continuously compounded rates we have $\ln P_t^{(n)} = \ln M - n R_t^{(n)}$ and substituting in (9.29) this gives the forward difference equation:

$$n R_t^{(n)} = (n-1) E_t R_{t+1}^{(n-1)} + r_t + T_t^{(n)} \tag{9.30}$$

Leading (9.30) one period:

$$(n-1) R_{t+1}^{(n-1)} = (n-2) E_{t+1} R_{t+2}^{(n-2)} + r_{t+1} + T_{t+1}^{(n-1)} \tag{9.31}$$

Taking expectations of (9.31) using $E_t E_{t+1} = E_t$ and substituting in (9.30)

$$n R_t^{(n)} = (n-2) E_t R_{t+2}^{(n-2)} + E_t(r_{t+1} + r_t) + E_t(T_{t+1}^{(n-1)} + T_t^{(n)}) \tag{9.32}$$

Continually substituting for the first term on the RHS of (9.32) and noting that $(n-j) E_t R_{t+j}^{(n-j)} = 0$ for $j = n$ we obtain:

$$R_t^{(n)} = E_t R_t^{*(n)} + \Phi_t^{(n)} \tag{9.33}$$

where

$$R_t^{*(n)} = (1/n) \sum_{i=0}^{n-1} r_{t+i} \tag{9.34a}$$

$$\Phi_t^{(n)} = (1/n) \sum_{i=1}^{n-1} T_{t+i}^{(n-i)} \tag{9.34b}$$

Hence the n-period long rate equals a weighted average of expected future short rates r_{t+i} plus the average risk premium on the n-period bond until it matures, $\Phi_t^{(n)}$. The variable $R_t^{*(n)}$ is referred to as the *perfect foresight rate* since it is a weighted average of the outturn values for the one-period short rates, r_{t+i}. Subtracting r_t from both sides of (9.34) we obtain an equivalent expression:

$$S_t^{(n,1)} = E_t S_t^{*(n,1)} + E_t \Phi_t^{(n)} \tag{9.35}$$

where

$$S_t^{(n,1)} = R_t^{(n)} - r_t \tag{9.36a}$$

$$E_t S_t^{*(n,1)} = \sum_{i=1}^{n-1} (1 - i/n) E_t \Delta r_{t+i} \tag{9.36b}$$

Equation (9.35) states that the actual spread $S_t^{(n,1)}$ between the n-period and one-period rate, equals a weighted average of expected *changes* in short rates plus a term premium.

The variable $S_t^{*(n,1)}$ is known as the perfect foresight *spread*. As we shall see in Chapter 14, the variables in (9.35), namely $R_t^{(n)}$ and r_{t+i}, are usually found to be non-stationary whereas Δr_{t+i} and $S_t^{(n,1)}$ are found to be stationary $I(0)$ variables. Hence econometric tests on (9.35) can be based on standard distributions (whereas those on (9.33) cannot). Equations (9.33) and (9.35) are general expressions for the term structure relationship but they are non-operational unless we assume a specific form for the term premium.

The PEH applied to spot yields assumes investors are risk neutral, that is, they are indifferent to risk and base their investment decision only on *expected* returns. The inherent variability or uncertainty concerning returns is of no consequence to their investment decisions. In terms of equations (9.33) and (9.35) the PEH implies $\Phi^{(n)} = 0$ for all n. We can impart some economic intuition into the derivation of (9.33) when we assume a zero term premium. To demonstrate this point we revert to using per-period rates rather than continuously compounded rates, but we retain the same notation so that $R_t^{(n)}$ and r_t are now per-period rates.

Consider investing A in a (zero coupon) bond with n years to maturity. The terminal value (TV) of the investment is:

$$TV_n = \$A(1 + R_t^{(n)})^n \tag{9.37}$$

where $R_t^{(n)}$ is the (compound) rate on the n-period long bond (expressed at an annual rate). Next consider the alternative strategy of reinvesting $A and any interest earned, in a series of 'rolled-over' *one-period* investments, for n years. Ignoring transactions costs the *expected* terminal value $E_t(TV)$ of this series of one-period investments is:

$$E_t(TV) = \$A(1 + r_t)(1 + E_t r_{t+1})(1 + E_t r_{t+2})\ldots(1 + E_t r_{t+n-1}) \tag{9.38}$$

where r_{t+i} is the rate applicable between periods $t + i$ and $t + i + 1$. The investment in the long bond gives a known terminal value since this bond is held to maturity. Investing in a series of one-year investments gives a terminal value which is subject to uncertainty, since the investor must guess the future values of the one-period spot yields, r_{t+j}. However, under the PEH risk is ignored and hence the terminal values of the above two alternative investment strategies will be equalised:

$$(1 + R_t^{(n)})^n = (1 + r_t)(1 + E_t r_{t+1})(1 + E_t r_{t+2})\ldots(1 + E_t r_{t+n-1}) \tag{9.39}$$

The equality holds because if the terminal value corresponding to investment in the long bond exceeds the *expected* terminal value of that on the sequence of one-year investments, then investors would at time t buy long bonds and sell the short bond. This would result in a rise in the current market price of the long bond and given a fixed maturity value, a fall in the long (spot) yield R_t. Simultaneously, sales of the short bond would cause a fall in its current price and a rise in r_t. Hence the equality in (9.39) would be quickly (instantaneously) restored.

We could *define* the expected 'excess' or 'abnormal' profit on a $1 investment in the long bond over the sequence of rolled-over short investments as:

$$E_t(AP_t) \equiv R_t^{(n)} - E_t(r'_{t+j}) \tag{9.40}$$

where $E_t(r'_{t+j})$ represents the RHS of (9.39). The PEH applied to *spot yields*, therefore, implies that the *expected* excess or abnormal profit is zero. We can go through the whole taxonomy of models in terms of $E_t(AP_t)$ in the same way as we did for holding period yields. These are summarised in Table 9.1 and need no further comment here.

Taking logarithms of (9.39) and using the approximation $\ln(1 + z) \approx z$ for $|z| < 1$ we obtain the approximate linear relationship

$$R_t^{(n)} = (1/n)[r_t + E_t r_{t+1} + E_t r_{t+2} + \cdots E_t r_{t+2}] \tag{9.41}$$

In general when testing the PEH one should use continuously compounded spot rates since then there is no linearisation approximation involved in (9.41)[6].

The PEH forms the basis for an analysis of the (spot) yield curve. For example, viewed from time t, if short rates are expected to rise (i.e. $E_t r_{t+j} > E_t r_{t+j-1}$) for all j) then from (9.41) the long rate $R_t^{(n)}$ will be above the current short rate r_t. The yield curve — a graph of $R_t^{(n)}$ against time to maturity — will be upward sloping since $R_t^{(n)} > R_t^{(n-1)} > \ldots r_t$. Since expected future short rates are influenced by expectations of inflation (Fisher effect) the yield curve is likely to be upward sloping when inflation is expected to increase in future years. If there is a liquidity premium that depends only on the term to maturity n, and $T^{(n)} > T^{(n-1)} > \ldots$, then the basic qualitative shape of the yield curve will remain as described above. However, if the term premium varies other than with 'n', for example varies over time, then the direct link between $R_t^{(n)}$ and the sequence of future short rates in broken.

PEH: Tests Using Different Maturities

Early tests were based on equation (9.41) and include variance bounds and regression-based tests. So far, we have analysed the expectations hypothesis only in terms of the n-period spot rate $R_t^{(n)}$ and a sequence of *one-period* short rates. However, the hypothesis can also be expressed in terms of the relationship between $R_t^{(n)}$ and *any* m-period rate $R_t^{(m)}$ (for which $s = n/m$ is an integer):

$$R_t^{(n)} = (1/s) \sum_{i=0}^{s-1} E_t R_{t+im}^{(m)} \tag{9.42}$$

Two rearrangements of (9.42) can be shown to imply that the spread $S_t^{(n,m)} = (R_t^{(n)} - R_t^{(m)})$ is an optimal predictor of future changes in *long* rates and the spread is an optimal predictor of (a weighted average of) future changes in *short* rates. We consider each of these in turn using convenient values of (n, m) for expositional purposes.

Spread Predicts Changes in Long Rates

Consider equation (9.42) for $n = 6$, $m = 2$:

$$R_t^{(6)} = (1/3)[E_t(R_t^{(2)} + R_{t+2}^{(2)} + R_{t+4}^{(2)})] \tag{9.43}$$

this may be shown to be equivalent to[7]

$$E_t R_{t+2}^{(4)} - R_t^{(6)} = (1/2)S_t^{(6,2)} \tag{9.44}$$

Hence if $R_t^{(6)} > R_t^{(2)}$ then the PEH predicts that, on average, this should be followed by a rise in the long rate between t and $t + 2$. The intuition behind this result can be seen by noting that (9.44) is just a rearrangement of the relationship that the expected HPY on a six-period bond, between t and $t+2$, should equal the known risk-free return on the two-period bond[8]. Equation (9.44) under RE suggests a regression test of the expectations hypothesis.

$$R_{t+2}^{(4)} - R_t^{(6)} = \alpha + \beta[S_t^{(6,2)}/2] + \eta_{t+2} \tag{9.45}$$

where we expect $\beta = 1$. Under RE, $S_t^{(6,2)}$ is independent of η_{t+1} and therefore OLS on (9.45) yields consistent estimates (although a GMM correction to the standard errors is required if there is heteroscedasticity in the error term, or if η_{t+2} is serially correlated due to the use of overlapping observations). For any (n, m), equation (9.44) can be shown to be:

$$E_t R_{t+m}^{(n-m)} - R_t^{(n)} = [m/(n-m)]S_t^{(n,m)} \tag{9.46}$$

The Spread Predicts Future Changes in Short Rates

Equation (9.43) may be rearranged to give[9]

$$E_t S_t^{(6,2)^*} = S_t^{(6,2)} \tag{9.47a}$$

where

$$S_t^{(6,2)^*} = (2/3)\Delta^2 R_{t+2}^{(2)} + (1/3)\Delta^2 R_{t+4}^{(2)} \tag{9.47b}$$

and $\Delta^m Z_t = Z_t - Z_{t-m}$. The term $S_t^{(6,2)^*}$ is the perfect foresight spread. Equation (9.47) implies that the actual spread $S_t^{(6,2)}$ is an optimal (best) predictor of a weighted average of future *two-period* changes in the short rate $R_t^{(2)}$. Hence if $S_t^{(6,2)} > 0$ then agents expect on average that future (two-period) short rates should rise. Note that although $S_t^{(6,2)}$ is an optimal predictor this does not necessarily imply that it forecasts the RHS of (9.47b) accurately. If there is substantial 'news', between periods t and $t+4$, then $S_t^{(6,2)}$ may be a rather poor predictor. However, it is optimal in the sense that, under the expectations hypothesis, no variable other than S_t can improve one's forecast of future changes in short rates. The fact that S_t is an optimal predictor will be used in Chapter 14 when we examine the VAR methodology. The generalisation of (9.47) is

$$E_t S_t^{(n,m)^*} = S_t^{(n,m)} \tag{9.48a}$$

where

$$S_t^{(n,m)^*} = \sum_{i=1}^{s-1} (1 - i/s)\Delta^{(m)} R_{t+im}^{(m)} \tag{9.48b}$$

and equation (9.48) suggests a straightforward regression-based test of the expectations hypothesis (under RE) based on:

$$S_t^{(n,m)^*} = \alpha + \beta S_t^{(n,m)} + \omega_t \tag{9.49}$$

Under the EH we expect $\beta = 1$ and if the term premium is zero $\alpha = 0$. Since $S_t^{(n,m)}$ is (by RE) independent of information at time t, then OLS yields unbiased estimates of the parameters (but GMM estimates of the covariance matrix may be required — see above). Note, however, that if the term premium is time varying and correlated with the spread then the parameter estimates in (9.49) will be biased.

Even if long and short rates are non-stationary then the variables in (9.46) and (9.48) are likely to be stationary. Hence standard distributions can be used in testing and this is a decided statistical 'plus' for these formulations. It is perhaps worth bearing in mind that for $n = 2m$ (e.g. six-month and three-month bonds) the two regressions (9.46) and (9.48) are equivalent. Also if (9.46) holds *for all* (n, m) then so will (9.48). However, if (9.46) is rejected for some subset of values of (n, m) then equation (9.48) doesn't necessarily hold and hence it provides independent information on the validity of the PEH.

In early empirical work the above two formulations were mainly undertaken for $n = 2m$, in fact usually for three- and six-month pure discount bonds (e.g. Treasury bills) on which data are readily available. Hence the two regressions are statistically equivalent. Results from equations (9.46) and (9.48) are, however, available for other maturities (i.e. $n \neq 2m$) and some of these tests are reported in the next chapter.

Variance Bounds Tests on Spot Yields

Shiller (1988) uses an equation similar to (9.33) to perform a very simple volatility test for the expectations hypothesis. In the extreme case where agents have *perfect foresight* then future expected short rates would equal their *ex-post* outturn values. If we *define* the *perfect foresight long rate* as:

$$R_t^* = \frac{1}{n}[r_t + r_{t+1} + r_{t+2} + r_{t+n-1}] \tag{9.50}$$

then under the PEH equation (9.33) and RE (i.e. $r_{t+i} = E_t r_{t+i} + \eta_{t+i}$) we have

$$R_t^* = R_t + \omega_t \tag{9.51}$$

where

$$\omega_t = (1/n) \sum_{i=1}^{n-1} \eta_{t+i}$$

and $E(\eta_{t+1}|\Omega_t) = 0$. Using past data we can construct the perfect foresight long rate for each year of any sample of data. Under RE, agents' forecasts are unbiased and hence the *sum* of the forecast errors ω_t should be close to zero, for large n. Hence for long-term bonds we expect the perfect foresight rate R_t^* to track the broad swings in the *actual* long rate R_t and as we shall see in the next chapter Shiller's evidence on US data is consistent with this hypothesis.

Clearly, as we found for stock prices, a more sophisticated method of testing for excess volatility is available. Under the RE the forecast error ω_t is independent of Ω_t and hence it is independent of R_t. Hence from (9.51) we have:

$$\text{var}[R_t^*] \geqslant \text{var}[R_t] \tag{9.52}$$

since by RE, $\text{cov}(R_t, \omega_t) = 0$ and $\text{var}(\omega_t) \geqslant 0$. These inequalities also apply if we assume a constant term premium $T_t^{(n)} = T^{(n)}$. Thus, if (i) the expectations or liquidity preference hypothesis (as applied to spot yields) is correct, (ii) agents have RE, (iii) the term premium depends only on n (i.e. is time invariant), then the variance of the actual long rate should be less than the variability in the perfect foresight long rate.

It is also the case that the expected (abnormal) profit should be independent of information at time t. In this linear framework the expected abnormal profit is given by $R_t - E_t R_t^*$.

Under RE, in the regression

$$R_t^* = a + bR_t + c\Omega_t + \varepsilon_t \tag{9.53}$$

we expect $c = 0$. (This is analogous to regression tests on using P_t and P_t^* in the stock market.) If interest rates are non-stationary $I(1)$ variables then the unconditional population variances in (9.52) are undefined but the variance bound inequality can be expressed in terms of the variables in (9.48) which are likely to be stationary. Hence we have

$$\mathrm{var}(S_t^*) \geqslant \mathrm{var}(S_t) \tag{9.54}$$

and in a regression context we have

$$S_t^* = a + bS_t + c\Omega_t + \varepsilon_t \tag{9.55}$$

where we expect $b = 1$, $c = 0$ if the expectations hypothesis is true.

9.2.2 Using the Yield to Maturity

The tests described above are based on spot yields for pure discount (zero coupon) bonds either expressed as continuously compounded rates or as per-period rates. As we have already noted the calculation of (approximate) spot yields from published data on *yields to maturity* is often not undertaken. There is generally much more published data on yields to maturity so it would be useful if our tests of the term structure could be recast in terms of the yield to maturity. In a pioneering article this has been done by Shiller (1979) and the results are summarised below.

The basis of Shiller's approximations can be presented heuristically as follows. The price of an n-period coupon paying bond is a *non-linear* function of the yield to maturity (equation (9.10)) and therefore so is the holding period yield $H_{t+1}^{(n)}$.

$$H_{t+1}^{(n)} = f(R_{t+1}^{(n-1)}, R_t^{(n)}, C) \tag{9.56}$$

where $R_t^{(n)}$ is the *yield to maturity* (i.e. the superscript 'y' is dropped) and $f(\cdot)$ is a non-linear function. Shiller linearises (9.56) around the point

$$R_t^{(n)} = R_{t+1}^{(n-1)} = \bar{R} = C \tag{9.57}$$

where $\bar{R}$ is the mean value of the yield to maturity. For bonds selling at or near par (redemption) value this gives an *approximate* expression for the holding period yield denoted $\tilde{H}_t^{(n)}$ where

$$\tilde{H}_t^{(n)} = \frac{R_t^{(n)} - \gamma_n R_{t+1}^{(n-1)}}{(1 - \gamma_n)} \tag{9.58}$$

where

$$\gamma_n = \gamma(1 - \gamma^{n-1})/(1 - \gamma^n) \text{ and}$$
$$\gamma = 1/(1 + \bar{R})$$

Equation (9.58) is an (approximate) identity which defines the HPY in terms of the yield to maturity. We now add the economic hypothesis that the excess holding period yield equals the one-period rate plus a time invariant term premium (Shiller uses the symbol Φ_n for $T^{(n)}$).

$$E_t \tilde{H}_t^{(n)} = r_t + \phi_n \tag{9.59}$$

From (9.58) and (9.59) we obtain a forward recursive equation for $R_t^{(n)}$ which when solved with terminal condition $R_{t+n-1}^{(1)} = r_{t+n-1}$, where r_t is the one-period spot rate, gives Shiller's approximation formula for the term structure in terms of the yield to maturity:

$$R_t^{(n)} = \frac{1 - \gamma}{(1 - \gamma^n)} \sum_{k=0}^{n-1} \gamma^k E_t r_{t+k} + \Phi_n \tag{9.60}$$

$$= E_t(R_t^*) + \Phi_n \tag{9.61}$$

where $\Phi_n = f(\gamma, \gamma^n, \phi^n)$ and R_t^* is the perfect foresight long rate. Hence the yield to maturity on a coupon bond is equal to a weighted average of expected future short rates r_{t+k} where the weights decline geometrically (i.e. $\gamma^k < \gamma^{k-1} < \ldots$). The term Φ_n is constant for any bond of maturity n and may be interpreted as the average of the one-period term premia, over the life of the long bond. For the expectations hypothesis $\Phi_n = \Phi$ for all n and for the pure expectations hypothesis $\Phi = 0$. However, in testing alternative theories of the term structure the precise form for any *constant* term premium is of minor significance and the term premium only plays a key role when we assume it is time varying (see Chapter 17).

The RHS of (9.60) with $E_t r_{t+k}$ replaced by actual *ex-post* values r_{t+k} is the perfect foresight long rate (yield to maturity) $R_t^{(n)*}$ and the usual variance bounds tests and regression tests of $R_t^{(n)}$ on $R_t^{(n)*}$ may be examined. Shiller (1979) also shows that when using the approximation for the holding period yield $\tilde{H}_t^{(n)}$, the variance bounds test is:

$$\operatorname{var} \tilde{H}_t^{(n)} \leqslant a^2 \operatorname{var}(r_t) \tag{9.62a}$$

where $a = (1 - \gamma^2)^{-1/2}$. Note that for $\bar{R} = 0.064$ then $\gamma = 0.94$ and $a^2 = 8.6$, so that the variance of $\tilde{H}_{t+1}^{(n)}$ can exceed that of the short rate. Equation (9.62a) puts an upper bound on $\operatorname{var} \tilde{H}_{t+1}^{(n)}$ (whereas (9.19) imposes a lower bound). If r_t is non-stationary $I(1)$, then $\operatorname{var}(r_t)$ is undefined but in this case Shiller (1989) provides an equivalent expression in terms of the stationary series Δr_t, namely:

$$\operatorname{var}(\tilde{H}_{t+1}^{(n)} - r_t) \leqslant c^2 \operatorname{var}(\Delta r_t) \tag{9.62b}$$

where $c = 1/\bar{R}$.

9.3 SUMMARY

Often, for the novice, the analysis of the bond market results in a rather bewildering array of terminology and test procedures. An attempt has been made to present these ideas in a clear and concise fashion and the conclusions are as follows:

- The one-period HPY on coupon paying bonds consists of a capital gain plus a coupon payment. This is very similar to stocks. Hence the rational valuation formula also applies to bonds. In an efficient market the bond price can be viewed as the present value of known future coupon payments (plus the redemption value), discounted at the expected future one-period spot rates of return. These expected one-period future spot rates for $t = 1, 2, \ldots n$ (if these are not observable in the market, for large n) may be viewed as consisting of a risk-free rate plus a term premium.

- The 'return' on zero coupon bonds of different maturities is measured by the spot yield. Theories of the term structure imply that *continuously compounded* long rates are a specific linear weighted average of (continuously compounded) expected future short rates. This *linear* relationship applies as an approximation if one uses (compounded) spot yields and a similar approximate relationship applies if one uses yields to maturity.

- The yield to maturity, although widely quoted in the financial press, is a somewhat misleading measure of the 'return' on a bond particularly when one wishes to examine the shape and movements in the yield curve.

- Alternative theories of the term structure are, in the main, concerned with whether term premia are (i) zero, (ii) constant over time and for all maturities, (iii) constant over time but differ for different maturities, (iv) depend on the proportion of wealth held in 'long debt'. These assumptions give rise to the pure expectations hypothesis, the expectations hypothesis, the liquidity preference hypothesis and the market segmentation hypothesis, respectively. In addition, term premia may be time varying (this is discussed in Chapter 14).

- The key element in the expectations hypothesis is that the long rate is a *specific* (geometric) weighted average of expected future short rates which can be approximated by a linear relationship. Agents are risk neutral and equalise expected returns over all investment horizons, using all available relevant information to predict future short rates. Hence, no abnormal profits can be made by switching between longs and shorts and the EMH under risk neutrality holds.

- The expectations hypothesis (plus RE) applied to HPYs implies that the *ex-post* excess holding period yield $(H_{t+1}^{(n)} - r_t)$ is independent of information at time t, Ω_t.

- The expectations hypothesis applied to (continuously compounded) spot yields implies that the variance of the perfect foresight long rate

$$R_t^* = (1/n)E_t \sum_i^n r_{t+i}$$

should exceed the variance of the actual long rate R_t.

- The expectations hypothesis implies that the spread $S_t^{(n,m)}$ between the n-period (spot) yield $R_t^{(n)}$ and the m-period spot yield $R_t^{(m)}$ is an optimal predictor of both the future change in the long rate and future changes in short rates and gives rise to the following regression tests:

$$R_{t+m}^{(n-m)} - R_t^{(n)} = \alpha + \beta[m/(n-m)]S_t^{(n,m)} + \gamma\Omega_t + \varepsilon_t$$

$$S_t^{(n,m)*} = \alpha + \beta S_t^{(n,m)} + \gamma\Omega_t + \eta_t$$

where the perfect foresight spread

$$S_t^{(n,m)*} = (1/s) \sum_{i=0}^{s-1} \Delta^m R_{t+im}^{(m)}$$

for $s = n/m$, an integer. Under the EH plus RE we expect $\beta = 1$ and $\gamma = 0$. A constant, non-zero term premium implies $\alpha \neq 0$.

Having set out the framework for a rather large number of possible tests of the EMH we are now in a position to examine illustrative empirical results, in the next chapter.

ENDNOTES

1. Strictly the sequence of future *one-period* required returns should be denoted $k(n, t)$, $k(n - 1, t + 1)$, etc. but for ease of exposition k_t, k_{t+1}, etc. are used.
2. Any complications that arise from Jensen's inequality are ignored.
3. When market determined spot rates exist then riskless arbitrage ensures the price of the bond is given by (9.3). Note that $rs_t^{(i)}$ is the spot rate applicable between period t and $t + i$, whereas k_{t+i} is the *one-period* rate of return between $t + i$ and $t + i + 1$. The two formulae give the same price for the bond when, for example, for $n = 2$:

$$(1 + rs^{(1)}) = (1 + k_0) \tag{i}$$

$$(1 + rs^{(2)})^2 = (1 + k_0) \cdot E_t(1 + k_1) \tag{ii}$$

which implies

$$E_t(1 + k_1) = (1 + rs^{(2)})^2 / (1 + rs^{(1)}) \tag{iii}$$

where k_1 is the *one-period* rate applicable between periods 1 and 2. Some readers will recognise (iii) as the pure expectations hypothesis. So-called general equilibrium models of interest rate determination also deal with these issues but such models are beyond the scope of this book (e.g. Cox et al (1981) and Brennan and Schwartz (1982)).
4. In discussing the various theories of the term structure, problems that arise from Jensen's inequality are ignored. In fact, the EH expressed in terms of the one-period HPY and in terms of the long rate as a weighted average of expected short rates are not generally equivalent. However, after linearisation the equivalence holds (see Cox et al (1981), McCulloch (1990) and Shiller et al (1983)).
5. For notational simplicity the subscript 'c' to denote continuously compounded rates is not used. Later it is noted that, subject to an element of approximation, our key formulae hold for both continuously compounded rates and for discrete compounded rates. This analysis also goes through for HPYs for $m > 1$ periods, that is for any n, m (with n/m an integer). See Shiller et al (1983).
6. In terms of *continuously compounded* rates the same analysis yields

$$A \exp(R_t^{(n)} \cdot n) = E_t[A \exp(r_t) \cdot \exp(r_{t+1}) \ldots \exp(r_{t+n-1})] \tag{i}$$

where $R_t^{(n)}$, r_{t+i} are continuously compounded rates. Taking logarithms the linear relationships (ignoring Jensen's inequality) holds exactly for these continuously compounded (spot) rates:

$$R_t^{(n)} = (1/n)E_t[r_t + r_{t+1} + r_{t+2} + \cdots r_{t+n-1}]$$

7. The derivation of (9.44) in the text requires careful attention to subscripts and super-
    scripts. We have

$$R_t^{(6)} = (1/3)[(R_t^{(2)} + E_t R_{t+2}^{(2)} + E_t R_{t+4}^{(2)}]$$ (1)

Moving (1) two periods forward, the six-period bond becomes a four-period bond:

$$R_{t+2}^{(4)} = (1/2)(E_{t+2} R_{t+2}^{(2)} + E_{t+2} R_{t+4}^{(2)})$$ (2)

Applying the law of iterated expectations to (2), that is $E_t(E_{t+2} R_{t+j}) = E_t R_{t+j}$, we
have:

$$E_t R_{t+2}^{(4)} = (1/2)(E_t R_{t+2}^{(2)} + E_t R_{t+4}^{(2)})$$ (3)

Substituting for the RHS of (3) in (1):

$$R_t^{(6)} = (1/3)R_t^{(2)} + (1/3)(2E_t R_{t+2}^{(4)})$$

$$E_t R_{t+2}^{(4)} = (3/2)R_t^{(6)} - (1/2)R_t^{(2)}$$

$$E_t R_{t+2}^{(4)} - R_t^{(6)} = (1/2)(R_t^{(6)} - R_t^{(2)}) = (1/2)S_t^{(6,2)}$$

8. Use will be made of continuously compounded rates with a maturity value of $1
    since this makes the algebra more transparent. We have:

$$\ln P_t^{(6)} = -6R_t^{(6)}$$ (1)

$$\ln P_{t+2}^{(4)} = -4R_{t+2}^{(4)}$$ (2)

$$\ln P_t^{(2)} = -2R_t^{(2)}$$ (3)

where we have used $\ln(1) = 0$. The (logarithmic) HPY on holding the six-period
bond from t to $t+2$ is

$$E_t \ln(P_{t+2}^{(4)}/P_t^{(6)}) = -4E_t R_{t+4}^{(4)} + 6R_t^{(6)}$$ (4)

The safe return on the two-period bond is

$$\ln(1/P_t^{(2)}) = -2R_t^{(2)}$$ (5)

Equating (4) and (5) and rearranging we obtain equation (9.44) in the text.

9. $$R_t^{(6)} = (1/3)[R_t^{(2)} + E_t R_{t+2}^{(2)} + E_t R_{t+4}^{(2)}]$$ (1)

Substracting $R_t^{(2)}$ from both sides and rearranging:

$$S_t^{(6,2)} = (-2/3)R_t^{(2)} + (1/3)[E_t R_{t+2}^{(2)} + E_t R_{t+4}^{(2)}]$$ (2)

$$= (2/3)[E_t R_{t+2}^{(2)} - R_t^{(2)}] + (1/3)[E_t R_{t+4}^{(2)} - E_t R_{t+2}^{(2)}]$$ (3)

The RHS of (3) is equal to $E_t S_t^{(6,2)*}$, that is equation (9.47b) in the text.

10
Empirical Evidence on the Term Structure

The previous chapter dealt with the wide variety of possible tests of the EMH in the bond market which can be broadly classified as regression-based tests and variance bounds tests. These two types of test procedure can be applied to spot yields, yields to maturity, bond prices and holding period yields (HPY). This chapter provides illustrative (rather than exhaustive) examples of these tests. At the end of this chapter some broad conclusions are reached on whether such tests support the EMH but the reader should not accept these conclusions as definitive, given the wide variety of tests not reported. As always, the EMH requires an economic model of expected (excess) returns on bonds and any failure of the EMH may be due to having the wrong economic model of (equilibrium) returns. In general the theories outlined in the previous chapter and the tests discussed in this chapter assume a time invariant term premium — models which relax this assumption are presented in Chapter 17. The stationarity of the variables used in particular tests is of importance, as noted when applying variance bounds and regression tests on stock prices. The issue of stationarity is noted in this chapter but is discussed in more detail in Chapter 14 on the VAR methodology. After presenting a brief account of some stylised facts for bond returns and the quality of data used, the following will be discussed:

- We investigate the term structure at the short end of the market, namely between three-month and six-month bills. These are 'pure discount' or 'zero coupon bonds' and this enables us to use quoted spot rates of interest.

- We examine bonds at the long end of the maturity spectrum. In particular we analyse the relationship between actual long rates and the perfect foresight long rate and undertake the appropriate variance bounds and regression based tests. We then repeat these tests using bond prices.

- Again for long maturity bonds, we examine the variance bounds inequalities for one-period HPYs and examine whether the zero-beta CAPM can explain the behaviour of HPYs.

A word about notation in this chapter. When using the symbol R_t it is not intended explicitly to distinguish between spot rates and yields to maturity as this distinction should be clear from the context/data being discussed. Where no ambiguity will arise, the superscript 'n' on R_t and H_t will be dropped in order to simplify the notation a little.

10.1   THE BEHAVIOUR OF RATES OF RETURN

In Figure 10.1 which graphs *yields to maturity* for Germany, we see that the short rate (i.e. three-month interbank rate) is more volatile than long rates (i.e. on 10-year bonds). For the most part long rates are higher than short rates but there are periods when the reverse is the case.

Table 10.1 presents results for Germany across the whole term structure. The yield to maturity rises monotonically as the term to maturity increases (column 1) as does the yield spread $(R_t^{(n)} - r_t)$ (column 7). The *one-month* holding period return $H_{t+1}^{(n)}$ and the excess holding period return $(H_{t+1}^{(n)} - r_t)$ both increase with maturity (columns 3 and 5) and the volatility of the price of 'long-maturity bonds' is greatly in excess of that for short-maturity bonds (column 4). Thus for Germany the results are quite straightforward. It appears that in order to willingly hold long-term bonds both a higher yield spread $(R_t^{(n)} - r_t)$ or a higher excess holding period yield $(H_{t+1}^{(n)} - r_t)$ is required *on average* over the 1967–1986 period and this is broadly consistent with the liquidity preference hypothesis. However, agents who hold long bonds in order to obtain a higher average expected excess HPY also experience increased 'risk', as measured in terms of the *ex-post* standard deviation (of bond prices). For example, when holding a 10-year bond rather than a 5-year bond the investor receives an average additional HPY of about 20 percent $(= 1.62/1.34)$ but the standard deviation increases by about 43 percent $(= 24.01/14.86)$ (Table 10.2, columns 5 and 6). As we shall see in Chapter 17, the above evidence is not

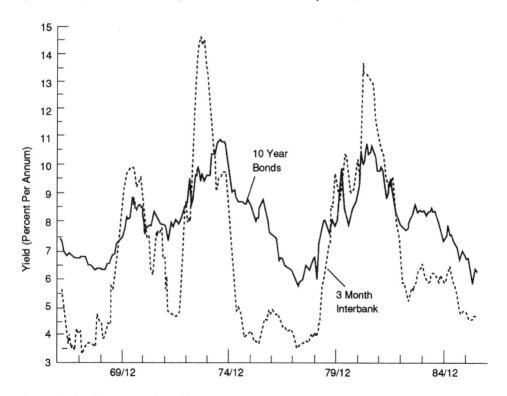

Figure 10.1   Government Securities Yields: Germany (Secondary Market — Percent per Annum). Reproduced by permission of Joseph Bisignano

Table 10.1 Summary Market Yield and One-Period Holding Yield Statistics: Germany (January 1967–May 1986)

Maturity	Market Yield		Holding Period Return			Excess Holding Period Yield[a]		Yield Spread	
	Mean	Variance	Mean	Variance	Standard Deviation	Mean	Standard Deviation	Mean	Standard Deviation
Three-month Interbank	6.78	8.06	–	–	–	–	–	–	–
1 Year	6.82	3.97	6.90	26.49	4.79	0.12	0.048	0.50	1.20
2 Year	7.27	2.92	7.44	62.10	7.77	0.66	0.50	0.74	1.46
3 Year	7.51	2.44	7.76	108.80	10.42	0.98	0.74	0.89	1.62
4 Year	7.66	2.17	7.97	162.29	12.78	1.19	0.89	0.99	1.74
5 Year	7.76	1.97	8.12	218.57	14.86	1.34	0.99	1.07	1.82
6 Year	7.84	1.83	8.24	293.0	17.21	1.46	1.07	1.11	1.88
7 Year	7.89	1.71	8.31	326.1	18.18	1.53	1.11	1.15	1.93
8 Year	7.93	1.61	8.36	373.81	19.47	1.58	1.15	1.17	1.97
9 Year	7.95	1.53	8.39	423.01	20.72	1.61	1.17	1.18	2.01
10 Year	7.96	1.49	8.40	569.76	24.01	1.62	1.18		2.03

(a) Holding period yield less three-month interbank rate.
Reproduced by permission of Joseph Bisignano.

necessarily in conflict with equilibrium asset returns models such as the CAPM since here it is the *ex-ante, conditional* variance that determines returns and not *ex-post* measures.

For the UK the results are not so uniform as for Germany. Excess HPYs do not increase monotonically with term to maturity (Table 10.2, column 5) although yield spreads do (column 7). For the USA, results are even more non-uniform (Table 10.3). The excess HPY (column 5) for the USA shows no clear pattern and although the yield spread is higher at the long end than the short end of the market, it does not rise monotonically. However, for very short maturities between two months and 12 months McCulloch (1987) has shown that for US Treasury bills the excess holding period yield $H_{t+1}^{(n)} - r_t^{(1)}$ rises monotonically from 0.032 percent per month (0.38 percent per annum) for $n = 2$ to 0.074 percent per month (0.89 percent per annum) for $n = 12$ months. (Although there is a 'blip' in this monotonic relationship for the 9-/10-month horizon, see McCulloch (1987)). Thus, for the UK there is no additional reward, in terms of the excess HPY (over the one-month return) to holding long bonds rather than short bonds although there is a greater yield spread on long bonds. The latter conclusions also broadly apply to the USA for long horizons but for short horizons there is monotonicity in the term structure (McCulloch, 1987) which is consistent with the LPH. There are therefore systematic differences between the behaviour of 'returns' in these countries.

A much longer series for yields to maturity on long bonds for the USA (albeit on corporate bonds which carry some default risk) and on a perpetuity (i.e. the Consol yield) for the UK are given in Figures 10.2(a) and 10.2(b), together with a representative short rate. The data for yields on the two long bonds appear stationary up until about 1950 when yields rise steeply. *Current period* short rates (for both the USA and the UK) appear to be more volatile than long rates so that changes in the spread $S_t = (R_t - r_t)$ are probably dominated by changes in r_t rather than in R_t.

According to the expectations hypothesis the perfect foresight spread R_t^* is a long weighted (moving) average of future short rates r_t and hence should be a smoother series than r_t. It appears from Figures 10.3(a) and 10.3(b) for the USA and the UK, respectively, that R_t^* 'tracks' R_t fairly well, as we would expect if the expectations or liquidity preference hypotheses (with a time invariant term premium) hold. However, we require more formal test procedures than the quick 'data analysis' given above.

Quality of Data

The 'quality' of the data used in empirical studies varies considerably. This can make comparisons of similar tests on data from a particular country done by different researchers or cross-country comparisons somewhat hazardous.

For example, consider data on the yield to maturity on 'five-year bonds'. This could be an *average* of yields on a number of bonds with four to six years' maturity or for maturities between five years and five years plus 11 months. The data used by researchers might represent either opening or closing rates (on a particular day of the month) and may be 'bid' or 'offer' rates, or an average of the two rates. The next issue concerns 'timing'. If we are trying to compare the return on a three-year bond with the rolled-over investment on three one-year bonds, then the yield data on the long bond for time t must be measured at exactly the same time as that for the short rate and the investment horizons should coincide exactly. In other words the rates should represent actual dealing rates on which one could undertake each investment strategy.

Table 10.2 Summary Market Yield and One-period Holding Yield Statistics: United Kingdom (January 1961–August 1986)

Maturity	Market Yield		Holding Period Return			Excess Holding Period Yield		Yield Spread	
	Mean	Variance	Mean	Variance	Mean	Standard Deviation	Mean	Standard Deviation
91 Day	8.45	10.44	–	–	–	–	–	–
5 Year	9.45	9.09	8.60	906.68	0.152	29.58	0.998	1.08
10 Year	9.99	9.89	8.80	1579.62	0.350	39.3	1.54	2.31
20 Year	10.14	9.96	8.62	2608.88	0.172	50.74	1.70	1.78

Reproduced by permission of Joseph Bisignano.

Table 10.3 Summary Market Yield and One-period Holding Yield Statistics: United States

Sample Period	Maturity	Market Yield		Holding Period Return		Excess Holding Period Yield		Yield Spread	
		Mean	Variance	Mean	Variance	Mean	Standard Deviation	Mean	Standard Deviation
Jan. 1960–Aug. 1986	3 Month	6.32	9.16	–	–	–	–	–	–
Jan. 1960–Aug. 1986	6 Month	6.50	8.72	6.49	17.9	0.17	2.76	0.18	0.23
Jan. 1960–Aug. 1986	1 Year	6.99	10.14	6.97	51.52	0.64	6.20	0.67	0.48
Jan. 1978–Aug. 1986	2 Year[a]	10.79	5.79	11.01	271.9	1.42	16.15	1.19	1.00
Jan. 1960–Aug. 1986	3 Year	7.28	9.35	7.12	220.8	0.79	14.43	0.95	0.90
Jan. 1960–Aug. 1986	5 Year	7.40	9.14	7.09	399.3	0.76	19.72	1.07	1.07
July 1969–Aug. 1986	7 Year[a]	9.08	6.38	8.94	737.0	1.22	27.05	1.37	1.39
Jan. 1960–Aug. 1986	10 Year	7.48	8.94	6.77	779.4	0.44	27.77	1.15	1.25
Jan. 1960–Aug. 1986	20 Year	7.50	9.04	6.28	1388.7	-0.04	37.20	1.17	1.35
Mar. 1977–Aug. 1986	30 Year	10.67	4.16	10.84	2194.6	1.61	46.96	1.44	1.77

Reproduced by permission of Joseph Bisignano.

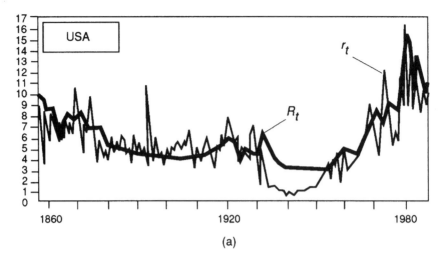

(a)

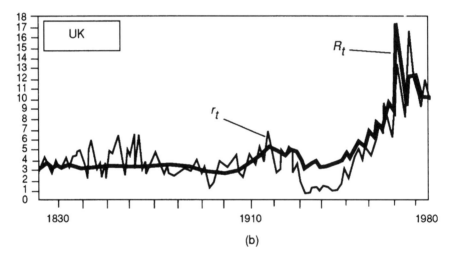

(b)

Figure 10.2 Long Term (R_t) and Short Term (r_t). (a) US Long-term Corporate Bond Yields R_t and US Four to Six-month Commercial Paper Rate r_t (Biannual Data 1857-1 to 1988-1); (b) UK Consolidated Yield R_t and UK Three-month Bank Bill Rate r_t (Annual Data 1842 to 1987). *Source*: Shiller, (1989) *Market Volatility*. © 1989 by the MIT Press. Reproduced by permission of MIT Press

Bond prices are required to measure HPYs. However, if data on bond prices are not available (e.g. on a monthly basis) researchers often approximate them from published data on yields to maturity (R_t). The simplest case here is a perpetuity where the bond price $P_t = C/R_t$ (where $C =$ coupon payment), but for redeemable bonds the calculation is more complex and the approximation may not necessarily be accurate enough to adequately test the particular hypothesis in question. As we noted in the previous chapter, tests of the expectations hypothesis in principle require data on spot yields. The latter are usually not available for maturities greater than about two years and have to be estimated from data on yields to maturity: this can introduce further approximations. These data problems

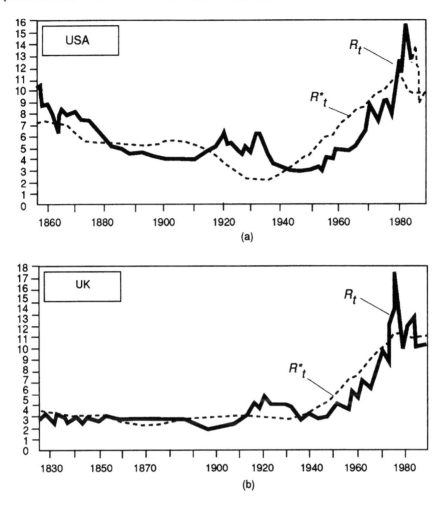

Figure 10.3(a) and (b) Long Rates R_t and the Perfect Foresight Long Rate R_t^*: USA and UK. *Source*: Shiller, (1989) *Market Volatility*. © 1989 by the MIT Press. Reproduced by permission of MIT Press

must be borne in mind when assessing empirical results but in what follows we will not dwell on these issues.

10.2 PURE DISCOUNT BONDS

A great deal of empirical work has been undertaken using three- and six-month bills. These are pure discount bonds (zero coupon bonds), their rates of return are spot yields which are continuously quoted and are readily available for most industrialised countries. The term structure relationship under the EH and risk neutrality is extremely simple. For quarterly data, the six-month rate R_t is a weighted average of three-month rates $r_{t+j}(j = 0, 1)$:

$$R_t = \lambda r_t + (1 - \lambda)E_t r_{t+1} + \phi \tag{10.1}$$

where $\lambda = 1/2$ and ϕ is a constant (additive) term premium. Using RE (i.e. $r_{t+1} = E_t r_{t+1} + \varepsilon_{t+1}$) and rearranging we have the following *equivalent* representations:

$$(r_{t+1} - R_t) = a_0 + a_1(R_t - r_t) + \varepsilon_{t+1} \tag{10.2}$$

where $a_0 = -\phi/(1 - \lambda)$ and $a_1 = \lambda/(1 - \lambda)$, or

$$\Delta r_{t+1} = b_0 + b_1(R_t - r_t) + \varepsilon_{t+1} \tag{10.3}$$

where $b_0 = -\phi/(1 - \lambda)$ and $b_1 = 1/(1 - \lambda)$, or

$$R^h_{t+1} = c_0 + c_1 r_t - \varepsilon_{t+1} \tag{10.4}$$

where $c_0 = 2\phi$, $c_1 = 1$ and $R^h_{t+1} = 2R_t - r_{t+1}$. Since the variables on the RHS of all three equations are dated at time t they are uncorrelated with the RE forecast error ε_{t+1} and hence OLS on these regression equations yields consistent parameter estimates (but a GMM correction to the covariance matrix may be required for 'correct' standard errors). Under risk neutrality we expect

$$H_0 : a_1 = 1 \quad \text{in (10.2)}$$
$$H_0 : b_1 = 2 \quad \text{in (10.3)}$$
$$H_0 : c_1 = 1 \quad \text{in (10.4)}$$

Regressions using either of the above three equations give similar inferences as the estimated parameters are *linear* transformations of each other. It may not be immediately obvious but the reader should also note that the above three regressions have been discussed in the previous chapter. For example, (10.3) is equivalent to a regression of the perfect foresight spread $S_t^{(6,3)*} = (1/2)\Delta r_{t+1}$ on the actual spread $S_t^{(6,3)} = R_t - r_t$ except for the scaling factor of 2. (See equation (9.4) Chapter 9.) Equation (10.2) is a regression of the change in the long rate on the spread (since the six-month bond becomes a three-month bond after three-months then $r_{t+1} - R_t$ is equivalent to $R_{t+1}^{(3)} - R_t^{(6)}$ in the notation of equation (9.46) of Chapter 9). Because $n = 2m$ the perfect foresight regression (equation (10.3)) yields identical inferences to the 'change in the long rate' equation (10.2), and hence here we need not explicitly consider the latter. It can also be easily demonstrated[1] that under the null of the EH, equation (10.4) is a regression of the HPY on r_t (as in equation (9.17), Chapter 9).

Various researchers have used one of the above equivalent formulations to test the EH + RE on three- and six-month Treasury bills. On US quarterly data, 1963(1)–1983(4), Mankiw (1986) finds $a_1 = -0.407$ ($se = 0.4$) which has the wrong sign. Simon (1989) using US weekly data on Treasury bills, 1961–1988, finds $b_1 = 0.04$ ($se = 0.43$). Although for one of the subperiods chosen, namely the 1972–1979 period, Simon finds $b_1 = 1.6$ ($se = 0.34$) and hence b_1 is not statistically different from 2. Both studies find that the expectations hypothesis is rather strongly rejected. The long–short spread ($R_t - r_t$) is of little or no use in predicting changes in short rates for most subsamples in Simon's study and the value of b_1 is rather unstable (it ranges between -0.33 and 0.98 in the various subperiods examined).

Jones and Roley (1983) using weekly data on newly issued US Treasury bills paid particular attention to matching exactly the investment horizon of the two, three-month investments with the six-month investment. Using weekly data a representative result for equation (10.4) is

$$R^h_{t+1} = \underset{(0.58)}{0.66} + \underset{(0.088)}{0.973} \; r_t \tag{10.5}$$

2 January 1970–13 September 1979, $\overline{R}^2 = 0.75$, SEE $= 0.98$,
W(1) $= 0.09$ ($\cdot$) $=$ standard error

where R^h_{t+1} is (a linear transformation of the) holding period yield (see footnote 1). The Wald test (a type of t test) for the restriction $c_1 = 1$ is not rejected, thus supporting the EH + RE (W(1) $= 0.09$, critical value $= 3.8$). However, some fairly strong caveats are in order. First, a statistical point. It is likely that r_t is non-stationary but R^h_{t+1} being the HPY is not. This would lead to a non-stationary error term and hence the statistics such as $\overline{R}^2$, standard errors and the Wald statistic have non-standard distributions and give misleading inferences. (This type of statistical problem was not prominent in the literature until after this article was published.) Second, Jones and Roley find that if additional variables Ω_t known at time t are added to equation (10.5) they are sometimes statistically significant. In particular, net inflows of foreign holdings of US Treasury bills are found to be statistically significant, although others such as the unemployment rate, the stock of three- and six-month bills (i.e. market segmentation hypothesis) are not. Thus one can be critical of the results on statistical grounds and it appears that there is a failure of the RE orthogonality condition.

Mankiw (1986) seeks to explain the failings of the EH by considering the possibility that the expectations of r_{t+1} by market participants as a whole consists of a weighted average of the rationally expected rate $(E_t r_{t+1})$ of the smart money traders and a simple naive myopic forecasting scheme (i.e. noise traders) based simply on the current short rate. If $\tilde{r}^e_{t+1}$ denotes the market's average expectation then Mankiw assumes:

$$\tilde{r}^e_{t+1} = wr_t + (1 - w)(E_t r_{t+1}) \tag{10.6}$$

where $0 < w < 1$. The EH then becomes

$$R_t = (1/2)r_t + (1/2)\tilde{r}^e_{t+1} + \phi \tag{10.7}$$

Substituting (10.6) in (10.7) and rearranging gives an equation similar to (10.3) but where $b_1 = (1 + w)/(1 - w) > 1$. However, incorporating this mixed expectations scheme does not rescue the expectations hypothesis since Mankiw finds that b_1 is negative.

The study of Mankiw (1986) fails to rescue the EH by assuming that the market expectation is a weighted average of the expectations of the smart money and noise traders. In a later paper by Mankiw and Miron (1986) they examine the EH and investigate why the EH using three- and six-month bills fails so abysmally post-1915 but appears to perform much better in the period 1890–1914. As with previous studies, estimating (10.3) on four subperiods (regimes) between 1915 and 1979, Mankiw and Miron find β is approximately zero and the R^2 is very low (< 0.06). For 1890–1914 (quarterly data) and using the interest rate data for time loans by banks they find a distinct improvement:

$$\Delta r_{t+1} = \underset{(0.14)}{-0.57} + \underset{(0.18)}{1.51} \; (R_t - r_t) \tag{10.8}$$

The R-squared $= 0.40$ and although $\beta > 0$, one still cannot accept the null that $\beta = 2$. They suggest that the reason for the improvement in the performance of the EH in the pre-1915 period, which is prior to the setting up of the Federal Reserve, is that $E_t \Delta r_{t+1}$ is more predictable. After 1915 the Federal Reserve attempted to smooth interest rates which can be represented as

$$E_t \Delta r_{t+1} = 0 \tag{10.9}$$

that is, r_{t+1} follows a random walk (strictly speaking, a martingale). If we add a term premium T_t to the EH we have from (10.3):

$$E_t \Delta r_{t+1} = -2T_t + \beta(R_t - r_t) \tag{10.10}$$

where $\beta = 2$. Using (10.9) and (10.10) we see that

$$(R_t - r_t) = T_t \tag{10.11}$$

Hence post-1915 the spread would have no predictive power for future changes in interest rates and would merely mimic movements in the term premium. More formally, econometricians will recognise that in (10.10) if we exclude T_t then the (OLS) estimate of the coefficient on $(R_t - r_t)$ will be biased.

The relationship between the *estimate* of $\hat{\beta}$ and the *variance* of $E_t(\Delta r_{t+1})$ is given in Figure (10.4). When Δr_{t+1} is unpredictable we have:

$$E_t \Delta r_{t+1} = 0 \quad \text{and} \quad \sigma^2(E_t \Delta r_{t+1}) = 0 \tag{10.12}$$

hence plim $\hat{\beta} = 0$. The estimated value of $\hat{\beta}$ approaches its true value of 2 as the variance of $E_t \Delta r_{t+1}$ increases. Mankiw and Miron show that in a simple predictive equation for Δr_{t+1}

$$\Delta r_{t+1} = \theta_1(L)r_t + \theta_2(L)R_t \tag{10.13}$$

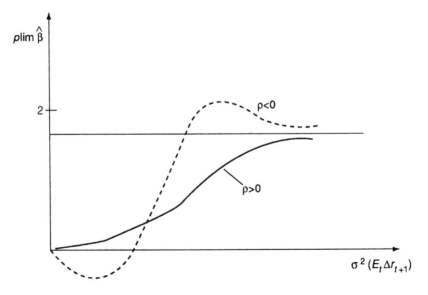

Figure 10.4 $\rho =$ Correlation Coefficient between T_t and $E_t \Delta r_{t+1}$. *Source*: Mankiw and Miron (1986). © 1986 by the President and Fellows of Harvard College.

the R-squared decreases from 0.4 for the 1890–1914 period to around zero for the post-1915 period thus confirming the above conjecture that the EH performs better in the pre-1915 period because interest rates are more predictable.

The Spread as an Optimal Predictor

Tests of the EH (with a constant term premium) between n-period and m-period spot yields are based on the fact that the spread $S_t^{(n,m)}$ is an optimal predictor of both future changes in short rates (the perfect foresight spread) and changes in long rates, as represented in the following two equations:

$$S_t^{(n,m)*} = \alpha + \beta S_t^{(n,m)} + \gamma \Omega_t + \varepsilon_t \tag{10.14}$$

$$R_{t+m}^{n-m} - R_t^{(n)} = \alpha' + \beta'[m/(n-m)S_t^{(n,m)}] + \gamma'\Omega_t + \eta_t \tag{10.15}$$

where

$$S_t^{(n,m)*} = (1/s) \sum_{i=0}^{s-1} \Delta^m R_{t+im}^{(m)}$$

is the perfect foresight spread. Under the EH we expect $\beta = \beta' = 1$ and if additional information known at time t is included we expect $\gamma = \gamma' = 0$.

Campbell and Shiller (1991) use monthly US data from January 1952 to February 1987. They used the McCulloch (1990) pure discount (zero coupon) bond yields on US government securities which included maturities of 0, 1, 2, 3, 4, 5, 6 and 9 months and 1, 2, 3, 4, 5 and 10 years. They find little or no support for the EH at the short end of the maturity spectrum. Regressing the perfect foresight spread on the actual spread. Campbell and Shiller obtained slope coefficients β ranging between 0 and 0.5 for maturities up to two years. For maturities greater than two years, the beta coefficients increase substantially and are around 1 for maturities of four, five and 10 years. Campbell and Shiller conclude therefore on the basis of this test, that the EH holds at the long end of the maturity spectrum but not at the short end. Regressing the change in long-term interest rates on the predicted spread yields negative β' coefficients which are statistically significantly different from unity. The latter results hold for the whole maturity spectrum and over various subperiods and hence reject the EH.

Cuthbertson (1996) uses London Interbank (offer) rates with maturities of 7 days, 1 month, 3 months, 6 months and 1 year to test the EH at the short end of the term structure in the UK. The data was sampled weekly (Thursdays, 4 pm) and ranged from 8 January 1981 to 13 February 1992. Using equation (10.14) Cuthbertson could not reject the null, H_0: $\beta = 1$, $\gamma = 0$ which is consistent with the EH for the UK at the short end of the maturity spectrum. (See also Hurn et al 1996 and Cuthbertson et al (1996a).)

On balance the above results suggest that the EH has some validity. The spread is of some use in forecasting over *long* horizons (i.e. a weighted average of short rates over the life n of the bond) but it gives the wrong signals over *short* horizons (i.e. the change in the long rate between t and $t + m$, where m may not be large). The latter may be because of the substantial 'noise' element in changes in long rates.

These results can be summarised on the term structure using pure discount bonds as follows:

- For the US the expectations hypothesis does not perform well at the short end of the maturity spectrum (i.e. less than four years). In the 1950–1990 period the spread predicts that the change in the long rate is in the opposite direction to that predicted by theory and it is not an unbiased predictor of the perfect foresight spread.

- Pre-1915 the EH performs somewhat better in the US but is still rejected on formal statistical tests. Also for the US, in the 1950–1990 period the spread is a much better (i.e. an unbiased) predictor of future changes in short rates over long horizons rather than short horizons.

- Failure of the EH at the short end of the maturity spectrum may be due to data deficiencies or to the presence of a time varying term premium.

More complex tests of the EH are provided in Chapter 14 but now we turn to tests of the EH based on coupon paying bonds with a long term to maturity.

10.3   COUPON PAYING BONDS: BOND PRICES AND THE YIELD TO MATURITY

If the EH + RE holds and the term premium depends only on n (i.e. is time invariant) then the variance of the actual long rate should be less than the variability in the perfect foresight long rate. Hence the variance ratio:

$$\text{VR} = \text{var}(R_t^{(n)}) / \text{var}(R_t^{(n)*})$$ (10.16)

should be less than unity. However, in initial variance bounds tests by Shiller (1979) using US and UK (1956–1977) data on yields to maturity 1966–1977 and by Pesando (1983) on Canadian bonds, these researchers find that the VR exceeds unity. This result was confirmed by Singleton (1980) who provided a formal *statistical* test of (10.16) (i.e. he computed appropriate standard errors for VR) (also, see Scott 1991, page 613)

If we assume that a *time varying* term premium $T_t^{(n)}$ can be added to EH then the violation of the variance bounds test could be due to variability in $T_t^{(n)}$. If this is the case, the variability in the term premium would have to be large in order to reverse the empirical results based on the variance bounds tests reported above.

However, there are some severe econometric problems with the early variance bounds studies on long rates discussed above. First, if the interest rate series have stochastic trends (i.e. are non-stationary) then their variances are not defined and the usual test statistics are inappropriate. Second, even assuming stationarity Flavin (1983) demonstrates that there may be substantial small sample bias in the usual test statistics used. To overcome the latter problem Shiller (1989, Chapter 13) used two very long data sets for the USA (1857–1988) and the UK (1824–1987) to compare R_t and the long moving average of short rates, namely the perfect foresight spread R_t^*. Graphs of R_t and R_t^* are shown in Figures 10.3(a) and 10.3(b) and 'by eye' it would appear that the variability in R_t and R_t^* are roughly comparable and indeed the variance ratio (VR) for both the US and the UK is only mildly violated.

However, the apparent non-stationarity of R_t towards the end of the sample could imply that sample variances are a poor measure of population variances. To counteract the latter, we can look at the following regression which uses a transformation of the variables which are more likely to be stationary:

$$R_t^* - R_{t-1} = \alpha + \beta(R_t - R_{t-1}) + v_t$$ (10.17)

Shiller finds:

$$\text{US: } \hat{\beta} = 1.156 \ (se = 0.253)$$

$$\text{UK: } \hat{\beta} = 0.347 \ (se = 0.178)$$

For the USA we can accept the EH hypothesis, since $\hat{\beta}$ is not statistically different from unity but for the UK, the EH is rejected at conventional significance levels. Overall on this long date set for the USA using the yields to maturity, the EH (with constant term premium) holds up quite well but the results for the UK are not as supportive of the EH.

10.3.2 Bond Prices

Scott (1991) has conducted variance bounds tests using bond *prices*. The method is analogous to that of variance bounds tests on stock prices. The *perfect foresight* bond price (for term to maturity n) is given by:

$$P_t^* = \frac{C}{(1 + k_{t+1})} + \frac{C}{(1 + k_{t+1})(1 + k_{t+2})} + \cdots \frac{C + M}{\prod_0^{n-1}(1 + k_{t+i})} \tag{10.18}$$

where k_{t+i} = time varying discount rate, C = coupon payment and the redemption value is M (see equation (9.6)). In Scott's 'simple model' k_{t+i} equals the short-term interest rate r_{t+i}, while in his 'second model' the discount rate is equal to r_{t+i} plus a term premium that declines as term to maturity decreases. Scott calculates the perfect foresight bond price given in (10.18) for short-, medium- and long-term US Treasury bonds (monthly data, 1932–1985) and compares these series with the series for actual bond prices at these maturities. Since $P_t^* = P_t + \eta_t$ where η_t is the RE forecast error of future discount rates, we expect $\text{var}(P_t) \leqslant \text{var}(P_t^*)$. Scott finds that the variance bounds test on bond prices is not violated for US data. It is also the case that in a regression of P_t^* on P_t we expect a coefficient of unity and hence in:

$$[P_t^* - P_t] = a + bP_t + e_t \tag{10.19}$$

we expect $b = 0$. Using US Treasury bond data, Scott finds that $b = 0$ for all the maturities he examined and his results are very supportive of the EH (with a time invariant term premium).

10.3.3 Holding Period Yields

For HPYs the variance bound inequalities using Shiller's approximation formula are

$$\text{var}(\tilde{H}_{t+1}) \leqslant a^2 \, \text{var}(r_t) \tag{10.20a}$$

$$\text{var}(\tilde{H}_{t+1}) \leqslant b^2 \, \text{var}(\Delta r_t) \tag{10.20b}$$

where a is a known constant and $b = 1/\overline{R}$ (see Chapter 9). For the US and UK data used in Figures 10.2(a) and 10.2(b) Shiller (1989, page 223) finds:

$$\text{USA: } \quad \sigma(\tilde{H})/a\sigma(r) = 1.14 \quad 1857\text{--}1987$$

$$\text{UK: } \quad \sigma(\tilde{H})/a\sigma(r) = 1.57 \quad 1824\text{--}1986$$

$$\text{UK: } \quad \sigma(\tilde{H})/a\sigma(r) = 1.13 \quad 1924\text{--}1930$$

The results are therefore supportive of the EH (with a time invariant term premium) for the USA over the whole sample but for the UK, the EH only appears to hold for the 1924–1930 period, when short rates appeared to be stationary. Bisignano (1987, Table 17) found that this particular variance bounds test was broadly accepted for Germany while for other countries (USA, UK, Canada) the variance ratio often greatly exceeded unity and is of the order 3–4 for maturities greater than five years. The above variance inequalities may also be calculated using $\sigma(\Delta r_t)$ rather than $\sigma(r_t)$ as the benchmark. For US and UK data Shiller (1989, page 269) finds that (10.20b) is not violated and hence stationarity of r_t is a key issue in interpreting these results.

Next we discuss evidence on the zero-beta CAPM where the betas are assumed constant over time, but may vary for bonds of different maturities. There is a separate regression for $E_t H_{t+1}^{(n)}$ for each maturity band (i.e. for $n = 1, 2, 3, \ldots$) and the assumption of RE allows the use of actual returns $H_{t+1}^{(n)}$ in place of the unobservable expected returns. Bisignano (1987) checks that the chosen zero-beta portfolio (which consists of a set of bills) has returns that are uncorrelated (orthogonal) with the return on the market bond portfolio, R_{t+1}^m. The results for the model were most favourable for Germany. For example, for five-year and 10-year bonds Bisignano (Table 22) finds:

$$H_{t+1}^{(5)} = 0.739\, R_{t+1}^z + 0.249\, R_{t+1}^m \qquad (10.21)$$
$$(3.1) \qquad\qquad (3.58)$$

$$1978(2)\text{--}1985(12) \ R^2 = 0.137, \ DW = 1.93$$

$$H_{t+1}^{(10)} = 0.646\, R_{t+1}^z + 0.332\, R_{t+1}^m$$
$$(1.69) \qquad\qquad (2.90)$$

$$1978(2)\text{--}1985(2) \ R^2 = 0.089, \ DW = 2.26$$

where the coefficient on R^m is the beta for the bond of maturity n. In general the results for Germany show that (i) systematic (non-diversifiable) risk as measured by beta rises with maturity (i.e. as n increases, $\beta^{(n)}$ increases), (ii) all $\beta^{(n)}$s are less than unity and (iii) the *sum* of the two estimated coefficients on the $E_t R_{t+1}^z$ and $E_t R_{t+1}^m$ in equation (10.21) equal unity as suggested by the theory. The above results hold when White's (1980) correction for heteroscedasticity is implemented (although no test or correction for high order serial correlation appears to have been undertaken). For the UK and USA the estimate of the $\beta^{(n)}$s is also statistically significant and rises with term to maturity n. Thus when we consider a portfolio model which explicitly includes a risk premium, which depends on term to maturity, we find that *expected* holding period yields do have a systematic pattern. This is in contrast to the *ex-post* average HPY, which for the UK and USA do not exhibit systematic behaviour. But this is perfectly consistent, since the theory deals with expected returns at a point in time, conditional on other variables and *not* for long-term sample averages of actual returns. For five- and 10-year bonds for the USA the betas are $\beta^{(5)} = 0.71$, $\beta^{(10)} = 0.92$ and hence the risk premium for the USA is about 2–3 times that for Germany.

The above evidence suggests that holding period returns are broadly in conformity with the zero-beta CAPM. Hence expected HPYs on long bonds depend on the riskiness of such bonds where the latter varies with the term to maturity. Chapter 17 extends the CAPM model to allow for a time varying term premium (as well as one that depends on term to maturity), that is we consider the case where $T = T(n, z_t)$.

10.4 SUMMARY

The following broad conclusions follow from the evidence on the bond market discussed in this chapter:

- For spot yields on three- and six-month bills (i.e. pure discount bonds) the US evidence tends not to support the EH. For US spot yields on longer-term bonds (i.e. $n > 4$ years) the spread tends to be an unbiased predictor for future changes in short-term rates thus supporting the EH at the long end of the maturity spectrum. For the UK the latter test is broadly supported by the data, even at the short end.

- For longer maturity coupon paying bonds, regression and variance bounds tests based on the yield to maturity, the holding period yield and bond prices tend to support the EH on US data. On UK data variance bounds tests on HPYs and long rates are less supportive of the EH yet the latter does not appear to be grossly at odds with the data.

- There is some evidence that the (zero-beta) CAPM may provide a useful model of holding period yields.

Coupon paying bonds with long maturities are rather like stocks (except their periodic payment is known and largely free of default risk). We therefore have something of a paradox in that long-term bonds broadly conform to the EMH whereas stocks do not, yet both types of asset are traded in competitive markets. Similarly, on the evidence before us, short maturity bonds (bills) do not conform to the EMH based on the US data. One tentative hypothesis to explain the different results for long-term bonds and stocks is that noise traders are more active in the latter than in the former market. It may also be the case that the greater volatility in short rates relative to long rates noted in Section 10.1 may imply that agents perceive that taking positions at the short end is fairly risky and hence a time varying risk premium could explain the failure of the EH and the EMH at the short end. The modelling of time varying risk premia is examined in Chapter 17.

APPENDIX 10.1 IS THE LONG RATE A MARTINGALE?

In this appendix we briefly examine (i) the conditions under which the long rate is a martingale and (ii) the use of forward rates in testing hypotheses about the term structure.

Is the Long Rate a Martingale?

In some of the early empirical work on the term structure researchers focused on whether the long rate behaved as a martingale. This evidence will not be examined in detail but the basic ideas in this important early strand in the term structure literature will be set out. To investigate the conditions under which long-term interest rates exhibit a martingale property, that is $E_t(R_{t+1}|\Omega_t) = R_t$ consider the EH applied to spot yields:

$$R_t^{(n)} = \frac{1}{n}[r_t + E_t r_{t+1} + E_t r_{t+2} + \ldots + E_t r_{t+n-1}] + T_t^{(n)} \tag{1}$$

where a term premium $T_t^{(n)}$ on the n-period bond has been included. Leading (1) one-period forward the n-period rate at $t + 1$ is given by:

$$R_{t+1}^{(n)} = \frac{1}{n}[r_{t+1} + E_{t+1} r_{t+2} + \ldots + E_{t+1} r_{t+n}] + T_{t+1}^{(n)} \tag{2}$$

Note that in moving from (1) to (2) we are examining the behaviour of two (different) bonds which both have a term to maturity of n periods at t *and* at $t + 1$. This is conceptually different to the derivation of $(\cdot)$ in the text where we examine the *same* bond whose maturity changes from n to $n - 1$ as we move from t to $t + 1$. Subtracting (1) from (2):

$$R_{t+1}^{(n)} - R_t^{(n)} = \frac{1}{n}[r_{t+1} - E_t r_{t+1}]$$

$$+ \frac{1}{n}[[E_{t+1} r_{t+2} - E_t r_{t+2}] + [E_{t+1} r_{t+3} - E_t r_{t+3}] + \ldots]$$

$$+ \frac{1}{n}[E_{t+1} r_{t+n} - r_t]$$

$$+ [T_{t+1}^{(n)} - T_t^{(n)}]$$

$$= n^{-1}[A + B + C + D] \tag{3}$$

where $A = $ RE forecast error: $\eta_{t+1} = r_{t+1} - E_t r_{t+1}$, $B = $ revisions to forecasts: $\omega_{t+1}^{(i)} = E_{t+1} r_{t+i} - E_t r_{t+i}$, $C = E_{t+1} r_{t+n} - r_t$ and $D = $ change in the term premium: $T_{t+1}^{(n)} - T_t^{(n)}$.

There is no *guarantee* that 'C' is either a constant or zero. However, for large n, the term C/n *may* be small relative to the *sum* of the other terms, although this is not guaranteed. Strictly speaking we need to *assume* a transversality condition, such that $C/n \to 0$. If the term premium is constant *and* the term 'C' is small (i.e. approaches zero) then we can write (3) as

$$R_{t+1}^{(n)} - R_t^{(n)} = \mu_{t+1} \tag{4}$$

where μ_{t+1} is the weighted sum of error terms $\{\eta_{t+1}, \omega_{t+1}^{(i)}\}$ in (3) and hence $E_t(\mu_{t+1}|\Omega_t) = 0$. It follows immediately from (4) that under these conditions $R_t^{(n)}$ is a martingale, that is $E_t R_{t+1}^{(n)} - R_t^{(n)} = 0$.

According to (3) the *only* reason we get a change in $R^{(n)}$ between t and $t + 1$ is:

(i) a non-zero forecast error for the short rate at $t + 1$ (term 'A'),

(ii) *revisions* to expectations between t and $t + 1$, about short rates in one or more future periods, that is term B (e.g. 'news' of a credible counterinflationary policy might imply a decrease in r_{t+j} in future periods and hence a decrease in some or all of the $(E_{t+1} r_{t+j} - E_t r_{t+j})$ terms,

(iii) a change in the agent's views about $E_{t+1} r_{t+n}$ (i.e. term 'C'),

(iv) a change in the agent's perceptions of the term premium required on long-term bonds (i.e. term 'D').

The first three items in the above list involve the arrival of new information or 'news' and, therefore, the monetary authorities cannot *systematically* influence long rate. At best, the authorities can only cause 'surprise' changes in the long rate by altering expectations of future short rates (e.g. by instituting a tough anti-inflation package). If the authorities could systematically influence the term premium then it would have some leverage on long rates. However, it is difficult to see how the authorities might accomplish this objective by, for example, open market operations. Hence an often cited implication of the above analysis is that under the EH + RE the authorities cannot 'twist' the yield curve.

Empirical tests of the martingale hypothesis are based on (4) and usually involve a regression of $\Delta R_{t+1}^{(n)}$ on information dated at time t or earlier Ω_t. In general $\Delta R_{t+1}^{(n)}$ is found to depend on variables in Ω_t although the explanatory power is low (e.g. Pesando (1983) using US data). However, as $R_t^{(n)}$ is *close to* a martingale process this is consistent with the evidence that long rates tend to broadly conform to the EH (with a time invariant term premium).

APPENDIX 10.2 FORWARD RATES

This chapter has tested various hypotheses about the term structure. These hypotheses can also be formulated in terms of implicit forward rates. We can now briefly discuss how such implicit forward rates are calculated and how they are used in tests of various hypotheses about the term structure. (The concepts used will also be useful in analysing the forward foreign exchange market in Part 4.) The methodology employed is shown by using simple illustrative examples and closely follows the notation in Fama (1984).

Consider the purchase of a two-period (zero coupon) bond. Such a purchase *automatically locks you in* to a fixed interest rate in the second period. At time 't' the investor knows $R(1, t)$ the one-year spot interest rate, and $R(2, t)$ the two-year spot rate (expressed at an annual rate). Hence he can calculate the *implicit* interest rate he is receiving between years 1 and 2. Denote $F(x, y : t)$ as the forward rate applicable for years $t + y$ to $t + x$. Then the forward rate between years $t + 1$ and $t + 2$ is given by:

$$[1 + R(2, t)]^2 = [1 + R(1, t)][1 + F(2, 1 : t)] \tag{1}$$

$F(2, 1 : t)$ is the *implicit forward rate* you 'lock in' when purchasing a two-year bond. Rearranging (1):

$$F(2, 1 : t) = [(1 + R(2, t))^2/(1 + R(1, t))] - 1 \tag{2}$$

For example, if you purchase a two-year bond at $R(2, t) = 10$ percent per annum and $R(1, t) = 9$ percent per annum then you must have '*locked in*' to a forward rate of 11.009 percent per annum in the second year. Note that (4) is an 'identity', there is no economic or market behaviour involved. If we let lower case letters denote *continuously compounded* rates (i.e. $r(n, t) = \ln[1 + R(n, t)]$) then (1) and (2) can be expressed as linear relationships and

$$f(2, 1 : t) = 2r(2, t) - r(1, t) \tag{3}$$

For a three-period horizon we have

$$3r(3, t) = r(1, t) + 2f(3, 1 : t) \tag{4}$$

where $f(3, 1 : t)$ is the implicit forward rate for the years $t + 1$ to $t + 3$ and hence applies to an investment horizon of $3 - 1 = 2$ years. Note also that

$$3r(3, t) = 2r(2, t) + f(3, 2 : t) \tag{5}$$

Equations (4) and (5) can be used to calculate the implicit forward rates $f(3, 1 : t)$, $f(3, 2 : t)$ from the observed spot rates. Implicit forward rates can be calculated for any horizon using the appropriate recursive formulae if data on spot rates are available. From the above equations the following recursive equation is seen to hold:

$$f(x, y : t) = [x/(x - y)]r(x, t) - [y/(x - y)]r(y, t) \tag{6}$$

We now return to the two-period case, and examine variants of the expectations hypothesis (EH), in terms of forward rates. If the EH plus a risk premium $T(2, t)$ holds then

$$2r(2, t) = r(1, t) + E_t r(1, t + 1) + T(2, t) \tag{7}$$

Comparing (3) and (7) we see that

$$f(2, 1 : t) = E_t r(1, t + 1) + T(2, t) \tag{8}$$

Hence the implicit forward rate is equal to the *market's expectation* of the return on a one-period bond, starting one period from now, plus the term premium. If $T(2, t) = 0$ then (8) is consistent with the pure expectations hypothesis. The PEH therefore implies that the implicit forward rate is an unbiased predictor of the expected future spot rate. Subtracting $r(1, t)$ from both sides of (6) we see that the EH also implies that the forward premium $f(2, 1 : t) - r(1, t)$ is an unbiased predictor of the expected *change* in interest rates. If we assume RE, $r(1, t + 1) = E_t r(1, t + 1) + \eta_{t+1}$, then (8) implies:

$$r(1, t + 1) - r(1, t) = [f(2, 1 : t) - r(1, t)] - T(2, t) + \eta_{t+1} \tag{9}$$

Tests of the PEH (i.e. $T = 0$), or the EH ($T = $ constant) or the LPH (i.e. $T = T^n$), all of which assume a time invariant term premium, are usually based on regressions of the form:

$$r(1, t + 1) - r(1, t) = \alpha + \beta[f(2, 1 : t) - r(1, t)] + \eta_{t+1} \tag{10}$$

where we expect $\alpha = -T$ and $\beta = 1$. Thus under the pure expectations hypothesis we expect the forward premium to be an unbiased predictor of change in the future spot rate (i.e. $\beta = 1$ *and* $\alpha = 0$). Under a constant term premium we also expect that no other variables dated t or earlier are statistically significant in (10). Note, however, that if T is non-constant and correlated with the forward premium, then OLS on (10) yields inconsistent (biased) estimates. Similar equations to (10) apply to implicit forward rates over different horizons.

Mishkin (1988) examines equations like (10) for short horizons, namely for two- to six-month horizons, using data on US Treasury bills over the period 1959–1982. He finds that for one-month ahead forecasts $\hat{\beta} = 0.40$ *(se* $= 0.11$*)* and $R^2 = 0.11$ but as the horizon is extended (i.e. for $r(1, t + m) - r(1, t)$, $m = 3, 4, 5, 6$) the forward premium generally has little or no predictive power (i.e. $\hat{\beta} \approx 0$ statistically). In all cases Mishkin finds he can reject H_0: $\beta = 1$ and this is consistent with the regression tests reported in the main text, which tend to reject the expectations hypothesis on US data at the very short end of the maturity spectrum. Fama (1987) presents results for longer horizons using (approximate) spot rates on US Treasury bills from one to five years' maturity. He finds that one can reject H_0: $\beta = 0$ for horizons greater than one year, although in most cases he also finds H_0: $\beta \neq 1$ is rejected. Hence the EH (with a constant term premium) is found to be invalid. However, the forecast power of regressions like (10) improve as the horizon is lengthened. For example, for four-year changes in one-year spot rates $r(1, t + 4) - r(1, t)$ the forward premium explains 0.48 percent of the variability in the dependent variable (see Figure 10.A1) and we do not reject H_0: $\hat{\beta} = 1$. The above results using forward rates are consistent with those presented in this chapter, namely that at the very short end (less than four years) the EH performs badly but improves somewhat at longer maturities. For further evidence on these types of tests and the use of the term premium to forecast inflation, see inter alios Mishkin (1988, 1990) and Fama (1987).

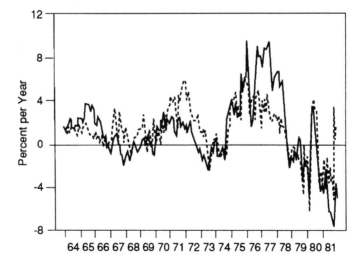

Figure 10.A1 Four-year Change in Spot Rate (Solid Line) and Forecast Change (Dashed Line) using the Forward-Spot Spread. *Source*: Fama and Bliss (1987). Reproduced by permission of the American Economic Association

The Peso problem might apply to equation (10) and could result in $\beta \neq 1$ even though the EH with a time invariant term premium holds. For example, if investors think that the authorities might increase interest rates, even though they assert they have a 'fixed interest rate' policy, then this will be reflected in a positive forward premium $f(2, 1 : t) - r(1, t) > 0$. However, if in the *sample of data*, the monetary authorities do not alter interest rates, then on average, $\Delta r_{t+1} = 0$ and equation (10) will not yield an estimate of $\hat{\beta} = 1$ in the sample.

The presence of the Peso problem implies that the forward rate is a biased predictor of $E_t r(1, t + 1)$ within the sample period examined. The Peso problem may be viewed either as a finite sample problem or a 'missing variable'. If we had a long enough data set it is (just) conceivable that over the whole sample, positive and negative 'Peso effects' would cancel. Alternatively, one could also argue that we obtain the result $\beta \neq 1$ because the 'missing variable' in the regression equation (10) is a term premium which might vary over time as the *perceived future* behaviour of the monetary authorities alters. If the variability in the term premium is correlated with the forward premium, then the OLS estimate of β is biased.

ENDNOTE

1. This is most easily demonstrated using continuously compounded spot rates. We have:

$$\ln P_t^{(3)} = \ln M - (1/4)r_t \tag{1}$$

$$\ln P_t^{(6)} = \ln M - (1/2)R_t \tag{2}$$

The logarithmic HPY is

$$h_{t+1}^{(6)} = \ln P_{t+1}^{(3)} - \ln P_t^{(6)} = (1/2)R_t - (1/4)r_{t+1} \tag{3}$$

The null hypothesis is that the HPY is equal to the risk-free (three-month) rate:

$$h_{t+1}^{(6)} = (1/4)r_t \tag{4}$$

Using (3) and (4):

$$2R_t - r_{t+1} = r_t \tag{5}$$

Equation (5) is equivalent to (10.4) in the text under the null of the EH. A similar equation to (5) can be derived using simple interest rates (i.e. $R_t^{(6)} = 2(M - P_t^{(6)})/(P_t^{(6)}, r_t = 4(M - P_t^{(3)})/P_t^{(3)}$ if we use the approximation $(1 + r_{t+1}/4) \approx r_{t+1}/4$. This is left as a simple exercise for the reader.

FURTHER READING

Most basic texts on financial markets and portfolio theory provide an introduction to alternative measures of bond returns together with theories and evidence on the term structure. More practitioner based are Fabozzi (1993) and Cooke and Rowe (1988) for the USA and for the UK, Bank of England (1993). At a more technical level, an overview of tests of the term structure can be found in Section II of Shiller (1989), particularly Chapters 12, 13 and 15, and Melino (1988).

——— PART 4 ———
The Foreign Exchange Market

The behaviour of the exchange rate particularly for small open economies that undertake a substantial amount of international trade has been at the centre of macroeconomic policy debates for many years. There is no doubt that economists' views about the best exchange rate system to adopt have changed over the years, partly because new evidence has accumulated as the system has moved through various exchange rate regimes. It is worthwhile briefly outlining the main issues.

After the Second World War the Bretton Woods arrangement of 'fixed but adjustable exchange rates' applied to most major currencies. As capital flows were small and often subject to government restrictions, the emphasis was on price competitiveness. Countries that had faster rates of inflation than their trading partners were initially allowed to borrow from the International Monetary Fund (IMF) to finance their trade deficit. If a 'fundamental disequilibrium' in the trade account developed then after consultation the deficit country was allowed to fix its exchange rate at a new lower parity. After a devaluation, the IMF would also usually insist on a set of austerity measures, such as cuts in public expenditure to ensure that real resources (i.e. labour and capital) were available to switch into export growth and import substitution. The system worked relatively well for a number of years and succeeded in avoiding the re-emergence of the use of tariffs and quotas that had been a feature of 1930s protectionism.

The US dollar was the anchor currency of the Bretton Woods system and the dollar was initially linked to gold at a fixed price of $35 per ounce. The system began to come under strain in the middle of the 1960s. Deficit countries could not persuade surplus countries to mitigate the competitiveness problem by a revaluation of the surplus countries' currency. There was an asymmetric adjustment process which invariably meant the deficit country had to devalue. The possibility of a large step devaluation allowed speculators a 'one way bet' and encouraged speculative attacks on those countries that were perceived to have poor current account imbalances even if it could be reasonably argued that these imbalances were temporary. The USA ran large current account deficits which increased the amount of dollars held by third countries. (The US extracted seniorage by this means.) Eventually, the amount of externally held dollars exceeded the value of gold in Fort Knox when valued at the 'official price' of $35 an ounce. At the official price, free convertibility of dollars into gold became impossible. A two-tier gold market developed (with the free market price of gold very much higher than the official price) and eventually convertibility of the dollar into gold was suspended by the US authorities. By the early 1970s the pressures on the system were increasing as international capital became more mobile and differential inflation rates between countries increased and caused large deficits and surpluses on current account. By 1972 most major industrial countries had *de facto* left the Bretton Woods system, and floated their currencies.

In part, the switch to a floating exchange rate regime had been influenced by monetary economists. They argued that control of the domestic money supply would ensure a desired inflation and exchange rate path. In addition, stabilising speculation by rational agents would ensure that large persistent swings in the real exchange rate and hence in price competitiveness could be avoided by an announced credible monetary policy (usually in the form of money supply targets). Some of these monetary models of exchange rate determination will be evaluated in Chapter 13.

Towards the end of the 1970s a seminal paper by Dornbusch (1976) showed that if FOREX dealers are rational, yet goods prices are 'sticky', then exchange rate overshooting could occur. Hence a contractionary monetary policy could result in a loss of price competitiveness over a substantial period with obvious deflationary consequences for real trade, output and employment. Although in long-run equilibrium the economy would move to full employment and lower inflation, the loss of output in the transition period could be more substantial in the Dornbusch model than in earlier (non-rational) monetary models, which assume that prices are 'flexible'.

The volatile movement in nominal and real exchange rates in the 1970s led Europeans to consider a move back towards more managed exchange rates which was eventually reflected in the workings of the Exchange Rate Mechanism (ERM) from the early 1980s. European countries that joined the ERM agreed to try and keep their bilateral exchange rates within announced bands around a central parity. The bands could be either wide (± 6 percent) or narrow (± 2.5 percent). The Deutschmark (DM) became the anchor currency. In part the ERM was a device to replace national monetary targets with German monetary policy, as a means to combat inflation. Faced with a fixed exchange rate against the DM, a high inflation country has a clear signal that it must quickly reduce its rate of inflation to that pertaining in Germany. Otherwise, unemployment would ensue in the high inflation country which would then provide a 'painful mechanism' for reducing inflation. The ERM has a facility for countries to realign their (central) exchange rates in the case of a fundamental misalignment. However, when a currency hits the bottom of its band because of a random speculative attack, all the Central Banks in the system may try and support the weak currency by coordinated intervention on the FOREX market.

The perceived success of the ERM in reducing inflation and exchange rate volatility in the 1980s led the G10 countries to consider a policy of coordinated intervention (i.e. the Plaza and Louvre accords) to mitigate 'adverse' persistent movements in their own currencies. The latter was epitomised by the 'inexorable' rise of the US dollar in 1983–1985 which seemed to be totally unrelated to changes in economic fundamentals. Recently some economists have suggested a more formal arrangement for currency zones and currency bands for the major currencies, along the lines of the rules in the ERM.

Very recently the ERM itself has come under considerable strain. Increasing capital mobility and the removal of all exchange controls in the ERM countries facilitated a speculative attack on the Italian lira, sterling and the franc around 16 September 1991 (known as Black Wednesday). Sterling and the lira left the ERM and allowed their currencies to float. About one year later, faced with further currency turmoil, most ERM bands were widened to $\pm$ 15 percent.

The move to a single European currency and a currency union (EMU) has been thrown into some confusion by the events of Black Wednesday. The reasons for a move to monetary union in Europe are complex but one is undoubtedly the desire to 'remove' the problem of floating or quasi-managed exchange rates. One of the main tasks in this part of the book is to examine why there is such confusion and widespread debate about the desirability of floating exchange rates. It is something of a paradox that economists are usually in favour of 'the unfettered market' in setting 'prices' but in the case of the exchange rate, perhaps *the* key 'price' in the economy, there are such divergent views.

This section of the book provides the analytic tools and ideas which will enable the reader to understand why there is a wide diversity of views on what drives the exchange rate. We discuss the following topics:

- the interrelationships between covered and uncovered interest parity, purchasing power parity and real interest rates
- testing for efficiency in the spot and forward markets and whether market participants are rational when setting FOREX 'prices'
- whether economic fundamentals drive the exchange rate and under what conditions exchange rate overshooting might occur
- the impact of 'news' on the volatility of exchange rates, the so-called Peso problem and the influence of noise traders in the FOREX market

11
Basic Arbitrage Relationships in the FOREX Market

This chapter outlines the basic concepts needed to analyse behaviour in the FOREX market. These concepts are first dealt with sequentially, in isolation, before discussing the inter-relationship between them.

11.1 COVERED AND UNCOVERED INTEREST PARITY (CIP)

There are two main types of 'deal' on the foreign exchange (FOREX) market. The first is the 'spot' rate, which is the exchange rate quoted for immediate delivery of the currency to the buyer (actually, delivery is two working days later). The second is the forward rate, which is the guaranteed price agreed today at which the buyer will take delivery of currency at some future period. For most major currencies, the highly traded maturities are for one to six months hence and, in exceptional circumstances, three to five years ahead. The market-makers in the FOREX market are mainly the large banks.

The relationship between spot and forward rates can be derived as follows. Assume that a UK corporate treasurer has a sum of money, £A, which he can invest in the UK or the USA for one year, at which time the returns must be paid to his firm's UK shareholders. Assume the forward transaction is riskless. Therefore, for the treasurer to be indifferent as to where the money is invested it has to be the case that returns from investing in the UK equal the returns in sterling from investing in the USA. The return from investing in the UK will be $A(1 + r)$ where r is the UK rate of interest. The return in sterling from investing in the USA can be evaluated using the spot exchange rate S (£/\$) and the forward exchange rate F for one year ahead. Converting the A pounds into dollars will give us A/S dollars which will increase to $(A/S)(1 + r^*)$ dollars in one year's time if r^* is the US rate of interest. If the forward rate for delivery in one year's time is F (£/\$) then the UK corporate treasurer can 'lock in' an exchange rate today and receive, *with certainty*, £$(A/S)(1 + r)F$ in one year's time. (We ignore default risk.) Equalising returns we have:

$$A(1 + r) = (A/S)(1 + r^*)F \tag{11.1}$$

which becomes

$$\frac{F}{S} = \frac{1 + r}{1 + r^*} \tag{11.2}$$

or

$$f - s = r - r^*\tag{11.3}$$

where $f = \ln(F)$ and $s = \ln(S)$ and we have used the approximation $\ln(1 + r^*) = r^*$, where r is measured as a decimal. The above equations represent the 'covered-interest parity' (CIP) condition which is an equilibrium condition based on riskless arbitrage. If CIP doesn't hold then there are forces which will restore equilibrium. For example, if $r > r^*$ and $f = s$ then US residents would purchase UK securities pushing their price up and interest rates down. US residents would also have to buy sterling spot and sell dollars forward, hence spot sterling would appreciate (i.e. s falls) and f would rise thus tending to restore equality in (11.3). In fact, because the transaction is riskless, FOREX dealers will tend to quote a forward rate that is equal to $s + r^* - r$. Use of the forward rate eliminates risk from future exchange rate changes as the forward rate is agreed today, even though the transaction takes place in (say) one year's time.

Uncovered Interest Parity (UIP)

We can repeat the above scenario but this time assuming the UK corporate treasurer is willing to take a guess on the exchange rate that will prevail in one year's time S_{t+1}^e when he converts his dollar investment back into sterling. If the corporate treasurer is risk neutral, he is concerned only with the expected return from the two alternative investments and he will continue to invest in the US rather than the UK until *expected returns* are equalised

$$S_{t+1}^e / S_t = (1 + r_t)/(1 + r_t^*)\tag{11.4}$$

or approximately:

$$s_{t+1}^e - s_t = r_t - r_t^*\tag{11.5}$$

where $s_{t+1} = \ln S_{t+1}$. The above relationship is the condition for equilibrium on the capital account under the assumption of risk neutrality. The UK corporate treasurer knows that he is taking a risk because the value of the exchange rate in one year's time is uncertain; however, he ignores this risk when undertaking his portfolio allocation decision.

We could of course relax the risk neutrality assumption by invoking the CAPM. For the UK treasurer the risk-free rate is r and the expected return on the 'round trip' risky investment in the US capital market is

$$1 + E_t R_{it+1} = E_t S_{t+1}^e (1 + r_t^*)/S_t\tag{11.6}$$

The CAPM then predicts

$$E_t R_{it+1} - r_t = \beta_i [E_t R_{t+1}^m - r_t]\tag{11.7}$$

where β_i is the beta of the foreign investment (which depends on the covariance between the market portfolio and the US portfolio) and $E_t R_{t+1}^m$ is the expected return on the market portfolio of assets held in *all* the different currencies and assets. The RHS of (11.7) is a measure of the risk premium as given by the CAPM. Loosely speaking, relationships like (11.7) are known as the International CAPM (or ICAPM) and this 'global CAPM' is looked at briefly in Chapter 18. For the moment notice that in the context of UIP and the CAPM, if we assume $\beta_i = 0$ then (11.7) reduces to UIP.

Returning to the UIP condition (11.5) it is obvious that if this does *not* hold there is an incentive for risk neutral speculators to switch funds between countries. If the latter happens very quickly (or the threat of it happening is prevalent) then UIP will be maintained at all times. Clearly, the UIP condition assumes that the market is dominated by risk neutral speculators and that neither risk averse 'rational speculators' nor noise traders have a perceptible influence on market prices.

11.2 PURCHASING POWER PARITY (PPP)

PPP is an equilibrium condition in the market for tradeable goods and forms a basic building block for several models of the exchange rate based on economic fundamentals. It is a 'goods arbitrage' relationship. For example, if applied solely to the domestic economy it implies that a 'Lincoln Continental' should sell for the same price in New York City as in Washington DC (ignoring transport costs between the two cities). If prices are lower in New York then demand would be relatively high in New York and low in Washington DC. This would cause prices to rise in New York and fall in Washington DC, hence equalising prices. In fact the *threat* of switch in demand would be sufficient for well-informed traders to make sure that prices in the two cities were equal. PPP applies the same arbitrage argument across countries, the only difference being that one must convert one of the prices to a 'common currency' for comparative purposes.

If domestic tradeable goods are perfect substitutes for foreign goods and the goods market is 'perfect' (i.e. there are low transactions costs, perfect information, perfectly flexible prices, no artificial or government restrictions on trading, etc.), then 'middlemen' or arbitrageurs will act to ensure that the price is equalised in a common currency. The PPP view of price determination assumes that domestic (tradeable) goods prices will be subject to arbitrage and will therefore equal the price in domestic currency units of the foreign goods. If the foreign currency price is P^* dollars and the exchange rate measured as the domestic currency per unit of foreign currency (say sterling per dollar) is S, then the price of a foreign import in domestic currency (sterling) is (SP^*). Domestic producers of a close (perfect) substitutes for the foreign good and arbitrageurs in the market will ensure that *domestic* (sterling) prices P equal the import price in the domestic currency, SP^*:

$$P = SP^* \quad \text{(strong form)}$$

or

$$p = s + p^* \tag{11.8}$$

$$\dot{P} = \dot{S} + \dot{P}^* \quad \text{(weak form)}$$

or

$$\Delta p = \Delta s + \Delta p^* \tag{11.9}$$

where lower case letters indicate logarithms (i.e. $p = \ln P$, etc). If domestic prices were higher than P^*S, then domestic producers would be priced out of the market. Alternatively, if they sold at a price lower than SP^* they would be losing profits since they believe they can sell all they can produce. This is the usual perfect competition assumption, here applied to domestic and foreign firms.

PPP may also be viewed as an equilibrium condition for the current account of the balance of payments (for given levels of domestic demand and world trade). This is simply because if PPP holds over time then it means that there are no profitable opportunities for domestic residents to switch demand from tradeable goods of the foreign country (i.e. imports) to domestically produced substitutes (or vice versa).

The *real exchange rate* is a measure of the price competitiveness or the price of domestic relative to foreign goods. The price of imports into the domestic economy, say the UK, is P^*S in the domestic currency (sterling). This can be compared with the price of goods produced domestically in the UK, P, to give the real exchange rate S^r as:

$$S^r = P^*S/P \tag{11.10}$$

A similar argument applies had we considered the price of exports *from* the UK in units of the foreign currency P/S and compared this with the price of competing goods in the US, P^*. It follows from the definition of the real exchange rate that if PPP holds then the real exchange rate or price competitiveness remains constant.

If goods arbitrage were the only factor influencing the exchange rate then the exchange rate would have to obey PPP:

$$s = p - p^* \tag{11.11}$$

or

$$\Delta s = \Delta p - \Delta p^* \tag{11.12}$$

Hence movements in the exchange rate would *immediately* reflect differential rates of inflation and the latter is often found to be the case in countries suffering from hyper-inflation (e.g. some Latin American countries, economies in transition in Eastern Europe and Russia around 1990). In contrast, one might expect goods arbitrage to work rather imperfectly in moderate inflationary periods in complex industrial economies with a wide variety of heterogeneous tradeable goods. Hence PPP may hold only in the very long run in such economies.

There have been a vast number of empirical tests of PPP with only the latest ones using the statistical technique of cointegration (see Chapter 20). Time does not allow an examination of these studies in detail and the reader is referred to a recent comprehensive study by Ardeni and Lubian (1991) who examine PPP for a wide range of currencies of industrialised nations (e.g. USA, Canada, UK, France, Italy). They find no evidence that relative prices and the exchange rate are 'linked' when using monthly data over the post-1945 period. However, for annual data over the longer time span of 1878–1985 they do find that PPP holds although deviations from PPP (i.e. changes in the real exchange rate) can persist for a considerable time. Hence if we were to plot the PPP exchange rate denoted S_t^P where:

$$S_t^P = P/P^* \tag{11.13}$$

against the actual exchange rate S_t then although there is some evidence from cointegration analysis that S_t and S_t^P move together in the long run, we find that they can also deviate substantially from each other over a run of years. It follows that the *real* exchange rate is far from constant (see Figures 11.1 and 11.2).

The evidence found by Ardeni and Lubian reflects the difficulties in testing for long-run equilibrium relationships in aggregate economic time series even with a very long span of data. Given measurement problems in forming a representative index of tradeable

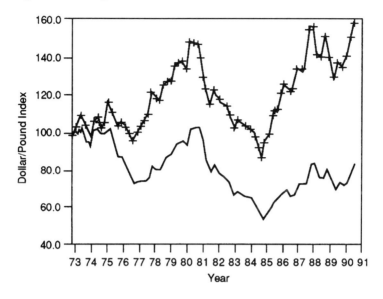

Figure 11.1 The Evolution of the Dollar-Pound Nominal (———) and Real (+ + +) Exchange Rate, 1973–1991. *Source*: Pilbeam (1992). Reproduced by permission of Macmillan Press Ltd

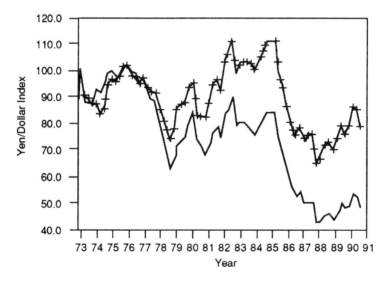

Figure 11.2 The Evolution of the Yen-Dollar Nominal (———) and Real (+ + +) Exchange Rate, 1973–1991. *Source*: Pilbeam (1992). Reproduced by permission of Macmillan Press Ltd

goods, it is unlikely that we will be able to get more definitive results in the near future. One's view might therefore be that the forces tending to produce PPP are rather weak although in the very long term there is some tendency for PPP to hold (see Grilli and Kaminsky (1991) and Fisher and Park (1991)). The very long run here could be 10–15 years. Hence in the models of exchange rate determination discussed in Chapter 13, PPP is often taken as a *long-run* equilibrium condition.

The above empirical results may be put into context when one considers an alternative approach to PPP working via the wage–price inflationary spiral. Appendix 11.1 shows that a rise in foreign (import) prices or a depreciation of the domestic currency raises production costs for the domestic industry and hence domestic prices and wages. The resulting equation which explains domestic prices is

$$\dot{P} = \left[\frac{b_1}{1 - b_1}\right][f + b_1(\dot{\chi}_w - \dot{\chi}_p) + a_2(y - \overline{y})] + (\dot{P} + \dot{S}) \tag{11.14}$$

where $y - \overline{y}$ = deviation of output from its natural rate, f = 'wage push' factors, $\dot{\chi}_w$ = exogenous growth in real wages, $\dot{\chi}_p$ = growth in labour productivity. It follows that PPP will hold if:

$$b_1(\dot{\chi}_w - \dot{\chi}_p) + f + a_2(y - \overline{y}) = 0 \tag{11.15}$$

Hence PPP holds either when output is at its natural rate or 'wage push' factors are zero or real wages grow at the rate of labour productivity. One can see that the factors in (11.15) involve rather complex, slowly varying long-term economic and sociopolitical forces and this may account for the difficulty in empirically establishing PPP, even in a very long span of data.

11.3 INTERRELATIONSHIPS BETWEEN CIP, UIP AND PPP

Forward Rate Unbiasedness and Real Interest Parity

If CIP and UIP hold simultaneously then this implies that the forward rate is an unbiased predictor of the future spot rate (see Table 11.1). The latter condition is referred to as the forward rate unbiasedness (FRU) property:

$$f_t = E_t s_{t+1} \tag{11.16}$$

Note that unbiasedness holds regardless of the expectations formation process for $E_t s_{t+1}$ (i.e. one need not assume rational expectations) but it does require risk neutrality (so that

Table 11.1 Relationship between CIP, UIP, FRU, RIP and PPP

Covered Interest Parity (CIP)	Forward Rate Unbiasedness (FRU)
$f_t - s_t = (r - r^*)_t$	$f_t = s^e_{t+1}$

Uncovered Interest Parity (UIP)

$s^e_{t+1} - s_t = (r - r^*)_t$

Real Interest Rate Parity (RIP) (Fisher Hypothesis)	Purchasing Power Parity (PPP)
$r_t - \Delta p^e_t = r^*_t - \Delta p^{*e}_t$	$s_{t+1} = p^e_{t+1} - p^{*e}_{t+1}$ $\Delta s^e_{t+1} = \Delta p^e_{t+1} - \Delta p^{*e}_{t+1}$

Real Exchange Rate

$c_t = p_t - p^*_t - s_t$

(i) $\Delta s^e_{t+1} = E_t s_{t+1} - s_t$.

UIP holds). However, for the market to be informationally efficient, agents must use all available information in forecasting $E_t s^e_{t+1}$ in the UIP relationship and hence we need to assume RE. If *any* two of the relationships from the set UIP, CIP and FRU are true then the third will also be true.

We could have started with FRU. Under risk neutrality, if (11.16) did not hold there would be (risky) profitable opportunities available by speculating in the forward market. In an efficient market (with risk neutrality) such profits should be instantaneously eliminated so that (11.16) holds at all times. Whether (11.16) holds because there is active speculation in the forward market or because CIP holds *and* all speculation occurs in the spot market so that UIP holds doesn't matter for the EMH. The key feature is that there are no unexploited profitable opportunities.

If UIP holds and there is perfect goods arbitrage in tradeable goods in all time periods then:

$$\Delta s^e_{t+1} = s^e_{t+1} - s_t = (r - r^*)_t \tag{11.17}$$

$$\Delta s^e_{t+1} = \Delta p^e_{t+1} - \Delta p^{*e}_{t+1} \tag{11.18}$$

It follows that

$$r_t - \Delta p^e_{t+1} = r^*_t - \Delta p^{*e}_{t+1} \tag{11.19}$$

and hence

$$PPP + UIP \Rightarrow \text{Real Interest Rate Parity (RIP)}$$

Again, it is easily seen from Table 11.1 that if *any* two conditions from the set of UIP, PPP and RIP are true then the third is also true.

11.4 SUMMARY

In the real world one would accept that CIP holds as here arbitrage is riskless. One might tentatively accept that UIP could hold in all time periods since financial capital is highly mobile and speculators (i.e. FOREX dealers in large banks) may act as if they are risk neutral (after all it's not their money they are gambling with, but the banks'). Hence one would then expect FRU to hold in all periods. In contrast, given relatively high information and adjustment costs in goods markets one might expect PPP to hold only over a relatively long time period (say, 5–10 years). Indeed in the short run movements in the real exchange rate are substantial. Hence even under risk neutrality (i.e. UIP holds) one might take the view that *expected* real interest rate parity would only hold over a rather long horizon. Note that it is *expected* real interest rates that are equalised. However, if over a run of years agents are assumed *not* to make systematic errors when forecasting price and exchange rate changes then, on average, real interest rates would be equalised in actual *ex-post* data.

The RIP condition also goes under the name of the international Fisher hypothesis. It may be considered as an arbitrage relationship based on the view that 'capital' (i.e. investment funds) will flow between countries to equalise the expected *real* return in each country. One assumes that a representative basket of goods (with prices p and p^*) in each country gives equal utility to the international investor (e.g. a 'Harrods' hamper' in the UK is perceived as equivalent to a 'Sak's hamper' in New York). International investors then switch funds via purchases of financial assets or by direct investment to where they yield the highest expected return in real terms. This arbitrage leads to an equalisation of expected real rates of return. Note that the investor's returns accrue in terms of the consumption goods of one particular country (currency). If he obtains his real returns in the UK say, but wishes to consume US goods (e.g. a Ford Mustang produced in the US), he will have to exchange sterling for dollars at the end of the investment period. However, if PPP holds over his investment horizon then he can obtain the same purchasing power (or set of goods) in the US as he can in the UK.

From what has been said above and one's own casual empiricism about the real world it would seem highly likely that CIP holds at most, if not at all, times. Agents in the FOREX market are unlikely to 'miss' any *riskless* arbitrage opportunities. On UIP one might accept that it is the best approximation one can get of behaviour in this 'risky market': FOREX dealers do take quite large open speculative positions, at least in the main currencies, almost minute by minute. FOREX dealers who are 'on the margin' and actively making the market may mimic risk neutral behaviour. Provided funds are available (i.e. no credit limits) one might then expect UIP to hold in actively traded FOREX markets. However, since information processing is costly one might expect UIP and even CIP to hold only in actively traded markets. In 'thin' markets (e.g. for the Indian rupee) CIP and UIP may not hold at all times. Because 'goods' are heterogeneous and because here information and search costs are relatively high, then PPP is likely to hold, at best, in the very long run. Hence so will RIP.

It is worth emphasising that all the relationships given in Table 11.1 are *arbitrage equilibrium conditions*. There is no direction of causality implicit in any of these relationships. They are merely 'no profit' conditions under the assumption of risk neutrality. Thus in the case of UIP it cannot be said that interest differentials 'cause' expectations of changes in the exchange rate (or vice versa). Of course our model can be expanded to include other equations where we explicitly *assume* some causal chain. For example, suppose we assert (on the basis of economic theory and evidence about government behaviour) that exogenous changes in the money supply by the central bank 'cause' changes in domestic interest rates. Then, given the UIP condition, the money supply also 'causes' a change in the expected rate of appreciation or depreciation in the exchange rate. The exogenous change in the money supply influences both domestic interest rates *and* the expected change in the exchange rate. Here 'money' is causal (by assumption) and the variables in the UIP relationship are jointly and simultaneously determined.

In principle when testing the validity of the three relationships UIP, CIP and FRU or the three conditions UIP, PPP and RIP we need only test any two (out of three), since if any two hold, the third will also hold. However, because of data availability and the different quality of data for the alternative variables (e.g. F_t is observable/published frequently, but P_t and P_t^* are available only infrequently and may be subject to index number measurement problems) evidence on all three relationships in each set have been investigated by researchers.

APPENDIX 11.1   PPP AND THE WAGE–PRICE SPIRAL

In the wages version of the expectations augmented Phillips curve, wage inflation, $\dot{w}$, is determined by price inflation, $\dot{p}$, and excess demand $(y - \bar{y})$. To this we can add the possibility that workers may push for a particular growth in real wages $\dot{\chi}_w$ based on their perceptions of their productivity. There may also be other forces f (e.g. minimum wage laws, socio-economic forces) which may influence wages. It is often assumed that prices are determined by a mark-up on unit wage costs and domestic import prices of raw materials; hence our wage–price model is

$$\dot{W} = \dot{x}_w + \alpha_1 \dot{P} + \alpha_2(y - \bar{y}) + f \tag{1}$$

$$\dot{P} = b_1(\dot{W} - \dot{x}_p) + b_2 \dot{P}_m \tag{2}$$

A dot over a variable indicates a percentage change and $\dot{x}_p$ is the trend growth rate of labour productivity. Imports are assumed to be predominantly homogeneous tradeable goods (e.g. agricultural produce, oil, iron ore, coal) or imported capital goods. Their foreign price is set in world markets and translated into domestic prices by the following (identity):

$$\dot{P}_m = \dot{P}^* + \dot{S}$$

Substituting (1) into (2) we obtain

$$\dot{P} = (1 - \alpha_1 b_1)^{-1}[b_1(\dot{x}_w - \dot{x}_p) + b_2 \dot{P}_m + \alpha_2 b_1(y - \bar{y}) + b_1 f] \tag{3}$$

Equation (3) is the *price* expectations augmented Phillips curve (PEAPC) which relates price inflation to excess demand $(y - \bar{y})$ and other variables. If we make the reasonable assumptions that *in the long run* there is no money illusion ($\alpha_1 = 1$, that is a vertical long run PEAPC) and there is homogeneity with respect to total costs ($b_1 + b_2 = 1$) then (3) becomes

$$\dot{P} = \frac{b_1}{1 - b_1}[f + b_1(\dot{x}_w - \dot{x}_p) + a_2(y - \bar{y})] + (\dot{P}^* + \dot{S}) \tag{4}$$

If we assume that in the long run the terms in square brackets are zero then the long-run secular influences on domestic prices are P^* and S, and PPP will hold, that is:

$$\dot{P} = \dot{P}^* + \dot{S}$$

A rise in foreign prices P^* or a depreciation of the domestic currency (S rises) leads to a rise in domestic prices (via equation (2)) which in turn leads to higher wage inflation (via equation (1)). The strength of the wage–price feedback as wage rises lead to further price rises, etc., depends on the size of α_1 and b_1. Under the homogeneity assumptions $\alpha_1 = 1$ and $b_1 + b_2 = 1$, the strength of the feedback is such that PPP holds in the long run. That is to say, a 1 percent depreciation of the domestic currency (or rise in foreign prices) eventually leads to a 1 percent rise in the aggregate domestic price index, *ceteris paribus*. Of course, PPP will usually not hold in the short run in this model either because of money illusion $\alpha_1 < 1$ or less than full mark up of costs $b_1 + b_2 < 1$ or because of the influence of the terms in square brackets in equation (4).

12

Testing CIP, UIP and FRU

In this chapter we discuss the methods used to test covered and uncovered interest parity and the forward rate unbiasedness proposition, and find that there is strong evidence in favour of covered interest parity for most maturities and time periods studied. The evidence in favour of uncovered interest parity is somewhat mixed although the possibility of making supernormal profits from speculation in the spot market seems remote. Tests of the unbiasedness of the forward rate generally find against the hypothesis and we explore some tests using survey data to ascertain whether this is due to a failure of risk neutrality or RE. Since only two out of the three conditions CIP, UIP and FRU are independent then the simultaneous finding of a failure of both FRU and UIP is logically consistent. The tests discussed in this chapter may be viewed as 'single equation tests'. More complex tests of UIP and FRU are possible in a multivariate (VAR) framework which also take account of the non-stationarity in the data. The latter test procedures are discussed in Part 5.

12.1 COVERED INTEREST ARBITRAGE

Let us consider whether it is possible, in practice, to earn riskless profits via covered interest arbitrage. In the real world the distinction between bid and offer rates both for interest rates and for forward and spot rates is important when assessing potential profit opportunities. In the strictest definition an arbitrage transaction requires no capital: the agent borrows the funds. Consider a UK investor who borrows £A in the Eurosterling market at an offer rate $r_£^0$. At the end of the period the amount owing will be

$$C = A \left[1 + r_£^0 \frac{D}{365} \right] \tag{12.1}$$

where A = amount of borrowed (£s), C = amount owed at end of period (£s), $r_£^0$ = offer rate (proportionate) on Eurosterling loan and D = number of days funds are borrowed.

Now consider the following set of transactions. The investor takes his £A and exchanges sterling for dollars at the bid rate S^b in the spot market. He invests these dollars in a Eurodollar deposit which pays the bid rate $r_\$^b$. He simultaneously switches these dollars into sterling at the forward rate F^0 (on the offer side). All these transactions take place instantaneously. The amount of sterling he will receive *with certainty* at the end of D days is given by

$$R = \frac{A \cdot F^0[1 + r_\$^b(D/360)]}{S^b} \tag{12.2}$$

Note that the convention in the USA and followed in (12.2) is to define 'one year' as 360 days when reducing annual interest rates to their daily equivalent. The *percentage excess return* ER to investing £A in US assets and switching back into sterling on the forward market is therefore given by

$$ER(£ \to \$) = 100 \left[\frac{R - C}{A}\right] = 100 \left[\frac{F^0}{S^b}\left[1 + r_\$^b \frac{D}{360}\right] - \left[1 + r_£^0 \frac{D}{365}\right]\right] \tag{12.3}$$

which is independent of A. Looking at the covered arbitrage transaction from the point of view of a US resident we can consider the covered arbitrage return from moving out of $s into sterling assets at the spot rate, investing in the UK and switching back into dollars at the current forward rate. This must be compared with the rate of return he can obtain by investing in dollar denominated assets in the US. A similar formula to that given in (12.3) ensues and is given by

$$ER(\$ \to £) = 100 \left[\frac{S^0}{F^b}\left[1 + r_£^b \frac{D}{365}\right] - \left[1 + r_\$^0 \frac{D}{360}\right]\right] \tag{12.4}$$

Given riskless arbitrage one would expect that $ER(£ \to \$)$ and $ER(\$ \to £)$ are both zero. Covered arbitrage involves no 'price risk', the only risk is credit risk due to failure of the counterparty to provide either the interest income or deliver the forward currency. If we are to adequately test the CIP hypothesis we need to obtain absolutely simultaneous 'dealing' quotes on the spot and forward rates and the two interest rates. There have been many studies looking at possible profitable opportunities due to covered interest arbitrage but not all use simultaneous dealing rates. However, Taylor (1987, 1989a) has looked at the CIP relationship in periods of 'tranquillity' and 'turbulence' in the foreign exchange market and he uses simultaneous quotes provided by foreign exchange and money market brokers. We will therefore focus on this study. The rates used by Taylor represent firm offers to buy and sell and as such they ought to represent the best rates (highest bid, lowest offer) available in the market, at any point in time. In contrast, rates quoted on the Reuters screen are normally 'for information only' and may not be actual trading rates. Taylor uses Eurocurrency rates and these have very little credit counterparty risk and therefore differ only in respect of their currency of denomination.

Taylor also considers brokerage fees and recalculates the above returns under the assumption that brokerage fees on Eurocurrency transactions represent about 1/50th of 1 percent. For example, the interest cost in borrowing Eurodollars taking account of brokerage charges is

$$r_\$^0 + 1/50 \tag{12.5}$$

While the rate earned on any Eurodollar deposits is reduced by a similar amount

$$r_\$^b - 1/50 \tag{12.6}$$

Taylor estimates that brokerage fees on spot and forward transactions are so small that they can be ignored. In his 1987 study Taylor looked at data collected every 10 minutes on the trading days of 11, 12 and 13 November 1985. This yielded 3500 potential arbitrage opportunities and he found that after allowing for brokerage costs there were no profitable covered arbitrage opportunities. The results therefore strongly support covered interest parity and the efficient markets hypothesis. In his second study, Taylor (1989a) re-examined the same covered interest arbitrage relationships but this time in periods of 'market turbulence' in the FOREX market. The historic periods chosen were the 1967 devaluation of sterling in November of that year, the 1972 flotation of sterling in June of that year as well as some periods around the General Elections in both the UK and the US in the 1980s. The covered interest arbitrage returns were calculated for maturities of 1, 2, 3, 6 and 12 months. The general thrust of the results are as follows:

- In periods of 'turbulence' there were *some* profitable opportunities to be made.

- The size of the profits tend to be smaller in the floating rate period than in the fixed rate period of the 1960s and became smaller as participants gained experience of floating rates, post 1972.

- The frequency, size and persistence over successive time periods of profitable arbitrage opportunities increases as the time to maturity of the contract is lengthened. That is to say there tended to be larger and more frequent profit opportunities when considering a 12-month arbitrage transaction than when considering a one-month covered arbitrage transaction.

Let us take a specific example. In November 1967, £1m arbitraged into dollars would have produced only £473 profit, however just after the devaluation of sterling (i.e. a period of turbulence) there were sizeable riskless returns of about £4000 and £8000 on riskless arbitrage at the three-month and six-month maturities, respectively. Capital controls (on UK sterling outflows) which were in force in the 1960s cannot account for these results since Eurosterling deposits/loans were not subject to such controls. Clearly the market is not always perfectly efficient in that riskless profitable opportunities are not immediately arbitraged away. In periods of turbulence, returns are relatively large and sometimes persist over a number of days at the long end of the maturity spectrum, while at the short end of the maturity spectrum profits are much smaller.

The reason for small yet persistent returns over a one-month horizon may well be due to the fact that the opportunity cost of traders' time is positive. There may not be enough traders in the market who think it is worth their time and effort to take advantage of *very small* profitable opportunities. Given the constraint of how much time they can devote to one particular segment of the market they may prefer to investigate and execute trades with larger expected returns, even if the latter are risky (e.g. speculation on the *future* spot rate by taking positions in specific currencies). It may even be more worthwhile for them to fill in their dealers' pads and communicate with other traders rather than take advantage of very small profitable opportunities.

The riskless returns available at the longer end of the market are quite large and represent a clear violation of market efficiency. Taylor puts forward several hypotheses as to why this may occur, all of which are basically due to limitations on the credit positions dealers can take in the foreign exchange market.

Market-makers are generally not free to deal in any amount with any counterparty that they choose. Usually the management of a bank will stipulate which other banks it is willing to trade with (i.e. engage in credit risk), together with the maximum size of liabilities which the management of the bank consider is prudent to have outstanding with any other bank, at any point in time. Hence there is a kind of liquidity constraint on covered arbitrage. Once the credit limit is 'full', no further business can be conducted with that bank (until outstanding liabilities have been unwound). This tends to create a preference for covered arbitrage at the short end of the market since funds are 'freed up' relatively frequently.

Banks are also often unwilling to allow their foreign exchange dealers to borrow substantial amounts from other banks at long maturities (e.g. one year). For example, consider a UK foreign exchange dealer who borrows a large amount of dollars from a New York bank for covered arbitrage transactions over an annual period. If the UK bank wants dollar loans from this same New York bank *for its business customers* it may be thwarted from doing so because it has reached its credit limits with the New York bank. If so, foreign exchange dealers will retain a certain degree of slackness in their credit limits with other banks and this may limit covered arbitrage at the longer end of the maturity spectrum.

Another reason for self-imposed credit limits on dealers is that Central Banks often require periodic financial statements from banks and the Central Bank may consider the short-term gearing position of the commercial bank when assessing its 'soundness'. If foreign exchange dealers have borrowed a large amount of funds for covered arbitrage transactions, this will show up in higher short-term gearing. Taylor also notes that some of the larger banks are willing to pay up to 1/16th of 1 percent above the market rate for Eurodollar deposits as long as these are in blocks of over $100m. They do so largely in order to save on the 'transactions costs' of the time and effort of bank staff. Hence Taylor recognises that there may be some mismeasurement in the Eurodollar rates he uses and hence profitable opportunities may be more or less than found in his study.

Taylor finds relatively large covered arbitrage returns in the fixed exchange rate period of the 1960s, however in the floating exchange rate period these were far less frequent and much smaller. For example, in Table 12.1 we see that in 1987 there were effectively no profitable opportunities in the one-month maturities from sterling to dollars. However, at the one-year maturity there are riskless arbitrage opportunities from dollars into sterling on both the Monday and Tuesday. Here $1m would yield a profit of around $1500 at the one-year maturity.

Taylor's study does not take account of any differential taxation on interest receipts from domestic and foreign investments and this may also account for the existence of persistent profitable covered arbitrage at maturities of one year. It is unlikely that market participants are influenced by the perceived relative risks of default between say Eurosterling and Eurodollar investments and hence this is unlikely to account for arbitrage profits even at the one-year maturities. Note that one cannot adequately test CIP between assets

Table 12.1 Covered Arbitrage: Percentage Excess Returns (1987)

	1 month		6 month		1 year	
	(£ → $)	($ → £)	(£ → $)	($ → £)	(£ → $)	($ → £)
Monday 8/6/87 (12 noon)	−0.043	−0.016	−0.097	−0.035	−0.117	−0.162
Tuesday 9/6/87 (12 noon)	−0.075	−0.064	−0.247	+0.032	−0.192	0.150

Source: Taylor (1989), Table 3.

with different risk characteristics (either 'market price risk' or credit risk). For example, studies that compare covered transactions between Eurosterling deposits and US corporate bonds are unlikely to be very informative about market efficiency in the forward market.

Note that CIP can hold even if no trades actually take place. It is the *threat* of riskless arbitrage that ensures CIP. This is in part reflected in the fact that if one goes to a bank for a forward quote it calculates the forward rate it will offer by using the CIP relationship. That is to say it checks on the values of $r_£$, $r_\$$ and S_t and then quotes a rate F_t calculated as

$$F = S\frac{(1 + r_£)}{(1 + r_\$)} \tag{12.7}$$

where the bid–offer distinction has been ignored. Looking at potentially profitable trades using data on which market-makers may have undertaken actual trades is clearly a useful way of testing CIP. However, many early studies of CIP used the logarithmic approximation and ran a regression:

$$(f - s)_t = a + b(r_£ - r_\$)_t + \varepsilon_t \tag{12.8}$$

The null of CIP is

$$H_0 : a = 0, \; b = 1$$

and if there are transactions costs these may show up as $a \neq 0$. Since $(r_\$ - r_£)_t$ is endogenous then 2SLS or IV rather than OLS should be used when estimating (12.8). However, these regression tests of CIP have a number of acute problems. The regressions generally do not distinguish between bid and offer rates and do not *explicitly* (or carefully) take account of transactions costs. Also if the logarithmic form is used then (12.8) is only an approximation. In early studies the rates used are not sampled contemporaneously. For these reasons these regression tests are not reported (see Cuthbertson and Taylor (1987) and MacDonald (1988) for details).

12.2 UNCOVERED INTEREST PARITY AND FORWARD RATE UNBIASEDNESS

With perfect capital mobility (i.e. foreign and domestic assets are perfect substitutes, instantaneous market clearing, zero transactions costs) and a zero risk premium (or risk neutrality) then the uncovered speculative return is zero:

$$s_t^e - s_{t-1} - d_{t-1} = 0 \tag{12.9}$$

where $d_{t-1} = r_{t-1} - r_{t-1}^*$, the uncovered interest differential and $s_t = \ln S_t$. Equation (12.9) holds if the spot market is 'efficient' and hence eliminates knowable opportunities for supernormal profit (providing there is a zero risk premium). Assuming RE, $s_t = s_t^e + u_t$, hence:

$$s_t = s_{t-1} + d_{t-1} + u_t \tag{12.10}$$

Equation (12.10) has the testable implication that the current spot rate depends upon the previous period's spot rate and the uncovered interest differential, with a unit coefficient on each variable. The orthogonality property of RE implies that no other variables known at time $t - 1$ or earlier should influence s_t (other than s_{t-1} and d_{t-1}).

Early empirical work tested equation (12.10) by regressing $(s_t - s_{t-1} - d_{t-1})$ on a wide variety of economic variables available at time $t - 1$ or earlier. Frankel (1979a) found that for the DM/$ rate on quarterly data over the 1970s that all additional variables tried were insignificant. Hacche and Townend (1981) using monthly data on the sterling effective rate (July 1972–February 1980) found that the interest rate coefficients, when included as independent variables, have unit coefficients; but lagged values of the change in the exchange rate and a measure of credit expansion are also significant. Hence the RE forecast error u_t is not independent of all information at time $t - 1$ or earlier and the joint hypothesis of zero risk premium and the EMH fails; similar results were obtained for the £/$ rate. Cumby and Obstfeld (1981) using weekly data (July 1974–June 1978) on six major currencies against the dollar found that lagged values of the dependent variable $(s_t - s_{t-1} - d_{t-1})$ of up to 16 weeks are statistically significant for all six currencies. The RE forecast error is therefore serially correlated, contrary to part of the maintained hypothesis.

Our interim conclusions concerning the validity of UIP + RE is that not all aspects of the maintained hypothesis hold and this may be due either to a (variable) risk premium, or a failure of RE or risk neutrality.

Testing FRU

First some stylised facts. A graph of the 30-day forward rate F and the actual spot rate led by 30 days S_{t+1} for the $/DM (using weekly data) is shown in Figure 12.1. It is obvious that the broad trends in the $/DM *actual future* spot rate are picked up by the current forward rate. This is the case for most currencies since the root mean square of the prediction error, $S_{t+1} - F_t$, is of the order of 2–2.5 percent against the dollar

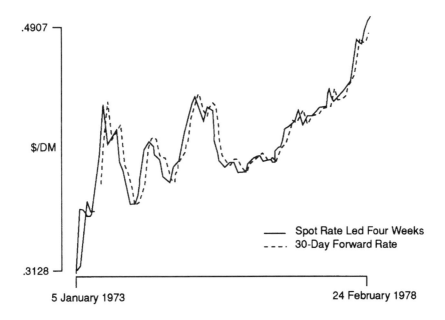

Figure 12.1 Forward Rate (30 Days) and Spot Rate (Led Four Weeks): Dollar–Deutschmark. *Source*: Frankel (1980). Reproduced by permission of the *Southern Economic Journal*

Table 12.2 Prediction Errors of Four-Week Forward Rates

	Currency against \$	(1) Percent, RMS Prediction Error $= \dfrac{\sqrt{\Sigma(s_{t+1} - f)^2}}{n}$	(2) Percent, RMS Change in Spot Rate $= \dfrac{\sqrt{\Sigma(s_{t+1} - s)^2}}{n}$	(3) Percent of Changes in Spot Rate Predicted by Forward Rate
1.	Deutschmark	2.10	2.12	2.2
2.	French franc	2.21	2.09	−11.4
3.	Pound sterling	2.18	2.23	6.0
4.	Italian lira	2.76	2.53	−18.8
5.	Swiss franc	2.51	2.61	7.4
6.	Dutch guilder	2.10	2.0	−10.0
7.	Japanese yen	1.84	1.84	0

Source: Frankel (1980), *Southern Economic Journal*, April.
Date Period: weekly data 5 July 1974–4 April 1978 (193 data points).

for the currencies shown in Table 12.2. This is particularly true for those currencies that experience a trend in the exchange rate (e.g. Japan and the UK). The four-week variability in the spot rate in column 2 of Table 12.2 is about 2–2.5 per cent for most currencies. The forward market does not predict *changes* in the spot rate at all accurately.

For example, only 2 percent of the changes in the \$/DM rate are predicted by the forward rate (column 3). In some cases this percentage is negative indicating that the forward rate is a worse predictor than the contemporaneous spot rate. The large size of these prediction errors does not necessarily imply a failure of market efficiency since all alternative predictors of S_{t+1}, given information at time t, may give even larger forecast errors.

It is clear from Figure 12.1 that a regression of S_{t+1} on F_t will produce (positively) serially correlated residuals since F_t provides a run of under- and overpredictions of S_{t+1}. If the \$/DM future spot rate S_{t+1} is lagged one period, the solid line would shift to the right and would nearly coincide with F_t. Hence the *current* forward rate appears to be more highly correlated with the *current* spot rate than with the future spot rate. This suggests that variables or news that influence S_t also impinge upon F_t.

If the forward market conforms to the EMH and speculators are risk neutral then the forward rate is an unbiased predictor of the (logarithm of the) expected future spot rate, s_{t+1}^e. If we incorporate an additive risk premium rp_t and invoke RE then

$$f_t = s_{t+1}^e + rp_t \tag{12.13}$$

$$s_{t+1} = s_{t+1}^e + u_{t+1} \tag{12.14}$$

Risk neutrality implies $rp_t = 0$. The risk premium is the expected profit margin of the speculator and may also capture any transactions costs (e.g. manpower costs) associated with the forward contract. RE implies:

$$E_t(u_{t+1}|\Omega_t) = 0 \tag{12.15}$$

which includes the assumption that u_{t+1} is serially uncorrelated. The simplest assumption to make concerning the risk premium is that it consists of a positive constant α plus a 'white noise' random element v_t:

$$rp_t = \alpha + v_t \tag{12.16}$$

Combining (12.13), (12.14) and (12.16) we obtain

$$s_{t+1} = \alpha + f_t + (u_{t+1} - v_t) \tag{12.17}$$

One test of the EMH interpretation of the forward market utilises a regression equation of the form:

$$s_{t+1} = \alpha + \beta f_t + \gamma \Lambda_t + \varepsilon_{t+1} \tag{12.18}$$

where Λ_t is a subset of the complete information set available at time t. If the EMH is true we expect $\alpha < 0$, $\beta = 1$, $\gamma = 0$ and ε_t to be serially uncorrelated. Λ_t may contain any relevant economic variables including values of the lagged dependent variable (s_t, s_{t-1}) or lagged forecast errors ($s_t - f_{t-1}$). A slightly weaker test of the EMH *assumes* $\gamma = 0$ and tests for $\beta = 1$ in the regression $s_{t+1} = \alpha + \beta f_t + \varepsilon_t$, which excludes Λ_t.

There is an important econometric point to be made here. ε_{t+1} in the estimating equation (12.18) is equal to $u_{t+1} - v_t$, but v_t influences the risk premium rp_t *and* f_t via equation (12.13). Hence ε_{t+1} and f_t in equation (12.18) are correlated, and OLS yields an inconsistent estimator. This is the so-called 'errors in variables' problem in econometrics. 'Correct' (i.e. asymptotically unbiased) estimates may be obtained using an instrumental variables technique such as 2SLS. (A correction to the covariance matrix and the standard errors because of the presence of heteroscedasticity can be made using a GMM estimator.)

Alternative formulations of the unbiasedness property to equation (12.18) are sometimes used. For example, unbiasedness also implies that the forward premium/discount $(f - s)$ is an unbiased predictor of the future *change* in the spot rate. Subtracting s_t from both sides of (12.13) and using (12.14):

$$(s_{t+1} - s_t) = (f_t - s_t) + u_{t+1} \tag{12.19}$$

A test of unbiasedness is then a test of $\alpha = \gamma_1 = 0$, $\beta = 1$ and that ε_t is white noise in the regression:

$$\Delta s_{t+1} = \alpha + \beta (f - s)_t + \gamma_1 \Lambda_t + \varepsilon_{t+1} \tag{12.20}$$

Some early studies used the 'levels version' (12.18) of the unbiasedness hypothesis. However, if s_{t+1} and f_t are $I(1)$ the usual test statistics in (12.18) are invalid. Looking at equation (12.20) we see that if (s, f) are $I(1)$ but s_{t+1} and f_t are cointegrated with cointegration parameter $(1, -1)$, that is $s_{t+1} = f_t + \varepsilon_{t+1}$ with $\varepsilon_{t+1} \sim I(0)$ then the variables in (12.19) are $I(0)$. The latter carries over to (12.20) if the variables in Λ_t are either $I(0)$, or $I(1)$ but cointegrate among themselves or if $\gamma_1 = 0$. In general (12.20) is to be preferred to (12.18) under the assumption of cointegration between s and f, since the error term is stationary and hence the usual test statistics are valid.

Early Tests

Frankel (1982a) reports a regression of the *change* in the spot rate Δs_{t+1} on the forward premium/discount $(f - s)_t$ and other variables known at time t (e.g. Δs_t). He is not able to reject the null hypothesis that $\alpha = \gamma_1 = 0$, $\beta = 1$ and ε_t is not serially correlated (see equation (11.27)). However, the 'power' of this test is rather low since one can also accept the joint hypothesis $\alpha = \gamma_1 = \beta = 0$. The latter result should come as no surprise since we noted that the forward premium/discount explains little of the change in the spot rate (see column 3, Table 11.2). MacDonald (1983) tests the unbiasedness property by allowing for any contemporaneous correlation between errors *across a set of equations* for $i = 1, 2, \ldots$ currencies of the form $s_{it+1} = \alpha + \beta f_{it} + \varepsilon_{it+1}$. If news events which are reflected in ε_{it} impinge upon more than one currency (which seems likely) then the ε_{it+1} for the set of currencies will be contemporaneously correlated (i.e. $E(\varepsilon_{it}, \varepsilon_{jt}) \neq 0$). Using Zellner's (1971) seemingly unrelated regression procedure (SURE) yields more efficient estimates of the standard errors of the parameters α and β. For example, MacDonald, using a SURE estimator, finds that for quarterly data over the period 1972(1)–1979(4) for six major currencies against the dollar only sterling and the Canadian dollar pass the joint hypothesis that $\alpha = 0$, $\beta = 1$. Rejection of the null hypothesis appears to be mainly due to $\alpha \neq 0$ rather than $\beta \neq 1$, and is more severe when Zellner's estimation method is used, compared with the more favourable results in his OLS regressions. However, this study does not address econometric problems associated with the non-stationarity of the data.

Notwithstanding the above empirical results, the balance of the evidence from many single equation studies is that there is a strong negative correlation between the forward premium and the subsequent change in the exchange rate (e.g. Fama (1984) and Meese and Roghoff (1983)). In fact the coefficient on the forward premium $fp_t = (f - s)_t$ is often nearer -1 than the 'unbiasedness value' of $+1$. This could be due to a failure of rational expectations or of risk neutrality. Following Fama (1984) we now maintain the assumption of RE while relaxing the assumption of risk neutrality to see if the latter may be the cause of the 'failure' of FRU.

12.3   FORWARD RATE: RISK AVERSION AND RATIONAL EXPECTATIONS

Risk averse speculators in the forward market will require compensation (i.e. a risk premium payment) for holding a net forward position in foreign exchange. Hence

$$f_t = rp_t + s_{t+1}^e \tag{12.21}$$

or

$$fp_t = rp_t + \Delta s_{t+1}^e \tag{12.22}$$

where $s_{t+1}^e = E_t s_{t+1}$, $\Delta s_{t+1}^e = s_{t+1}^e - s_t$, $fp_t = f_t - s_t$, and rp_t is an ad-hoc additive risk premium which may be time varying. Under RE equation (12.22) becomes:

$$f_t - s_{t+1} = rp_t - \varepsilon_{t+1} \tag{12.23}$$

where $\varepsilon_{t+1} = s_{t+1} - s_{t+1}^e$ is the RE forecast error. Suppose we now assume a very specific 'model' for the risk premium, namely that it depends (linearly) only on the forward premium fp_t:

$$rp_t = \delta_1 + \beta_1 fp_t \tag{12.24}$$

Under the null of RE but with a time varying risk premium given by (12.24) we have, substituting (12.24) in (12.23) (Fama, 1984):

$$f_t - s_{t+1} = \delta_1 + \beta_1 fp_t - \varepsilon_{t+1} \tag{12.25}$$

If the risk premium depends on the forward premium then we expect $\beta_1 \neq 0$. Note, however, that equation (12.25) embodies a rather restricted form of the risk premium since it is assumed that it depends only on fp_t and not on any other variables (there is therefore a possibility of omitted variables bias in (12.25)).

Now assume the 'usual' null hypothesis of FRU + RE and a *constant* risk premium

$$s_{t+1} - s_t = \delta_2 + \beta_2 fp_t + \varepsilon_{t+1} \tag{12.26}$$

We expect $\beta_2 = 1$ for unbiasedness and a time invariant risk premium implies $\delta_2 =$ constant. After some tedious algebra (see Appendix 12.1) Fama (1984) is able to show that the difference between β_1 and β_2 is given by:

$$\beta_1 - \beta_2 = [\mathrm{var}(rp_t) - \mathrm{var}(\Delta s^e_{t+1})]/\mathrm{var}(fp_t)$$

$$= [\mathrm{var}\,(\text{risk premium}) - \mathrm{var}\,(\text{expectations})]/\mathrm{var}(fp_t) \tag{12.27}$$

A positive value for $(\beta_1 - \beta_2)$ indicates that the variance of the risk premium is greater than the variance of expectations about s^e_{t+1}. However, it can be seen from (12.22) that if rp_t is highly variable then the forward premium will be a poor predictor of the expected change in the spot rate and this is what we find in the usual 'unbiasedness single equation regression' (12.26). Therefore $\beta_1 - \beta_2$ provides a quantitative guide to the relative importance of the time variation in the risk premium under the maintained hypothesis that RE holds.

Studies of the above type (e.g. Fama 1984) which estimate equations (12.25) and (12.26) usually find that $\beta_1 - \beta_2$ is positive. The latter usually arises because empirically β_2 is less than zero while β_1 is usually positive. Fama (1984) finds a range for $\beta_1 - \beta_2$ of 1.6 (for Japanese yen) to 4.2 (for Belgian francs). Fama's result that $\beta_1 > 0$ indicates that variations in the forward premium cause variations in the risk premium (see equations (12.22), (12.24) and (12.25)) while $\beta_2 < 0$ implies that unbiasedness does not hold (see equation (12.26)). Thus the overall conclusion from this work is that under the null of RE, the FRU proposition fails because the (linear additive) risk premium is 'highly' time varying.

It is worth repeating that a limitation of the above analysis is that the potentially time varying risk premium rp_t is assumed to depend only on the time varying forward premium fp_t. Also the risk premium is an ad-hoc linear addition in equation (12.13) and is not based on any well-founded economic theory.

The weakness of the above analysis is that it *assumes* that RE holds so that any violation of the null hypothesis is attributed to a time varying risk premium. What we require is a method which allows the failure of FRU to be apportioned between a violation of RE and variations in the risk premium.

Forward Rate: The Separation of RE and Risk Using Survey Data

As we have seen the joint null of 'FRU + RE + risk neutrality' is rejected by a large number of empirical studies (using a variety of regression techniques). By using survey data on agents' expectations of the future spot rate, Frankel and Froot (1986) show how one can apportion the rejection of the null between that due to a failure of RE and that due to a failure of risk neutrality. Consider the usual forward premium regression

$$\Delta s_{t+1} = \alpha + \beta fp_t + \varepsilon_{t+1} \tag{12.28}$$

where $\Delta s_{t+1} = s_{t+1} - s_t$, fp_t is the forward premium $(f_t - s_t)$ and $\varepsilon_{t+1} = E_t s_{t+1} - s_{t+1}$ is the RE forecast error. The OLS regression coefficient β is given by

$$\beta = \text{cov}(\Delta s_{t+1}, fp_t)/\text{var}(fp_t) \tag{12.29}$$

It is easy to show that

$$\beta = 1 - \beta_{\text{RE}} - \beta_{\text{RN}} \tag{12.30}$$

where

$$\beta_{\text{RE}} = -\text{cov}(\varepsilon_{t+1}, fp_t)/\text{var}(fp_t) \tag{12.31}$$

$$\beta_{\text{RN}} = 1 - \text{cov}(\Delta s^e_{t+1}, fp_t)/\text{var}(fp_t) \tag{12.32}$$

and

$$\Delta s^e_{t+1} = s^e_{t+1} - s_t$$

Under the assumption of RE, the forecast error ε_{t+1} is independent of the information set Ω_t and hence of fp_t so that $\beta_{\text{RE}} = 0$. Also, regardless of how expectations are formed then under FRU the expected rate of appreciation Δs^e_{t+1} will equal the forward premium fp_t, so that $\text{cov}(\Delta s^e_{t+1}, fp_t) = 1$ and hence $\beta_{\text{RN}} = 0$ (i.e. risk neutrality holds). If RE *and* risk neutrality hold then $\beta_{\text{RE}} = \beta_{\text{RN}} = 0$ and hence from (12.30), $\beta = 1$, as one would expect.

If we have survey data on s^e_{t+1} we can construct a data series for $\varepsilon_{t+1} = s_{t+1} - s^e_{t+1}$ along with the sample analogues of β_{RE} and β_{RN}. The latter provide evidence on the importance of the breakdown of either RE or risk neutrality in producing the result $\beta \neq 1$.

First, let us remind ourselves of some problems, outlined in Chapter 5, that arise in using survey data to test economic hypotheses. The first question that arises is whether the data is qualitative (e.g. respondents answer 'up', 'down', or 'same') or quantitative (e.g. respondents answer 'the exchange rate for sterling in 91 days will be 2.5 DM/£'). If qualitative date is used then the different methods which are used to transform the data yield different *quantitative* results for s^e_{t+1}. Hence we can have different sets of quantitative data purporting to measure the same expectations. Also, if we have quantitative data this may be either for individuals or for averages (or median value) over a group of individuals. In principle, RE applies to an individual's expectations and not to an average taken over a set of individuals.

There is also the question of whether the respondents are likely to give correct, thoughtful answers and whether the individuals surveyed remain as a fixed cohort or change over time. Also, when dealing with the FRU proposition the individual's estimate of s^e_{t+1} must be taken at the same time as f_t (and s_t). Finally there is the problem of whether the horizon of the survey data (on s^e_{t+1}) exactly matches the outturn figure for s_{t+1}. These problems bedevil attempts to draw very firm conclusions from studies based on survey data. Different conclusions by different researchers may be due to such 'quality differences' in the survey data used.

Let us return to the study by Frankel and Froot (1986, 1987, 1989) who use quantitative survey data on US respondents. They calculate β_{RE} and β_{RN} and using (12.30) they find that $\beta \neq 1$ (in fact β is negative) and that this is primarily attributed to a failure of RE (i.e. β_{RE} is non-zero). This broad conclusion holds over five (main) currencies and over horizons of 1, 3 and 6 months, for data from the mid 1970s and 1980s. MacDonald and

Torrance (1988) using quantitative data on UK respondents in 1985/86 also obtain similar results to Frankel and Froot.

Taylor (1989b) uses *qualitative* survey data on UK respondents which he transforms into quantitative data for the period 1981–1985. He finds the opposite of the above results, namely that the failure of $\beta \neq 1$ is mainly due to $\beta_{RN} \neq 0$. However, this evidence is fairly weak since for three out of the four exchange rates studied $\beta_{RE} = \beta_{RN} = 0$ and in only one case is $\beta_{RN} > 0$. In fact, $\beta_{RN} = 1.4(t = 0.15)$ for the sterling effective rate, but it is difficult to interpret results using the effective rate since this is a 'basket' of currencies (each of which has a set of bilateral forward rates).

On balance then there appears to be fairly strong evidence based on regressions using survey data (in particular see Froot and Frankel (1989)) that

- the forward premium is a biased predictor of subsequent changes in the exchange rate
- most of the bias is due to systematic forecast errors and very little to *variations* in the risk premium
- the *average* risk premium is non-zero but it is time invariant and in particular it does not vary with the forward discount

The failure of RE may be due to the fact that agents are 'irrational' and therefore *do* make systematic forecast errors. However, it could equally be due to the fact that agents take time to learn about new exchange rate processes and while they are learning, they make systematic errors because they do not know the true model. This learning could persist for some time if either the fundamentals affecting the exchange rate are continually changing or if the influence of noise traders on the market varies over time. Alternatively there may be a 'Peso problem' and a failure of FRU may occur even when agents are rational in the general sense of the word — namely they are doing the best they can with the information available.

12.4 EXCHANGE RATES AND NEWS

A prominent feature of the movement in bilateral exchanges is their extreme volatility. Weekly changes are extremely volatile with monthly and quarterly changes less so. Causal empiricism tell us that 'news', for example new money supply figures or new data on the current account position, can lead foreign exchange dealers to buy and sell currencies and influence spot and forward rates. Newspaper headlines such as 'Dollar falls because of unexpectedly high money supply figures' are not uncommon. The implication here is that if the published money supply figures had been *as expected* the exchange rate would have remained unchanged. It is the 'new information' contained in the money supply figures that leads FOREX dealers to change their view about future exchange rates, hence to buy and sell 'today' on the basis of this 'news'. On the other hand, *expected* events that are later confirmed may already be incorporated in the current exchange rate — an implication of an efficient market. For example, another headline might be 'Exchange rate improves as President *announces* lower monetary targets for the future'. The emphasis here is that expected future events may influence the exchange rate today.

We shall use the term 'news' as a shorthand solely for unexpected events. Our task in this section is to examine whether the above commonsense notions concerning the behaviour of the foreign exchange market may be formally incorporated in the exchange rate models discussed previously. The volatility of exchange rates may then be explained by news and changing expectations of future events.

Why are Exchange Rate Movements Volatile?

Two stylised facts about exchange rate volatility have a bearing on the analysis that follows. We have noted that the *predicted change* in the exchange rate, given by the forward premium fp_t, gives a poor forecast of Δs_{t+1} on a month-to-month basis. The variance of the actual change in the spot exchange rate can often exceed that for the forward discount by a factor of 20 (Frankel, 1982a). This suggests that the bulk of exchange rate changes Δs_{t+1} are due to 'new information' which by definition could not have been anticipated and reflected in the forward discount fp_t which prevailed in the previous period.

Second, *contemporaneous* spot and forward rates move very closely together. For example, for the \$/£, \$/DM and \$/yen exchange rates the correlation between the *contemporaneous* spot rate and one-month forward rate exceeds 0.99 and correlations between the corresponding *percentage changes* in spot and forward rates exceed 0.96 for these three currencies.

Direct Tests of the News Hypothesis in Spot and Forward Markets

Our first problem is how to measure news or unexpected events. There are three main approaches, one using survey data on expectations, another public forecasts and the third, RE and regression analysis.

Expectations data exist for prices, inflation and output for a number of industrial countries. Data on interest rate expectations are also available for the US (see Holden et al (1985)). Usually, but not always, data on expectations are qualitative. However, there are methods for transforming the data into a quantitative figure for expectations (Carlson and Parkin, 1975 and Pesaran, 1987).

Whether we think that economic fundamentals influence the exchange rate depends on our model of exchange rate determination. However, given a time series of survey data on expectations of relevant variables, $E_{t-1}X_t$, the unexpected or 'news' variables are simply given by $(X_t - E_{t-1}X_t)$. Public forecasts of X_t (from, for example, the Central Bank, Treasury or City forecasters) can be used in a similar manner to form variables representing 'news'.

If neither survey data on expectations nor forecast data are available, we can construct pseudo expectations series $E_{t-1}X_t$ and 'news' variables $(X_t - E_{t-1}X_t)$ using regression analysis. For any variable X_t we can assume agents make a forecast of X_t using past values of X_t itself and past values of other relevant economic variables Z_t:

$$X_t = \theta_1(L)X_{t-1} + \theta_2(L)Z_{t-1} + \varepsilon_t \tag{12.33}$$

where $\theta_i(L)$ are polynomials in the lag operator. Equation (12.33) can be viewed as a reduced form of a 'complete' economic model. After estimating (12.33) the predictions $\hat{X}_t$ can be taken as a proxy for agents' expectations, $E_{t-1}X_t$. The residual from (12.33), namely $\hat{\varepsilon}_t$, is a measure of the surprise of news about X_t, so $\hat{\varepsilon}_t$ is a proxy for $(X_t - E_{t-1}X_t)$.

Let us now turn to a general representation of models of the exchange rate which we designate:

$$s_t = \beta X_t + \omega_t \tag{12.34}$$

and hence

$$E_{t-1}s_t = \beta E_{t-1}X_t \tag{12.35}$$

where X_t is a set of fundamental economic variables that are thought to influence s_t (ω_t is a white noise error). For example, in some monetary models, X_t includes relative money supplies, relative real output and relative interest rates (see Chapter 13). From (12.34) and (12.35):

$$s_t = s_t^e + \beta'(X_t - E_{t-1}X_t) + \omega_t = s_t^e + \text{news} + \omega_t \tag{12.36}$$

where $s_t^e = E_{t-1}s_t$. Thus the forecast error $(s_t - s_t^e)$ is composed of an unobservable random component ω_t and unexpected changes ('news') in the fundamental variables X_t that determine s_t. If expectations are rational, $(X_t - E_{t-1}X_t)$ will be orthogonal (uncorrelated) with any other variables (at $t-1$ or earlier), and with error term ω_t.

Equation (12.36) can only be made operational if we have a model for s_{t+1}^e. The relationship between s_t and X_t should come from some relevant economic theory. In practice there may be several competing hypotheses about the determinants of s_t. Tests of the hypothesis that 'news' influences the spot (or forward) rate is always tested jointly with a hypothesis about the determination of the equilibrium expected exchange rate s^e and the expectations generating equation (12.33). Hence, different researchers choosing different models for s_t^e and $E_{t-1}X_t$ often obtain different results when testing the 'news' hypothesis.

Perhaps the simplest and most straightforward models of the determination of s_t^e involve risk neutrality and RE. UIP with a constant risk premium rp implies s_t^e and is determined by:

$$s_t^e = s_{t-1} + d_{t-1} + rp \tag{12.37}$$

If we assume FRU (or UIP + CIP) then s_t^e is given by:

$$s_t^e = f_{t-1} + rp' \tag{12.38}$$

Substituting the above expressions for s_t^e in equation (12.36) we obtain:

$$(s_t - s_{t-1} - d_{t-1}) = rp + \beta'(X_t - E_{t-1}X_t) + \omega_t \tag{12.39}$$

$$s_t - f_{t-1} = rp' + \gamma'(X_t - E_{t-1}X_t) + \omega_t \tag{12.40}$$

The above equations may be viewed as models embodying UIP + RE and FRU + RE, respectively, but where one is attempting to explain *some* of the RE forecast error in terms of surprises in specific economic variables X_t. If the EMH in the spot and forward markets holds then one would expect β and γ to be non-zero and for any variables dated at time $t-1$ or earlier to have zero coefficients when added to either of these equations.

If one uses a specific economic model based on fundamentals then s_t^e in (12.36) is replaced by the appropriate economic variables βX_t. For example, in monetary models of exchange rate determination X_t would include relative money supplies in the domestic and foreign country (see Chapter 13). In this case economic theory would indicate the 'sign' one would expect on β and hence on the surprise variables $(X_t - E_{t-1}X_t)$ in the regression (12.36).

The main problem with studies of this type is that there is no general agreement on a theory about the economic 'fundamentals' that determine the expected (equilibrium) exchange rate s_t^e. Hence there is no agreement on what variables to include as 'surprises'

$(X_t - E_{t-1}X_t)$ and often no agreement as to what the 'sign' on these variables should be *a priori*. Also to the extent that one may not be able to 'model' or quantify some major 'news' items (e.g. political rumour of a change in policy) one might expect the *observed* news items to provide little additional explanation. Finally, what is considered an important news item in one period may not be viewed as important at another time period, suggesting that the coefficients β and γ may not be statistically significant over all subsamples of the data and may appear unstable over time.

It follows from the above that these 'news regressions' are unlikely to yield great insights. In general, the news items (e.g. surprises in interest rates, money supplies, oil prices) that are found to be statistically significant (e.g. Frenkel (1981), Copeland (1984)) still leave much of the variation in the dependent variable in equation (12.36), (12.39) or (12.40) unexplained — that is there is still a lot of 'noise' or 'news' in exchange rate movements which is not explained at all.

Often in these studies lagged news items (e.g. $(X_{t-1} - E_{t-2}X_{t-1})$) are found to be significant. This is a refutation of RE since these lagged forecast errors are known at time $t - 1$. Such results are indicative of market inefficiency.

12.5 PESO PROBLEMS AND NOISE TRADERS

In previous sections we have noted that the simplifying assumptions of risk neutrality and RE are not consistent with the empirical results on FRU and speculation in the spot market via the UIP relationship. This section examines two reasons for the apparent empirical failure of these relationships and the high volatility exhibited by the spot rate. First, it is shown how the Peso problem can complicate the interpretation tests of the EMH in spot and forward markets. Second, a study of chartists, a particular form of noise trader in the FOREX market allow us to ascertain whether their behaviour might cause destabilising exchange rate movements and nullify the EMH.

Peso Problem

The apparent failure of the EMH in empirical tests may be illusory because of an issue known as the Peso problem. The Peso problem leads the researcher to measure expectations incorrectly, hence forecasts may appear biased and not independent of information at time t.

The Peso problem arises from the behaviour of the Mexican peso in the mid 1970s. Although the peso was on a notionally fixed exchange rate against the US dollar, it traded consistently at a forward discount for many years, in anticipation of a devaluation (which eventually occurred in 1976). Prima facie, the fact that the forward rate for the peso was persistently below the outturn value for the spot rate (in say three months' time) implies persistent profitable arbitrage opportunities for risk neutral speculators.

The Peso problem arises from the fact that there could be unobservable (and hence unquantifiable) events which *may* occur in the future, but in our sample of data never actually do occur. It is completely rational for an investor in forming his expectations to take account of factors that are unobservable to the econometrician. However, if the event never occurs in the sample of data examined by the econometrician, then he may erroneously infer that the agent's expectations are biased. Hence the econometrician may believe that he has unearthed a refutation of RE but in fact he has not. This is most easily seen by noting that under the RE and risk neutrality $\Delta s_{t+1} = (f - s)_t + \eta_{t+1}$. However, in a short sample of data on the peso in the mid 1970s one would find $(f - s)_t \neq 0$, yet $\Delta s_{t+1} = 0$: an apparent violation of the unbiasedness proposition. To illustrate the problem further, let us consider the Peso problem in a fairly simple way. Suppose UIP holds and US and Mexican interest rates are always equal and constant, then

$$E_t s_{t+1} = s_t \tag{12.41}$$

where s_t is measured as dollars per peso. If the Mexican government's fixed exchange rate policy is entirely credible (call this 'regime 1') and has been adhered to for a number of years then $s_{t+1}^e = s_{t+1} = s_t$ for all time periods in regime 1. Hence under 'complete credibility' expectations are correct in all time periods.

Now suppose that Mexican investors begin to think the government's commitment to a fixed exchange rate has weakened and that there is a non-zero probability π_2 that the peso will be devalued and a probability $(1 - \pi_2)$ that it will remain 'fixed'. Call this period 'partial credibility'. A rational investor would then have an expectation given by

$$E_t s_{t+1} = \pi_2 s_{t+1}^{(2)} + (1 - \pi_2) s_{t+1}^{(1)}$$
$$= \pi_2 (s_{t+1}^{(2)} - s_{t+1}^{(1)}) + s_{t+1}^{(1)} \tag{12.42}$$

where $s_{t+1}^{(1)}$ = exchange rate under the fixed exchange rate, regime 1, $s_{t+1}^{(2)}$ = new exchange rate under the devaluation, regime 2, that is $s_{t+1}^{(2)} > s_{t+1}^{(1)} = s_t^{(1)}$. Suppose, however, that during the 'partial credibility' period the Mexican government does *not* alter the exchange rate. The outturn data will therefore be $s_{t+1}^{(1)} = s_t^{(1)}$, the existing fixed parity. Hence even *survey data* collected over this partial credibility period (which accurately measures $E_t s_{t+1}$), will not equal the (constant) outturn value $s_t^{(1)}$

$$E_t s_{t+1} = \pi_2 s_{t+1}^{(2)} + (1 - \pi_2) s_t^{(1)} \neq s_t^{(1)} \tag{12.43}$$

The *ex-post* forecast error in the 'partial credibility' period using (12.42) is

$$\tilde{w}_{t+1} = s_t^{(1)} - E_t s_{t+1} = \pi_2 (s_t^{(1)} - s_{t+1}^{(2)}) < 0 \tag{12.44}$$

where we have used $s_{t+1}^{(1)} = s_t^{(1)}$. Hence the *ex-post* forecast error, which is observable if we have survey data on expectations, is non-zero and biased. Also if $s_t^{(1)}$ varies slightly then a regression of $\tilde{w}_{t+1}$ on the actual exchange rate $s_t^{(1)}$ will in general yield a non-zero coefficient. The latter coefficient will equal π_2, if $s_{t+1}^{(2)}$ is constant over the sample period and may be 'close to' π_2 if $s_{t+1}^{(2)}$ varies only slightly over time (i.e. some omitted variables bias will ensue). Hence we have an apparent refutation of the informational efficiency assumption of RE because the forecast error is not independent of information at time t. Notice that even if π_2, the probability of the unobserved event, is small the 'bias' in the forecast error $\tilde{w}_{t+1}$ can still appear large if the potential change in s under the new regime is thought to be large (i.e. $s_t^{(1)} - s_{t+1}^{(2)}$ is large).

Now let us consider the problems caused when we try to test for FRU. If investors think a devaluation of the peso is likely then $s_{t+1}^{(2)} > s_t^{(1)}$ and hence from (12.43) we see that $E_t s_{t+1} > s_t^{(1)}$ (remember that s_t is in units of pesos per US dollar and hence an increase in 's' is a devaluation of the peso). Under FRU and risk neutrality, speculation in the forward market ensures

$$f_t = E_t s_{t+1} \tag{12.45}$$

and hence $f_t > s_t^{(1)}$ and f_t will be persistently above the constant outturn value for the spot rate (i.e. peso at forward discount).

Suppose we had a longer data set which included a period when the Mexican government announced a fixed exchange rate but that agents then believe that this announced rate might be abandoned in favour of a *revaluation* of the peso. The above analysis would again apply but in this 'favourable partial credibility period' (regime 3) the systematic forecast errors $\tilde{w}_t^*$ would now be *positive* (and not negative as under regime 2). Hence with a long enough data set where 'unfavourable' and 'favourable' unobserved events occur equally often, our data set would conform to the RE postulates of unbiased forecast errors and forecast errors that are independent of Ω_t.

The Peso problem therefore arises because one is testing a hypothesis with a limited data set, in which there are unobservable yet *non-random* variables (i.e. the probability of changes in government policy). Thus the *average* of the outturn values for s_t are not an accurate representation of agents' true expectations. The RE assumption

$$s_{t+1} = E_t s_{t+1} + u_{t+1}$$

where u_{t+1} is random around zero, does not hold in the 'short', partial credibility data set.

The only way one can in principle get round the Peso problem when investigating FRU is to use accurate survey data on expectations to test $E_t s_{t+1} = f_t$. However, in practice, analysing survey data has its own problems. It is possible that Peso problems are fairly prevalent and in any actual data set we have, they do not cancel out. Peso problems that involve an equal frequency of positive and negative 'events' with probabilities π_i or size of shifts ($s^{(j)} - s^{(i)}$) that just exactly cancel out in the data set available to the researcher seems unlikely. Clearly a longer data set is likely to mitigate this problem but perhaps not irradicate it entirely. However, for advocates of RE, the apparent failure of RE in statistical tests can always be attributed to 'hidden' Peso problems.

Noiser Traders

If one were to read the popular press then one would think that foreign exchange dealers were speculators, par excellence. In the 1980s, young men in striped shirts, wearing primary coloured braces were frequently seen on television, shouting simultaneously into two telephones in order to quickly execute buy and sell orders for foreign currencies. The obvious question which arises is, are these individuals purchasing and selling foreign exchange on the basis of news about fundamentals or do they in fact 'chase trends'? If the latter, the question then arises as to whether they can have a pervasive influence on the price of foreign exchange. As we have seen there have been a large number of technically sophisticated tests of market efficiency in the foreign exchange market both in terms of spot speculation (UIP) and speculation in the forward market (FRU). However, there has been remarkably little work done on the techniques used by actual foreign exchange dealers and whether these might cause movements in exchange rates which are *not* related to news about fundamentals. An exception here is the study by Allen and Taylor (1989a) who look at a particular small segment of the foreign exchange market and undertake a survey of chartists' behaviour. Chartists study only the price movements in the market and base their view of the future solely on past price changes. Chartists believe that they can recognise patterns in past price movements which can be used to predict future movements and hence generate profitable trading strategies. This, of course, would not be the case in an efficient market.

Individual chartists use a variety of methods to predict future price changes. For example, they might use moving averages of past prices to try and predict future prices. They may have very high frequency graphs of say minute-by-minute price movements and they attempt to infer systematic patterns in these graphs. Consider, for example, the idealised pattern given in Figure 12.2 which is known as 'the head and shoulders reversal pattern'. On this graph is drawn a horizontal line called 'the shoulder'. Once the pattern reaches point D, that is a peak below the neckline, the chartist would assume this signals a full trend reversal. He would then sell the currency believing that it would fall in the future and he could buy it back at a lower price. As another example, consider Figure 12.3, the so-called 'symmetric triangle' indicated by the oscillations converging on the point at A. To some chartists this would signal a future upward movement. Clearly the interpretation of such graphs is subjective. For chartists as a group to influence the market, most chartists must interpret the charts in roughly the same way, otherwise all the chartists would do would be to introduce some random noise into prices but no trends. It is well known that chartists also use survey data on 'market sentiment'. For example, if 'sentiment' is reported to be optimistic about the German economy, the chartists may well try and step in early and buy DMs.

The data set on which the Allen and Taylor study is based is rather small. The survey was conducted on a panel of chartists (between 10 and 20 responded every week) over the period June 1988–March 1989. They were telephoned every Thursday and asked for their expectations with respect to the sterling–dollar, dollar–mark and dollar–yen exchange rates for one and four weeks ahead, yielding about 36 observations per chartist per currency. The survey also asked the chartists about the kind of information they used in making their forecasts and who the information was passed on to (e.g. actual traders).

It was found that at the shortest horizons, say intra-day to one week, as much as 90 percent of the respondents used some chartist input in forming their exchange rate

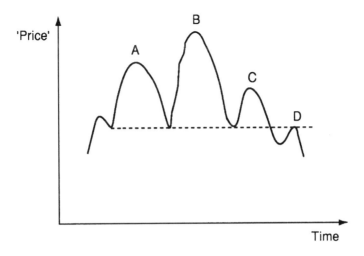

Figure 12.2 Head and Shoulders. *Source*: Allen and Taylor (1989b).

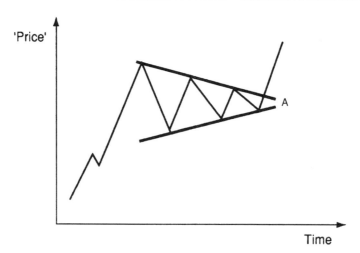

Figure 12.3 Symmetric Triangle. *Source*: Allen and Taylor (1989b).

expectations. As the time horizon lengthens to three months, six months or one year the weight given to fundamentals increases and 85 percent of the respondents judged that over these longer horizons 'fundamentals' were more important than chart analysis. However, the chart analysis was always seen as complementary to the analysis based on fundamentals and therefore it is possible that chart analysis influences exchange rates even at these longer horizons.

If one looks *ex post* at the accuracy of the chartists' forecasts taken as a whole, then Figure 12.4 for the DM/$, four-week ahead forecasts are fairly typical of the results for other currencies. In general Allen and Taylor find:

- There is a tendency for the forecasts to miss turning points. On a rising or falling market the chartists' expectations underestimate the extent of the rise or fall.

- Prediction errors are noticeably greater at the four-week horizon than at the one-week horizon. Individual chartist's forecasts for four-week ahead predictions are generally unbiased but they are biased for the one-week ahead predictions.

- For all the chartists taken as a whole, they correctly predict the change in the exchange rate over one-week and four-week horizons approximately 50 percent of the time. This is what one would accept if their forecasts were purely due to chance.

However, the above result for *all* chartists neglects the possibility that *individual* chartists might in fact do well and do consistently well over time. In fact there are differences in forecast accuracy among the chartists and there are some chartists who are systematically 'good'. However, one cannot read too much into the last result since the time period of the survey is fairly short and in a random sample of individuals one would always expect that a certain percentage would do 'better than average' (e.g. 5 percent of the population).

Again taking chartists as a whole, Allen and Taylor assess whether they outperform alternative methods of forecasting. For example, some alternatives examined are forecasts based on the random walk and ARIMA forecasts or forecasts based upon a VAR (using exchange rates, the interest rate differential and the relative stock market performance).

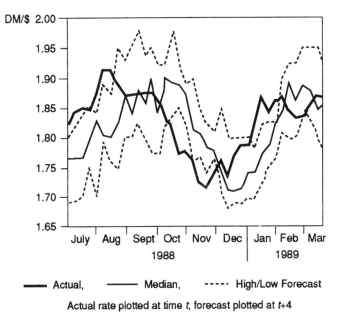

Figure 12.4 Deutschmark: Four Weeks Ahead Chartist Forecasts. *Source*: Allen and Taylor (1989b)

The results here are mixed. However, few individual forecasters (apart from forecaster 'M') beat the random walk model. In most cases the ARIMA and VAR forecasts were worse than predictions of 'no change' based on a random walk and often most chartists failed to beat these statistical forecasting models. However, overall there is not much in it. All of the statistical forecasting methods and the chartists' forecasts had approximately the same root mean squared errors for one-week and four-week ahead forecasts with, on balance, the random walk probably doing best. However, there were some chartists (e.g. chartist 'M') who consistently outperformed all other forecasting methods.

Since Allen and Taylor have data on expectations they can correlate changes in expectations with past changes in the actual exchange rate. Of particular interest is whether chartists have bandwagon expectations. That is to say when the exchange rate increases between $t-1$ and t, does this lead all chartists to revise their expectations upwards. Allen and Taylor tested this hypothesis but found that for all chartists as a group, bandwagon expectations did not apply. Thus chartist advice does not appear to be intrinsically destabilising in that they do not over-react to recent changes in the exchange rate. Allen and Taylor also investigate whether chartists have adaptive or regressive expectations. These are essentially mean reverting expectations and there were some chartists who approximated this behaviour. Thus chartists may cause short-run deviations from fundamentals. Overall the results seem to suggest there are agents in the market who make systematic forecasting errors but there appears to be no bandwagon or explosive effect from this behaviour and at most chartists might influence short-run deviations of the exchange rate from fundamentals. The Allen and Taylor study did not examine whether chartists' forecasts actually resulted in profitable trades, they merely looked at the accuracy of chartists' forecasts. However, a number of studies have been done (Goodman, 1979, 1980, Levich, 1980 and Bilson, 1981) which have looked at *ex-post* evaluations of forecasting services, *some* of which were provided by technical analysts (e.g. chartists). A major finding of these studies is that certain foreign exchange advisory services do consistently outperform the forward rate as a predictor of the future spot rate. In particular Goodman finds that 'technical advice' is consistently superior to both the forward rate and other econometric models based on fundamentals, in forecasting the future spot rate.

12.6 SUMMARY

For the topics covered in this chapter the main conclusions are:

- Riskless arbitrage opportunities in the FOREX market sometimes do appear at relatively long horizons (one year) but for the most part there are no large persistent profitable opportunities and covered interest parity holds.
- Evidence suggests that UIP and FRU do not hold but one cannot conclusively say that this is due to a failure of the assumption of risk neutrality or RE. A tentative conclusion might be that rejection lies more with the assumption that agents use RE at all times.
- The addition of explicit variables to proxy 'news' does not appear to add a great deal to the predictability of the future change in spot rates given either the interest differential (UIP) or the forward discount (FRU).
- Because of a presumption of frequent and possibly substantial government intervention in the forward and spot markets, Peso problems are likely to be present. However, they are virtually impossible to quantify and this makes it difficult to interpret whether the 'negative' results when testing UIP and FRU do imply a rejection of the EMH.
- Noise traders probably do influence spot rates but such behaviour, based on results from chartists' expectations, are likely to have only a short-run impact on freely floating spot rates and chartists' behaviour is unlikely to be destabilising, independently of other traders' behaviour.

Hence, no definitive results emerge from the tests outlined in this chapter on the behaviour of forward and spot rates and this in part accounts for governments switching their policy stance with regard to exchange rates. Sometimes the authorities take the view that the market is efficient and hence refrain from intervention while at other times they believe the market is dominated by (irrational) noise traders and hence massive intervention is sometimes undertaken. A 'half-way house' is then provided when the authorities suggest that rules for concerted intervention are required to keep the exchange rate within preannounced bands, as in the exchange rate mechanism of the European Monetary System. A logical development of the view that free market exchange rates are excessively volatile and that governments cannot prevent fundamental and persistent misalignments is the move towards a common currency, as embodied in the Maastricht Treaty for European countries.

APPENDIX 12.1 DERIVATION OF FAMA'S DECOMPOSITION OF THE RISK PREMIUM IN THE FORWARD MARKET

If we include an additive time varying risk premium rp_t in the FRU hypothesis we obtain:

$$f_t = rp_t + s_{t+1}^e \tag{1a}$$

or equivalently:

$$fp_t = rp_t + \Delta s^e_{t+1} \tag{1b}$$

where $\Delta s^e_{t+1} = s^e_{t+1} - s_t$, $s^e_{t+1} = E_t s_{t+1}$ and $fp_t = f_t - s_t$. Under RE:

$$s_{t+1} = s^e_{t+1} + \varepsilon_{t+1} \tag{2}$$

and (1a) and (1b) become

$$f_t = rp_t + s_{t+1} - \varepsilon_{t+1} \tag{3a}$$

$$fp_t = rp_t + \Delta s_{t+1} - \varepsilon_{t+1} \tag{3b}$$

Assume that rp_{t+1} depends linearly on the forward premium

$$rp_{t+1} = \delta_1 + \beta_1 fp_t \tag{4}$$

Under null hypothesis of RE, FRU and a time varying risk premium we have from (3a) and (4)

$$(f_t - s_{t+1}) = \delta_1 + \beta_1 fp_t - \varepsilon_{t+1} \tag{5}$$

Now consider the 'usual' null hypothesis of FRU + RE but with a *constant* risk premium

$$\Delta s_{t+1} = \delta_2 + \beta_2 fp_t + \varepsilon_{t+1} \tag{6}$$

For unbiasedness we require $\beta_2 = 1$ and a constant risk premium implies $\delta_2 = -rp_t = $ constant.
    Under their respective null hypotheses OLS provides consistent estimators of β_1 and β_2 in equations (5) and (6):

$$\beta_1 = \text{cov}(f_t - s_{t+1}, fp_t)/\text{var}(fp_t) \tag{7}$$

$$\beta_2 = \text{cov}(\Delta s_{t+1}, fp_t)/\text{var}(fp_t) \tag{8}$$

Substitute for $f_t - s_{t+1}$ from (3a) and for fp_t from (1b) in equation (7):

$$\beta_1 = \text{cov}(rp_t - \varepsilon_{t+1}, \Delta s^e_{t+1} + rp_t)/\text{var}(fp_t) \tag{9}$$

Under RE, the forecast error ε_{t+1} is independent of information at time t including rp_t. Also Δs^e_{t+1} is independent of ε_{t+1} under RE. Hence (9) reduces to

$$\beta_1 = [\text{cov}(rp_t, \Delta s^e_{t+1}) + \text{var}(rp_t)]/\text{var}(fp_t) \tag{10}$$

Equation (2), the RE condition, may be rewritten

$$\Delta s_{t+1} = \Delta s^e_{t+1} + \varepsilon_{t+1} \tag{11}$$

where $\Delta s_{t+1} = s_{t+1} - s_t$ and $\Delta s^e_{t+1} = s^e_{t+1} - s_t$. If we now substitute for Δs_{t+1} from (11) and for fp_t from (1b) in equation (8) we obtain:

$$\beta_2 = \text{cov}(\Delta s^e_{t+1} + \varepsilon_{t+1}, rp_t + \Delta s^e_{t+1})/\text{var}(fp_t) \tag{12}$$

Under RE, ε_{t+1} is independent of rp_t and Δs^e_{t+1} hence:

$$\beta_2 = [\text{cov}(rp_t, \Delta s^e_{t+1}) + \text{var}(\Delta s^e_{t+1})]/\text{var}(fp_t) \tag{13}$$

Substracting (13) from (10) we then obtain (12.27) in the text

$$\beta_1 - \beta_2 = [\text{var}(rp_t) - \text{var}(\Delta s^e_{t+1})]/\text{var}(fp_t) \tag{14}$$

13
The Exchange Rate and Fundamentals

There are a large number of alternative models based on 'economic fundamentals' that have been used to analyse movements in the spot exchange rate. This chapter, however, sketches only the main ideas. It is probably correct to say that monetary models in their various forms have dominated the theoretical and empirical exchange rate literature and we discuss a number of these such as the flex-price and sticky-price monetary models and the Frankel real interest rate model. As we shall see these models have been far from successful in explaining movements in exchange rates. Indeed, there is no consensus among economists on the appropriate set of economic fundamentals that influence exchange rates and this in part is why policy makers have sought to limit exchange rate movements by cooperative arrangements such as Bretton Woods and the ERM in Europe (and in the latter case to consider proposals for a move towards a common currency). The flex-price monetary model (FPMM) concentrates on the current rather than the capital account and assumes prices are flexible and output is exogenously determined by the supply side of the economy. Under floating rates the FPMM model predicts a close relationship between rapid monetary growth and a depreciating exchange rate (and vice versa) — which, for example, is broadly consistent with events in Italy, the UK, Germany and Japan in the first half of the 1970s and in some Latin American countries in the 1970s and 1980s. In fact, in terms of its predictions the text book Mundell–Fleming model under the assumption of a full employment level of output yields similar results to the FPMM.

Unfortunately, the FPMM failed adequately to explain the large swings in the *real* exchange rate (or competitiveness) that occurred in a number of small, open economies, such as those of the UK, the Netherlands and Italy in the second half of the 1970s and early 1980s. The FPMM takes 'money' as the only asset of importance and hence ignores other asset flows in the capital account of the balance of payments. Once we recognise the importance of capital flows, which have obviously increased due to the gradual dismantling of exchange controls, we have to address the question of expectations. Speculative short-term capital flows respond to relative interest rates between the domestic and foreign country but also depend upon expectations about exchange rate movements. The sticky-price monetary model (SPMM) invokes the rational expectations hypothesis to deal with exchange rate expectations and it is usually assumed that capital account flows are perfectly mobile. Price adjustment in the goods market is slow and is determined by excess demand working via the price expectations augmented Phillips curve (PEAPC). The combination of sticky prices (or sluggish output response) and high capital mobility implies that changes in monetary and fiscal policy can cause 'large' swings in the nominal and real exchange rate and possibly lead to exchange rate overshooting.

A recurring theme in the exchange rate literature concerns the response of the exchange rate to a change in domestic interest rates. The FPMM model predicts that a depreciation ensues after a *rise* in domestic interest rates, while the SPMM model yields the opposite conclusion. The real interest rate monetary model (RIMM) clarifies this exchange rate–interest rate nexus and also yields insights into why exchange rate movements appear to be 'excessively' volatile.

Finally, a defect in the SPMM is its implicit assumption of the perfect substitutability of domestic and foreign assets and failure to analyse explicitly the stock flow interactions arising from current account imbalances. This is remedied in the portfolio balance model of exchange rates (PBM).

13.1 FLEX-PRICE MONETARY MODEL

The FPMM model relies on the PPP condition and a stable demand for money function. The (logarithm) of the demand for money may be assumed to depend on (the logarithm of) real income, y, the price level, p, and the level of the (bond) interest rate, r. We assume a similar 'foreign' demand for money function. Monetary equilibria in the domestic and foreign country are given by:

$$m^s = p + \phi y - \lambda r \tag{13.1}$$

$$m^{s*} = p^* + \phi^* y^* - \lambda^* r^* \tag{13.2}$$

where foreign variables are starred. In the FPMM model the domestic interest rate is exogenous — a rather peculiar property. This assumption implies that the domestic interest rate is rigidly linked to the exogenous world interest rate because of the assumption of 'perfect capital mobility' and a *zero* expected change in the exchange rate. Given that output is also assumed fixed at the full employment level (the neoclassical supply curve) then any excess money can only influence the 'perfectly flexible' domestic price level, one for one: hence the 'neutrality of money' holds.

Equilibrium in the traded goods 'market' (i.e. the current account) ensues when prices in a common currency are equalised: in short when PPP holds. Using lower case letters to denote logarithms, the PPP condition is:

$$s = p - p^* \tag{13.3}$$

The world price, p^*, is exogenous to the domestic economy, being determined by the world money supply. The domestic money supply determines the domestic price level and hence the exchange rate is determined by *relative* money supplies. Algebraically, substituting (13.1) and (13.2) into (13.3) gives

$$s = (m^s - m^{s*}) - \phi y + \phi^* y^* + \lambda r - \lambda^* r^* \tag{13.4}$$

Possible transmission mechanisms underlying (13.4) are (i) an increase in the domestic money supply leads to an increased demand for *foreign* goods (and assets), an excess demand for foreign currency and a depreciation in the domestic currency. (The latter increases import prices in domestic currency and domestic producers' 'arbitrage' domestic prices upwards to match the new level of import prices of tradeable goods.) Alternatively, (ii) excess money balances cause an excess demand for *domestic* goods, followed by a rise in domestic prices via the Phillips curve. This is followed by a switch to relatively cheap foreign goods causing downward pressure on the domestic exchange rate. It is probably (i) that is closest to the spirit of the FPMM price-arbitrage approach.

It is worth noting that the effect of either a change in output or the domestic interest rate on the exchange rate in the FPMM is contrary to that found in a Keynesian model. A higher level of output or lower domestic interest rates in the FPMM model causes an increase in the domestic demand for money. The latter allows a lower domestic price level to achieve money market equilibrium, and hence results in an *appreciation* in the exchange rate (see, for example, Frenkel et al (1980) and Gylfason and Helliwell (1983)). Now, a rise in nominal interest rates may ensue either because of a tight monetary policy or because of an increase in the expected rate of inflation, π. The Fisher hypothesis states that real rates of interest Ψ are constant in the long run:

$$r = \Psi + \pi \qquad (13.5)$$

Adding this relationship to the FPMM of equation (13.4) we see that a high expected rate of domestic inflation is associated with a high nominal interest rate and a depreciation in the domestic exchange rate (i.e. s has a 'high' value). Thus the interest rate–exchange rate relationship appears somewhat less perverse when the Fisher hypothesis is added to the FPMM model to yield what one might term the *hyperinflation* FPMM. The latter terminology arises because r is dominated by changes in π in hyperinflations (e.g. as in Germany in the 1920s). This is all very well but one might be more disposed to view the rate of depreciation (i.e. the *change* in s) as depending on the expected rate of inflation as in the Frenkel (1979) 'real interest' model discussed below.

The FPMM as presented here may be tested by estimating equations of the form (13.4) for the exchange rate or by investigating the stability of the PPP relationship and the demand for money functions. As far as equation (13.4) is concerned it worked reasonably well empirically in the early 1970s floating period for a number of bilateral exchange rates (see Bilson (1978)), but in the late 1970s the relationship performed badly other than for countries with high inflation (e.g. Argentina and Brazil). The increase in *capital* mobility in the 1970s may account for the failure of the FPMM model. Although there are difficulties in testing the PPP relationship it has been noted that it too does not appear to hold in the latter half of the 1970s (see also Frenkel (1981)).

13.2 STICKY-PRICE MONETARY MODEL (SPMM)

In the latter half of the 1970s the FPMM ceased to provide an accurate description of the behaviour of exchange rates for a number of small open economies. For example, in the UK over the period 1979–1981 the sterling *nominal* effective exchange rate (i.e. the rate against a basket of currencies) *appreciated* substantially even though the UK money supply grew rapidly relative to the growth in the 'world' money supply. However, more startling, the *real* exchange rate (i.e. price competitiveness or the terms of trade) appreciated by about 40 percent over this period and this was followed by an equally sharp fall over the 1981–1984 period. The FPMM can only explain changes in the real exchange rate by *differential short-run* lags in the response of the nominal exchange rate and the domestic (and foreign) price level to changes in relative money supplies. Faced with the kind of evidence cited above these lags appeared to be highly variable or, in other words, the FPMM failed to explain this phenomenon adequately. Large volatile swings in the real exchange rate may lead to large swings in net trade (i.e. real exports less real imports) with consequent multiplier effects on domestic output and employment. The SPMM provides an explanation of exchange rate overshooting (Dornbusch, 1976) and short-run changes in real output, as occurred in the very severe recession of 1979–1982 in the UK. The SPMM is able to resolve the conundrum found in the FPMM where one obtains the counterintuitive result that a rise in domestic interest rates leads to a depreciation in the domestic currency. In the SPMM if the rise in nominal rates is unexpected and hence constitutes a rise in *real* interest rates the conventional result, namely an appreciation in the exchange rate, ensues.

Like the FPMM the SPMM is 'monetarist' in the sense that the neutrality of money is preserved in the long run by invoking a vertical neoclassical supply curve for output (or equivalently a vertical long-run Phillips curve). However, PPP holds only in the long run and hence short-run changes in the real net trade balance are allowed. Key elements in the SPMM are the assumption of a conventional, stable demand for money function and uncovered interest parity. Agents in the foreign exchange market are assumed to form (Muth) rational expectations about the future path of the exchange rate: they immediately act on any new information and this is what makes the exchange rate 'jump' and undergo frequent changes. In addition, in SPMM the capital account and the money market 'clear' in all periods, but the goods market, where prices are sticky, does not. It is this combination of 'flex-price' and 'fix-price' markets that can produce exchange rate overshooting.

13.3 DORNBUSCH OVERSHOOTING MODEL

We now look at a simplified account of the Dornbusch (1976) model beginning with a description of the main behavioural assumptions, followed by an analysis of the impact of a tight monetary stance on the economy. (For a detailed account see Cuthbertson and Taylor (1987).)

The uncovered interest parity (open-arbitrage) relationship expresses the condition for equilibrium in the capital account. Foreign exchange speculators investing abroad *expect* a return of $r^* + \mu$ percent, where $r^* = $ foreign interest rate and $\mu = $ expected *appreciation* of the *foreign* currency (depreciation in the domestic currency). With perfect capital mobility and risk neutrality, equilibrium in the capital account requires:

$$r = r^* + \mu \tag{13.6}$$

Expectations about the exchange rate are assumed to be regressive. If the actual rate lies below the long-run equilibrium rate, $\bar{s}$, then agents expect the actual rate to rise towards the long-run rate; that is, for the spot rate of the domestic currency rate to *depreciate* in the future:

$$\mu = \theta(\bar{s} - s) \quad 0 < \theta < 1 \tag{13.7}$$

where s and $\bar{s}$ are in logarithms. This expectations generating equation may be made fully consistent with rational expectations in that the regressive formula allows expectations to be correct *ex post*, given the other equations in the Dornbusch model. Equilibrium in the money market implies

$$m^s = \lambda r + \phi y + p \tag{13.8}$$

In the goods market, aggregate demand (AD) is given by

$$AD = \delta(s - p + p^*) - \sigma r + \gamma y + \gamma' \tag{13.9}$$

The first term represents the impact of the real exchange rate on *net* trade volumes, the second ($-\sigma r$) the investment schedule, the third (γy) the consumption function *and* expenditure effects on imports and the final term (γ') exogenous demand factors such as government expenditure. The 'supply side' is represented by a vertical long-run Phillips curve: the rate of inflation responds to excess demand in the goods market; prices adjust slowly to equilibrium ($0 < \Pi < 1$),

$$\dot{p} = \Pi(AD - \bar{y}) = \Pi[\delta(s - p + p^*) - \sigma r + \gamma y + \gamma' - \bar{y}] \tag{13.10}$$

where $\bar{y}$ is the full employment level of output.

Flexible Prices: Long Run

Consider a reduction of 1 percent in the money supply. If prices are perfectly flexible, a fall of 1 percent in the price level will restore money market equilibrium (with an unchanged level of interest rates). In addition, if the exchange rate appreciates by 1 percent, the *real* exchange rate remains constant and real aggregate demand continues to match aggregate supply. In the long run, the interest rate is unchanged and therefore real investment is unchanged and uncovered interest parity still holds. It follows from the latter that (immediately *after* the 'long-run' appreciation), the exchange rate is *expected* to remain constant in the future. Thus, as prices in the SPMM are *not* sticky *in the long run*, then after a monetary contraction the exchange rate will be higher in order to maintain price competitiveness (PPP).

Fixed Prices: Short-Run Overshooting

In contrast, now assume prices and output are sticky in the short run. With y and p 'sticky', a decrease in the money supply requires a rise in the bond rate, r, to 'clear' the money market ($dr = -(1/\lambda)dm^s$, equation (13.8)). The rise in r causes a potential capital inflow, which can be arrested only if the domestic exchange rate is expected to depreciate, thus re-establishing uncovered interest parity. According to equation (13.7) an *expected* depreciation of the domestic currency requires the *actual* spot rate immediately to appreciate above its long equilibrium value; hence the exchange rate 'overshoots' its long-run value.

It is useful to present a simplified account of the mathematics behind this result. Because of the vertical Phillips curve, output is fixed in the long run and the neutrality of money implies $dp = dm$. As PPP also holds in the long run, $d\bar{s} = d\bar{p} = d\bar{m}^s$ (where a bar over a variable indicates its long-run value). Turning to the short run, assume p and y are fixed so that any short-run disequilibrium in the money market is taken up by adjustments in r:

$$dr = -dm^s/\lambda \tag{13.11}$$

To preserve uncovered interest parity in the short run the *expected* appreciation in the exchange rate μ must equal the interest differential dr (note that $dr^* = 0$):

$$d\mu = dr = -dm^s/\lambda \tag{13.12}$$

From the expectations equation (13.7) and using (13.12) above, the *short-run* change in the exchange rate is:

$$ds = d\bar{s} - d\mu/\theta = [1 + (\theta\lambda)^{-1}] dm^s \tag{13.13}$$

Since $\theta\lambda > 0$ the initial change in the spot rate of $[1 + (\theta\lambda)^{-1}] dm^s$ exceeds the 'unit' long-run change: $d\bar{s} = dm^s$.

It is clear that 'overshooting' is in part due to the restrictive channels through which monetary policy is forced to operate. Initially all adjustment in the money market is via the interest rate and only in the long run does the price level equilibrate the money market and the interest rate return to its original level. Although it is not immediately apparent from the above analysis, the assumption of risk neutrality is of equal importance in this respect. Note that, in contrast to the prediction of the FPMM, the response of the exchange rate to the interest rate is as one might intuitively expect: an unanticipated jump in the interest rate (consequent on a fall in the money supply) leads to an appreciation of the domestic currency.

13.4 FRANKEL REAL INTEREST DIFFERENTIAL MODEL (RIDM)

Frankel (1979) provides a general model for analysing the impact of changes in the interest rate on the exchange rate and he refers to this as the 'real interest differential model'. It provides a Dornbusch relationship with respect to the nominal interest rate ($\partial s/\partial r < 0$) and a hyperinflation FPMM with respect to the expected rate of inflation ($\partial s/\partial \pi > 0$). Also, the exchange rate may overshoot its long-run equilibrium value.

Frankel's model assumes uncovered arbitrage but modifies the Dornbusch expectations equation for the exchange rate by adding a term reflecting relative expected secular inflation ($\pi - \pi^*$). The expectations equation is

$$s^e - s = \theta(\bar{s} - s) + (\pi - \pi^*) \tag{13.14}$$

and uncovered interest parity yields

$$s^e - s = r - r^* \tag{13.15}$$

The expected rate of depreciation ($s^e - s$) depends upon the deviation of the exchange rate from its equilibrium value, which as we know gives Dornbusch-type results. In addition, if $s = \bar{s}$, the expected rate of depreciation is given by the expected inflation differential between the domestic and foreign currency: as we shall see this term generates hyperinflation FPMM results. Frankel asserts that the expectations equation is a plausible, expectations generating mechanism *per se* but it may also be shown to be consistent with *rational* expectations. (We do not deal with this aspect.)

Combining equations (13.14) and (13.15) and rearranging we have

$$\bar{s} - s = (1/\theta)[(r - \pi) - (r^* - \pi^*)] \tag{13.16}$$

The movement in the spot rate around its equilibrium value is determined by the relative *real* interest differential. Further, in long-run equilibrium, $s = \bar{s}$, which implies $\bar{r} - \bar{r} = \pi - \pi^*$; hence, the term in square brackets may be rewritten as $[(r - r^*) - (\bar{r} - \bar{r}^*)]$. It is only when a tight monetary policy raises the nominal interest differential $(r - r^*)$ above its long-run level $(\bar{r} - \bar{r}^*)$, given by relative expected inflation, that the 'current' exchange rate appreciates above its long-run equilibrium level $(\bar{s} - s > 0)$.

We now assume that PPP holds in the long run and with the usual demand for money functions (with $\phi = \phi^*$, $\lambda = \lambda^*$ for simplicity) we obtain an expression for the *long-run* exchange rate (as in the FPMM model):

$$\bar{s} = \bar{p} - \bar{p}^* = \bar{m} - \bar{m}^* - \phi(\bar{y} - \bar{y}^*) + \lambda(\bar{r} - \bar{r}^*)$$
$$= (\bar{m} - \bar{m}^*) - \phi(\bar{y} - \bar{y}^*) + \lambda(\pi - \pi^*) \tag{13.17}$$

where we have used $\bar{r} - \bar{r}^* = \pi - \pi^*$ (the 'international Fisher effect' which is implicit in the hyperinflation FPMM). The crucial elements in the Frankel model are the expectations equation (13.14) and the distinction between the short-run and long-run determinants of the exchange rate. Substituting for $\bar{s}$ from (13.16) in (13.17) we obtain Frankel's ('reduced-form') exchange rate equation:

$$s = \bar{m} - \bar{m}^* - \phi(\bar{y} - \bar{y}^*) - (1/\theta)(r - r^*) + [(1/\theta) + \lambda](\pi - \pi^*)$$
$$s = \bar{m} - \bar{m}^* - \phi(\bar{y} - \bar{y}^*) + \alpha(r - r^*) + \beta(\pi - \pi^*) \tag{13.18}$$

where $\alpha = -(1/\theta)$ and $\beta = (1/\theta) + \lambda$. We can now characterise our three competing models in terms of the parameters α and β.

It is evident from Table 13.1 that in the Frankel model we obtain a Dornbusch-type result $(\partial s/\partial r < 0)$ if interest rates increase while inflation expectations remain constant. This situation is likely to correspond to an *unanticipated* change in the money supply which has an immediate impact on interest rates (to 'clear' the money market) but is not immediately perceived as permanent and hence does not influence π. On the other hand, an *equal* increase in the nominal interest rate, r, and inflationary expectations π cause a depreciation in the exchange rate $(\beta + \alpha > 0)$ — a FPMM-type result. Hence, by adding an ancillary assumption to the Dornbusch-type model, namely equation (13.14), an *anticipated* increase in the money supply is likely to lead to an expected depreciation and (the Frankel model then predicts) an actual depreciation. Implicitly the Frankel model highlights the possible differential response of the exchange rate to anticipated and unanticipated changes in the money supply and interest rates.

Table 13.1 The Frankel Real Interest Rate Model

Model	Parameters
Frankel	$\alpha < 0$, $\beta > 0$; $|\beta| > |\alpha|$
FPMM	$\alpha > 0$, $\beta = 0$
FPMM–hyperinflation	$\alpha = 0$, $\beta > 0$
Dornbusch–SPMM	$\alpha < 0$, $\beta = 0$

The Portfolio Balance Model

The current and capital account monetary models which have been the subject matter of the preceding sections make at least two important simplifying assumptions: domestic and foreign assets are perfect substitutes and any wealth effects of a current account surplus or deficit are negligible. The portfolio balance model of exchange rates explores the consequences of explicitly relaxing these assumptions (see, e.g., Branson (1977), Isard (1978) and Dornbusch and Fischer (1980)). The level of the exchange rate in the portfolio balance model (PBM) is determined, at least in the short run, by supply and demand in the markets for all financial assets (i.e. money, domestic and foreign bonds). In the PBM a surplus (deficit) on the current account represents a rise (fall) in net domestic holdings of foreign assets. The latter affects the level of wealth and hence the desired demand for assets which then affects the exchange rate. Thus, the PBM is an inherently dynamic model of exchange rate adjustment which includes behavioural interactions in asset markets, the current account, the price level and the rate of asset accumulation. The reduced form equations used in testing the PBM therefore include stocks of assets other than money. For example, domestic and foreign bonds and stocks of overseas assets held by domestic and foreign residents (usually measured by the cumulative current account position) influence the exchange rate.

A General Framework

The above models can be presented in a common framework suitable for empirical testing by invoking the UIP condition as a key link to the 'fundamentals' in each model. To see this, note that the UIP condition in logarithms is:

$$E_t s_{t+1} - s_t = r_t - r_t^* \tag{13.19}$$

Now assume that some model of the economy based on fundamentals z_t implies that the interest differential depends on these fundamentals:

$$r_t - r_t^* = \gamma' z_t \tag{13.20}$$

From the above:

$$s_t = E_t s_{t+1} - \gamma' z_t \tag{13.21}$$

and by repeated forward recursion and using the law of iterated expectations

$$s_t = -\sum_{i=0}^{n-1} \gamma' E_t z_{t+i} + E_t s_{t+n} \tag{13.22}$$

Hence movements in the current spot rate between t and $t+1$ are determined by revisions to expectations or 'news' about future fundamentals z_{t+i}. In this RE model the exchange rate is volatile because of the frequent arrival of news. The fundamentals, z_t in equation (13.22), vary slightly depending on the economic model adopted. For the flex-price monetary model FPMM we have

$$s_t = p_t - p_t^* = (m - m^*)_t - \alpha(y - y^*)_t + \beta(r - r^*)_t \tag{13.23}$$

substituting for $r - r^*$ from the UIP condition and rearranging we have

$$s_t = [1/(1+\beta)]z_t + [\beta/(1+\beta)]E_t s_{t+1} \tag{13.24}$$

where $z_t = (m - m^*)_t - \alpha(y - y^*)_t$. By repeated forward substitution

$$s_t = [1/(1+\beta)]\sum_{i=0}^{\infty} [\beta/(1+\beta)]^i E_t z_{t+i} \tag{13.25}$$

where we have imposed a transversality condition. In the Dornbusch SPMM (De Grauwe et al, 1993) inertia is introduced into the system because prices respond with a lag to excess demand X_t in the goods market

$$p_t - p_{t-1} = \delta X_t \tag{13.26}$$

and excess demand is high when the real exchange rate depreciates (i.e. s_t increases):

$$X_t = q_1(s_t + p_t^* - p_t) \tag{13.27}$$

Using UIP and the money demand equations this gives rise to a similar form to (13.25) except that there is now inertia in the exchange rate:

$$s_t = \theta_1 s_{t-1} + \lambda \sum_{j=0}^{\infty} \theta_2 E_{t-1} z_{t+j} \qquad (\theta_1, \theta_2) < 1 \tag{13.28}$$

where z_t depends on current and lagged values of the money supply and output.

The portfolio balance model (PBM) may also be represented in the form (13.28) by noting that here we can amend the UIP condition to incorporate a risk premium which depends on relative asset holdings in domestic B_t and foreign bonds B_t^*.

$$r_t - r_t^* = E_t s_{t+1} - s_t + f(B_t/B_t^*) \tag{13.29}$$

The resulting equation (13.29) for the exchange rate now has relative bond holdings in the vector of fundamentals, z_t.

Forecasts of the future values of the fundamentals z_{t+j} depend on information at time t and hence equation (13.29) can be reduced to a purely backward looking equation in terms of the fundamentals (if we ignore any implicit cross-equation RE restrictions) and this is often how such models are empirically tested in the literature as we shall see below. However, one can also exploit the full potential of the forward terms in (13.28) which imply implicit cross-equation restrictions, if one is willing to posit an explicit set of forecasting equations for the fundamental variables. This is done in Chapter 15 for the FPMM to illustrate the VAR methodology as applied to the spot rate in the FOREX market.

13.5 TESTING THE MODELS

As one can see from the above analysis, tests of SPMM involve regressions of the spot rate on relative money stocks, interest rates, etc. and tests of the PBM also include other asset stocks. If we ignore hyperinflation periods, then these models have not proved successful in predicting movements in bilateral spot rates, particularly in post 1945 data. Some of the models do work reasonably well over short subperiods but not over the whole period. Meese (1990) provides a useful 'summary table' of the performance of such models. He estimates a general equation which, in the main, subsumes all of the above theories:

$$s_t = a_0 + a_1(L)(m - m^*)_t + a_2(L)(y - y^*)_t + a_3(L)(r - r^*)_t + a_4(L)(\pi - \pi^*)_t$$
$$+ a_5(L)(F - F^*)_t + e_t \tag{13.30}$$

where F = stock of foreign assets held by domestic residents and F^* = stock of domestic assets held by foreign residents. Meese (1990) repeats the earlier tests of Meese and

Roghoff (1983) by running equation (13.30) up to time period t and then using it to forecast out-of-sample for horizons of 1, 6 and 12 months. New data is then added and the estimation and forecasting process is repeated. The forecasts based on the structural equations use actual future values of the RHS variables. He then compares the root mean square forecast errors from (13.30) with those from a benchmark provided by the 'no-change' prediction of the random walk model of the exchange rate. It is clear from Table 13.2 that the forecasts using the economic fundamentals in (13.30) are in all cases worse than those of the random walk hypothesis.

Meese (1990) dismisses the reasons for the failure of these models based on fundamentals as mismeasurement of variables, inappropriate estimation techniques or even omitted variables (since so many alternatives have been tried). He suggests that the failure of such models may be due to weakness in their underlying relationships such as the PPP condition, and the instability found in money demand functions and the mounting evidence from survey data on expectations that agents' forecasts do not obey the axioms of rational expectations. He notes that non-linear models (e.g. chaotic models) that involve regime changes (e.g. Peso problem) and models that involve noise traders may provide some insights into the determination of movements in the spot rate but research in these areas is only just beginning.

A novel approach to testing monetary models of the exchange rate is provided by Flood and Rose (1993). They compare the volatility in the exchange rate and in economic fundamentals for periods of 'fixed rates' (e.g. Bretton Woods, where permitted exchange

Table 13.2 Root Mean Square Error (RMSE) Out-of-Sample Forecast Statistics — November 1980 through June 1984 (44 Months)

Exchange Rate	Horizon (Months)	Random Walk	Models[a]	
			1	2
log(DM/$)	1	3.1	3.1	3.2
	6	7.9	8.4	8.5
	12	8.7	11.1	11.4
log(yen/$)	1	3.5	3.3	3.5
	6	7.8	7.0	7.7
	12	9.0	7.5	8.7

RMSE Out-of-Sample Forecast Statistics – November 1976 through June 1981 (56 Months)

Exchange Rate	Horizon (Months)	Random Walk	Forward Rate	Models[a]	
				1	2
log(DM/$)	1	3.22	3.20	3.65	3.50
	6	8.71	9.03	12.03	9.95
	12	12.98	12.60	18.87	15.69
log(yen/$)	1	3.68	3.72	4.11	4.20
	6	11.58	11.93	13.94	11.94
	12	18.31	18.95	20.41	19.20

(a) Model 1: Equation (13.30) with $a_5 = 0$. Model 2: Equation (13.30) with all parameters freely estimated. Both models are sequentially estimated by either generalised least squares or instrumental variables with a correction for serial correlation. RMSE is just the average of squared forecast errors for each of the three prediction horizons.

Source: Meese (1990).

rate fluctuations were ±1 percent) and floating rates. Not surprisingly exchange rates are far more volatile in the floating rate periods. If the monetary models are correct then one should also observe a dramatic increase in volatility in some of the economic fundamentals (e.g. relative money supplies) when a previously fixed exchange rate is floated. For nine industrialised (OECD) countries, Flood and Rose find that although the conditional volatility of bilateral exchange rates against the dollar alters dramatically across these exchange rate regimes, none of the economic fundamentals experience a marked change in volatility. Hence one can legitimately conclude that the economic fundamentals in the monetary models (e.g. money supply, interest rates, inflation rates, output) do not explain the volatility in exchange rates. (It is worth noting, however, that the latter conclusion may not hold in the case of extreme hyperinflations where the variability in relative inflation rates (i.e. fundamentals) across regimes might alter substantially.)

A more formal exposition of the Flood and Rose methodology in testing the FPMM may be obtained from equation (13.4) with $\phi = \phi^*$, $\lambda = \lambda^*$ and substituting for $r - r^*$ from the UIP condition

$$s_t = \mathrm{TF}_t + \lambda(s^e_{t+1} - s_t) \tag{13.31}$$

where $\mathrm{TF}_t = (m - m^*)_t - \phi(y - y^*)_t$ is 'traditional fundamentals'. Equation (13.4) defines 'virtual fundamentals' (VF) as $\mathrm{VF}_t = s_t - \lambda(r - r^*)_t$. Now, under the FPMM, equation (13.4), we expect the variability in virtual fundamentals VF_t to equal the variability in traditional fundamentals TF_t. To obtain a time series for TF_t and VF_t all one requires is a representative value for the structural parameters of the demand for money function λ and ϕ. As reported above, Flood and Rose find that while the volatility of VF increases dramatically in the floating rate period, the volatility of fundamentals TF_t changes very little. (This result is invariant to reasonable values of λ and ϕ and also holds when they consider the SPMM.) Flood and Rose speculate that since few macroeconomic variables undergo dramatic changes in volatility, which coincide with changes in exchange rate regimes, then it is unlikely that *any* exchange rate model based only on economic fundamentals will prove adequate. For nine OECD countries, they also correlate the average monthly variance of the exchange rate over successive two-year horizons $\sigma^2(S)$ against the variance of various macroeconomic variables. They find that there is no correlation between $\sigma^2(S)$ and either the variability in the money supply or interest rates, or FOREX reserves or stock prices and only a rather weak negative correlation with the variance of output. Hence in moving from a floating exchange rate regime to a fixed rate, the reduced volatility in the exchange rate is *not* reflected in an increase in volatility of other macroeconomic variables. (A similar result is found by Artis and Taylor (1994) for European countries which moved from a floating rate into the Exchange Rate Mechanism in the 1980s.) The balance of the argument on fixed versus floating based on the above evidence would seem to favour some kind of target bands rather than a pure floating regime. The evidence also suggests that there is some change in the trading behaviour of agents when there is a move from flexible to 'fixed' rates (e.g. do noise traders transfer to other 'unrestricted' speculative markets? does the credibility of the fixed rate policy play an important role in influencing expectations and hence trading activity?).

Rational Bubbles

We noted in Chapter 7 that there are not only severe econometric difficulties in testing for rational bubbles but such tests are contingent on having the correct equilibrium model of asset returns. Rejection of the no-bubbles hypothesis may well be due to misspecification of the underlying model involving fundamentals. The latter is particularly acute for monetary models of the exchange rate since these provide a rather poor statistical representation of movements in the spot exchange rate. The FPMM with a *deterministic* bubble term results in an equation for the spot rate of the form:

$$s_t = (1+\beta)^{-1} \sum_{i=0}^{\infty} \beta/(1+\beta)E_t z_{t+i} + B_0[(\beta+1)/\beta)]^t \qquad (13.32)$$

where z_t = set of monetary variables and B_0 = value of bubble at $t = 0$. The null of no bubbles is $H_0: B_0 = 0$. However, if the z_t variables are a poor representation of the true fundamentals then the estimate of B_0 may be different from zero, as it is the only other candidate left to help explain the dependent variable. Testing $B_0 = 0$ in (13.32) is also problematic because of the 'exploding regressor' problem. However, the test due to West (1987a) avoids the latter problem and provides a test for any form of bubble whether stochastic or deterministic.

Meese (1986) uses the FPMM as his maintained fundamentals model for the $/DM exchange rate (1973–1982) and rejects the no-bubbles hypotheses. West (1987b) uses a second type of West (1988a) test and augments the FPMM of Meese to include money demand errors which may pick up other potential 'fundamentals'. He finds against the presence of bubbles for the $/DM rate (1974–1984).

The Peso problem poses an additional difficulty when testing for bubbles in the foreign exchange market. It is widely believed that the monetary authorities frequently intervene in the FOREX market and that the authorities often try and mitigate large swings in (real and) nominal exchange rates (e.g. Plaza and Louvre agreements in the 1980s). Market participants are likely to form expectations of such events and these expectations are unlikely to be measured correctly by the econometrician. The latter, coupled with the poor performance empirically of exchange rate models based on fundamentals, implies that there is little one can say with any degree of certainty about the presence or otherwise of rational bubbles in spot exchange rates.

Random Walk Reappears

The failure of structural models of the spot rate led researchers to fall back on producing parsimonious *statistical* representations. To a reasonable approximation, daily bilateral exchange rates follow a martingale

$$E_{t-1}s_t - s_{t-1} = 0 \qquad (13.33)$$

where the forecast error $\eta_t = S_t - E_{t-1}S_t$ has a non-constant variance (Baillie and Bollerslev, 1989 and Baillie and McMahon, 1989). Hence the model is:

$$s_t = s_{t-1} + \eta_t \qquad (13.34)$$

and the time varying variance of η_t denoted σ_t^2 seems to be well approximated by an autoregressive structure of the form

$$\sigma_t^2 = \alpha_0 + \alpha_1 \sigma_{t-1}^2 + \alpha_2 \eta_{t-1}^2 \qquad (13.35)$$

which is known as a GARCH(1,1) process (see Chapter 20). In a recent study Mark (1995) has re-examined the usefulness of 'fundamentals' in explaining changes in the (log) exchange rate over short and long horizons. Mark (1995) takes the monetary model as determining fundamentals $z_t = (m - m^*) - \alpha(y - y^*)$, which should be linked to the spot rate s_t in the long run. If the exchange rate adjusts slowly to disequilibrium in the fundamentals then:

$$s_{t+k} - s_t = \delta_k + \beta_k(s_t - z_t)$$

Mark finds that the R^2 in the above regression and the value of β_k increases as the horizon k increases from 1 to 16 quarters. (He uses quarterly data on the US dollar against the Canadian dollar, Deutschmark, yen and Swiss franc, 1973–1991.) Also, out-of-sample forecasts at long horizons ($k = 16$) outperform the random walk for DM, yen and Swiss franc. The above analysis is not a test of a 'fully specified' monetary model but demonstrates that 'monetary fundamentals' may provide a useful predictor of the exchange rate, over long horizons (although not necessarily over short horizons). The above exchange rate equation is a simple form of error correction model, with an error correction term $(s - z)_t$. This model is re-examined in the context of cointegration in Chapter 15. Clearly, if one is looking for a purely statistical representation one may also consider non-linear models (e.g. Engel and Hamilton (1990)), neural networks (e.g. Trippi and Turban (1993)) and chaos models of the exchange rate. Below we briefly discuss the latter.

13.6 CHAOS AND FUNDAMENTALS

The RE hypothesis when applied to models of speculative prices and returns results in an Euler equation which can contain an exogenous bubble term (De Grauwe et al, 1993). The model is therefore not fully self-contained because we need to select the solution either with or without the bubble and this choice is *not* determined by the model but requires and ad-hoc assumption using information which is exogenous to the model. So there is, in a sense, an ad-hoc element in RE models; they are not 'complete' models of the expectations process.

RE models of the exchange rate attribute the volatility in the spot rate to the arrival of new information or news. However, using high frequency data the study by Goodhart (1989) finds that most exchange rate movements appear to occur in the absence of observable news. Add to this evidence from cointegration studies that for many currencies there is no long-run (cointegrating) relationship between the spot rate and economic fundamentals (e.g. Boothe and Glassman (1987) and Baillie and Selover (1987)) then models based on fundamentals begin to look rather weak. There is also evidence that at short horizons (e.g. one month) the spot rate is positively autocorrelated whereas at longer horizons there is significant negative serial correlation (Cutler et al, 1989) which is indicative of NT with extrapolative predictions at short horizons and with fundamentals more predominant at longer horizons. Finally, there is evidence using survey data that expectations are not rational and they may exhibit bandwagon effects at short horizons with mean reversion at longer horizons (Frankel and Froot, 1988 and Takagi, 1991). Also, Froot and Ito (1989) demonstrate that the chain rule of RE doesn't apply, in that the forward iteration of expectations over short horizons do not equal those for the equivalent long horizons.

An eclectic view of the evidence on exchange rate behaviour therefore provides a number of anomalies relative to the central paradigm of a model based on economic fundamentals in which *all* agents use RE. Models of chaos suggest that apparent random behaviour may not be due solely to 'shocks' or noise and point to the possibility that *non-linear deterministic* dynamic models may lie behind observed movements in exchange rates. Chaotic models do not necessarily rule out RE but given that they have only recently been applied to economic problems, these chaotic models have concentrated on possible non-linearities rather than in applying RE to such models (which analytically would be very difficult because the mathematical expectations operator cannot evaluate expressions such as $E(x_t/y_t)$ which appear in the non-linear systems).

The spirit in which we approach models of chaos is one where we hope they can begin to provide alternative insights into the somewhat anomalous behaviour of the exchange rate (and other asset prices) rather than provide a complete theory of such movements.

This section examines the contribution that chaos theory can make in accounting for the empirical results discussed earlier, which seem to indicate a failure of fundamentals in explaining movements in the spot rate and for an apparent failure of RE and market efficiency. The work of De Grauwe et al (1993) is used extensively to show how a specific illustrative chaotic model can provide a starting point, at least, into the apparent anomalous behaviour of the FOREX market. This is done using the sticky-price monetary model (SPMM) to determine the equilibrium exchange rate as viewed by the smart money (SM) and is combined with the model of heterogeneous expectations by noise traders (NT) and SM presented in Section 8.3 which provides further non-linearities in the model. The model gives rise (under certain parameter values) to chaotic behaviour of the exchange rate. It is then possible to show that the *simulated* exchange rate series from this chaos model:

- approximates a random walk

- yields a regression in which the forward premium is a biased predictor of the future change in the exchange rate

- yields a regression of the exchange rate on fundamentals (i.e. money supply) in which the economic fundamentals provide a poor predictor of future movements in the exchange rate.

All of the above empirical results are observed in the real world data and hence the chaotic model is at least capable of mimicking the behaviour of real world data in the FOREX market. The final part of this section briefly outlines the results of some tests for chaos and for the presence of non-linearity in relationships in the FOREX market.

Sticky-Price Monetary Model

We have already discussed this model so we can be brief. In the *long run* the exchange rate is governed by PPP

$$S_t^* = P_t^*/P_t^{f*} \tag{13.36}$$

where P_t^* is the domestic *steady state* price level. Changes in the real exchange rate lead to changes in real (excess) demand (i.e. net trade) and hence in the rate of inflation:

$$P_t/P_{t-1} = [(S_t/P_t^f)/P_t]^k \quad k > 0 \tag{13.37}$$

The parameter k measures the speed of adjustment of prices to excess demand and as full employment is assumed, equilibrium is realised through price changes. The standard domestic money demand function is equal to the exogenous supply

$$M_t = M_t^d = Y_t^a P_t (1 + r_t)^{-c} \tag{13.38}$$

and the expected change in the *market* exchange rate is determined by UIP:

$$E_t(S_{t+1}/S_t) = (1 + r_t)/(1 + r_t^f) \tag{13.39}$$

In this model (unlike that in Section 8.3) the exchange rate has a feedback effect on the domestic price level via equation (13.37). The steady state is defined as $P_t^f = 1$, $r_t^f = 0$, $Y_t = 1$ and $E_t S_{t+1} = S_t$. Hence from the UIP condition $r_t = 0$ and from (13.38), $P_t^* = M_t^s$. The solution for the model at time t is found by substitution for P_t from (13.37) in (13.38) and then solving for $(1 + r_t)$ and substitution in the UIP condition (13.39) to give

$$S_t = X_t^{\theta_1} E_t(S_{t+1})^{\theta_2} \tag{13.40}$$

where

$$X_t = M_t Y_t^{-a} P_{t-1}^{-(1/(1+k))} \tag{13.41}$$

and θ_1, θ_2 are functions of the other structural parameters (and $0 < \theta_2 < 1$). Hence the spot rate is determined by the fundamentals that comprise X_t. The term $E_t(S_{t+1})$ is the *market's* expectation and provides an important non-linearity in the model. The market's expectation is determined by a weighted average of the behaviour of NT and SM (see Section 8.3).

$$E(S_{t+1}/S_{t-1}) = f(S_{t-1}, S_{t-2}, \ldots)^{m_t} (S_{t-1}^*/S_{t-1})^{(1-m_t)\alpha} \tag{13.42}$$

where the weight given to noise traders is

$$m_t = 1/(1 + \beta(S_{t-1} - S_{t-1}^*)^2) \tag{13.43}$$

Equations (13.42), (13.43) and (13.40) yield the following non-linear equation for the exchange rate

$$S_t = (X_t)^{\theta_1} (S_{t-1})^{\phi_1} (S_{t-2})^{\phi_2} (S_{t-3})^{\phi_3} (S_{t-4})^{\phi_4} \tag{13.44}$$

The above representation assumes an exogenous money supply but we can also solve the model under the assumption of interest rate smoothing

$$(M_t^s/M_{t-1}^s) = [(1 + r_t)/(1 + r_{t-1})]^\Psi \tag{13.45}$$

where $\Psi(> 0)$ measures the intensity of interest rate smoothing. The simulated path of the exchange rate under interest rate smoothing for a given chaotic solution is shown in Figure 13.1 and has the general random pattern that we associate with real world exchange rate data. De Grauwe et al then take this simulated data and test for a random walk (strictly, a unit root).

$$S_t = \alpha S_{t-1} + \varepsilon_t$$

and find that they cannot reject $\alpha = 1$ (for a wide variety of parameters of the model which result in chaotic solution). Hence a pure deterministic 'fundamentals model' can mimic a stochastic process with a unit root.

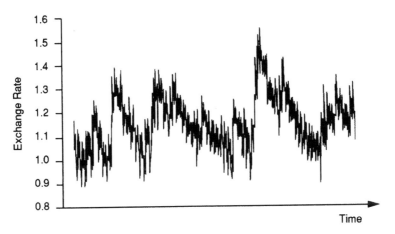

Figure 13.1 Chaotic Exchange Rate Model with Money. *Source*: De Grauwe et al (1993). Reproduced by permisssion of Blackwell Publishers

If covered interest parity holds, the forward premium $(F/S)_t$ is equal to the interest differential $(1 + r_t)/(1 + r_t^f)$. De Grauwe et al use the simulated values of the interest differential as a measure of $(F/S)_t$ and regress the latter on the simulated values of (S_{t+1}/S_t):

$$(S_{t+1}/S_t) = a + b(F/S)_t$$

They find $b < 0$ which is also the case with actual real world data. Hence in a chaotic model the forward premium is a biased forecast of the change in the spot rate even when we have risk neutrality at the *level of the market* (i.e. UIP holds). The above paradox is resolved when we recognise the heterogeneity of expectations of the NT and SM. A rise in domestic interest rates r_t leads to an immediate appreciation of the current spot rate of the domestic currency (i.e. S_t falls as in the Dornbusch model) and via covered interest parity a rise in $(F/S)_t$. However, if the market is dominated by NT they will extrapolate the current appreciation which tends to lead to a further appreciation in the domestic currency next period (i.e. $E_tS_{t+1} - S_t$ falls). The domination by extrapolative NT, however, means that on average a rise in $(F/S)_t$ is accompanied by a fall in $E_tS_{t+1} - S_t$. If there were *only* SM in the market then UIP indicates that the spot rate would depreciate (i.e. $E_tS_{t+1} - S_t$ increases) in future periods after a rise in r_t as in the Dornbusch model.

De Grauwe et al also simulate the model when stochastic shocks are allowed to influence the money supply (which is now assumed to be exogenous). The money supply is assumed to follow a random walk and the error term therefore represents 'news'. Over a long time period the simulated data for S_t broadly moves with that for the money supply as our fundamentals model would indicate and a simple (OLS cointegrating) regression confirms this:

$$S_t = 0.02 + 0.09\, M_t$$
$$(0.5)\quad (32.8)$$

In the simulated data the variability in S_t is much greater than that for M_t. The simulated data is then split into several subperiods of 50 observations each and the regression $S_t = \alpha + \beta M_t$ is run. De Grauwe et al find that the parameters α and β are highly unstable, the equation forecasts badly out-of-sample and has a RMSE that exceeds that for a random walk. Therefore over a short period the simulated 'chaotic data' mimics the results found using actual data by Meese and Roghoff. However, the chaotic data still exhibits some predictive features. For example, a purely AR(3) model when estimated on the simulated data using 50 data points forecasts better than either the random walk or the structural model. Thus, data from a chaotic system can be modelled and may yield reasonable forecasts over short horizons. These results provide a prima facie case for the statistical success of error correction models over static models or purely AR models, if the real world exhibits chaotic behaviour. The static structural regression $S_t = \alpha + \beta M_t^s$ mimics the long-run fundamentals and the *linear* AR(3) model mimics the non-linear dynamics. Of course, the (linear) error correction model is not the correct representation of the true non-linear chaotic model but it may provide a reasonably useful approximation for any finite set of data.

Chaotic models applied to economic phenomena are in their infancy so one cannot expect definitive results at present. However, they do suggest that non-linearities in economic relationships might be important and the latter may yield chaotic behaviour. In addition one can always add stochastic shocks to any non-linear system which will tend to increase the noise in the system. Hence although much of economic theory has been founded on linear models or linear approximations to non-linear models to ensure tractability and closed form solutions, it may be that such approximations can mask important non-linearities in behavioural responses (see Pesaran and Potter (1993)).

A key question not yet tackled is whether *actual* data on exchange rates exhibit chaotic behaviour. The obvious difficulty in discriminating between a chaotic deterministic process and a purely linear stochastic process has already been noted. There are several tests available to detect chaotic behaviour but they require large amounts of data (i.e. say 20 000 data points) to yield reasonably unambiguous and clear results. De Grauwe et al (1993) use several tests on daily exchange rate data but find only weak evidence of chaotic behaviour for the yen/dollar, pound sterling/dollar daily exchange rate data and no evidence at all for chaotic behaviour in the DM/dollar exchange rate over the 1972–1990 period. This may be due to insufficient data or because the presence of any stochastic 'noise' masks the detection of chaos. They then test for the presence of non-linearities in this exchange rate data. Using two complementary test statistics (Brock et al, 1987 and Hinich, 1982) they find that for six major bilateral rates, they could not reject the existence of non-linear structures for any of the bilateral rates using daily and weekly *returns* (i.e. the percentage change in the exchange rate) and for monthly data they only reject non-linearity in one case, namely the pound sterling/yen rate. Of course, non-linearity is necessary for chaotic behaviour but it is not sufficient: the presence or otherwise of chaotic behaviour depends on the precise parameterisation of the non-linear relationship. Also the above tests do not tell us the precise form of the non-linearity in the dynamics of the exchange rate, merely that some form or other of non-linearity appears to be present. We are still left with the somewhat Herculean task of specifying and estimating a non-linear structural model of the exchange rate.

13.7 SUMMARY

It is important that the reader is aware of the attempts that have been made to explain movements in spot exchange rates in terms of economic fundamentals, not least because these models have to some extent helped to shape key economic policy decisions as noted in the opening remarks.

It would seem unlikely that any minor refinements to the traditional monetary models discussed in Sections 13.1–13.4 would lead to dramatic improvements in their statistical performance. At present it would appear to be the case that *formal* tests of the various models lead one to reject them. Over short horizons, say up to about one year, monetary fundamentals generally do not help predict changes in the spot rate. Over longer horizons of four years fundamentals do provide some predictive power for some currencies (Mark, 1995). The latter is consistent with the view that purchasing power parity and the (demand for) money–income nexus hold in the long run (i.e. the relevant variables are cointegrated). However, on balance it must be recognised that there exists a great deal of uncertainty regarding the underlying determinants of the spot exchange rate in industrialised countries with moderate inflation. The concepts and ideas which underlie these models (e.g. PPP, UIP relative money supplies) do still play a role in guiding policy makers, not least because they have little else to go on other than their 'hunch' about the appropriate interest rate–exchange rate nexus to apply in particular circumstances. The absence of firm policy implications which arise because of the statistical inadequacy of structural models has resulted in policy makers trying to mitigate the severity of wide swings in the real exchange rate by coordinated Central Bank intervention, a move towards currency zones and even the proposal to adopt a common currency.

The lack of success of 'pure fundamentals' models in explaining movements in the spot exchange rate has recently led researchers to consider non-linear models that may result in chaotic behaviour. The underlying theory in these models usually involves both rational traders and some form of noise-trader behaviour. They are not models that involve all agents being rational and maximising some well-defined objective function. Nevertheless, their ad-hoc assumptions are usually plausible. The main conclusions to emerge from this literature as applied to exchange rates are:

- Deterministic non-linear models are capable of generating apparently persistent random and irregular time series which broadly resemble those in real world data. The addition of 'news' or random 'shocks' provides additional random impulses.

- The empirical evidence on exchange rates is ambivalent on the presence of purely (deterministic) chaos. However, it does quite strongly indicate the presence of non-linearities in the data generation process.

- The challenge now is to produce coherent theoretical models that are capable of generating chaotic or behavioural non-linear models that are subject to random shocks. Non-linear structural (fundamental) models need not necessarily rule out the use of expectations. However, models involving the interaction of NT and SM, which are not fully (Muth) rational, also seem worthy of further analysis.

- Non-linear theoretical models will need to be tested against the data and this may provide further econometric challenges.

The problem with chaotic models and indeed non-linear stochastic models is that often small changes in parameters values can lead to radically different behaviour or forecasts for the exchange rate. Given that econometric parameter estimates from non-linear models are frequently subject to some uncertainty, the range of possible forecasts from such models becomes potentially quite large. If such models are not firmly rooted in economic theory then their predictions and policy implications might not carry great weight. However, on purely academic grounds there may be further insights to be obtained from such models.

FURTHER READING

Macroeconomics texts such as Cuthbertson and Taylor (1987) and Burda and Wyplosz (1993) provide an overview of theories of the determination of spot exchange rates, at an intermediate level. Other intermediate texts which deal exclusively with exchange rates are Copeland (1994) who also has a useful chapter on chaos, and MacDonald (1988) who provides copious references to the empirical literature. MacDonald and Taylor (1992) and Taylor (1995) in their survey articles concentrate on what might loosely be described as macroeconomic models of the exchange rate. Froot and Thaler (1990) survey the anomalies literature in the FOREX market while De Grauwe et al (1993) is a very accessible account of chaos theory applied to the FOREX market.

PART 5
Tests of the EMH using the VAR Methodology

Tests of the EMH in the FOREX market and for stocks and bonds outlined in earlier chapters have in part been concerned with the informational efficiency assumption implied by rational expectations. Empirical work centres on whether information at time t or earlier can be used to predict returns and hence enable investors to earn abnormal profits. The variance bounds approach tests whether asset prices equal their fundamental value. The anomalies literature frequently seeks to test for the existence of profitable trading rules in the market. All of these tests are, of course, conditional on a specific economic theory (or ad-hoc hypothesis) concerning the determination of equilibrium expected returns.

This part of the book examines some relatively sophisticated tests of the EMH applied to stocks, bonds and the FOREX market which have recently appeared in the literature. The generic term for these tests is the 'VAR methodology'. Some readers will probably be aware that tests of the informational efficiency requirement of the EMH result in restrictions on the parameters of the model under investigation (see Chapter 5). The model in this instance usually consists of a hypothesis about equilibrium returns plus an explicit forecasting equation (or equations) which is used to mimic the predictions for the unobservable rational expectations of agents. Early tests of these cross-equation restrictions were undertaken by estimating the model both with and without the restrictions imposed and then seeing how far the 'fit' of the model deteriorated when the restrictions are imposed. A likelihood ratio test was often invoked to provide the actual metric for the test statistic. The VAR methodology tests these same RE restrictions but, as we shall see, need only estimate the unrestricted model and this is usually computationally much simpler.

In testing the EMH on asset prices in previous chapters we have used variance bounds *inequalities*. In the VAR methodology these variance inequalities are replaced by variance *equalities*. For example, consider the expectations hypothesis EH of the term structure. Using the VAR methodology we can obtain a best predictor of future changes in short-term interest rates $E_t \Delta r_{t+j}$: call this prediction S'_t. Under the EH + RE the predictions S'_t should mimic movements in the actual spread between long and short rates S_t. Hence the variance of S_t should equal the variance of the best forecast S'_t. Hence the VAR methodology provides two 'metrics' for evaluating the PEH + RE, first a set of (cross-equation) restrictions on the estimated parameters of the VAR prediction equations and second a comparison of movements in the actual spread S_t with the forecast spread S'_t which is a form of variance equality. In addition because the VAR approach pays great attention to the use of stationary variables it mitigates some of the problems of non-stationarity encountered in Shiller-type variance bounds (inequality) tests on yields and asset price levels.

So far we have concentrated on the econometrics of the tests using the VAR methodology. However, it is important to note that the (cross-equation) parameter restrictions referred to above do have an economic interpretation. Only if these restrictions hold is it the case that investors make zero abnormal profits and that the (RE) forecast errors are independent of the information set used by agents. The latter conditions are of course at the heart of the EMH and informational efficiency.

Some readers may find the material in Chapter 14 more difficult than that in earlier chapters. However, it is my contention that the material is not analytically difficult although the algebra sometimes seems a little voluminous and on first reading it may be difficult to see the wood for the trees. The latter is in part due to a desire to guide the reader from simple specific cases to the more complex general case which appears in the burgeoning literature in this area. Your perseverance will have a high payoff in fully understanding the literature in this area. To aid the exposition a simplified overview of the main analytic issues is presented first.

Overview

To throw some light on where we are headed in relation to tests already discussed in earlier chapters consider, by way of example, our much loved RVF for stock prices P_t and the expectations hypothesis for the long rate R_t (using spot yields):

$$P_t = V_t \equiv \sum_{i=1}^{\infty} \gamma^i E_t D_{t+i} \qquad \gamma = 1/(1+k) \tag{1}$$

$$R_t = \text{TV}_t \equiv (1/n) \sum_{i=0}^{n-1} E_t r_{t+i} \tag{2}$$

The 'fundamental value' V_t denotes the DPV of expected future dividends and the discount rate γ is assumed constant $(0 < \gamma < 1)$. TV is the expected terminal value of a series of rolled-over one-period investment in short bonds. Under the EMH the actual stock price equals V_t and the long rate equals TV_t, otherwise profitable (risky) trades are possible and abnormal profits can be made.

The regression-based tests and the variance bounds tests of the EMH result from applying the RE assumption:

$$D_{t+1} = E_t D_{t+1} + \eta_{t+1} \tag{3}$$

$$r_{t+1} = E_t r_{t+1} + v_{t+1} \tag{4}$$

to (1) and (2), respectively, where η_{t+1} and v_{t+1} represent 'news' or 'surprises'. The above equations imply that stock prices only change because of the arrival of new information between t and $t+1$ hence stock *returns* (i.e. basically the change in stock prices) are unforecastable using information available at time t or earlier (Ω_t). Similarly, for bonds, (2) and (4) imply that the excess return from investing in the long bond rather than a sequence of short bonds, namely $R_t - \text{TV}_t$, depends only on news and the expected or average excess return is zero.

The variance bounds inequality for stocks arises because when $E_t D_{t+i}$ in (1) is replaced by $D_{t+i} - \eta_{t+i}$ using (3) then a weighted average of the forecast errors η_{t+j} is introduced into the RHS of (1) so we have

$$P_t^* = P_t + \omega_t \tag{5}$$

where P_t^* is the perfect foresight price calculated using *ex-post* actual values of D_{t+j}. Since by RE, P_t is uncorrelated with ω_t, yet $\text{var}(\omega_t)$ must be greater than zero we obtain the usual variance bounds inequality. A similar argument applies to the term structure equation (2). Hence the variance bounds tests do not seek to provide *explicit forecasting schemes* for the unobservable expectations $E_t D_{t+i}$ and $E_t r_{t+i}$ but merely assume forecasts are unbiased and that forecast errors are independent of Ω_t. (This is the 'errors in variables' approach which will be familiar to econometricians.)

In contrast, the methodology in Chapter 14 seeks to provide explicit forecasting equations for D_{t+i} and r_{t+i} based on regressions using a limited information set Λ_t. These forecasting equations we may term *weakly rational* since they do not necessarily use the full information set Ω_t as used by agents. However, given explicit forecasts of dividends and assuming we know γ then we can calculate the RHS of (1) and provide an explicit *forecast* for V_t which we denote V_t'. For ease of exposition it is useful at this point to assume the econometrician has discovered the 'true' forecasting model for D as used by agents, namely an AR(1) process:

$$D_{t+1} = \alpha D_t + \eta_{t+1} \tag{6}$$

By the chain rule of forecasting:

$$E_t D_{t+i} = \alpha^i D_t \tag{7}$$

and the best forecast of the DPV of future dividends using the true information set in (6) we denote P_t' where:

$$P_t' = \sum_{i=1}^{\infty} (\gamma\alpha)^i D_t = \alpha\gamma D_t / (1 - \gamma\alpha) \tag{8}$$

Knowing γ and having an estimate of α from the regression (6) *a time series* for P_t' can be constructed. (As we shall see P_t' is referred to as the 'theoretical price': it is the best estimate of the DPV of 'fundamentals' given by our theoretical valuation model.) If the RVF and (6) are 'true' then we expect (i) P_t and P_t' to move together over time and to be highly correlated, (ii) the variance ratio, defined as:

$$\text{VR} = \text{var}(P_t) / \text{var}(P_t') \tag{9}$$

to equal unity and (iii) in the regression

$$P_t = \beta_0 + \beta_1 P_t' + u_t \tag{10}$$

we expect $\beta_0 = 0$, $\beta_1 = 1$. By positing the 'true' expectations scheme for D_t and estimating this relationship, we have been able to move from a variance bounds *inequality* to a relationship between P_t and P_t' based on a *variance equality*[1]. The relationship between P_t and P_t' allows the three 'metrics' in (i) to (iii) to be used to assess the validity of the EMH based on the RVF plus RE.

It should be obvious that similar considerations apply to the term structure relationship. If the 'true' model for r_{t+1} is $r_{t+1} = \beta r_t + \varepsilon_{t+1}$ then we can use this in (2) to calculate the best prediction TV'_t for the RHS of (2) where $TV'_t = f(\beta r_t)$.

In general the econometrician will not know the 'true' forecasting equation for dividends and (6) will be an approximation. In this case we do not expect P_t to equal the forecast P'_t exactly. The reason is that the equation chosen by the econometrician to forecast D_{t+i} may be based on a limited information set ($\Lambda_t \subset \Omega_t$) and therefore the econometrician's forecasting equation will not equal the true (rational) expectations forecast, as formulated by investors. Clearly the closer (6) is to the 'true' equation the more we expect the conditions (i)–(iii) to hold[1]. Also, even if the econometrician knew the form of the true model to forecast D_{t+j} his estimates would be subject to sampling error and hence the conditions (i)–(iii) would hold, for *any given sample*, only within the usual statistical confidence limits.

It was stated above that conditions (i)–(iii) will hold even with a limited information set. In fact, this is only true if the forecasting equation for D_{t+j} depends on P_t and in the term structure model if forecasts of r_{t+j} depend on R_t. The key element in obtaining the results (i)–(iii) with a *limited information* set is that the LHS variable in the appropriate efficient markets relationship (e.g. P_t or R_t) is used in the forecasting equations for the RHS variables (i.e. D_{t+j} or r_{t+j}). This then constitutes a VAR system which will be analysed in much of the rest of this section of the book.

From AR to VAR

Let us return to our story of trying to predict r_{t+i} and assume that r_{t+1} depends on r_t and R_t:

$$r_{t+1} = \beta_1 r_t + \beta_2 R_t + \varepsilon_{t+1} \tag{11}$$

Having estimated (11), we now wish to use it to forecast $E_t r_{t+2}$ so that we can substitute this value in the RHS of (2) in order to calculate TV_t. We see that

$$E_t r_{t+1} = \beta_1 r_t + \beta_2 R_t$$

$$E_t r_{t+2} = \beta_1 E_t r_{t+1} + \beta_2 E_t R_{t+1}$$

Hence:

$$E_t r_{t+2} = \beta_1 [\beta_1 r_t + \beta_2 R_t] + \beta_2 E_t R_{t+1} \tag{12}$$

The values of (r_t, R_t) are known at time t; however we do not have a value for $E_t R_{t+1}$ and hence we cannot as yet obtain an explicit forecast for $E_t r_{t+2}$. What we need is a forecasting equation for R_{t+1} and so assume (somewhat arbitrarily) this is of the *same general form* as that for r_{t+1} in (11), that is:

$$R_{t+1} = \psi_1 r_t + \psi_2 R_t + v_{t+1} \tag{13}$$

Now, having estimated (13) we can obtain an expression for $E_t R_{t+1}$ in terms of variables known at time t, namely:

$$E_t R_{t+1} = \Psi_1 r_t + \Psi_2 R_t \tag{14}$$

Equations (11) and (14) taken together are known as a vector autoregression (VAR) (of order 1) and they allow one to calculate *all* future values of $E_t r_{t+i}$ to input into (2) to calculate TV'_t. Shiller calls the variable TV'_t the *theoretical long rate:* it is the best forecast of the RHS of (2). Given the *theoretical model* of the expectations hypothesis in (2), then the actual long rate R_t should move in unison with TV'_t.

It can now be illustrated why the use of a VAR implies that $R_t = TV'_t$, even when the econometrician uses only a limited information set $\Lambda_t (\subset \Omega_t)$. The reason is that $E_t r_{t+j}$ depends on R_t (as well as r_t). Hence *all* future values of r_{t+j} depend on R_t (and r_t), that is $TV'_t = f_1(\beta, \Psi)R_t + f_2(\beta, \Psi)r_t$ where f_1 and f_2 depend on the estimated parameters of the VAR. The expectations hypothesis then implies $R_t = TV'_t$ which can only hold if $f_1(\beta, \Psi) = 1$ (and $f_2(\beta, \Psi) = 0$). But if $f_1 = 1$ (and $f_2 = 0$) then $TV'_t = R_t$ which naturally must move one-for-one with actual R_t. Hence even with a limited information set we expect the correlation between R_t and TV'_t to equal unity and $VR = \text{var}(R_t)/\text{var}(TV'_t)$ to also equal unity. This basic insight is elaborated below.

Turning briefly to the RVF for stock prices, note that if we allow *both* D_t and the discount factor $\gamma_t = 1/(1 + k_t)$ to vary over time then a VAR in D_t and k_t is required to forecast all future values of $E_t D_{t+i}$ and $E_t k_{t+i}$ so that we can calculate our forecast V'_t of the RHS of (1). There is an additional problem, namely the RHS of (1) is non-linear in k_t and D_t. As we shall see in Chapter 16, linearisation of the RVF provides a solution to this technical problem.

There is another way that the VAR methodology can be used to test the EMH and this involves so-called cross-equation restrictions between the parameters of each of the VAR equations (11) and (14), respectively. However, a brief explanation of these tests is not possible here and they are discussed below.

If the reader thought at the end of the last chapter that he had probably already been given a near exhaustive (or exhausting!) set of tests of the various versions of the EMH, then it must be apparent from the above that he is sadly mistaken. These 'new' tests based on the VAR methodology have some advantages over the variance bounds tests and tests based on the predictability of returns. But the VAR methodology also has some potential drawbacks. It does not explicitly deal with time varying risk premia (this is the subject of Chapter 17). It relies on *explicit* (VAR) equations to generate expectations, which are linear with constant parameters and which are assumed to provide a good approximation to the forecasts actually used by investors. In contrast, all the variance bounds tests require is the somewhat weaker assumption that whatever forecasting scheme is used, forecast errors are independent of Ω_t. Hence to implement the variance bounds tests, the econometrician/researcher does not have to know the explicit forecasting model (equation) used by investors.

We discuss the VAR methodology first with respect to the bond market in Chapter 14 since concepts and algebra are simpler than for FOREX and stock markets which are discussed in the following chapters. At the outset the reader should note that although the above examples of the VAR methodology have been conducted in terms of the *levels* of the stock price and dividends and the *levels* of the long rate and short rates for the EH, in actual empirical work, transformations of these variables are used in order to try and ensure stationarity of the variables. In the case of bonds we have already seen that the EH equation (2) can be rewritten in terms of the long–short spread $S_t = R_t - r_t$ and *changes* in the short rates Δr_{t+j}. For stocks the RVF is non-linear in dividends and the time varying discount factor and therefore the transformation is a little more complex involving the (logarithm of the) dividend price ratio and the (logarithm of the) change in dividends. These issues are dealt with at the appropriate point in each chapter.

14

The Term Structure and the Bond Market

This chapter outlines a series of procedures used in testing the EMH in the bond market using the VAR methodology. For the bond market the VAR algebra is somewhat easier than for the stock market but some readers may still find the material difficult. Use will be made of the simplest cases to illustrate points of interest: extending the analysis to the general case is usually straightforward but it involves even more tedious and complex algebra. In the rest of the chapter we discuss:

- How cross-equation parameter restrictions arise from the EMH and RE.
- The relationship between the likelihood ratio test and the Wald test of restrictions, using the VAR methodology.
- How the parameter restrictions ensure that (i) investors do not systematically make abnormal profits and (ii) that investors (RE) forecast errors are independent of information at time t used by agents in making the forecasts.
- Illustrative empirical results at the short and long end of the maturity spectrum for government bonds, using the VAR methodology are presented.

Beginning with the simplest model of the EH of the term structure, the forecasting scheme for the short rate is assumed to be univariate. The analysis is repeated for a vector autoregressive system (VAR) in terms of the spread $S_t = R_t - r_t$ and the change in short rates Δr_t. It is then shown how the cross-equation parameter restrictions can be represented in matrix notation, so that any VAR equation can be used to provide forecasts of the theoretical spread S'_t and hence allow the comparison between S'_t and the actual spread S_t using variance ratios and correlation coefficients. Finally, a brief survey of empirical work in this area is examined.

14.1 CROSS-EQUATION RESTRICTIONS AND INFORMATIONAL EFFICIENCY

The pure expectations hypothesis (PEH) implies that the two-period interest rate R_t is given by:

$$R_t = (r_t + r^e_{t+1})/2 \qquad (14.1)$$

or equivalently that the long–short spread $S_t = (R_t - r_t)$ provides an optimal forecast of future changes in the short rate (where $\Delta r_{t+1}^e = r_{t+1}^e - r_t$):

$$S_t = \Delta r_{t+1}^e / 2 \tag{14.2}$$

AR Forecasting Scheme

Using (14.2) a test of the PEH + RE is possible if we assume a weakly rational *expectations generating equation* for Δr_{t+1}^e which depends only on its own past values. For example:

$$\Delta r_{t+1} = a_1 \Delta r_t + a_2 \Delta r_{t-1} + \omega_{t+1} \tag{14.3}$$

(where we exclude a constant term to simplify the algebra). Agents are assumed to use the limited information set $\Lambda_t = (\Delta r_t, \Delta r_{t-1})$ to forecast future changes in interest rates:

$$\Delta r_{t+1}^e = a_1 \Delta r_t + a_2 \Delta r_{t-1} \tag{14.4}$$

and the forecast error $\omega_{t+1} = \Delta r_{t+1} - \Delta r_{t+1}^e$ is independent of Λ_t under RE. We can show that under the null that the PEH + RE is true then equations (14.2) and (14.3) imply a cross-equation restriction. Substituting (14.4) in (14.2)

$$S_t = (a_1/2)\Delta r_t + (a_2/2)\Delta r_{t-1} \tag{14.5}$$

If the PEH is true then (14.3) and (14.5) are true and it can be seen that the coefficients in these two equations are not independent. 'By eye' one can see, for example, that the ratio of the coefficients on Δr_t and Δr_{t-1} in each equation are $a_i/(a_i/2) = 2$ (for $i = 1, 2$). Consider the joint estimation of (14.3) and (14.5) *without any restrictions* on the parameters:

$$S_t = \pi_1 \Delta r_t + \pi_2 \Delta r_{t-1} + v_{t+1} \tag{14.6}$$

$$\Delta r_{t+1} = \pi_3 \Delta r_t + \pi_4 \Delta r_{t-1} + \omega_{t+1} \tag{14.7}$$

If the PEH + RE is true then (14.3) and (14.5) hold and hence we expect

$$\pi_3 = a_1, \quad \pi_4 = a_2$$
$$\pi_1 = a_1/2, \quad \pi_2 = a_2/2 \tag{14.8}$$

An error term has been added to the unrestricted equation (14.6) for the spread. This arises either because S_t might be measured with error or given our limited information set $\Lambda_t (\subset \Omega_t)$, the error term picks up the difference between forecasts by the econometrician based on $\Lambda_t = (r_t, r_{t-1})$ and the true forecasts which use the complete information set $\Omega_t^{(2)}$.

The econometrician obtains estimates of *four* coefficients π_1 to π_4 but there are only two underlying parameters, a_1, a_2, in the model. Hence there are two implicit restrictions in the model and from (14.8) these are easily seen to be:

$$\frac{\pi_3}{\pi_1} = 2 = \frac{\pi_4}{\pi_2} \tag{14.9}$$

These restrictions can be tested by comparing the log-likelihood values from estimates of the unrestricted equations (14.6) and (14.7) in which the coefficients π_i are freely estimated with those from the same two equations with the restrictions imposed. In the estimated *restricted equation system* we impose $\pi_3 = 2\pi_1$ and $\pi_4 = 2\pi_2$ in (14.7) which becomes:

$$\Delta r_{t+1} = 2\pi_1 \Delta r_t + 2\pi_2 \Delta r_{t-1} + w^r_{t+1} \tag{14.10}$$

while the form of equation (14.6) is unchanged:

$$S_t = \pi_1 \Delta r_t + \pi_2 \Delta r_{t-1} + v^r_{t+1} \tag{14.11}$$

The likelihood ratio test compares the 'fit' of the unrestricted two-equation system with that of the restricted system. The variance–covariance matrix of the unrestricted system (assuming each error term is white noise but they may be a contemporaneous correlation, i.e. $\sigma_{wv} \neq 0$) is:

$$\Sigma_u = \begin{bmatrix} \sigma^2_w & \sigma_{wv} \\ \sigma_{wv} & \sigma^2_v \end{bmatrix} \tag{14.12}$$

The variances and covariances of the error terms are calculated from the residuals from each equation (e.g. $\sigma^2_v = \Sigma \hat{v}^2_t/n$, $\sigma_{wv} = \Sigma \hat{w}_t \hat{v}_t/n$). The restricted system has covariance matrix Σ_r of the same form as (14.12) but the variances and covariances are calculated using the residuals from the restricted regressions (14.10) and (14.11), that is $\hat{w}^r$ and $\hat{v}^r$, respectively.

The likelihood ratio test is computed as

$$LR = n \cdot \ln[(det\Sigma_r)/(det\ \Sigma_u)] \tag{14.13}$$

where n = number of observations and 'det' indicates the determinant of the covariance matrix

$$det\ \Sigma = \sigma^2_w \sigma^2_v - (\sigma_{wv})^2 \tag{14.14}$$

If the restrictions hold in the data then we do not expect much change in the residuals and hence $det[\Sigma_r] \approx det[\Sigma_u]$ so that $LR \approx 0$. Conversely, if the data do not comply with the restrictions we expect the 'fit' to be worse and for the restricted residuals to be larger (on average) than their equivalent unrestricted counterparts. Hence $[\sigma^2_w]_r > [\sigma^2_w]_u$ and

$$det[\Sigma_r] > det[\Sigma_u]$$

and LR will be large. It may be shown that LR is distributed with a (central) chi squared distribution (χ^2) under the null, with q degrees of freedom (where q = number of parameter restrictions). Thus we reject the null if $LR > \chi^2_c(q)$ where χ_c is the critical value. (For a formal derivation of the likelihood ratio test see Harvey (1981) and Cuthbertson et al (1992)).

Interpretation of the RE Restrictions

The two *estimated equations* (14.10) and (14.11) with the restrictions imposed are easily seen to be consistent with the zero abnormal profit condition. Under the PEH the (abnormal) profit AP from investing long rather than short is:

$$AP = 2R_t - (r_t + r_{t+1}) = 2S_t - \Delta r_{t+1} \tag{14.15}$$

For the *expected* abnormal profit to be zero we require:

$$E_t(AP) = 2E(S_t|\Lambda_t) - E(\Delta r_{t+1}|\Lambda_t) \tag{14.16}$$

Using (14.10) and (14.11) in (14.16):

$$E_t(\text{AP}) = 2(\pi_1 \Delta r_t + \pi_2 \Delta r_{t-1}) - (2\pi_1 \Delta r_t + 2\pi_2 \Delta r_{t-1}) = 0 \tag{14.17}$$

Hence when the restrictions on the forecasting equation (14.10) for Δr_{t+1} are imposed, the expected profit, conditional on Λ_t is zero. Using the restricted equation system it is also easy to see that $S_t = \Delta r^e_{t+1}/2$ regardless of the particular values of the π_is. Put another way, the restrictions on the π_is are such that the PEH always holds. Of course had we used the unrestricted equation (14.6) to forecast Δr_{t+1} then since the latter depends on π_3 and π_4, the above relationships would not hold.

The above cross-equation restrictions may be given further intuitive appeal by noting that they also imply that the (RE) forecast error is independent of the limited information set assumed, that is they enforce the error orthogonality property of RE. The forecast error is:

$$\Delta r_{t+1} - E(\Delta r_{t+1}|\Omega_t) = (\pi_3 \Delta r_t + \pi_4 \Delta r_{t-1} + \omega_{t+1}) - 2S_t \tag{14.18}$$

where we have assumed the PEH hypothesis (14.2) holds. Substituting from (14.6) for S_t:

$$\Delta r_{t+1} - \Delta r^e_{t+1} = (\pi_3 - 2\pi_1)\Delta r_t + (\pi_4 - 2\pi_2)\Delta r_{t-1} + (\omega_{t+1} - 2v_{t+1}) \tag{14.19}$$

Hence the *expected value* of the forecast error will *not* be independent of information at time t or earlier unless:

$$\pi_3 - 2\pi_1 = \pi_4 - 2\pi_2 = 0 \tag{14.20}$$

But the above are just a simple rearrangement of the cross-equation restrictions (14.9). In fact this example is so simple algebraically that the restrictions in (14.9) are 'cross-equation' but they are not non-linear.

Cross-Equation Restrictions: Addition of the Spread

A dispassionate commentator might remark that the AR forecasting scheme assumed is very simple and that investors might use many more variables than this to forecast future interest rates. The Campbell–Shiller VAR methodology recognises this and points to the most obvious additional variable that investors might use. Given that investors are supposed to believe in the PEH, then from (14.2) a variable that should be useful in predicting Δr_{t+1} should be the spread S_t itself. Hence, we now augment (14.7) with S_t and obtain a new expectations generating equation:

$$\Delta r_{t+1} = \pi_3 \Delta r_t + \pi_4 \Delta r_{t-1} + \pi_5 S_t + \omega_{t+1} \tag{14.21}$$

where $\pi_3 = a_1$, $\pi_4 = a_2$, $\pi_5 = b_1$. Proceeding as before and substituting the *forecast* for Δr_{t+1} in the PEH equation (14.2), we obtain:

$$S_t = (a_1/2)\Delta r_t + (a_2/2)\Delta r_{t-1} + (b_1/2)S_t \tag{14.22}$$

Wald Test

Campbell and Shiller note a very straightforward way of estimating the restrictions implicit in the model. Since S_t appears on both sides of (14.22), then the equation can only hold (for all values of the variables) if:

$$1 = b_1/2, \quad 0 = a_1/2, \quad 0 = a_2/2 \tag{14.23}$$

(or equivalently $\pi_5 = 2$, $\pi_3 = \pi_4 = 0$) which we obtain by equating coefficients on the left-hand and right-hand side variables. But these restrictions can be *directly* obtained by simply performing the regression on the expectations generating equation (14.21) and performing a Wald test based only on the estimation of the *unrestricted* estimates from (14.21), namely $b_1 = 2$, $a_1 = a_2 = 0$ (or $\pi_5 = 2$, $\pi_3 = \pi_4 = 0$). In this simple example we have linear restrictions so the Wald test is the same as a t test on a set of coefficients. The benefit in using the Wald test is that one doesn't have to run an additional regression on the *restricted* equation system as we did when we performed the likelihood ratio test[3].

Essentially the Wald test implies that only S_t is useful in forecasting Δr_{t+1} and its coefficient in (14.21) should equal 2. This is because the PEH (14.2) implies S_t is the optimal forecast of Δr_{t+1}^e. Hence any *additional* variables in the expectations generating equation (14.21), namely Δr_t, Δr_{t-1}, should be zero as suggested by the Wald test.

It is also straightforward to show that the restrictions imply that the forecast error $\Delta r_{t+1} - \Delta r_{t+1}^e$ is independent of all information at time t or earlier (use equations (14.2) and (14.21)) and that expected (abnormal) profits $E_t(AP) = E(\Delta r_{t+1}) - 2S_t$ are zero (equation (14.21) says it all).

Summary: Cross-Equation Restrictions

(i) By assuming an expectations generating equation for Δr_{t+1} one can test the joint hypothesis of the PEH + RE by running *both* the unrestricted and (the implied) restricted equations and applying a likelihood ratio test. The disadvantage of this procedure (in more complex cases) is that the *restricted* equation has to be formulated algebraically and then estimated: sometimes this can be rather difficult to implement.

(ii) The Campbell–Shiller methodology uses a Wald test which only requires one to estimate the *unrestricted* parameter estimates in the expectations generation equation.

(iii) Whichever test is used the (non-linear) restrictions on the π_i ensure that (a) expected (abnormal) profits are zero, (b) the PEH holds, that is $S_t = 2\Delta r_{t+1}^e$ at all times and (c) that the forecast error for Δr_{t+1} is independent of the variables in the information set at time t or earlier.

(iv) In the above tests one has to posit an *explicit* expectations generating equation for Δr_{t+1}^e, and if the latter is incorrectly specified then tests of the PEH + RE might fail not because the PEH is incorrect, but because agents use a different forecasting scheme for Δr_{t+1}^e, resulting in biased parameter estimates.

It is interesting to compare the above tests involving cross-equation restrictions with a direct test of the PEH which we discussed in Chapter 10 which only invokes the unbiasedness and orthogonality properties of RE

$$r_{t+1} = E_t r_{t+1} + \eta_{t+1} \tag{14.24}$$

Substituting in the term structure relationship (14.2) and adding Ω_t gives

$$S_t^* = a + bS_t + c\Omega_t + \eta_{t+1} \tag{14.25}$$

where $S_t^* = \Delta r_{t+1}/2$ is the 'perfect foresight spread'. Under the null of PEH + RE we expect $a = c = 0$ and $b = 1$. The interesting contrast between these two types of test is that the regression test using S_t^* does *not* require an *explicit* forecasting scheme for Δr_{t+1}. All we require is that the RE forecast error is unbiased and hence independent of Ω_t under the null. The latter conditions are less stringent than having to posit an *explicit* expectations scheme[4]. As we often have little guidance about the appropriate form for the equation for Δr_{t+1} a direct test based on (14.25) may be seen as a positive feature in testing the PEH. However, using only a single equation test may result in some loss of 'statistical efficiency' compared with estimating a two-equation system and using the cross-equation tests or the Wald test approaches. These issues are explored further in Section 14.3 when we discuss conflicting results from empirical work in this area.

14.2 THE VAR APPROACH

In the previous example we only had to make a one-period ahead forecast of short rates. When multiperiod forecasts are required we need an equation to forecast future values of the spread S_t. The latter can be done by using the Campbell–Shiller vector autoregression (VAR) approach which involves matrix notation. As before, this approach is illustrated using a simple example. The PEH applied to a three-period horizon gives:

$$R_t = \tfrac{1}{3}(r_t + r_{t+1}^e + r_{t+2}^e) \tag{14.26}$$

which may be reparameterised to give:

$$S_t = \tfrac{2}{3}\Delta r_{t+1}^e + \tfrac{1}{3}\Delta r_{t+2}^e \tag{14.27}$$

where $S_t = R_t - r_t$ is the long–short spread, $\Delta r_{t+1}^e = (r_{t+1}^e - r_t)$ and $\Delta r_{t+2}^e = (r_{t+2}^e - r_{t+1}^e)$. Now assume that both S_t and Δr_t may be represented as a bivariate vector autoregression of order one (for simplicity):

$$S_{t+1} = a_{11}\Delta r_t + a_{12}S_t + \omega_{1t+1} \tag{14.28}$$

$$\Delta r_{t+1} = a_{21}\Delta r_t + a_{22}S_t + \omega_{2t+1} \tag{14.29}$$

or in vector notation:

$$\mathbf{z}_{t+1} = \mathbf{A}\mathbf{z}_t + \boldsymbol{\omega}_{t+1} \tag{14.30}$$

where $\mathbf{z}_{t+1} = (S_{t+1}, \Delta r_{t+1})'$, $\mathbf{A}$ is the (2×2) matrix of coefficients a_{ij}, and $\boldsymbol{\omega}_{t+1} = (\omega_{1t+1}, \omega_{2t+1})'$. From (14.30) the optimal prediction of future $\mathbf{z}$'s using the chain rule for forecasting is:

$$E_t \mathbf{z}_{t+1} = \mathbf{A}\mathbf{z}_t \tag{14.31}$$

$$E_t \mathbf{z}_{t+2} = E_t \mathbf{z}_{t+1} = \mathbf{A}^2 \mathbf{z}_t \tag{14.32}$$

Now let $\mathbf{e1}' = (1, 0)$, and $\mathbf{e2}' = (0, 1)$ be 2×1 selection vectors. It follows that:

$$S_t = \mathbf{e1}'\mathbf{z}_t \tag{14.33}$$

$$E_t \Delta r_{t+1} = \mathbf{e2}'\mathbf{z}_{t+1}^e = \mathbf{e2}'\mathbf{A}\mathbf{z}_t \tag{14.34}$$

$$E_t \Delta r_{t+2} = \mathbf{e2}'\mathbf{z}_{t+2}^e = \mathbf{e2}'\mathbf{A}^2 \mathbf{z}_t \tag{14.35}$$

Substituting the above in the PEH equation (14.27):

$$S_t = \mathbf{e1}'\mathbf{z}_t = \left(\tfrac{2}{3}\mathbf{e2}'\mathbf{A} + \tfrac{1}{3}\mathbf{e2}'\mathbf{A}^2\right)\mathbf{z}_t \tag{14.36}$$

If (14.36) is to hold for all values of $\mathbf{z}_t$ then the following non-linear restrictions between the coefficients a_{ij} must hold:

$$f(\mathbf{a}) = \mathbf{e1}' - \mathbf{e2}'\left(\tfrac{2}{3}\mathbf{A} + \tfrac{1}{3}\mathbf{A}^2\right) = 0 \tag{14.37}$$

where the $f(\mathbf{a})$ has been defined as the set of restrictions. Hence a test of the PEH plus the forecasting scheme represented by the VAR simply requires one to estimate the *unrestricted* VAR equations and apply a Wald test based on the restrictions in (14.37).

Wald Test

It is worth giving a brief account of the form of the Wald test at this point. After estimating our 2×2 VAR we have an estimate of the variance–covariance matrix of the *unrestricted* VAR system which as previously we denote

$$\Sigma = \begin{bmatrix} \sigma_w^2 & \sigma_{wv} \\ \sigma_{wv} & \sigma_v^2 \end{bmatrix} \tag{14.38}$$

The variance–covariance matrix of the non-linear function $f(\mathbf{a})$ in (14.37) is given by:

$$\mathrm{var}[f(\mathbf{a})] = f_a(\mathbf{a})' \Sigma f_a(\mathbf{a})$$

where $f_a(\mathbf{a})$ is the first derivative of the restrictions with respect to the a_{ij} parameters. The Wald statistic is:

$$W = f(\mathbf{a})\{\mathrm{var}[f(\mathbf{a})]\}^{-1} f(\mathbf{a})' \tag{14.39}$$

There is little intuitive insight one can obtain from the general form of the Wald test (but see Buse 1982). However, the larger is the variance of $f(\mathbf{a})$ the smaller is the value of W. Hence the more imprecise the estimates of the A matrix the smaller is W and the more likely one is 'to pass' the Wald test (i.e. not reject the null). In addition if the restrictions hold exactly then $f(\mathbf{a}) \approx 0$ and $W \approx 0$. It may be shown that under the standard conditions for the error terms (i.e. no serial correlation or heteroscedasticity, etc.) then W is distributed as central χ^2 under the null with r degrees of freedom, where $r = $ number of restrictions. If W is less than the critical value χ_c^2 then we do not reject the null $f(\mathbf{a}) = 0$. The VAR–Wald test procedure is very general. It can be applied to more complex term structure relationships and can be implemented with high order lags in the VAR. Campbell and Shiller show that under the PEH, in general, the spread between n-period and m-period bond yields $(n > m)$ denoted $S_t^{(n,m)}$ may be represented:

$$S_t^{(n,m)} = E_t \sum_{l=1}^{k-1} (1 - i/k)\Delta^m r_{t+im}^{(m)} \tag{14.40}$$

where $\Delta^m r_t = r_t - r_{r-m}$ and $k = n/m$ (an integer). For example, for $n = 4$, $m = 1$, $S_t^{(4,1)} = R_t^{(4)} - r_t^{(1)}$ and:

$$S_t^{(4,1)} = E_t \left[\tfrac{3}{4}\Delta r_{t+1}^{(1)} + \tfrac{2}{4}\Delta r_{t+2}^{(1)} + \tfrac{1}{4}\Delta r_{t+3}^{(1)}\right] \tag{14.41}$$

A VAR of higher order is of the form:

$$S_{t+1} = [a_{11}S_t + a_{12}\Delta r_t] + [a_{13}S_{t-1} + a_{14}\Delta r_{t-1}]$$
$$+ [a_{15}S_{t-2} + a_{16}\Delta r_{t-2}] + \cdots + \omega_{1t+1}$$

$$\Delta r_{t+1} = [a_{21}S_t + a_{22}\Delta r_t] + [a_{23}S_{t-1} + a_{24}\Delta r_{t-1}]$$
$$+ [a_{25}S_{t-2} + a_{26}\Delta r_{t-2}] + \cdots + \omega_{2t+1}$$

However, having obtained estimates of the a_{ij} in the usual way, we can rearrange the above 'high lag' system into a first order system. For example, suppose we have a VAR of order $p = 2$, then in matrix notation this is equivalent to:

$$\begin{bmatrix} S_{t+1} \\ \Delta r_{t+1} \\ S_t \\ \Delta r_t \end{bmatrix} = \begin{bmatrix} a_{11} & a_{12} & a_{13} & a_{14} \\ a_{21} & a_{22} & a_{23} & a_{24} \\ 1 & 0 & 0 & 0 \\ 0 & 1 & 0 & 0 \end{bmatrix} \begin{bmatrix} S_t \\ \Delta r_t \\ S_{t-1} \\ \Delta r_{t-1} \end{bmatrix} + \begin{bmatrix} \omega_{1t+1} \\ \omega_{2t+1} \\ 0 \\ 0 \end{bmatrix} \qquad (14.42)$$

Equation (14.50) is known as the *companion form* of the VAR and may be compactly written:

$$\mathbf{Z}_t = \mathbf{A}\mathbf{Z}_{t-1} + \boldsymbol{\omega}_{t+1} \qquad (14.43)$$

where $\mathbf{Z}'_{t+1} = [S_{t+1}, \Delta r_{t+1}, S_t, \Delta r_t]$. Given the $(2p \times 1)$ selection vectors $\mathbf{e1}' = [1, 0, 0, 0]$, $\mathbf{e2} = [0, 1, 0, 0]$ we have:

$$S_t^{(n,m)} = \mathbf{e1}'\mathbf{Z_t} \qquad (14.44a)$$

$$\Delta r_t^{(m)} = \mathbf{e2}'\mathbf{Z_t} \qquad (14.44b)$$

$$E_t\Delta r_{t+j}^{(m)} = \mathbf{e2}'\mathbf{A}^j\mathbf{Z_t} \qquad (14.44c)$$

where in our example $n = 4$, $m = 1$, $p = 2$. If (14.44) are substituted into the general PEH equation (14.40), Campbell and Shiller demonstrate that the VAR non-linear restrictions are given by:

$$f(\mathbf{a}) = \mathbf{e1}' - \mathbf{e2}'\mathbf{A}[\mathbf{I} - (m/n)(\mathbf{I} - \mathbf{A}^n)(\mathbf{I} - \mathbf{A}^m)^{-1}](\mathbf{I} - \mathbf{A})^{-1} = 0 \qquad (14.45)$$

which for our example gives

$$f^*(\mathbf{a}) = \mathbf{e1}' - \mathbf{e2}'\mathbf{A}[\mathbf{I} - (1/4)(\mathbf{I} - \mathbf{A}^4)(\mathbf{I} - \mathbf{A})^{-1}](\mathbf{I} - \mathbf{A})^{-1} = 0 \qquad (14.46)$$

and this restriction can be tested using the Wald statistic outlined above.

Interpretation

Let us return to the three-period horizon PEH to see if we can gain some insight into how the non-linear restrictions in (14.36) arise. We proceed as before and determine the optimal forecasts of Δr_{t+1} and Δr_{t+2} from the VAR. We have from (14.29) at time $t + 2$ and (14.28):

$$E_t(\Delta r_{t+2}) = a_{21}(E_t\Delta r_{t+1}) + a_{22}(E_tS_{t+1}) \qquad (14.47)$$

$$E_tS_{t+1} = a_{11}\Delta r_t + a_{12}S_t \qquad (14.48)$$

Using the above equations and (14.29):

$$E_t(\Delta r_{t+2}) = a_{21}(a_{21}\Delta r_t + a_{22}S_t) + a_{22}(a_{11}\Delta r_t + a_{12}S_t)$$
$$= (a_{21}^2 + a_{22}a_{11})\Delta r_t + a_{22}(a_{21} + a_{12})S_t \tag{14.49}$$

Using (14.29) and (14.49) in the PEH equation (14.27):

$$S_t = \tfrac{2}{3}(a_{21}\Delta r_t + a_{22}S_t) + \tfrac{1}{3}[(a_{21}^2 + a_{22}a_{11})\Delta r_t + a_{22}(a_{21} + a_{12})S_t]$$

$$S_t = \left[\tfrac{2}{3}a_{21} + \tfrac{1}{3}(a_{21}^2 + a_{22}a_{11})\right]\Delta r_t + \left[\tfrac{2}{3}a_{22} + \tfrac{1}{3}a_{22}(a_{21} + a_{12})\right]S_t$$

$$S_t = f_1(\mathbf{a})\Delta r_t + f_2(\mathbf{a})S_t \tag{14.50}$$

Equating coefficients on both sides of (14.50) the non-linear restrictions are:

$$0 = f_1(\mathbf{a}) = \tfrac{2}{3}a_{21} + \tfrac{1}{3}(a_{21}^2 + a_{22}a_{11}) \tag{14.51a}$$

$$1 = f_2(\mathbf{a}) = \tfrac{2}{3}a_{22} + \tfrac{1}{3}a_{22}(a_{21} + a_{12}) \tag{14.51b}$$

It has been rather tedious to derive these conditions by the long-hand method of substitution and it is far easier to do so in matrix form as derived earlier since we also obtain a general form for the restrictions (suitable for programming for any values of n, m and p). The matrix restrictions in (14.37) must be equivalent to those in (14.51). Clearly the non-linear element comes from the $\mathbf{A}^2$ term while the left-hand side of (14.51) corresponds to the vector $\mathbf{e}1$. It is left as a simple exercise for the reader to show that for:

$$\mathbf{A} = \begin{bmatrix} a_{11} & a_{12} \\ a_{21} & a_{22} \end{bmatrix}$$

the restrictions in (14.51) are equivalent to those in (14.37). As before, the non-linear cross-equation restrictions (14.51) ensure that

(i)   Expected (abnormal) profits based on information $\mathbf{Z}_t$ in the VAR are zero.

(ii) The PEH equation (14.27) holds for all values of the variables in the VAR.

(iii) The error in forecasting Δr_{t+1}, Δr_{t+2} using the VAR is independent of information at time t or earlier (i.e. of S_{t-j}, Δr_{t-j} for $j \geq 0$). The latter is the orthogonality property of RE.

It is now straightforward to demonstrate how difficult it can become to formulate and estimate the restricted model and hence perform a likelihood ratio test of the restrictions, even for the three-period horizon case. The unrestricted VAR consists of (14.28) + (14.29). To obtain the restricted VAR we have to use (14.51) to obtain a_{21} and a_{22} in terms of all the other a_{ij}s and then substitute these (two) expressions in (14.29) which together with the (unchanged) equation (14.28) constitute the restricted model. The algebraic manipulations required become horrendous as either the horizon in the PEH or the lag length of the VAR is increased.

The Advantages of the VAR Approach

(i)   To test the PEH + RE restrictions we need only estimate the unrestricted coefficients in the VAR. The Wald test on the parameters of the VAR can be formulated for the general case of any n and m (for which $k = n/m$ is an integer).

(ii) Joint estimation of the two-equation VAR yields more (statistically) efficient estimators than any single equation testing procedure. The VAR can be estimated by OLS (i.e. stacked OLS or SURE) with a GMM correction to the standard errors if heteroscedasticity is present in ω_t.

The disadvantages are:

(i) An explicit forecasting scheme for $(S_t, \Delta r_t)$ is required which may be misspecified, and hence statistical results are biased.

(ii) The Wald test may have poor small sample properties and it is not invariant to the precise way the non-linear restrictions are formed (e.g. Gregory and Veall (1985)). Hence the Wald test may reject the null hypothesis of the PEH + RE because of only 'slight deviations' in the data from the null hypothesis. For example, if $f_2(a) = 1.03$ in (14.51) but the standard error on $f_2(a)$ was 0.003 one would reject the null (on a t test) but an economist would still say that the data largely supported the PEH. Campbell and Shiller (1992) recognise that the Wald test restrictions may be rejected and yet the PEH + RE may provide a 'reasonable model' of the behaviour of interest rates.

Further Testable Implications of the PEH Using the VAR Methodology — The Theoretical Spread S'_t

Campbell and Shiller (1992) suggest some additional 'metrics' for measuring the empirical success of the PEH and these are outlined for the three-period horizon model of the PEH (i.e. $n = 3, m = 1$):

$$S_t = \tfrac{2}{3}\Delta r^e_{t+1} + \tfrac{1}{3}\Delta r^e_{t+2} \tag{14.52}$$

We have seen that the RHS of (14.52) may be represented as a linear prediction using the estimated VAR. If we denote the RHS as the *theoretical spread* S'_t then:

$$S'_t = \mathbf{e2'} \left(\tfrac{2}{3}\mathbf{A} + \tfrac{1}{3}\mathbf{A}^2\right) \mathbf{z}_t = f(\mathbf{A})\mathbf{z}_t = f_1(a)\Delta r_t + f_2(a)S_t \tag{14.53}$$

The theoretical spread is the econometricians' 'best shot' at what the true (RE) forecast of (the weighted average of) future changes in short-term interest rates will be. If the PEH (14.52) is correct then $f_2(\mathbf{a}) = 1$ and $f_1(\mathbf{a}) = 0$ and hence $S'_t = S_t$ and therefore the *actual* spread S_t should be highly correlated with the theoretical spread. In the data set, the latter restrictions will (usually) not hold exactly and hence we expect S'_t from (14.53) to broadly move with the actual spread. Under the null hypothesis of the PEH + RE the following 'statistics' provide useful metrics against which we can measure the success of the PEH.

(i) The correlation coefficient corr(S_t, S'_t) between S_t and S'_t should be close to unity and in a regression

$$S'_t = \alpha + \beta S_t + v_t \tag{14.54}$$

we expect $\alpha = 0$ and $\beta = 1$.

(ii) Because the VAR contains the spread then either the *variance ratio* or the ratio of standard deviations:

$$\text{VR} = \text{var}(S_t)/\text{var}(S'_t)$$

$$\text{SDR} = \sigma(S_t)/\sigma(S'_t) \tag{14.55}$$

should both be close to unity. Sometimes the SDR is referred to as the 'variance ratio' since both give similar inferences.

(iii) It follows that in a graph of S_t and S'_t against time, the two series should broadly move in unison.

(iv) The PEH equation (14.52) implies that S_t is a sufficient statistic for future changes in interest rates and hence S_t should 'Granger cause' changes in interest rates. The latter implies that in the VAR equation (14.29) explaining Δr_{t+1}, then S_t and its own lagged values should, as a group, contribute in part to the explanation of Δr_{t+1} (so-called block exogeneity tests can be used here).

(v) Suppose R_t and r_t are $I(1)$ variables. Then Δr_{t+j} is $I(0)$ and if the PEH is correct then from (14.27) the spread $S_t = R_t - r_t$ must also be $I(0)$. Hence R_t and r_t must be cointegrated, with a cointegration parameter of unity. That is, given a long time series R_t and r_t should broadly move together.

It is worth noting that if the econometrician had the 'true' RE forecasting scheme used by investors then S_t and S'_t would be equal in all time periods. The latter statement does not imply that rational agents do not make forecasting errors, they do. However, S_t is set in the market with reference to the *expected* value of future interest rates. Therefore, if we have an equation that predicts the expected values actually used by agents in the market, then $S_t = S'_t$ for all t.

Perfect Foresight Spread

It is convenient here to remind the reader of a test of the PEH + RE based on the perfect foresight spread S^*_t, although it must be stressed that this test has nothing to do with the VAR methodology. The logic of this test using S_t and S^*_t is set out in Chapter 9 and is summarised here for the three-period case. The test does not use an explicit forecasting equation for $E_t\Delta r_{t+j}$ but merely invokes the unbiasedness and orthogonality assumptions of RE:

$$\Delta r_{t+j} = E_t(\Delta r_{t+j}|\Omega_t) + \eta_{t+j} \tag{14.56}$$

Substituting in equation (14.27) and rearranging:

$$\left[\tfrac{2}{3}\Delta r_{t+1} + \tfrac{1}{3}\Delta r_{t+2}\right] = S_t + \left[\tfrac{2}{3}\eta_{t+1} + \tfrac{1}{3}\eta_{t+2}\right] \tag{14.57}$$

Now define the LHS of (14.57) as the perfect foresight spread S^*_t and note that this implies $\text{var}(S^*_t) \leqslant \text{var}(S_t)$. Also, in the single equation regression:

$$S^*_t = a + bS_t + c\Omega_t + \eta^*_{t+1} \tag{14.58}$$

under the null hypothesis of PEH + RE, we expect $H_0 : a = c = 0$, $b = 1$. The RHS variables in (14.58) are dated at t or earlier and are independent of the RE forecast errors. Hence OLS on (14.58) provides unbiased estimates. However, η^*_{t+1} is MA (1) and may also be heteroscedastic, so the standard errors from OLS are invalid but correct standard errors are available using a GMM correction to the covariance matrix (see Chapter 20).

One word of warning. Do not confuse the perfect foresight spread S^*_t with the theoretical spread S'_t used in the VAR methodology. The perfect foresight spread S^*_t is a constructed variable which 'replaces' the expectations variables by their actual values. It is the spread that would ensue *if* agents forecast with 100 percent accuracy. On the other hand the theoretical spread is an *explicit* forecast of future interest rates based on the econometricians' best guess of the variables investors might actually use when forecasting the future.

At this point the reader will no doubt like to refresh his memory concerning the various concepts presented for evaluating the EH before moving on to illustrative empirical results in this area.

14.3 EMPIRICAL EVIDENCE

In his study using the VAR methodology. Taylor (1992) uses *weekly* data (Wednesday 3 pm rates) on three-month Treasury bills and yields to maturity on 10-, 15- and 20-year UK government bonds (over the period January 1985–November 1989) and finds strongly against the EH under rational expectations. Using the VAR methodology, he finds (i) spreads do not Granger cause changes in interest rates (ii) the variance ratios (VR) are in excess of 1.5 for all maturities and they are (statistically) in excess of unity and (iii) the VAR cross-equation restrictions are strongly violated.

MacDonald and Speight (1991) use quarterly data for 1964–1986 on a representative single government 'long bond' (i.e. over 15 years to maturity for five OECD countries). For the UK, the VAR restrictions, Granger causality and variance ratio test generally indicate rejection of the PEH (although correlation coefficient between S_t and S_t' is 'high' for the UK at 0.87). For other countries, Belgium, Canada, the USA and West Germany, the results are mixed but in general the Wald test is rejected and the variance ratios are in excess of 1.5 (except for the UK where it is found to be 1.29). However, no standard errors are given for the variance ratios and so formal statistical tests cannot be undertaken. (See also Mills (1991) who undertakes similar tests on UK data over a long sample period, namely 1871–1988.)

Campbell and Shiller (1992) use *monthly* data on US government bonds for maturities of up to five years including maturities for 1, 2, 3, 4, 6, 9, 12, 14, 36, 48 and 60 months for the period 1946–1987. Their data are therefore towards the short end of the maturity spectrum for bonds. Generally speaking they find little or no support for the EH at maturities of less than one year, from the regressions of the perfect foresight spread S_t^* on the actual spread S_t, their β values being in the region 0–0.5, rather than close to unity. Similarly the values of $\mathrm{corr}(S_t, S_t')$ are relatively low being in the range 0–0.7 and the values of VR are in the range 2–10 for maturities of less than one year. At maturities of four and five years Campbell and Shiller (1992) find more support for the EH since the variance ratio (VR) and the correlation between S_t and S_t' are close to unity. However, Campbell and Shiller do not directly test the VAR cross-equation restrictions but this has been done subsequently by Shea (1992) who in general finds they are rejected.

Cuthbertson (1996) considers the PEH of the term structure at the very short end of the maturity spectrum and is therefore able to use spot rates. (See also Cuthbertson et al (1995) for results using data on German spot rates.) His data consist of London Interbank (offer) rates for maturities of 1, 4, 13, 26 and 52 weeks. The complete data set is sampled *weekly* (Thursdays, 4 pm rates) beginning on the second Thursday in January 1981 and ending on the second Thursday of February 1992 giving a total of 580 data points. The one-week

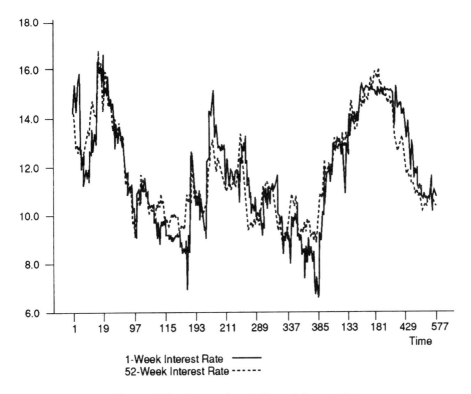

Figure 14.1 One-week and 52-week Interest Rates.

and 52-week yields are graphed in Figure 14.1: these rates move closely together in the long run (i.e. appear to be cointegrated) but there are also substantial movements in the spread, $S_t^{(52,1)}$.

The regressions of the perfect foresight spread $S_t^{*(n,m)}$ on the actual spread $S_t^{(n,m)}$ and the limited information set Λ_t (consisting of five lags of $S_t^{(n,m)}$ and $\Delta R_t^{(m)}$) are shown in Table 14.1. In all cases we do not reject the null that information available at time t or earlier does not incrementally add to the predictions of future interest rates, thus supporting the PEH + RE. In all cases, except that for $S_t^{(4,1)}$ (the four-week/one-week spread), we also do not reject the null $H_0 : \beta = 1$, thus in general providing strong support for PEH + RE. The rejection of the null for $S_t^{(4,1)}$ may be due to the short investment period and a slight misalignment of investment horizons, since four one-week investments may not always fall on a Thursday four weeks hence.

Cuthbertson's results from the VAR models for $S_t^{(n,m)}$ and $\Delta R_t^{(m)}$ indicate that $S_t^{(n,m)}$ Granger causes $\Delta R_t^{(m)}$: a weak test of the PEH. (There is also Granger causality from $\Delta R_t^{(m)}$ to $S_t^{(n,m)}$ indicating substantial feedback in the VAR regressions.) Cuthbertson also finds that for all maturities there is a strong correlation (Table 14.2, column 4) between the actual spread S_t and the predicted or theoretical spread S_t' from the forecasts using the VAR. The variance ratio (VR) = var(S_t)/ var(S_t') yields *point* estimates (column 3) are within two standard deviations of unity in 5 out of 8 cases. Hence on the basis of these two statistics we can broadly accept the PEH under weakly rational expectations.

Table 14.1 Perfect Foresight Spread: $S_t^{*(n,m)} = \alpha + \beta S_t^{(n,m)} + \gamma H_t + \eta_t^*$

(%)	Coefficients		Marginal	Significance	Levels
(n, m)	α (s.e. α)	β (s.e. β)	$H_0: \beta = 1$	$H_1: \alpha = 0, \beta = 1$	$H_2: \gamma = 0$
(26,13)	0.033 (0.14)	0.97 (0.23)	88	83	89
(52,26)	−0.018 (0.13)	1.32 (0.44)	47	74	96
(52,13)	0.019 (0.10)	1.22 (0.30)	46	73	65
(52,4)	−0.064 (0.25)	1.17 (0.21)	42	58	39
(4,1)	−0.069 (0.02)	0.73 (0.06)	<0.01	<0.01	40
(13,1)	−0.166 (0.06)	0.98 (0.07)	82	2.0	64
(26,1)	−0.133 (0.12)	1.02 (0.10)	0.86	40	20
(52,1)	−0.164 (0.25)	1.09 (0.15)	54	52	22

The regression coefficients reported in columns 2 and 3 are from regressions with $\gamma = 0$ imposed. The whole sample period is from the second Thursday January 1981 to the 2nd Thursday February 1992. After allowing for leads and lags this yields 540 observations (when $\gamma = 0$ is imposed) and 524 (when $\gamma \neq 0$). The method of estimation is GMM with a correction for heteroscedasticity and moving average errors of order $(m - n - 1)$, using Newey and West (1987) declining weights to guarantee positive semi definiteness. The last three columns are marginal significance levels for the null hypothesis stated. For $H_2 : \gamma = 0$ the reported results are for an information set which includes five lags of the change in short rates and of the spread (longer lags gave qualitatively similar results).

Table 14.2 Tests of the PEH using Weakly Rational Expectations

(1)	(2)	(3)	(4)
Spread	Wald Statistic, W(.)	$\text{var}(S_t) / \text{var}(S_t')$	$R^2(S_t, S_t')$
(n, m)	[.] = critical value (5%)	(.) = std. error	(.) = std. error
(26,13)	W(6) = 26.3 [12.6]	0.84 (0.44)	0.979 (0.014)
(52,26)	W(6) = 10.3 [12.6]	0.37 (0.20)	0.994 (0.005)
(52,13)	W(4) = 6.3 [9.5]	0.50 (0.20)	0.999 (0.001)
(52,4)	W(4) = 7.3 [9.5]	0.61 (0.18)	0.999 (0.001)
(4,1)	W(8) = 29.9 [15.5]	1.82 (0.42)	0.977 (0.015)
(13,1)	W(8) = 27.3 [15.5]	1.18 (0.26)	0.995 (0.003)
(26,1)	W(8) = 16.5 [15.5]	1.00 (0.25)	0.997 (0.002)
(52,1)	W(8) = 10.2 [15.5]	0.86 (0.23)	0.998 (0.002)

Wald statistics and standard errors are heteroscedastic robust.

By way of illustration the graph of S_t and S_t' from Cuthbertson (1996) is given for $(n, m) = (4, 1)$ in Figure 14.2. The R^2 of 0.98 indicates that the lagged spread predicts the direction of change in future interest rates but the point estimate of the variance ratio (= 1.8) suggests that the *quantitative* impact of $(S_t, \Delta R_t^{(m)})$ on future changes in interest rates is too small relative to that required by the PEH under rational expectations. The Wald test of the restrictions of the VAR coefficients is rejected at short horizons. In contrast, Hurn et al (1993) using *monthly* LIBOR rates (1975–1991) find that the Wald tests are not rejected. Shea (1992) notes that, particularly when using overlapping data, the Wald test rejects too often when the EH is true and this may, in part, account for the different results in these two studies.

Given that long rates R_t and short rates r_t are found in all of the above studies to be $I(1)$, then a weak test of the PEH + RE is that R_t and r_t are cointegrated with a cointegration parameter of unity. This is always found to be the case in the studies cited so that the spread $S_t = R_t - r_t$ is $I(0)$ for all maturities (m and n).

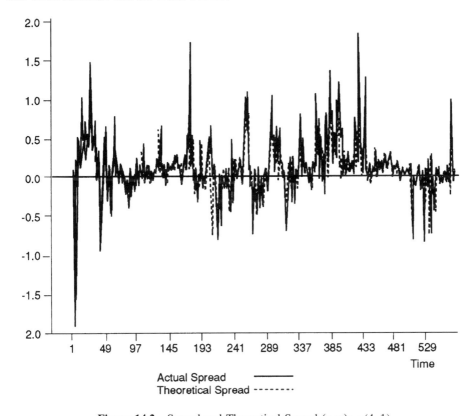

Figure 14.2 Spread and Theoretical Spread (n,m) = (4, 1).

While it is often found to be the case that, *taken as a pair*, any two interest rates are cointegrated and each spread $S_t^{(n,m)}$ is stationary, this cointegration procedure can be undertaken in a more comprehensive fashion. If we have q interest rates which are $I(1)$ then the EH implies (see equation (14.40)) that $(q - 1)$ linearly independent spreads $S_t^{(n,m)}$ are cointegrated. We can arbitrarily normalise on $m = 1$, so that the cointegrating vectors are $S_t^{(2,1)} = R_t^{(2)} - R_t^{(1)}$, $S_t^{(3,1)} = R_t^{(3)} - R_t^{(1)}$, etc. The so-called Johansen (1988) procedure allows one to estimate all of these cointegrating vectors simultaneously in a VAR of the form (see Chapter 20):

$$\Delta\mathbf{X}_t = \theta(L)\Delta\mathbf{X}_{t-1} + \boldsymbol{\alpha}_1'(R^{(2)} - \beta_1 R^{(1)})_{t-1} + \boldsymbol{\alpha}_2'(R^{(3)} - \beta_2 R^{(1)})_{t-1} \cdots$$

$$+ \boldsymbol{\alpha}_{q-1}'(R^{(q)} - \beta_q R^{(1)})_{t-1} \tag{14.59}$$

where $\mathbf{X}_t = (R^{(1)}, R^{(2)}, \ldots R^q)_t$. One can then test to see if the number of cointegrating vectors in the system equals $q - 1$ and then test the joint null $H_0 : \beta_1 = \beta_2 = \ldots \beta_{q-1} = 1$. Both are tests of the PEH. Shea (1992) and Hall et al (1992) find that although one does not reject the presence of $q - 1$ cointegrating vectors on the US data, nevertheless it is frequently the case that not all the β_i are found to be unity. Putting subtle statistical issues aside, a key consideration in interpreting these results is whether the VAR is an adequate representation of the data generation process for interest rates (e.g. are the parameters constant over the whole sample period). If the VAR is acceptable and some

β_i are numerically (and statistically) far from unity then the EH is rejected for the *whole* maturity spectrum. However, the EH may still hold for some subset of yields (e.g. at the very short end — see Cuthbertson (1996) and Cuthbertson et al (1995) and over some time periods (see Hall et al (1992)). The above results may be summarised as follows:

(i)   For the most part, long and short rates are cointegrated, with a cointegration parameter close to or equal to unity.

(ii) Spreads do tend to Granger cause future changes in interest rates for most maturities.

(iii) The perfect foresight spread S_t^* is correlated with the actual spread S_t with a coefficient which is often close to unity and is independent of other information at time t or earlier.

(iv) The theoretical spread S_t' (i.e. the predictions from the unrestricted VAR regressions) is usually highly correlated with the actual spread although the variance ratio (VR) is quite often not equal to unity.

(v)   the cross-equation restrictions on the VAR parameters are often rejected.

In broad terms, we can probably have less confidence in the PEH + RE as we move from the results of test (i) to test (v). Although note that the failure of the Wald test may not imply a severe rejection of the EH, if the model is supported by the other tests.

Why Such Divergent Results?

Can we account for those divergent results as far as the PEH is concerned? Usually stronger support for the PEH is given by the perfect foresight regressions in comparison with those from the VAR approach (particularly the rejection of the VAR cross-equation restrictions). One reason for this is that the perfect foresight regressions which use (14.59) implicitly allow potential *future* events (known to agents but not to the econometrician) to influence expectations, whereas the VAR approach requires an *explicit* information set known both to agents *and* the econometrician at time t or earlier. The market for short-term instruments is often heavily influenced by the government's monetary policy stance and in 'second guessing' the timing of interest rate changes by central banks. In periods of government intervention (influence) any purely 'backward-looking' regressions might be thought to provide poor predictors of future changes in interest rates: however, the rational expectations assumption $r_{t+j} = E_t r_{t+j} + \omega_{t+j}$ only requires unbiasedness and may suffer less from this effect. Hence on this count one might expect the perfect foresight regressions to perform better than the VAR approach and to yield relatively greater support for the PEH hypothesis (if it is indeed true).

The above institutional detail might also explain why we find a high R^2 between the actual spread S_t and the predicted theoretical spread S_t' using the VAR but the point estimate of the variance ratio $VR = var(S_t)/ var(S_t')$ is often in excess of unity at short horizons. The high R^2 implies that for *most time periods* the correlation between S_t and S_t' is high and this may be due to relatively 'long periods' when there is little or no government intervention in the market. However, on the (relatively few) occasions when government pronouncements and actions are expected to impinge upon the market in the *near future*, one might expect the VAR to underpredict future changes in short rates and hence var(S_t) to be greater than var(S_t'). (Such points would then be represented by the large 'spikes' in Figure 14.2.)

The most dramatic failure of the PEH occurs with the rejection of the VAR restrictions. Now it can be easily shown (see Campbell and Shiller (1987)) that rejection of the VAR restrictions implies either (i) information ($\mathbf{H}_t \subset \Omega_t$) at time t or earlier (other than S_t) influences future changes in short rates, or (ii) the influence of the current spread S_t on future changes in interest rates via the chain rule of forecasting is less than required by the PEH. But in contrast to (i), *single equation* perfect foresight regressions often reject the null that $\mathbf{H}_t$ influences future changes in interest rates. Hence rejection of the VAR restrictions is probably due to the 'low weight' given to S_{t-j} in the (VAR) regressions for $\Delta R_t^{(m)}$. Why might the latter occur? Two reasons are suggested. First, if agents use alternative (non-regression) forecasting schemes (e.g. chartists, see Allen and Taylor (1989)) the VAR methodology breaks down. Second, if agents actually do use the VAR regression methodology for forecasting in financial markets, one would expect them to utilise almost minute-by-minute observations (S_t, ΔR_t): hence forecasts based on (even) weekly data seem unlikely adequately to mimic such behaviour.

The frequency of the data collection, the extent to which rates are recorded contemporaneously (i.e. are they recorded at the same time of day?) and any approximations used in calculating yields might explain the conflicting results in each of the above studies. For example, Campbell and Shiller (1991) use *monthly* data and for maturities of *less than one year* their results are less supportive of the PEH + RE than Cuthbertson (1996). One might conjecture that this may be due to (i) the *weekly* data used in Cuthbertson means that the information set used in the VAR more closely approximates that used by agents and (ii) Cuthbertson uses data on pure discount instruments as opposed to Campbell and Shiller's data which uses McCulloch's (1987) approximation for yields on pure discount bonds based on interpolation, using cubic splines. (If the latter approximations are less severe the longer the term to maturity, this may account for Campbell and Shiller's relatively more favourable results for the EH at longer maturities.)

Holding Period Yield

Taylor (1992) also tests the various term structure theories using excess holding period yields (over 13 weeks) ($H_{t+13}^{(n)} - r_t$) and in particular he tests two variants. First, he finds against the proposition that the excess holding period yield (HPY) depends on a time-varying term premium (which is modelled using a GARCH process, see Chapter 17). Second, he tests the market segmentation hypothesis by running the regression:

$$(H_{t+13}^{(n)} - r_t) = \alpha + \beta(PD)_t + \varepsilon_{t+13} \tag{14.60}$$

where PD is the amount of debt of maturity n outstanding as a proportion of total government debt. Taylor finds $\beta > 0$ for maturities $n = 10$, 15 and 20 years, which supports the market segmentation hypothesis at the relatively long end of the maturity spectrum.

Taylor's (1992) results using UK weekly data for *long* maturities support the market segmentation hypothesis. However, the results in Cuthbertson (1996) and Hurn et al (1993) suggest that for maturities of *less than one year* the PEH plus an assumption of 'rational' or 'weakly rational' expectations broadly characterises behaviour of agents in the UK interbank market. The above seemingly contradictory results are not necessarily inconsistent. In the UK specialist agents (basically the corporate treasury departments of large companies and money brokers) deal almost exclusively at the short maturities and large changes in portfolio composition may not be required to equalise expected yields. In contrast, the long-bond market is dominated by insurance companies and pension funds which are likely to pay greater attention to the maturity composition of their portfolios (given the relatively fixed payments required on their liabilities). In short, UK pension funds and insurance companies have a desired long-run portfolio which they will only alter at the margin in response to changes in relative yields (Friedman and Roley, 1979 and Barr and Cuthbertson, 1991). The latter are brought about when the authorities change the composition of government debt across the maturity spectrum.

14.4 SUMMARY

Throughout this chapter interim summaries have been provided, since for some readers the material may appear, on first reading, somewhat complex. Therefore a brief summary is all that is required here.

(i)   The VAR methodology provides a series of statistical tests based on a comparison of the actual spread S_t and the 'best' forecast of future changes in interest rates given by the perfect foresight spread, S_t^*.

(ii) The 'metrics' provided by the VAR approach include a variance ratio test and a test of cross-equation restrictions on the parameters of the VAR. Only if the latter hold will the zero expected profit condition of the EH (with zero transactions costs) and the orthogonality conditions of the RE hypothesis hold.

(iii) If the spread and the change in interest rates are stationary then standard test procedures can be used.

(iv) Empirical results from the VAR methodology must be viewed as complementary to those based on variance bounds inequalities discussed in Chapter 10. Empirical results on the validity of the EH, using the VAR methodology, are somewhat mixed as is often the case in applied work.

On balance the VAR approach suggests that for the UK, the EH (with a time invariant term premium) provides a useful model of the term structure at the short end (i.e. for maturities of less than one year) but not at the long end of the maturity spectrum and vice versa for US data.

All of the tests in this chapter assume a time invariant risk premium but models which relax this assumption are the subject of Chapter 17.

ENDNOTES

1. The issues discussed here are quite subtle. Consider the following identity for the RE forecast using *all* relevant information, Ω_t:

$$E(D_{t+j}|\Omega_t) = E(D_{t+j}|\Lambda_t) + [E(D_{t+j}|\Omega_t) - E(D_{t+j}|\Lambda_t)]$$
$$= E(D_{t+j}|\Lambda_t) + \varepsilon_{t+1}$$

where ε_{t+1} is the *revision* to expectations as more information becomes available and under RE has a zero mean value and is independent of the limited information set Λ_t. Therefore, the econometrician's forecast of V_t differs from the agent's forecast by a weighted average of ε_{t+j} and hence

$$P_t = E(V_t|\Omega_t) = E(V_t|\Lambda_t) + f(\varepsilon_{t+j})$$
$$P_t = P'_t + f(\varepsilon_{t+j})$$

Hence we expect P'_t and P_t to have *some* correlation and for $\hat{\beta}_1$ in (10) to be unity but for $VR > 1$.

2. How the error term arises in (14.6) can be demonstrated by using the result from footnote 1, namely:

$$E(\Delta r_{t+1}|\Omega_t) = E(\Delta r_{t+1}|\Lambda_t) + \varepsilon_{t+1}$$

Substituting in the PEH, $S_t = E(\Delta r_{t+1}|\Omega_t)/2$ we have:

$$S_t = (1/2)E(\Delta r_{t+1}|\Lambda_t) + \varepsilon_{t+1}/2$$
$$= (a_1/2)\Delta r_t + (a_2/2)\Delta r_{t-1} + v_{t+1}$$

where $v_{t+1} = (\varepsilon_{t+1}/2)$ and $E(v_{t+1}|\Lambda_t) = 0$ and v_{t+1} is independent of $\Lambda_t = (\Delta r_t, \Delta r_{t-1})$.

3. The restricted equation in this simple case is trivial and is given by the regression of $(\Delta r_{t+1} - 2S_t)$ on a constant. The log-likelihood from this restricted regression is then compared with that from the unrestricted equation (14.21) with a constant term.

4. Note that in this simple example the two types of test become identical, if we let Ω_t in (14.25) 'contain' Δr_t and Δr_{t-1} only. However, in general the two approaches do differ.

15
The FOREX Market

The previous chapter dealt with the VAR methodology in some detail. Broadly speaking, the VAR approach can be applied to any theoretical model involving multiperiod forecasts and which is linear in the variables. Not surprisingly, therefore, it can also be used to test efficiency in the forward and spot markets using the uncovered interest parity (UIP) and forward rate unbiasedness (FRU) conditions outlined in Chapter 12. This chapter briefly outlines how the VAR methodology can be applied in these cases and

- illustrates the VAR methodology applied to FRU and UIP
- discusses some practical matters in choosing the appropriate VAR
- presents some recent empirical tests of FRU and UIP and provides an illustrative example of tests of a forward-looking version of the flex-price monetary model of the spot rate, using the VAR methodology

15.1 EFFICIENCY IN THE FOREX MARKET

The Forward Market

Chapter 12 analysed tests of forward market unbiasedness, $E_t s_{t+1} = f_t$, based on single equation tests for any one pair of currencies (or a *set* of single equations in order to increase the statistical efficiency of the tests using a ZSURE estimator). Our tests of FRU will now be extended, in a statistical sense at least, by considering a VAR system in order to forecast over multiperiod horizons. The first equation is:

$$\Delta s_{t+1} = a_{11}\Delta s_t + a_{12} f p_t + w_{1t+1} \tag{15.1}$$

where w_{1t+1} is white noise and independent of the RHS variables and $fp_t = (f - s)_t$, the forward premium. In the *one period case* when the forward rate refers to delivery at time $t + 1$, then the test of FRU is very simple. Under the null of risk neutrality and RE we expect

$$H_0 : a_{11} = 0, a_{12} = 1 \tag{15.2}$$

The above equation then reduces to the unbiasedness condition for the forward rate:

$$E_t s_{t+1} = f_t \tag{15.3}$$

which may be equivalently expressed as

$$E_t \Delta s_{t+1} = (f - s)_t \tag{15.4}$$

Note that H_0 also implies that the forecast error based on the VAR:

$$\Delta s_{t+1} - E_t \Delta s_{t+1} = a_{11} \Delta s_t + (a_{12} - 1)(f - s)_t + w_{1t+1} \tag{15.5}$$

is independent of the limited information set $\Lambda_t = (\Delta s_t, f p_t)$. In the *one step* ahead case we require only equation (15.1) to test FRU. However, we now consider a two step ahead prediction (which is easily generalised to the case of m step ahead predictions).

Two-Period Case

Suppose we have quarterly data but are considering forward rates f_t for six months ahead, hence FRU is:

$$E_t s_{t+2} - s_t = E_t \Delta_2 s_{t+2} = f p_t \tag{15.6}$$

To forecast two periods ahead we use *the identity*

$$E_t \Delta_2 s_{t+2} = E_t \Delta s_{t+2} + E_t \Delta s_{t+1} \tag{15.7}$$

Leading (15.1) one period forward, to forecast $E_t \Delta s_{t+2}$ we require a forecast of $E_t(f p_{t+1})$. Hence we require an equation to determine $f p$ which can be taken to be

$$f p_{t+1} = a_{21} \Delta s_t + a_{22} f p_t + w_{2t+1} \tag{15.8}$$

Equations (15.1) and (15.8) are a simple bivariate vector autoregression (VAR). If (s_t, f_t) are $I(1)$ variables but (s_t, f_t) have a cointegrating parameter $(1, -1)$ then $f p_t = f_t - s_t$ is $I(0)$ and all the variables in the VAR are stationary. Such stationary variables may be represented by a unique infinite moving average (vector) process which may be inverted to yield an autoregressive process (see Hannan (1970) and Chapter 20). A first order system consisting of equations (15.1) and (15.8) can be used as an illustration.

It can be shown that the FRU hypothesis (15.4) implies a set of non-linear cross-equation restrictions among the parameters a_{ij} and these non-linear restrictions ensure that the two-period forecast error implicit in (15.6) is independent of information $\Lambda_t = (\Delta s_t, f p_t)$. For illustrative purposes these restrictions are derived by 'substitution' and then shown how they appear in matrix form and how we can easily incorporate a VAR of high order and use it to forecast over any horizon. Using (15.7), (15.1) and (15.8) it is easy to see that

$$
\begin{aligned}
E_t \Delta_2 s_{t+2} &= E_t \Delta s_{t+2} + E_t \Delta s_{t+1} \\
&= a_{11}(a_{11} \Delta s_t + a_{12} f p_t) + a_{12}(a_{21} \Delta s_t + a_{22} f p_t) \\
&\quad + (a_{11} \Delta s_t + a_{12} f p_t)
\end{aligned} \tag{15.9}
$$

Collecting terms and equating the resulting expression for $E_t \Delta_2 s_{t+2}$ with $f p_t$

$$E_t \Delta_2 s_{t+2} = \theta_1 \Delta s_t + \theta_2 E f p_t = f p_t \tag{15.10}$$

where

$$\theta_1 = a_{11}^2 + a_{12} a_{21} + a_{11} \tag{15.11a}$$

$$\theta_2 = a_{11} a_{12} + a_{12} a_{22} + a_{12} \tag{15.11b}$$

It is clear that (15.10) can only hold for all values of Δs_t and fp_t if:

$$\theta_1 = 0 \text{ and } \theta_2 = 1 \tag{15.11c}$$

The forecast error for the spot rate between t and $t + 2$ is given by

$$\Delta_2 s_{t+2} - E_t \Delta_2 s_{t+2} \tag{15.12}$$

which given (15.6) and the VAR (15.10) is given by:

$$\theta_1 \Delta s_t + \theta_2 fp_t - fp_t + \eta_{t+1} \tag{15.13}$$

where η_{t+1} depends on w_{it+1} $(i = 12)$. If θ_1 and θ_2 are *unrestricted* then the expected value of the forecast error will in general depend on $(\Delta s_t, fp_t)$, that is information at time t. It is only if $\theta_1 = 0$ and $\theta_2 = 1$ that the orthogonality property of RE holds. In the previous chapter we noted that these restrictions can be tested using a likelihood ratio test of the restricted versus unrestricted VAR. From (15.11) we see that the restrictions can be rearranged to give

$$a_{21} = -a_{11}(1 + a_{11})/a_{12} \tag{15.14}$$

$$a_{22} = [1 - a_{12}(1 + a_{11})]/a_{12} \tag{15.15}$$

Hence the restricted VAR is

$$\Delta s_{t+1} = a_{11} \Delta s_t + a_{12} fp_t \tag{15.16}$$

$$fp_{t+1} = \left[\frac{-a_{11}(1 + a_{11})}{a_{12}} \right] \Delta s_t + \left[\frac{1 - a_{12}(1 + a_{11})}{a_{12}} \right] fp_t \tag{15.17}$$

The individual coefficients (a_{11}, a_{12}) in equation (15.17) are constrained to take on the same value in (15.16). The log-likelihood value from the restricted system (15.16) + (15.17) can be compared with that from the unrestricted system (15.1) + (15.8). As noted in the previous chapter if the difference in log-likelihoods is large ('small') then the restrictions are rejected (not rejected).

The problem with the above is that the restrictions have to be worked out and explicitly programmed into the VAR equations which are estimated subject to *non-linear* estimation techniques. Both these tasks can become 'complex' when the VAR has a large number of lags or the forecast horizon in the FRU equation is large. As we have already noted, a computationally simpler procedure is to estimate the unrestricted (linear in parameters) VAR and undertake a Wald test directly on the unrestricted a_{ij} coefficient estimates. It can now be quickly demonstrated how the above problem (with lag length $p = 1$) can be represented in matrix form and how it can be generalised. The matrix form of the unrestricted VAR is:

$$\mathbf{z}_{t+1} = \mathbf{A}\mathbf{z}_t + \mathbf{w}_{t+1} \tag{15.18}$$

where

$$\mathbf{z}_{t+1} = (\Delta s_{t+1}, fp_{t+1})$$

$$\mathbf{A} = \{a_{ij}\} \quad (2 \times 2)$$

Let $\mathbf{e1'} = (1, 0)$ and $\mathbf{e2'} = (0, 1)$ so that:

$$\Delta s_t = \mathbf{e1'z}_t \tag{15.19}$$

$$fp_t = \mathbf{e2'z}_t \tag{15.20}$$

It follows that

$$E_t\mathbf{z}_{t+2} = E_t\mathbf{Az}_{t+1} = \mathbf{A}^2\mathbf{z}_t \tag{15.21}$$

$$E_t(\Delta_2 s_{t+1}) = E_t(\Delta s_{t+2} + \Delta s_{t+1}) = \mathbf{e1'}(\mathbf{A}^2 + \mathbf{A})\mathbf{z}_t \tag{15.22}$$

Hence the FRU hypothesis (15.6) implies:

$$\mathbf{e1'}(\mathbf{A} + \mathbf{A}^2)\mathbf{z}_t = \mathbf{e2'z}_t$$

$$\mathbf{e2'} - \mathbf{e1'}(\mathbf{A} + \mathbf{A}^2) = 0 \tag{15.23}$$

where

$$\mathbf{A}^2 = \begin{pmatrix} a_{11}^2 + a_{12}a_{21}, & a_{11}a_{12} + a_{12}a_{22} \\ a_{21}a_{11} + a_{22}a_{21}, & a_{21}a_{12} + a_{22}^2 \end{pmatrix} \tag{15.24}$$

It is easy to see that (15.23) are the same restrictions as were worked out earlier 'by substitution'. A Wald test of (15.23) is easily constructed. The procedure can be generalised to include any lag length VAR since a pth order VAR can always be written with the $\mathbf{A}$ matrix in companion form, as a first order system. A forward prediction of Δs_{t+m} for any horizon m is given by

$$E_t\Delta_m s_{t+m} = \sum_{i=1}^{m} E_t\Delta s_{t+i} \tag{15.25}$$

and hence FRU for an m-period forward rate $fp_t^{(m)}$ is

$$E_t\Delta_m s_{t+m} = \sum_{i=1}^{m} \mathbf{e1'A}^i\mathbf{z}_t = fp_t^{(m)} \tag{15.26}$$

The FRU restrictions for an m-period horizon are:

$$f(\mathbf{A}) = \mathbf{e2'} - \mathbf{e1'}\sum_{i=1}^{m} \mathbf{A}^i = 0 \tag{15.27}$$

which can be tested using the Wald procedure. We can also use the VAR predictions to yield a series for the theoretical forward premium for m periods,

$$fp_t^{(m)'} = \sum_{i=1}^{m} \mathbf{e1'A}^i\mathbf{z}_t$$

(see equations (15.10) and (15.26)) which can then be compared to the actual forward premium (using graphs, variance ratios and correlation coefficients).

The Spot Market and Forward Market
The uncovered interest parity (UIP) condition can be applied over a multiperiod horizon and the VAR approach used in exactly the same way as described above. The multiperiod

UIP condition is:

$$E_t \Delta_m s_{t+1} = E_t(s_{t+m} - s_t) = (r - r^*)_t \tag{15.28}$$

For example, if we have quarterly data then the interest differential on one-year bonds should equal the expected change in the exchange rate over the subsequent four quarters (i.e. $m = 4$). The above UIP equation is similar to the FRU equation (15.26) except we have $(r_t - r_t^*)$ on the RHS and not $fp_t^{(m)}$. However, it should be obvious that the analysis for a VAR in Δs_t and $(r_t - r_t^*)$ goes through in exactly the same fashion as for FRU. If the cross-equation restrictions on the parameters of the VAR are not rejected then we do not reject the multiperiod UIP condition. What about testing FME and UIP together? This is easy too. Consider the trivariate VAR where $z'_{t+1} = (\Delta s, fp, r - r^*)_{t+1}$. Having obtained the unrestricted estimates $\mathbf{A}$ (and put them in companion form) we will have two sets of restrictions of the form

$$\sum_{i=1}^{m} \mathbf{e1}' \mathbf{A}^i - \mathbf{e2}' = 0 \qquad \text{FRU} \tag{15.29}$$

$$\sum_{i=1}^{m} \mathbf{e1}' \mathbf{A}^i - \mathbf{e3}' = 0 \qquad \text{UIP} \tag{15.30}$$

where the vectors $\mathbf{eJ}$ have unity in the Jth element and zeros elsewhere ($J = 1, 2, 3$). We can test each restriction separately, thus testing FRU or UIP only, or test them both together (i.e. a joint test of FRU + UIP). Of course, if we accept that covered interest parity holds then rejection of either *one* of FRU or UIP should imply rejection of the other.

How Big Can a VAR Get?

We noted in Chapter 14 that if we have unbiased estimates of the true parameters of the VAR then adding additional variables will not, *in principle*, rescue tests of the EMH, if they have failed the Wald test on a limited information set. The key assumption, however, is unbiased parameter estimates. We noted that with a finite sample, 'bias' is possible and hence additional variables may make a difference to the Wald test of the VAR restrictions. It is convenient at this point to elaborate on these arguments surrounding the appropriate 'size' of the VAR since it is a key element in evaluating empirical work.

The reader will have noticed that FRU can be tested in a VAR that contains three variables $(\Delta s, fp, r_t - r_t^*)$ or two variables $(\Delta s, fp)$. Which is better? In fact, why not greatly expand the number of variables in the information set (e.g. add stock returns, long-term interest rates, etc.) even when testing just the FRU.

The first thing to note is that a VAR of m variables can always be reduced to one in q variables, where $q < m$, and in fact we can even reduce the system to $q = 1$, that is an autoregressive equation. To illustrate this consider the 3×3 VAR system discussed above, with lag length $p = 1$ for ease of exposition

$$\Delta s_t = a_{11} \Delta s_{t-1} + a_{12} fp_{t-1} + a_{13} d_{t-1} + w_{1t} \tag{15.31}$$

$$fp_t = a_{21} \Delta s_{t-1} + a_{22} fp_{t-1} + a_{23} d_{t-1} + w_{2t} \tag{15.32}$$

$$d_t = a_{31} \Delta s_{t-1} + a_{32} fp_{t-1} + a_{33} d_{t-1} + w_{3t} \tag{15.33}$$

where $d_t = (r - r^*)_t$. For $|a_{33}| < 1$, the last equation may be written

$$d_t = (1 - a_{33}L)^{-1}[a_{31}\Delta s_{t-1} + a_{32}fp_{t-1} + w_{3t}] \qquad (15.34)$$

Hence d_t is a function of lagged values of Δs_{t-1}, fp_{t-1} (and a MA error in w_{3t}). Substituting (15.34) for d_{t-j} in the RHS of the first two equations (15.31) and (15.32) with Δs_t and fp_t as dependent variables we obtain *two* equations for Δs_t and fp_t depending only on their own lagged values. Similarly we could now repeat the procedure for fp_t obtaining $fp_t = g(\Delta s_{t-j})$ and substitute out for this in the equation with Δs_t as the dependent variable, giving an ARMA model for Δs_t (see Chapter 20).

Statistically, the choice between a univariate model or a multivariate VAR depends on a trade-off between the statistical requirements of lack of serial correlation and heteroscedasticity in the errors, the overall 'fit' of the equations and parsimony (i.e. the 'best' explanation with the smallest number of parameters). Test statistics are available to decide among these various criteria (e.g. Akaike and Schwartz criteria) but judgement is usually required even when using purely statistical tests. This is because the statistical criteria are likely to conflict. For example, maximising a parsimony criterion like the Akaike information criterion might result in serially correlated errors.

To the above statistical criteria an economist might have prior views (based on theory and gut instinct) about what are the key variables to include in a VAR. However, as a VAR is a reduced form of the structural equations of the whole economy there is always likely to be a rather disparate set of alternative variables one might include in a VAR. Hence empirical results based on any *particular* VAR are always open to attack on the grounds that the VAR may not be 'the best' possible representation of the data. In particular, the stability of the parameters of the VAR is crucial in interpreting the validity or otherwise of the Wald test of the cross-equation restrictions (see Hendry (1988) and Cuthbertson (1991)).

15.2   RECENT EMPIRICAL RESULTS

One can see that the VAR methodology is conducive to testing several variants of the same basic idea, namely RE cross-equation restrictions. Recent studies recognise the importance of the cointegration literature when formulating the variables to include in the VAR. (They not only include difference variables in the VAR but also the 'levels' or cointegrating $I(0)$ variables such as fp_t and $(r - r^*)_t$ in the above examples). Recent studies are virtually unanimous in finding rejection of the VAR restrictions when testing the FRU hypothesis and the UIP hypothesis — under the maintained hypothesis of a time invariant (constant) risk premium. The rejection of FRU and UIP is found to hold at several horizons (e.g. 3, 6, 9 and 12 months), over a quite wide variety of alternative information sets, across different currencies and over several time spans of data (see, for example, Hakkio (1981), Baillie and McMahon (1989), Levy and Nobay (1986), MacDonald and Taylor (1987, 1988) and Taylor (1989c)).

Term Structure of Forward Premia

Some studies have combined tests of *covered* interest parity with the EH of the term structure of interest rates applied to both domestic and foreign interest rates. The VAR methodology is again useful for multiperiod forecasts. By way of illustration consider the *covered* interest parity (CIP) relationships (in logarithms) for three- and six-month interest rates and forward rates but using *monthly* data:

$$fp_t^{(3)} = f_t^{(3)} - s_t = d_t^{(3)} \tag{15.35}$$

$$fp_t^{(6)} = f_t^{(6)} - s_t = d_t^{(6)} \tag{15.36}$$

where $d_t^{(i)} = r_t^{(i)} - r_t^{*(i)}$ ($i = 3, 6$). If the pure expectations hypothesis of *interest rates* holds in both the domestic and foreign country then

$$d_t^{(6)} = (d_t^{(3)} + E_t d_{t+3}^{(3)})/2 \tag{15.37}$$

where the subscript $t + 3$ applies because monthly data is used. The above equations imply a term structure of forward premia which involves forecasts of the forward premium:

$$fp_t^{(6)} = \left[fp_t^{(3)} + E_t fp_{t+3}^{(3)} \right] /2 \tag{15.38}$$

Equation (15.38) is conceptually the same as that for the term structure of spot yields on zero coupon bonds, discussed in Chapter 14. Clearly, given any VAR involving $fp_t^{(6)}$ and $fp_t^{(3)}$ (and any other relevant variables one wishes to include in the VAR) then (15.38) will imply the, by now, familiar set of cross-equation restrictions.

There have been a number of VAR studies applied to (15.38) and they usually resoundingly reject the pure expectations hypothesis of the term premia in forward rates (e.g. MacDonald and Taylor (1990)). Since there is strong independent evidence that *covered* interest parity holds for most time periods and most maturities, then rejection of the restrictions implicit in the VAR parameters applied to (15.38) is most likely due to a failure of the expectations hypothesis of the term structure of interest rates to hold in the domestic and foreign countries.

The Spot Rate, Fundamentals and the VAR Approach

In our analysis of the flex-price monetary model FPMM in Chapter 13 we saw that the spot rate may be represented as a forward convolution of fundamental variables:

$$s_t = (1 + \beta)^{-1} \sum_{i=0}^{\infty} [\beta/(1 + \beta)]^i E(x_{t+i}|\Omega_t) \tag{15.39}$$

where

$$x_t = (m_t - m_t^*) - (\gamma y_t - \gamma^* y_t^*) \tag{15.40}$$

Subtracting x_t from both sides of (15.39)

$$q_t = s_t - x_t = \sum_{i=1}^{\infty} \theta^i E_t(\Delta x_{t+i}|\Omega_t) \tag{15.41}$$

where $\theta_i = \beta/(1 + \beta)$, $E_t \Delta x_{t+1} = E_t x_{t+1} - x_t$ and $E_t \Delta x_{t+i} = E_t(x_{t+i} - x_{t+i-1})$ for $i > 1$. Equation (15.41) is now in a similar algebraic form to that outlined for the EH of the term structure in Chapter 14. We may somewhat loosely refer to $q_t = s_t - x_t$ as the 'exchange rate spread'. Hence, we can apply the same test procedures to (15.41) as in our earlier analysis.

If the economic fundamentals in x_t are $I(1)$ then Δx_{t+i} in (15.41) is $I(0)$ and we also expect s_t and x_t to be cointegrated and hence q_t to be $I(0)$. If we form a VAR in $\mathbf{z}_t = (q_t, \Delta x_t)'$ then it is easy to see that (15.41) implies

$$\mathbf{e1}'\mathbf{z}_t = \sum_{i=1}^{\infty} \theta^i \mathbf{e2}'\mathbf{A}^i \mathbf{z}_t = \mathbf{e2}'\theta\mathbf{A}(\mathbf{I} - \theta\mathbf{A})^{-1}\mathbf{z}_t \tag{15.42}$$

Hence the Wald restrictions implied by this version of the FPMM are:

$$\mathbf{e1}' - \mathbf{e2}'\theta\mathbf{A}(\mathbf{I} - \theta\mathbf{A})^{-1} = 0 \tag{15.43}$$

or

$$\mathbf{e1}'(\mathbf{I} - \theta\mathbf{A}) - \mathbf{e2}'\theta\mathbf{A} = 0 \tag{15.44}$$

Equation (15.44) is a set of linear restrictions which imply that the RE forecast error for the spot rate is independent of any information available at time t other than that given by the variables in x_t. We can also define the 'theoretical exchange rate spread' q_t' as

$$q_t' = \mathbf{e2}'\theta\mathbf{A}(\mathbf{I} - \theta\mathbf{A})^{-1}\mathbf{z}_t \tag{15.45}$$

and compare this with the actual spread q_t. To implement the VAR methodology we need to have estimates of γ, γ^* to form the variable $q_t = s_t - x_t$ and estimates of β to calculate θ. An implication of the FPMM is that

$$s_t = (m_t - m_t^*) - (\gamma y_t - \gamma^* y^*) + (\beta r - \beta^* r^*) \tag{15.46}$$

is a cointegrating relationship (given that all the variables are $I(1)$). Estimates of $(\gamma, \gamma^*, \beta_1, \beta^*)$ may be obtained by a (multivariate) estimation procedure known as the Johansen procedure (see Chapter 20). The variables $q_t = s_t - x_t$ and Δx_t can then be constructed and used in the VAR.

MacDonald and Taylor (1993) provide a good illustration of the implementation of this procedure. Note that by using (15.41) we take explicit account of the possible non-stationarity in the data. Hence one avoids possible spurious regression problems found in earlier tests of the FPMM which used levels of trended variables. We also avoid the specification error found in earlier studies that used only first differences of the variables and ignored any cointegrating relationships among the $I(1)$ variables. MacDonald and Taylor use monthly data January 1976–December 1990 on the DM/\$ rate. From the Johansen procedure they find they do not reject the null that the coefficients on relative money supplies and relative income are unity for the 'home' (Germany) and 'foreign' (USA) variables and that the interest rate coefficients are nearly equal and opposite:

$$s_t = (m - m^*)_t + (y_t - y_t^*) + 0.049r - 0.050r_t \tag{15.47}$$

They take $\beta = \beta^* = 0.05$ and the variable denoted x_t above is taken to be $x_t = (m - m^*)_t - (y_t - y_t^*)$. MacDonald and Taylor find that the Wald tests in (15.43) and (15.44) decisively reject the RE cross-equation restrictions and there is excess volatility in the spot rate. The variance of the actual spread q_t exceeds the variance of the theoretical spread q_t' given by (15.45) by a factor greater than 100 (when $\beta = 0.05$) (although no standard errors are given).

MacDonald and Taylor note that the presence of a cointegrating vector (15.46) implies that the spot rate may be represented as a dynamic error correction model (ECM) (see Chapter 20) and they impose the restrictions in (15.47) on $q_t = s_t - x_t$ and run a second-stage regression to estimate the short-run dynamic response of s_t. Their preferred ECM is:

$$\Delta s_t = \underset{(0.003)}{0.005} + \underset{(0.07)}{0.24\Delta s_{t-2}} - \underset{(0.23)}{0.42\Delta_2\Delta m_t} - \underset{(0.34)}{0.79\Delta y_t} - \underset{(0.003)}{0.008\Delta^2 r_t^*} - \underset{(0.013)}{0.025q_{t-1}}$$

$$(15.48)$$

where $R^2 = 0.14$, $SE = 3.2$ percent, $(\cdot)$ = standard error. Equation (15.48) passes all the usual diagnostic tests, although note that the R^2 of 14 percent indicates that most of the variation in Δs_t is not explained by the equation. They then perform a 'rolling regression' and use (15.48) to forecast over different horizons as the estimated parameters are updated. They find that the RMSE for the ECM are *slightly* less than those from the random walk, 'no change' forecasts for horizons of 1, 2, 3, 6, 9 and 12 months. This is in contrast to some of the earlier results in Meese and Roghoff (1983). However, note that most of the statistical explanation in (15.48) appears to be due to the ad-hoc dynamic terms and little of the statistical explanation seems due to the long-run error correction term. The forecasts are likely to be dominated by the difference terms, which probably approximate a random walk themselves, hence the reason why the reported RMSEs are approximately the same as those for the random walk model[1]. The MacDonald and Taylor study is a valiant attempt to test correctly a sophisticated version of the FPMM but the model is barely an improvement on the random walk in predicting monthly movements in the DM/$ spot rate.

15.3 SUMMARY

Tests of risk neutrality and RE based on FRU and UIP over multiperiod forecast horizons are easily accomplished using the VAR methodology. The VAR methodology can also be applied to forward-looking models of the spot rate based on economic fundamentals such as relative money supply growth. The main results using this methodology in the FOREX market suggest

- the FOREX market is not efficient under the maintained hypothesis of risk neutrality and RE since both FRU and UIP fail the VAR tests
- the FPMM applied to the $/DM rate indicates that this model does not fit the data particularly well, the VAR restrictions do not hold, the spot rate is excessively volatile (relative to its 'theoretical' counterpart) and the model performs little better than a random walk. However, as noted in Chapter 13 'monetary fundamentals' provide some predictive content for *long horizon* changes in the exchange rate

These results imply that the FOREX market is inefficient under risk neutrality and RE. This may be because of a failure of RE or because there exists a sizeable time varying risk premium. The latter is examined in Chapter 18. Alternatively, there could be elements of irrational behaviour in the market caused by 'fads' or by the mechanics of the trading process itself. However, relatively sophisticated tests described in this chapter have not rescued the abysmal performance of 'formal' fundamentals models of the spot rate and efficiency in the FRU and UIP relationships is rejected.

ENDNOTE

1. MacDonald and Taylor (1994) also consider other variants of the FPMM with similar results to those reported above. Note that the 'low' t statistic on the ECM term is indicative that s_t may not be cointegrated with the fundamentals (see Banerjee et al (1993)).

16
Stock Price Volatility

It was seen in Chapter 6 that a definitive interpretation of the results from several types of variance bounds test on stock prices is dogged by the stationarity issue, namely the appropriate method of 'detrending' the series for the actual price P_t and the perfect foresight price P_t^*. However, in the previous two chapters we have noted that the VAR procedure tackles this problem head on by explicitly testing for stationarity in the variables and it also allows several alternative metrics for assessing the validity of the EMH.

It would be useful if we could apply the VAR methodology to stock prices. In general, the rational valuation formula (RVF) is non-linear in dividends and the required rate of return (or discount factor); however, a linear approximation is possible. This linear approximation also results in a transformation such that the 'new' variables are likely to be stationary. Hence the cointegration methodology can be used in setting up the VAR. In applying the VAR methodology to stocks a comparison can be made of a time series of the 'theoretical' (log) stock price p_t' (or log dividend price ratio δ_t')[1] with the actual (log of the) stock price p_t to ascertain whether the latter is excessively volatile. Results from the VAR methodology can be compared with earlier tests on excess volatility which compared $\text{var}(P_t)$ with the variance of the perfect foresight price $\text{var}(P_t^*)$. The VAR methodology also gives rise to cross-equation parameter restrictions, similar to those found when testing the EMH in the bond and FOREX markets.

It was noted that Fama and French (1988) and others found that long horizon *returns* (e.g. over several years) are 'more forecastable' than short horizon returns (e.g. over a month or one year). Using the linearisation of the RVF it is possible to derive a formula for long horizon returns and the VAR methodology then provides complementary evidence to that of Fama and French.

The RVF assumes that stock prices change only on the arrival of new information or news about 'fundamentals': that is the future course of either dividends or discount rates. An interesting question is whether the observed volatile movements in stock prices are due solely to news. To answer this question a key element is whether one-period returns are *persistent*. 'Persistent' means that the arrival of news about *current* returns has a strong influence on all future returns and hence on all future discount rates. If persistence is high then it can be shown that news about returns can have a large effect on stock *prices* even if one-period returns are barely predictable. This theme is developed further in the next chapter when the degree of persistence in a time varying risk premium is investigated. However, in this chapter the key aims are to:

- develop a range of tests of the rational valuation formula (RVF) for stock prices using the VAR methodology and to provide illustrative examples of these test procedures

- demonstrate the relationship between tests using the VAR methodology and those for long horizon returns such as Fama and French and those using Shiller volatility tests, based on the perfect foresight price

- show that although one-period *returns* are hardly predictable this may nevertheless imply that stock *prices* deviate significantly and for long periods from their fundamental value, that is there is excess volatility in stock prices

- examine the relationship between stock price volatility and the degree of persistence in one period returns

Some of the analysis in deriving the above results is rather tedious and perhaps less intuitively appealing than either the VAR methodology applied to the term structure of interest rates or volatility tests on stock prices. An attempt has been made to add some intuition where possible and deal with some of the algebraic manipulations in Appendix 16.1. However, for the reader who has fully mastered the VAR material in the previous chapters there are no major new conceptual issues presented in this chapter.

16.1 THEORETICAL ISSUES

We begin with an overview of the RVF and rearrange it in terms of the dividend price ratio, since the latter variable is a key element in the VAR approach as applied to the stock market. We then derive the Wald restrictions implied by the RVF and the rational expectations assumption and show that these restrictions are equivalent to a key proposition of the EMH, namely that one-period *excess returns* are unforecastable.

16.1.1 Linearisation of Returns and the RVF

We define P_t = stock price at the *end* of period t, D_{t+1} = dividends paid *during* period $t + 1$, H_{t+1} = one period holding period return from the *end* of period t to the *end* of period $t + 1$. All variables are in real terms. Define h_{t+1} as

$$h_{t+1} \equiv \ln(1 + H_{t+1}) = \ln[(P_{t+1} + D_{t+1})/P_t] \tag{16.1}$$

The one-period return depends positively on the capital gain (P_{t+1}/P_t) and on the dividend yield (D_{t+1}/P_t). Equation (16.1) can be linearised to give (see Appendix 16.1)

$$h_{t+1} \approx \rho p_{t+1} - p_{t+1} + (1 - \rho)d_{t+1} + k \tag{16.2}$$

where lower case letters denote logarithms (e.g. $p_t = \ln P_t$), $\rho = \overline{P}/(\overline{P} + \overline{D})$ is a linearisation parameter and empirically is calculated to be around 0.94 from the sample data, while k is a linearisation constant (and for our purposes may be largely ignored). Equation (16.2) is an approximation but we will treat it as an accurate approximation. Note that like (16.1), equation (16.2) implies that the (approximate) one-period holding period yield depends positively on the capital gain (i.e. p_{t+1} relative to p_t) and the level of (the logarithm of) dividends d_{t+1}. If we define the (log) dividend price ratio as[2]

$$\delta_t = d_t - p_t \tag{16.3}$$

then equation (16.2) becomes

$$h_{t+1} = \delta_t - \rho\delta_{t+1} + \Delta d_{t+1} + k \tag{16.4}$$

Equation (16.4) for the one-period return undoubtedly looks a little strange and is not terribly intuitive. It is an (approximate) identity with no economic content as yet. It implies that if we wish to forecast one period *returns* we need to forecast the future dividend price ratio δ_{t+1} and the growth in dividends during period $t + 1$. It follows that to forecast h_{t+1} then δ_t and Δd_t must be included in the VAR. The observant reader might also notice that (16.4) is a forward difference equation in δ_t and since $\delta_t = d_t - p_t$ it can be solved forward to yield an expression for the (logarithm of the) price *level* of the stock: a sort of RVF in logarithms. Before we do this however it is worth undertaking a brief digression to explain how the dividend price ratio is related to the discount rate and the *growth* in dividends in the 'usual' RVF of Chapter 4. This will provide the intuition we need to understand the RVF in terms of δ_t which appears below, in equation (16.8). The RVF in the levels of the variables is

$$\frac{P_t}{D_t} = E_t\left[\frac{(D_{t+1}/D_t)}{(1+r_t)} + \frac{(D_{t+2}/D_t)}{(1+r_t)(1+r_{t+1})} + \frac{(D_{t+3}/D_t)}{(1+r_t)(1+r_{t+1})(1+r_{t+2})} + \cdots\right] \tag{16.5}$$

where we have divided through by D_t to give a price dividend ratio. Next we note that, for example:

$$\frac{D_{t+2}}{D_t} = \left[\frac{D_{t+2}}{D_{t+1}}\right]\left[\frac{D_{t+1}}{D_t}\right] \approx \Delta d_{t+2}\Delta d_{t+1} \tag{16.6}$$

where we have used the logarithmic approximation for the rates of growth of dividends. From (16.5) and (16.6) we see that the RVF is consistent with the following:

(i) the current price-dividend ratio is positively related to all future growth rates of dividends Δd_{t+j},

(ii) the current price dividend ratio is negatively related to all future discount factors r_{t+j}.

We can, of course, invert equation (16.5) so that the current dividend price ratio (or dividend yield) is qualitatively expressed as:

$$(D_t/P_t) = f(\Delta d^e_{t+j}, r^e_{t+j}) \quad f_1 < 0, f_2 > 0 \tag{16.7}$$

Since (16.7) is just a rearrangement of the RVF formula then intuitively we have

(i) when dividends are expected to grow, *ceteris paribus*, the current price will be high and hence the dividend price ratio will be low,

(ii) where future discount rates are expected to be high, the current price will be low and hence the current dividend price ratio will be high.

We can obtain the same 'rearrangement' of the RVF as (16.7) but one which is linear in the parameters, by solving (16.4) in the usual way using forward recursion (and imposing a transversality condition) (see Campbell and Shiller 1988):

$$\delta_t = \sum_{j=0}^{\infty} \rho^j(h_{t+j+1} - \Delta d_{t+j+1}) - k/(1-\rho) \tag{16.8}$$

where h_{t+j} the one-period return is 'equivalent to' the one-period discount factor r_{t+j} in (16.5) above. In fact, since (16.4) is an identity then (16.8) is also an identity (subject to the linear approximation). A rather subtle point can now be made which will introduce an economic input to equations (16.4) and (16.8) and make the latter a linearised version of the RVF which, of course, does embody economic behaviour. From Chapter 4 it will be recalled that if we assume the economic hypothesis that investors have a required (or desired) expected one-period return equal to r_t then we can derive the RVF (16.5) with a time varying discount rate (equal to r_t). Similarly suppose the (log) expected (real) rate of return required by investors *to willingly hold stocks* is denoted r^e_{t+j} then[3]:

$$E_t h_{t+j} = r^e_{t+j} \tag{16.9}$$

Then from (16.4)

$$\delta_t - \rho \delta^e_{t+1} + \Delta d^e_{t+1} + k = r^e_{t+1} \tag{16.10}$$

(note the superscript 'e' on δ_{t+1}). Solving (16.10) forward

$$\delta_t = \sum_{j=0}^{\infty} \rho^j [r^e_{t+j+1} - \Delta d^e_{t+j+1})] + k/(1 - \rho) \tag{16.11}$$

Equation (16.11) is now the linear logarithmic approximation to the RVF given in (16.7) and it can be seen that the same negative relationship between δ_t and Δd_{t+j} and the same positive relationship between δ_t and r^e_{t+j} holds as in the 'exact' RVF of (16.5). Virtually the same result is obtained if one takes expectations of the identity (16.4) and solves recursively to give:

$$\delta_t = \sum_{j=0}^{\infty} \rho^j [h^e_{t+j+1} - \Delta d^e_{t+j+1}] - k/(1 - \rho) \tag{16.12}$$

where $E_t \delta_t = \delta_t$ as δ_t is known at time t. The only difference here is that h^e_{t+j} must be interpreted as the expected one-period *required* rate of return on the stock. In the empirical work to be discussed below much of the analysis concentrates on using forecasting equations for the 'fundamentals' on the RHS of (16.12), namely one-period returns and dividend growth, and then using (16.12) to give *predicted values* for the dividend price ratio which we denote δ'_t. The predicted series δ'_t can then be compared with the actual values δ_t. A forecast for the (log of the) stock *price* is obtained using the identity (16.3), namely $p'_t = d_t - \delta'_t$ and the latter can then be compared with movements in the actual stock price.

Gordon's Growth Model

Further intuitive appeal can be provided for equation (16.11) for the dividend price ratio version of the RVF by going back to Gordon's dividend growth model (see Chapter 4). If the required rate of return r_t and expected growth in dividends g are both constant then the usual RVF gives the dividend price ratio (see Chapter 4) as:

$$(D/P) = r - g \tag{16.13}$$

Equation (16.12) can therefore be seen to be a *dynamic* version of Gordon's model with the required rate of return and dividend growth varying, period by period. In the Poterba and Summers (1986) model of stock prices, examined in the next chapter, they analyse the RVF under the assumption that dividend growth is constant: they concentrate on the variability in future discount rates due to a time varying risk premium. In principle, equation (16.12) is an extension of the Poterba–Summers approach since both dividends and the discount rate are allowed to vary over time. So the question that we can now examine is whether the EMH can explain movements in stock prices based on the RVF, when we allow both time varying dividends and time varying discount rates. Let us first draw a parallel with our earlier analysis of the expectations hypothesis (EH) of the term structure.

Spreads, Dividend Yields and All That

A useful intuitive interpretation of (16.12) can be obtained by comparing it with a similar expression from the expectations hypothesis (EH) of the term structure. The EH implies that the spread $S_t^{(n,m)} = R_t^{(n)} - R_t^{(m)}$ is an optimal linear forecast and should Granger cause future changes in interest rates

$$S_t^{(n,m)} = \Sigma w_i \Delta R_{t+im}^{(m)} \tag{16.14}$$

where w_i is a set of known constants. Equation (16.11) is the equivalent relationship for stock prices. The spread is replaced by the (log) dividend price ratio δ_t and future changes in interest rates are replaced by $(r_{t+j} - \Delta d_{t+j})$.

16.2 STOCK PRICE VOLATILITY AND THE VAR METHODOLOGY

Even when measured in real terms, stock prices and dividends are likely to be non-stationary but the dividend price ratio and the variable $(r_{t+j} - \Delta d_{t+j})$ are more likely to be stationary so that the VAR methodology and standard statistical results may be applied to (16.12). If the RVF is correct we expect δ_t to Granger cause $(r_{t+j} - \Delta d_{t+j})$ and because the RVF equation (16.12) is linear in future variables we can apply the variety of tests to (16.11) used when analysing the EH with the VAR methodology. This can now be done. The vector of variables in the agents information set is taken to be

$$\mathbf{z}_t = [\delta_t, rd_t]' \tag{16.15}$$

where $rd_t = r_t - \Delta d_t$. Taking a VAR lag length of one for illustrative purposes we have:

$$\mathbf{z}_{t+1} = \begin{bmatrix} \delta_{t+1} \\ rd_{t+1} \end{bmatrix} = \begin{bmatrix} a_{11} & a_{12} \\ a_{21} & a_{22} \end{bmatrix} \begin{bmatrix} \delta_t \\ rd_t \end{bmatrix} + \begin{bmatrix} w_{1t+1} \\ w_{2t+1} \end{bmatrix}$$

$$\mathbf{z}_{t+1} = \mathbf{A}\mathbf{z}_t + \mathbf{w}_{t+1} \tag{16.16}$$

Defining $\mathbf{e1} = (1, 0)'$ and $\mathbf{e2}' = (0, 1)'$ it follows that

$$\delta_t = \mathbf{e1}'\mathbf{z}_t \tag{16.17a}$$

$$E_t rd_{t+j} = \mathbf{e2}' E_t \mathbf{z}_{t+j} = \mathbf{e2}' (\mathbf{A}^j \mathbf{z}_t) \tag{16.17b}$$

Substituting (16.17) in (16.11)

$$\mathbf{e1}'\mathbf{z}_t = \sum_{j=0}^{\infty} \rho^j \mathbf{e2}' \mathbf{A}^{j+1} \mathbf{z}_t = \mathbf{e2}' \mathbf{A} (\mathbf{I} - \rho \mathbf{A})^{-1} \mathbf{z}_t \qquad (16.18)$$

If (16.18) is to hold for all $\mathbf{z}_t$ then the *non-linear* restrictions (we ignore the constant term since all data is in deviations from means) are:

$$\mathbf{f(a)} = \mathbf{e1}' - \mathbf{e2}' \mathbf{A} (\mathbf{I} - \rho \mathbf{A})^{-1} = \mathbf{0} \qquad (16.19)$$

Post-multiplying by $(\mathbf{I} - \rho \mathbf{A})$ this becomes a *linear* restriction

$$\mathbf{e1}'(\mathbf{I} - \rho \mathbf{A}) - \mathbf{e2}' \mathbf{A} = \mathbf{0} \qquad (16.20)$$

These restrictions can be evaluated using a Wald test in the usual way[4]. Thus if the RVF formula is true and agents use RE we expect the restrictions in (16.19) or (16.20) to hold. The restrictions in (16.20) are

$$(1, 0) = (\rho a_{11}, \rho a_{12}) + (a_{21}, a_{22})$$

that is

$$1 = \rho a_{11} + a_{21} \qquad (16.21a)$$
$$0 = \rho a_{12} + a_{22} \qquad (16.21b)$$

One Period Returns are not Forecastable

There is little or no direct intuition one can glean from the linear restrictions (16.21) but it is easily shown that they imply that expected one-period *real excess* returns $E_t(h_{t+1} - r_{t+1})$ are unforecastable or equivalently that abnormal profit opportunities do not arise in the market. Using (16.4) and ignoring the constant:

$$E(h_{t+1} - r_{t+1}|\Omega_t) = \delta_t - \rho E_t \delta_{t+1} + E_t(\Delta d_{t+1} - r_{t+1})$$
$$= \delta_t - \rho E_t \delta_{t+1} - E_t(rd_{t+1}) \qquad (16.22)$$

From (16.16)

$$E_t \delta_{t+1} = a_{11} \delta_t + a_{12} rd_t$$
$$E_t(rd_{t+1}) = a_{21} \delta_t + a_{22} rd_t$$

and

$$E_t(h_{t+1} - r_{t+1}|\Omega_t) = \delta_t - \rho[a_{11}\delta_t + a_{12}rd_t] - (a_{21}\delta_t + a_{22}rd_t)$$
$$= (1 - \rho a_{11} - a_{21})\delta_t - (a_{22} + \rho a_{12})rd_t \qquad (16.23)$$

Hence given the VAR forecasting equations, the expected excess one-period return is predictable from information available at time t unless the linear restrictions given in the Wald test (16.21) hold[5]. The economic interpretation of the non-linear Wald test is discussed later in the chapter.

The 'Theoretical' Dividend Price Ratio and the 'Theoretical' Price Level

We can define the RHS of (16.18) as the theoretical spread δ_t' and use our unrestricted VAR estimates to obtain a time series for δ_t'

$$\delta_t' = \sum_{j=0}^{\infty} \rho^j (r_{t+j+1}^e - \Delta d_{t+j+1}^e) = \mathbf{e}2'\mathbf{A}(\mathbf{I} - \rho\mathbf{A})^{-1}\mathbf{z}_t \tag{16.24}$$

Under the RVF + RE, in short the EMH, we expect movements in the actual dividend price ratio δ_t to mirror those of δ_t' and we can evaluate this proposition by (i) a graph of δ_t and δ_t', (ii) SDR $= \sigma(\delta_t)/\sigma(\delta_t')$ should equal unity and (iii) the correlation coefficient corr(δ_t, δ_t') should equal unity. Instead of working with the dividend price ratio we can use the identity $p_t' = d_t - \delta_t'$ to derive a series for the theoretical price *level* given by the EMH and compare this with the actual stock price using the metrics in (i)–(iii) above.

Further Implications of the VAR Approach

The constructed variable p_t' embodies the investor's best forecast of the DPV of future dividends using time varying rates of return (discount) and given the information set *assumed* in the VAR. It is therefore closely related to the expected value of the perfect foresight price $E_t P_t^*$ in the original Shiller volatility tests. The difference between the two is that P_t^* is calculated without recourse to *specific* expectations equations for future fundamental variables but merely invokes the RE unbiasedness assumption (i.e. $D_{t+j} = E_t D_{t+j} + \eta_{t+j}$). Put another way, EP_t^* is an unconditional expectation and does not require an explicit model for the behaviour of dividends whereas p_t' is *conditional on* a specific statistical model for dividends.

It is worth briefly analysing the relationship between the (log of the) perfect foresight price $p_t^* = \ln(P_t^*)$ and the (log of the) theoretical price p_t', in part so that we are clear about the distinction between these two allied concepts. In so doing we are able to draw out some of the strengths and weaknesses of the VAR approach compared with the Shiller variance bounds tests and regression tests based on P_t^* that we discussed in Chapter 6. The log-linear identity (16.2) (with h_{t+1} replaced by r_{t+1}) can be rearranged to give

$$p_t = \rho p_{t+1} + (1 - \rho)d_{t+1} - r_{t+1} + k \tag{16.25}$$

Solving (16.25) by recursive forward substitution gives a log-linear expression for the DPV of *actual* future dividends and discount rates which we denote p_t^*.

$$p_t^* = (1 - \rho) \sum_{j=0}^{\infty} \rho^j d_{t+j+1} - \sum_{j=0}^{\infty} \rho^j r_{t+j+1} + k/(1 - \rho) \tag{16.26}$$

Equation (16.26) uses actual (*ex-post*) values and is the log-linear version of equation (16.24) in Chapter 6 and hence p_t^* represents the (log of the) perfect foresight price[6]. Under the EMH we have the equilibrium condition

$$p_t = E(p_t^*/\Omega_t) \tag{16.27}$$

Under RE agents use all available information Ω_t in calculating $E_t p_t^*$ but the theoretical price p_t' only uses the limited information contained in the VAR which is chosen by the econometrician. Investors 'in reality' might use more information than is in the VAR. Does this make the VAR results rather 'weak' relative to tests based on the perfect foresight price p_t^* and Shiller's variance inequalities? In one sense yes, in another sense no.

First, the VAR contains δ_t and that is why Shiller's variance bound inequality var(P_t) < var(P_t^*) is transformed into an equality, namely $p_t = p_t'$ in the VAR methodology. What is more, even if we add more variables to the VAR we still expect the coefficient on δ_t to be unity. To see this, note that from (16.24)

$$\delta_t' = \mathbf{e2}'\mathbf{f}(\mathbf{a}) \qquad \mathbf{z}_t = [\delta_t, rd_t] \tag{16.28}$$

$$f(\mathbf{a}) = \mathbf{A}(\mathbf{I} - \rho\mathbf{A})^{-1} \tag{16.29}$$

For VAR lag length of one, f(**a**) is a (2×2) matrix which is a non-linear function of the a_{ij}s of the VAR[7]. Denote the second row of f(**a**) as the 2×1 vector $[f_{21}(\mathbf{a}), f_{22}(\mathbf{a})] = $ **e2**$'f(\mathbf{a})$ where f_{21} and f_{22} are scalar (non-linear) functions of the a_{ij} parameters. Then from (16.28) we have

$$\delta_t' = f_{21}(\mathbf{a})\delta_t + f_{22}(\mathbf{a})rd_t \tag{16.30}$$

Since under the EMH $\delta_t = \delta_t'$ we expect the scalar coefficient $f_{21}(\mathbf{a}) = 1$ and that for $f_{22}(\mathbf{a}) = 0$. These restrictions hold even if we add additional variables to the VAR. All that happens if we add a variable x_t to the VAR system is that we obtain an additional term $f_3(\mathbf{a})x_t$ and the EMH implies that $f_3(\mathbf{a}) = 0$ (in addition to the above two restrictions).

Thus if the VAR restrictions are rejected on a limited information set they should also be rejected when a 'larger' information set is used in the VAR. The latter is true as a matter of logic and should be found to be true if we have a large enough sample of data. In this sense the use of a limited information set is not a major drawback. However, in a *finite* data set we know that variables incorrectly omitted from the regression by the econometrician, yet used by agents in forecasting, can result in 'incorrect' (i.e. biased or inconsistent) parameter estimates. Therefore a larger information set may provide additional information on the validity of the hypothesis.

Thus while Shiller variance bounds tests based on the perfect foresight price may suffer from problems due to non-stationarity in the data, the results based on the VAR methodology may suffer from omitted variables bias or other specification errors (e.g. wrong functional form). Although there are diagnostic tests available (e.g. tests for serial correlation in the error terms of the VAR, etc.), as a check on the statistical validity of the VAR representation it nevertheless could yield misleading inferences in finite samples.

We are now in a position to gain some insight into the economic interpretation of the Wald test of the non-linear restrictions in (16.19), which are equivalent to those in (16.30) for our two-variable VAR. If the non-linear restrictions are rejected then this *may* be due to $f_{22}(a) \neq 0$. If so, then rd_t influences

$$\sum_{j=0}^{\infty} \rho^j (r_{t+j+1}^e - \Delta d_{t+j+1}^e)$$

To the extent that the (weighted) sum of one-period returns is a form of multiperiod return then violation of the non-linear restrictions is indicative that the (weighted) return over a long horizon is predictable. This argument will not be pushed further at this point since it is dealt with explicitly below in the section on multiperiod returns.

We can use the VAR methodology to provide yet another metric for assessing the validity of the RVF + RE in the stock market. This metric is based on splitting the term

$r_t - \Delta d_t$ into its component elements so that

$$\mathbf{z}_t = (\delta_t, \Delta d_t, r_t)'$$

We can then decompose the RHS of (16.24) into:

$$\delta_t = \delta'_{dt} + \delta'_{rt} \tag{16.31}$$

where:

$$\delta'_{rt} = \mathbf{e3}'\mathbf{A}(\mathbf{I} - \rho\mathbf{A})^{-1}\mathbf{z}_t \tag{16.32}$$

$$\delta'_{dt} = -\mathbf{e2}'\mathbf{A}(\mathbf{I} - \rho\mathbf{A})^{-1}\mathbf{z}_t \tag{16.33}$$

Hence, we expect corr($\delta_t - \delta'_{dt}, \delta'_{rt}) = 1$. If this correlation coefficient is substantially less than one then it implies that the variation in real expected returns δ'_{rt} is not sufficiently variable to explain the movements in the dividend price ratio, corrected for the influence of future dividend forecasts $\delta_t - \delta'_{dt}$.

As we shall see in Section 16.4 a variance decomposition based on (16.31) is also useful in examining the influence of the *persistence* in expected returns on the dividend price ratio δ_t and hence on stock prices ($p_t = d_t - \delta_t$). The degree of persistence in expected returns is modelled by the size of certain coefficients in the $\mathbf{A}$ matrix of the VAR. We can use (16.31) to decompose the variability in δ_t as follows:

$$\text{var}(\delta_t) = \text{var}(\delta'_{dt}) + \text{var}(\delta'_{rt}) + 2\,\text{cov}(\delta'_{dt}, \delta'_{rt}) \tag{16.34}$$

where the RHS terms can be shown to be functions of the $\mathbf{A}$ matrix of the VAR. However, this analysis will not be pursued here and in this section the covariance term does not appear since we compare δ_{rt} with $\delta_t - \delta'_{dt}$.

Summary

We have covered rather a lot of ground but the main points in our application of the VAR methodology to stock prices and returns are:

(i)   We can obtain a linear approximation to the one-period return which may then be solved forward to give an expression for the current (log) dividend price ratio δ_t in terms of expected future dividend growth rates Δd_{t+j} and a sequence of expected *required* one-period returns on the stock (denoted r_{t+j} or h_{t+j})

$$\delta_t = E_t \sum_{j=0}^{\infty} \rho^j(h_{t+j+1} - \Delta d_{t+j+1}) + k/(1 - \rho) \tag{16.35}$$

(ii) Using a simple transformation of the dividend price ratio, namely $p_t = d_t - \delta_t$, we can obtain the linearised version of the RVF:

$$p_t = E_t \left[(1 - \rho) \sum_{j=0}^{\infty} \rho^j d_{t+j+1} - \sum_{j=0}^{\infty} \rho^j r_{t+j+1} + k/(1 - \rho) \right] \tag{16.36}$$

(iii) Analysis of the dividend price ratio using (16.35) or the price level using (16.36) is equivalent but use of (16.35) in estimation enables one to work with variables that are more likely to be stationary than those in (16.36), thus enabling use of the cointegration/VAR methodology and standard statistical tests.

(iv) The dividend price model (16.35) implies a set of cross-equation restrictions on the parameters of the VAR. These cross-equation restrictions ensure that one-period excess returns are unforecastable and that RE forecast errors are independent of information at time t.

(v) From the VAR we can calculate the 'theoretical' dividend price ratio δ'_t and the theoretical stock price $p'_t (= d_t - \delta'_t)$. Under the null of the EMH + RE we expect $\delta_t = \delta'_t$ and $p_t = p'_t$. In particular, the coefficient on δ_t (or p_t) from the VAR when weighted appropriately (see equation (16.30)) should equal unity, with all other variables having a zero weight.

(vi) We can compare δ_t and δ'_t (or p_t and p'_t) graphically or by using the standard deviation ratio SDR $= \sigma(\delta_t)/\sigma(\delta'_t)$ or by looking at the correlation coefficient of δ_t and δ'_t: these provide alternative 'metrics' on the success or otherwise of the RVF + RE. δ_t is a sufficient statistic for future changes in $r_t - \Delta d_t$ and hence should, at a minimum, Granger cause the latter variable.

(vii) A measure of the *relative* strength of the variation in expected dividends (δ'_{dt}) and the variation in expected future returns (δ'_{rt}) in contributing to the variability in stock prices (δ'_t) can be obtained from the VAR.

16.3 EMPIRICAL RESULTS

The results are illustrative. They are not a definitive statement of where the balance of the evidence lies. Empirical work has concentrated on the following issues:

(i) The choice of alternative models for expected one-period holding returns, that is the variables r_{t+j} (or h_{t+j}).

(ii) How many variables to include in the VAR, the appropriate lag length and the stability of the parameter estimates.

(iii) How to interpret any conflicting results between the alternative 'metrics' used, such as the predictability of one-period returns in a single equation study, and the correlation, variance ratio statistics and Wald tests of the VAR methodology.

16.3.1 The RVF and Predictability of Returns

The first study we examine was undertaken by Campbell and Shiller (1988), who use annual data on an aggregate US stock index and associated dividends for the period 1871–1986. They use four different assumptions about the one-period *required* rates of return r_{t+j} which are:

(i) Required *real* returns are constant (i.e. $r_t = $ constant).

(ii) Required nominal (or real) returns equal the nominal (or real) Treasury bill (or commercial paper) rate $r_t = r^c_t$.

(iii) Required real returns are proportional to consumption growth (consumption is multiplied by a constant which is a measure of the coefficient of relative risk aversion, α), that is $r_t = \alpha \Delta c_t$.

(iv)   Required real returns depend on a risk premium that equals the coefficient of relative risk aversion times the (conditional) variance of stock returns:

$$r_t = \alpha \sigma_t^2$$

Hence in the VAR 'r_t' is replaced by one of the above alternatives. Note that (ii) is the usual assumption of no-risk premium, (iii) is based on the intertemporal consumption CAPM of expected returns while (iv) has a risk premium loosely based on the CAPM for the market portfolio (although the risk measure used, σ_t^2, equals squared *ex-post* returns and is a relatively crude measure of the conditional variance of stock returns, see Chapter 17).

Results are qualitatively unchanged regardless of the assumptions (i)–(iv) chosen for required returns and therefore comment is made mainly on results under assumption (i), that is constant real returns (Campbell and Shiller, 1988, Table 4). The variables δ_t, r_t and Δd_t are found to be stationary $I(0)$ variables. In a *single equation* regression of (approximate) log returns on the information set δ_t and Δd_t (r_t doesn't appear because it is assumed constant) we have:

$$h_t = 0.141\delta_t - 0.012\Delta d_t \qquad (16.37)$$
$$\quad (0.057) \quad (0.12)$$

1871–1986, $R^2 = 0.053$ (5.3 percent), $(\cdot) =$ standard error.

Only the dividend price ratio is statistically significant in explaining annual (one-period) real returns but the degree of explanatory power is low ($R^2 = 5.3$ percent).

In the VAR (with lag length $= 1$) using $z_{t+1} = (\delta_{t+1}, \Delta d_{t+1})$ the variable δ_{t+1} is highly autoregressive, and most of the explanatory power ($R^2 = 0.515$) comes from the term δ_t (coefficient $= 0.706$, s.e. $(\delta_t) = 0.066$) and little from Δd_t. The change in real dividends Δd_{t+1} is partly explained by Δd_t but the dividend price ratio δ_t is also statistically significant with the 'correct' negative sign (see equation (16.35)). Hence δ_t Granger causes Δd_t, a weak test of the RVF. If we take the estimated **A** matrix of the VAR and use (16.28) to calculate $f_{21}(\mathbf{a})$ and $f_{22}(\mathbf{a})$ of (16.30) then Campbell and Shiller find:

$$\delta_t' = 0.636\delta_t - 0.097\Delta d_t \qquad (16.38)$$
$$\quad (0.123) \quad (0.109)$$

Under the null of the RVF + RE we expect the coefficient on δ_t to be unity and that on Δd_t to be zero: the former is rejected although the latter is not. From our theoretical analysis we noted that if $\delta_t' \neq \delta_t$ then *one-period returns* are predictable and therefore the VAR results are consistent with single equation regressions on the predictability of returns such as those found in Fama and French (1988). The Wald test of the cross-equation restrictions is rejected as is the result that the standard deviation ratio is unity since

$$\text{SDR} = \sigma(\delta_t')/\sigma(\delta_t) = 0.637 \text{ (s.e.} = 0.12) \qquad (16.39)$$

However, the correlation between δ_t and δ_t' is very high at 0.997 (s.e. $= 0.006$) and is not statistically different from unity. It appears therefore as if δ_t and δ_t' move in the same direction but the variability in actual δ_t is about 60 percent (i.e. $1/0.637 = 1.57$) larger than its rationally expected value δ_t' under the EMH. That is the dividend price ratio and hence stock prices are too volatile to be explained by fundamentals even when we allow dividends and the discount rate to vary over time.

Using the single equation regression (16.37) the null that one-period returns are unforecastable is rejected at a 4.5 percent significance level; however, using the VAR methodology the Wald test of $\delta_t = \delta'_t$ is rejected at a much higher level of 0.5 percent suggesting that a multivariate approach is more useful. Note that δ'_t is a weighted average of *all* future one-period returns r_{t+j} and hence approximates a long-horizon return. The strong rejection of the Wald test is therefore consistent with the Fama and French results, where non-predictability is more strongly rejected for long rather than short-horizon returns. We return to this issue below.

The results also make clear that even though one-period returns are barely predictable nevertheless this may imply a fairly gross violation of the equality $\delta_t = \delta'_t$ (or $p_t = p'_t$). Hence the actual stock price is *substantially* more volatile than predicted by the RVF, even when one-period returns are largely unpredictable.

The correlation between $(\delta_t - \delta'_{dt})$ and δ'_{rt} for VAR lag lengths that exceed unity is generally found to be low. The correlations are in the region zero to 0.6 under all of the alternative assumptions about required returns investigated (e.g. required returns proportional to consumption growth, required returns equal the real interest rate, etc.). Hence a tentative conclusion would be that expected future returns are not sufficiently volatile to explain the variability in actual stock prices. Variability of the stock price is mostly due to variability in expected dividends although even the latter is not sufficiently variable to explain stock price variability 'fully' (i.e. $\text{var}(\delta_t) > \text{var}(\delta'_t)$ and $\text{var}(p_t) > \text{var}(p'_t)$).

In a second study Campbell and Shiller (1988, Chapter 8) extend the information set in the VAR to include not only δ_t and Δd_t but also the (log) earnings price ratio e_t where $e_t = \bar{e}_t - p_t$ and $\bar{e}_t = $ long moving average of the log of real earnings. The motivation for including e_t is that financial analysts often use forecasts of earnings in order to predict future price movements and hence future returns on the stock. Indeed Campbell and Shiller find that the earnings yield is the key variable in determining returns h_{t+1} and statistically it works better than the dividend price ratio. The VAR now includes the three 'fundamental' variables $z_{t+1} = (\delta_{t+1}, \Delta d_{t+1}, e_{t+1})'$ but the basic VAR analysis remains unchanged.

Campbell and Shiller (1988) consider two hypotheses for expected or required one-period real returns. First, they assume required returns are constant and second, that excess returns are constant. Excess returns equal $h_{t+1} - r_t$ where r_t is the short-term interest rate. There is therefore no time varying risk premium incorporated in the analysis. Results are broadly similar for both of the above assumptions about required returns. The predicted and actual values for (δ_t, δ'_t) and (p_t, p'_t) over the period 1901–1986 for an aggregate US stock price index are shown in Figures 16.1 and 16.2.

It is clear particularly after the late 1950s that there is a substantial divergence between the actual and theoretical series thus rejecting the RVF + RE. There is excess volatility in stock prices and they often diverge substantially from their fundamental values p'_t as given by the RVF. The latter is the case even though actual one-period (log) returns h_t and the theoretical return h'_t are highly correlated (e.g. $\text{corr}(h_t, h'_t) = 0.915$, s.e. $= 0.064$, see Shiller (1989), Table 8.2). The reason for the above results can be seen by using (16.24) and $p'_t = d_t - \delta'_t$ to calculate the theoretical price:

$$p'_t = 0.256 p_t + 0.776 e_t + 0.046 d_t - 0.078 d_{t-1} \qquad (16.40)$$

Hence p_t only has a weight of 0.256 rather than unity in determining p'_t and the *long-run* movements in p'_t (in Figure 16.2) are dominated by the 'smooth' moving average of

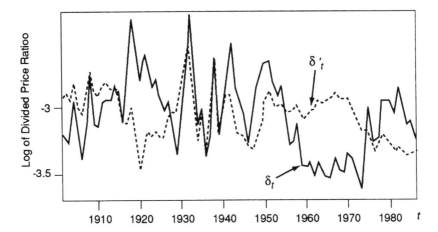

Figure 16.1 Log-Dividend Price Ratio δ_t (Solid Line) and Theoretical Counterpart δ'_t (Dashed Line), 1901–1986. *Source*: Shiller (1989). Reproduced by permission of the American Finance Association

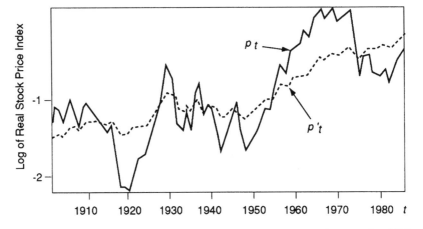

Figure 16.2 Log Real Stock Price Index p_t (Solid Line) and Theoretical Log Real Price Index p'_t (Dashed Line), 1901–1986. *Source*: Shiller (1989). Reproduced by permission of the American Finance Association

earnings e_t. However, in the short run p_t is highly volatile and this causes p'_t to be highly volatile. By definition, one-period *returns* depend heavily on price changes, hence h_t and h'_t are highly correlated. (It can be seen in Figure 16.2 that *changes* in p_t are highly correlated with *changes* in p'_t, even though the *level* of p_t is far more volatile than p'_t.)

The Campbell and Shiller results are largely invariant to whether required real returns or required excess returns over the commercial paper rate are used as the time varying discount rate. Results are also qualitatively invariant in various subperiods of the whole data set 1927–1986 and for different VAR lag lengths. However, Monte Carlo studies (Campbell and Shiller, 1989 and Shiller and Belratti, 1992) demonstrate that the Wald test may reject too often under the null that the RVF fundamentals' model is true, when the VAR lag length is long (e.g. greater than 3). Notwithstanding the Monte Carlo results. Campbell and Shiller (1989) note that in none of their 1000 simulations are the rejections of the Wald test as 'strong' or the lack of correlation between (δ_t, δ_t') or (p_t, p_t') or (h_{1t}, h_{1t}') as low as in the actual data set. This suggests that although biases exist in the VAR approach, the violations produced with the *actual* data set are much worse than one would expect if the null hypothesis of the EMH were true.

Using UK aggregate data on stock prices (monthly, 1965–1993 and annual 1918–1988) Cuthbertson and Hayes (1995) find similar results to Campbell and Shiller except for the case where returns depend on volatility and here they find stronger evidence than Campbell and Shiller (1988) in favour of the RVF. The Wald test of the non-linear restrictions, the variance ratio between δ_t and δ_t' and their correlation coefficient are consistent with the RVF, when 'volatility' is included in the VAR.

An interesting disaggregated study by Bulkley and Taylor (1992) uses the predictions from the VAR, namely the theoretical price, in an interesting way. First, a VAR is estimated recursively 1960–1980 for each company i and the predictions P_{it}' are obtained. For each year of the recursive sample, the gap between the theoretical value P_{it}' and the actual price P_{it} are used to help predict returns R_i over one to 10-year horizons (with corrections for company risk variables) z_k:

$$R_i = \alpha + \gamma_0 (P_i'/P_i) + \sum_{k=1}^{m} \gamma_k z_k \qquad (16.41)$$

Contrary to the EMH, they find that $\gamma_0 \neq 0$. They also rank firms on the basis of the top/bottom 20 and top/bottom 10, in terms of the value of (P_i'/P_i) and formed portfolios of these companies. The *excess* returns on these portfolios over one to 10-year horizons are given in Figure 16.3. For example, holding the top 20 firms as measured by the P_i'/P_i ratio for three years would have earned returns in excess of those on the S&P index, of over 7 percent per annum. They also find that excess returns cumulated over five years suggest mispricing of the top 20 shares of a (cumulative) 25 percent. This evidence therefore rejects the EMH.

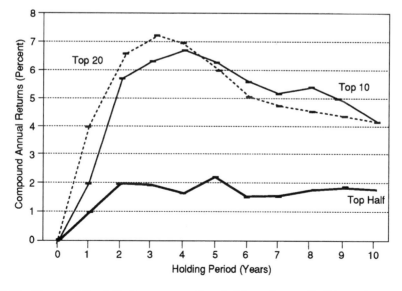

Figure 16.3 Excess of Portfolio Returns over Sample Mean. *Source*: Bulkley and Taylor (1992). Reproduced by permission of Elsevier Science

16.3.2 Shiller Volatility Tests and Multiperiod Returns

The survey of empirical work on stock prices in Chapter 6 includes tests of Shiller's volatility inequalities and the Fama and French long-horizon regressions. A tentative connection was made between the results from these two approaches noting that $P_t - P_t^*$ (where $P_t^* = $ perfect foresight price) is like a very long-horizon return. Hence a regression of $P_t - P_t^*$ on the information set Ω_t should yield zero coefficients if long-horizon returns are unforecastable. Fama and French use actual long-horizon returns over N periods R_{t+N}^N and find that these are predictable using past returns, particularly for returns measured over a three to five year horizon. Fama and French use univariate AR models in their tests.

Campbell and Shiller (1988, Chapter 8) are able to apply their linearised formula for *one-period* returns to yield *multiperiod* returns and the latter can be shown to imply cross-equation restrictions on the coefficients in the VAR. Hence using the VAR methodology one can examine the Fama and French 'long-horizon' results in a multivariate framework. First, we define a *sequence* of *one-period* holding period returns, H_{1t+j} for successive time periods t to $t + 1$, $t + 1$ to $t + 2$, etc.:

$$1 + H_{1,t+1} = (P_{t+1} + D_{t+1})/P_t$$

$$1 + H_{1,t+2} = (P_{t+2} + D_{t+2})/P_{t+1} \tag{16.42}$$

The *two-period* compound return from t to $t + 2$ is defined as

$$(1 + H_{2,t}) = (1 + H_{1,t+1})(1 + H_{1,t+2})$$

hence in general the *i*-period return from t to $t + i$ is

$$(1 + H_{i,t}) = (1 + H_{1,t+1})(1 + H_{1,t+2})(1 + H_{1,t+3})\ldots(1 + H_{1,t+i})$$

Using lower case letters to denote logarithms and letting $h_t^* = \ln(1 + H)$ we have:

$$h_{it}^* = \sum_{j=0}^{i-1} h_{1,t+j+1} \tag{16.43}$$

Equation (16.43) is unbounded as the horizon i increases, so Campbell and Shiller prefer to work with a *weighted average* of the i period log return:

$$h_{i,t} = \sum_{j=0}^{i-1} \rho^j h_{1,t+j+1} \tag{16.44}$$

Using (16.44) and the identity (16.4) for one-period returns h_{1t+1} we have[8]

$$h_{i,t} = \sum_{j=0}^{i-1} \rho^j (\delta_{t+j} - \rho\delta_{t+1+j} - \Delta d_{t+j+1} + k)$$

$$h_{i,t} = \delta_t - \rho^i \delta_{t+i} + \sum_{j=0}^{i-1} \rho^j \Delta d_{t+j+1} + k(1 - \rho^i)/(1 - \rho) \tag{16.45}$$

Equation (16.45) is an (approximate) identity which defines the multiperiod return $h_{i,t}$ from period t to $t + i$ in terms of δ_t, δ_{t+i} and Δd_{t+j}. It doesn't have a great deal of direct intuitive appeal but we can briefly try and interpret the first three terms (the linearisation constant, the last term, is of no consequence). The one-period return depends on the current dividend price ratio (see (16.4)) and this accounts for the first term in (16.45). The multiperiod return must depend on dividends arising from t to $t + i$ and given that we have anchored d_t with the term $\delta_t(= d_t - p_t)$ it must therefore depend on the *growth* in dividends — this is the third term on the RHS of (16.45). The second term is of decreasing importance as the return horizon increases (since $\rho^i \delta_{t+i} \to 0$ if δ is stationary and $0 < \rho < 1$). It appears because returns over a finite horizon depend on the terminal (selling) price at $t + i$ and hence on δ_{t+i}.

We are now in a position to see how a multivariate forecasting equation based on a VAR may be compared with the Fama and French 'long-horizon', single equation regressions. A VAR in $\mathbf{z}_t = (\delta_t, \Delta d_t)$ can be used to *forecast* the RHS of (16.45) which is the *theoretical return over i periods* denoted $h'_{i,t}$. We can then compare the actual i period return h_{it} with h'_{it} using graphs, the variance ratio test and the correlation between $h_{i,t}$ and $h'_{i,t}$.

Although (16.45) can be used to provide a forecast of h_{it} from a VAR based on δ_t and Δd_t, equation (16.45) does not provide a Wald test of restrictions on the $\mathbf{A}$ matrix, since $h_{i,t}$ is not in the information set. However, a slight modification can yield a Wald test for multiperiod returns. We again introduce the behavioural hypothesis that expected *one-period excess* returns are constant[9]

$$E(h_{1,t} - r_{t+1}) = c \qquad (16.46)$$

It follows that

$$E(h_{it}|\Omega_t) = \sum_{j=0}^{i-1} \rho^j E_t r_{t+j+1} + c(1 - \rho^i)/(1 - \rho) \qquad (16.47)$$

Taking expectations of (16.45) and equating the RHS of (16.45) with the RHS of (16.47) we have the familiar difference equation in δ_t which can be solved forward to give the dividend ratio model for *i period* returns

$$\delta_t = \sum_{j=0}^{i-1} \rho^j E_t(r_{t+j+1} - \Delta d_{t+j+1}) + \rho^i E_t \delta_{t+i} + (c - k)(1 - \rho^i)/(1 - \rho) \qquad (16.48)$$

If we ignore the constant term, (16.48) is a similar expression to that obtained earlier (see (16.12)) except that the summation is over i periods rather than to infinity[10]. It is the dynamic Gordon model over i periods. Campbell and Shiller (1988) use (16.48) to form a Wald test of multiperiod returns for different values of $i = 1, 2, 3, 5, 7, 10$ years and also for an infinite horizon. For $\mathbf{z}_t = (\delta_t, rd_t, e_t)'$ these restrictions are:

$$\mathbf{e1}'(\mathbf{I} - \rho^i \mathbf{A}^i) = \mathbf{e2}' \mathbf{A}(\mathbf{I} - \rho \mathbf{A})^{-1}(\mathbf{I} - \rho^i \mathbf{A}^i) \qquad (16.49)$$

For $i = 1$ (or $i = \infty$) the above reduces to

$$\mathbf{e1}'(\mathbf{I} - \rho \mathbf{A}) = \mathbf{e2}' \mathbf{A} \qquad (16.50)$$

which is the case examined in detail in section 16.2. If (16.50) holds then post-multiplying by $(\mathbf{I} - \rho \mathbf{A})^{-1}(\mathbf{I} - \rho^i \mathbf{A}^i)$ we see that (16.49) also holds *algebraically* for *any* i. This is a manifestation of the fact that if one-period returns are unforecastable then so are i-period returns. Campbell and Shiller for the S&P index 1871–1987 find that the Wald test is rejected only at about the 2 to 4 percent level for $i = 1$ but these tests are rejected much more strongly for $i > 3$ (i.e. at a level of 0.2 percent or less). This mirrors the Fama and French single equation results that multiperiod returns are more forecastable than single-period returns. Again, Cuthbertson et al (1995) on UK data find similar results to the above for constant real and expected returns. But they find evidence that multiperiod returns are not forecastable when a measure of volatility is allowed to influence current returns.

Perfect Foresight Price and Multiperiod Returns

It can now be shown that if the (log-linearisation of the) multiperiod return $h_{i,t}$ is fore-castable then this implies that the Shiller variance bound inequality is also likely to be violated. Because of the way the (weighted) multiperiod return $h_{i,t}$ was defined in (16.45) it is the case that $h_{i,t}$ remains finite as $i \to \infty$:

$$\lim_{i \to \infty} h_{i,t} = (1 - \rho) \sum_{j=0}^{\infty} \rho^j d_{t+j+1} - p_t + k/(1 - \rho)$$

$$= \ln P_t^{**} - \ln P_t + k/(1 - \rho) \tag{16.51}$$

The first term on the RHS of (16.51) has been written as $\ln P_t^{**}$ because it is the logarithmic equivalent of the perfect foresight price P_t^* in Shiller's volatility tests. If $h_{i,t}$, the i-period return is predictable based on information at time t (Ω_t), then it follows from (16.51) that in a regression of $(\ln P_t^{**} - \ln P_t)$ on Ω_t we should also find that Ω_t is statistically significant. Therefore $\ln P_t^{**} \neq \ln P_t + \varepsilon_t$ and the Shiller variance bound could be violated. It is also worth noting that the above conclusion also applies over finite horizons. Equation (16.45) for $h_{i,t}$ for finite i is a log-linear representation of $\ln P_{it}^* - \ln P_t$ when P_{it}^* is computed under the assumption that the terminal perfect foresight price at $t + i$ equals the actual price P_{t+i}. The variable $\ln P_{it}^*$ is a close approximation to the variable used in the volatility inequality tests undertaken by Mankiw et al (1991) where they calculate the perfect foresight price over different investment horizons. Hence tests on h_{it} for finite i are broadly equivalent to the volatility inequality of Mankiw et al reported in Chapter 6. The two sets of results give broadly similar results but with Campbell and Shiller (1988) rejecting the EMH more strongly than Mankiw et al .

Summary

(i) An earnings price ratio e_t helps to predict the return on stocks ($h_{i,t}$), particularly for returns measured over several years and it outperforms the dividend price ratio.

(ii) Actual one-period returns h_{1t}, stock prices p_t and the dividend price ratio δ_t are all too volatile (i.e. their variability exceeds that for their theoretical counterparts h_{1t}', p_t' and δ_t') to conform to the fundamental valuation model, under rational expectations. This applies under a wide variety of assumptions for required expected returns.

(iii) Although h_{1t} is 'too variable' relative to its theoretical value h_{1t}', nevertheless the correlation between h_{1t} and h_{1t}' is high (at about 0.9, in the constant discount rate case). Hence the variability in returns is *in part at least* explained by variability in fundamentals (i.e. of dividends or earnings). Movements in stock prices may therefore be described as an overreaction but it seems to be an overreaction to fundamentals such as earnings or dividends and not to fads or fashions. The latter evidence is broadly consistent with the recent ideas of intrinsic bubbles (Chapter 7).

(iv)   Violation of excess volatility tests on the level of stock prices (from Shiller's (1981) early work), that is $\text{var}(P_t) > \text{var}(P_t^*)$ is consistent with the view that long-horizon returns are forecastable. Failure of the Wald restrictions on the VAR in the multi-period horizon case (equations (16.49) and (16.50)) can be shown to be broadly equivalent to a violation of Shiller's variance bounds tests for $j \to \infty$ and refu-tation of the hypothesis that multiperiod returns are not predictable (as found by Fama and French (1988) and Mankiw et al (1991)).

On balance, the above results support the view that the EMH in the form of the RVF + RE does not hold for the stock market. Long-horizon returns (i.e. 3–5 years) are predictable although returns over shorter horizons (e.g. 1 month–1 year) are barely predictable. Never-theless it appears to be the case that there can be a quite large and persistent divergence between actual stock prices and their theoretical counterpart as given by the RVF. Thus evidence therefore tends to reject the EMH under several alternative models of equilib-rium returns. The results from the VAR analysis are consistent with those from Shiller's work using variance inequalities (see Chapter 6). The rejections of the EMH reported in this chapter are also somewhat stronger than those found by Mankiw et al (1993) using variance bounds and regression-based tests on long-horizon returns.

16.4   PERSISTENCE AND VOLATILITY

This section demonstrates how the VAR analysis can be used to examine the relationship between the predictability and persistence of one-period returns and their implications for the volatility in stock prices. We have noted that monthly returns are not very predictable and single equation regressions have a very low R^2 of around 0.02. Persistence in a univariate model is measured by how close the autoregressive coefficient is to unity. This section also shows that if expected one-period returns are largely unpredictable, yet are persistent, then news about returns can still have a large impact on stock prices. Also by using a VAR system we can simultaneously examine the relative contribution of news about dividends, news about future returns (discount rates) and their interaction on the variability in stock prices.

We begin with a heuristic analysis of the impact of news and persistence on stock prices based on the usual RVF, and then examine the problem using the Campbell–Shiller linearised formulae for one-period returns and the RVF, first using an AR(1) model and then using a VAR system. Finally, some illustrative empirical results using the VAR methodology are presented.

16.4.1   Persistence and News

Campbell (1991) considers the impact on stock prices of (i) changes in expected future discount rates (required returns) and (ii) changes in expected future dividends. A key element in Campbell's analysis is the degree of persistence in future dividends and discount rates. The starting point is the rational valuation formula

$$P_t = E_t \sum_{j=1}^{\infty} \left[\prod_{i=0}^{j-1}(1 + h_{t+i})^{-1} \right] D_{t+j} \tag{16.52}$$

Persistence in h_t can be represented by an AR(1) model

$$h_{t+1} = \beta_0 + \beta h_t + \varepsilon_{t+1} \tag{16.53}$$

where β close to unity represents a high degree of persistence. A 'shock' or news about returns is represented by ε_{t+1}. If β is close to unity then an increase in ε_{t+1} causes not only h_{t+1} to increase but also causes all subsequent $h_{t+j}(j = 2, 3, 4, \ldots)$ to increase quite substantially. As P_t depends inversely on *all future* values then a small change in ε_{t+1} may cause a very large change in the current price P_t, if $\beta \approx 1$. Hence persistence in expected returns can cause substantial volatility in stock prices even if news about current discount rates ε_{t+1} is rather small. To introduce a stochastic element into dividend behaviour assume an AR(1) model:

$$D_{t+1} = \alpha_0 + \alpha D_t + v_{t+1} \tag{16.54}$$

Using (16.54) current 'good news' about dividends (i.e. $v_{t+1} > 0$) will therefore cause a substantial rise in current price if $\alpha \approx 1$: this is 'persistence' again. It is possible that 'good news' about dividends (i.e. $v_{t+1} > 0$) may be accompanied by 'bad news', and hence higher discount rates (i.e. $\varepsilon_{t+1} > 0$). These two events have offsetting effects on P_t. It is conceivable that the current price may hardly change at all if these two events are strongly positively correlated (and the degree of persistence is similar). Put somewhat loosely, the effect of news on P_t is a weighted non-linear function which depends on revisions to future dividends, revisions to future discount rates and the covariance between the revisions to dividends and discount rates. The effect on P_t is:

  (i)   positive, for positive news about dividends,

 (ii)   negative, for news which generates increases in future discount rates,

(iii)   the effects from (i) or (ii) on the current price P_t are mitigated to the extent that upward revisions to future dividends are offset by upward revisions to future discount rates (i.e. if ε_{t+1} and v_{t+1} are positively correlated).

Let us now turn to the impact of the *variability* in dividends and discount rates on the variability in stock prices. We know that for $|\beta| < 1$ and $|\alpha| < 1$ we can rewrite (16.53) and (16.54) as an infinite moving average:

$$h_{t+m} = [\beta_0/(1 - \beta)] + \varepsilon_{t+m} + \beta \varepsilon_{t+m-1} + \beta^2 \varepsilon_{t+m-2} + \ldots$$

$$D_{t+m} = [\alpha_0/(1 - \alpha)] + v_{t+m} + \alpha v_{t+m-1} + \alpha^2 v_{t+m-2} + \ldots \tag{16.55}$$

The variance of r_{t+m} and D_{t+m} conditional on information at time t is therefore:

$$\text{var}(h_{t+m}|\Omega_t) = \sigma_\varepsilon^2(1 + \beta^2 + \beta^4 + \ldots)$$

$$\text{var}(D_{t+m}|\Omega_t) = \sigma_v^2(1 + \alpha^2 + \alpha^4 + \ldots) \tag{16.56}$$

and the covariance is:

$$\text{cov}(h_{t+m}, D_{t+m}|\Omega_t) = \sigma_{\varepsilon v}(1 + \alpha\beta + (\alpha\beta)^2 + \ldots)$$

$$= \rho_{\varepsilon v}\sigma_\varepsilon\sigma_v(1 + \alpha\beta + (\alpha\beta)^2 + \ldots) \tag{16.57}$$

where we have assumed that ε_{t+1} and v_{t+1} are contemporaneously correlated with correlation coefficient $\rho_{\varepsilon v}$. From (16.52) the variability in P_t is a non-linear sum of the above variances and covariances. For given values of σ_v and σ_ε, the variance of P_t is larger:

(i)   the larger the persistence in dividends, *ceteris paribus* (i.e. $\alpha \approx 1$),
(ii) the larger the persistence in the discount rate, *ceteris paribus* (i.e. $\beta \approx 1$),
(iii) the smaller is $\rho_{\varepsilon v}$ (i.e. as ρ moves from +1 towards -1).

In case (iii) if $\rho_{\varepsilon v} < 0$ then the influence of positive news about dividends ($v_{t+1} > 0$) is accompanied by news about future discount rates which reduces h_{t+m} (i.e. $\varepsilon_{t+1} < 0$). Since P_t depends positively on D_{t+m} and inversely on h_{t+m} then two effects reinforce each other and the variance of prices is large.

Linearisation

The problem with the above largely intuitive analysis is that the effects working via (16.52) are non-linear. However, Campbell (1991) makes use of the log-linear version of the *one-period* holding period return h_{t+1}.

$$h_{t+1} = k + \delta_t - \rho \delta_{t+1} + \Delta d_{t+1} \tag{16.58}$$

Solving (16.58) forward we obtain the linearised version of the RVF in terms of δ_t:

$$\delta_t = \sum_{j=0}^{\infty} \rho^j (h_{t+j+1} - \Delta d_{t+j+1}) - k/(1 - \rho) \tag{16.59}$$

From (16.58) and (16.59) the surprise or forecast error in the one-period expected return can be shown to be (see Appendix 16.1):

$$h_{t+1} - E_t h_{t+1} = [E_{t+1} - E_t] \sum_{j=0}^{\infty} \rho^j \Delta d_{t+j+1} - [E_{t+1} - E_t] \sum_{j=1}^{\infty} \rho^j h_{t+1+j} \tag{16.60}$$

which in more compact notation is:

$$v_{t+1}^h = \eta_{t+1}^d - \eta_{t+1}^h \tag{16.61}$$

$$\begin{bmatrix} \text{unexpected returns} \\ \text{in period } t+1 \end{bmatrix} = \begin{bmatrix} \text{news about future} \\ \text{dividend growth} \end{bmatrix} - \begin{bmatrix} \text{news about future} \\ \text{expected returns} \end{bmatrix}$$

The LHS of (16.61) is the unexpected capital gain $p_{t+1} - E_t p_{t+1}$ (see appendix). The terms η_{t+1}^d and η_{t+1}^h on the RHS of (16.61) represent the DPV of 'revisions to expectations'. Under RE such revisions to expectations are caused solely by the arrival of news or new information. Equation (16.61) is the key equation used by Campbell. It is nothing more than a rearrangement (and linearisation) of the expected return identity (or equivalently of the rational valuation formula). It simply states that a favourable outturn for the *ex-post* return h_{t+1} over and above that which had been expected $E_t h_{t+1}$ must be due to an upward revision in expectations about the growth in future dividends Δd_{t+j} or a downward revision in future discount rates h_{t+j}. If the revisions to expectations about either the growth in dividends or the discount rate are *persistent* then any news in these items will have a substantial effect on unexpected returns ($h_{t+1} - E_t h_{t+1}$) and hence on the variance of the latter.

The RHS of (16.60) is a weighted sum of two stochastic variables Δd_{t+j} and h_{t+1+j}. The variance of the unexpected return $\text{var}(v_{t+1}^h)$ can be written:

$$\text{var}[v_{t+1}^h] = \text{var}[\eta_{t+1}^d] + \text{var}[\eta_{t+1}^h] - 2\,\text{cov}[\eta_{t+1}^d, \eta_{t+1}^h] \tag{16.62}$$

As we shall see below, the news about unexpected returns can be split into the separate 'news' elements on the RHS of (16.62) once we assume some form of stochastic process for h_{t+1} (and any other variables that influence h_{t+1}): that is a VAR system. The log-linear approximation allows us to consider the implications of the RVF when expected returns and expected dividends vary through time. Campbell suggests a measure of the persistence in expected returns:

$$P_h = \sigma(\eta^h_{t+1})/\sigma(u_{t+1}) \tag{16.63}$$

where u_{t+1} is the innovation at time $t + 1$ in the one-period ahead expected return, that is

$$u_{t+1} = [E_{t+1} - E_t]h_{t+2} \tag{16.64}$$

so that u_{t+1} is a revision to expectations over one period only. P_h is therefore defined as:

$$P_h = \frac{\text{standard error of news about the DPV of } \textit{all future } \text{returns}}{\text{standard error of news about } \textit{one-period ahead } \text{expected returns}}$$

P_h may be interpreted as follows. Using (16.63) we see that an innovation in the one-period expected return u_{t+1} of 1 percent will lead to a P_h percent change in all future discount rates η^h_{t+j} and hence via (16.61) a P_h percent unexpected capital loss.

Univariate Case

It is useful to consider a simple case to demonstrate the importance of persistence in explaining the variability in stock prices. Suppose *expected* returns follow an AR(1) process:

$$E_{t+1}h_{t+2} = \beta E_t h_{t+1} + u_{t+1} \tag{16.65}$$

The degree of persistence depends on how close β is to unity. For this AR(1) model it can be shown that

$$P_h = \rho/(1 - \rho\beta) \approx 1/(1 - \beta) \quad \text{(for } \rho \approx 1) \tag{16.66}$$

$$\text{var}(\eta^h_{t+1})/\text{var}(v^h_{t+1}) = (1 + \beta)R^2/(1 - \beta)(1 - R^2) \tag{16.67}$$

where $R^2 =$ the fraction of the variance of stock returns h_{t+1} that is predictable and $v^h_{t+1} = h_{t+1} - E_t h_{t+1}$. For β close to unity it can be seen that the P_h statistic is large, indicating a high degree of persistence. In an earlier study Poterba and Summers (1988) found that $\beta = 0.5$ in their AR univariate model for returns. They then calculated that the stock price response to a 1 percent innovation in news about returns is approximately 2 percent. This is consistent with that given by Campbell's P_h statistic in (16.66).

We can now use equation (16.67) to demonstrate that even if one-period stock returns h_{t+1} are largely unpredictable (i.e. R^2 is low) then as long as expected returns are persistent, the impact of news about future returns on stock prices can be large. Taking $\beta = 0.9$ and a value for R^2 in a forecasting equation for one-period returns as 0.025 we have from (16.67) that:

$$\text{var}(\eta^h_{t+1}) = 0.49 \, \text{var}(v^h_{t+1}) \tag{16.68}$$

Also

$$\text{var}(P_{t+1} - E_t P_{t+1}) \equiv \text{var}(v^h_{t+1})$$

Hence, in this case news about future returns $\text{var}(\eta^h_{t+1})$ explains 49 percent of the variance of v^h_{t+1} and hence 49 percent of the variability in stock prices. Therefore the predictability of stock returns can be quite low, yet if the persistence in returns is high then news about returns can explain a large proportion of the variability in (unexpected) returns and stock price movements.

Campbell is able to generalise the above univariate model by using a multivariate VAR system. If we have one equation to explain returns h_{t+1} and another to explain the growth in dividends Δd_{t+1} then the covariance between the error terms in these two equations provides a measure of the covariance term in (16.62). We can also include any additional variables in the VAR that are thought to be useful in predicting either returns or the growth in dividends. Campbell (1991) uses a (3×3) VAR system. The variables are the monthly (real) return h_{t+1} on the value weighted New York Stock Exchange index, the dividend price ratio δ_t and the relative bill rate rr_t. (The latter is defined as the difference between the short-term Treasury bill rate and its one-year backward moving average: the moving average element 'detrends' the $I(1)$ interest rate series.) The VAR for these three variables $\mathbf{z}_t = (h_t, \delta_t, rr_t)$ in companion form is:

$$\mathbf{z}_{t+1} = \mathbf{A}\mathbf{z}_t + \mathbf{w}_{t+1} \qquad (16.69)$$

where $\mathbf{w}_{t+1}$ is the forecast error $(\mathbf{z}_{t+1} - E_t\mathbf{z}_{t+1})$. We can now go through the usual 'VAR hoops' using (16.69) and (16.60) to decompose the variance in the unexpected stock return v^h_{t+1} into that due to the DPV of news about expected dividends and news about expected discount rates (returns). Using the VAR it is easily seen that:

$$\eta^h_{t+1} = [E_{t+1} - E_t] \sum_{j=1}^{\infty} \rho^j h_{t+1+j}$$

$$= \mathbf{el}' \sum_{j=1}^{\infty} \rho^j \mathbf{A}^j \mathbf{w}_{t+1} = \rho(\mathbf{I} - \rho\mathbf{A})^{-1}\mathbf{el}'\mathbf{A}\mathbf{w}_{t+1} \qquad (16.70)$$

Since v^h_{t+1} is the first element of $\mathbf{w}_{t+1}$, that is $\mathbf{el}'\mathbf{w}_{t+1}$, we can calculate η^d_{t+1} from the identity:

$$\eta^d_{t+1} = v^h_{t+1} + \eta^h_{t+1} = (\mathbf{el}' + \rho(\mathbf{I} - \rho\mathbf{A})^{-1}\mathbf{el}'\mathbf{A})\mathbf{w}_{t+1} \qquad (16.71)$$

Given estimates of the $\mathbf{A}$ matrix from the VAR together with the estimates of the variance–covariance matrix of forecast errors $\mathbf{\Psi} = E(\mathbf{w}_{t+1}\mathbf{w}'_{t+1})$ we now have all the ingredients to work out the variances and covariances in the variance decomposition. The variances and covariances are functions of the $\mathbf{A}$ matrix and the variance–covariance matrix $\mathbf{\Psi}$. The persistence measure P_h can be shown (see Appendix 16.1) to be:

$$P_h = \sigma(\boldsymbol{\lambda}'\mathbf{w}_{t+1})/\sigma(\mathbf{el}'\mathbf{A}\mathbf{w}_{t+1}) = (\boldsymbol{\lambda}'\mathbf{\Psi}\boldsymbol{\lambda})/(\mathbf{el}'\mathbf{A}\mathbf{\Psi}\mathbf{A}'\mathbf{el}) \qquad (16.72)$$

where $\boldsymbol{\lambda}' = \rho(I - \rho\mathbf{A})^{-1}\mathbf{el}'\mathbf{A}$ and $\sigma(\cdot)$ indicates the standard deviation of the terms in parentheses.

16.4.2 Results

An illustrative selection of results from Campbell (1991) is given in Table 16.1 for monthly data over the period 1952(1)–1988(12). In the VAR equation for returns, h_{t+1}

is influenced by variables other than lagged returns h_t, namely by the dividend price ratio and the relative bill rate. Thus a univariate model for h_{t+1} is inadequate and hence any theoretical results based on an AR representation are likely to be misleading. (Note, however, that for an earlier period, 1927(1)–1951(12), one can accept that h_{t+1} is an AR(1) model with a low R^2 of 0.0281.) Equation (ii), Table 16.1, indicates that the dividend price ratio is strongly autoregressive with a lagged dependent variable of 0.98. This is a near unit root which might affect statistical inferences based on tests which assume the dividend price ratio is stationary (see below). The relative bill rate, equation (iii), is determined by its own lagged value and by the dividend price ratio. The R^2 from the VAR equation for monthly returns h_{t+1} has a relatively low R^2 of 0.065 compared with those for dividend yield ($R^2 = 0.96$) and the relative bill rate ($R^2 = 0.55$). The persistence measure is calculated to be $P_h = 5.7$ (s.e. $= 1.5$) indicating that a 1 percent positive innovation in the expected return leads to a capital loss of around 6 percent, *ceteris paribus*. (However, persistence is smaller in the earlier 1927(1)–1951(12) period with $P_h = 3.2$, s.e. $= 2.4$.) News about future returns var(η^h) account for over 75 percent of the variance of unexpected returns with news about dividends accounting for about 13 percent (Table 16.2). This leaves a small contribution due to the negative covariance term of about 10 percent. News about expected future returns are negatively correlated with news about cash flows thus amplifying the volatility of stock returns to new information about these two 'fundamentals'. This is similar to the 'overreaction to fundamentals' found in other studies of the predictability of stock returns. However, here the effect is small and not statistically significant.

Campbell (1991) notes that these VAR results need further analysis and he considers the sensitivity of the variance decomposition to the VAR lag length, possible omitted

Table 16.1 VAR Results for US Monthly Stock Returns 1952(1)–1988(2)

Dependent Variable	h_t (s.e.)	(D/P) (s.e.)	rr_t (s.e.)	R^2
(i) h_{t+1}	0.048 (0.060)	0.490 (0.227)	−0.724 (0.192)	0.065
(ii) $(D/P)_{t+1}$	−0.001 (0.003)	0.980 (0.011)	0.034 (0.009)	0.959
(iii) rr_{t+1}	0.013 (0.012)	−0.017 (0.058)	0.739 (0.052)	0.548

h_{t+1} is the log real stock return over a month, (D/P) is the ratio of total dividends paid in the previous year to the current stock price and rr_t is the one-month Treasury bill rate minus a one-year backward moving average. Standard errors and test statistics are corrected for heteroscedasticity.
Source: Campbell (1991, Table 1, Panel C, p. 166).

Table 16.2 Variance Decomposition for Real Stock Returns 1952(1)–1988(12)

R_h^2	var(η^d)/ var(v^h)	var(η^h)/ var(v^h)	$-2\,\text{cov}(\eta^d, \eta^h)$	corr(η^d, η^h)
0.065 [0.000]	0.127 (0.016)	0.772 (0.164)	0.101 (0.153)	−0.161 (−0.256)

R^2 is the fraction of the variance of monthly real stock returns which is forecast by the VAR and [·] is the marginal significance level for the joint significance of the VAR forecasting variables. (·) = standard error. The VAR lag length is one.
Source: Campbell (1991, Table 2, p. 167).

variables in the VAR, and unit roots in the dividend price equation, which are likely to effect the small sample properties of the asymptotic test statistics used. He finds:

(i)   The above results are largely invariant to the lag length of the VAR either when using monthly returns or returns measured over three months.

(ii) The variance of news about future returns is far less important (and that for future dividend is more important) when the dividend price ratio is excluded from the VAR.

(iii) Performing a Monte Carlo experiment with h_{t+1} independent of any other variables and a unit root imposed in the dividend price equation has 'a devastating effect' on the bias in the variance decomposition statistics reported in Table 16.2. With the artificially generated series where h_{t+1} is unforecastable then unexpected stock returns are moved entirely by news about future dividends. Hence, $\mathrm{var}(\eta^d_{t+1})/\mathrm{var}(v^h_{t+1})$ should equal unity and the R-squared for the returns equation should equal zero. For the whole sample 1927–1980 the latter results are strongly violated, although they are not rejected for the post-war period.

(iv) Because of the sensitivity of the results to the presence of a unit root Campbell tests the actual dividend data and is able to reject the null of a unit root. He also notes that even when d_t has a unit root, none of the Monte Carlo runs indicates a greater degree of predictability of stock returns than that found in the actual post-1950s data.

Cuthbertson et al (1995) repeat the Campbell analysis on UK annual data 1918–1993 for the value-weighted BZW equity index. They include a wide array of variables in the VAR, the key ones being the dividend price ratio and a measure of volatility. There is some evidence that persistence in volatility helps to explain persistence in expected returns. The contribution of the news about future returns to the movement in current returns is about four times that of news about dividends (with the covariance term being statistically insignificant). These results broadly mirror those of Campbell (1991) on US data.

Campbell (1991) and Cuthbertson et al (1995) have shown that there is some evidence to support the view that in post-1950s data, stock returns in a multivariate VAR system do appear to be (weakly) predictable and reasonably persistent. News concerning current one-period returns does influence future returns and hence the variability in stock prices. These time varying, predictable stock returns in the post-war data imply that the RVF with a constant discount rate is likely to be a misleading basis for examination of the EMH. Of course, this analysis does not provide an economic model of why expected returns $E_t h_{t+1}$ depend on dividends and the relative bill rate, but merely provide a set of statistical correlations that need to be explained. However, although Campbell's and Cuthbertson et al (1995) results show that the variability in stock prices is unlikely to be solely due to news about future cash flows the *relative* importance of news about dividends and news about returns is difficult to pin down precisely. The results from the variance decomposition depend on the particular information set chosen (and whether dividends have a unit root).

Summary

A summary of the key results has already been provided, so briefly the main conclusions are as follows:

- The VAR methodology and the linearisation of the RVF allows one to investigate the relationship between one-period returns, multiperiod returns and the volatility of stock prices within a common theoretical framework that also explicitly deals with the issue of stationarity of the data.

- Under a variety of assumptions about the determination of one-period returns the evidence strongly suggests that stock prices do not satisfy the RVF and the informational efficiency assumption of RE. These rejections of the EMH seem conclusive and more robust than those found in the variance bounds literature (see Chapter 6).

- Although monthly returns are barely predictable, the VAR approach indicates that returns at long horizons are predictable. (Thus complementing the Fama and French (1988) results).

- There is some persistence in one-period returns so that although the latter are hardly predictable, nevertheless news about current returns can have quite a strong influence on future returns and hence on stock prices. Thus there is some influence from fundamentals such as dividends and returns on stock prices but the quantitative effect of this relationship is not sufficient to rescue the RVF.

This chapter has examined the RVF under the assumption of time varying discount rates which depend on the risk-free rate, the growth in consumption and the variance of stock prices. The latter two variables can be interpreted in terms of a time varying risk premium. However, the measure of variance used in this chapter is relatively crude, being an unconditional variance. The next chapter examines the role of time varying *conditional* variances in explaining asset returns.

APPENDIX 16.1   RETURNS, VARIANCE DECOMPOSITION AND PERSISTENCE

This appendix does three things. It shows how to derive the Campbell–Shiller linearised formula for stock returns and the dividend price ratio. It then shows how these equations give rise to Campbell's variance decomposition and the importance of persistence in producing volatility in stock prices. Finally, it demonstrates how a VAR can provide empirical estimates of the degree of persistence.

1. Linearisation of Returns

The one-period, *real* holding period return is:

$$H_{t+1} = \frac{P_{t+1} - P_t + D_{t+1}}{P_t} \tag{1}$$

where P_t is the *real* stock price at the end of period t and D_{t+1} is the *real* dividend paid during period $t+1$. (Both the stock price and dividends are deflated by some general price level, for example the consumer price index.) The natural logarithm of (one plus) the real holding period return is noted as h_{t+1} and is given by:

$$h_{t+1} = \ln(1 + H_{t+1}) = \ln(P_{t+1} + D_{t+1}) - \ln(P_t) \tag{2}$$

If lower case letters denote logarithms then (2) becomes:

$$h_{t+1} = \ln[\exp(p_{t+1}) + \exp(d_{t+1})] - p_t \tag{3}$$

The first term in (3) is a non-linear function in p_{t+1} and d_{t+1}. It is linearised by taking a first-order Taylor series expansion around the geometric mean of P and D:

$$\log[\exp(p_{t+1}) + \exp(d_{t+1})] = k + \rho p_{t+1} + (1 - \rho)d_{t+1} \tag{4}$$

where

$$\rho = P/(P + D) \tag{5}$$

and therefore ρ is a number slightly less than unity and k is a constant.

Using (3) and (4):

$$h_{t+1} = k + \rho p_{t+1} + (1 - \rho)d_{t+1} - p_t \tag{6}$$

Adding and subtracting d_t in (6) and defining $\delta_t = d_t - p_t$ as the log dividend price ratio, we have:

$$h_{t+1} = k + \delta_t - \rho\delta_{t+1} + \Delta d_{t+1}$$

Equation (7) can be interpreted as a linear *forward difference equation* in δ:

$$\delta_t = -k + \rho\delta_{t+1} + h_{t+1} - \Delta d_{t+1} \tag{8}$$

Solving (8) by the forward recursive substitution method and assuming the transversality condition holds:

$$\delta_t = \sum_{j=0}^{\infty} \rho^j[h_{t+j+1} - \Delta d_{t+j+1}] - k/(1 - \rho) \tag{9}$$

Equation (9) states that the log dividend price ratio can be written as the discounted sum of all future returns minus the discounted sum of all future dividend growth rates less a constant term. If the current dividend price ratio is high because the current price is low then it means that in the future either required returns h_{t+j} are high or dividend growth rates Δd_{t+j} are low, or both.

Equation (9) is an identity and holds almost exactly for *actual* data. However, it can be treated as an *ex-ante* relationship by taking expectations of both sides of (9) conditional on the information available at the end of period t:

$$\delta_t = \sum_{j=0}^{\infty} \rho^j[E_t(h_{t+j+1}) - E_t(\Delta d_{t+j+1})] - k/(1 - \rho) \tag{10}$$

It should be noted that δ_t is known at the *end of period* t and hence its expectation is equal to itself.

2. Variance Decomposition

To set the ball rolling note that we can write (10) for period $t + 1$ as:

$$\delta_{t+1} = \sum_{j=0}^{\infty} \rho^j[E_{t+1}(h_{t+j+2}) - E_{t+1}(\Delta d_{t+j+2})] - k/(1 - \rho) \tag{11}$$

From (8) we have:

$$h_{t+1} - \Delta d_{t+1} - k = \delta_t - \rho\delta_{t+1} \tag{12}$$

Substituting from (10) and (11) and rearranging we obtain:

$$h_{t+1} - \Delta d_{t+1} - k = E_t h_{t+1} + \sum_{j=1}^{\infty} \rho^j E_t(h_{t+j+1}) - \sum_{j=0}^{\infty} \rho^j E_t \Delta d_{t+j+1} - k/(1 - \rho)$$

$$- \sum_{i=0}^{\infty} \rho^{i+1} E_{t+1}(h_{t+i+2}) + \sum_{i=0}^{\infty} \rho^{i+1} E_{t+1}(\Delta d_{t+i+2}) + k\rho/(1 - \rho) \tag{13}$$

The constant terms involving k and ρ cancel out in (13). Substituting $j = i + 1$ in the last two summations on the right hand side of (13) and rearranging we obtain:

$$h_{t+1} - E_t h_{t+1} = \sum_{j=1}^{\infty} \rho^j E_t(h_{t+j+1}) - \sum_{j=0}^{\infty} \rho^j E_t(\Delta d_{t+j+1}) - \sum_{j=1}^{\infty} \rho^j E_{t+1}(h_{t+j+1})$$

$$+ \sum_{j=1}^{\infty} \rho^j E_{t+1}(\Delta d_{t+j+1}) + \Delta d_{t+1} \tag{14}$$

Rearranging (14) we obtain our key expression for unexpected or abnormal returns:

$$h_{t+1} - E_t h_{t+1} = (E_{t+1} - E_t) \sum_{j=0}^{\infty} \rho^j \Delta d_{t+1+j} - (E_{t+1} - E_t) \sum_{j=1}^{\infty} \rho^j h_{t+1+j} \tag{15}$$

Equation (15) is the equation used by Campbell (1991) to analyse the impact of persistence in expected future returns on the behaviour of current unexpected returns $h_{t+1} - E_t h_{t+1}$. Each term in (15) can be written as:

$$u_{t+1}^h = \eta_{t+1}^d - \eta_{t+1}^h \tag{16}$$

$$\begin{bmatrix} \text{unexpected returns} \\ \text{in period } t+1 \end{bmatrix} = \begin{bmatrix} \text{news about future} \\ \text{dividend growth} \end{bmatrix} - \begin{bmatrix} \text{news about future} \\ \text{expected returns} \end{bmatrix}$$

From (16) we have

$$\text{var}(v_{t+1}^h) = \text{var}(\eta_{t+1}^d) + \text{var}(\eta_{t+1}^h) - 2\,\text{cov}(\eta_{t+1}^d, \eta_{t+1}^h) \tag{17}$$

The variance of unexpected stock returns in (17) comprises three separate components: the variance associated with the news about cash flows (dividends), the variance associated with the news about future returns and a covariance term. Given this variance decomposition, it is possible to calculate the relative importance of these three components in contributing to the variability of stock returns. Using (6) it is also worth noting that for $p \approx 1$ and no surprise in dividends:

$$h_{t+1} - E_t h_{t+1} \approx p_{t+1} - E_t p_{t+1}$$

where P_t is the stock price.

Campbell also presents a measure of the persistence of expected returns. This is defined as the ratio of the variability of the innovation in the expected present value of *future returns* (i.e. standard error of η_{t+1}^h) to the variability of the innovation in the *one-period ahead* expected return. If we define u_{t+1} to be the innovation at time $t+1$ in the one-period ahead expected return we have:

$$u_{t+1} = (E_{t+1} - E_t)h_{t+2} \tag{18}$$

and P_h the measure of persistence of expected returns is defined as:

$$P_h = \sigma(\eta_{t+1}^h)/\sigma(u_{t+1}) \tag{19}$$

Expected return follows an AR(1) process

The expected stock return needs to be modelled in order to carry out the variance decomposition (17) and to calculate the measure of persistence (19). For exposition purposes Campbell is followed and initially it is assumed that the expected stock return follows a univariate AR(1) model. The calculation is then repeated using h_{t+1} in the VAR representation. The AR(1) model for expected returns is:

$$E_{t+1} h_{t+2} = \beta E_t h_{t+1} + u_{t+1} \tag{20}$$

Using (20), the expected value of h_{t+2} at time t is:

$$E_t h_{t+2} = \beta E_t h_{t+1} \tag{21}$$

where we have used $E_t E_{t+1} = E_t$ and $E_t u_{t+1} = 0$. Equation (20) minus (21) gives:

$$(E_{t+1} - E_t)h_{t+2} = u_{t+1} \tag{22}$$

Leading (21) one period and taking expectations at time t we have:

$$E_t h_{t+3} = \beta E_t h_{t+2} = \beta^2 E_t h_{t+1} \tag{23}$$

and similarly:

$$E_{t+1} h_{t+3} = \beta E_{t+1} h_{t+2} = \beta(\beta E_t h_{t+1} + u_{t+1}) \tag{24}$$

Subtracting (23) from (24) we obtain:

$$(E_{t+1} - E_t)h_{t+3} = \beta u_{t+1}$$

In general, therefore, we can write:

$$(E_{t+1} - E_t)h_{t+j+1} = \beta^{j-1} u_{t+1} \tag{25}$$

Using the definition of news about future returns, in (15) and (16) and using (25), we have:

$$\eta^h_{t+1} = \sum_{j=1}^{\infty} \rho^j \beta^{j-1} u_{t+1} = \rho u_{t+1}/(1 - \rho\beta) \tag{26}$$

Hence the variance of discounted unexpected returns is an exact function of the variance of one-period unexpected returns:

$$\mathrm{var}(\eta^h_{t+1}) = [\rho/(1 - \rho\beta)]^2 \, \mathrm{var}(u_{t+1}) \tag{27}$$

Using (27), the measure of persistence P_h in (19) is seen to be

$$P_h = \rho/(1 - \rho\beta) \approx 1/(1 - \beta)$$

Hence if β is close to unity which we can interpret as a high degree of persistence in the AR(1) model, then P_h will also be large. Since $p_{t+1} - E_t p_{t+1} = -\eta^h_{t+1}$ (when $\eta^d = 0$) and $\eta^h = [\rho/(1 - \rho\beta)]u_{t+1} \approx [1/(1 - \beta)]u_{t+1}$ then for the AR(1) case $p_{t+1} - E_t p_{t+1} = P_h \cdot u_{t+1}$. Hence a 1 percent increase in u_{t+1} leads to a P_h percent increase in η^h and hence a P_h percent unexpected capital loss.

For the AR(1) case it can now be shown that even if we can only explain a small proportion of the variability in one-period returns h_{t+1} (i.e. returns are difficult to forecast), yet if returns are persistent, then news about returns can be very important in explaining stock price volatility. In short, the more persistent are expected returns, the more important is the variance of news about future returns $\mathrm{var}(\eta^h_{t+1})$ in explaining unexpected returns $v^h_{t+1} - E_t h_{t+1}$ (or unexpected capital gains or losses, $p_{t+1} - E_t p_{t+1}$).

R^2 can be defined as the fraction of the variance of stock returns which is predictable so we have:

$$R^2 = \mathrm{var}(E_t h_{t+1})/\mathrm{var}(h_{t+1}) \tag{28}$$

$$1 - R^2 = \mathrm{var}(v^h_{t+1})/\mathrm{var}(h_{t+1}) \tag{29}$$

$$R^2/(1 - R^2) = \mathrm{var}(E_t h_{t+1})/\mathrm{var}(v^h_{t+1}) \tag{30}$$

Also from (20) the variance of $E_t h_{t+1}$ is:

$$\mathrm{var}(E_t h_{t+1}) = \mathrm{var}(u_{t+1})/(1 - \beta^2) \tag{31}$$

Substituting (31) in (30) and solving for $\mathrm{var}(u_{t+1})$, we obtain:

$$\mathrm{var}(u_{t+1}) = (1 - \beta^2) \, \mathrm{var}(v^h_{t+1})R^2/(1 - R^2) \tag{32}$$

Using (32), equation (27) can be written as:

$$\text{var}(\eta_{t+1}^h)/\text{var}(v_{t+1}^h) = (1 - \beta^2)[\rho/(1 - \rho\beta)]^2 R^2/(1 - R^2) \tag{33a}$$

$$\approx [(1 + \beta)/(1 - \beta)]R^2/(1 - R^2) \tag{33b}$$

The left-hand side of (33) is one of the components of the variance decomposition that we are interested in and represents the importance of variance of discounted expected future returns relative to variance of unexpected returns (see equation (17)).

For monthly returns, a forecasting equation with $R^2 \approx 0.025$ is reasonably representative. The variance ratio (VR) in (33b) for $\beta = 0.5$ or 0.75 or 0.9 is VR = 0.08 or 0.18 or 0.49, respectively. Hence for a high degree of persistence but a low degree of predictability, news about future returns can still have a large (proportionate) effect on unexpected returns $\text{var}(v_{t+1}^h)$.

3. The VAR Model, Variance Decomposition and Persistence

The above univariate case neglects any *interaction* between news about expected returns and news about dividends, that is the covariance term in (17). At a minimum an equation is required to explain dividend growth. The covariance between the forecast errors (i.e. news) for dividend growth and those for returns can then be examined, and other variables in the VAR that it is thought might help in forecasting these two fundamental variables can be included. It is possible then to model the expected return along with some other forecasting variables in the context of a VAR model and carry out the variance decomposition for this multivariate case.

This section assumes the $(m \times 1)$ vector $\mathbf{z}_{t+1}$ contains h_{t+1} as its first element. The other variables in $\mathbf{z}_{t+1}$ are known at the end of period $t + 1$ and are used to set up the following VAR model:

$$\mathbf{z}_{t+1} = \mathbf{A}\mathbf{z}_t + \mathbf{w}_{t+1} \quad E(\mathbf{w}_{t+1}\mathbf{w}_{t+1}') = \mathbf{\Psi} \tag{35}$$

where $\mathbf{A}$ is the companion matrix. The first element in $\mathbf{w}_{t+1}$ is v_{t+1}^h. First note that:

$$E_{t+1}\mathbf{z}_{t+j+1} = \mathbf{A}^{j+1}\mathbf{z}_t + \mathbf{A}^j\mathbf{w}_{t+1} \tag{36}$$

$$E_t\mathbf{z}_{t+j+1} = \mathbf{A}^{j+1}\mathbf{z}_t \tag{37}$$

Subtracting (37) from (36) we get:

$$(E_{t+1} - E_t)\mathbf{z}_{t+j+1} = \mathbf{A}^j\mathbf{w}_{t+1} \tag{38}$$

Since the first element of $\mathbf{z}_t$ is h_t, if we premultiply both sides of (38) by $\mathbf{el}'$ (where $\mathbf{el}'$ is an $l \times m$ row vector containing 1 as its first element with all other elements equal to zero) we obtain:

$$(E_{t+1} - E_t)h_{t+j+1} = \mathbf{el}'\mathbf{A}^j\mathbf{w}_{t+1} \tag{39}$$

and hence:

$$\eta_{t+1}^h = (E_{t+1} - E_t)\sum_{j=1}^{\infty} \rho^j h_{t+1+j} = \mathbf{el}'\sum_{j=1}^{\infty} \rho^j \mathbf{A}^j \mathbf{w}_{t+1}$$

$$= \mathbf{el}'\rho\mathbf{A}(\mathbf{I} - \rho\mathbf{A})^{-1}\mathbf{w}_{t+1} = \lambda'\mathbf{w}_{t+1} \tag{40}$$

where $\lambda' = \mathbf{el}'\rho\mathbf{A}(\mathbf{I} - \rho\mathbf{A})^{-1}$ is a non-linear function of the parameters of the VAR. Since the first element of $\mathbf{w}_{t+1}$ is v_{t+1}^h, using (16) and (40) we can write:

$$\eta_{t+1}^d = \mathbf{el}'[\mathbf{I} + \rho\mathbf{A}(\mathbf{I} - \rho\mathbf{A})^{-1}]\mathbf{w}_{t+1} = \gamma'\mathbf{w}_{t+1} \tag{41}$$

It can be seen from (40) and (41) that both unexpected future returns and unexpected future dividends can be written as linear combinations of the VAR error terms where each error term is multiplied by a non-linear function of the VAR parameters. Setting $j = 1$ in (39) and using (18) we obtain:

$$(E_{t+1} - E_t)h_{t+2} = u_{t+1} = \mathbf{el}'\mathbf{A}\mathbf{w}_{t+1} \tag{42}$$

Equations (40) to (42) can be used to carry out the variance decomposition and to calculate the measure of persistence P_h given the VAR model. In particular we have:

$$\text{var}(\eta^h_{t+1}) = \lambda' \Psi \lambda \tag{43}$$

$$\text{var}(\eta^d_{t+1}) = \gamma' \Psi \gamma \tag{44}$$

$$\text{var}(v^h_{t+1}) = \mathbf{el}' \Psi \mathbf{el} \tag{45}$$

$$\text{cov}(\eta^h_{t+1}, \eta^d_{t+1}) = \lambda' \Psi \gamma \tag{46}$$

$$\text{var}(u_{t+1}) = \mathbf{el}' \mathbf{A} \Psi \mathbf{A}' \mathbf{el} \tag{47}$$

$$P_h = (\lambda' \Psi \lambda)/(\mathbf{el}' \mathbf{A} \Psi \mathbf{A} \mathbf{el}) \tag{48}$$

Once the 'A' parameters of the VAR and the covariance matrix Ψ have been estimated the required variances and covariances can easily be calculated. One can use OLS to estimate each equation in the VAR individually, but Campbell suggests the use of the Generalised Method of Moments (GMM) estimator due to Hansen (1982) to correct for any heteroscedasticity that may be present in the error terms. The GMM point estimates of parameters are identical to the ones obtained by OLS, although the GMM variance–covariance matrix of all the parameters in the model will be 'corrected' for the presence of heteroscedasticity (White, 1984).

The standard errors of the variance statistics in (43)–(48) can be calculated as follows. Denote the vector of all parameters in the model by θ (comprising the non-redundant elements of $\mathbf{A}$ and Ψ) and the heteroscedasticity adjusted variance–covariance matrix of the estimate of these parameters by $\mathbf{V}$. Suppose, for example, we are interested in calculating the *standard error* of P_h. Since P_h is a non-linear function of θ its variance can be calculated as:

$$\text{var}(P_h) = \left[\frac{\partial P_h}{\partial \theta}\right]' \mathbf{V} \left[\frac{\partial P_h}{\partial \theta}\right] \tag{49}$$

The derivatives of P_h with respect to the parameters θ can be calculated numerically. The standard error of P_h is then the square root of $\text{var}(P_h)$.

ENDNOTES

1. Note the change in notation in this chapter: δ_t is *not* the discount factor, as was used in earlier chapters.

2. The usual convention of dating the price variables P_t as the price at the end of the period is followed. In Campbell and Shiller (1989) and Shiller and Beltratti (1992) price variables are dated at the beginning of period, hence equation (16.3) is then $\delta_t = d_{t-1} - p_t$ but Campbell (1991) for example, uses 'end of period' variables.

3. Here r_t represents *any* economic variables that are thought to influence the expected one-period return. In some models r_t is the nominal risk-free rate while for the CAPM, for example, r_t would represent a conditional variance. Note that in earlier chapters k_t was used in place of r_t.

4. As noted in Chapter 15 the Wald statistic is not invariant to the form of the (non-linear) restriction even though they may be algebraically equivalent.

5. In matrix form the restriction may be expressed as follows using (16.17a) and (16.17b):

$$\delta_t = \mathbf{el}' \mathbf{z}_t \tag{16.17a}$$

$$E_t(rd_{t+1}) = \mathbf{e2}' \mathbf{A} \mathbf{z}_t \tag{16.17b}$$

$$E_t(h_{t+1} - r_{t+1}) = E_t[\delta_t - \rho \delta_{t+1} - rd_{t+1}] \tag{16.4}$$

Substituting from (16.17) in (16.4) and using $E_t(\delta_{t+1}) = \mathbf{el}'E_t\mathbf{z}_{t+1} = \mathbf{el}'\mathbf{Az}_t$:

$$E_t(h_{t+1} - r_{t+1}) = [\mathbf{el}' - \rho\mathbf{el}'\mathbf{A} - \mathbf{e2}'\mathbf{A}]\mathbf{z}_t$$
$$= [\mathbf{el}'(\mathbf{I} - \rho\mathbf{A}) - \mathbf{e2}'\mathbf{A}]\mathbf{z}_t$$

which is independent of $\mathbf{z}_t$ only if the term in square brackets is zero. The latter is easily seen to be given by equation (16.20).

6. Clearly (16.26) can also be obtained from (16.8) and then using $p_t^* = d_t - \delta_t$.

7. Since a VAR of any order can be written as a first-order system (the companion form) the analysis of the 2×2 case is not unduly restrictive.

8. Equation (16.45) arises by successive substitution. For example

$$h_{2t} = h_{1t} + \rho h_{1t+1}$$

which using (16.4) gives

$$h_{2t} = \delta_t - \rho^2\delta_{t+2} + \Delta d_t + \rho\Delta d_{t+1} + k + \rho k$$

One can see that the intermediate values of δ, in this case δ_{t+1}, do not appear. Hence only δ_t and δ_{t+i} appear in the expression for h_{it}.

9. The algebra goes through for any model of expected returns (e.g. when real returns are constant or depend on consumption growth).

10. Equation (16.48) collapses to the infinite horizon RVF (16.12) as i goes to infinity.

FURTHER READING

The VAR methodology is relatively recent and hence the only major source of overview material is to be found in Shiller (1989) in Sections II and III on the stock and bond markets. Mills (1993) also provides some examples from the finance literature. Recent articles employing this methodology are numerous and include Cuthbertson (1996), Cuthbertson et al (1996) on UK and German short-term rates, and Engsted (1993) for Danish short rates. Recent examples of the cointegration approach for bills/bonds are Cuthbertson et al (1996) and Engsted and Tanggaard (1994a,b).

Campbell and Mei (1993), Campbell and Ammer (1993) and Cuthbertson et al (1995) extend the Campbell (1991) variance decomposition approach to disaggregated stock returns and macroeconomic factors.

PART 6
Time Varying Risk Premia

One of the recent growth areas in empirical research on asset prices has been in the modelling of time varying risk premia. To an outside observer it may seem strange that financial economists have only recently focused on the most obvious attribute of holding stocks and long-term bonds, namely that they are risky and that perceived riskiness is likely to vary substantially over different historical periods. As we have seen in earlier chapters the consumption CAPM provides a model with a time varying risk premium but unfortunately this model does not appear adequately to characterise the data on asset returns and asset prices. In part, the reason for the delay in economic models 'catching up' with the perfectly acceptable intuitive idea of a time varying risk premium was the lack of appropriate statistical tools. The recent arrival of so-called ARCH models has allowed models in which the risk premium depends on time varying variances and covariances to be explored more fully. As we saw in Chapter 3, the basic CAPM plus an assumption that agents' perceptions of future riskiness is persistent results in equilibrium returns being variable and in part predictable. With the aid of ARCH models, the validity of the CAPM can be examined under the assumption that equilibrium returns for bonds and stocks depend on a time varying risk premium determined by conditional variances and covariances.

Chapter 17 is concerned primarily with testing the one-period CAPM model of stock returns, and will look at how persistence in the risk premium can, in principle, lead to the large swings in stock *prices* which are observed in the data. However, estimates of the degree of persistence in the risk premium may be sensitive to the inclusion of other economic variables in the equation for stock returns, such as the dividend price ratio, the risk-free interest rate and the volume of trading in the market. In earlier chapters we also noted that the presence of noise traders may also influence stock returns. Hence Chapter 17 examines how robust is the relationship between expected returns and time varying variances, when additional variables are included in the returns equation.

Chapter 18 begins by noting the rather close similarities between the mean-variance model of asset demands encountered in Chapter 3 and the one-period CAPM. This brings together a strand in the monetary economics literature, namely the mean-variance model with the CAPM model which is usually found in the finance literature. We can then explore how the basic CAPM can be reinterpreted to yield the result that equilibrium returns depend on a (weighted) function of variances, covariances *and* asset shares. When foreign assets are included in the analysis this model is often referred to as the international CAPM. The difficulties in estimating this form of the CAPM are documented and empirical results under the assumption of a time varying risk premium are reported. These results using the 'asset shares' formulation of the CAPM provide complementary evidence to that in Chapter 17 which uses the standard form of the CAPM.

Chapter 19 examines the validity of the basic CAPM applied to the bond market and in particular the determination of the one-period holding period yield on bills (zero coupon bonds) and long-term bonds using ARCH models to examine the role of time varying risk premia.

The reader will have noted that we do not proposed to analyse explicitly the possible impact of time varying risk premia in the FOREX market, in particular on the spot rate. This is because in this strand of the literature foreign assets are treated as part of the general portfolio choice problem. The return to holding foreign assets equals the return in the local currency plus the expected change in the exchange rate. The change in the spot rate is therefore subsumed in the 'returns' variables. Similarly, the (conditional) variances and covariance of the exchange rate are subsumed in those for the returns. In essence the international CAPM implicitly models the expected change in the exchange rate and the (time varying) covariances associated with it. Of course data availability on the returns to various types of foreign asset may limit the scope of the analysis.

17
Risk Premia: The Stock Market

This chapter begins with a summary of the empirical analysis undertaken by Schwert (1989) who looked at possible sources for the time varying volatility found in data on stock returns. He examined how far the conditional volatility in stock returns depends on its own past volatility and also on the volatility in other economic variables (fundamentals) such as bond volatility and the volatility in real output. The remainder of this chapter is concerned with the measurement and influence of risk premia on stock returns and stock prices. If perceptions of risk are persistent then an increase in risk today will increase perceptions of risk in many future periods. The discount factors in the rational valuation formula (RVF) for stock prices depend on the risk premium. Hence if risk is persistent, a small increase in perceived risk might cause a large fall in stock prices. The latter is the basic intuition behind the Poterba-Summers (1988) model to explain the volatility in stock prices. The Poterba-Summers model is discussed under various assumptions about the precise form one might assume for the time varying risk premium.

For the market portfolio, the CAPM indicates that risk is proportional to the conditional variance of forecast errors, but the model gives no indication of how 'risk' might evolve over time. ARCH and GARCH models assume that a good statistical representation of movements in risk is that 'risk tomorrow' is some weighted average of 'risk' in earlier periods. The CAPM plus any ARCH models provide an explicit model for the expected return on stocks which depends on a time varying risk premium. It seems reasonable to ask whether this 'joint model' is sufficient to explain stock returns or whether additional variables (e.g. dividend price ratio) remain a statistically important determinant of returns. The model of Attanasio and Wadhwani is discussed, which addresses this more complex test of the EMH, together with how the 'smart money plus noise-trader' theoretical model of De Long et al (1990) may be implemented and this also provides a handle on the behaviour of the serial correlation in returns found by Poterba and Summers (1988) and others in the earlier work described in Chapter 6. Analysis of the above models allows us to present in a fairly intuitive way a variety of ARCH models of conditional volatility. To summarise, the key aims in this chapter are:

- to examine the economic variables that might influence changes in stock market volatility over time
- to measure the degree of persistence in the risk premium on stock returns and its impact on changes in stock prices
- to ascertain the importance of time varying risk premia in determining stock returns

17.1   WHAT INFLUENCES STOCK MARKET VOLATILITY?

The rational valuation (DPV) formula for stock prices is

$$P_t = E_t \left[\sum_{j=1}^{\infty} \gamma_{t+j} D_{t+j} \right] \tag{17.1}$$

$$\gamma_{t+j} = 1 \Big/ \prod_{i=1}^{j} (1 + r_{t+i} + rp_{t+i})$$

where r_t = risk-free rate, rp_t = risk premium. Stock price volatility therefore depends on the volatility in future dividends and discount rate (and any covariance between these). The return R_{t+1} to holding stocks depends on future price *changes* and hence the volatility of returns depends on the same factors as for stock prices. Expected future dividends may in principle depend on many economic variables, indeed on any variables that influence the future profitability of companies (e.g. inflation, output growth). The discount rate depends on the risk-free rate of return r_t and on changing perceptions of the riskiness of stocks, rp_t. Schwert (1989) does not ask what *causes* volatility in stock *returns* but seeks to establish on a purely empirical basis what economic variables are *correlated* with the volatility in returns. He is also interested in whether volatility in stock returns influences other economic variables. It may be the case for instance that changes in stock return volatility lead to changes in the volatility of fixed investment and output. If the latter is deemed to be undesirable, one might then wish to seek ways to curb stock price volatility.

Schwert examines *conditional* volatilities, that is the volatility in stock returns, conditional on having obtained the best forecast possible for stock returns. If the best forecast for stock returns is denoted $E(R_{t+1}|\Omega_t)$ then $\varepsilon_{t+1} = (R_{t+1} - E_t R_{t+1})$ is the conditional forecast error. If $E_t \varepsilon_{t+1} = 0$ then the conditional variance of the forecast error of returns is $\mathrm{var}(\varepsilon_{t+1}|\Omega_t) = E_t(R_{t+1} - E_t R_{t+1})^2$. To obtain a measure of $\mathrm{var}(\varepsilon_{t+1})$ or its standard error we need to model the 'best' forecasting scheme for R_{t+1}.

Schwert uses a fairly conventional approach to measuring conditional volatility. He assumes that the best forecast of *monthly* stock returns R_{t+1} is provided by an AR model (we exclude monthly dummies):

$$R_{t+1} = \sum_{j=0}^{m} \alpha_j R_{t-j} + \varepsilon_{t+1} \tag{17.2}$$

Schwert finds that the (absolute values) of the residuals $\hat{\varepsilon}_{t+1}$ from (17.2) exhibit serial correlation. Hence there is some predictability in $|\varepsilon_t|$ itself, which he models using a further autoregression:

$$|\hat{\varepsilon}_{t+1}| = \sum_{j=1}^{s} \rho_j |\hat{\varepsilon}_{t-j+1}| + u_{t+1} \tag{17.3}$$

As we shall see in Section (17.2.2), equation (17.3) is a form of autoregressive conditional heteroscedasticity (ARCH) in the forecast errors. From the ARCH regression we obtain estimates of the ρ_j. The *predictions* from (17.3), that is

$$\varepsilon_{t+1}^* = \sum_{j=1}^{s} \hat{\rho}_j |\hat{\varepsilon}_{t-j+1}|$$

then provide a time varying estimate of the *conditional* standard deviation of the forecast errors for stock returns. The above method is used by Schwert to obtain the conditional volatility of other economic time series. He uses equations (17.2) and (17.3) on monthly data for stock returns (an aggregate index), for bond returns, inflation, short-term interest rates, the growth in industrial production (output) and monetary growth.

The *sum* of the ρ_j in (17.3) is a measure of *persistence* in volatility. It is the size of (the sum of the) ρ_j that is important and not the number of lagged values of ε_{t-j} in determining the degree of persistence. To see this let $s = 1$ and let $\rho_1 = \rho$. By recursive substitution in (17.3) we have (ignore the fact that ε is an absolute value):

$$\varepsilon_{t+2} = \rho\varepsilon_{t+1} + u_{t+2} = \rho(\rho\varepsilon_t + u_t) + u_{t+2}$$

$$\varepsilon_{t+3} = \rho\varepsilon_{t+2} + u_{t+3} = \rho^3\varepsilon_t + \rho^2 u_t + \rho u_{t+2} + u_{t+3}$$

Hence:

$$\varepsilon_{t+n} = \rho^n\varepsilon_t + \rho^{n-1}u_t + \rho^{n-2}u_{t+1} + \rho^{n-3}u_{t+2} + \ldots u_{t+n} \qquad (17.4)$$

Thus, given a starting point at time t (i.e. ε_t) then ε_{t+n} is determined by a weighted (moving) average of the white noise error terms u_{t+j}. If ρ is close to unity (e.g. 0.95) then a positive 'shock' at time t (i.e. $u_t > 0$) will still have a strong effect on ε_{t+n} even after n periods, since ρ^{n-1} is still fairly large. For example, for $\rho = 0.95$ a unit shock at time t (i.e. $u_t = 1$) has an impact on ε_{t+12} of 0.54 after 12 months and an impact on ε_{t+24} of 0.3 after 24 months. However, if $\rho = 0.5$ the impact of u_t on ε_{t+12} is very near zero. A high value of ρ therefore implies a 'long memory'. For ρ close to unity, shocks at time t continue to influence ε_{t+n} in many future periods and even though these effects 'die out' (i.e. the effect on ε at $t + j$ is greater than at $t + j - 1$), nevertheless they persist for many periods and 'die out' extremely slowly. Since ε_{t+n} is a long moving average of the errors u_{t-j} (if ρ is close to 1) then even though each u_{t+j} is white noise, nevertheless ε_{t+n} will exhibit long swings. Once ε_t becomes 'large' (small) it tends to stay large (small) for some considerable time.

All the series examined by Schwert for the US are found to exhibit persistence in volatility over the period 1859–1987 with each $\Sigma\rho_j$ in the region of 0.8–0.85. Hence, in principle, the persistence in stock return volatility is mirrored by persistence in the volatility of the fundamentals.

We now turn to the possible relationship between the conditional volatility of stock prices $\hat{\varepsilon}_{t+1}$ and the conditional volatility of the economic fundamentals ε_{it} where $i =$ conditional volatility of output, bond rates, inflation, etc. Schwert runs a regression of stock return volatility $|\hat{\varepsilon}_t|$ on its own lagged values and also on lagged values of the $|\varepsilon_{it}|$ for the fundamental variables. Any 'reverse influence', that is from stock volatility to volatility in fundamentals such as output, can be obtained from an equation with output volatility as the dependent variable. In fact Schwert generally estimates the stock return volatility equation together with the 'reverse regressions' in a vector autoregressive (VAR) system.

Schwert's results are mixed. He finds little evidence that volatility in economic fundamentals (e.g. output, inflation) has a discernible influence on stock return volatility (and the impact is not stable over time). However, there is a statistically significant effect from interest rate and corporate bond rate volatility on stock volatility. Also some other 'non-volatility' economic variables do influence the monthly conditional stock return volatility. These include the debt equity ratio (leverage) which has a positive impact, as does trading activity in the month. The latter is measured by the growth rate in the number of trades or buy/sell orders or the number of trading days in the month. (As we shall see in Section 17.2.2 the impact of the volume of trades on stock return volatility found by Schwert is consistent with the results of Lamoureux and Lastrapes (1990a) who use an ARCH model for volatility.) Stock volatility is also shown to be higher during recessions than in economic booms. Examination of the results from the 'reverse regressions' reveals that there is some weak evidence that volatility in stock returns has incremental explanatory power for the volatility in output.

It must be said that much of the movement in stock return volatility in Schwert's study is not explained by the fundamental economic variables examined. The R-squared values in Schwert's report regressions are usually in the region of 0.0–0.3. Hence much of the monthly conditional volatility in the forecast errors of stock returns is due to 'unobservables'. It is possible that the presence of 'fads' due to the actions of noise traders in the market may be associated with these unmeasurable elements of stock price volatility. Although stock return volatility cannot be adequately explained by volatility in the economic fundamentals considered by Schwert, this in itself does not throw much light on the relative importance of the smart money versus noise-trader view of the working of the stock market.

17.2 THE IMPACT OF RISK ON STOCK RETURNS

We have seen in the previous section that the variance of the forecast error in returns is highly persistent and hence predictable. Future values of the variance of forecast errors depend on the known current variance. If the perceived risk premium on stocks is adequately measured by the conditional variance, then it follows that the future risk premium is, in part, predictable. An increase in variance will increase the perceived riskiness of stocks in all future periods. Since the risk premium is an element of the discount factor, which determines the stock price (i.e. DPV of future dividends), then persistence in the risk premium could lead to a change in the discount factors for all future periods and hence a large change in the level of stock prices.

17.2.1 The Poterba–Summers Model

Poterba and Summers (1988) investigate whether changes in investors' perceptions of risk are large enough to account for the very sharp movements in stock *prices* that are actually observed. First, a somewhat stylised account is presented of the central argument of Poterba and Summers. The market portfolio of stocks is taken to be the S&P stock market index. Stock prices may vary if forecasts of expected dividends are revised or if the discount factor changes: Poterba and Summers concentrate on the behaviour of the latter. The discount factor δ_t can be considered to be made up of a risk-free rate plus a risk premium, that is $\delta_t = 1/(1 + r_t + rp_t)$ and the stock price is determined by the RVF, equation (17.1):

$$P_t = E_t(\delta_{t+1}D_{t+1}) + E_t(\delta_{t+1}\delta_{t+2}D_{t+2}) + E_t(\delta_{t+1}\delta_{t+2}\delta_{t+3}D_{t+3}) + \ldots \quad (17.5)$$

Poterba and Summers argue that the growth in future dividends is fairly predictable and they concentrate instead on the volatility and persistence of the risk premium rp_t. If investors thought that the risk premium would increase tomorrow, then this would cause a fall in stock prices today, since the discount factor δ_{t+1} has increased and the DPV of next periods dividends is lower. However, if this increase in risk did *not* persist in future periods, the fall in stock prices would be quite small. This is easily seen from equation (17.5). The stock price is the discounted present value of future dividends using *all* the discount factors for *all* future periods. If only the next periods risk premium rp_{t+1} increases, this effects only the δ_{t+1} terms on the right hand side of equation (17.5) and not the other discount factors δ_{t+2}, δ_{t+3}, etc. However, now consider the case when there is *persistence* in the risk premium. This means that should investors believe that the risk premium will increase tomorrow, then they would also expect it to increase in subsequent periods. Hence a change in risk premium today has a large effect on stock prices since if rp_t increases then δ_{t+1}, δ_{t+2}, δ_{t+3}, etc. are *all* expected to increase.

The key element in Poterba and Summers' view of why stock prices are highly volatile is that there can be 'shocks' to the economy in the *current* period which alter the perceived risk premium for *many future periods*. Thus the rational valuation formula for stock prices with a time varying and persistent risk premium may explain the large observed movements in stock prices. If this model can explain the actual movements in stock prices, then as it is based on rational behaviour, stock prices cannot be *excessively* volatile.

Poterba and Summers use a linearised approximation to the RVF and they are able to show exactly how the stock price responds to a surprise increase in the perceived riskiness of stocks. The response depends crucially on the *degree of persistence* exhibited by agents' perceptions of changes in the conditional volatility of the forecast error in stock returns. If, on average, the degree of persistence in volatility is 0.5, then an increase in volatility of 10 percent is followed (on average) in subsequent periods by volatility increases of 5, 2.5, 1.25, 0.06, 0.03, etc. percent. Under the latter circumstances Poterba and Summers calculate that a 1 percent increase in volatility leads to only a 1.2 percent fall in stock prices. However, if the degree of persistence is 0.99 then the stock price would fall by over 38 percent for every 1 percent increase in volatility: a sizeable effect. Given that stock prices often do undergo sharp changes over a very short period of time, then for the Poterba–Summers model to 'fit the facts' we need to find a high degree of persistence in agents' perceptions of volatility.

Poterba–Summers: Empirical Results

Poterba and Summers treat all variables in the RVF in real terms and consider P_t as the real stock price of the market portfolio which uses the S&P index over the period 1928–1984. As Poterba and Summers wish to focus on the impact of the risk premium on P_t they assume

(i)   real dividends grow at a constant rate g, so that the 'unobservable' $E_t(D_{t+j})$ is equal to $(1 + g)^j D_t$ and

(ii) the real risk-free rate is constant ($r_t = r$).

The CAPM (Merton, 1973 and 1980) suggests that the risk premium on the *market portfolio* is proportional to the conditional variance of forecast errors on equity returns $E_t \sigma_{t+1}^2$

$$E_t R_{t+1} = r_t + \lambda E_t \sigma_{t+1}^2 = r_t + rp_t$$

where λ is the market price of risk. Hence:

$$rp_t = \lambda E_t \sigma_{t+1}^2$$

In Merton's intertemporal CAPM, λ depends on a weighted average of different consumers' relative risk aversion parameters which are assumed to be constant. Poterba and Summers assume (and later verify empirically) that volatility can be represented by ARMA model(s) and here we assume an AR(1) process:

$$\sigma_{t+1}^2 = \alpha_0 + \alpha_1 \sigma_t^2 + v_{t+1} \qquad 0 > \alpha_i > 1 \qquad (17.6)$$

where v_{t+1} is a white noise error. The latter provides the mechanism by which we may (randomly) switch from a period of high volatility to one of low volatility as v_t moves from positive to negative. If α_1 is small, the degree of persistence in volatility is small. For example, if $\alpha_1 = 0$, σ_t^2 is a constant ($= \alpha_0$) plus a zero mean random error v_t and hence exhibits no persistence. Conversely if α_1 is close to 1, for example $\alpha_1 = 0.9$, then if v_t increases by 10, this results in a sequence of future values of σ^2 of 9, 8.1, 6.4, etc. in future periods and hence σ_t^2 is highly persistent. If σ_t^2 follows an AR(1) process then so will rp_t:

$$rp_t = \lambda \alpha_0 + \lambda \alpha_1 rp_{t-1}$$

To make the problem tractable Poterba and Summers linearise (17.1) around the mean value of the risk premium $\overline{rp}$. This linearisation allows one to calculate the *percentage* response of P_t to the *percentage* change in σ_t^2:

$$\frac{\partial[\ln P_t]}{\partial[\ln(\sigma_t^2)]} = \frac{-\overline{rp}}{[1 + \overline{r} + \overline{rp} - \alpha_1(1 + g)]} \qquad (17.7)$$

Thus the response of P_t to a change in volatility σ_t^2 increases with the degree of persistence α_1. Poterba and Summers compute an *unconditional* volatility measure for the variance of *monthly* stock returns based on the average *daily* change in the S&P composite index over a particular month. Hence for month t:

$$\hat{\sigma}_t^2 = \sum_{i=1}^{m} s_{ti}^2 / m \qquad (17.8)$$

where s_{ti} = daily change in the stock index in month t and m = number of trading days in the month. They then investigate the persistence in $\hat{\sigma}_t^2$ using a number of alternative ARMA models (under the assumption that $\hat{\sigma}_t^2$ may be either stationary or non-stationary). For example, for the AR(1) model they obtain a value of α_1 in the range 0.6–0.7. (They also use estimates of σ^2 implied by option prices which give estimates of *ex-ante* or forward-looking volatilities. Here they also find that there is little persistence in volatility.) The values of the remaining variables are

(i) $\overline{r}$ = average real return on Treasury bills = 0.4 percent per annum = 0.035 percent per month,

(ii) g = average growth rate of real dividends = 0.01 percent per annum = 0.00087 percent per month,

(iii) $\overline{rp}$ = mean risk premium = average value of $(ER^m - r)$ = 0.006 per month (which implies a value of $\lambda = \overline{rp}/\sigma^{-2}$ of 3.5).

Substituting all these values in (17.7) Poterba and Summers find that a 50 percent increase in volatility ($\hat{\sigma}^2$) depresses the share price by only a minuscule 0.7 percent (and the largest effect they find empirically is a fall of 11 percent). Hence within the Poterba and Summers framework the measured persistence in volatility is too low to explain the observed sharp movements in stock prices.

17.2.2 Volatility and ARCH Models

Chou (1988) notes that there are some problems with the Poterba–Summers empirical estimation of the time varying variance σ_t^2. He notes that the Poterba–Summers measure of the variance remains constant within a given horizon (i.e. a month) and is then assumed to vary over longer horizons (i.e. the AR model of equation (17.8) for σ^2). It is therefore not a correct measure of the conditional variance. Chou repeats the Poterba–Summers analysis using an explicit model of *conditional* variances based on a GARCH(1,1) model which is explained briefly below and more fully in Chapter 20. Note also that the Poterba–Summers estimation technique being a two-step procedure yields inconsistent estimates of the parameters (see Pagan and Ullah (1988)). Chou, as in Poterba and Summers, assumes expected returns on the market portfolio are given by the CAPM (plus RE):

$$(R_{t+1} - r_t) = \lambda[E_t\sigma_{t+1}^2] + \varepsilon_{t+1} \tag{17.9}$$

where R_{t+1} = return on the market portfolio, r_t = risk-free rate. Taking expectations of (17.9) it is easy to see that the best forecast of the excess return depends on the best forecast of the conditional variance

$$(E_tR_{t+1} - r_t) = \lambda[E_t\sigma_{t+1}^2] \tag{17.10}$$

The conditional forecast error is therefore

$$R_{t+1} - E_tR_{t+1} = \varepsilon_{t+1} \tag{17.11}$$

and the conditional variance of the forecast error is

$$E_t(R_{t+1} - E_tR_{t+1})^2 = E_t(\varepsilon_{t+1}^2) = E_t(\sigma_{t+1}^2) \tag{17.12}$$

We assume $\varepsilon_{t+1} \sim N(0, \sigma_{t+1}^2)$ and hence has a time varying variance. According to the CAPM the expected excess return varies directly with the time varying variance of forecast errors: large forecast errors (i.e. more risk) require compensation in the form of higher expected returns. It remains to describe the time path of the conditional variance. Chou assumes a GARCH(1,1) model in which the conditional variance at $t + 1$ is a weighted average of last periods conditional variance σ_t^2 and the forecast error (squared) ε_t^2:

$$\sigma_{t+1}^2 = \alpha_0 + \alpha_1\varepsilon_{t+1}^2 + \alpha_2\sigma_t^2 \tag{17.13}$$

The GARCH(1,1) model is a form of adaptive expectations in the second moment of the distribution. The best guess of σ_{t+1}^2 at time t (i.e. $E_t\sigma_{t+1}^2$) is given by the RHS of (17.13). The *expected value* of the variance for time $t + 1$ is:

$$E_t\sigma_{t+1}^2 = \alpha_0 + (\alpha_1 + \alpha_2)\sigma_t^2 \tag{17.14}$$

By recursive substitution and the law of iterated expectations the conditional variance for all future periods $t + s$ is:

$$E_t \sigma_{t+s}^2 = \frac{\alpha_0[1 - (\alpha_1 + \alpha_2)^5]}{1 - (\alpha_1 + \alpha_2)} + (\alpha_1 + \alpha_2)^s \sigma_t^2 \qquad (17.15)$$

The α_i are constrained to be non-negative so that the conditional variance is always non-negative. If $(\alpha_1 + \alpha_2) = 1$ then a change in the current variance σ_t^2 has a one-for-one effect on *all* future expectations. If $\alpha_1 + \alpha_2 < 1$ then the influence of σ_t^2 on $E_t \sigma_{t+s}^2$ dies away exponentially. Thus $(\alpha_1 + \alpha_2)$ measures the degree of *persistence* in the conditional variance. If $\alpha_1 + \alpha_2 \geqslant 1$ then the *un*conditional variance $\alpha_0/[1 - (\alpha_1 + \alpha_2)]$ is not defined and we have a non-stationary (explosive) series in the conditional variance. Equations (17.9) + (17.13) taken together are often referred to as a 'GARCH in mean' or GARCH-M model. Chou (1988) estimates these two equations simultaneously, using the maximum likelihood method. His data is for *weekly* returns (Tuesday–Tuesday closing prices) on the NYSE value weighted stock price index (with dividends assumed to be reinvested) over the period 1962–1985 (1225 observations). The price index and weekly returns are shown in Figures 17.1 and 17.2. The crashes of 1974 and 1982 are clearly visible in Figure 17.1 and periods of tranquillity and turbulence in returns are noticeable in Figure 17.2.

Chou finds that the estimate of the market price of risk (or index of relative risk aversion) λ over various subperiods is not well determined statistically and borders on being statistically insignificant. However, it has plausible point estimates in the range 3–6 (Poterba and Summers obtain a value of 3.5 and Merton (1973) finds a value of 3.2). The value of $\alpha_1 + \alpha_2$ is very stable over subperiods and is around 0.98 indicating substantial

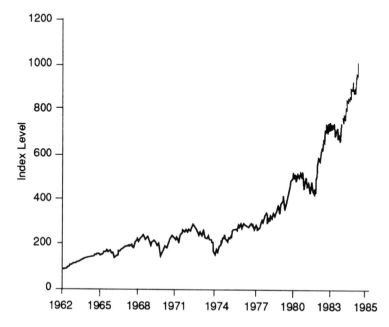

Figure 17.1 NYSE: Stock Index. *Source*: Chou (1988). Reproduced by permission of John Wiley and Sons Ltd

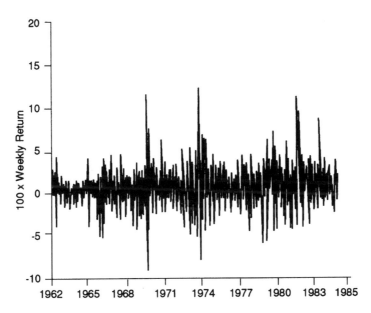

Figure 17.2 NYSE: Weekly Stock Returns. *Source*: Chou (1988). Reproduced by permission of John Wiley and Sons Ltd

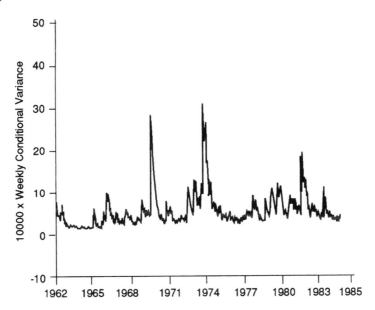

Figure 17.3 NYSE: Variance of Stock Returns. *Source*: Chou (1988). Reproduced by permission of John Wiley and Sons Ltd

persistence in the conditional variance (Figure 17.3). It follows from our previous discussion that observed sharp falls in stock *prices* can now be explained using the RVF and the Poterba–Summers framework. Indeed, when $\alpha_1 + \alpha_2 = 1$ (which is found to be largely acceptable on statistical grounds by Chou) then stock prices move tremendously and the elasticity $d(\ln P_t)/d(\ln \sigma_t^2)$ can be as high as (minus) 60.

Chou re-estimates his GARCH(1.1) model for different 'return horizons' using returns over (for example) $N = 5, 20, 50$ and 250 trading days. He finds the estimates of $\alpha_1 + \alpha_2$ are very stable at around 0.95 in all of these variants. As a point of comparison Chou calculates the Poterba–Summers measure of variance (see equation (17.8)) using different values of N. He then estimates $\sigma^2_{Nt+1} = \alpha_0 + \alpha_1 \sigma^2_{Nt} + v_{t+1}$ for these various values of N. He finds that α_1, the degree of persistence, varies tremendously increasing from near zero for $N = 5$ (working) days to $\alpha_1 = 0.6$ for $N = 20$ days (i.e. one month) and to $\alpha_1 = 0.9$ for $N = 250$ days (i.e. one year). This suggests that the Poterba–Summers method may not have correctly captured the true degree of persistence. Note, however, that Chou's experiment should really have used a closer measure of σ^2 to that used by Poterba and Summers, namely

$$\sigma^2_{Nt} = \Sigma(R^N - \overline{R}^N)^2 / N \tag{17.16}$$

For daily data over one month as used by Poterba and Summers, $\overline{R}$ will be close to zero but over longer horizons (i.e. N increases), $\overline{R}$ is likely to be non-zero because of bull and bear markets. Hence the above measure is more representative of the Poterba–Summers approach and may not yield such sensitivity in the estimate of α_1, as found in Chou's experiment. However, Chou's use of a GARCH model is preferable on *a priori* grounds as it correctly estimates a measure of *conditional* variance.

As a counterweight to the above result by Chou consider a slight modification of Chou's model as used by Lamoureux and Lastrapes (1990). They assume that conditional volatility is influenced both by past forecast errors (GARCH) and by the volume of trading (VOL) (i.e. number of buy/sell orders undertaken during the day):

$$\sigma^2_{t+1} = \alpha_0 + \alpha_1 \varepsilon^2_t + \alpha_2 \sigma^2_t + \gamma \text{VOL}_t \tag{17.17}$$

They model *daily* returns (price changes) and hence feel it is realistic to assume constant expected returns μ:

$$R_{t+1} = \mu + \varepsilon_{t+1} \tag{17.18}$$

$$\varepsilon_{t+1} \sim N(0, \sigma^2_{t+1}) \tag{17.19}$$

They estimate $(17.17) + (17.18)$ for 20 actively traded companies using about one year of daily data (for 1981 or 1982). When γ is set to zero they generally find a similar result to Chou, namely strong, persistent GARCH effects (i.e. $\alpha_1 + \alpha_2 \approx 0.8$–$0.95$). However, the residuals ε_{t+1} are non-normal and hence strictly these results are statistically invalid given the assumption (17.19). When VOL$_t$ is added they find that $\alpha_1 = \alpha_2 = 0$ but $\gamma \neq 0$ and the residuals are now normally distributed. Hence conditional volatility σ^2_{t+1} is not determined by past forecast errors but by the volume of trading (i.e. the persistence in VOL accounts for the persistence in σ^2_{t+1}). They interpret VOL as measuring the arrival of new information and therefore conjecture that in general GARCH effects in other studies are really measuring the persistence in the arrival of new information. Thus on this data set, the Chou model is shown to be very sensitive to the specification change of introducing VOL$_t$ into the GARCH process. Note that volatility (risk) is still time varying but its degree of persistence is determined by the persistence in trading volume. There are some caveats to add to the results of Lamoureux and Lastrapes. In particular, as their model uses data on individual firms a correct formulation of the CAPM should include the covariance between asset i and the market return. This makes the model far more complex particularly as far as estimation and identification is concerned, but it is possible that the results from the GARCH equation may be different to those described above. The sensitivity of the GARCH equation (and the CAPM) to specification changes is examined further below.

17.2.3 CAPM, Noise Traders and Volatility

The empirical analysis above has highlighted the potential sensitivity of asset return equations to assumptions about the equilibrium model determining returns and to the precise parameterisation of any time varying conditional variances. Below we continue to explore the ability of the CAPM to explain equilibrium asset returns but use alternative specifications of the GARCH process. We then examine a model in which noise traders have an influence on equilibrium returns.

The CAPM and Dividends

The study by Attanasio and Wadhwani (1990) starts with the empirical observation that, from previous work, it is known that the expected excess return on an aggregate stock market index (which is assumed to proxy the market portfolio) depends on the previous period's dividend price ratio. The latter violates the EMH under constant expected excess returns. Previous work in this area often assumed *a constant* risk premium but then sometimes interpreted the presence of the dividend yield as *indicative* of a time varying risk premium. Attanasio and Wadhwani suggest that if we explicitly model the time varying risk premium then we may find that the dividend yield $(= Z_t)$ does *not* influence expected returns. If so, this would support the CAPM version of the EMH. If we assume the CAPM is the correct equilibrium pricing model:

$$[R^m_{t+1} - r_t] = \lambda E_t[\sigma^2_{t+1}] + \delta Z_t + \varepsilon_{t+1} \tag{17.20}$$

then we expect $\lambda > 0$ and $\delta = 0$. The time varying conditional variance of the market return is given by the variance of ε_{t+1} which is assumed to be determined by the following GARCH(1,2) model (with the dividend yield added)

$$\sigma^2_{t+1} = \alpha_0 + \alpha_1 \sigma^2_t + \alpha_2 \varepsilon^2_t + \alpha_3 \varepsilon^2_{t-1} + \pi Z_t \tag{17.21}$$

where α_i and π are constrained to be non-negative. The GARCH model implies that the expected variance for period $t + 1$, that is $E_t \sigma^2_{t+1}$, depends on a weighted average of last periods of the variance σ^2_t and the two most recent forecast errors squared $(\varepsilon^2_{t+1}, \varepsilon^2_t)$. In addition, equation (17.21) *explicitly* allows the dividend yield to affect the conditional variance — this is not a violation of the CAPM and the EMH. Using monthly data January 1953–November 1988 on an aggregate US stock price series, a representative result is (Attanasio and Wahwani 1990, Table 2, page 10):

$$[R^m_{t+1} - r_t] = -0.035 + 0.55Z_t - 4.05r_t + 22.3\sigma^2_{t+1} \tag{17.22}$$
$$(0.025) \quad (0.39) \quad (1.05) \quad (11.3)$$

$$53(1)-88(11), R^2 = 0.059, (\cdot) = \text{standard error}$$

$$\sigma^2_{t+1} = \alpha_0 + 1.5(10^{-2})\varepsilon^2_t + 2.2(10^{-2})\varepsilon^2_{t-1} + 0.87\sigma^2_t + 5.310^{-2}Z_t \tag{17.23}$$
$$(2.9.10^{-2}) \quad (4.0.10^{-2}) \quad (0.06) \quad (2.4.10^{-2})$$

In the CAPM equation (17.22) the conditional variance is found to be significant and the dividend yield (Z_t) is not, thus supporting the CAPM. However, in (17.22) results are reported when Attanasio and Wadhwani also include the short rate which is statistically significant in the excess returns equation. The latter rejects the CAPM model of equilibrium returns (under the assumption of RE).

In the GARCH equation (17.23), the dividend yield Z_t has a statistically significant effect on the conditional variance and this would explain why previous researchers who assumed a constant risk premium found Z_t significant in the CAPM returns equation (17.22). Note that there is also considerable persistence in the conditional variance since $\alpha_1 + \alpha_2 + \alpha_3 = 0.91$.

Noise Traders, Risk and Serial Correlation in Stock Returns

Noise traders are now introduced into the market who (by definition) do not base their asset decisions on fundamental value. Positive feedback traders buy after a price rise and sell after a price fall (e.g. use of 'stop-loss' orders or 'portfolio insurers'). This gives rise to *positive* serial correlation in returns, since price rises are followed by an increase in demand and further price rises next period. Negative feedback traders pursue the opposite strategy, they 'buy low' and 'sell high'. Hence a price fall would be followed by a price rise if these traders dominated the market. (The latter would also be true for investors who assign a *constant share* of market value wealth to each asset, since a price fall on asset i will lead to a fall in its 'value share' in the portfolio and hence lead to additional purchases and a subsequent price rise.) The demand for stocks by noise traders N_t (as a proportion of the total market value of stocks) may be represented

$$N_t = \gamma R_{t-1} \tag{17.24}$$

with $\gamma > 0$, indicating positive feedback traders and $\gamma < 0$, indicating negative feedback traders and R_{t-1} is the holding period return in the previous period. Let us assume that the demand for shares by the smart money is determined by a (simple) mean-variance model (Section 3.2).

$$S_t = [E_t R_t - \alpha]/\mu_t \tag{17.25}$$

where S_t = proportion of stock held by smart money, α = expected rate of return for which demand by the smart money is zero, μ_t = measure of the perceived riskiness of shares. We assume μ_t is a positive function of the conditional variance σ_t^2 of stock prices (i.e. $\mu = \mu(\sigma)^2$). Thus the smart money holds more stock the higher the expected return and the smaller the riskiness of stocks. If the smart money holds all the stocks, then $S_t = 1$ and rearranging (17.25) we have the CAPM for the market portfolio: the excess return $(E_t R_t - \alpha)$ and depends on a risk premium, which is proportional to the conditional variance of stock prices, $\mu_t = c\sigma^2$. Equilibrium in the market requires all shares to be held:

$$S_t + N_t = 1 \tag{17.26}$$

Substituting (17.24) and (17.25) in (17.26) rearranging and using the RE assumption $R_t = E_t R_t + \varepsilon_t$ we have:

$$R_t = \alpha + \mu(\sigma_t^2) - \gamma\mu(\sigma_t^2)R_{t-1} + \varepsilon_t \tag{17.27}$$

Thus in a market with smart money and noise traders the serial correlation in R_t will depend on the type of noise trader. Somewhat paradoxically a positive feedback trader (i.e. $\gamma > 0$) results in *negative* serial correlation in R_t (for any given constant level of risk σ_t^2) and vice versa. A linear form for $\mu(\sigma_t^2)$ in equation (17.27) gives

$$R_t = \alpha + \theta\sigma_t^2 + (\gamma_0 + \gamma_1\sigma_t^2)R_{t-1} + \varepsilon_t \qquad (17.28)$$

The direct impact of feedback traders at a constant level of risk is given by the sign of γ_0. However, suppose γ_0 is positive (i.e. positive serial correlation in R_t) but γ_1 is negative. Then as risk σ_t^2 increases the coefficient on R_{t-1}, namely $\gamma_0 + \gamma_1\sigma_t^2$, could change sign and the serial correlation in stock returns would move from positive to negative, as risk increases. This would suggest that as volatility increases the market becomes more dominated by positive feedback traders, who interact in the market with the smart money, resulting in overall negative serial correlation in returns.

Sentana and Wadhwani (1992) estimate the above model using US daily data 1855–1988, together with a complex GARCH model of the time varying conditional variance. Their GARCH model allows the number of non-trading days to influence conditional variance (French and Roll, 1986) although in practice this is not found to be statistically significant. The conditional variance is found to be influenced differentially by positive and negative forecast errors. *Ceteris paribus*, a unit negative forecast error leads to a larger change in conditional variance than does a positive forecast error.

The switch point for the change from positive serial correlation in returns to negative serial correlation is $\sigma_t^2 > (-\gamma_0/\gamma_1)$ and they find $\gamma_0 = 0.09$, $\gamma_1 = -0.01$ and the switch point is $\sigma_t^2 > 5.8$. Hence when volatility is low stock returns at very short horizons (i.e. daily) exhibit *positive* serial correlation but when volatility is high returns exhibit negative autocorrelation. This model therefore provides some statistical support for the view that the relative influence of positive and negative feedback traders may vary with the degree of risk but it doesn't explain why this might happen. As is becoming familiar in such studies of aggregate stock price returns, Sentana and Wadhwani also find that the conditional variance exhibits substantial persistence (with the sum of coefficients on the GARCH parameters being close to unity). In the empirical results θ is not statistically different from zero, so that the influence of volatility on the mean return on stocks only works through the non-linear interaction variable $\gamma_1\sigma_t^2 R_{t-1}$. Thus the empirical results are not in complete conformity with the theoretical model.

17.3 SUMMARY

In the past 10 years there has been substantial growth in the number of empirical studies examining the volatility of stock returns, particularly those which use ARCH and GARCH processes to model conditional variances and covariances. Illustrative examples of this work have been provided and in general terms the main conclusions are:

- Only a small part of the conditional volatility in stock prices is explained by the volatility in economic fundamentals or by other economic variables (such as the level of gearing).

- There is considerable support for the view that the conditional variance of the forecast errors of stock returns are persistent although ARCH models being purely ad hoc do not provide theoretical reasons why this is so.

- The high degree of persistence in conditional volatility implies that the substantial observed movements in stock prices may be consistent with the RVF with a time varying risk premium.

- On balance the evidence suggests that equilibrium returns on an aggregate stock market index are influenced by agents' changing perceptions of risk. Hence the CAPM with time varying conditional variances would appear to be an improvement on the assumption that equilibrium returns are constant. Nevertheless the CAPM with time varying returns does not provide a complete explanation of equilibrium returns (e.g. the volume of trading may influence expected returns).

- It is possible that noise traders as well as smart money influence the expected return on an aggregate stock market index, even after making allowance for time varying risk premia.

18

The Mean Variance Model and the CAPM

This chapter is concerned with two main topics: first, the relationship between the mean-variance model of asset demands and the CAPM, and second, tests of the CAPM which use a formulation based on asset shares. The strengths and weaknesses of the latter approach are assessed in relation to the tests of the CAPM outlined in the previous chapter. The focus of the empirical work is on testing a set of implied restrictions on the parameters of the CAPM and on the importance or otherwise of time varying risk premia.

18.1 THE MEAN-VARIANCE MODEL

There is a strong tradition in monetary economics of optimising models which seek to determine an investor's desired demand for individual assets in a portfolio. This section generalises on the results from the mean-variance model of asset demands (MVMAD) discussed in Section 3.2. The MVMAD (or one version of it) predicts that investor's equilibrium demand for a single risky asset (as a share of total wealth) depends on a set of *expected* returns and the variances and covariances of the forecast errors of returns, which represent the riskiness of these assets. Hence we have

$$\mathbf{x}_t^* = \rho^{-1} \mathbf{\Sigma}_t^{-1} (E_t \mathbf{R}_{t+1} - \mathbf{r}_t) \tag{18.1}$$

where $\mathbf{x}_t^* = (n \times 1)$ vector of n *risky* asset shares, $\mathbf{\Sigma}_t = (n \times n)$ matrix of forecast errors of returns comprising the variance–covariance terms (σ_{ij}), $E_t \mathbf{R}_{t+1} - \mathbf{r}_t$ is an $(n \times 1)$ vector of *expected* excess returns, $r_t = $ risk-free rate and $\rho = $ coefficient of *relative* risk aversion. The demand (share) of the $(n + 1)^{\text{th}}$ *risk-free* asset is derived from the budget constraint

$$x_{n+1} = 1 - \sum_{i=1}^{n} x_i \tag{18.2}$$

The MVMAD (or rather one version of it) assumes that investors choose the optimal values of asset shares x_i^* in order to maximise a function that depends on expected return, risk and a measure of the individual's aversion to risk. The latter sounds very similar to the objective function in the CAPM. The obvious question is whether these two strands in the literature are interrelated. The answer is that they are but the correspondence is not one-for-one. The MVMAD is based on expected utility theory. One can assume that utility depends positively on end-of-period wealth or alternatively on expected return: choosing the former we have the maximand:

$$\max E_t[U(W_{t+1})] \tag{18.3}$$

The budget constraint for end-of-period wealth is:

$$W_{t+1} = W_t + W_t \mathbf{x}_t' \mathbf{R}_{t+1} + W_t \left[1 - \sum_1^n x_i \right] r_t \tag{18.4}$$

The first term on the RHS of (18.4) is initial wealth, the second term is the return per \$ on the portfolio multiplied by initial wealth and the final term is the receipts from holding the risk-free asset. If asset returns are normally distributed and we assume a constant *absolute* risk aversion utility function then maximising (18.3) subject to (18.4) reduces to:

$$\max[E_t R_{t+1}^p - \rho^* \sigma_p^2] \text{ or } \min[\rho^* \sigma_p^2 - E_t R_{t+1}^p] \tag{18.5}$$

where $E_t R_{t+1}^p = \Sigma x_i (E_t R_{it+1}) =$ expected return on the portfolio, $\sigma_p^2 =$ variance of the portfolio and $\rho =$ risk aversion parameter. There is much debate in the asset demand mean-variance literature (see, for example, Cuthbertson (1991b) and Courakis (1989) for an overview) about whether specific utility functions can give rise to asset demands for desired asset *shares* x_i^*, which are independent of initial wealth. Another consideration is whether the model expressed in terms of maximising end-of-period utility from *real* wealth (or *real* returns) yields a similar functional form for asset demand functions when the problem is conducted in terms of end-of-period *nominal* wealth (or nominal returns).

The reader will have noted from the CAPM that it is crucial that asset demands and equilibrium asset returns are independent of the level of initial wealth. If equilibrium returns are not independent of initial wealth then the theory is somewhat circular since equilibrium asset returns then depend on initial wealth which itself depends on *existing* asset returns. Hence if the mean-variance model of *asset demands* is to yield results similar to the CAPM it must (at a minimum) yield desired asset demands in dollar terms A_i that are proportional to initial wealth and hence asset *shares* that are independent of wealth. To choose a particular functional form for the utility function which yields such asset demand functions is not straightforward and the current state of the literature suggests that this can only be achieved as an approximation and results are only valid for small changes around the initial point.

We will sidestep these theoretical issues somewhat and assume that, to a reasonable approximation, a version of the mean variance model of asset *demands* based on (18.3) and (18.4) does yield asset demands in terms of equilibrium asset shares of the form (18.1). Frequently this type of model assumes that the 'constant' ρ in (18.1) is the coefficient of *relative* risk aversion. In general ρ *does* depend on the level of wealth but the assumption made is that for small changes in the variables ρ may be considered to be (broadly) constant. Having obtained the mean-variance asset demand functions it is then usually assumed that *desired* asset supplies $\mathbf{x}_t^s$ (e.g. for government bonds, equity, corporate bonds and foreign assets) are *exogenous*. Market equilibrium is given by $\mathbf{x}_t^s = \mathbf{x}_t^*$. Letting $\mathbf{x}_t$ denote the market equilibrium (which also equals the actual stock of assets outstanding) and inverting (18.1) we have

$$(E_t \mathbf{R}_{t+1} - \mathbf{r}_t) = \rho \Sigma_t \mathbf{x}_t \tag{18.6}$$

The above equation, somewhat confusingly, is often referred to as the CAPM or if international assets are included in the vector $\mathbf{x}_t$, the international CAPM (or I-CAPM). Note that even if all investors have the same expectations about σ_{ij} they are unlikely to have similar risk-return preferences and hence the risk aversion parameter ρ is an aggregate over all individuals, which will in general depend on the distribution of wealth.

It is worth noting that the MVMAD only deals with the demand side of the market. If supply side decisions are governed by a *set* of economic variables $\mathbf{z}_t$ (e.g. supply of government bonds is determined by the budget deficit and corporate bonds by the initial gearing position of firms) then market equilibrium becomes:

$$\mathbf{x}_t^s(\mathbf{z}_t) = \rho^{-1}\boldsymbol{\Sigma}^{-1}(E_t\mathbf{R}_{t+1} - \mathbf{r}_t)$$

Hence in general

$$(E\mathbf{R}_{t+1} - \mathbf{r}_t) = \rho\boldsymbol{\Sigma}\mathbf{x}^s(\mathbf{z}_t) \tag{18.7}$$

and equilibrium expected returns depend not only on $\{\sigma_{ij}\}$ but also on a set of variables $\mathbf{z}_t$. Equation (18.7) is the basis of the so-called structural or portfolio approach to the determination of asset returns which occurs frequently in the monetary economics literature. In this approach a *set* of asset demand *and* asset supply equations are estimated and then these resulting equations are solved algebraically to yield the reduced form equations for expected and actual returns given in (18.7) (Friedman, 1979). Alternatively, monetary economists estimate the reduced form equation (18.7) directly: that is they regress excess or relative returns on a whole host of potential economic variables represented by $\mathbf{z}_t$ in (18.7) (e.g. budget deficit, changes in wealth, inflation).

The CAPM Revisited

At present the reader must be somewhat bewildered since the RHS of (18.6) appears to be nothing like the CAPM equation which for asset i is:

$$E_tR_{it+1} - r_t = \beta_iE_t(R_{t+1}^m - r)$$

$$= \lambda\operatorname{cov}(R_i, R^m)_{t+1} \tag{18.8}$$

where $E_tR_{t+1}^m =$ expected return on the market portfolio and

$$\lambda = (E_tR_{t+1}^m - r_t)/\sigma_m^2 = \text{market price of risk} \tag{18.9}$$

However, (18.6) does reduce to something close to (18.8) as can be seen in the following illustrative case of three risky assets. Writing (18.6) in full:

$$\begin{bmatrix} R_{1t+1} - r_t \\ R_{2t+1} - r_t \\ R_{3t+1} - r_t \end{bmatrix} = \rho \begin{bmatrix} \sigma_{11} & \sigma_{12} & \sigma_{13} \\ \sigma_{21} & \sigma_{22} & \sigma_{23} \\ \sigma_{31} & \sigma_{32} & \sigma_{33} \end{bmatrix} \begin{bmatrix} x_{1t} \\ x_{2t} \\ x_{3t} \end{bmatrix} \tag{18.10}$$

where $\sigma_{ii} \equiv \sigma_i^2, \sigma_{12} = \sigma_{21}$. It follows that

$$E_tR_{1t+1} - r_t = \rho(\sigma_{11}x_{1t} + \sigma_{12}x_{2t} + \sigma_{13}x_{3t})$$

$$E_tR_{2t+1} - r_t = \rho(\sigma_{21}x_{1t} + \sigma_{22}x_{2t} + \sigma_{23}x_{3t})$$

$$E_tR_{3t+1} - r_t = \rho(\sigma_{31}x_{1t} + \sigma_{32}x_{2t} + \sigma_{33}x_{3t}) \tag{18.11}$$

We now note that for a three-asset world the definition of $\text{cov}(R_i, R^m)$ is:

$$\text{cov}(R_i, R^m) = x_1\sigma_{i1} + x_2\sigma_{i2} + x_3\sigma_{i3} \quad (i = 1, 2, 3) \tag{18.12}$$

Hence (18.11) may be rewritten:

$$E_t(R_{it+1} - r_t) = \rho\,\text{cov}(R_i, R^m)_{t+1} \tag{18.13}$$

Thus the standard CAPM (18.8) and the mean-variance model of asset demands with exogenous supply (18.10) are equivalent providing $\rho = \lambda$. Now unfortunately ρ and λ are not quite the same thing. However, both ρ and λ are similar in that they are both measures of risk. In broad terms ρ measures the curvature of the individual's utility function while $1/\lambda$ measures the additional return on the market portfolio per unit of market risk. This is about as far as we can go in terms of drawing on the common elements in the two approaches.

To summarise, the MVMAD with an exogenous supply of assets yields an equation for equilibrium asset returns that is very similar to that given by the CAPM. They only differ in their measure of overall risk. The MVMAD uses a measure of risk (ρ) which depends on the curvature of the utility function while the CAPM uses a measure (λ) which depends on the additional return on the *market* portfolio to compensate for market risk (σ_m^2).

Both the mean-variance asset demand approach and the standard CAPM are *one-period problems*. The investor is only concerned with (wealth) at the end of the first period and all future periods are ignored. However, Lintner (1971) has shown that in a multiperiod minimisation problem of the form (18.5) that λ is equal to the harmonic mean of each agent's coefficient of relative risk aversion.

Summary: MVMAD and the CAPM

We have concentrated on the relationship between the MVMAD which appears in the monetary economics literature and the CAPM of the finance literature. The main conclusions are:

(i) The MVMAD is usually couched in terms of maximising the expected value of utility from end-of-period wealth. Under certain restrictive assumption about the form of the utility function this may be reduced to a maximand (or minimand) in terms of portfolio variance and portfolio expected return as in the CAPM.

(ii) Unlike the CAPM, the MVMAD has asset demands that depend on the risk preferences of individuals and are in general not independent of initial wealth.

(iii) The MVMAD is usually inverted to give an equation for asset returns (as in the CAPM) on the assumption that asset supplies are exogenous. The latter is a strong assumption unlikely to hold in practice.

(iv) Both the CAPM and the MVMAD (with exogenous asset supplies) indicate that asset returns depend on (a) $\text{cov}(R_i, R^m)$ or equivalently (b) Σx_t, where $\Sigma = \{\sigma_{ij}\}$.

(v) The weakness of the MVMAD is that it requires the researcher to assume an explicit utility function and equilibrium prices depend on individuals' preferences and the distribution of wealth, represented by the average coefficient of risk aversion ρ across agents in the market.

(vi) The tractability of the CAPM arises from the fact that the maximand is *not* defined in terms of utility but only in terms of σ_p^2 and $E_t R_{t+1}^p$. It therefore allows equilibrium asset returns and equilibrium asset shares to be independent of initial wealth and investor preferences (and hence the same for all investors).

18.2 TESTS OF THE CAPM USING ASSET SHARES

We now want to explore *an alternative method* of presenting and testing the CAPM which is often discussed in the literature. For each asset i we have:

$$E_t R_{it+1} - r_t = \lambda \operatorname{cov}(R_i, R^m) \tag{18.14}$$

using the definition of $\operatorname{cov}(R_i, R^m)$ we have:

$$E_t R_{it+1} - r_t = \lambda \left(x_i \sigma_{ii} + \sum_{\substack{j=1 \\ i \neq j}}^{n} x_j \sigma_{ij} \right) \tag{18.15}$$

For illustrative purposes consider again the case of $n = 3$ assets then (18.15) is seen to be

$$E_t \begin{bmatrix} R_{1t+1} - r_t \\ R_{2t+1} - r_t \\ R_{3t+1} - r_t \end{bmatrix} = \lambda \begin{bmatrix} \sigma_{11} & \sigma_{12} & \sigma_{13} \\ \sigma_{21} & \sigma_{22} & \sigma_{23} \\ \sigma_{31} & \sigma_{32} & \sigma_{33} \end{bmatrix} \begin{bmatrix} x_{1t} \\ x_{2t} \\ x_{3t} \end{bmatrix} \tag{18.16}$$

or in matrix form

$$E_t \mathbf{R}_{t+1} - \mathbf{r}_t = \lambda \boldsymbol{\Sigma} \mathbf{x}_t \tag{18.17}$$

First assume the σ_{ij} are constant (and note that $\sigma_{ij} = \sigma_{ji}$). The CAPM then predicts that the expected excess return on asset i depends only on a weighted average of (risky) asset shares x_{it} (which are equilibrium/desired asset shares in the CAPM). We have noted how economists often like to test the implications of a theory by testing restrictions on parameters. Are there any restrictions in the system (18.16)? Writing out (18.16) in full:

$$(R_{1t+1} - r_t) = (\lambda\sigma_{11})x_{1t} + (\lambda\sigma_{12})x_{2t} + (\lambda\sigma_{13})x_{3t} = \lambda(\boldsymbol{\Pi}_1' \mathbf{x_t}) + \varepsilon_{1t} \tag{18.18a}$$

$$(R_{2t+1} - r_t) = (\lambda\sigma_{21})x_{1t} + (\lambda\sigma_{22})x_{2t} + (\lambda\sigma_{23})x_{3t} = \lambda(\boldsymbol{\Pi}_2' \mathbf{x_t}) + \varepsilon_{2t} \tag{18.18b}$$

$$(R_{3t+1} - r_t) = (\lambda\sigma_{31})x_{1t} + (\lambda\sigma_{32})x_{2t} + (\lambda\sigma_{33})x_{3t} = \lambda(\boldsymbol{\Pi}_3' \mathbf{x_t}) + \varepsilon_{3t} \tag{18.18c}$$

Assume for the moment that λ is known so that we can use $(R_{it+1} - r_t)/\lambda$ as dependent variables in (18.18). Suppose we run the *unrestricted* regressions in (18.18) and obtain six 'unrestricted coefficients'

$$\boldsymbol{\Pi}_1' = (\Pi_{11}, \Pi_{12}, \Pi_{13}), \ \boldsymbol{\Pi_2} = (\Pi_{21}, \Pi_{22}, \Pi_{23}), \ \boldsymbol{\Pi_3} = (\Pi_{31}, \Pi_{32}, \Pi_{32})$$

In matrix notation

$$E_t \mathbf{R}_{t+1} - \mathbf{r}_t = \lambda(\boldsymbol{\Pi}' \mathbf{x}_t) \tag{18.19}$$

If the CAPM with constant σ_{ij} is true then from (18.18) we expect

$$\frac{\Pi_{12}}{\Pi_{21}} = \frac{\sigma_{12}}{\sigma_{21}} = 1 \text{ or } \Pi_{12} = \Pi_{21} \tag{18.20}$$

and in our (3×3) system we also expect

$$\Pi_{13} = \Pi_{31} \text{ and } \Pi_{23} = \Pi_{32} \tag{18.21}$$

These restrictions, of course, arise from the fact that the variance–covariance matrix $\boldsymbol{\Omega}$ is symmetric.

Restrictions on the Variance–Covariance Matrix

Tests of the above restrictions are rarely conducted since there is another more complex set of restrictions for the CAPM implicit in (18.18) which logically subsumes the above restrictions. If we add the assumption of rational expectations:

$$R_{it+1} = E_t(R_{it+1}|\Omega_t) + \varepsilon_{it+1} \tag{18.22}$$

and

$$E(\varepsilon_{it+1}|\Omega_t) = 0$$

where Ω_t is the information set available at time t. Then from (18.22) the variance–covariance matrix of forecast errors is:

$$E_t(\mathbf{R}_{t+1} - E_t\mathbf{R}_{t+1})^2 = E_t \begin{pmatrix} \varepsilon_1\varepsilon_1, & \varepsilon_1\varepsilon_2, & \varepsilon_1\varepsilon_3 \\ \varepsilon_2\varepsilon_2, & \varepsilon_2\varepsilon_2, & \varepsilon_2\varepsilon_3 \\ \varepsilon_3\varepsilon_1, & \varepsilon_3\varepsilon_2, & \varepsilon_3\varepsilon_3 \end{pmatrix} = E(\varepsilon\varepsilon') \tag{18.23}$$

Substituting (18.23) in (18.16) we obtain a regression equation in terms of actual *ex-post* excess returns

$$(\mathbf{R}_{t+1} - \mathbf{r}_t) = \lambda \boldsymbol{\Sigma}\mathbf{x}_t + \boldsymbol{\varepsilon}_t \tag{18.24}$$

where $\boldsymbol{\varepsilon}'_t = (\varepsilon_{1t}, \varepsilon_{2t}, \varepsilon_{2t})$. However, from the derivation of the theoretical CAPM we know that

$$\boldsymbol{\Sigma} = \{\sigma_{ij}\} \quad \text{where } \sigma_{ij} = E[(R_i - ER_i)(R_j - ER_j)] \tag{18.25}$$

But under RE comparing (18.25) and (18.23) we see that

$$\boldsymbol{\Sigma} = E(\varepsilon\varepsilon') \tag{18.26}$$

Thus the CAPM + RE imposes the restriction that the *estimated* parameters Π_i in the regression of the excess returns on the x_{it} (i.e. equation (18.19)) should equal the regression *estimates* of the variance–covariance matrix of regression residuals $E(\varepsilon\varepsilon')$. The unrestricted set of equations (18.19) can be estimated using SURE or maximum likelihood and yield a value for Π which does not equal $E(\varepsilon\varepsilon')$. The regression can then be recomputed imposing the restrictions that the Π_{ij} equal their appropriate $E(\varepsilon_i\varepsilon_j)$. This will worsen the 'fit' of the equations but if the restrictions are statistically acceptable the 'fit' shouldn't worsen appreciably (or the estimates of the Π_{ij} alter in the two sets of regressions). This is the basis of the likelihood ratio test of these restrictions.

The elements Π_{ij} are determined exclusively by the estimates of the $E(\varepsilon_i\varepsilon_j)$ and therefore the regression also provides ('identifies') an estimate of λ, the market price of risk. The estimate for λ (or ρ) can be compared with estimates obtained from other studies. Also note that because the regression package automatically *imposes* $E(\varepsilon\varepsilon')$ to be symmetric, then, under the restriction that $\Pi = E(\varepsilon\varepsilon')$, Π is also *automatically* symmetric.

The test that $\Pi = E(\varepsilon\varepsilon')$ is therefore also a test that symmetry holds in the Π matrix (*plus* the stronger restriction that *each* $\Pi_{ij} = E(\varepsilon_i\varepsilon_j)$). It is in this sense that our earlier tests (18.21) are subsumed in this more general test.

Difficulties in Estimating the 'Asset Shares' Form of the CAPM

The above restriction $\Pi = E(\varepsilon\varepsilon')$ undoubtedly provides a 'strong test' of the CAPM but in practice we face the usual difficulties with data, estimation and interpretation. Some of these are as follows:

(i)   The returns R_{it+1} in the CAPM are holding period returns (e.g. over one month) and these are not always available, particularly for foreign assets (e.g. some studies use monthly Eurocurrency rates to approximate the monthly holding period return on government bonds).

(ii) The shares x_{it} according to the CAPM are equilibrium holdings at *market value*. Often data on x_{it} for marketable assets (e.g. for government bonds) are only available at the issue price and not at market value.

(iii) There is the question of how many assets one should include in the empirical study. Under the CAPM investors who hold the market portfolio hold *all* assets (including real estate, land, gold, etc.). Clearly, given a finite data set, to include a large number of assets would involve a loss of degrees of freedom and multicollinearity problems would probably arise.

(iv) If either any important asset shares are excluded or if the asset shares included are measured with error then this may result in biased parameter estimates. In principle the measurement error problem can be mitigated by applying a form of instrumental variables. A measure of omitted variables bias can be ascertained by trying different sets of x_{it} and comparing the sensitivity of results obtained. In a similar vein, omitted variables bias might show up as temporal instability in the parameter estimates (Hendry, 1988). Often in empirical studies these 'refinements' to the estimation procedure are not undertaken.

Under the assumption of constant σ_{ij} (the so-called *static* CAPM) it is invariably found that the restrictions $\Pi = E(\varepsilon\varepsilon')$ are rejected. Also as the variability in the x_{it} is usually rather low relative to the variability in $(R_{it+1} - r_t)$, the fit of these CAPM relationships is very poor (Frankel, 1982, Engel and Rodrigues, 1989, Giovannini and Jorion, 1989 and Thomas and Wickens, 1993). Finally these studies find that λ (or ρ) is often negative (rather than positive) and is extremely poorly determined statistically. Indeed usually one does not reject λ(or ρ) $= 0$ statistically. The CAPM then reduces to the hypothesis that expected excess returns are zero (or equal a constant)

$$E_t R_{it+1} - r_t = \alpha_i$$

In the context of international assets with a known own currency nominal return (e.g. Eurocurrency rates) this amounts to uncovered interest parity (for $\alpha_i = 0$). Thus although expected excess returns are found to depend on asset shares x_{it} the restrictions on the parameters Π_{ij} do not conform to the *static* CAPM (i.e. constant σ_{ij}) and the fit of the equations is rather poor.

Time Varying Variances and Covariances

The next obvious step in the analysis is to investigate whether the conditional covariances (i.e. the regression estimates of $\hat{\sigma}_{ij} = \sum_t \hat{\varepsilon}_{it}\hat{\varepsilon}_{jt}/n$) are constant or whether they vary over time. A particularly simple form of non-constancy (but by no means the only one) is the ARCH model

$$\hat{\sigma}^2_{ijt+1} = \beta_0 + \beta_1 \hat{\sigma}^2_{ijt} \quad \text{(for all } i \text{ and } j) \tag{18.27}$$

Thomas and Wickens (1993) find little evidence of time varying variances and covariances for a diverse set of assets which include foreign as well as domestic assets. However, if a subset of assets, for example only 'national' assets or only equities, are included in the CAPM model then ARCH effects are found to be present. Other empirical studies often do not *test* for ARCH effects but *assume* they may be present and then recompute the above model and test the time varying covariance restrictions $\Pi_t = E(\varepsilon_i \varepsilon_j)_t$.

As far as estimation is concerned the introduction of ARCH effects can cause fairly horrendous computational requirements as the number of parameters can be very large. For example, with seven risky assets each *single* σ_{ijt+1} can in principle depend on all the other seven *lagged values* of σ_{ijt} for the other assets (and a constant). Thus for a first-order ARCH model for asset 1 *only* we have:

$$(\sigma_{1j})^2_{t+1} = \beta_i + \sum_{j=1}^{7} \theta_j \sigma^2_{1jt} \tag{18.28}$$

Equation (18.28) for asset 1 includes individual terms for $\sigma_{11}, \sigma_{12}, \sigma_{13}, \ldots, \sigma_{17}$, and other similar equations are needed for σ_{2j}, σ_{3j}, etc. (of course remembering that $\sigma_{ij} = \sigma_{ji}$). For higher-order ARCH processes additional lagged terms also need to be estimated. Such is the computational task (and loss of degrees of freedom) that usually only first-order ARCH processes are used and sometimes only *own lagged* covariances are embodied in the ARCH process:

$$(\sigma^2_{ij})_{t+1} = \beta_1 + \theta_{ij}(\sigma^2_{ij})_t \tag{18.29}$$

Since we are now allowing the Σ matrix in (18.24) to vary over time (as well as the x_t), naturally the *time varying covariance* CAPM 'fits' better but again the CAPM restriction that (schematically) $\Pi_t = \Sigma_t$ is invariably rejected (e.g. Giovannini and Jorion (1989) and Thomas and Wickens (1993). Also it is often the case that the point estimate of λ (or ρ) is negative and again the null hypothesis that is zero is easily accepted. The latter is a rejection of the CAPM.

An alternative method of 'modelling' the time varying variances in the CAPM is to assume that the variances σ_{ij} are (linearly) related to a small set of macroeconomic variables z_{it}. Engel and Rodrigues (1989), who use the government debt of six countries as the 'complete set' of assets in the portfolio, assume z_{it} is either 'surprises' in oil prices or surprises in the US money supply (the data series for these 'surprises' are residuals from ARIMA models). They find that both surprises in oil prices and in the US money supply help to explain the relative rates of return on this international portfolio of government bonds. However, the CAPM restriction that $\Sigma_t = \Pi_t$ is still rejected (and λ or ρ is statistically zero).

There is an additional potential weakness of the above reported tests of the CAPM. This is that they only consider returns of over one month. Now while in principle the

CAPM should be true for all holding periods, it would seem that transactions costs and information costs for *some* participants in the market would at certain times be important and may prevent the CAPM holding over short horizons. For these agents (who are intramarginal for very short but not at *all* horizons) it might be better to consider longer horizon returns, for example, for 3, 6 months or even 1–2 years. In this case a low-order ARCH process might also be a better representation than for one-month returns.

All the above studies only consider the one-period CAPM model. The conventional CAPM and the MVMAD yield expressions for equilibrium returns under the assumption that agents are concerned only with one-period returns (or next periods wealth in the case of the MVMAD). Merton (1973) in his intertemporal CAPM has demonstrated that with constant preferences (e.g. constant relative risk aversion parameter ρ) and some additional restrictions, the CAPM yields a constant price of risk (λ):

$$1/\lambda = (E_t R_{t+1}^m - r_t)/\sigma_m^2$$

for the *entire* market portfolio. However, in Merton's model the price of risk is not constant for *components* of the market portfolio (Chou et al, 1989, page 4). It is clear therefore that in an intertemporal CAPM one would not expect the 'price of risk' to be constant for returns on subsets of the portfolio. However, the latter is precisely the assumption made in much empirical work. Put another way, a weakness of the above empirical studies is that they assume that the portfolios chosen are good representations of the market portfolio (i.e. the 'errors in variables' problem is not acute). The next section discusses a model which relaxes the assumption that the price of risk is constant and hence attempts to tackle this potential omitted variables problem.

Time Varying Price of Volatility

The CAPM for asset i may be written

$$(E_t R_{it+1} - r_t) = \Psi_t \, \text{cov}(R_i, R^m)_t \tag{18.30}$$

where we shall refer to Ψ_t as the *price of volatility* and allow it to be time varying. (This term is chosen because the *price of risk* λ is usually assumed to be a constant.) Following Chou et al (1989) suppose we approach the problem of the potential mismeasurement of the market portfolio by assuming it consists of an observable stock return R^s and an *unobservable component* with return R^u. The variances are σ_s^2 and σ_u^2, and the covariance between the stock return and the unobservable return is σ_{su}. The CAPM for the stock portfolio (we omit t subscripts on the σ_{ij} terms):

$$\begin{aligned} E_t R_{t+1}^s - r_t &= \Psi_t [x_t \sigma_s^2 + (1 - x_t)\sigma_{su}] \\ &= \Psi_t [x_t + (1 - x_t)\beta_t^u]\sigma_s^2 \\ &= \Psi_t \theta_t \sigma_s^2 \end{aligned} \tag{18.31}$$

where $\beta_t^u = (\sigma_{su}/\sigma_s^2)_t$, $\theta_t = x_t + (1 - x_t)\beta_t^u$, and x_t is share of equities in the true market portfolio. Hence, β_t^u is the unobserved but possibly time varying CAPM beta between the stock portfolio and the unobserved part of the true market portfolio. Under RE equation (18.31) becomes:

$$R_{t+1}^s - r_t = \Psi_t \theta_t \sigma_s^2 + \varepsilon_{t+1} \tag{18.32}$$

In a number of empirical studies of the CAPM the market portfolio is known to be a subset of the total set of assets available to the investor. Hence we have a situation like that in (18.32) which reduces to the 'standard CAPM' equation

$$R^s_{t+1} - r_t = \alpha\sigma^2_s + \varepsilon_{t+1} \tag{18.33}$$

where α is constant only if:

(i) $x_t = 1$, that is the true market portfolio consists only of stocks, or

(ii) $(\sigma_{su})_t = (\sigma^2_s)_t$, that is the (conditional) covariances between the 'omitted assets' and the included assets (stocks) are equal for all time periods, and

(iii) Ψ_t the price of volatility is constant.

Any time variation found in α in an equation of the form (18.33) will be due to the breakdown of one or all of the above assumptions. A number of studies find that a time varying *own variance* σ^2_s can help to explain movements in *own* expected excess returns but 'the linkage' is unstable (i.e. α is time varying). This is consistent with the omitted variables interpretation of equation (18.33). A purely *statistical* method of modelling time variation in α which is reasonably general is to assume α follows a random walk

$$\alpha_t = \alpha_{t-1} + v_t \tag{18.34}$$

If $\sigma^2_v = 0$ then this reduces to a model with a constant value for Ψ. Using weekly returns data on US stocks, Chou et al (1989) first estimate equation (18.33) with a constant value of α and a GARCH(1,1) model for σ^2_s

$$\sigma^2_{st+1} = a_0 + a_1(\sigma^2_s)_t + a_2\varepsilon^2_t \tag{18.35}$$

The regression *over subperiods* reveals that α does vary over time. Using the random walk model for α, the time variation in α is found to be substantial (when they use monthly returns data). There is also *persistence* in σ^2_s since a_1 is about 0.84 and a_2 about 0.13, and both coefficient estimates are very statistically significant. Having obtained their time series for α_t, from (18.34), Chou et al investigate whether α_t depends on a number of macroeconomic variables that might be thought to influence x_t, β^u_t and Ψ_t (in equation (18.31)).

From (18.31) one can see that if Ψ is constant the unobservable variables x_t, β^u_t appear as cross-products of the form $(z_t\sigma^2_{st})$ where $z_t = x_t$ or β^u_t. Hence we can approximate the general relationship (18.32) as

$$(R^s_{t+1} - r_t) = q_1(\sigma^2_s)_t + q_2(z_t\sigma^2_{st}) + \varepsilon_{t+1} \tag{18.36}$$

When (18.36) is estimated together with the GARCH(1,1) model for the time varying risk element σ^2_{st}, Chou et al find that for z_t = rate of inflation, the coefficient q_2 is statistically significant and fairly stable. Unfortunately for the CAPM, however, the coefficient q_1 on σ^2_s becomes negative and statistically insignificant. (Other variables such as the real rate of interest and the ratio of the value of the NYSE stock price index to consumption are tried as measures of x_1, but are not usually statistically significant or stable.)

The above study while ingenious in its statistical approach does not yield much additional insight into the behaviour of asset returns other than to show that the basic CAPM even with a time varying *variance* (but no covariances) is inadequate. The use of additional variables such as the rate of inflation to proxy the 'unobservables' only meets with limited success. In fact the model then begins to resemble a rather general APT model where expected returns may depend on a set of economic variables and in particular on the (own) variance σ^2_{st} and inflation.

18.3 SUMMARY

The main conclusions from the empirical work that uses a version of the CAPM in terms of asset shares are:

(i) Expected excess returns are only weakly related to changes in asset shares even when time varying covariances are introduced into the CAPM. In addition, the CAPM restrictions $\Pi = \Sigma$ appear to fail even when Π and Σ are assumed to be time varying.

(ii) Estimates of λ (or ρ) tend to be very imprecise and statistically we can accept that $\lambda = 0$. The CAPM therefore fails and risk neutrality applies.

(iii) The results differ somewhat depending on what is chosen to constitute the market portfolio. For example, some researchers use only *domestic* assets or only world *bond* holdings, rather than a wider set of assets.

(iv) Equity returns may well depend on time varying covariances but *not* in the restrictive form given in the standard CAPM. Also, there is some evidence (albeit rather shaky) that the statistical significance of any time varying risk premia effects may be due to a few *dramatic periods* of turbulence.

(v) Additional assumptions such as differential transactions costs, heterogeneous expectations formation and differential taxation across investors are required to save the CAPM, in the face of the evidence presented above.

(vi) Tests of the CAPM which use the excess market return $ER^m_{t+1} - r_t$ as the RHS variable may be subject to less measurement error than using the x_{it} as RHS variables. Hence tests on the former which we discussed in the previous chapter may be more informative about the validity of the CAPM.

———————— 19 ————————
└ Risk Premia and the Bond Market ┘

In Chapter 10 when examining empirical evidence on the term structure the term (risk) premium on bonds was allowed to vary depending only on the term to maturity. This gives rise to various hypotheses applied to holding period yields (HPYs), spot yields and yields to maturity. This chapter deals exclusively with the determination of one-period HPYs on bonds of various maturities, where the term premium is allowed to vary over time. The procedure is as follows.

- We begin with studies which deal with the short end of the term structure, namely the choice between six-month and three-month bills. We look first at studies which use rather ad-hoc measures of a time varying risk premium, and then move on to examine fairly simple ARCH models of conditional variances.

- Next we turn to the modelling of time varying term premia on long-term bonds. We begin with the study by Mankiw (1986) who attempts to correlate various measures of risk with the yield spread. We then return to the CAPM. As a benchmark we see how far (variants of) the CAPM with *time invariant* betas can explain excess HPYs on long-term bonds. Here the risk premium may vary with the excess return on a benchmark portfolio such as the market portfolio and the zero beta portfolio.

- The CAPM does not rule out the possibility that conditional variances and covariances in asset returns are time varying (i.e. the betas are time varying). We therefore analyse some empirical work that utilises *a set* of ARCH and GARCH equations to model these time varying risk premia on long-term bonds.

- Finally we examine the possible interdependence between the risk premia on bonds and that on stocks.

19.1   TIME VARYING RISK: PURE DISCOUNT BONDS

In Chapters 10 and 14 we saw that the expectations hypothesis applied to zero coupon (or pure discount) bonds at the short end of the maturity spectrum received some empirical support both from single equation studies and studies using the VAR methodology. However, empirical anomalies still remain (e.g. violation of the VAR parameter restrictions under the null of the EH + RE). For example, Simon (1989) using weekly data on three-month (13 weeks) and six-month bills ran the following regression:

$$\Delta^{13} r_{t+13} = \beta_0 + \beta(R - r)_t + \eta_{t+13} \tag{19.1}$$

where R_t = (spot) yield on six-month bill (annual rate), r_t = (spot) yield on three-month bill (annual rate) and $\Delta^{13} r_{t+13} = r_{t+13} - r_t$. Under risk neutrality, the EH + RE implies that $\beta = 2$. Simon (1989) using weekly data on US Treasury bills finds that the coefficient on $(R_t - r_t)$ is substantially less than 2 over subsamples of data from 1961–1988 and hence he rejects the EH + RE (see Section 10.2). In this section we examine work by Simon (1989), Jones and Roley (1983) and a pioneering study by Engle et al (1987) all of which attempt to apply models involving time varying risk premia to the bill market.

In the article referred to above, Simon (1989) tries to improve the model by introducing a time varying risk premium. The *expected excess* one-period holding period yield (HPY) when investing in six-month bills rather than three-month bills is *defined as*[1]:

$$E_t y_{t+13} = E_t H_{t+13} - r_t = 2R_t - E_t r_{t+13} - r_t \tag{19.2}$$

The holding period in this case is three months (13 weeks). Given our definition of y_{t+13} the RE forecast error η_{t+13} may be written:

$$\eta_{t+13} = y_{t+13} - E_t y_{t+13} \tag{19.3}$$

Over a three-month holding period, the six-month bill constitutes the risky asset since its selling price in three months' time is unknown (and is, of course, directly related to $E_t r_{t+13}$ in (19.2) since after three months has elapsed the six-month bill 'becomes' a bill with only three months to maturity). If we denote the risk premium as θ_t then the excess yield on the risky six-month bill (held for three months) is determined by:

$$E_t y_{t+13} = \phi + \theta_t \tag{19.4}$$

Simon assumes that the risk premium is proportional to the square of the excess HPY:

$$\theta_t = \alpha E_t (2R_t - r_t - r_{t+13})^2 \tag{19.5}$$

Substituting (19.5) in (19.4) using (19.2) and the RE condition (19.3) and rearranging we have:

$$\Delta^{13} r_{t+13} = a + b_1 (R_t - r_t) + b_2 E_t (2R_t - r_t - r_{t+13})^2 + \eta_{t+13} \tag{19.6}$$

where we expect $b_1 = 2$, $b_2 < 0$. (Strictly $b_1 = 2$ should be imposed so that the LHS variable is a holding period yield.) Equation (19.6) has to be estimated by IV because of the errors in variables problem introduced when we replace the expected value in (19.6) by its *ex-post* value. Because of the use of overlapping data the error term in (19.6) is MA(12) and may also be heteroscedastic. Simon (1989) 'corrects' for these problems by using an estimation technique known as two-step two-stage least squares (see Chapter 20). Simon's most favourable result is:

$$\Delta r_{t+13}^{13} = 0.06 + 1.6 (R - r)_t - 0.47 (2R_t - r_t - r_{t+1})^2 \tag{19.7}$$
$$\phantom{\Delta r_{t+13}^{13} = } (0.18) \quad (0.34) \qquad\qquad (0.06)$$

1972–1979 (weekly data), $R^2 = 0.48$, $(\cdot) = $ standard error

The last term indicates the presence of a time varying risk premium and the coefficient on the yield spread $(R_t - r_t)$ is not statistically different from 2. A similar result to the above is found for the 1961–1971 period but for the post-1982 period (ending in 1988) the risk premium term is statistically insignificant and there is some variability in the coefficient on $(R - r)_t$ (here, point estimates range from 1.6 to 4.4 over various subperiods). The model is therefore an improvement on the risk neutrality assumption that underlies the EH + RE but unstable coefficients remain a problem.

Jones and Roley (1983) also test the hypothesis that the excess one-period HPY of six-month over three-month US Treasury bills depends on a time varying risk premium θ_t. Here θ_t is measured by a weighted average of the change in the absolute value of the short rate which again is a rather ad-hoc measure of risk[2]

$$\theta_t = (1/8) \sum_{i=0}^{7} |r_{t-13i} - r_{t-13i+1}| \tag{19.8}$$

Using weekly data for Fridays over the period January 1970–September 1979 and ensuring that the three-month return exactly matches the holding period of the six-month investment they find

$$2R_t - r_{t+13} = -1.0 \quad + 0.97 r_t + 0.75 \theta_t \tag{19.9}$$
$$(0.86) \quad (0.08) \quad (0.31)$$

$$1970\text{-}1979, \bar{R}^2 = 0.79, \text{ SEE} = 0.90$$

The coefficient on r_t is not statistically different from unity so that the LHS of equation (19.9) can be rewritten in terms of the excess yield y_{t+13} (see (19.2)). Jones and Roley also test to see if any additional variables at time t influence the excess yield. They find that an unemployment variable and the stock of *domestically* held three- or six-month bills are statistically insignificant. However, they find that flows of *foreign* holdings of US Treasury bills are just statistically significant at conventional significance levels (suggesting some market segmentation). Hence, θ_t does not provide an 'exhaustive explanation' of excess yields and strictly speaking the RE information efficiency assumption is violated. However, too much weight should not be attached to the result that elements of the complete information set Ω_t are statistically significant because if one undertakes enough permutations of additional variables, some are bound to be found to be significant at conventional significance levels (i.e. Type I errors occur).

Shiller et al (1983, page 199) in commenting on the Jones–Roley measure of the risk premium θ_t in (19.8) note that their proxy is not well grounded in any economic theory. Shiller et al also find that when the Jones–Roley sample period is extended to include the period 1979–1982, when the Federal Reserve targeted the monetary base and the volatility of short rates increased sharply, then θ_t is much less significant. Also θ_t is found to be statistically insignificant if the ratio of the flow of short debt to long debt is added to equation (19.9) (see Shiller et al (1983), Table 4) which suggests some form of market segmentation rather than 'risk'. Hence, the excess HPY on six-month over three-month bills does not appear to be a stable function of the ad-hoc risk premium θ_t used by Jones and Roley.

ARCH Model

The problem with the above studies is that the risk premium is rather ad hoc and is not given by the conditional variance of forecast errors. In a pioneering study Engle et al (1987) utilise the ARCH approach to model time varying risk in the bill market. The expected excess yield $E_t y_{t+1}$ of long bills over short bills is assumed to be determined by the *conditional* variance of the returns:

$$E_t y_{t+1} = \beta + \delta E_t[\text{var}(y_{t+1}|\Omega_t)] \tag{19.10}$$

Invoking RE we have $y_{t+1} = E_t y_{t+1} + \varepsilon_{t+1}$. We take $\varepsilon_{t+1} \sim N(O, \sigma^2_{t+1})$ and therefore $\text{var}(y_{t+1}|\Omega_t)$ in (19.10) may be replaced by:

$$E_t \text{var}(y_{t+1}|\Omega_t) = E_t(y_{t+1} - E y_{t+1}|\Omega_t)^2 = E_t \varepsilon^2_{t+1} = E_t \sigma^2_{t+1} \tag{19.11}$$

Hence not surprisingly the conditional variance of the excess yield is the same as the conditional variance of the rational expectations forecast error. Thus (19.10) may be rewritten:

$$y_{t+1} = \beta + \delta(E_t \sigma^2_{t+1}) + \varepsilon_{t+1} \tag{19.12}$$

Equation (19.12) has the intuitive interpretation that the larger the variance of the forecast errors, the larger the 'reward' in terms of the excess yield that agents require in order willingly to hold long bills rather than short bills. Thus in periods of turbulence (i.e. σ^2_{t+1} is high) investors require a higher expected excess yield and vice versa.

Equation (19.12) may be viewed as being derived from an 'inverted' mean-variance model of asset demands, where there is only one risky asset. The demand function for the risky 'six-month' asset is:

$$A^d_t = \frac{E_t y_{t+1}}{c(E_t \sigma^2_{t+1})} \tag{19.13}$$

where c is a coefficient of risk aversion. If asset supplies 'A' are fixed and relatively constant (or slowly varying) then equilibrium gives

$$E_t y_{t+1} = A c E_t \sigma^2_{t+1} \tag{19.14}$$

which is similar to (19.12) with $\beta = 0$ and $\delta = Ac$. In this model there is only *one* risky asset, namely the return over three months on the six-month bill. Therefore, equation (19.12) may also be viewed as a very simple form of the CAPM where 'risk' is measured by the conditional variance of the *single* risky asset. The correspondence between the CAPM and the mean-variance model of asset demands has been noted in previous chapters.

To make (19.12) operational we require a model of the time varying variance. Engle et al assume a simple ARCH model in which σ^2_{t+1} depends on past (squared) forecast errors:

$$\sigma^2_{t+1} = \alpha_0 + \alpha_1 \left[\sum_{i=0}^{4} w_i \varepsilon^2_{t-i} \right] \tag{19.15}$$

where the w_i are declining (arithmetic) weights set at $w_i = (4/10, 3/10, \ldots,$ etc.) with $\Sigma w_i = 1$, and α_0 and α_1 are to be estimated. We can 'get a handle' on the sign we expect on α_1 by assuming *past* forecast errors ε^2_{t-i} have been constant $(= \sigma^2$ say). In these circumstances we would envisage agents expecting next period's forecast error $E_t \sigma^2_{t+1}$ to be equal to this constant value σ^2. For the latter to hold in (19.15) we require $\alpha_0 = 0$, $\alpha_1 = 1$. Equation (19.12) given (19.15) is often referred to as an 'ARCH in mean' model. A representative result from Engle et al (1987) using quarterly data, 1959–1985, on US three- and six-month bills is:

$$y_{t+1} = -0.024 + 0.687 \, [E_t\sigma^2_{t+1}] + \varepsilon_{t+1} \qquad (19.16a)$$
$$\phantom{y_{t+1} = } (1.2) \quad (5.2)$$

$$\sigma^2_{t+1} = 0.0023 + 1.64 \left(\sum_{i=0}^{4} w_i\varepsilon^2_{t-i} \right) \qquad (19.16b)$$
$$\phantom{\sigma^2_{t+1} = } (1.0) \quad (6.3)$$

The excess yield responds positively to the expected variance of forecast errors ($\delta = 0.687$) and the variance of forecast errors depends on past forecast errors although the coefficient α_1 is somewhat greater than unity. Engle et al then include the yield spread $(R_t - r_t)$ in equation (19.16a) since in earlier studies this had been found to help predict the excess yield at $t + 1$. The idea here is that the yield spread might *not* influence y_{t+1} once allowance is made for time varying risk and hence the RE assumption would then not be violated. Unfortunately, both σ^2_{t+1} and $(R - r)_t$ are statistically significant in explaining y_{t+1} and therefore the RE information efficiency assumption is still violated in this model.

The results of Engle et al appear to demonstrate strong effects of the conditional variance on equilibrium returns. Tzavalis and Wickens (1993) demonstrate that this result is sensitive to the data period chosen and in particular whether the period of extreme volatility in interest rates in 1979–1982, when monetary base targeting was in operation, is included. Broadly speaking Tzavalis and Wickens (using monthly data) reproduce Engle et al's results using a GARCH(1,1) model but then include a dummy variable DV_t taking the value unity over the months 1979(10)–1982(9) and zero elsewhere. They find that when DV_t is included, the degree of persistence in volatility falls, that is $\alpha_1 + \alpha_2$ in the GARCH process (17.13) is of the order of 0.3 rather than 0.9 and the dummy variable is highly significant and positive. In addition, the expected HPY is no longer influenced by the conditional variance, that is we do not reject the null that $\delta = 0$ in equation (19.10). The dummy variable merely increases the average level of volatility in the 1979–1982 period and the reasons for such an exogenous shift has no basis in economic theory. Therefore, based on intuitive economic arguments one might still favour the model without the dummy variable and take the view that persistence is high when volatility is high. Hence, there may be a threshold effect. In periods of high volatility, volatility is highly persistent and influences expected equilibrium returns. In contrast, in periods of low volatility, persistence is much lower and the relatively low value of the conditional variance does not have a perceptible impact on equilibrium returns. Intuitively the above seems plausible (cf. the effect of inflation on money demand or consumption in periods of high and low inflation) but clearly this non-linear effect requires further investigation.

19.2 TIME VARYING RISK: LONG-TERM BONDS

This section begins with the study by Mankiw (1986) who tries to explain the dependence of the excess HPY on long bonds in terms of a time varying term premium, and then examines the behaviour of the CAPM with constant betas as a benchmark for later studies which allow betas to be time varying.

Under the EH with constant term premium the excess one-period holding period yield $(H_t - r_t)$ on a bond of any maturity should be independent of information at time t. A number of researchers have found that this hypothesis is resoundingly rejected for a

Table 19.1 Regression of Excess Holding Return on the Yield Spread, US, Canada, UK and Germany, 1961(1)–1984(4)[a]

Independent Variables	US	Canada	UK	Germany
Constant	−6.12	−5.20	−2.28	−0.95
	(2.27)	(3.04)	(3.59)	(3.25)
Yield Spread	4.99	3.40	1.51	1.87
	(1.58)	(1.62)	(1.40)	(1.48)
Summary Statistics				
$\bar{R}^2$	0.086	0.034	0.002	0.006
Durbin Watson	2.17	1.96	2.23	1.57
Standard Error of Estimate	20.4	23.9	28.1	25.8

Data from OECD, *Main Economic Indicators*, various issues.
(a)   The dependent variable is the excess holding period return between long and short bonds, $H_{t+1} - r_t$. The yield spread is defined as $R_t - r_t$, where R_t is the long rate and r_t is the short rate. Standard errors are in parentheses.
Source: Mankiw (1986).

number of different countries. For example, Mankiw (1986) finds that for the USA, the UK, Canada and Germany (Table 19.1), the excess HPY on long bonds depends on the yield spread. When the data for all the countries are pooled he obtains:

$$(H_{it+1} - r_{it}) = -3.28 + 2.04 \ (R_{it} - r_{it}) \qquad (19.17)$$
$$(2.01) \quad (0.66)$$

where $(\cdot) = $ standard error and $H_{t+1} = (P_{t+1} - P_t + C)/P_t$ is the one-period holding period yield on the long-term bond. He conjectures, as many have done, that the spread $(R_t - r_t)$ could be a proxy for a time varying (linear additive) term premium θ_t where

$$(H_{t+1} - r_t) = \alpha + \beta\theta_t + \varepsilon_t \qquad (19.18)$$

and θ_t depends on $(R - r)_t$. If one had a direct measure of the risk premium θ_t then one could include this in (19.17) along with the spread and if θ_t is correctly measured one would expect the coefficient on $(R - r)_t$ to be zero. However, Mankiw argues that if θ_t is subject to measurement error this would bias the coefficient estimates in such a regression. He decides instead to investigate the regression

$$\theta_t = \delta_0 + \delta_1(R - r)_t + v_t \qquad (19.19)$$

using alternative variables to measure risk. Since θ_t appears on the LHS of (19.19) the parameters δ_i are not subject to measurement error. If $\delta_1 \neq 0$, the argument would be that $(R - r)_t$ influences $(H - r)_t$ in (19.17) because $(R - r)_t$ is correlated with the independently measured risk premium θ_t. As alternative measures of θ_t Mankiw (1986) uses (i) the absolute value of the percentage change in the price of the long bond, (ii) the covariance between the HPY and the growth of consumption as suggested by the consumption CAPM (see Chapter 4) and (iii) the covariance between the HPY and the excess return on the market portfolio of *stocks*. In (iii) the tentative view is that the excess return on the stock market might be a good proxy for consumption growth for investors who are likely to hold bonds (i.e. predominantly the wealthy). Hence (iii) can also be loosely interpreted in terms of the consumption CAPM.

Mankiw uses a fairly simple measure for the covariance terms. For example, the consumption covariance $CC_{t+1}^{(n)}$ for an n-period bond is defined as:

$$CC_{t+1}^{(n)} = (g_{t+1}^c - \overline{g})(H_{t+1}^{(n)} - \overline{H}^{(n)}) \tag{19.20}$$

where $g_{t+1}^c = C_{t+1}/C_t$ and C_t = real consumption. Mankiw therefore assumes that the (conditional) *expected* values for consumption growth and holding period yields are constant and equal to their sample values.

Unfortunately for all four countries studied, Mankiw finds that for risk measures (i) and (iii) the coefficient δ_1 in (19.19) is statistically insignificantly different from zero. For risk measure '(ii)' the null that $\delta_1 = 0$ is not rejected for three out of four countries and in the one case where δ_1 is significant it has the wrong sign (i.e. it is negative). Hence Mankiw finds that these proxy variables for a time varying term premium do not rescue the expectations hypothesis.

Bisignano (1987) examines whether the zero-beta CAPM with the addition of a growth term in consumption (i.e. consumption CAPM) can provide an acceptable statistical explanation of holding period yields. Here, excess HPYs are time varying because of the variation in 'market returns' and consumption covariability: however, the betas vary only with term to maturity. The equation to be estimated is:

$$H_{t+1}^{(n)} = [1 - \beta^{(n)}]R_{t+1}^z + \beta^{(n)}R_{t+1}^m + a^{(n)}CC_{t+1}^{(n)} + v_{t+1} \tag{19.21}$$

where R^z = holding period return on a zero-beta portfolio of bonds and R^m = holding period return on a market portfolio of bonds. The two hypotheses to be tested are

$$H_0^1 : \beta^{(n)} \neq 0, \quad a^{(n)} = 0 \text{ (zero-beta CAPM)}$$

$$H_0^2 : \beta^{(n)} = 0 \quad a^{(n)} \neq 0 \text{ (consumption CAPM)}$$

The market return R_{t+1}^m is measured by the Saloman Brothers world *bond* portfolio index and the zero-beta portfolio comprises a portfolio of short-term assets (such that the correlation between R^m and R^z is zero). From equation (19.21), we see that if we *define* the risk premium θ_t as $E_t(H^{(n)} - R^z)_{t+1}$ then

$$\theta_t = \beta^{(n)}(R^m - R^z)_{t+1} + a^{(n)}CC_{t+1}^{(n)} \tag{19.22}$$

For Germany Bisignano (1987, Table 27) reports the following results for five-year and 10-year bonds:

$$H_{t+1}^{(5)} = 0.74R_{t+1}^z + 0.26R_{t+1}^m - 125.6CC_{t+1}^{(5)}$$
$$\quad (10.7) \qquad (3.8) \qquad\quad (2.3)$$

$$78(2)\text{-}85(11), R^2 = 0.182, \text{ DW} = 1.78, (\cdot) = t \text{ statistic}$$

$$H_{t+1}^{(10)} = 0.64R_{t+1}^z + 0.367R_{t+1}^m - 246.5CC_{t+1}^{(10)} \tag{19.23}$$
$$\quad (5.75) \qquad (3.2) \qquad\quad (2.1)$$

$$78(2)\text{-}85(11), R^2 = 0.133, \text{ DW} = 2.2, (\cdot) = t \text{ statistic}$$

There is therefore some support for this 'two-factor model', namely that *both* the market return R_{t+1}^m and the consumption covariability term CC_{t+1} help in explaining excess holding period yields. However, the consumption term is relatively less well determined statistically and the additional explanatory power provided by this term is not particularly great. Bisignano (1987) estimates the zero-beta CAPM (i.e. imposes $a^{(n)} = 0$ in equation (19.23)) for a number of countries and for several different maturities between one and 20 years. In general, for Germany, the USA, Japan, the UK and Canada he finds $\beta^{(n)}$ is statistically significant and rises with term to maturity n. For example, for the USA, $\beta^{(1)} = 0.21$ ($t = 4.2$) and $\beta^{(20)} = 1.28$ ($t = 5.4$) (Table 23) indicating greater systematic risk for long bonds than for short bonds. Thus there is some support here for the zero-beta CAPM as an explanation of time varying excess HPYs on bonds even when the betas are assumed to be time invariant. Below Bisignano's model is extended by allowing the conditional covariance between $H_t^{(n)}$ and R_t^m, that is $\beta^{(n)}$, to vary not only with term to maturity but also over time.

ARCH and GARCH Models

In the CAPM risk is measured either by the asset's beta or by its covariance with the market portfolio. ARCH or GARCH processes can be used to model time varying risk premia. After setting out the model we look at some recent illustrative empirical results using this approach. We shall see that implementation of ARCH models often involves estimating a large number of parameters and in fact the estimation procedure is also highly non-linear which can create additional (convergence) problems. Because of these technical difficulties particularly when working with a finite data set, we shall see that researchers have simplified the estimation problem in various ways. First, there is usually some limitation on the number of asset returns considered (e.g. just returns on domestic bonds rather than domestic and foreign bonds) and second, the parameters of the GARCH process are usually restricted in some way (e.g. using low order rather than high order lags).

The theoretical model of the bond market outlined below incorporates bonds of varying maturities and also allows for time varying risk premia. The basic model used is the CAPM and hence time varying premia are modelled via time varying covariances. In turn, these covariances are modelled by an ARCH or GARCH process. For a bond of maturity n, the CAPM + RE implies that the excess (HPY) yield $y_{t+1}^{(n)} = [H_{t+1}^{(n)} - r_t]$ is given by:

$$y_{t+1}^{(n)} = \lambda[E_t \, \text{cov}[H_{t+1}^n, R_{t+1}^m]] + \varepsilon_{t+1}^{(n)} \qquad (19.24)$$

where λ is the market price of risk. For the *market portfolio* the excess HPY is proportional to the market price of risk and the *variance* of the excess yield on the market portfolio:

$$y_{t+1}^{(m)} = \lambda[E_t \, \text{var}[R_{t+1}^m]] + u_{t+1}^m \qquad (19.25)$$

where we assume $u_{t+1}^m \sim N(0, \sigma_{mt+1}^2)$. From (19.25) the conditional variance of the market excess HPY, $\text{var}(y^m|\Omega_t)$, is equal to $E_t[u_{t+1}^m]^2 = E_t\sigma_{mt+1}^2$. Hence (19.25) can be rewritten:

$$y^{(m)} = \lambda E_t(\sigma_m^2)_{t+1} + u_{t+1}^m \qquad (19.26)$$

From (19.24) $[y_{t+1}^{(n)} - E y_{t+1}^{(n)}] = \varepsilon_{t+1}^n$ and from (19.25) $[y_{t+1}^{(m)} - E y_{t+1}^{(m)}] = u_{t+1}^m$. Hence the *conditional covariance* of $H_{t+1}^{(n)}$ and R_{t+1}^m is given by $\text{cov}(H_{t+1}^{(n)}, R_{t+1}^m) = E_t[u_{t+1}^m \varepsilon_{t+1}^n] = \sigma_{mn}^2$. We can therefore rewrite (19.24) as:

$$y_{t+1}^{(n)} = \lambda E_t[u_{t+1}^m \varepsilon_{t+1}^n] + \varepsilon_{t+1}^n \qquad (19.27)$$

or

$$y_{t+1}^{(n)} = \lambda E_t(\sigma_{mn}^2)_{t+1} + \varepsilon_{t+1}^n \qquad (19.28)$$

Equation (19.26) for the market portfolio and (19.28) for bonds of maturity n therefore constitute our model of equilibrium assets returns. Estimation of (19.26) and (19.28) requires expressions for the variance and covariances of the error terms. A GARCH(1,1) model implies that agents forecast future variances/covariances (i.e. 'risk') on the basis of *past* variances and covariances. For an n-period bond its *own* variance (σ_n^2) and its covariance with the market σ_{nm}^2 may be represented by the following two GARCH(1,1) equations:

$$\sigma_{nt+1}^2 = \alpha_0 + \alpha_1\sigma_{nt}^2 + \alpha_2(\varepsilon_t^n)^2 \qquad (19.29)$$

$$[\sigma_{nm}^2]_{t+1} = \delta_0 + \delta_1[\sigma_{nm}^2]_t + \delta_2\varepsilon_t^n u_t^m \qquad (19.30)$$

The GARCH variance for the *market* forecast errors σ_m^2 is

$$[\sigma_m^2]_{t+1} = \gamma_0 + \gamma_1[\sigma_m^2]_t + \gamma_2(u_t^m)^2 \qquad (19.31)$$

The above equations are just a replication of the GARCH equations examined previously. Each equation implies that the conditional variance (or covariance) is a weighted average of the previous period's conditional variance (covariance) and last period's actual forecast error (or covariance of forecast errors with the market). The degree to which investors believe that a period of turbulence will *persist* in the future is given by the size of $\alpha_1 + \alpha_2$ (or $\delta_1 + \delta_2$, etc.). If $\alpha_1 + \alpha_2 = 0$ then the variance $\sigma_{nt+1}^2 = \alpha_0$ and it is not time varying. If $\alpha_1 + \alpha_2 = 1$ then a forecast error at time t, ε_t^n will influence the investor's perception of the amount of risk in *all* future periods. If $0 < (\alpha_1 + \alpha_2) < 1$ then shocks to volatility only influence perceptions of future risk, for a finite number of future periods.

The illustrative empirical application of the above model is provided by Hall et al (1992) who estimate the above model for bonds of several maturities and for a number of different countries. For each country, they assume that the market portfolio consists *only* of domestic bonds (i.e. does not contain any foreign bonds) and HPYs are measured over one month. For the *market portfolio* of bonds there is evidence of a GARCH effect as γ_1, γ_2 are non-zero. However, the conditional variance σ_{mt+1}^2 does not appear to explain, statistically at least, much of the variation in the excess market yields $E_t R_{t+1}^m - r_t$ since in equation (19.26) λ is only statistically different from zero for Japan and France (and we can accept $\lambda = 0$ for the UK, Canada, the USA and Germany). In general Hall et al also find that the *covariance* terms do not influence HPYs on bonds of maturity n (for $n = 1$-3, 3-5, 5-7, 7-9, 10-15, and greater than 15 years) in a number of countries (e.g. the UK, Japan, the USA and Germany).

Hall et al also test to see whether information at time t, namely lagged excess HPYs $(H - r)_{t-j}$ and the yield spread $[R_t^{(n)} - r_t]$, influence the excess yield $E_t y_{t+1}^n$ in equation (19.28). This is a test of whether the CAPM with time varying risk premia together with RE provides a complete explanation of excess yields. In addition, Hall et al include the conditional *(own) variance* of the n-period bond σ_n^2 alongside the covariance term σ_{nm} in equation (19.28). If the CAPM is correct the own-variance σ_n^2 should *not* influence the HPY.

In the majority of cases they reject the hypothesis that the lagged HPY and the yield spread are statistically significant. Hence Mankiw's (1986) results where the excess HPY on long bonds depends on the yield spread is refuted in the Hall et al study, when a time varying term premium is included. However, particularly at the short end of the market (e.g. 1–3 year bonds) Hall et al find that the time varying *own-variance* σ_n^2 is far more important quantitatively and statistically than the time varying covariance term σ_{nm}, thus rejecting the CAPM.

There are many potential candidates to explain the rather mixed results across maturities and countries found in the Hall et al study. Candidates include:

(i)   an approximation to HPYs is used,

(ii)   holding periods other than one month are not investigated and the one-period or 'static' CAPM is not invariant to the choice of the length of the holding period,

(iii) the market portfolio is taken to be all *domestic* bonds (e.g. no foreign bonds or any equities are included),

(iv) there are a large number of parameters to estimate from a relatively limited data set and therefore Hall et al assume that the parameters in the different GARCH equations for variances and covariances are equal (i.e. $\alpha_i = \delta_i = \gamma_i$, for $i = 1, 2$). This saves on degrees of freedom and mitigates possible difficulties in maximising a highly non-linear likelihood function but may impose invalid restrictions. In fact, even when these restrictions are imposed the likelihood function may not be well determined (i.e. may be rather 'flat').

Despite some restrictive assumptions in the Hall et al study it does suggest that time varying risk premia (which exhibit persistence) do exist in bond markets but they are rather difficult to pin down empirically and the effects are not uniform across bonds of different maturities and different countries. The study does highlight the difficulties in using the ARCH procedure to obtain a tractable model of the CAPM with time varying variances and covariances. The number of parameters to be estimated and the non-linearity of the maximisation procedure on a limited (and perhaps somewhat poor) data set imply that any results are likely to involve wide margins of error and they may not be terribly robust to slight specification changes.

19.3   INTERACTION BETWEEN STOCK AND BOND MARKETS

The CAPM determines the expected returns on *each and every* asset if agents are to retain them in their 'equilibrium' portfolio. In the CAPM, all agents hold the market portfolio of *all* assets in proportion to market value weights. However, we know that most gains from diversification may be obtained by holding around 20 assets. Given transactions cost, costs of collecting and monitoring information, as well as the need to hedge projected outflows of cash against maturing assets, then holding a subset of the market portfolio makes sense for some individuals and institutions. An investor might therefore focus his attention on the choice between *blocks* of assets and be relatively unconcerned about the specific set of assets within a particular 'block'. Thus the investor might focus his decision on the returns from holding a 'block' of six-month bills, a 'block' of long bonds and a 'block' of stocks. Over a three-month holding period the return on the above assets is uncertain.

The above simplification is used by Bollerslev et al (1988) in simultaneously modelling the HPY on these three broad classes of asset using the CAPM. They also utilise a useful decomposition of the CAPM covariance term. It is easily shown that if we have three broad assets categories that constitute the market portfolio, then

$$\text{cov}[H^{(1)}, R^m] = \text{cov}\left[H^{(1)}, \sum_1^3 w_j H^{(j)}\right]$$

$$= w_1 \text{cov}[H^{(1)} H^{(1)}] + w_2 \text{cov}[H^{(1)}, H^{(2)}] + w_3 \text{cov}[H^{(1)}, H^{(3)}]$$

$$= w_1 \sigma_{11t} + w_2 \sigma_{12t} + w_3 \sigma_{13t} \tag{19.32}$$

where w_i = value weight of each asset in the market portfolio. Thus we can split the 'single' CAPM covariance term on the LHS of (19.32) into the above three components. The estimating equations for the excess HPYs on the three assets y_{it+1} ($i = 1, 2, 3$) are of the form:

$$y_{it+1} = \alpha_i + \lambda \left[\sum_{j=1}^3 w_j \sigma_{ijt}\right] \tag{19.33}$$

where the w_j are known and λ is the market price of risk, which according to the CAPM should be the same across all assets. Bollerslev et al estimate three excess HPY equations of the form (19.32): one for six-month bills, another for 20-year bonds, and one for a stock market index. They model the three time varying variance and covariance terms using a GARCH(1,1) model (but with no restrictions on the parameters of the GARCH procedure) of the form:

$$\sigma_{ijt+1} = \alpha_{ij} + \beta_{ij} \sigma_{ijt} + \gamma_{ij} \varepsilon_{it} \varepsilon_{jt}$$

The broad thrust of the results are:

(i)   The excess holding period yield on the three assets does depend on the time varying conditional covariances since $\lambda = 0.499$ (se = 0.16).

(ii) Conditional variances and covariances are time varying and are adequately modelled using the GARCH(1,1) model. Persistence in conditional variance is greatest for bills, then for bonds and finally for stocks ($\alpha_1 + \alpha_2$ equals 0.91, 0.62 and 0.55, respectively).

(iii) Although the CAPM does *not* imply that conditional covariances should explain all of the movement in *ex-post* excess HPYs (because the arrival of 'news' causes a divergence between y_{t+1} and $E_t y_{t+1}$) one can see that *actual* HPYs vary much more than the expected HPY given by the *prediction* from (19.32) (see Figure 19.1) for bills (the graphs for bonds and stocks are qualitatively similar).

The CAPM with GARCH time varying volatilities does reasonably well empirically in explaining HPYs and when the *own variance* from the GARCH equations is added to (19.32) it is statistically insignificant (as one would expect under the CAPM). However, the CAPM does not provide a 'complete' explanation of excess HPYs. For example, when the lagged excess HPY, for asset i, is added to the CAPM equation for asset i, it is found to be statistically highly significant — this rejects the simple static CAPM formulation. Also when a 'surprise consumption' variable is added to the CAPM equations, it is usually statistically significant. This indicates rejection of the simple one-factor CAPM and suggests the consumption CAPM might have additional explanatory power.

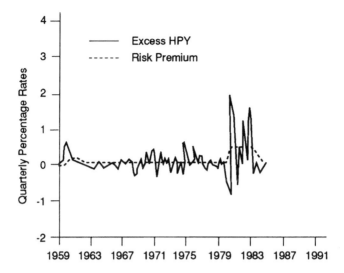

Figure 19.1 Risk Premia for Bills. *Source*: Bollerslev et al (1988). 'A Capital Asset Pricing Model with Time Varying Covariances', *Journal of Political Economy*, 96(1), Fig. 1, pp. 1116–1131. Reproduced by permission of University of Chicago Press

The Bollerslev et al model of expected returns in equation (19.32) is very similar to that of Thomas and Wickens (1993) described in Chapter 18. The difference between the two approaches is that Thomas and Wickens consider a wider set of assets (e.g. including foreign bonds and stocks), they allow the shares w_i to vary and they test (and reject) the additional restriction that the elements σ_{ij} are equal to the variance–covariance matrix of error terms. However, the less restrictive model of Bollerslev et al does appear to work better empirically.

19.4 SUMMARY

There appears to be only very weak evidence of a time varying term premium for short-term zero coupon bonds (bills). As the variability in the price of bills is in most periods smaller than that of long-term bonds (or equities) this result is perhaps not too surprising. When the short-term bill markets experience severe volatility (e.g. USA, 1979–1982) then the evidence of persistence in time varying term premia and the impact of the conditional variance on expected return is much stronger.

Holding period yields on long-term bonds do seem to be influenced by time varying conditional variances and covariances but the stability of such relationships are open to question. While ARCH and GARCH models provide a useful statistical basis for modelling time varying second moments the complexity of some of the parameterisations is such that precise parameter estimates are often not obtained in empirical work. In some studies the conditional second moments appear to be highly persistent. If, in addition, they are thought to affect required returns then shocks to variances and hence to risk premia can have a strong impact on bond prices. However, such results are sometimes found to be sensitive to specification changes in the ARCH process.

It was noted in Chapter 17 that generally speaking the above points also apply to empirical work on stock returns. However, there is perhaps somewhat stronger evidence for stocks of persistence in time varying volatilities and that volatility affects equilibrium returns, than there is for bonds. However, as far as stock returns are concerned it is still an open question as to whether the time series behaviour of conditional volatility is different in periods of 'high and low' volatility.

ENDNOTES

1. This is most easily demonstrated assuming continuously compounded rates. For a fixed maturity value M on a zero coupon bond we have:

$$\ln P_t^{(3)} = \ln M - (1/4)r_t \tag{1}$$

$$\ln P_t^{(6)} = \ln M - (1/2)R_t \tag{2}$$

Hence:

$$H_{t+13} \equiv \ln P_{t+13}^{(3)} - \ln P_t^{(6)} = (1/2)R_t - (1/4)r_{t+13} \tag{3}$$

The *excess* HPY is:

$$H_{t+13} - (1/4)r_t \tag{4}$$

and substituting from (3) in (4) we see that the expected excess HPY is given by $2R_t - E_t r_{t+13} - r_t$ as in the text.

2. Given that for continuously compounded rates on zero coupon bonds, $\ln P_t^{(n)} = \ln M - nR_t^{(n)}$ the absolute change in interest rates on an n-period bond is proportional to the percentage change in the price of the bond.

FURTHER READING

The recent literature in this area tends to be very technical, covering a wide variety of ARCH/GARCH-type models as well as non-parametric and stochastic volatility models. Cuthbertson et al (1992) and Mills (1993) provide brief overviews of the use of ARCH and GARCH models in finance. Overviews of the econometric issues are given in Pagan and Schwert (1990), Bollerslev et al (1992), with Bollerslev (1986) and Engle (1995) being the most accessible of these four sources.

PART 7
Econometric Issues in Testing Asset Pricing Models

This section of the book presents a brief overview of the key concepts used in the econometric analysis of time series data on financial variables. Since these concepts and techniques are widely used in the finance literature dealing with discrete time models, the material is included in order to make the book as self-contained as possible. The treatment of these topics is fairly brief and concentrates on the use to which these techniques can be put rather than detailed proofs. Nevertheless, it should provide a concise introduction to this complex subject matter.

First, an analysis is given of univariate time series covering topics such as autoregressive and moving average representations, stationarity and non-stationary, conditional and unconditional forecasts and the distinction between deterministic and stochastic trends. Then the extension of these ideas in a multivariate framework (Section 20.2) and the relationship between structural economic models, VARs and the literature on cointegration and error correction models are considered. Section 20.3 presents the basic ideas behind ARCH and GARCH models and their use in modelling time varying variances and covariances. Attention will not be given to detailed estimation issues of ARCH models (for this see Bollerslev (1986)) but on the economic interpretation of these models. Section 20.4 outlines some basic issues in estimating models which invoke the rational expectations assumption, a key hypothesis in many of the tests reported in the rest of this book. Again the aim is not a definitive account of these active research areas but to present an overview which will enable the reader to understand the basis of the empirical results reported elsewhere in the book.

20
Economic and Statistical Models

20.1 UNIVARIATE TIME SERIES

An 'economic model' can be defined as one that has some basis in economic theory. Economic theory usually yields 'static equilibrium' or 'long-run' relationships. For example, if purchasing power parity (PPP) holds then the log of the nominal exchange rate y is linked to the price of domestic goods relative to the price of foreign goods $x_t = \ln P_t - \ln P_t^*$. If we assume instantaneous adjustment we have:

$$y_t = \beta_1 + \beta_2 x_t + \varepsilon_t \tag{20.1}$$

where ε_t is a random error term which is often taken to be white noise (see below). Under PPP, we expect $\beta_2 = 1$. However, it may be possible to obtain a 'good' representation of the behaviour of a variable y_t without recourse to any economic theory. For example, a purely statistical model of the exchange rate y_t is the *univariate autoregressive model* of order 1, that is AR(1):

$$y_t = \alpha + \beta y_{t-1} + \varepsilon_t \tag{20.2}$$

It may be the case that *some* economic theory is consistent with equation (20.2) but the purely statistical or time series modeller would not be concerned or probably not be aware of this. Clearly then the 'statistical modeller' and 'economic modeller' might end up with the same statistical representation of the data. However, their motivation and criteria as to whether the representation is 'adequate' may well be different. Both the statistical and the economic modellers require that their models adequately characterise the data. However, the economic modeller will also generally require that his model is in conformity with some economic theory.

Whether one is a statistical modeller or an economic modeller it is useful to classify the data one is using in various ways. To set the ball rolling consider the following univariate autoregressive model of order 1, AR(1), for y_t:

$$y_t = \beta y_{t-1} + \varepsilon_t \tag{20.3}$$

where ε_t is a zero-mean random variable with constant variance σ^2, and ε_t is uncorrelated with any other variable in the sequence $\{\varepsilon_{t-j}, j = \pm 1, \pm 2, \ldots\}$

$$E\varepsilon_t = 0 \qquad \forall t \tag{20.4a}$$

$$\text{var}(\varepsilon_t) = E(\varepsilon_t^2) = \sigma^2 \qquad \forall t \tag{20.4b}$$

$$\text{cov}(\varepsilon_t, \varepsilon_{t-j}) = 0 \qquad \forall j \neq 0 \text{ and } t \tag{20.4c}$$

The above properties denote a (zero-mean) *white noise* process. If in addition ε_t has a normal distribution then it is called Gaussian white noise.

The Lag Operator

We can represent (20.3) as:

$$(1 - \beta L)y_t = \varepsilon_t \tag{20.5}$$

L is the lag operator, such that $L^m y_t \equiv y_{t-m}$ and $(1 - \beta L)$ is said to be a polynomial (or order 1) in the lag operator. An equivalent representation of (20.5) is:

$$y_t = (1 - \beta L)^{-1}\varepsilon_t \tag{20.6a}$$

$$= [1 + \beta L + (\beta L)^2 + (\beta L)^3 + \cdots]\varepsilon_t \tag{20.6b}$$

$$y_t = \varepsilon_t + \beta\varepsilon_{t-1} + \beta^2\varepsilon_{t-2} + \beta^3\varepsilon_{t-3} + \cdots \tag{20.6c}$$

y_t is therefore an infinite geometrically weighted average of the error term ε_t. We could also have obtained (20.6c) by repeated 'back substitution':

$$y_t = \beta(\beta y_{t-2} + \varepsilon_{t-1}) + \varepsilon_t \tag{20.7a}$$

$$y_t = \beta^2(\beta y_{t-3} + \varepsilon_{t-2}) + \beta\varepsilon_{t-1} + \varepsilon_t \tag{20.7b}$$

$$y_t = \beta^n y_{t-n} + \varepsilon_t + \beta\varepsilon_{t-1} + \beta^2\varepsilon_{t-2} + \cdots \tag{20.7c}$$

As long as $|\beta| < 1$ then $\beta^n \to 0$ as $n \to \infty$ and the term $\beta^n y_{t-n}$ becomes insignificant. The lag operator is a convenient shorthand and is useful in manipulating certain expressions. For example

$$(1 - \beta L)^{-1}\varepsilon_t = (1 + \beta L + \beta^2 L^2 + \cdots)\varepsilon_t$$

$$= \varepsilon_t + \beta\varepsilon_{t-1} + \beta^2\varepsilon_{t-2} + \cdots \tag{20.8a}$$

It is obvious that y_t in (20.7c) depends on current and all past values of $\varepsilon_{t-j}(j > 1)$, however y_t is uncorrelated with *future* values of $\varepsilon_{t+j}(j \geqslant 1)$.

Stationarity

If $|\beta| < 1$ then y_t is a stationary series. Broadly speaking a stationary series has a *constant* mean and variance and the correlation between values y_t and y_{t-j} depends only on the *time difference* 'j'. Thus the mean, variance and (auto-) correlation for any lag 'j' are independent of time. A stationary series tends to return often to its mean value and the variability of the series doesn't alter as we move through time (Figure 20.1).

The condition for stationarity $|\beta| < 1$ can be seen intuitively by noting that if we have a starting value y_0 then subsequent values of y in periods 1, 2, ... are βy_0, $\beta^2 y_0$, etc. plus the random error terms ε_1, $(\beta\varepsilon_1 + \varepsilon_2)$, $(\beta^2\varepsilon_1 + \beta\varepsilon_2 + \varepsilon_3)$, etc. If $|\beta| < 1$ then the deterministic part of y, namely $\beta^n y_0$, approaches zero and the weighted average of the ε_is are also finite (and eventually they tend to cancel out as the ε_is are random around zero). Hence y_{t+n}:

$$y_{t+n} = \beta^n y_t + \varepsilon_{t+n} + \beta\varepsilon_{t+n-1} + \beta^2\varepsilon_{t+n-2} + \cdots$$

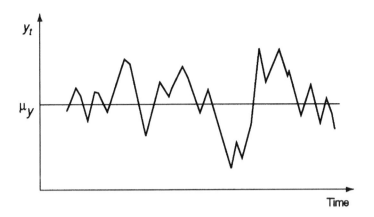

Figure 20.1 Stationary Series.

remains finite. More formally a process is 'weakly' or 'covariance' stationary if:

$$E y_t = \mu \qquad \text{(20.9a)}$$

$$\text{var}(y_t) = \sigma^2 \qquad \text{(20.9b)}$$

$$\text{cov}(y_t, y_{t-j}) = \gamma_j \qquad \text{(20.9c)}$$

where all the RHS population 'moments' are independent of time t and have finite values. If in addition y_t is normally distributed then the process represented by (20.9a) to (20.9c) is *strongly stationary*. However, the distinction between weak and strong stationarity is not important in what follows so 'stationarity' is used to mean 'weak' or 'covariance' stationary. A white noise error term ε_t is a very specific type of stationary series where the mean and covariance are zero.

All the usual hypothesis testing procedures in statistics are based on the assumption that the variables used in constructing the tests are stationary. For a non-stationary series the distribution of 'conventional' test statistics may not be well behaved. The statistical properties of tests on non-stationary series generally involve substantial changes to aspects of the 'conventional' tests (e.g. special tables of critical values). To illustrate the case of a non-stationary series consider:

$$y_t = \alpha + \beta y_{t-1} + \varepsilon_t \qquad \text{(20.10)}$$

where $\beta = 1$ and ε_t is white noise. This is known as a *random walk with drift*. The drift parameter is α and the model is:

$$\Delta y_t = \alpha + \varepsilon_t \qquad \text{(20.11)}$$

The *growth* in y_t (assume y_t is in natural logarithms) is a constant ($= \alpha$) plus a white noise error. The realisation of (20.10) is shown in Figure 20.2. Clearly y_t has a mean which increases over time and hence the *level* of y_t is non-stationary.

If $\alpha = 0$ and $\beta = 1$ we have a *random walk without drift*. The realisation of y_t is shown in Figure 20.2 and y_t is non-stationary because the (unconditional) variance of y_t gets larger as $n \to \infty$ and therefore is not independent of time.

$$y_t = (1 - L)^{-1} \varepsilon_t = \varepsilon_t + \varepsilon_t + \varepsilon_{t-1} + \varepsilon_{t-2} + \cdots \qquad \text{(20.12a)}$$

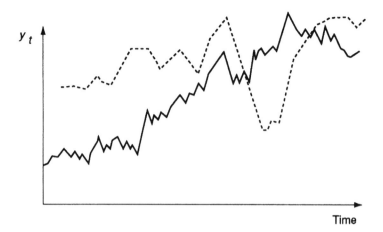

Figure 20.2 Non-Stationary Series. Random Walk with Drift(————), Random Walk with Zero Drift(-----)

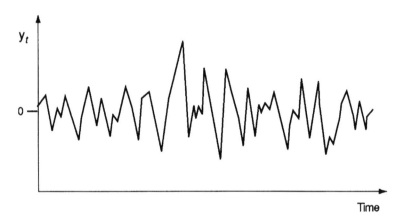

Figure 20.3 MA(I) Series ($y_t = \varepsilon_t - 0.5\varepsilon_{t-1}$).

$$E y_t = 0 \tag{20.12b}$$

$$\text{var}(y_t) = E\left[\sum_1^n \varepsilon_t^2 + 2\sum_{t \neq s} \varepsilon_t \varepsilon_s\right] = n\sigma^2 \tag{20.12c}$$

Hence var$(y_t) \to \infty$ as $n \to \infty$.

Moving Average Process

Another simple time series representation of y_t is the moving average process of order 1, MA(1):

$$y_t = \varepsilon_t + \lambda\varepsilon_{t-1} = (1 + \lambda L)\varepsilon_t \tag{20.13}$$

a realisation of which is shown in Figure (20.3). An equivalent representation is:

$$(1 + \lambda L)^{-1} y_t = \varepsilon_t$$

$$y_t = -\sum_{j=1}^{\infty}(-\lambda)^j y_{t-j} + \varepsilon_t \qquad (20.14)$$

provided $|\lambda| < 1$. Comparing (20.13) and (20.14) we note that an MA(1) process (with $|\lambda| < 1$) may be represented as an infinite autoregressive process. For $|\lambda| < 1$ the MA(1) process is said to be 'invertible'. Similarly, comparing (20.3) and (20.6c) an AR(1) process may be represented as an infinite moving average process (for $|\beta| < 1$).

ARIMA Process

If a series is non-stationary, then differencing often produces a stationary series. For example, if the level of y_t is a random walk with drift then Δy_t is stationary (see equation (20.11)). Any stationary stochastic time series y_t can be approximated by a mixed *autoregressive moving average* (ARMA) process of order (p, q), that is ARMA(p, q):

$$y_t = \phi_1 y_{t-1} + \phi_2 y_{t-2} + \cdots \phi_p y_{t-p} + \varepsilon_t + \theta_1 \varepsilon_{t-1} + \theta_2 \varepsilon_{t-2} + \cdots \theta_q \varepsilon_{t-q} \quad (20.15a)$$

$$\phi(L)y_t = \theta(L)\varepsilon_t$$

where ϕ (L) and θ (L) are polynomials in the lag operator:

$$\phi(L) = 1 - \phi_1 L - \phi_2 L^2 - \phi_3 L^3 - \cdots - \phi_p L^p \qquad (20.15b)$$

$$\phi(L) = 1 + \theta_1 L + \theta_2 L^2 + \cdots + \theta_q L^q \qquad (20.15c)$$

The *stationarity condition* then is that the roots of ϕ (L) lie *outside* the unit circle (i.e. all the roots of ϕ (L) are greater than one in absolute value). A similar condition must be placed on θ (L) to ensure *invertibility* (i.e. that the MA(q) part may be written in terms of an infinite autoregression on y, see equation (20.14)).

If a series needs differencing d times (for most economic time series $d = 1$ or 2 is sufficient) to yield a stationary series then $\Delta^d y_t$ can be modelled as an ARMA (p, q) process or equivalently the level of y_t is an ARIMA(p, d, q) model. For example, Granger (1966) demonstrates that many economic time series (e.g. GDP, consumption, income) may be adequately represented by a purely statistical ARIMA(0,1,1) model:

$$\Delta y_t = \delta + \varepsilon_t + \theta \varepsilon_{t-1} \qquad (20.16)$$

Autocorrelation Function: Correlogram

The properties of univariate time series models may be summarised by the (population) autocorrelation function and its sample analogue, the correlogram. The (population) autocorrelation between y_t and $y_{t-\tau}(\tau = 0, \pm 1, \pm 2, \ldots)$ is

$$\rho_\tau = \gamma_\tau / \gamma_0 \qquad (20.17a)$$

where γ_τ is the *autocovariance function* at lag τ.

$$\gamma_\tau = \text{cov}(y_t, y_{t-\tau}) \qquad (20.17b)$$

$$\gamma_0 = \text{var}(y_t) \qquad (20.17c)$$

By definition $\rho_0 = 1$. There is a value of ρ_τ for each lag τ, and the autocorrelations are dimensionless. The sign of ρ_τ indicates whether y_t and $y_{t-\tau}$ are positively or negatively correlated. The *sample* autocorrelations are:

$$\hat{\rho}_\tau = c_\tau / c_0 \quad (\tau = 1, 2, 3 \ldots) \tag{20.18a}$$

where c_τ is the sample autocovariance:

$$c_\tau = n^{-1} \sum_{t=\tau+1}^{n} (y_t - \bar{y})(y_{t-\tau} - \bar{y}) \quad (\tau = 0, 1, 2, \ldots) \tag{20.18b}$$

A plot of $\hat{\rho}_\tau$ against τ is called the correlogram. The correlogram is useful in helping to classify the type of ARIMA model that might best characterise the data. A correlogram that approaches zero as τ increases indicates a stationary series, whereas a 'flat' correlogram indicates that the series must be differenced at least once to yield a stationary series. For example, if y_t is a random walk with drift, equation (20.10), then y_t and the first difference of this series, Δy_t, have correlograms like those of Figure 20.4. The correlograms for the stationary AR(1) model (with $0 < \beta < 1$) and the MA(1) model (with $0 < \lambda < 1$) as represented by equations (20.3) and (20.13), respectively, have the distinctive shapes shown in Figure 20.5. Hence a researcher wishing to model y_t as a univariate time series could immediately *identify* from the correlograms in Figure 20.5 what type of model to estimate. When y_t is generated by a more complex ARMA(p, q) process then the shape of the correlogram can only be taken as indicative of the type of ARMA model to estimate. The information given by the shape of the correlogram and the appropriate choice of univariate 'time series' model forms the basis of Box–Jenkins or time series modelling.

Forecasts and the Variance of Forecast Errors

This section demonstrates the relationship between unconditional forecasts and conditional forecasts and their associated forecast error variances using a simple stationary AR(1) model

$$y_t = \alpha + \beta y_{t-1} + \varepsilon_t \qquad |\beta| < 1 \tag{20.19}$$

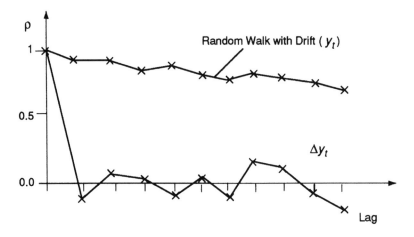

Figure 20.4 Correlogram for Random Walk with Drift (y_t) and for Δy_t.

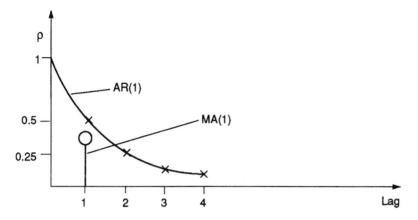

Figure 20.5 Correlogram for AR(1) ($y_t = 0.5y_{t-1} + \varepsilon_t$) and MA(1) ($y_t = \varepsilon_t + 0.5\varepsilon_{t-1}$).

where ε_t is $N(0, \sigma^2)$ and ε_t is uncorrelated with y_{t-1}. For $|\beta| < 1$ we have from (20.19) by back substitution:

$$y_t = (\alpha + \alpha\beta + \alpha\beta^2 + \cdots) + \beta^m y_{t-m} + \varepsilon_t + \beta\varepsilon_{t-1} + \beta^2\varepsilon_{t-2} + \cdots$$

$$y_t = \frac{\alpha}{1 - \beta} + \varepsilon_t + \beta\varepsilon_{t-1} + \beta^2\varepsilon_{t-2} + \cdots \tag{20.20}$$

where for $|\beta| < 1$, the term $\beta^m y_{t-m}$ approaches zero. At time t the *unconditional mean* of y_t from (20.20) is:

$$E y_t = \mu \tag{20.21}$$

where $\mu = \alpha/(1 - \beta)$ and we have used $E_t\varepsilon_{t-j} = 0$ ($j \geqslant 0$). We can interpret the unconditional (population) mean of y_t as the best forecast of y_t when we have no information about previous values of y. Alternatively, it is the 'average value' around which y_t oscillates in the population. Now let us calculate the *unconditional variance* of y_t. Using (20.20) and (20.21) we can easily see that

$$(y_t - \mu) = \alpha + \beta y_{t-1} + \varepsilon_t - \alpha/(1 - \beta) = \beta(y_{t-1} - \mu) + \varepsilon_t \tag{20.22}$$

Hence

$$E(y_t - \mu)^2 = \beta^2 E(y_{t-1} - \mu)^2 + \text{var}(\varepsilon_t) + 2\beta \, \text{cov}(y_{t-1} - \mu, \varepsilon_t) \tag{20.23}$$

For a stationary series $\text{var}(y_t) = \text{var}(y_{t-1})$ and because ε_t is uncorrelated with $(y_{t-1} - \mu)$ the last term is zero, hence the unconditional variance of y_t is:

$$\text{var}(y_t) = \sigma^2/(1 - \beta^2) \tag{20.24}$$

It is also useful to derive this variance from (20.20)

$$\text{var}(y_t) = E(y_t - \mu)^2 = E\left[\sum_{i=1}^{\infty} \beta^i \varepsilon_{t-i}\right]^2$$

$$= \sigma^2(1 + \beta^2 + \beta^4 + \beta^6 + \cdots)$$

where we have $E(\varepsilon_t \varepsilon_{t-i}) = 0$ for $i \neq 0$ and $E(\varepsilon_t^2) = \sigma^2$ for all t. Hence for $|\beta| < 1$ we again have

$$\text{var}(y_t) = \sigma^2/(1 - \beta^2) \tag{20.25}$$

The unconditional variance is the 'best guess' of the variance without any knowledge of recent past values of y. In the non-stationary case $\beta = 1$ and the unconditional mean and variance are infinite (undefined). This is clear from equations (20.21) and (20.25) and is the mathematical equivalent of the statement that 'a random walk series can wander anywhere'.

Conditional Mean and Variance: Stationary Series

In calculating the conditional mean and variance we have to be precise about the dating of the information set Ω. If we have information at t or earlier (i.e. on y_{t-j} or ε_{t-j}, $j \geq 0$) then the conditional mean of y_t is denoted $E(y_t|\Omega_t)$ or $E_t y_t$ for short. From (20.19) the conditional mean in the AR(1) model for different forecast horizons is obtained by forward substitution:

$$E_t y_{t+1} = \alpha + \beta y_t$$

$$E_t y_{t+2} = \alpha(1 + \beta) + \beta^2 y_t$$

$$E_t y_{t+m} = \alpha(1 + \beta + \beta^2 + \beta^{m-1}) + \beta^m y_t \tag{20.26}$$

The conditional variance, given information at time t, for different forecast horizons m is defined as

$$\text{var}(y_{t+m}|\Omega_t) = E\left[y_{t+m} - E(y_t|\Omega_t)\right]^2 \tag{20.27}$$

By successive substitution:

$$y_{t+2} = \alpha + \beta y_{t+1} + \varepsilon_{t+2} = \alpha + \beta(\alpha + \beta y_t + \varepsilon_{t+1}) + \varepsilon_{t+2}$$
$$= \alpha(1 + \beta) + \beta^2 y_t + \beta \varepsilon_{t+1} + \varepsilon_{t+2}$$

and

$$y_{t+3} = \alpha + \beta y_{t+2} + \varepsilon_{t+3}$$
$$= \alpha(1 + \beta + \beta^2) + \beta^3 y_t + (\beta^2 \varepsilon_{t+1} + \beta \varepsilon_{t+2} + \varepsilon_{t+3})$$

$$y_{t+m} = \alpha \sum_{i=0}^{m-1} \beta^i + \beta^m y_t + \sum_{i=0}^{m-1} \beta^i \varepsilon_{t+m-i} \tag{20.28}$$

Using (20.6), (20.7) and (20.8) the conditional variances at various forecast errors are

$$\text{var}(y_{t+1}|\Omega_t) = \sigma^2$$

$$\text{var}(y_{t+3}|\Omega_t) = (1 + \beta^2 + \beta^4)\sigma^2$$

$$\text{var}(y_{t+m}|\Omega_t) = (1 + \beta^2 + \beta^4 + \cdots \beta^{2m-2})\sigma^2 \tag{20.29}$$

We can immediately see by comparing (20.25) and (20.29) that the conditional variance is always less than the unconditional variance at all forecast horizons. Of course as $m \to \infty$

the conditional variance (20.29) approaches the unconditional variance $\sigma^2/(1 - \beta^2)$. Conditional variances are smaller than the unconditional variance because the former uses the information in the stochastic behaviour in (20.19) in forecasting future values of y_{t+m}.

Conditional Mean and Variance: Non-Stationary Series

The above analysis is repeated with $\beta = 1$. After 'm' periods the expected value of y_{t+m} is

$$E_t y_{t+m} = y_t + \alpha m \tag{20.30}$$

Since y_t is a fixed starting point (which we can set to zero), the (conditional) expected value of y_{t+m} is a deterministic time trend 'αm' (cf. $y_t = a + bt$). However, the *stochastic* behaviour of the RW ($\beta = 1$) with drift ($\alpha \neq 0$) is given by

$$y_{t+m} = \alpha m + y_t + (\varepsilon_{t+m} + \varepsilon_{t+m} + \cdots \varepsilon_{t+1}) \tag{20.31}$$

and is often referred to as a *stochastic trend*. This is because in addition to the deterministic trend element 'αm', there is a stochastic moving average error. For the random walk without drift ($\alpha = 0$) the best *conditional* forecast of *all* future values of y is simply the current value y_t.

Unlike the stationary case, the influence of past errors on y_{t+m} does not diminish as $m \to \infty$ since the $\Sigma \varepsilon_{t+i}$ terms are not 'weighted' by $|\beta| < 1$ (see (20.31)). The conditional variance of the forecasts can be obtained from (20.29) by setting $\beta = 1$ and is given by:

$$\text{var}(y_{t+m}|\Omega_t) = m\sigma^2 \tag{20.32}$$

As m increases the variance increases and approaches infinity as the forecast horizon $m \to \infty$. The conditional variance for a random walk series is explosive.

Deterministic and Stochastic Trends

A deterministic trend is given by

$$y_t = \alpha + \beta t + \varepsilon_t \tag{20.33}$$

where t takes the values 1, 2, 3 ..., etc. The dependent variable y_t in (20.33) is non-stationary since its mean rises continuously over time. The mean of y_t is $\alpha + \beta t$ and hence is independent of other economic variables, even when considering a forecast into the distant future. The conditional forecast error is σ^2 and it does not increase the longer the forecast horizon. Our stochastic trend for the RW with drift may be written

$$y_t = y_0 + \beta t + (\varepsilon_t + \varepsilon_{t-1} + \cdots + \varepsilon_1)$$

Hence the stochastic trend has an infinite memory: the initial historic value of y at $t = 0$ (i.e. y_0) has an influence on all future values of y. The implications of deterministic and stochastic trends in forecasting are very different as are the properties of test statistics applied to these two types of series. We need some statistical tests to discriminate between these two hypotheses. Appropriate 'detrending' of a deterministic trend involves a regression of y_t on 'time' but for a stochastic trend (i.e. random walk) 'detrending' involves taking first differences of the series (i.e. using Δy_t).

If a series is detrended incorrectly then incorrect inferences based on a statistical analysis of the 'detrended' series are very likely to be misleading. For example, if a random walk with drift is regressed on time (i.e. $t = 1, 2, 3, \ldots$), a very high R^2 (which approaches 1 as the sample size increases) is obtained even though there is in reality no deterministic time trend present (this is often referred to as the spurious regression problem). Also if a random walk series is detrended using a deterministic trend and hence the new detrended series is $y_t - \hat{\beta}t$ then the autocorrelation function will (spuriously) indicate positive correlation at low lags and a cyclical pattern at high lags.

Summary

It may be useful to summarise briefly the main points dealt with so far, these are:

- A stationary series is one that has a mean, variance and autocovariances in the population (of data) that are independent of time and are finite. The population mean and variance are constant and the covariance between y_t and y_{t-m} depends only on the lag length 'm' (and is constant for any *given* lag length). Since the population moments (i.e. mean, variance and covariance) are constant, they can usually be consistently estimated by their sample analogues.

- A graph of a stationary series (for the population of data) has no discernible 'long' upward or downward trend, the series frequently crosses its mean value (μ) and the variability of the series around the mean value is, *on average*, a constant deviation (which is finite).

- A non-stationary series is one that either has its population mean or its variance or its autocovariances which vary over time. In some special cases the population (unconditional) mean, variance (or even covariance) may approach plus or minus infinity (i.e. be undefined).

- The simplest form of non-stationary series is the random walk with drift (with a Gaussian error)

$$y_t = \alpha + \beta y_{t-1} + \varepsilon_t \quad \text{where } \beta = 1$$
$$(1 - \beta L)y_t = \alpha + \varepsilon_t$$

The non-stationary series y_t is said to have a unit root in the lag polynomial, that is $(1 - \beta L)$ has $\beta = 1$. If $\alpha = 0$ the best conditional forecast of y_{t+m} based on information at time t, for all horizons 'm', is simply the current value y_t. For $\alpha \neq 0$ the best conditional forecast of y_{t+m} is αm.

- Stochastic trends and deterministic trends have different time series properties and must be modelled differently.

- It may be shown that any stationary stochastic series y_t may be represented by an infinite moving average of white noise errors (plus a deterministic component, which will be ignored). This is Wold's decomposition theorem. If the moving average component is invertible then the y_t may also be represented by an infinite autoregression. A finite lag ARMA(p, q) process may provide a parsimonious approximation to the infinite lag AR or MA process.

- The unconditional mean of a stationary series may be viewed as the long-run value to which the series settles down. The unconditional variance gives a measure of the size of movements around the unconditional mean. The conditional mean uses the information in the time series process to help forecast future values of y_t and this results in the conditional variance of the forecast errors being smaller than the unconditional variance.

20.2   MULTIVARIATE TIME SERIES MODELS

This section generalises the results for the univariate time series models discussed above to a multivariate framework. In particular, it will show how a multivariate system may be reduced to a univariate system. Since the real world is a multivariate system the arguments concerning the appropriate choice of multivariate system to use in practical situations will be discussed and a brief look taken of the relationship between a structural *economic* model and a multivariate time series representation of the data. Finally a multivariate system where some variables may be cointegrated will be examined.

It is convenient at this point to summarise the results of the univariate case. Wold's decomposition theorem states that any stationary stochastic series y_t may be represented as a univariate infinite moving average of white noise errors (plus a deterministic component, which we ignore throughout, for simplicity of exposition):

$$y_t = \sum_{i=0}^{\infty} \theta_i \varepsilon_{t-i} = \theta(L)\varepsilon_t \quad (\theta_0 = 1) \tag{20.34}$$

where $\theta(L) = (1 + \theta_1 L + \theta_2 L^2 + \cdots)$. If $\theta(L)$ is invertible then y_t may also be represented as an infinite univariate autoregression, from (20.33):

$$\theta^{-1}(L)y_t = \varepsilon_t$$

or

$$y_t = f(y_{t-j}) + \varepsilon_t \tag{20.34a}$$

A stationary series may also be represented as an ARMA (p, q) model:

$$\phi(L)y_t = \theta(L)\varepsilon_t \tag{20.35}$$

As y_t is stationary the roots of $\phi(L)$ lie outside the unit circle and (20.35) may be transformed into an infinite MA model

$$y_t = \phi^{-1}(L)\theta(L)\varepsilon_t = g(\varepsilon_{t-j}) \tag{20.36}$$

or if $\theta(L)$ is invertible then (20.35) may also be transformed into an infinite lag AR model plus a white noise error

$$\theta^{-1}(L)\phi(L)y_t = \varepsilon_t$$

or

$$y_t = f(y_{t-j}) + \varepsilon_t \tag{20.37}$$

Hence we have a number of alternative equivalent representations of any univariate time series y_t. By using a matrix formulation we will see that the above alternative representations apply to a multivariate system.

Vector Representations

We can generalise the single equation ARMA model by considering a system of equations where each variable y_{it} depends on lags of itself y_{it-m} and of all other variables y_{jt-m} and a moving average of white noise errors. For any set of stationary variables (we will consider only three for illustrative purposes) the vector autoregressive moving average model (VARMA) is

$$\phi_{11}(L)y_{1t} = \phi_{12}(L)y_{2t} + \phi_{13}(L)y_{3t} + \theta_{11}(L)\varepsilon_{1t} + \theta_{12}(L)\varepsilon_{2t} + \theta_{13}(L)\varepsilon_{3t}$$

$$\phi_{22}(L)y_{2t} = \phi_{21}(L)y_{1t} + \phi_{23}(L)y_{3t} + \theta_{21}(L)\varepsilon_{1t} + \theta_{22}(L)\varepsilon_{2t} + \theta_{23}(L)\varepsilon_{3t}$$

$$\phi_{33}(L)y_{3t} = \phi_{32}(L)y_{2t} + \phi_{31}(L)y_{1t} + \theta_{31}(L)\varepsilon_{1t} + \theta_{32}(L)\varepsilon_{2t} + \theta_{33}(L)\varepsilon_{3t} \quad (20.38)$$

where $\phi_{11}, \phi_{22}, \phi_{33}$ are of the form $\phi_{11} = (1 - \phi_{11}^{(1)}L - \phi_{11}^{(2)}L^2 - \cdots)$ Hence each equation is of the form

$$y_{1t} = f_1[(y_{1t-1}, y_{1t-2}, \ldots), (y_{2t-1}, y_{2t-2}, \ldots), (y_{3t-1}, y_{3t-2}, \ldots), \text{ error terms}]$$

The above equations can be represented in matrix form as:

$$\mathbf{\Phi}(L)\mathbf{Y}_t = \mathbf{\Theta}(L)\varepsilon_t \quad (20.39)$$

where $\mathbf{Y}_t = (y_{1t}, y_{2t}, y_{3t})$ and $\varepsilon_t = (\varepsilon_{1t}, \varepsilon_{2t}, \varepsilon_{3t})$ and $\mathbf{\Phi}(L)$ and $\mathbf{\Theta}(L)$ are conformable matrices which depend on the ϕ_{ij} and θ_{ij} parameters, respectively.

The VARMA equation system (20.39) is consistent with Wold's decomposition theorem if all the roots of $\mathbf{\Phi}(L)$ lie outside the unit circle, since (20.39) implies:

$$\mathbf{Y}_t = \mathbf{\Phi}^{-1}(L)\mathbf{\Theta}(L)\varepsilon_t$$

Hence each y_{it} can be represented as an infinite moving average of current and past white noise errors ε_t. Since any linear combination of $(\varepsilon_{1t}, \varepsilon_{2t}, \varepsilon_{3t})$ can also be represented in terms of a MA of a *single* error, say, v_{it}, then each y_{it} can be written:

$$y_{it} = f(v_{it}, v_{it-1}, v_{it-2}, \ldots) \quad (20.40)$$

It is also straightforward to see that if $\mathbf{\Theta}(L)$ is invertible then:

$$\mathbf{\Theta}^{-1}(L)\mathbf{\Phi}(L)\mathbf{Y}_t = \varepsilon_t \quad (20.41)$$

and hence any set of variables $y_{it} (i = 1, 2, 3)$ may be represented as an infinite vector autoregression plus a linear combination of white noise errors $\varepsilon_{it} (i = 1, 2, 3)$. That is each y_{it}, take y_{1t} as an example, is of the form

$$y_{1t} = \alpha_1(L)y_{1t-1} + \alpha_2(L)y_{2t-1} + \alpha_3(L)y_{3t-1} + v_{1t} \quad (20.42)$$

where v_{1t} is a linear combination of white noise errors at time t and hence is itself white noise. The above representation is known as a vector autoregression (VAR) and in matrix notation is:

$$\mathbf{Y}_t = \mathbf{A}(L)\mathbf{Y}_{t-1} + \mathbf{v}_t \quad (20.43)$$

Can we Reduce the Size of the VARMA System?

It can now be demonstrated how

- a 'large' VARMA or VAR system can be reduced to a 'smaller' VARMA or VAR system
- a VARMA or VAR system can be reduced to a univariate system

To simplify the algebra consider reducing a simple 2×2 system to a univariate system. We begin with a VARMA (2×2) model:

$$y_{1t} = \phi_{11}y_{1t-1} + \phi_{12}y_{2t-1} + \theta_1(L)\varepsilon_{1t} \tag{20.44}$$

$$y_{2t} = \phi_{21}y_{1t-1} + \phi_{22}y_{2t-1} + \theta_2(L)\varepsilon_{2t} \tag{20.45}$$

and will only derive the univariate equation for y_{1t}. From (20.45) we can obtain y_{2t} only as a function of y_{1t-j} (and the error terms):

$$y_{2t} = (1 - \phi_{22}L)^{-1}[\phi_{21}y_{1t-1} + \theta_2(L)\varepsilon_{2t}]$$

$$y_{2t} = f(y_{1t-j}, \varepsilon_{2t-j}) \tag{20.46}$$

Substituting for y_{2t-1} from (20.46) in (20.44) we have

$$y_{1t} = \phi_{11}y_{1t-1} + \phi_{12}[f(y_{1t-j-1}, \varepsilon_{2t-j-1})] + \theta_1(L)\varepsilon_{1t}$$

or

$$y_{1t} = g(y_{1t-j}, \varepsilon_{2t-j-1}, \varepsilon_{1t-j}) \tag{20.47}$$

Equation (20.47) is a univariate ARMA model for y_{1t}. As we have seen the ARMA model can be further reduced to an infinite autoregression or moving average model (if stationarity and invertibility apply). The results of this section can be summarised as follows. A set of k stationary stochastic variables $y_{1t}, y_{2t}, \ldots y_{kt}$ can be represented as

(i) a $(k \times k)$ VARMA system,

(ii) a smaller $(k - l) \times (k - l)$ VARMA system,

(iii) an infinite vector autoregressive VAR series with white noise errors $\beta(L)\mathbf{Y}_t = \varepsilon_t$ so that each y_{it} depends only on lags of itself y_{it-j} and lags of all the other variables $y_{k,t-j}$ (and a white noise error).

(iv) The set of k variables can be reduced to a set of univariate ARMA equations for each of the y_{it}:
$$\phi(L)y_{it} = \theta(L)\varepsilon_{it} \quad (i = 1, 2, \ldots k)$$

(v) The univariate ARMA representation can be transformed into an infinite moving average representation (Wold's decomposition theorem) or an infinite univariate autoregression (assuming invertibility and stationarity).

What are the Advantages and Disadvantages of Alternative Time Series Representations?

All of the time series representations we have discussed assume that any series y_{it} can be represented as a *linear function* of either its own lags, lags of other variables or the error terms. If the world is 'non-linear' then clearly the linear form can at best be an approximation to the true non-linear system. Some non-linear time series models have been analysed in the literature (e.g. a simple bi-linear model

$$\alpha(L)y_t = \Theta(L)\varepsilon_t + \sum_k \sum_l \gamma_{kl} y_{t-k}\varepsilon_{t-l})$$

However, this approach has not as yet featured greatly in the economic analysis of asset prices and will not be discussed further.

Temporal Stability

A key issue in using time series models is temporal stability in the parameters. There is a danger when investigating a VARMA or VAR system that it is 'too small' to capture the 'true' constant parameters out there in the real world. Suppose, for the sake of argument, that the VARMA equation (20.44) for y_{1t} has stable parameters when considered as a function of lagged values of y_{1t}, y_{2t}. However, suppose that equation (20.45) for y_{2t} has some unstable parameters (even one will do). When we substitute for y_{2t} from (20.45) in (20.44) and reduce the system to a univariate form (either AR or MA) then this 'smaller' system for y_{1t} has 'new' parameters that incorporate the parameters of equation (20.45) for y_{2t}. Hence if the latter are unstable, then the parameters of all 'smaller systems' (i.e. equation 20.47) will also be unstable.

To give a concrete example of the above, suppose y_{1t} and y_{2t} are prices and interest rates, respectively. Without loss, let us assume the errors in (20.44) and (20.45) are simply white noise, that is consist of ε_{1t} and ε_{2t} only. Equation (20.45), for interest rates, we can interpret as the monetary authorities reaction function. If the authorities have a feedback rule whereby an *increase* in the price level causes the authorities to raise interest rates over successive time periods then we have:

$$y_{2t} = \phi_{21} y_{1t-1} + \phi_{22} y_{2t-1} + \varepsilon_{2t} \tag{20.48}$$

with $\phi_{21}, \phi_{22} > 0$. Suppose that after some time the monetary authorities decide against a feedback rule for the interest rate and simply try and gradually lower interest rates. Equation (20.48) now becomes:

$$y_{2t} = \phi_{22} y_{2t-1} + \varepsilon_{2t} \tag{20.49}$$

with $0 < \phi_{22} < 1$. Hence the parameters of the equation for y_{2t}, the interest rate, are time varying over the two different monetary regimes. A researcher who estimates a *univariate* system for either y_{1t} or y_{2t} over the *whole data set* would find that the parameters are unstable. If he ignores this temporal instability then his estimates of the parameters will be biased and he will not have 'discovered' the true constant parameters of the system in the two distinct regimes. Any tests based on the 'smaller system' (e.g. restrictions on the parameters, forecast tests) will be incorrect. On the other hand the multivariate equation (20.44) for y_{1t} has stable parameters (although that for y_{2t} does not). Hence the danger in representing the 'real world' by time series models which involve a relatively small number of variables is that the 'omitted variables' which have been 'substituted out' to yield the smaller system of equations may have non-constant parameters: hence the smaller system will also have non-constant parameters.

To represent a series either as an *infinite* VAR or AR model, or an *infinite* VMA or MA model, is impossible in a *finite* data set. One approximates such models with lags of a finite order. There are diagnostic tests (e.g. tests for serial correlation in the errors of a

VAR system) that can be used to assess whether the finite lag approximation is likely to be an adequate representation of the data. But clearly this finite sample approximation may also cause the estimated model to be a poor representation of the 'true' underlying model.

Structural and Statistical Models Revisited

This section draws some comparisons between a structural economic model which is derived from economic theory (or theories) and the purely time series representations discussed above. As we shall see a structural economic model can be reduced to a purely time series representation. The transformation to a time series representation usually implies restrictions on the parameters but a pure time series modeller would ignore these and merely estimate an unrestricted time series representation.

A macroeconomic model usually consists of a set of equations that may represent the behaviour of economic agents, identities or technical identities or equilibrium conditions. Shown below is a stylised model with three endogenous variables

y_{1t} = rate of wage inflation (percent per annum)

y_{2t} = rate of domestic price inflation in the UK (percent per annum)

y_{3t} = percentage deviation of output from its long-run trend (i.e. from its 'natural rate' or non-accelerating rate of inflation (NAIRU))

y_{3t} is called 'cyclical output' from now on. The exogenous variables in the model are:

x_{1t} = percentage change in import prices (in domestic currency)

x_{2t} = trades union power

x_{3t} = government expenditure

The first equation in the model is a wages version of the expectations augmented Phillips curve. Wage inflation y_{1t} is assumed to depend on price inflation y_{2t}, cyclical output y_{3t} and trades union power x_{2t}. The second equation models price inflation y_{2t} using a cost mark-up equation. Price inflation y_{2t} depends on wage inflation y_{1t} and import price inflation x_{1t}. (These two equations are used in the chapter on exchange rates.) The final equation expresses equilibrium in the goods market. Real output y_{3t} increases as real income rises and hence is positively related to wage increases y_{1t} but it is negatively related to domestic price inflation y_{2t}. Government expenditure x_{3t} directly adds to demand and hence influences real output. The three-equation economic model is then

$$y_{1t} = a_{11}y_{2t} + a_{13}y_{3t} + g_{12}x_{2t} + [\alpha_{11}(L)y_{2t} + \alpha_{12}(L)y_{3t} + \gamma_{12}(L)x_{2t}] + \varepsilon_{1t}$$

$$y_{2t} = a_{21}y_{1t} + g_{21}x_{1t} + [\alpha_{21}(L)y_2 + \alpha_{22}(L)y_2 + \gamma_{21}x_1] + \varepsilon_2.$$

$$y_{3t} = a_{31}y_{1t} + a_{32}y_{2t}$$

(50)

Lagged values have been inclu... ...ion because it is probable that y... ...ver time, rather than instantaneou... ...is a *structural simultaneous equa*... ...hat one endogenous variable y_{it}

The reader will have noted that not all the variables of the system appear in all the equations: this is because economic theory usually suggests some exclusion restrictions (e.g. y_{3t} doesn't appear in the equation determining y_{2t}). In order to make it possible *in principle* to estimate a unique set of parameters of the model, the system needs to be 'identified'. Space constraints prevent us from discussing the concept of identification in detail. However, unless the system is identified, estimates of the parameters are meaningless since *any* linear combination of the three equations is equally valid statistically (and clearly an arbitrary linear combination would not in general conform to one's theoretical priors). We will assume that the three-equation system in (20.50) is identified, so this is not a problem here.

Notice that in a three-equation system we can only solve (algebraically) for three unknowns (y_{1t}, y_{2t}, y_{3t}) in terms of the 'knowns' (x_{1t}, x_{2t}, x_{3t}). The economist states *a priori* which of the variables are *not* determined within the model: these are called exogenous variables. Finally, note that economic theory would usually imply that the y_{it} are explained by the RHS variables except for an additive white noise process ε_{it}. (In fact we can relax this assumption and assume the ε_{it} are ARMA processes and what follows would still be valid.) The differences between the 'structural economic model' in (20.50) and the VARMA time series model are:

(i)   the presence of *current dated* variables on the RHS of the structural model for y_{it} and x_{it},

(ii) the presence of lagged exogenous variables $x_{it-j} (i = 1, 2, 3)$,

(iii) some 'exclusion restrictions' on the variables in the structural model (i.e. y_{3t} doesn't appear in equation (20.50)),

(iv) the economic model involves a structure that is determined by the economic theory under consideration.

Taking up the last point we see, for example, that agents alter y_{1t} only in response to changes in y_{2t}, y_{3t} or x_{2t} (and their lags) and *not directly* because of changes in x_{1t} or x_{3t}. Economic theory would usually suggest that the behavioral parameters should be constant over time.

From a Structural Model to a VARMA or VAR System

The structural model in (20.50) can be compactly written in matrix notation

$$\mathbf{A}_0 \mathbf{Y}_t = \mathbf{A}_1 \mathbf{X}_t + \mathbf{A}_2(L) \mathbf{Y}_{t-1} + \mathbf{A}_3(L) \mathbf{X}_{t-1} + \boldsymbol{\varepsilon}_t$$

or

$$\mathbf{Y}_t = \mathbf{A}_0^{-1}(\mathbf{A}_1 \mathbf{X}_t + \mathbf{A}_2(L) \mathbf{Y}_{t-1} + \mathbf{A}_3(L) \mathbf{X}_{t-1} + \boldsymbol{\varepsilon}_t) \tag{20.51}$$

Equation (20.51), which is known as the 'final form', expresses $\mathbf{Y}_t$ as a function of lagged values of $\mathbf{Y}_t$ and current and lagged values of $\mathbf{X}_t$. We know that any covariance stationary series may be given a *purely statistical* representation in the form of a VARMA model. If we apply this to $\mathbf{X}_t$ we have

$$\mathbf{X}_t = \mathbf{B}(L) \mathbf{X}_{t-1} + \boldsymbol{\Theta}(L) \mathbf{v}_t \tag{20.52}$$

If $\mathbf{X}_t$ is stationary all the roots of $\mathbf{B}(L)$ lie outside the unit circle and hence

$$\mathbf{X}_t = (I - \mathbf{B}(L))^{-1} \boldsymbol{\Theta}(L) \mathbf{v}_t$$

and

$$A_3(L)X_t = A_3(L)(I - B(L))^{-1}\Theta(L)v_t \qquad (20.53)$$

Substituting from (20.52) for X_t and $A_3(L)X_{t-1}$ in (20.51), we see that Y_t is 'reduced to' a VARMA model of the form

$$Y_t = \psi(L)Y_{t-1} + \lambda(L)\eta_t \qquad (20.54)$$

where the final term is a moving average of the white noise errors ε_t and v_t. Hence given a VARMA statistical representation of the stationary series X_t, any structural simultaneous equations model can be represented as a VARMA model. It follows from our earlier discussion that the structural model can be further reduced to the 'simpler' VAR and ARMA models outlined in the 'summary' above.

In general, the fact that the A_i matrices of the structural model have restrictions given by economic theory (i.e. some elements are zero) often implies some restrictions on the derived VARMA equations. These restrictions can usually be tested. However, if we ignore such restrictions then any VARMA model may be viewed as an *unrestricted representation* of a structural economic model. Note that the VARMA model for any y_{it} will usually depend on lags of *all* the other $y_{jt} (i \neq j)$ variables even though the structural equation for y_{it} might exclude a particular y_{jt}.

Some modellers advocate starting with a structural model based on some economic theory, which usually involves some *a priori* (yet testable) restrictions on the parameters. One can then analyse this model with a variety of statistical tests. Others (e.g. Sims (1980)) feel that the *a priori* knowledge required to identify the structural model (e.g. exclusion restrictions) are so 'incredible' that one should start with an *unrestricted* VARMA model and simplify this model only on the basis of various *statistical* tests (e.g. exclusion restrictions and Granger causality tests, see below). These 'simplification restrictions' of Sims would not be suggested by economic theory but one would simply trade off 'fit' against parsimony on purely statistical grounds (e.g. by using the Akaike information criteria).

Expectations Variables Added

If we add an expectations variable for one particular variable, for example $E_t y_{it+q}$ (where $q = 1$, or 2, or 3, etc.) to the structural economic model then we have additional problems of interpretation and identification (the latter are particularly problematic, e.g. see Pesaran (1987)). However, since expectations are formed with information available at time t or earlier then it must be true that

$$E_t y_{it+q} = f(\Omega_t) = f(\Psi(L)y_t, \lambda(L)X_t) \qquad (20.55)$$

We can therefore (assuming suitable transversality conditions hold, see Cuthbertson and Taylor (1987) and Pesaran (1987)) substitute out for $E_t y_{t+q}$ in terms of current and past observable values of the variables in the system. Hence the structural model with expectations can be reduced to one without expectations and is of the general form (20.51). In fact as we have noted, the assumption of RE usually implies some additional restrictions on the A_i matrices of the structural model. In general, therefore, the addition of expectations variables still allows us to express any set of time series variables Y_t as a multivariate VARMA, VAR or VMA model or as a univariate ARMA, AR or MA representation.

Problems

Again the key potential problem in moving from *a conditional structural model* for any y_{it} to a purely time series representation is whether the x_{it} variables can be adequately represented by a *linear* VARMA time series model $\mathbf{B}^*(L)\mathbf{X}_t = \Theta(L)\mathbf{v}_t$ *with constant parameters*. If either of these conditions does not hold then the resulting linear VARMA time series model for y_{it} will be misspecified and have unstable parameters.

On the other hand suppose the world is linear but the *a priori* restrictions (e.g. exclusion restrictions) imposed on the structural model by the economic theorist are incorrect 'in reality': in this case the VARMA representation may provide a superior statistical representation of the data.

The aim of the above is to point out the relationship between these two broad approaches to modelling time series. Both have acute potential problems, both require an enormous amount of judgement in deciding which approach is 'reasonable' in any given circumstances. It is certainly this author's view that economic theory ought to play some role in this decision process but there are no clear-cut infallible 'rules' one can apply: 'beauty and truth' in applied economics are usually in the eye of the beholder.

Stationarity and Non-Stationarity in Systems: Cointegration

This section deals with the issue of cointegration and discusses how non-stationary series can yield 'spurious regressions' and how one can test to see if individual variables are non-stationary. Having found that a set of variables is non-stationary it is now possible to outline how the Johansen procedure can be used to determine whether a set of non-stationary series are 'linked together' in the long run, that is cointegrated. Finally, the relationship between the Johansen procedure, the Box Jenkins methodology, error correction models and Granger causality is briefly discussed.

We have noted that any single series can be classified as stationary or non-stationary. We now consider possible relationships between *a set of* non-stationary variables. Two series x_t and y_t might be 'highly trended' because of a deterministic time trend ($y_t = \alpha_0 + \alpha_1 t + \varepsilon_t$) or because of a 'stochastic trend' (e.g. random walk with drift, $y_t = \alpha_0 + y_{t-1} + \varepsilon_t$). Cointegration deals with data that have stochastic trends. In general two series with stochastic trends will not be statistically related. For example, consider $x_t = \beta_0 + x_{t-1} + v_t$ and $y_t = \alpha_0 + y_{t-1} + \varepsilon_t$ where ε_t and v_t are statistically *independent* (white noise) errors. In the 'true' model there is *no* relationship between y_t and x_t. However, if we regress y_t on x_t in a *sample* of data then standard statistics (e.g. R^2, t statistics) will suggest that they are linearly related:

$$y_t = \hat{\delta}_0 + \hat{\delta}_1 x_t \tag{20.56}$$

This is usually referred to as the 'spurious regression' or 'nonsense regression' problem (Granger and Newbold, 1974). The R^2 and t statistics from such regressions are misleading. The t statistics for δ_i are not distributed as a Student's t distribution and cannot be used for testing hypotheses on the parameters δ_0, δ_1. The R^2 is often bimodal. Granger and Newbold noted that in these 'spurious regressions', $R^2 > \mathrm{DW}$ ($\mathrm{DW} = \mathrm{Durbin}\text{–}\mathrm{Watson}$ statistic). The DW was 'low' indicating positive serial correlation in the residuals.

Cointegration seeks to provide a correct method of estimating equations that contain a set of variables, some of which have stochastic trends. Such stochastic trends are frequently found in economic time series (e.g. stock prices, interest rates and dividends).

In principle, cointegration thus avoids the spurious regression problem. In addition cointegration indicates whether it is possible to model the non-stationary data in an error correction model.

Time series data (y_t, x_t) that need to be differenced once to yield a stationary series (e.g. the random walk) are said to be *integrated of order 1*, that is $I(1)$. There are now many tests available to ascertain whether an individual series is $I(1)$. We will only consider the Dickey–Fuller (DF) and augmented DF tests. The AR(1) model for any time series y_t is

$$y_t = \alpha_0 + \alpha_1 y_{t-1} + \varepsilon_t \tag{20.57}$$

where we take ε_t to be a stationary white noise series. If $\alpha_1 < 1$ (we take α_1 to be positive) then y_t is a stationary $I(0)$ series. However, if $\alpha_1 = 1$ then y_t is $I(1)$ since it needs to be differenced once to yield a stationary series:

$$\Delta y_t = \alpha_0 + \varepsilon_t \tag{20.58}$$

Thus Δy_t is stationary given that ε_t is stationary. Rearranging (20.57) we have:

$$\Delta y_t = \alpha_0 + \theta y_{t-1} + \varepsilon_t \tag{20.59}$$

where $\theta = \alpha_1 - 1$. If $\alpha_1 < 1$ then $\theta < 0$. Hence a test for stationarity is a test for $\theta < 0$. Dickey and Fuller (1979) show that the t statistic on θ in the OLS regression (20.59) can be used to test for $\theta < 0$. However, the critical value of the t statistic is not given by a Student's t distribution and requires special tables of critical values. The DF critical value for testing $\theta < 0$ is about 2.85 for reasonable sample sizes. Hence for y_t to be $I(0)$ we require $\theta < 0$ and $|t| > 2.85$ where $t = t$ statistic on θ. If y_t is found to be $I(1)$ then the series is differenced once and the DF test applied to the Δy_t series to see if it is $I(0)$. The augmented Dickey–Fuller test includes additional lagged difference terms of the form

$$\sum_{i=1}^{n} \Psi_i \Delta y_{t-i}$$

to remove any serial correlation that may be present in ε_t. (A deterministic time trend may also be included in (20.59).) Having ascertained that a set of variables are all integrated of the same order (we only consider $I(1)$ series) then we can proceed to see if these variables move together in the long run (i.e. have common stochastic trends). We consider the two variable case first.

In general a linear combination of $I(1)$ series that is $q_t = y_t - \beta' x_t$ is also $I(1)$ and therefore non-stationary. However, it is possible that the linear combination q_t is stationary and in this case y and x are said to be *cointegrated* with a *cointegration parameter*, β. If q_t is a stationary $I(0)$ variable then we can say that the stochastic trend in y_t is 'explained' by' the stochastic trend in $\beta' x_t$. Hence the two series move together over time, 'the gap' q_t between them is finite and the gap doesn't grow larger over time.

If we have two variables which are cointegrated then the cointegrating vector is unique. However, for any $r + 1$ variables there can be up to r *unique* cointegrating vectors. For illustrative purposes let us consider a three-variable system, where y_{1t}, y_{2t}, y_{3t} are all $I(1)$. Let us suppose that there are two unique cointegrating vectors, which without loss of generality we normalise on y_{1t} and y_{2t}. The Engle and Granger (1987) representation theorem states that cointegration implies that there exists a statistical representation of the data known as an *error correction model* (ECM) which is of the form:

$$\Delta y_{1t} = \alpha_{11}(y_{1t-1} - \delta_1 y_{3t-1}) + \alpha_{12}(y_{2t-1} - \delta_2 y_{3t-1})$$
$$+ \text{(terms in } \Delta y_{1t-j}, \Delta y_{2t-j}, \Delta y_{3t-j}) + \varepsilon_{1t}$$
$$\Delta y_{2t} = \alpha_{21}(y_{1t-1} - \delta_1 y_{3t-1}) + \alpha_{22}(y_{2t-1} - \delta_2 y_{3t-1})$$
$$+ \text{(terms in } \Delta y_{1t-j}, \Delta y_{2t-j}, \Delta y_{3t-j}) + \varepsilon_{2t}$$
$$\Delta y_{3t} = \alpha_{22}(y_{1t-1} - \delta_1 y_{3t-1}) + \alpha_{32}(y_{2t-1} - \delta_2 y_{3t-1})$$
$$+ \text{(terms in lagged } \Delta y_{1t-j}, \Delta y_{2t-j}, \Delta y_{3t-j}) + \varepsilon_{3t} \qquad (20.60)$$

The interesting features of the ECM are

(i)   The two cointegrating vectors *may*, in principle, appear in all the equations for the (3×3) system. The cointegrating parameters are δ_1 and δ_2.

(ii) All the variables in the error correction system are stationary $I(0)$ variables. The y_{it} $(i = 1, 2, 3)$ are $I(1)$ by assumption, hence Δy_{it} must be $I(0)$. The vectors $(y_{1t-1} - \delta_1 y_{3t-1})$ and $(y_{2t-1} - \delta_2 y_{3t-1})$ are stationary because the $I(1)$ series are cointegrated.

In fact (20.60) is nothing more than VAR where the non-stationary $I(1)$ variables have been 'transformed' into stationary series (i.e. into difference terms or cointegrating vectors) so that a VAR representation is permissible. The error terms $\varepsilon_{it}(i = 1, 2, 3)$ are given by:

$$\varepsilon_{it} = (\Delta y_{it} - \text{'linear combination of stationary variables'})$$

and hence are stationary. Since the error terms are stationary the usual statistical tests can be applied to the α_{ij} parameters of a VAR model in error correction form.

Before cointegration came on the scene the so-called Box–Jenkins methodology had been used in analysing statistical time series models. This methodology implied that any non-stationary $I(1)$ series be differenced *before* estimating and testing the VAR (or VARMA) model. Hence a VAR model which contains only the first differences of the $I(1)$ variables is used in the Box–Jenkins methodology. This ensured that the error terms in the equation were stationary and hence conformed to standard distribution theory. Standard statistical tests using 'standard tables' of critical values could then be used. However, cointegration analysis indicates that a VAR *solely* in first differences is misspecified, if there are some cointegrating vectors present among the $I(1)$ series. Put another way a VAR solely in first differences omits potentially important stationary variables (i.e. the error correction, cointegrating vectors) and hence parameter estimates may suffer from omitted variables bias. How acute the omitted variables bias might be depends on the correlation between the included 'differenced only' terms of the Box–Jenkins VAR and the omitted cointegration variables $(y_{it} - \delta_i y_{jt})$. If these correlations are low (high) then the omitted variables bias is likely to be low (high).

The parameters of the error correction model (20.60) can be estimated jointly using the Johansen procedure. This procedure also allows one to test for the number of unique cointegrating vectors in the system which involves non-standard critical values. (This is done for interest rates in Chapter 14.) One may be able to simplify the error correction system by *testing* to see if any of the weights on the error correction terms (i.e. the α_{ij}

parameters) are zero in any of the equations. One can also test for exclusion restrictions on the lagged difference terms which may then yield a more parsimonious statistical representation of the data.

Our simultaneous equations structural model can be reduced to an error correction system. For any variables that are $I(1)$ one can apply the Johansen procedure which will provide a set of unique cointegrating vectors (if any) and these variables are then included in the structural model in the form $(y_{it-1} - \delta'_i \mathbf{z}_{t-1})$.

Since the ECM is a VAR involving lags of stationary variables it can, like any VAR, be transformed to give the following alternative representations. First, a 'smaller' error correction system (e.g. 3×3 to a 2×2 system), or a VMA system. Also it can be reduced to a 'single-equation' ARMA, AR or MA model in exactly the same way as discussed above for the VAR with stationary variables. It follows that the 'dangers', particularly in terms of parameter stability of the resulting representations, will again be of key concern.

In general the choice between a 'large' VAR/ECM or a 'smaller' system is a trade-off between efficiency and bias. The larger system is less likely to suffer from omitted variables bias but the parameters may not be very precisely estimated (since one loses 'degrees of freedom' as the number of parameters to be estimated increases relative to the fixed sample of data). On the other hand, excluding some variables (i.e. parsimony) or starting with a very 'small' system may increase the precision of the estimated parameters but at a cost in terms of potential omitted variables bias and perhaps a loss of forecasting accuracy. With any real world finite data set one can apply a wide variety of tests to guide one's choice but ultimately a great deal of judgement is required.

Granger Causality

There is one widely used and simple test on a VAR which enables a more parsimonious representation of the data. To illustrate this consider a (3×3) VAR system in the *stationary* variables y_{1t}, y_{2t}, y_{3t}. The equation for y_{1t} is:

$$y_{1t} = \beta_1(L)y_{1t-1} + \beta_2(L)y_{2t-1} + \beta_3(L)y_{3t-1} + \varepsilon_{1t} \tag{20.61}$$

where sufficient lags have been included to ensure that ε_{1t} is white noise. One might wish to test the proposition that lags of y_{2t} *taken together* have no *direct* effect on y_{1t}. If the restriction that all the coefficients in $\beta_2(L)$ are zero is not rejected then we can conclude that y_2 does not Granger cause y_1. The terms in y_2 can then be omitted from the equation which explains y_1. A similar Granger causality test can be done for y_3 in equation (20.61). We can also apply Granger causality tests for the equations with y_{2t} and y_{3t} as dependent variables. Granger causality tests are often referred to as 'block exogeneity tests'. Note that Granger causality is a purely statistical view of causality: it simply tests to see if lags of y_{jt} have *incremental* explanatory power for y_{it} $(i \neq j)$.

In the VAR/ECM, lags of y also appear in the error correction term so that here one must also include the 'weights' α_{ij} in the Granger causality test. Otherwise the principle is the same as in the pure VAR case described above.

A good example of where economic theory suggests a test for Granger causality is the term structure of interest rates. Here the expectations hypothesis of the term structure suggests that the long rate R_t is directly linked to future short-term interest rates r_{t+j} $(j = 1, 2, 3, \ldots,$ etc). Hence the theory would imply that the long rate should Granger cause short rates. Similarly, according to the fundamental valuation equation, the price of a stock depends on future dividend payments and hence stock prices should Granger cause dividends.

Summary

The main conclusions of this section are as follows:

(i) A structural economic model can be represented as a purely vector time series model and the latter can be reduced to a univariate model. In using VAR models the issue of the temporal stability of the parameter is of key importance.

(ii) Cointegration deals with the relationships between non-stationary $I(1)$ variables. If a set of variables are cointegrated then any cointegrating vectors should be included in the VAR representation. Hence the VAR system purely in first differences of $I(1)$ variables may be misspecified.

(iii) The VAR cointegration framework has been extensively used in testing whether the EMH holds for speculative asset prices.

20.3 SIMPLE ARCH AND GARCH MODELS

This section outlines the basis of models of autoregressive conditional heteroscedasticity (ARCH) and the generalised ARCH (or GARCH) approach in modelling time varying risk premia. The emphasis is on the intuitive economic reasons for using these models rather than the details of the estimation procedures and algorithms. We begin with a very simple ARCH model and then build up to a generalised ARCH in mean model, involving conditional variances and covariances.

Simple ARCH Model

The basic idea behind ARCH models is that the *second moments* of the distribution may have an autoregressive structure. Consider an asset return model where we assume the expected excess return $E_t y_{t+1}$ is constant

$$E_t y_{t+1} = \Psi \tag{20.62}$$

Now assume RE

$$y_{t+1} = \Psi + \varepsilon_{t+1} \tag{20.63}$$

where $\varepsilon_{t+1} = y_{t+1} - E_t y_{t+1}$ is the RE forecast error. Many asset markets are characterised by periods of 'turbulence and tranquillity', that is to say large (small) forecast errors (of whatever sign) tend to be followed by further large errors (small) errors. There is therefore persistence in the variance of the forecast errors. The simplest formulation of this is

$$\sigma_{t+1}^2 = \text{var}(\varepsilon_{t+1}|\Omega_t) = w + \alpha \varepsilon_t^2 \tag{20.64}$$

If $\alpha < 1$ the *unconditional* variance of ε_t, denoted σ^2, is given by

$$\sigma^2 = w/(1 - \alpha) \tag{20.65}$$

and is a constant. However, the *conditional* variance given by (20.64) varies over time and ε_t^2 can be used to predict the variance next period σ_{t+1}.

Estimation of the two-equation system $(20.63) + (20.64)$ is fairly straightforward. If we assume normality, the log-likelihood (excluding the constant term) is:

$$l = -\tfrac{1}{2} \sum_t \ln \sigma_t^2 - \tfrac{1}{2} \sum_t (\varepsilon_t^2 / \sigma_t^2) \tag{20.66}$$

In terms of $(20.63) + (20.64)$ the likelihood may be expressed as:

$$l = -\frac{1}{2} \sum_t \ln(w + \alpha \varepsilon_{t-1}^2) - \frac{1}{2} \sum_t \left[\frac{\varepsilon_t^2}{w + \alpha \varepsilon_{t-1}^2} \right]$$

$$l = -\frac{1}{2} \sum_t \ln[w + \alpha(y_{t-1} - \Psi)^2] - \frac{1}{2} \sum_t \left[\frac{(y_t - \Psi)^2}{w + \alpha(y_{t-1} - \Psi)^2} \right] \tag{20.67}$$

The log-likelihood can therefore be expressed as a non-linear function of the unknown parameters w, α and β and the data series y_t. Standard optimisation routines can then be used to maximise the likelihood. In particular, one must ensure that the time varying variance is always positive. In this case this is easily done by replacing w and α in (20.63) by w^2 and α^2 which are always positive and hence σ_{t+1}^2 in (20.64) will always be positive.

GARCH Models

The ARCH process in (20.64) has a memory of only one period. We could generalise this process by adding lags of ε_{t-i}^2:

$$\sigma_{t+1}^2 = w + \alpha_1 \varepsilon_t^2 + \alpha_2 \varepsilon_{t-1}^2 + \cdots \tag{20.68}$$

but the number of parameters to estimate increases rapidly. A more parsimonious method of introducing a 'long memory' is the GARCH(1,1) process

$$\sigma_{t+1}^2 = w + \alpha \varepsilon_t^2 + \beta \sigma_t^2 \tag{20.69}$$

The GARCH process has the same structure as an AR(1) model for the error term except the AR(1) process applies to the variance. The unconditional variance denoted σ^2 (a constant) is:

$$\sigma^2 = w/[1 - (\alpha + \beta)] \tag{20.70}$$

for $(\alpha + \beta) < 1$. However, (20.69) can be rearranged to give

$$(1 - \beta L)\sigma_{t+1}^2 = w + \alpha \varepsilon_t^2$$

$$\sigma_{t+1}^2 = w(1 + \beta + \beta^2 + \cdots) + \alpha(1 + \beta L + (\beta L)^2 + \cdots)\varepsilon_t^2 \tag{20.71}$$

Hence σ_{t+1}^2 can be viewed as an infinite weighted average of all past squared forecast errors. The weights on ε_{t-j}^2 in (20.71) are constrained to be geometrically declining. With a little manipulation (20.71) may also be rewritten

$$(\sigma_{t+1}^2 - \sigma^2) = \alpha(\varepsilon_t^2 - \sigma^2) + \beta(\sigma_t^2 - \sigma^2) \tag{20.72}$$

Using either (20.69) or (20.72) we can take expectations of both sides and noting that $E_t \varepsilon_t^2 = \sigma_t^2$ we have (for equation (20.69))

$$\sigma_{t+1}^2 = w + (\alpha + \beta)\sigma_t^2 \tag{20.73}$$

and by forward substitution we have

$$\sigma_{t+m}^2 = w[1 + (\alpha + \beta) + (\alpha + \beta)^2 + \cdots] + (\alpha + \beta)^m \sigma_t^2 \tag{20.74}$$

Given a shock to ε_t^2 (i.e. $\sigma_t^2 > 0$) at time t then the *persistence* in changes in future values of σ_{t+j} depends on the size of $\alpha + \beta$. If $\alpha + \beta$ is close to unity then a shock at time t will persist for many future periods. For $\alpha + \beta = 1$ then any shock will lead to a permanent change in *all* future values of σ_{t+j}^2: hence shocks to the conditional variance are 'persistent'. For $\alpha + \beta = 1$ we have what is known as an *integrated* GARCH process (i.e. IGARCH). For IGARCH the conditional variance is non-stationary and the unconditional variance is unbounded. The statistical/distribution properties of IGARCH processes are currently the focus of much research in this literature.

One can generalise (20.69) to a GARCH(p, q) process where there are p lags of ε_t and q lags of σ_t^2. This allows the conditional variance to have an infinitely long memory (because of the σ_{t-j}^2 terms) but doesn't constraint the response of σ_{t+j}^2 to a shock in ε_t^2 to have geometrically declining weights. Given the acute non-linearities of the likelihood function and loss of degrees of freedom as the number of parameters in the GARCH process increases, researchers have often used fairly low-order GARCH(p, q) models and these have been found to fit the time varying volatility in the forecast errors of asset prices fairly well.

The likelihood function for (20.63) plus the GARCH(1,1) model is of the form (20.67). However, an arbitrary starting value for σ_t^2 is required to generate the terms in σ_{t+j}^2 in the likelihood function. ε_1 is given by $(y_1 - \Psi)$ and this together with a starting value σ_1^2 can be used to generate $\sigma_2^2 = w + \alpha_1 \varepsilon_1^2 + \beta \sigma_1^2$. Values of $\varepsilon_{t+1} = y_{t+1} - \Psi$ for $t = 1, 2, \ldots$ can be used to generate $\sigma_{t+1}^2 = w + \alpha_1 \varepsilon_t^2 + \beta \sigma_t^2 (t = 2, 3, \ldots)$ by recursive substitution for σ_t^2.

ARCH-M and GARCH-M Models

Suppose we now extend our economic model of asset pricing so that the expected return depends positively on the perceived riskiness of the asset or portfolio. Suppose that the riskiness can be adequately represented by the (conditional) 'own' variance of the forecast errors of returns σ_{t+1}^2. This model of expected returns can be represented by the 'ARCH in mean' equation:

$$y_{t+1} = \Psi_0 + \Psi_1 \sigma_{t+1}^2 + \varepsilon_{t+1} \tag{20.75}$$

Thus the expected return $E_t y_{t+1}$ is given by $(\Psi_0 + \Psi_1 \sigma_{t+1}^2)$ where σ_{t+1}^2 is the *expected* (conditional) variance (strictly we should write this as $E(\sigma_{t+1}^2 | \Omega_t)$ but do not do so for notational ease). The forecast error squared is

$$\varepsilon_{t+1}^2 = (y_{t+1} - \Psi_0 - \Psi_1 \sigma_{t+1}^2) \tag{20.76}$$

We assume that there is persistence in the variance of the conditional forecast errors which is either ARCH(p) or GARCH(1,1)

$$\text{ARCH} \quad \sigma_{t+1}^2 = w + \sum_{i=0}^{p} \alpha_i \varepsilon_{t-i}^2$$

$$\text{GARCH} \quad \sigma_{t+1}^2 = w + \alpha \varepsilon_t^2 + \beta \sigma_t^2 \tag{20.77}$$

After substituting (20.75) for ε_t in the likelihood function and using one of the above functions for σ_{t+1}^2 we obtain the likelihood in terms of the unknown parameters Ψ_0, Ψ_1, together with the unknown parameters α_i, β of the ARCH/GARCH process.

The ARCH-M or GARCH-M models can be generalised to include either additional variables z_{1t} in the expected return equation or additional variables z_{2t} that are thought to influence the conditional variance. For a GARCH(1,1) process this would consist of the following two equations:

$$y_{t+1} = \Psi_0 + \Psi_1\sigma_{t+1}^2 + \Psi_2'z_{1t} + \varepsilon_{t+1} \tag{20.78}$$

$$\sigma_{t+1}^2 = w + \alpha\varepsilon_t^2 + \beta\sigma_t^2 + \gamma'z_{2t} \tag{20.79}$$

For example, the APT suggests that the variables in z_{1t} could be macroeconomic variables such as the growth in output or the rate of inflation. Often the dividend price ratio is found to influence returns and this might also be included in (20.78). Economic theory is not particularly informative about the variables z_{2t} that might influence investors' perceptions of future volatility but clearly if volatility in prices is associated with new information arriving in the market then a market turnover variable might be included in z_{2t}. A dummy variable for days of the week when the market is open (i.e. $z_{2t} = 1$ for market open, and zero otherwise) can also be incorporated in the GARCH equation. It is also possible that elements of z_{2t} also appear in the equation for y_{t+1} (and a dummy variable for daily returns and the weekend effect are obvious candidates). So far we have assumed that the forecast errors ε_{t+1} are normally distributed, so that:

$$y_{t+1}|\Omega_t \sim N(\Psi'x_t, \sigma_{t+1}^2) \tag{20.80}$$

where the variables that influence y_{t+1} are subsumed in x_t. The conditional mean of y_{t+1} is $\Psi'x_t$ and the conditional variance is given by σ_{t+1}^2. However, we can assume any distribution we like for the conditional moments. For example, for daily data on stock returns or changes in exchange rates (i.e. the y_{t+1} variable) the conditional distribution often assumed is the Student's t distribution which has slightly fatter tails than the normal distribution. The likelihood is more complex algebraically than that given in equation (20.67) for the normal distribution but the principle behind the estimation remains unchanged. The terms in σ_t^2 and ε_t in the (new) likelihood equation are replaced by (non-linear) functions of the 'observables' y_t, x_t and the unknown parameters Ψ and (w, α, β) of the GARCH process. The likelihood can then be estimated in the usual fashion (e.g. see the maximisation options in the GAUSS, LIMDEP or RATS programmes) which often involves numerical (rather than analytic) techniques.

Although the *unconditional* distributions for many financial variables (e.g. daily changes in stock prices, interest rates or exchange rates) may be leptokurtic, it may be that the conditional distribution based on a model like the GARCH-M model in (20.78) + (20.79) may yield a distribution that is not leptokurtic.

Covariances and ARCH Models

To motivate the application of ARCH models to incorporate covariances consider the excess return y_{1t+1} on a particular portfolio (e.g. the return on a portfolio of shares held in various chemical firms). The CAPM plus RE implies that

$$y_{1t+1} = \Psi_0 + \Psi_1(\sigma_{1m}) + \varepsilon_{1t+1} \tag{20.81}$$

where σ_{1m} is the expected *covariance* between the return on asset 1 and the market portfolio. The term ε_{1t+1} is the (RE) forecast error in predicting the return on asset 1. To analyse the behaviour of the covariance term we require an equation to predict the return y_{mt+1} on the *market portfolio* and this is given by (Merton, 1973):

$$y_{mt+1} = \Psi_0^* + \Psi_1 \sigma_{mt+1}^2 + \varepsilon_{mt+1} \qquad (20.82)$$

Hence the return on the market portfolio is determined by the conditional variance of the market portfolio σ_m^2. The term Ψ_0^* should equal zero and Ψ_1 is the market price of risk. (Note that Ψ_1 appears in both (20.81) and (20.82) according to portfolio theory.) Any shocks that influence the return on the market portfolio are also likely to influence the return on asset 1. For example, this is because 'good news' about the economy may have an effect on the return on the stocks in portfolio 1 as well as all other stocks in the market portfolio. Hence ε_{1t} and ε_{mt} are likely to be correlated (i.e. their covariance is non-zero). If we assume a GARCH(1,1) process for the covariance we have

$$[\sigma_{1m}]_{t+1} = w + \alpha[\varepsilon_{1t}\varepsilon_{mt}] + \beta[\sigma_{1m}]_t \qquad (20.83)$$

There will also be an equation of the form (20.83) to explain the conditional *variances* for both σ_{1t+1}^2 and σ_{mt+1}^2 (see equation (20.79)). The parameters α and β in the GARCH covariance equation and in the two GARCH variance equations need not be the same. Hence the degree of persistence (i.e. the value of $\alpha + \beta$) can be different in each GARCH specification and generally speaking one's 'instinct' would be that the degree of persistence might well be different in each process. In practice, however, the (α, β) parameters are often *assumed* to be the same in each GARCH equation because otherwise it is difficult to get precise estimates of the parameters from the likelihood function which is highly non-linear in the parameters.

Clearly the GARCH-M model with variances and covariances involves a (2×1) vector of error terms $(\varepsilon_{1t}, \varepsilon_{mt})$ and the likelihood function in (20.66) is no longer appropriate. However, the principle is the same. Given starting values at $t = 0$ for σ_{1m}, σ_m^2 and σ_1^2 the GARCH equations can be used recursively to generate values for these variables at $t = 1, 2 \dots$ in terms of the unknown parameters. Similarly equations (20.81) and (20.82) provide a series for ε_{1t} and ε_{mt} to input into the likelihood, which is then maximised using numerical methods.

Summary

ARCH and GARCH models provide a fairly flexible method of modelling time-varying conditional variances and covariances. Such models assume that investors' perceptions of risk tomorrow depend on what their perception of risk has been in earlier periods. ARCH models are therefore autoregressive in the second moment of the distribution. An 'ARCH (or GARCH) in mean' model assumes that expected returns depend upon investors' perceptions of risk. A higher level of risk requires a higher level of expected returns. ARCH models allow this risk premium to vary over time and hence expected equilibrium returns also vary over time.

20.4 RATIONAL EXPECTATIONS: ESTIMATION ISSUES

Over the last 10 years the role of expectations formation in both theoretical and applied financial economics has been of central importance. At the applied level relatively few practitioners have adopted the full Muth rational approach which requires specification of a complete macromodel. Such 'full information methods' have generally been confined to estimating 'small models' (e.g. Taylor (1979)). Much applied work has concentrated on estimating 'single equations' that contain expectations variables. For example, in the pure expectations hypothesis of the term structure, the long rate on bonds depends on expectations about future short-term interest rates. The current price of stocks depends on expected future dividends and under risk neutrality the current forward rate is an unbiased predictor of the expected future spot rate of exchange.

In general the efficient markets literature is concerned with the proposition that agents use all available information to remove any known profitable opportunities in the market and this usually involves agents forming expectations about future events. To test the propositions outlined above we need a framework for modelling these unobservable expectations.

The literature on estimating expectations models is vast and can quickly become very complex. An attempt has been made to explain only the main (limited information) methods currently in use. We shall concentrate only on those problems introduced by expectations variables and will not analyse other econometric problems that might also arise (e.g. simultaneous equations problems). The reader is referred to intermediate econometrics text books for the basic estimation methods (e.g. OLS, IV, 2SLS, GLS) used in analysing time series data (e.g. Cuthbertson et al (1992) and Greene (1990)).

The rational expectations (RE) hypothesis has featured widely in the literature and we begin by discussing the basic axioms of RE which are crucial in choosing an appropriate estimation procedure. We also examine equations that contain multiperiod expectations. In the next section, we discuss the widely used 'errors in variables' method (EVM) of estimating structural equations under the assumption that agents have rational expectations. The use of auxiliary equations (e.g. extrapolative predictions) to generate a suitable proxy variable for the unobservable expectations series give rise to two-step procedures and the pitfalls involved in such an approach are also examined.

Problems which arise when the structural expectations equation has serially correlated errors will then be highlighted. The Generalised Method of Moments (GMM) estimator of Hansen (1982) and Hansen and Hodrick (1980) and the Two-Step Two-Stage Least Squares estimator (Cumby et al, 1983) provide solutions to this problem.

20.4.1 The Economics of Expectations Models and the RE Hypothesis

This section analyses the various ways in which expectations variables are utilised in the applied literature and the implications of the economic assumptions for the estimation issues discussed in a later section.

Usually the applied economist is interested in estimating the structural parameters of a single equation or set of equations containing expectations terms which forms a subset of a larger model. (In a 'full' Muth-RE model (Muth, 1961) we would have to specify the whole model.) The simplest *structural expectations equation* can be represented:

$$y_{1t} = bx_{t+j}^e + u_{1t} \tag{20.84}$$

where:

$$x_{t+j}^e = E[x_{t+j}|\Omega_{t-j}] \qquad j \geqslant 0 \tag{20.85}$$

and x_{t+j}^e is an expectations variable. E is the expectations operator conditional on the complete (relevant) information set available to the agent at time $t - j$ (i.e. Ω_{t-j}). For example, in a purchasing power parity price equation, Ex_{t+j} represents expected world prices and y_{1t} the domestic export price (in a common currency). If the forward rate of exchange is an unbiased estimate of the future spot rate then $y_{1t} = f_t$ and x_{t+j}^e is the expected future spot rate. In the absence of data on Ex_{t+j} (e.g. quantitative survey data) we must posit an auxiliary hypothesis for Ex_{t+j}. Whatever expectations scheme we choose, of key importance for the econometrics of the model are

(i)   the forecast horizon.
(ii) the dating and content of the information set used in making the forecast,
(iii) the relationship between the forecast error and the information set.

To develop these issues further it is useful to discuss the basic axioms of RE.

Basic Axioms of RE

If agents have RE they act as if they know the structure of the complete model to within a set of white noise errors (i.e. the axiom of correct specification). Forecasts are unbiased on average, with constant variance and successive (one-step ahead) forecast errors are uncorrelated with each other and with the information set used in making the forecast. Thus, the relationship between outturn x_{t+1} and the *one-step ahead* RE forecast $_tx_{t+1}^e$ using the complete information set Ω_t (or a subset Λ_t) is:

$$x_{t+1} = {}_tx_{t+1}^e + \omega_{t+1} \tag{20.86}$$

where

$$E[\omega_{t+1}|\Omega_t] = [\omega_{t+1}|\Lambda_t] = 0 \tag{20.87a}$$

$$E[\omega_{t+1}^2|\Omega_t] = \sigma_\omega^2 \tag{20.87b}$$

$$E[\omega_{t+1}\omega_{t+1-j}|\Omega_t] = 0 \quad j = 1, 2 : \ldots \infty \tag{20.87c}$$

The one-step ahead rational expectations forecast error ω_{t+1} is 'white noise' and an 'innovation', conditional on the complete information set Ω_t and is orthogonal to a subset of the complete information set $(\Lambda_t \subset \Omega_t)$.

The *k-step* RE forecast errors $(k > 1)$ *are* serially correlated and are MA($k - 1$). To demonstrate this in a simple case assume x_t is AR(1).

$$x_{t+1} = \phi x_t + \omega_{t+1} \quad E(\omega_{t+1}|\Omega_t) = 0 \tag{20.88}$$

Hence:

$$x_{t+j} = \phi^j x_t + \omega_{t+j} + \phi\omega_{t+j-1} + \phi^2\omega_{t+j-2} + \cdots \tag{20.89}$$

From (20.88) it is easy to see that:

$$[x_{t+1} - {}_tx_{t+1}^e] = \omega_{t+1} \tag{20.90}$$

while the two-period ahead forecast error is:

$$[x_{t+2} - {}_tx_{t+2}^e] = [\phi\omega_{t+1} + \omega_{t+2}] \tag{20.91}$$

The *one-step* ahead forecast error is an independent white noise process ω_{t+1} but the two-period ahead forecast error is MA(1): similarly the k-step ahead forecast error is MA($k - 1$). Note that *all* the multiperiod forecast errors

$$[x_{t+j} - {}_t x^e_{t+j}] \quad j \geqslant 1$$

are independent of (orthogonal to) the information set Ω_t (or Λ_t). There is one further property of RE that is useful in analysing RE estimators and that is the form of revisions to expectations. The *one-period revision* to expectations

$$[{}_{t+1} x^e_{t+j} - {}_t x^e_{t+j}]$$

depends only on new information arriving between t and $t + 1$ and hence from (20.89) is easily seen to be

$$[{}_{t+1} x^e_{t+j} - {}_t x^e_{t+j}] = \phi^{j-1} \omega_{t+1} \tag{20.92}$$

The two-period revision to expectations

$$[{}_{t+2} x^e_{t+j} - {}_t x^e_{t+j}]$$

will of course depend on ω_{t+1} and ω_{t+2} and be MA(1): one can generalise the result for k-period revisions to expectations.

Direct Tests of RE

Direct tests of the basic axioms of RE may involve multiperiod expectations and this immediately raises estimation problems. For example, *if monthly* quantitative survey data is available on the *one-year ahead* expectation, ${}_t x^e_{t+12}$, a test of the axioms often involves a regression of the form:

$$x_{t+12} = \beta_0 + \beta_1 [{}_t x^e_{t+12}] + \beta_2 \Lambda_t + \eta_t \tag{20.93}$$

where

$$H_0 : \beta_0 = \beta_2 = 0, \, \beta_1 = 1$$

Under the null, η_{t+12} is MA(11) and an immediate problem due to RE is the need to use some kind of Generalised Least Squares (GLS) estimator if efficiency is to be achieved. Of course, for one-period ahead expectations where data of the same frequency is available, the error term is white noise and independent of the regressors in (20.93): OLS therefore provides a best linear unbiased estimator.

An additional problem arises if the survey data on expectations is assumed to be measured with error. If the true RE expectation is ${}_t x^e_{t+12}$ and a survey data provides a measure ${}_t \tilde{x}^e_{t+12}$ where we assume a simple linear measurement model (Pesaran, 1985):

$$_t \tilde{x}^e_{t+12} = \alpha_0 + \alpha_1 [{}_t x^e_{t+12}] + \varepsilon_t \tag{20.94}$$

Then substituting for ${}_t x^e_{t+12}$ from (20.94) in (20.93):

$$x_{t+12} = \lambda_0 + \lambda_1 [{}_t \tilde{x}^e_{t+12}] + \beta_2 \Lambda_t + \zeta_t \tag{20.95}$$

where

$$\lambda_0 = [\alpha_1 \beta_0 - \beta_1 \alpha_0]/\alpha_1$$

$$\lambda_1 = \beta_1/\alpha_1$$

$$\zeta_t = \eta_t - [\beta_1/\alpha_1]\varepsilon_t$$

The additional problem in (20.94) is that now $_t\tilde{x}^e_{t+12}$ is correlated with ζ_t. This is because ε_t determines $_t\tilde{x}^e_{t+12}$. Hence some form of generalised IV estimator is required for consistency and asymptotic efficiency. As we shall see the orthogonality property between the RE forecast error and the information set (Λ_t or Ω_t) is frequently used in finding a suitable instrument set. However, it is not always simply the case that Λ_t provides a valid instrument set for the problem at hand.

The EVM and Extrapolative Predictors

In order to motivate our discussion of the estimation problems in the next two sections it is useful at this stage to summarise some of the problems encountered when estimating a structural expectations model: problems that arise include serial correlation and correlation between regressors and the error term. For illustrative purposes assume the structural model of interest is:

$$y_t = \delta_1[_tx^e_{t+1}] + \delta_2[_tx^e_{t+2}] + u_t \tag{20.96}$$

u_t is taken to be white noise and x_t is an exogenous expectations variable. Under the assumption of RE we have

$$x_{t+j} = {}_tx^e_{t+j} + \omega_{t+j} \tag{20.97}$$

A method of estimation widely used (and one of the main ones discussed in this chapter) is the errors in variables method (EVM), where we replace the unobservable $_tx^e_{t+1}$ by its realised value x_{t+j}. This method is consistent with agents being Muth rational, but could also be taken as a condition of the relationship between outturn and forecast without invoking Muth-RE. Substituting from (20.97) in (20.96)

$$y_t = \delta_1 x_{t+1} + \delta_2 x_{t+2} + \varepsilon_t \tag{20.98a}$$

$$\varepsilon_t = u_t - \delta_1\omega_{t+1} - \delta_2\omega_{t+2} \tag{20.98b}$$

Clearly from (20.97) x_{t+j} and w_{t+j} are correlated and hence plim $[x'_{t+j}\varepsilon_t]/T \neq 0 (j = 1, 2)$ and $E(\varepsilon\varepsilon') \neq \sigma^2_\varepsilon I$ because of the moving average error introduced by the RE forecast errors ω_{t+j}. Hence our RE model requires some form of instrumental variables estimation procedure with a correction for serial correlation. These two general problems form a main focus for this section.

20.4.2 The Errors in Variables Method EVM

The EVM is a form of IV or 2SLS approach. Under RE, the unobservable expectations variable $_tx^e_{t+j}$ is determined by the full relevant information set Ω_t. In the EVM a subset of the true information set $\Lambda_t(\subset \Omega_t)$ is sufficient to generate consistent estimates. However, first it is shown that OLS yields an inconsistent estimator.

One-Period Ahead Expectations: White Noise Structural Error

It is important to note that here we are dealing with a very specific expectations model. The simplest structural model embodying one-period ahead expectations is:

$$y_t = \beta x^e_{t+1} + u_t \tag{20.99}$$

Where u_t is white noise and x^e_{t+1} is assumed to be uncorrelated in the limit with u_t:

$$\text{plim}(x^e_{t+1}{}'u_t)/T = 0 \qquad (20.100)$$

If we assume rational expectations then

$$x_{t+1} = x^e_{t+1} + \omega_{t+1} \qquad (20.101)$$

and the RE forecast error ω_{t+1} is independent of the information set Ω_t (or Λ_t)

$$E(\Omega'_t\omega_{t+1}) = 0 \qquad (20.102)$$

Substituting (20.101) in (20.99) we obtain

$$y_t = \beta x_{t+1} + q_t \qquad (20.103)$$

$$q_t = (u_t - \beta\omega_{t+1}) \qquad (20.104)$$

Consider applying OLS to (20.103) we have:

$$\hat{\beta} = \beta + (x_{t+1}{}'x_{t+1})^{-1}(x_{t+1}{}'q_t) \qquad (20.105)$$

From (20.101):

$$\text{plim}(x_{t+1}{}'x_{t+1})/T = \text{plim}(x^e_{t+1}{}'x^e_{t+1})/T + \text{plim}(\omega_{t+1}{}'\omega_{t+1})/T \qquad (20.106)$$

on rewriting this more succinctly:

$$\sigma^2_x = \sigma^2_{xe} + \sigma^2_\omega \qquad (20.107)$$

From (20.101) and (20.104) and noting that x^e_{t+1} is uncorrelated in the limit with ω_{t+1}:

$$\text{plim}(x_{t+1}{}'q_t)/T = -\beta\,\text{plim}(\omega_{t+1}{}'\omega_{t+1})/T = -\beta\sigma^2_\omega \qquad (20.108)$$

Substituting these expressions in (20.105):

$$\text{plim}\,\hat{\beta} = \beta\left[1 - \frac{\sigma^2_\omega}{\sigma^2_{xe} + \sigma^2_\omega}\right] \qquad (20.109)$$

Thus the OLS estimator for β is inconsistent and is biased downwards. The bias is smaller the smaller is the variance of the 'noise' element σ^2_ω in forming expectations.

Instrumental Variables: 2SLS

OLS is inconsistent because of the correlation between the RHS variable x_{t+1} and the error term q_t which 'contains' the RE forecast error ω_{t+1}. The solution to this problem is to use instrumental variables, IV, on (20.103). However, to illustrate some additional nuances when applying IV consider the following model:

$$y_t = \alpha x^e_{1t+1} + \beta x_{2t} + u_t = Q^e\delta + u_t \qquad (20.110)$$

$$Q^e = \{x^e_{1t+1}, x_{2t}\} \quad \delta = (\alpha, \beta)' \qquad (20.111)$$

where x^e_{1t+1}, x_{2t} are asymptotically uncorrelated with u_t. Direct application of IV to (20.110) would require an instrument for x_{1t+1} from a subset of the information set

Λ_t *but including* x_{2t}:

$$\hat{x}_{1t+1} = \Lambda_t \hat{\Pi} \tag{20.112}$$

$$\hat{\Pi} = (\Lambda_t' \Lambda_t)^{-1}(\Lambda_t' x_{1t+1}) \tag{20.113}$$

The researcher is now faced with two options. Direct application of IV would utilise the instrument matrix

$$W_1 = \{\hat{x}_{1t+1}, x_{2t}\} \tag{20.114}$$

Where x_{2t} acts as its own instrument, giving

$$\delta_1 = (W_1' Q)(W_1' y) \tag{20.115}$$

$$\text{var}(\hat{\delta}_1) = \sigma^2 (W_1' Q)^{-1} \tag{20.116}$$

This is also the 2SLS estimator since in the first stage x_{1t+1} is regressed on *all* the predetermined (or exogenous variables) in (20.110) *and* the additional instruments in Λ_t. An alternative is to *replace* x_{1t+1}^e in (20.110) by $\hat{x}_{1t+1}$ and apply *OLS* to:

$$y_t = \alpha \hat{x}_{1t+1} + \beta x_{2t} + q_t^* \tag{20.117}$$

$$q_t^* = u_t - \alpha(x_{t+1} - x_{t+1}^e) - \alpha(\hat{x}_{t+1} + x_{t+1}) \tag{20.118}$$

This yields a 'two step estimator' but as long as x_{1t+1} is regressed on *all* the predetermined variables, then OLS on (20.114) is *numerically* equivalent to the 2SLS estimator $\hat{\delta}_1$ and is therefore consistent. However, there is a problem with this approach. The OLS residuals from (20.117) are:

$$e = y_t - \hat{\alpha}\hat{x}_{1t+1} - \hat{\beta}x_{2t} \tag{20.119}$$

but the correct (IV/2SLS) residuals use x_{1t+1} and not $\hat{x}_{1t+1}$ and are:

$$e_1 = y - \hat{\alpha}x_{1t+1} - \hat{\beta}x_{2t} \tag{20.120}$$

Hence the variance–covariance matrix of parameters from OLS on (20.117) are incorrect since $s^2 = e'e/T$ is an incorrect (inconsistent) measure of σ^2 (Pagan, 1984). The remedy is straightforward, however; one merely amends the OLS programme to produce the correct residuals e_1 in the second stage.

Extrapolative Predictors

Extrapolative predictors are those where the information set utilised by the econometrician is restricted to be lagged values of the variable itself, that is an AR (ρ) model

$$x_{1t+1} = \phi_1 x_{1t} + \phi_2 x_{1t-1} + \phi_2 x_{1t-2} + \cdots \phi_\rho x_{t-\rho} + \varepsilon_t \tag{20.121}$$

$$x_{1t+1} = \Phi(L)x_{1t} + \varepsilon_t \tag{20.122}$$

The maximum value of ρ is usually chosen so that ε_t is white noise. OLS applied to (20.121) yields one-step ahead predictions

$$\hat{x}_{1t+1}^* = \hat{\phi}(L)x_{1t} \tag{20.123}$$

The use of extrapolative predictors has proved popular in models with multiperiod expectations and in testing RE cross-equation restrictions (in the latter procedure a VAR rather than AR model is usually used).

For the moment consider using the extrapolative predictor either *as an instrument* for x^e_{1t+1} or to *replace* x^e_{1t+1} in (20.110). Using $\hat{x}^*_{1t+1}$ as an instrument for x^e_{1t+1} *and* including x_{2t} in the instrument matrix $\mathbf{W}_1$ gives consistent estimates. Now consider the 'two-step' method. Having obtain $\hat{x}^*_{1t+1}$ in the 'first stage', the second-stage regression consists of OLS on:

$$y_t = \alpha\hat{x}^*_{1t+1} + \beta x_{2t} + q^*_t \tag{20.124}$$

$$q_t = u_t + \alpha(x^e_{1t+1} - x_{1t+1}) - \alpha(\hat{x}_{1t+1} - x_{1t+1}) \tag{20.125}$$

Compared with the EVM/IV approach (see equations (20.103) and (20.104)) we have an additional term $(\hat{x}_{1t+1} - x_{1t+1})$ in the error term of our second-stage regression (20.124). The term $(x_{1t+1} - \hat{x}^*_{1t+1})$ is the residual from the first-stage regression (20.122).

The variable x_{2t} is part of the agent's information set, at time t, and may therefore be used by the agent in predicting x_{1t+1}. If so, then $(x_{1t+1} - \hat{x}^*_{1t+1})$ and the 'omitted variable' from the first-stage regression, namely x_{2t}, are correlated. Thus in (20.124) the correlation between the RHS variable x_{2t} and a component of the error term q^*_t implies that OLS on (20.124) yields inconsistent estimates of (α, β) (Nelson, 1975). This is usually expressed in the literature as follows: if x_{2t} Granger causes x_{1t+1} then the two-step estimator is inconsistent. This illustrates the danger in using extrapolative predictors and *replacing* x^e_{t+1} in the second-stage OLS regression, rather than using $\hat{x}^*_{1t+1}$ as an instrument and applying the IV formula. Viewed from the perspective of 2SLS, the inconsistency at the second stage (20.124) arises because in the first-stage regression, the researcher does not use *all* the predetermined variables in the model, he erroneously excludes x_{2t}. Somewhat paradoxically then, even if x_{2t} is not used by agents in forecasting x_{1t+1} it must be included in the first-stage regression if the two-step procedure is used: otherwise $(x_{1t+1} - \hat{x}_{1t+1})$ may be correlated with x_{2t}. Of course, if the two-step procedure is used and consistent estimates $(\hat{\alpha}, \hat{\beta})$ are obtained, the correct residuals calculated using x_{1t+1} and not $\hat{x}_{1t+1}$ (as in equation (20.120)) must be used in the calculation of standard errors.

20.4.3 Serially Correlated Errors and Expectations Variables

Up to this point in our discussion of appropriate estimators we have assumed white noise errors in the regression equation. We now relax this assumption. Serially correlated errors may arise because of multiperiod expectations or because of serially correlated structural errors. In either case, we see below that two broad solutions to the problem are possible. The first method uses the Generalised Method of Moments (GMM) approach of Hansen (1982) and 'corrects' the covariance matrix to take account of serially correlated errors. The second method is a form of Generalised Least Squares estimator under IVs and is known as the *Two-Step Two-Stage Least Squares* estimator (2S–2SLS) (Cumby et al, 1983). These two solutions to the problem are by no means exhaustive but have been widely used in the literature.

The GMM Approach

This approach is demonstrated by first considering serial correlation that arises in equations with multiperiod expectations and then moving on to consider serial correlation in the structural error.

Multiperiod Expectations

Suppose that the structural error u_t is white noise but we have multiperiod expectations (we restrict ourselves to two-period ahead expectations for ease of exposition):

$$y_t = \beta_1 x_{t+1}^e + \beta_2 x_{t+2}^e + u_t \tag{20.126}$$

$$x_{t+j}^e = E(x_{t+j}|\Omega_t) \quad (j = 1, 2) \tag{20.127}$$

RE implies:

$$x_{t+j} = x_{t+j}^e + \eta_{t+j} \quad (j = 1, 2) \tag{20.128}$$

and substituting (20.128) in (20.126) we have our estimating equation:

$$y_t = \beta_1 x_{t+1} + \beta_2 x_{t+2} + q_t \tag{20.129}$$

$$q_t = u_t - \beta_1 \eta_{t+1} - \beta_2 \eta_{t+2} \tag{20.130}$$

2SLS on (20.129) with instrument set Λ_t will yield consistent estimates of β_1, β_2. However, the usual formula for the variance of the IV estimator is incorrect in the presence of serial correlation and q_t is MA(1). Hansen and Hodrick (1980) suggest a 'correction' to the formula for the variance of the usual 2SLS estimator. Putting (20.129) in matrix notation:

$$\mathbf{y} = \mathbf{X}\boldsymbol{\beta} + \mathbf{q} \tag{20.131}$$

The 2SLS estimator for β is equivalent to OLS on

$$\mathbf{y} = \hat{\mathbf{X}}\mathbf{b}^* + \mathbf{q} \tag{20.132}$$

$$\hat{\mathbf{X}} = (\hat{x}_{t+1}, \hat{x}_{t+2}) \tag{20.133}$$

and $\hat{x}_{t+j}$ are the predictions from the regression of $x_{t+j}(j = 1, 2)$ on Λ_t. The 2SLS estimator is:

$$\mathbf{b}^* = (\hat{\mathbf{X}}'\hat{\mathbf{X}})^{-1}(\hat{\mathbf{X}}'\mathbf{y}) \tag{20.134}$$

with residuals:

$$\mathbf{e}^* = \mathbf{y} - \mathbf{X}\mathbf{b}^* \tag{20.135}$$

Note that in the calculation of $\mathbf{e}^*$ we use $\mathbf{X}$ and not $\hat{\mathbf{X}}$. To calculate the correct variance of β in the presence of an MA(1) error, note that the variance–covariance matrix is:

$$E(\mathbf{qq}') = \sigma_0^2 \begin{bmatrix} 1 & \rho_1 & 0 & \dots & \dots & & \dots 0 \\ \rho_1 & 1 & \rho_1 & 0 & \dots & & \vdots \\ 0 & \rho_1 & 1 & \rho_1 & & & \vdots \\ \vdots & & & \ddots & & & 0 \\ & & & & 1 & \rho_1 \\ 0 & \dots & \dots & \dots 0 & & \rho_1 & 1 \end{bmatrix} = \sigma_0^2 \Sigma \tag{20.136}$$

where ρ_1 is the correlation coefficient between the error terms. Since e_t^* are based on the consistent estimator $\mathbf{b}^*$, then consistent estimators of σ_0^2, σ_1^2 and ρ are given by the following 'sample moments:

$$\hat{\sigma}_0^2 = (n^{-1}) \sum_1^n e_t^{*2} \tag{20.137}$$

$$\hat{\sigma}_1^2 = (n^{-1}) \sum_{2}^{n} e_t^* e_{t-1}^* \tag{20.138}$$

$$\hat{\rho}_1 = (\hat{\sigma}_1/\hat{\sigma}_0)^2 \tag{20.139}$$

Knowing Σ we can calculate the correct formula for var($\mathbf{b}^*$) as follows. Substitute from (20.131) in (20.134):

$$\mathbf{b}^* = \boldsymbol{\beta} + (\hat{\mathbf{X}}'\hat{\mathbf{X}})^{-1}\hat{\mathbf{X}}'\mathbf{q} \tag{20.140}$$

Since $\text{plim}(T^{-1})(\hat{\mathbf{X}}'\mathbf{q}) = 0$, then b^* is consistent and the asymptotic variance of b^* is given by:

$$\text{var}(\mathbf{b}_*) = T^{-1}\,\text{plim}\left[\left[\hat{\mathbf{X}}'\hat{\mathbf{X}}\right]^{-1}\hat{\mathbf{X}}'\left[qq'\right]\hat{\mathbf{X}}\left[\hat{\mathbf{X}}'\hat{\mathbf{X}}\right]^{-1}\right]$$

$$\text{var}(\mathbf{b}_*) = \sigma_0^2\left[\hat{\mathbf{X}}'\hat{\mathbf{X}}\right]^{-1}\left[\hat{\mathbf{X}}'\hat{\boldsymbol{\Sigma}}\hat{\mathbf{X}}\right]\left[\hat{\mathbf{X}}'\hat{\mathbf{X}}\right]^{-1} \tag{20.141}$$

Above, we assume that the population moments are consistently estimated by their sample equivalents. Note that var($\mathbf{b}^*$), the Hansen–Hodrick correction to the covariance matrix for $\mathbf{b}^*$, reduces to the usual 2SLS formula for the variance when there is no serial correlation (i.e. $\Sigma = \sigma^2 \mathbf{I}$). The Hansen–Hodrick correction is easily generalised to the case where we have an MA(k) error, we merely have to calculate $\hat{\rho}_s (s = 1, 2, \ldots k)$ and substitute these estimates in Σ.

The Hansen–Hodrick correction to the standard errors can also be applied where estimation of β in (20.131) can proceed using OLS. In this case the Hansen–Hodrick estimate for var($\mathbf{b}$) is given by (20.141) but with $\mathbf{X}$ replacing $\hat{\mathbf{X}}$ and the elements of Σ are calculated using the consistent OLS residuals.

In the above derivation we have assumed that the error term is homoscedastic. However, if the error term is heteroscedastic, as is usually the case with financial data, then Σ can also be recomputed to take account of this problem.

A Two-Step Two-Stage Least Squares (2S–2SLS) Estimator

So far we have been able to obtain a consistent estimator of the structural parameter β_1 in (20.126) under RE by utilising IV/2SLS or the EVM. We have then 'corrected' the usual formula for the variance of the estimator using the Hansen–Hodrick formula. Although the Hansen–Hodrick correction yields a consistent estimator of the variance it is possible to obtain an asymptotically more efficient estimator which is also consistent. Cumby et al (1983) provide such an estimator which is a *specific form* of the class of generalised instrumental variables estimators. The formulae for this estimator look rather formidable. If our structural expectations equation after replacing any expectations variables by their outturn values is:

$$\mathbf{y} = \mathbf{X}\boldsymbol{\beta} + \mathbf{q} \tag{20.142}$$

with

$$E(\mathbf{qq}') = \sigma^2\boldsymbol{\Sigma} \quad \text{and} \quad \text{plim}[T^{-1}(\mathbf{X}'\mathbf{q})] \neq 0 \tag{20.143}$$

Then the 2S–2SLS estimator is:

$$\hat{\beta}_{g2} = [\mathbf{X}'\boldsymbol{\Lambda}(\boldsymbol{\Lambda}'\boldsymbol{\Sigma}\boldsymbol{\Lambda})^{-1}\boldsymbol{\Lambda}'\mathbf{X}]^{-1}[\mathbf{X}'\boldsymbol{\Lambda}(\boldsymbol{\Lambda}'\boldsymbol{\Sigma}\boldsymbol{\Lambda})^{-1}\boldsymbol{\Lambda}'\mathbf{y}] \tag{20.144}$$

$$\text{var}(\hat{\boldsymbol{\beta}}_{g2}) = \sigma^2 [\mathbf{X}'\mathbf{\Lambda}(\mathbf{\Lambda}'\mathbf{\Sigma}\mathbf{\Lambda})^{-1}\mathbf{\Lambda}'\mathbf{Q}]^{-1} \tag{20.145}$$

Where $\mathbf{\Lambda}$ is the information set available. Clearly to make this estimator operational we need a suitable instrument set $\mathbf{\Lambda}$ and an estimate of the variance–covariance matrix $\mathbf{\Sigma}$ of the error term. We have already discussed above how to choose an appropriate instrument set and how a 'consistent' set of residuals can be used to form $\mathbf{\Sigma}$. This 'first-stage' estimate of $\mathbf{\Sigma}$ can then be substituted in the above formulae, to complete the 'second stage' of the estimation procedure (see Cuthbertson (1990)).

In small or moderate size samples it is not possible to say whether the Hansen–Hodrick correction is 'better than' the 2S–2SLS procedure since both rely on asymptotic results. Hence, at present, in practical terms either method may be used. The one clear fact which emerges, however, is that the normal 2SLS estimator for $\text{var}(\hat{\beta})$ is incorrect and care must be taken in utilising Cochrane–Orcutt-type transformations to eliminate AR errors since this may result in an inconsistent estimator for β.

Summary

There are two basic problems involved in estimating structural (single) equations involving expectations terms (such as equation (20.126)) by the EVM. First, correlation between the *ex-post* variables x_{t+j} and the error term means that IV (or 2SLS) estimation must be used to obtain consistent estimates of the parameters. Second, the error term is likely to be serially correlated which means that the usual IV/2SLS formulae for the variances of the parameters are incorrect. Two avenues are then open. Either one can use the IV residuals to form the (non-scalar) covariance matrix ($\sigma^2\mathbf{\Sigma}$) and apply the 'correct' IV formula for $\text{var}(\mathbf{b}^*)$ (see equation (20.141)). Alternatively, one can take the estimate of $\sigma^2\mathbf{\Sigma}$ and apply a variant of Generalised Least Squares under IV, for example the 2S–2SLS estimator for $\text{var}(\beta_{g2})$ in equation (20.145).

FURTHER READING

There are a vast number of texts dealing with 'standard econometrics' and a particularly clear presentation and exposition is given in Greene (1990). More advanced analysis is provided in Harvey (1981), Taylor (1986) and Hamilton (1994) and in the latter, particularly noteworthy are the chapters on GMM estimation, unit roots and changes in regime. Cuthbertson et al (1992) give numerous applied examples of time series techniques as does Mills (1993), albeit somewhat tersely. A useful basic introduction to the Hendry 'general to specific' methodology is to be found in Charemza and Deadman (1992) with a more advanced and detailed account in Hendry (1995). ARCH and GARCH is covered in a series of articles in Engle (1995).

References

Allen, H.L. and Taylor, M.P. (1989a) 'Chart Analysis and the Foreign Exchange Market', *Bank of England Quarterly Bulletin*, Vol. 29, No. 4, pp. 548–551.

Allen, H.L. and Taylor, M.P. (1989b) 'Charts and Fundamentals in the Foreign Exchange Market', *Bank of England Discussion Paper No. 40*.

Ardeni, P.G. and Lubian, D. (1991) 'Is There Trend Reversion in Purchasing Power Parity', *European Economic Review*, Vol. 35, No. 5, pp. 1035–1055.

Artis, M.J. and Taylor, M.P. (1989) 'Some Issues Concerning the Long Run Credibility of the European Monetary System', in R. MacDonald and M.P. Taylor (eds) *Exchange Rates and Open Economy Macroeconomics*, Blackwell, Oxford.

Artis, M.J. and Taylor, M.P. (1994) 'The Stabilizing Effect of the ERM on Exchange Rates and Interest Rates: Some Nonparametric Tests', *IMF Staff Papers*, Vol. 41, No. 1, pp. 123–148.

Asch, S.E. (1952) *Social Psychology*, Prentice Hall, New Jersey, USA.

Attanasio, O. and Wadhwani, S. (1990) 'Does the CAPM Explain Why the Dividend Yield Helps Predict Returns?', *London School of Economics Financial Markets Group Discussion Paper No. 04*.

Azoff, E.M. (1994) *Neural Network Time Series Forecasting of Financial Markets*, J. Wiley, New York.

Baillie, R.T. (1989) 'Econometric Tests of Rationality and Market Efficiency', *Econometric Review*, Vol. 8, pp. 151–186.

Baillie, R.T. and Bollerslev, T. (1989) 'Common Stochastic Trends in a System of Exchange Rates', *Journal of Finance*, Vol. 44, No. 1, pp. 167–181.

Baillie, R.T. and McMahon, P.C. (1989) *The Foreign Exchange Market: Theory and Evidence*, Cambridge University Press, Cambridge.

Baillie, R.T. and Selover, D.D. (1987) 'Cointegration and Models of Exchange Rate Determination', *International Journal of Forecasting*, Vol. 3, pp. 43–52.

Banerjee, A., Dolado, J.J., Galbraith, J.W. and Hendry, D.F. (1993) *Co-integration, Error-Correction, and the Econometric Analysis of Non-Stationary Data*, Oxford University Press, Oxford.

Banerjee, A., Dolado, J.J., Hendry, D.F. and Smith, G.W. (1986) 'Exploring Equilibrium Relationships in Econometrics through Static Models: Some Monte Carlo Evidence', *Oxford Bulletin of Economics and Statistics*, Vol. 48, No. 3, pp. 253–277.

Bank of England (1993) *British Government Securities: The Market in Gilt Edged Securities*, Bank of England, London.

Barnett, W.A., Geweke, J. and Snell, K. (1989) *Economic Complexity: Chaos, Sunspots, Bubbles and Non-linearity*, Cambridge University Press, Cambridge.

Barr, D.G. and Cuthbertson, K. (1991) 'Neo-Classical Consumer Demand Theory and the Demand for Money, *Economic Journal*, Vol. 101, No. 407, pp. 855–876.

Barsky, R.B. and De Long, J.B. (1993) 'Why Does the Stock Market Fluctuate?', *Quarterly Journal of Economics*, Vol. 108, No. 2, pp. 291–312.

Batchelor, R.A. and Dua, P. (1987) 'The Accuracy and Rationality of UK Inflation Expectations: Some Qualitative Evidence', *Applied Economics*, Vol. 19, No. 6, pp. 819–828.

Baumol, W.J. and Benhabib, J. (1989) 'Chaos: Significance, Mechanism and Economic Applications', *Journal of Economic Perspectives*, Vol. 3, No. 1, pp. 77-105.

Becker, G.S. (1991) 'A Note on Restaurant Pricing and Other Examples of Social Influences on Price', *Journal of Political Economy*, Vol. 99, No. 5, pp. 1109-1116.

Bernstein, P.L. (1992) *Capital Ideas*, Macmillan, New York.

Bilson, J.F.O. (1978) 'The Monetary Approach to the Exchange Rate: Some Empirical Evidence', *IMF Staff Papers*, Vol. 25, pp. 48-77.

Bilson, J.F.O. (1981) 'The "Speculative Efficiency" Hypothesis', *Journal of Business*, Vol. 54, pp. 435-451.

Bisignano, J.R. (1987) 'A Study of Efficiency and Volatility in Government Securities Markets', *Bank for International Settlements*, Basle, mimeo.

Black, F. (1972) 'Capital Market Equilibrium with Restricted Borrowing', *Journal of Business*, Vol. 45, pp. 444-455.

Black, F., Jensen, M.C. and Scholes, M. (1972) 'The Capital Asset Pricing Model: Some Empirical Tests', in M.C. Jensen, (ed.) *Studies in the Theory of Capital Markets*, New York, Praeger.

Black, F. and Scholes, M. (1974) 'The Effects of Dividend Yield and Dividend Policy on Common Stock Prices and Returns', *Journal of Financial Economics*, Vol. 1, pp. 1-22.

Blake, D. (1990) *Financial Market Analysis*, McGraw-Hill, Maidenhead.

Blanchard, O.J. (1979) 'Speculative Bubbles, Crashes and Rational Expectations', *Economic Letters*, Vol. 3, pp. 387-389.

Blanchard, O.J. and Watson, M.W. (1982) 'Bubbles, Rational Expectations and Financial Markets', in P. Wachtel (ed.) *Crises in the Economic and Financial System*, Lexington, Massachusetts: Lexington Books, pp. 295-315.

Bollerslev, T. (1986) 'Generalised Autoregressive Conditional Heteroskedasticity', *Journal of Econometrics*, Vol. 31, pp. 307-327.

Bollerslev, T. (1988) 'On the Correlation Structure of the Generalised Conditional Heteroscedastic Process', *Journal of Time Series Analysis*, Vol. 9, pp. 121-131.

Bollerslev, T., Chou, R.Y. and Kroner, K.F. (1992) 'ARCH Modeling in Finance: A Review of the Theory and Empirical Evidence', *Journal of Econometrics*, Vol. 52, pp. 5-59.

Bollerslev, T., Engle, R.F. and Wooldridge, J.M. (1988) 'A Capital Asset Pricing Model with Time-varying Covariances', *Journal of Political Economy*, Vol. 96, No. 1, pp. 116-1131.

Boothe, P. and Glassman, P. (1987) 'The Statistical Distribution of Exchange Rates: Empirical Evidence and Economic Implications', *Journal of International Economics*, Vol. 2, pp. 297-319.

Branson, W.H. (1977) 'Asset Markets and Relative Prices in Exchange Rate Determination', *Sozial Wissenschaftliche Annalen*, Band 1.

Bremer, M.A. and Sweeney, R.J. (1988) 'The Information Content of Extreme Negative Rates of Return', *Working Paper*, Claremont McKenna College.

Brennan, M.J. (1973) 'A New Look at the Weighted Average Cost of Capital', *Journal of Business Finance*, Vol 30, pp. 71-85.

Brennan, M.J. and Schwartz, E.S. (1982) 'An Equilibrium Model of Bond Pricing and a Test of Market Efficiency', *Journal of Financial and Quantitative Analysis*, Vol. 17, No. 3, pp. 301-329.

Brock, W.A., Dechert, W.D. and Scheinkman, J.A. (1987) 'A Test for Independence Based on the Correlation Dimension', *SSRI Working Paper No. 8762*, Department of Economics, University of Wisconsin-Madison.

Bulkley, G. and Taylor, N. (1992) 'A Cross-Section Test of the Present-Value Model for US Stock Prices', *Discussion Paper in Economics No. 92/11*, University of Exeter (forthcoming in *Journal of Empirical Finance*).

Bulkley, G. and Tonks, I. (1989) 'Are UK Stock Prices Excessively Volatile? Trading Rules and Variance Bounds Tests', *Economic Journal*, Vol. 99, pp. 1083-1098.

Burda, M.C. and Wyplosz, C. (1993) *Macroeconomics: A European Text*, Oxford University Press, Oxford.

Burmeister, E. and McElroy, M.B. (1988). 'Joint Estimation of Factor Sensitivities and Risk Premia for the Arbitrage Pricing Theory', *Journal of Finance*, Vol. 43, 721-735.

Buse, A. (1982) 'The Likelihood Ratio, Wald and Lagrange Multiplier Test: An Expository Note', *American Statistician*, Vol. 36, No. 3, pp. 153-157.

Campbell, J.Y. (1991) 'A Variance Decomposition for Stock Returns', *Economic Journal*, Vol. 101, No. 405, pp. 157-179.

Campbell, J.Y. and Ammer, J. (1993) 'What Moves the Stock and Bond Markets? A Variance Decomposition for Long-term Asset returns', *Journal of Finance*, Vol. 48, 3–37.

Campbell, J.Y. and Mei, J. (1993) 'Where do Betas Come From? Asset Price Dynamics and the Sources of Systematic Risk', *Review of Financial Studies*, Vol. 6, 567–592.

Campbell, J.Y. and Shiller, R.J. (1984) 'A Simple Account of the Behavior of Long-term Interest Rates', *American Economic Review*, Vol. 74, pp. 44–48.

Campbell, J.Y. and Shiller, R.J. (1987) 'Cointegration and Tests of Present Value Models', *Journal of Political Economy*, Vol. 95, No. 5, pp. 1062–1088.

Campbell, J.Y. and Shiller, R.J. (1988) 'Stock Prices, Earnings, and Expected Dividends', *Journal of Finance*, Vol. 43, No. 3, pp. 661–676.

Campbell, J.Y. and Shiller, R.J. (1989) 'The Dividend-Price Ratio and Expectations of Future Dividends and Discount Factors', *Review of Financial Studies*, Vol. 1, pp. 195–228.

Campbell, J.Y. and Shiller, R.J. (1991) 'Yield Spreads and Interest Rate Movements: A Bird's Eye View', *Review of Economic Studies*, Vol. 58, pp. 495–514.

Carlson, J.A. and Parkin, J.M. (1975) 'Inflation Expectations', *Economica*, Vol. 42, pp. 123–138.

Cavaglia, S., Verschoor, W.F.C. and Wolff, C.C.P. (1993) 'Further Evidence on Exchange Rate Expectations', *Journal of International Money and Finance*, Vol. 12, pp. 78–98.

Cecchetti, S.G., Lam, P.-S. and Mark, N.C. (1990) 'Mean Reversion in Equilibrium Asset Prices', *American Economic Review*, Vol. 80, No. 3, pp. 398–418.

Charemza, W.W. and Deadman, D.F. (1992) *New Directions in Econometric Practice*, Edward Elgar, Aldershot.

Chen, N. (1983) 'Some Empirical Tests of the Theory of Arbitrage Pricing', *Journal of Finance*, Vol. 38, No. 5, pp. 1393–1414.

Chen, N., Roll, R. and Ross, S.A. (1986) 'Economic Forces and the Stock Market', *Journal of Business*, Vol. 59, 383–403.

Chou, R.Y. (1988) 'Volatility Persistence and Stock Valuations: Some Empirical Evidence Using GARCH', *Journal of Applied Econometrics*, Vol. 3, pp. 279–294.

Chou, R.Y., Engle, R. and Kane, A. (1989) 'Estimating Risk Aversion with a Time Varying Price of Volatility', *Discussion Paper*, Department of Economics, University of California, San Diego.

Clare, A., O'Brien, R., Thomas, S. and Wickens, M. (1993) 'Macroeconomic Shocks and the Domestic CAPM: Evidence from the UK Stock Market', *Discussion Paper 93-02*, Department of Economics, Brunel University, UK.

Clare, A.D. and Thomas, S.H. (1994) 'Macroeconomic Factors, the APT and the UK Stock Market', *Journal of Business Finance and Accounting*, Vol. 21, pp. 309–330.

Clare, A.D., Thomas, S.H. and Wickens, M.R. (1994) 'Is the Gilt-equity Yield Ratio Useful for Predicting UK Stock Returns?', *Economic Journal*, Vol. 104, 303–316.

Cooke, T.Q. and Rowe, T.D. (1988) *Instruments of the Money Market* (6th edition), Federal Reserve Bank of Richmond, Richmond, Virginia.

Copeland, L.S. (1984) 'The Pound Sterling/US Dollar Exchange Rate and the "News" ', *Economics Letters*, Vol. 15, pp. 109–113.

Copeland, L.S. (1994) *Exchange Rates and International Finance* (2nd edition), Addison-Wesley, Reading.

Courakis, A.S. (1989) 'Does Constant Relative Risk Aversion Imply Asset Demands that are Linear in Expected Returns?', *Oxford Economic Papers*, Vol. 41, pp. 553–566.

Cox, J.C., Ingersoll (Jr.), J.E. and Ross, S.A. (1981) 'A Re-examination of Traditional Hypotheses About the Term Structure of Interest Rates', *Journal of Finance*, Vol. 36, No. 4, pp. 769–799.

Cumby, R. (1990) 'Consumption Risk and International Equity Returns: Some Empirical Evidence', *Journal of International Money and Finance*, Vol. 9, pp. 182–192.

Cumby, R.E. and Obstfeld, M. (1981) 'A Note on Exchange-Rate Expectations and Nominal Interest Differentials: A Test of the Fisher Hypothesis', *Journal of Finance*, Vol. 36, No. 3, pp. 697–703.

Cumby, R.E., Huizinga, J. and Obstfeld, M. (1983) 'Two-Step Two-Stage Least Squares Estimation in Models with Rational Expectations', *Journal of Econometrics*, Vol. 21, pp. 333–355.

Cuthbertson, K. (1990) 'Modelling Expectations: A Review of Limited Information Estimation Methods', *Bulletin of Economic Research*, Vol. 42, No. 1, pp. 1–34.

Cuthbertson, K. (1991a) 'The Encompassing Implications of Feedforward Versus Feedback Mechanisms: A Reply to Hendry', *Oxford Economic Papers*, Vol. 43, No. 2, pp. 344–350.

Cuthbertson, K. (1991b) 'Modelling the Demand for Money', in C.J. Green and D.T. Llewellyn (eds) *Surveys in Monetary Economics, Volume I, Monetary Theory and Policy*, Blackwell, Oxford.

Cuthbertson, K. (1996) 'The Expectations Hypothesis of the Term Structure: The UK Interbank Market', *Economic Journal*, forthcoming, 1996.

Cuthbertson, K. and Hayes, S. (1995) 'Identifying Sources of Systematic Risk in the UK Stock Market', Department of Economics, University of Newcastle, mimeo.

Cuthbertson, K. and Taylor, M.P. (1987) *Macroeconomic Systems*, Blackwell, Oxford.

Cuthbertson, K., Hall, S.G. and Taylor, M.P. (1992) *Applied Econometric Techniques*, Harvester Wheatsheaf, Hemel Hemstead.

Cuthbertson, K., Hayes, S. and Nitzsche, D. (1994a) 'The Behaviour of UK Stock Prices and Returns: Is the Market Efficient?', *Newcastle Discussion Papers in Economics No. 94/05*, University of Newcastle.

Cuthbertson, K., Hayes, S. and Nitzsche, D. (1994b) 'Are German Money Market Rates Well Behaved?', *Newcastle Discussion Papers in Economics No. 94/04*, University of Newcastle.

Cuthbertson, K., Hayes, S. and Nitzsche, D. (1996a) 'The Behaviour of Certificate of Deposit Rates in the UK', *Oxford Economic Papers*, forthcoming.

Cuthbertson, K., Hayes, S. and Nitzsche, D. (1996b) 'Interest Rates in Germany and the UK: Cointegration and Error Correction Models', *Manchester School*, forthcoming.

Cutler, D.M., Poterba, J.M. and Summers, L.H. (1989) 'What Moves Stock Prices?', *Journal of Portfolio Management*, Vol. 15, 4–12.

Cutler, D.M., Poterba, J.M. and Summers, L.H. (1991) 'Speculative Dynamics', *Review of Economic Studies*, Vol. 58, 529–546.

De Bondt, W.F.M. and Thaler, R.H. (1985) 'Does the Stock Market Overreact?', *Journal of Finance*, Vol. 40, No. 3, pp. 793–805.

De Bondt, W.F.M. and Thaler, R.H. (1989) 'Anomalies: A Mean-Reverting Walk Down Wall Street', *Journal of Economic Perspectives*, Vol. 3, No. 1, pp. 189–202.

De Grauwe, P., Dewachter, H. and Embrechts, M. (1993) *Exchange Rate Theory: Chaotic Models of Foreign Exchange Markets*, Blackwell, Oxford.

De Long, J.B., Shleifer, A., Summers, L.H. and Waldmann, R.J. (1989) 'The Size and Incidence of the Losses from Noise Trading', *Journal of Finance*, Vol. 44, No. 3, pp. 681–696.

De Long, J.B., Shleifer, A., Summers, L.H. and Waldmann, R.J. (1990) 'Noise Trader Risk in Financial Markets', *Journal of Political Economy*, Vol. 98, No. 4, pp. 703–738.

Dhrymes, P.T., Friend, I. and Gultekin, N.B. (1984) 'A Critical Re-examination of the Empirical Evidence on the APT', *Journal of Finance*, Vol. 39, No. 2, June, pp. 323–346.

Diba, B.T. and Grossman, H.L. (1988) 'Explosive Rational Bubbles in Stock Prices?', *American Economic Review*, Vol. 78, No. 3, pp. 520–530.

Dickey, D.A. and Fuller, W.A. (1979) 'Distribution of the Estimators for Autoregressive Time Series with a Unit Root', *Journal of the American Statistical Association*, Vol. 74, No. 366, pp. 427–431.

Dickey, D.A., Jansen, D.W. and Thornton, D.L. (1991) 'A Primer on Cointegration with an Application to Money and Income', *Review (Federal Reserve Bank of St. Louis)*, Vol. 73, No. 2, pp. 58–78.

Dornbusch, R. (1976) 'Expectations and Exchange Rate Dynamic', *Journal of Political Economy*, Vol. 84, No. 6, pp. 1161–1176.

Dornbusch, R. and Fischer, S. (1980) 'Exchange Rates and the Current Account', *American Economic Review*, Vol. 70, No. 5, pp. 960–971.

Driffill, J. and Sola, M. (1994) 'Testing the Term Structure of Interest-Rates Using Stationary Vector Autoregression with Regime Switching', *Journal of Economic Dynamics and Control*, Vol. 18, No. 3/4, pp. 601–628.

Elton, E.J. and Gruber, M.J. (1993) *Modern Portfolio Theory and Investment Analysis* (4th edition), J. Wiley, New York.

Engel, C. and Hamilton, J.D. (1990) 'Long Swings in the Dollar: Are They in the Data and Do Markets Know It', *American Economic Review*, Vol. 80, No. 1, pp. 689–713.

Engel, C. and Morris, C.S. (1991) 'Challenges to Stock Market Efficiency: Evidence from Mean Reversion Studies', *Economic Review, Federal Reserve Bank of Kansas City*, Sept./Oct., pp. 21–35.

Engel, C. and Rodrigues, A.P. (1989) 'Tests of International CAPM With Time-Varying Covariances', *Journal of Applied Econometrics*, Vol. 4, pp. 119–138.

Engle, R.F. (1982) 'Autoregressive Conditional Heteroscedasticity with Estimates of the Variance of United Kingdom Inflation', *Econometrica*, Vol. 50, No. 4, pp. 987–1008.

Engle, R.F. (1995) *ARCH: Selected Readings*, Oxford University Press, Oxford.

Engle, R.F. and Bollerslev, T. (1986) 'Modelling the Persistence of Conditional Variances', *Econometric Review*, Vol. 5, No. 1, pp. 1–50.

Engle, R.F. and Granger, C.W.J. (1987) 'Co-integration and Error Correction: Representation, Estimation, and Testing', *Econometrica*, Vol. 55, No. 2, pp. 251–276.

Engle, R.F., Lilien, D.M. and Robins, R.P. (1987) 'Estimating Time Varying Risk Premia in the Term Structure: The ARCH-M Model', *Econometrica*, Vol. 55, No. 2, pp. 391–407.

Engsted, T. (1993) 'The Term Structure of Interest Rates in Denmark 1982-89: Testing the Rational Expectations/Constant Liquidity Premium Theory', *Bulletin of Economic Research*, Vol. 45, No. 1, pp. 19–37.

Engsted, T. and Tanggaard, C. (1993) 'The Predictive Power of Yield Spreads for Future Interest Rates: Evidence from the Danish Term Structure', The Aarhus School of Business, Denmark, mimeo.

Engsted, T. and Tanggaard, C. (1994a) 'Cointegration and the US Term Structure', *Journal of Banking and Finance*, Vol. 18, pp. 167–181.

Engsted, T. and Tanggaard, C. (1994b) 'A Cointegration Analysis of Danish Zero-Coupon Bond Yields', *Applied Financial Economics*, forthcoming.

Evans, G.W. (1991) 'Pitfalls in Testing for Explosive Bubbles in Asset Prices', *American Economic Review*, Vol. 81, No. 4, pp. 922–930.

Fabozzi, F. (1993) *Bond Markets: Analysis and Strategy* (2nd edition), Prentice Hall, New York.

Fama, E.F. (1970) 'Efficient Capital Markets: A Review of Theory and Empirical Work', *Journal of Finance*, Vol. 25, No. 2, pp. 383–423.

Fama, E.F. (1976) 'Forward Rates as Predictors of Future Spot Rates', *Journal of Financial Economics*, Vol. 3, pp. 361–377.

Fama, E.F. (1984) 'Forward and Spot Exchange Rates', *Journal of Monetary Economics*, Vol. 14, pp. 319–338.

Fama, E.F. (1990) 'Term-Structure Forecasts of Interest Rates, Inflation, and Real Returns', *Journal of Monetary Economics*, Vol. 25, No. 1, pp. 59–76.

Fama, E.F. and Bliss, R.R. (1987) 'The Information in Long-Maturity Forward Rates', *American Economic Review*, Vol. 77, No. 4, pp. 680–692.

Fama, E.F. and French, K.R. (1988a) 'Permanent and Temporary Components of Stock Prices', *Journal of Political Economy*, Vol. 96, 246–273.

Fama, E.F. and French, K.R. (1988b) 'Dividend Yields and Expected Stock Returns', *Journal of Financial Economics*, Vol. 22, 3–25.

Fama, E.F. and French, K.R. (1989) 'Business Conditions and Expected Returns on Stocks and Bonds', *Journal of Financial Economics*, Vol. 25, 23–49.

Fama, E.F. and MacBeth, J.D. (1974) 'Tests of the Multiperiod Two-Parameter Model', *Journal of Financial Economics*, Vol. 1, No. 1, pp. 43–66.

Fisher, E.O. and Park, J.Y. (1991) 'Testing Purchasing Power Parity Under the Null Hypothesis of Cointegration', *Economic Journal*, Vol. 101, No. 409, pp. 1476–1484.

Flavin, M.A. (1983) 'Excess Volatility in the Financial Markets: A Reassessment of the Empirical Evidence', *Journal of Political Economy*, Vol. 91, 246–273.

Flood, M.D. and Rose, A.K. (1993) 'Fixing Exchange Rates: A Virtual Quest for Fundamentals', *CEPR Discussion Paper No. 838.*

Flood, R.P. and Garber, P.M. (1980) 'Market Fundamentals Versus Price-Level Bubbles: The First Tests', *Journal of Political Economy*, Vol. 88, pp. 745–770.

Flood, R.P. and Garber, P.M. (1994) *Speculative Bubbles, Speculative Attacks and Policy Switching*, MIT Press, Cambridge, Massachusetts.

Flood, R.P., Garber, P.M. and Scott, L.O. (1984) 'Multi-Country Tests for Price-Level Bubbles', *Journal of Economic Dynamics and Control*, Vol. 84, No. 3, pp. 329–340.

Flood, R.P., Hodrick, R.J. and Kaplan, P. (1986) 'An Evaluation of Recent Evidence on Stock Market Bubbles', *NBER Working Paper No. 1971* (Cambridge, Massachusetts).

Fortune, P. (1991) 'Stock Market Efficiency: An Autopsy?', *New England Economic Review, Federal Reserve Bank of Boston*, March/April, pp. 17–40.

Frankel, J.A. (1979) 'On the Mark: A Theory of Floating Exchange Rates Based on Real Interest Differentials', *American Economic Review*, Vol. 69, No. 4, pp. 610–622.

Frankel, J.A. (1980) 'Tests of Rational Expectations in the Forward Exchange Market', *Southern Economic Review*, Vol. 46, No. 4, pp. 1083–1101.

Frankel, J.A. (1982a) 'A Test of Perfect Substitutability in the Foreign Exchange Market', *Southern Economic Review*, Vol. 49, No. 2, pp. 406–416.

Frankel, J.A. (1982b) 'In Search of the Exchange Risk Premium: A Six Currency Test Assuming Mean-Variance Optimization', *Journal of International Money and Finance*, Vol. 1, pp. 255–274.

Frankel, J.A. and Froot, K.A. (1986) 'The Dollar as an Irrational Speculative Bubble: The Tale of Fundamentalists and Chartists', *Marcus Wallenberg Papers on International Finance*, Vol. 1, pp. 27–55.

Frankel, J.A. and Froot, K.A. (1987) 'Using Survey Data to Test Standard Propositions Regarding Exchange Rate Expectations', *American Economic Review*, Vol. 77, No. 1, pp. 133–153.

Frankel, J.A. and Froot, K.A. (1988) 'Chartist, Fundamentalists and the Demand for Dollars', *Greek Economic Review*, Vol. 10, pp. 49–102.

French, K.R. and Roll, R. (1986) 'Stock Return Variances: The Arrival of Information and the Reaction of Traders', *Journal of Financial Economics*, Vol. 17, pp. 5–26.

French, K.R., Schwert, G.W. and Stambaugh, R.F. (1987) 'Expected Stock Returns and Volatility', *Journal of Financial Economics*, Vol. 19, pp. 3–29.

Frenkel, J.A. (1981a) 'Flexible Exchange Rates, Prices, and the Role of "News": Lessons from the 1970s', *Journal of Political Economy*, Vol. 89, No. 4, pp. 665–705.

Frenkel, J.A. (1981b) 'The Collapse of Purchasing Power Parity During the 1970s', *European Economic Review*, Vol. 16, pp. 145–165.

Frenkel, J.A. Gylfason, T. and Helliwell, J.F. (1980) 'A Synthesis of Monetary and Keynesian Approaches to Short-Run Balance-of-Payments Theory', *Economic Journal*, Vol. 90, pp. 582–592.

Friedman, B.M. (1979) 'Optimal Expectations of the Extreme Information Assumptions of "Rational Expectations" Macromodels', *Journal of Monetary Economics*, Vol. 5, 23–41.

Friedman, B.M. and Roley, V.V. (1979) 'Investors' Portfolio Behavior Under Alternative Models of Long-Term Interest Rate Expectations: Unitary, Rational, or Autoregressive', *Econometrica*, Vol. 47, No. 6, pp. 1475–1497.

Friend, I., Landskroner, Y. and Losq, E. (1976) 'The Demand for Risky Assets Under Uncertain Inflation', *Journal of Finance*, Vol. 11, No. 31, pp. 1287–1297.

Froot, K.A. and Frankel, J.A. (1989) 'Forward Discount Bias: Is it an Exchange Risk Premium?', *Quarterly Journal of Economics*, Vol. 104, No. 1, pp. 139–161.

Froot, K.A. and Ito, T. (1989) 'On the Consistency of Short-Run and Long-Run Exchange Rate Expectations', *Journal of International Money and Finance*, Vol. 8, Dec., pp. 487–510.

Froot, K.A. and Obstfeld, M. (1991) 'Intrinsic Bubbles: The Case of Stock Prices', *American Economic Review*, Vol. 81, No. 5, pp. 1189–1214.

Froot, K.A. and Thaler, R.H. (1990) 'Anomalies: Foreign Exchange', *Journal of Economic Perspectives*, Vol. 4, No. 3, pp. 179–192.

Garber, P.M. (1990) 'Famous First Bubbles', *Journal of Economic Perspectives*, Vol. 4, No. 2, pp. 35–54.

Gilles, C. and LeRoy, S.F. (1991) 'Econometric Aspects of the Variance-Bounds Tests: A Survey', *Review of Financial Studies*, Vol. 4, No. 4, pp. 753–791.

Giovannini, A. and Jorion, P. (1989) 'The Time Variation of Risk and Return in the Foreign Exchange and Stock Markets', *Journal of Finance*, Vol. 44, No. 2, pp. 307–325.

Gleick, J. (1987) *Chaos: Making a New Science*, Cardinal Books, London.

Goodhart, C. (1989) 'News and the Foreign Exchange Market', *London School of Economics Financial Market Group Discussion Paper No. 71*.

Goodman, S.H. (1979) 'Foreign Exchange Rate Forecasting Techniques: Implications for Business and Policy', *Journal of Finance*, Vol. 34, No. 2, pp. 415–427.

Goodman, S.H. (1980) 'Who's Better than the Toss of a Coin?', *Euromoney*, pp. 80–84.

Gordon, M.J. (1962). *The Investment, Financing and Valuation of the Corporation*, Irwin, Homewood Ill.

Granger, C.W.J. (1966) 'The Typical Spectral Shape of an Economic Variable', *Econometrica*, Vol. 34, No. 1, pp. 150–161.

Granger, C.W.J. and Newbold, P. (1974) 'Spurious Regressions in Econometrics', *Journal of Econometrics*, Vol. 2, pp. 111–120.

Greene, W.H. (1990) *Econometric Analysis*, Macmillan, New York.

Gregory, A.W. and Veall, M.R. (1985) 'Formulating Wald Tests of Nonlinear Restrictions', *Econometrica*, Vol. 53, No. 6, pp. 1465–1468.

Grilli, V. and Kaminsky, G. (1991) 'Nominal Exchange Rate Regimes and the Real Exchange Rate: Evidence from the United States and Great Britain, 1885–1986', *Journal of Monetary Economics*, Vol. 27, No. 2, pp. 191–212.

Grossman, S.J. and Shiller, R.J. (1981) 'The Determinants of the Variability of Stock Market Prices', *American Economic Review*, Vol. 71, 222–227.

Grossman, S.J. and Stiglitz, J.E. (1980) 'The Impossibility of Informationally Efficient Markets', *American Economic Review*, Vol. 66, pp. 246–253.

Gylfason, T. and Helliwell, J.F. (1983) 'A Synthesis of Keynsian, Monetary and Portfolio Approaches to Flexible Exchange Rates', *Economic Journal*, Vol. 93, No. 372, pp. 820–831.

Hacche, G. and Townend, J. (1981) 'Exchange Rates and Monetary Policy: Modelling Sterling's Effective Exchange Rate, 1972–80', in W.A. Eltis and P.J.N. Sinclair, *The Money Supply and the Exchange Rate*, Oxford University Press, Oxford, pp. 201–247.

Hakkio, C.S. (1981) 'Expectations and the Forward Exchange Rate', *International Economic Review*, Vol. 22, pp. 383–417.

Hall, A.D., Anderson, H.M. and Granger, C.W.J. (1992) 'A Cointegration Analysis of Treasury Bill Yields', *Review of Economic and Statistics*, Vol. 74, pp. 116–126.

Hall, S.G. (1986) 'An Application of the Granger and Engle Two-Step Estimation Procedure to United Kingdom Aggregate Wage Data', *Oxford Bulletin of Economics and Statistics*, Vol. 48, No. 3, pp. 229–239.

Hall, S.G. and Miles, D.K. (1992) 'Measuring Efficiency and Risk in the Major Bond Markets', *Oxford Economic Papers*, Vol. 44, pp. 599–625.

Hall, S.G., Miles, D.K. and Taylor, M.P. (1989) 'Modelling Asset Prices with Time-Varying Betas', *Manchester School*, Vol. 57, No. 4, pp. 340–356.

Hall, S.G., Miles, D.K. and Taylor, M.P. (1990) 'A CAPM with Time-varying Betas: Some Results', in S.G.B. Henry and K.D. Patterson (eds) *Economic Modelling at the Bank of England*, Chapman and Hall, London.

Hamilton, J.D. (1994) *Time Series Analysis*, Princeton University Press, Princeton, New Jersey.

Hannan, E.J. (1970) *Multiple Time Series*, Wiley, New York.

Hansen, L.P. (1982) 'Large Sample Properties of Generalised Method of Moments Estimators', *Econometrica*, Vol. 50, No. 4, pp. 1029–1054.

Hansen, L.P. and Hodrick, R.J. (1980) 'Forward Exchange Rates as Optimal Predictors of Future Spot Rates: An Econometric Analysis', *Journal of Political Economy*, Vol. 88, No. 5, pp. 829–853.

Harvey, A.C. (1981) *The Econometric Analysis of Time Series*, Philip Allan, Oxford.

Hausman, J.A. (1978) 'Specification Tests in Econometrics', *Econometrica*, Vol. 46, pp. 1251–1272.

Hendry, D.F. (1988) 'The Encompassing Implications of Feedback Versus Feedforward Mechanisms in Econometrics', *Oxford Economic Papers*, Vol. 40, No. 1, pp. 132–149.

Hendry, D.F. (1995) *Dynamic Econometrics*, Oxford University Press, Oxford.

Hinich, M.J. (1982) 'Testing for Gaussianity and Linearity of a Stationary Sequence', *Journal of Time Series*, Vol. 3, No. 3, pp. 169–176.

Hoare Govett (1991) 'UK Market Prospects for the Year Ahead', *Equity Market Strategy*, Hoare Govett, London.

Hodrick, R.J. (1987) *The Empirical Evidence of the Efficiency of Forward and Futures Foreign Exchange Markets*, Harwood, Chur, Switzerland.

Holden, K. (1994) 'Vector Autoregression Modelling and Forecasting', Discussion Paper 5/94, Centre for International Banking, Economics and Finance, Liverpool Business School, Liverpool John Moores University.

Holden, K., Peel, D.A. and Thompson, J.L. (1985) *Expectations Theory and Evidence*, Macmillan, Basingstoke.

Holloway, C. (1981) 'A Note on Testing an Aggressive Investment Strategy Using Value Line Ranks', *Journal of Finance*, Vol. 36, No. 3, pp. 711–719.

Hurn, A.S., Moody, T. and Muscatelli, V.A. (1996) 'The Term Structure of Interest Rates in the London Interbank Market', *Oxford Economic Papers*, forthcoming 1996.

Isard, P. (1978) 'Exchange Rate Determination: A Survey of Popular Views and Recent Models', *Princeton Studies in International Finance, No. 42.*

Ito, T. (1990) 'Foreign Exchange Rate Expectations: Micro Survey Data', *American Economic Review*, Vol. 80, No. 3, pp. 434–449.

Jensen, M.C. (1986) 'Agency Costs of Free Cash Flow, Corporate Finance, and Takeovers', *American Economic Review Papers and Proceedings*, Vol. 76, No. 2, pp. 323–329.

Jensen, M.C. (1978) 'Some Anomalous Evidence Regarding Market Efficiency', *Journal of Financial Economics*, Vol. 6, pp. 95–101.

Joerding, W. (1988) 'Are Stock Prices Excessively Sensitive to Current Information?', *Journal of Economic Behaviour and Organization*, Vol. 9, pp. 71–85.

Johansen, S. (1988) 'Statistical Analysis of Cointegration Vectors', *Journal of Economic Dynamics and Control*, Vol. 12, pp. 231–254.

Jones, D.S. and Roley, V.V. (1983) 'Rational Expectations and the Expectations Model of the Term Structure', *Journal of Monetary Economics*, Vol. 12, pp. 453–465.

Keane, S.M. (1983) *Stock Market Efficiency: Theory, Evidence and Implications*, Philip Allan, Oxford.

Keim, D.B. and Stambaugh, R.F. (1986) 'Predicting Returns in the Stock and Bond Markets', *Journal of Financial Economics*, Vol. 17, 357–390.

Keynes, J.M. (1936) *The General Theory of Employment, Interest, and Money*, Harcourt, Brace and World, New York.

Kirman, A.P. (1991) 'Epidemics of Opinion and Speculative Bubbles in Financial Markets', in M. Taylor (ed.) *Money and Financial Markets*, Macmillan, London.

Kirman, A.P. (1993) 'Testing for Bubbles', Discussion Paper, European University Institute, Florence.

Kirman, A. (1993) 'Ants, Rationality, and Recruitment', *Quarterly Journal of Economics*, Vol. 108, No. 1, pp. 137–156.

Kleidon, A.W. (1986) 'Variance Bounds Tests and Stock Price Valuation Models', *Journal of Political Economy*, Vol. 94, pp. 953–1001.

Kolb, R.W. (1995) *Investments* (4th edition), Kolb Publishing, Boulder.

Lamoureux, C.G. and Lastrapes, W.D. (1990a) 'Heteroscedasticity in Stock Return Data: Volume Versus GARCH Effects', *Journal of Finance*, Vol. 45, No. 1, pp. 221–229.

Lamoureux, C.G. and Lastrapes, W.D. (1990b) 'Persistence in Variance, Structural Change and the GARCH Model', *Journal of Business and Economic Statistics*, Vol. 8, 225–234.

Lee, C.M.C., Shleifer, A. and Thaler, R.H. (1990) 'Closed-End Mutual Funds', *Journal of Economic Perspectives*, Vol. 4, No. 4, pp. 153–164.

LeRoy, S.F. (1989) 'Efficient Capital Markets and Martingales', *Journal of Economic Literature*, Vol. 27, Dec., pp. 1583–1621.

LeRoy, S.F. and Parke, W.R. (1992) 'Stock Market Volatility: Tests Based on the Geometric Random Walk', *American Economic Review*, Vol. 82, No. 4, pp. 981–992.

LeRoy, S.F. and Porter, R.D. (1981) 'The Present-Value Relation: Tests Based on Implied Variance Bounds', *Econometrica*, Vol. 49, 555–574.

Levich, R.M. (1980) 'Analysing the Accuracy of Foreign Exchange Advisory Services: Theory and Evidence', Chapter 5 in Levich and Wihlborg (eds) *Exchange Risk and Exposure*, Lexington Books.

Levy, E. and Nobay, R. (1986) 'The Speculative Efficiency Hypothesis: A Bivariate Analysis', *Economic Journal*, Vol. 96, Conference Supplement, pp. 109–121.

Levy, H. (1978) 'Equilibrium in an Imperfect Market: A Constraint on the Number of Securities in the Portfolio', *American Economic Review*, Vol. 68, No. 4, pp. 643–658.

Levy, H. and Sarnat, M. (1984) *Portfolio and Investment Selection: Theory and Practice*, Prentice Hall, New York.

Lintner, J. (1971) 'The Aggregation of Investors' Diverse Judgements and Preferences in Purely Competitive Security Markets', *Journal of Finance and Quantitative Analysis*, Vol. 4, No. 4, pp. 347–450.

Litzenberger, R.H. and Ramaswamy, K. (1979) 'The Effect of Personal Taxes and Dividends on Capital Asset Prices: Theory and Empirical Evidence', *Journal of Financial Economics*, June, pp. 163–195.

Lo, A.W. and MacKinlay, A.C. (1988) 'Stock Market Prices do not Follow Random Walks: Evidence from a Simple Specification Test', *Review of Financial Studies*, Vol. 1, 41–66.

Lofthouse, S. (1994) *Equity Investment Management*, J. Wiley, New York.

Lucas, R.E. (1978) 'Asset Prices in an Exchange Economy', *Econometrica*, Vol. 46, pp. 1426–1446.

MacDonald, R. (1983) 'Some Tests of the Rational Expectations Hypothesis in the Foreign Exchange Market', *Scottish Journal of Political Economy*, Vol. 30, No. 3, pp. 235–250.

MacDonald, R. (1985) '"News" and the 1920s Experience with Floating Exchange Rates', *Economic Letters*, Vol. 17, pp. 379–383.

MacDonald, R. (1988) *Floating Exchange Rates: Theories and Evidence*, Unwin Hyman, London.

MacDonald, R. and Power, D. (1991) 'Persistence in UK Stock Market Returns', in M.P. Taylor (ed.) *Money and Financial Markets*, Basil Blackwell, Oxford.

MacDonald, R. and Speight, A.E.H. (1988) 'The Term Structure of Interest Rates in the UK', *Bulletin of Economic Research*, Vol. 40, No. 4, pp. 287–299.

MacDonald, R. and Speight, A.E.H. (1991) 'The Term Structure of Interest Rates Under Rational Expectations: Some International Evidence', *Applied Financial Economics*, Vol. 1, pp. 211–221.

MacDonald, R. and Taylor, M.P. (1987)

MacDonald, R. and Taylor, M.P. (1990) 'The Term Structure of Forward Premia: The Interwar Experience', *Manchester School*, Vol. 58, pp. 54–65.

MacDonald, R. and Taylor, M.P. (1989) 'Foreign Exchange Market Efficiency and Cointegration: Some Evidence from the Recent Float', *Economic Letters*, Vol. 29, No. 1, pp. 63–68.

MacDonald, R. and Taylor, M.P. (1992) 'Exchange Rate Economics — A Survey', *IMF Staff Papers*, Vol. 39, No. 1, pp. 1–57.

MacDonald, R. and Taylor, M.P. (1993) 'The Monetary Approach to the Exchange Rate: Rational Expectations, Long Run Equilibrium and Forecasting', *IMF Staff Papers*, Vol. 40, No. 1, pp. 89–107.

MacDonald, R. and Taylor, M.P. (1994) 'The Monetary Model of the Exchange Rate: Long Run Relationship, Short Run Dynamics and How to Beat the Random Walk', *Journal of International Money and Finance*, Vol. 13, No. 3, pp. 276–290.

MacDonald, R. and Torrance, T.S. (1988) 'On Risk, Rationality and Excessive Speculation in the Deutschmark United States Dollar Exchange Market: Some Evidence Using Survey Data', *Oxford Bulletin of Economics and Statistics*, Vol. 50, No. 2, pp. 107–123.

Malkiel, B.G. (1977) 'The Valuation of Closed-End Investment-Company Shares', *Journal of Finance*, Vol. 32, No. 3, pp. 847–859.

Malkiel, B.G. (1979) 'The Capital Formation Problem in the United States', *Journal of Finance*, Vol. 34, 291–306.

Mankiw, N.G. (1986) 'The Term Structure of Interest Rates Revisited', *Brookings Papers on Economic Activity*, Vol. 1, pp. 61–110.

Mankiw, N.G. and Miron, J.A. (1986) 'The Changing Behavior of the Term Structure of Interest Rates', *Quarterly Journal of Economics*, Vol. 101, No. 2, pp. 211–228.

Mankiw, N.G. and Shapiro, M.D. (1986) 'Risk and Return: Consumption Beta Versus Market Beta', *Review of Economics and Statistics*, Vol. 68, No. 3, pp. 452–459.

Mankiw, N.G. and Summers, L.H. (1984) 'Do Long-Term Interest Rates Overreact to Short-Term Interest Rates', *Brookings Papers on Economic Activity*, Vol. 1, pp. 223–242.

Mankiw, N.G., Romer, D. and Shapiro, M.D. (1985) 'An Unbiased Reexamination of Stock Market Volatility', *Journal of Finance*, Vol. 40, 677–687.

Mankiw, N.G., Romer, D. and Shapiro, M.D. (1991) 'Stock Market Forecastability and Volatility: A Statistical Appraisal', *Review of Economic Studies*, Vol. 58, pp. 455–477.

Mark, N.C. (1995) 'Exchange Rates and Fundamentals: Evidence on Long Horizon Predictability', *American Economic Review*, Vol. 85, No. 1, pp. 201–218.

Marsh, T.A. and Merton, R.C. (1986) 'Dividend Variability and Variance Bounds Tests for the Rationality of Stock Market Prices', *American Economic Review*, Vol. 76, 483–498.

McCulloch, J.H. (1971) 'Measuring the Term Structure of Interest Rates', *Journal of Business*, Vol. 44, pp. 19–31.

McCulloch, J.H. (1987) 'The Monotonicity of the Term Premium: A Closer Look', *Journal of Financial Economics*, Vol. 18, pp. 185–192.

McCulloch, J.H. (1990) 'U.S. Government Term Structure Data', in B. Friedman and F. Hahn (eds) *The Handbook of Monetary Economics*, North Holland, Amsterdam.

McElroy, M.B., Burmeister, E. and Wall, K.D. (1985) 'Two Estimators for the APT Model When Factors are Measured', *Economic Letters*, Vol. 19, pp. 271–275.

Meese, E. (1990) 'Currency Fluctuation in the Post-Bretton Woods Era', *Journal of Economic Perspectives*, Vol. 4, No. 1, pp. 117–134.

Meese, R.A. (1986) 'Testing for Bubbles in Exchange Markets: A Case of Sparkling Rates', *Journal of Political Economy*, Vol. 94, No. 2, pp. 345–373.

Meese, R.A. and Rogoff, K. (1983) 'Empirical Exchange Rate Models of the Seventies: Do They Fit Out of Sample?', *Journal of International Economics*, Vol. 14, pp. 3–24.

Mehra, R. and Prescott, E.C. (1985) 'The Equity Premium: A Puzzle', *Journal of Monetary Economics*, Vol. 15, 145–161.

Melino, A. (1988) 'The Term Structure of Interest Rates: Evidence and Theory', *Journal of Economic Surveys*, Vol. 2, No. 4, pp. 335–366.

Merton, R.C. (1973) 'An Intertemporal Capital Asset Pricing Model', *Econometrica*, Vol. 41, pp. 867–887.

Merton, R.C. (1980) 'On Estimating the Expected Return on the Market', *Journal of Financial Economics*, Vol. 8, pp. 323–361.

Merton, R.C. (1987) 'On the Current State of the Stock Market Rationality Hypothesis', in S. Fischer (ed.) *Macroeconomics and Finance: Essays in Honor of Franco Modigliani*, MIT Press, Cambridge, Massachusetts.

Miles, D. (1993) 'Testing for Short-termism in the UK Stock Market', *Economic Journal*, Vol. 103, pp. 1379–1396.

Mills, T.C. (1991) 'The Term Structure of UK Interest Rates: Tests of the Expectations Hypothesis', *Applied Economics*, Vol. 23, pp. 599–606.

Mills, T.C. (1993) *The Econometric Modelling of Financial Time Series*, Cambridge University Press, Cambridge.

Mishkin, F.S. (1988) 'The Information in the Term Structure: Some Further Results', *Journal of Applied Econometrics*, Vol. 3, No. 4, pp. 307–314.

Mishkin, F.S. (1990) 'What Does the Term Structure Tell us About Future Inflation?', *Journal of Monetary Economics*, Vol. 25, No. 1, pp. 77–95.

Muth, J.F. (1961) 'Rational Expectations and the Theory of Price Movements', *Econometrica*, Vol. 29, No. 3, pp. 315–335.

Nelson, C.R. (1975) 'Rational Expectations and the Estimation of Econometric Models', *International Economic Review*, Vol. 16, pp. 555–561.

Newey, W.K. and West, K.D. (1987) 'A Simple, Positive Semi-Definite, Heteroskedasticity and Autocorrelation Consistent Covariance Matrix', *Econometrica*, Vol. 55, No. 3, pp. 703–708.

Pagan, A.R. (1984) 'Econometric Issues in the Analysis of Regressions with Generated Regressors', *International Economic Review*, Vol. 25, No. 1, pp. 221–247.

Pagan, A.R. and Schwert, G.W. (1990) 'Alternative Models for Conditional Stock Volatility', *Journal of Econometrics*, Vol. 45, pp. 267–290.

Pagan, A.R. and Ullah, A. (1988) 'The Econometric Analysis of Models with Risk Terms', *Journal of Applied Econometrics*, Vol. 3, pp. 87–105.

Perron, P. (1988) 'Trends and Random Walks in Macroeconomic Time Series: Further Evidence from a New Approach', *Journal of Economic Dynamics and Control*, Vol. 12, 297–332.

Pesando, J.E. (1983) 'On Expectations, Term Premiums and the Volatility of Long-term Interest Rates', *Journal of Monetary Economics*, Vol. 12, No. 3, pp. 467–474.

Pesaran, M.H. (1985) 'Formation of Inflation Expectations in British Manufacturing Industries', *Economic Journal*, Vol. 95, No. 380, pp. 948–975.

Pesaran, M.H. (1987) *The Limits to Rational Expectations*, Blackwell, Oxford.

Pesaran, M.H. and Potter, S.M. (1993) *Nonlinear Dynamics, Chaos and Econometrics*, J. Wiley, New York.

Pesaran, M.H. and Timmermann, A. (1994) 'Forecasting Stock Returns: An Examination of Stock Market Trading in the Presence of Transaction Costs', *Journal of Forecasting*, Vol. 13, No. 4, pp. 335–367.

Pesaran, M.H. and Timmermann, A. (1995) 'Predictability of Stock Returns: Robustness and Economic Significance', *Journal of Finance*, Vol. L, No. 4, pp. 1201-1228.

Peters, E.E. (1991) *Chaos and Order in the Capital Market*, J. Wiley, New York.

Phillips, P.C.B. and Perron, P. (1988) 'Testing for a Unit Root in Time Series Regression', *Biometrika*, Vol. 75, No. 2, pp. 335-346.

Pilbeam, K. (1992) *International Finance*, Macmillan, Basingstoke.

Poon, S. and Taylor, S.J. (1991) 'Macroeconomic Factors and the UK Stock Market', *Journal of Business and Accounting*, Vol. 18, pp. 619-636.

Poterba, J.M. and Summers, L.H. (1986) 'The Persistence of Volatility and Stock Market Fluctuations', *American Economic Review*, Vol. 76, No. 5, pp. 1142-1151.

Poterba, J.M. and Summers, L.H. (1988) 'Mean Reversion in Stock Prices: Evidence and Implications', *Journal of Financial Economics*, Vol. 22, 26-59.

Reinganum, M.R. (1982) 'A Direct Test of Roll's Conjecture on the Firm Size Effect', *Journal of Finance*, Vol. 37, No. 1, pp. 27-35.

Reinganum, M.R. (1983) 'The Anomalous Stock Market Behavior of Small Firms in January: Empirical Tests for Tax-Loss Selling Effects', *Journal of Financial Economics*, Vol. 12, No. 1, pp. 89-104.

Roll, R. (1977) 'A Critique of Asset Pricing Theory's Tests', *Journal of Financial Economics*, Vol. 4, pp. 1073-1103.

Roll, R. and Ross, S.A. (1980) 'An Empirical Investigation of the APT', *Journal of Finance*, Vol. 35, No. 5, Dec., pp. 1073-1103.

Roll, R. and Ross, S.A. (1984) 'A Critical Re-examination of the Empirical Evidence on the APT: A Reply', *Journal of Finance*, Vol. 39, No. 2, pp. 347-350.

Ross, S.A. (1976) 'The Arbitrage Theory of Capital Asset Pricing', *Journal of Economic Theory*, Vol. 13, Dec., pp. 341-360.

Samuelson, P. (1965) 'Proof that Properly Anticipated Prices Fluctuate Randomly', *Industrial Management Review*, Vol. 6, pp. 41-49.

Schaefer, S.M. (1977) 'The Problem with Redemption Yields', *Financial Analysts Journal*, Vol. 33, No. July/Aug., pp. 59-67.

Schwert, G.W. (1989) 'Why Does Stock Market Volatility Change Over Time?', *Journal of Finance*, Vol. 44, No. 5, pp. 1115-1153.

Scott, L.O. (1985) 'The Present Value Model of Stock Market Prices: Regression Tests and Monte Carlo Results', *Review of Economics and Statistics*, Vol. 57, 599-605.

Scott, L.O. (1990) 'Asset Prices, Market Fundamentals, and Long-Term Expectations: Some New Tests of Present Value Models', unpublished, University of Georgia, Athens, Georgia.

Scott, L.O. (1991) 'Financial Market Volatility', *IMF Staff Papers*, Vol. 38, No. 3, pp. 347-365.

Sentana, E. and Wadhwani, S. (1992) 'Feedback Traders and Stock Return Autocorrelations: Evidence From a Century of Daily Data', *Economic Journal*, Vol. 102, No. 411, pp. 415-425.

Shanken, J. (1992) 'On the Estimation of Beta-Pricing Models', *Review of Financial Studies*, Vol. 5, pp. 1-33.

Shanken, J. and Weinstein, M. (1990) 'Macroeconomic Variables and Asset Pricing: Estimation and Tests', Working Paper, University of Rochester.

Sharpe, W. (1982) 'Factors on NYSE Security Returns 1931-79', *Journal of Portfolio Management*, Vol. 8, No. 2, pp. 5-19.

Shawky, J. (1982) 'An Update on Mutual Funds: Better Grades', *Journal of Portfolio Management*, Winter.

Shea, G.S. (1989) 'Ex-Post Rational Price Approximations and the Empirical Reliability of the Present-Value Relation', *Journal of Applied Econometrics*, Vol. 4, pp. 139-159.

Shea, G.S. (1992) 'Benchmarking the Expectations Hypothesis of the Term Structure: An Analysis of Cointegration Vectors', *Journal of Business and Economic Statistics*, pp. 347-365.

Sheffrin, S.M. (1983) *Rational Expectations*, Cambridge University Press, Cambridge.

Sherif, M. (1937) 'An Experimental Approach to the Study of Attitudes', *Sociometry*, Vol. 1, pp. 90-98.

Shiller, R.J. (1979) 'The Volatility of Long-Term Interest Rates and Expectations Models of the Term Structure', *Journal of Political Economy*, Vol. 87, No. 6, pp. 1190-1219.

Shiller, R.J. (1981) 'Do Stock Prices Move too Much to be Justified by Subsequent Changes in Dividends?', *American Economic Review*, Vol. 71, 421-436.

Shiller, R.J. (1984) 'Stock Prices and Social Dynamics', *Brookings Papers on Economic Activity*, Vol. 2, 457–498.

Shiller, R.J. (1989) *Market Volatility* MIT Press, Cambridge, Massachusetts.

Shiller, R.J. (1990) 'Speculative Prices and Popular Models', *Journal of Economic Perspectives*, Vol. 4, No. 2, pp. 55–65.

Shiller, R.J. and Beltratti, A.E. (1992) 'Stock Prices and Bond Yields', *Journal of Monetary Economics*, Vol. 30, 25–46.

Shiller, R.J., Campbell, J.Y. and Schoenholtz, K.J. (1983) 'Forward Rates and Future Policy: Interpreting the Term Structure of Interest Rates', *Brookings Papers on Economic Activity*, Vol. 1, pp. 173-217.

Shleifer, A. and Summers, L.H. (1990) 'The Noise Trader Approach to Finance', *Journal of Economic Perspectives*, Vol. 4, No. 2, pp. 19–33.

Shleifer, A. and Vishny, R.W. (1990) 'Equilibrium Short Horizons of Investors and Firms', *American Economic Review Papers and Proceedings*, Vol. 80, No. 2, pp. 148-153.

Simon, D.P. (1989) 'Expectations and Risk in the Treasury Bill Market: An Instrumental Variables Approach', *Journal of Financial and Quantitative Analysis*, Vol. 24, No. 3, pp. 357-365.

Sims, C.A. (1980) 'Macroeconomics and Reality', *Econometrica*, Vol. 48, No (Jan), pp. 1-48.

Singleton, K.J. (1980) 'Expectations Models of the Term Structure and Implied Variance Bounds', *Journal of Political Economy*, Vol. 88, No. 6, pp. 1159-1176.

Smith, P.N. (1993) 'Modeling Risk Premia in International Asset Markets', *European Economic Review*, Vol. 37, No. 1, pp. 159-176.

Summers, L.H. (1986) 'Does the Stock Market Rationally Reflect Fundamental Values?', *Journal of Finance*, Vol. 41, No. 3, pp. 591-601.

Takagi, S. (1991) 'Exchange Rate Expectations', *IMF Staff Papers*, Vol. 8, No. 1, pp. 156-183.

Taylor, J.B. (1979) 'Estimation and Control of a Macromodel with Rational Expectations', *Econometrica*, Vol. 47, pp. 1267-1286.

Taylor, M.P. (1987) 'Covered Interest Parity: A High-Frequency, High Quality Data Survey', *Economica*, Vol. 54, pp. 429-438.

Taylor, M.P. (1988) 'What Do Investment Managers Know? An Empirical Study of Practitioners Predictions', *Economica*, Vol. 55, pp. 185-202.

Taylor, M.P. (1989a) 'Covered Interest Arbitrage and Market Turbulence', *Economic Journal*, Vol. 99, No. 396, pp. 376-391.

Taylor, M.P. (1989b) 'Expectations, Risk and Uncertainty in the Foreign Exchange Market: Some Results Based on Survey Data', *Manchester School*, Vol. 57, No. 2, pp. 142-153.

Taylor, M.P. (1989c) 'Vector Autoregressive Tests of Uncovered Interest Rate Parity with Allowance for Conditional Heteroscedasticity', *Scottish Journal of Political Economy*, Vol. 36, No. 3, pp. 238-252.

Taylor, M.P. (1992) 'Modelling the Yield Curve', *Economic Journal*, Vol. 102, No. 412, pp. 524-537.

Taylor, M.P. (1995) 'The Economics of Exchange Rates', *Journal of Economic Literature*, Vol. 33, pp. 13-47.

Taylor, S. (1986) *Modelling Financial Time Series*, J. Wiley, New York.

Thaler, R.H. (1987) 'Anomalies: The January Effect', *Journal of Economic Perspectives*, Vol. 1, No. 1, pp. 197-201.

Thaler, R.H. (1994) *Quasi Rational Economics*, Russell Sage Foundation, New York.

Thomas, S.H. and Wickens, M.R. (1993) 'An International CAPM for Bonds and Equity', *Journal of International Money and Finance*, Vol. 12, No. 4, pp. 390-412.

Tirole, J. (1985) 'Asset Bubbles and Overlapping Generations', *Econometrica*, Vol. 53, No. 5, pp. 1071-1100.

Tobin, J. (1958) 'Liquidity Preference as Behaviour Towards Risk', *Review of Economic Studies*, Vol. 56, pp. 65-86.

Trippi, R.R. and Turban, E. (1993) *Neural Networks in Finance and Investing*, Irwin, Burr Ridge, IL.

Tzavalis, E. and Wickens, M. (1993) 'The Persistence of Volatility in the US Term Premium 1970-1986', *Discussion Paper No. 11-93*, London Business School, mimeo.

West, K.D. (1987a) 'A Specification Test for Speculative Bubbles', *Quarterly Journal of Economics*, Vol. 102, No. 3, pp. 553-580.

West, K.D. (1987b) 'A Standard Monetary Model and the Variability of the Deutschemark-Dollar Exchange Rate', *Journal of International Economics*, Vol. 23, pp. 57–76.

West, K.D. (1988a) 'Asymptotic Normality, when Regressors have a Unit Root', *Econometrica*, Vol. 56, No. 6, pp. 1397–1417.

West, K.D. (1988b) 'Dividend Innovations and Stock Price Volatility', *Econometrica*, Vol. 56, pp. 37–61.

White, H. (1980) 'A Heteroscedasticity-Consistent Covariance Matrix Estimator and a Direct Test for Heteroscedasticity', *Econometrica*, Vol. 48, pp. 55–68.

White, H. (1984) *Asymptotic Theory for Econometricians*, Academic Press, New York.

Wold, H. (1938) *A Study in the Analysis of Stationary Time Series*, Alquist and Wiksell, Upsala.

Zellner, A. (1971) *An Introduction to Bayesian Inference in Econometrics*, John Wiley, New York.

Index

Akaike information criterion, 339
Anomalies, 169, 185
Anti-inflation policy, 207, 250
Arbitrage, 63, 172, 259, 268–271
Arbitrage pricing theory (APT), 61–67, 74, 75,
    129, 401
Arbitrageurs, 174, 179
ARCH model, 43–45, 183, 202, 375–380,
    389, 398–415, 438–442
ARIMA models, 286, 287, 398, 420–442
ARMA models, 117, 126–127, 151–153, 161,
    339, 382, 421, 422, 426–437
Asset demand, 54–57
Augmented Dickey Fuller test (*see* Dickey-
    Fuller test)
Autocorrelation, 421, 422, 426
Autocovariance function, 422, 426
Autoregressive models (*see* ARMA models)

Bankruptcy, 177, 201
Bearish, 182, 183, 203, 204
Beta, 24, 41–46, 57–61, 70–73
Bid-ask spread (see also spread), 124, 173
Big-Bang, 174
Black Wednesday, 256, 257
Bond, 3–10, 178, 208, 211–227, 234, 250,
    297, 309, 311, 313, 375, 401, 402,
    407–41
    corporate, 207, 212, 237, 272, 379, 392,
        393
    coupon paying, 8, 212, 246, 249
    government, 189, 207, 212, 326, 392, 393,
        397, 398
    zero coupon, 212, 229, 234, 340, 402, 413,
        414
    pure discount, 7, 212, 213, 241, 245, 249,
        331, 402
Bond market, 207–214, 234, 249, 315, 332,
    344, 374, 376, 402–411
Bond price, 211–218, 246–247

Box Jenkins methodology, 422, 434, 436
Bretton Woods, 255, 256, 290, 299
Bubble, 156–168, 193, 195, 301, 302, 360
    collapsing, 157, 162, 163, 167, 168
    exogenous, 157, 161, 302
    explosive, 156, 162
    intrinsic, 157, 163–167, 360
    rational, 156–163, 167, 195, 300, 301
Budget constraint, 49, 223, 391, 392
Budget deficit, 393
Bullish, 182, 183, 203
BZW equity index, 367

Capital asset pricing model (CAPM), 22–76,
    82–88, 96, 97, 103, 122, 127–133,
    177, 178, 190, 221, 222, 248, 249, 260,
    373–377, 381–412
    consumption (*see* consumption CAPM)
    post-tax, 72, 73
    zero beta, 48–54, 69, 234, 248, 249, 408
Capital gain/loss, 345, 363, 364, 371
Capital market, 19, 187
Capital market line (CML), 37–39, 46
Capital mobility, 291–293
Central bank, 207, 266, 271, 280, 307, 330
Chaos, 169, 176, 195, 196, 205–294, 302–308
Chartists, 174, 179, 194, 198–201, 284–288,
    331
Chi-squared distribution (*see* distribution)
Closed end fund, 170–173, 185
Cochran-Orcutt transformation, 452
Cointegration, 162, 302, 328, 329, 335,
    434–438
Commercial paper, 353, 356
Consol (*see* Perpetuity)
Consumer Price Index, 368
Consumption, 294, 353, 355, 368, 374, 407,
    408
Consumption CAPM (CCAPM), 76, 83–88,
    128, 133–140, 408

Contagion, 190
Correlogram, 421, 422
Costs, 52, 53, 97, 106, 123–135, 169, 171, 175, 201, 205, 225, 261, 269–274, 332, 399, 411
Cost mark up equation, 431
Covariance conditional, 409–413, 438
Credit limit, 271
Currency, 255, 261, 292, 305–307, 376, 444

Data, 237, 277–284, 302, 328, 403, 444
Debt-equity ratio, 379
Detrending, 344, 425, 426
Devaluation, 270, 282, 283
Diagnostic test, 129, 342, 351, 430
Dickey Fuller test (DF test), 435
Discount factor, 136, 344, 373, 380, 381
Discount rate, 346–350, 360–367, 378
Discounted present value (DPV), 3–21, 76–88, 104–112, 136–147, 178, 188, 208–216, 311, 350, 363–365, 378–381
Distribution, 58, 71, 100, 111, 126, 152, 168, 182, 183, 321, 386, 392, 418, 419, 434, 441
Dividend, 9, 10, 346–352, 359–368, 372, 380–387, 434
Dividend price ratio, 346–354, 359, 360, 366–369, 375, 377, 387
Dornbusch overshooting model, 293–295
Dow Jones index, 130, 161
Duration, 217

Earnings, 360
Earnings price ratio, 355
Economic fundamentals (*see* fundamentals)
Economic model, 417, 427, 431, 432
Economic theory, 417, 431–433
Economic time series (*see* time series)
Efficiency (*see* informational efficiency)
Efficient frontier, 25, 29–33, 37
Efficient markets hypothesis (EMH), 44, 93–100, 105–129, 134, 143–152, 169–181, 194, 201, 208–215, 231–234, 249, 265, 269–288, 309–315, 338–368, 377, 387, 438
Efficient portfolio (*see* portfolio)
EMU 257
Employment, 207, 256, 293, 294, 303
Error correction model, 306, 342, 343, 434–437
Errors in variables method (EVM), 443–452
Estimation
    2 stage least squares (2SLS), 272, 275, 403, 443–452
    Generalised least squares, 443, 445, 452

GMM estimation, 146, 227, 242, 275, 324, 325, 373, 443, 449
Instrumental variable (IV), 272, 397, 403, 443–452
Maximum likelihood, 128, 396
Ordinary least squares (OLS), 149, 227, 242, 244, 253, 272, 276, 278, 284, 305, 324, 325, 373, 435, 443–451
Seemingly unrelated regression procedure (SURE), 276, 324, 334, 396
Euler equation, 77–85, 138, 154–167, 200, 302
Eurocurrency market, 268
Eurocurrency rate, 269, 271, 397
European Monetary System (EMS), 288
Excess holding period yield (*see* HPY)
Excess volatility (*see* volatility)
Exchange rate, 194, 200–207, 255–282, 290–307, 376, 417
    fixed/floating, 255–257, 271, 283, 300
    real, 262–265, 292, 298
Exchange Rate Mechanism (ERM), 256, 257, 290, 300
Exchange rate overshooting, 256, 257, 291–295
Expectations
    mathematical, 100–102, 114
    Rational (*see* Rational expectations)
    revision to, 363, 364
Expectations hypothesis (EH), 208–211, 219–232, 237, 240–252, 309–333, 339–340, 348, 403–408, 443
Extrapolative predictor, 447–449

Factor analysis *see* APT)
Fads, 175, 183, 185, 202, 342, 360
Fair game, 77, 94, 96, 100–104, 159
Federal Reserve, 244, 404
Feedback trader, 118–120, 179, 388, 389, 430
Fisher hypothesis, 226, 265, 292, 296
Flex-price monetary model, 290–301, 340–343
Forecast, 311–316, 323–335, 346–352, 355, 359, 360, 380, 410, 424, 425, 430, 437, 444, 449
    conditional, 422–426
    multiperiod, 320, 334, 339, 342
    unconditional, 415
Forecast error, 242, 250, 283, 310, 335, 336, 341, 353, 363, 365, 377–391, 403–410, 422, 427, 438–447
Forecasting
    chain rule of forecasting 311, 320, 331
Forecasting equation, 311, 312, 318, 325, 346, 359, 364

FOREX market, 176, 193, 251, 255–267, 270–284, 288, 298–303, 308, 309, 334–343, 344, 376
Forward discount, 279, 280–284, 288
Forward market, 257, 265, 272, 274, 280, 284, 288, 334, 337
Forward premium, 252, 253, 275–278, 289, 303, 305, 334–340
Forward rate, 251, 252, 259–268, 273–280, 288, 334–340
Forward rate unbiasedness (FRU), 264–268, 272–289, 334–342

GARCH model, 183, 301, 377, 383–389, 400, 406, 415, 438–442, 452
Gaussian error, 418, 426
Gearing, 190, 389, 393
Geometric random walk (see random walk)
Gordon's growth model, 135, 164, 347, 359
Granger causality, 325–330, 348–354, 433–438, 449

Herding, 156, 175, 176, 190, 202
Holding period return yield (HPY), 9, 10, 208–253, 331, 345, 353, 358, 368, 376, 397–414
Hyperinflation, 262, 292, 298, 300

Indifference curve, 3, 10–18, 38, 39, 50, 55–57
Inflation, 54, 108, 130, 207, 218, 226, 252, 256, 263–267, 272, 295, 300–307, 378, 393, 400–406, 431
Information set, 261, 312, 327, 330–341, 348–369, 386, 396, 404–411, 423, 426, 433, 443–452
Informational efficiency, 105–117, 138–142, 147–150, 159, 265, 283, 309–310, 315, 368, 404, 406
  semi strong form, 105
  strong form, 105
  weak form, 105, 117, 128, 133
Insider information, 105
Integrated GARCH (IGARCH) (see GARCH model)
Interest rate, 3–20, 33–73, 130, 207–212, 243, 244, 259–269, 290–298, 309, 315–333, 375–409
  continuously compounded, 3–8, 20, 211–233, 251, 414
  real, 104, 257, 290–293,
  risk free, 10–25, 33, 34, 48–65, 82–116, 121, 146, 214, 220–237

Interest rate parity
  covered (CIP), 260, 264–272, 281, 288, 338, 340
  real interest rate, 264–266
  uncovered (UIP), 260–268, 272, 273, 281–288, 293–300, 304–307, 334–342, 397
  testing, 268–289
Internal rate of return, 6–21
International Fisher hypothesis (see Fisher hypothesis)
International Monetary Fund (IMF), 255
Investment appraisal 6, 15–20

January effect, 123, 129, 169–173, 201
Johansen procedure, 434, 437

Lag operator, 418–421
Leverage, 379
Likelihood ratio test, 309, 315–319, 323, 333, 336, 396, 411
Linear combination
Linearisation, 363, 368
Liquidity preference hypothesis, 208, 211, 219–221, 228, 231–237, 252
Liquidity premium (see risk premium)
London Interbank Rate (LIBOR, LIBID), 245, 326–328

MA process (see also ARIMA model), 40, 123, 420–423, 437
Maastricht Treaty, 288
Marginal rate of substitution (MRS), 87, 88
Market psychology, 156, 285
Market segmentation hypothesis, 208, 211, 219–223, 231, 243, 331, 404
Markov switching model, 127, 166, 192
Martingale, 94, 99–104, 113, 159, 167, 191, 244, 249, 250, 301
Matrix
  companion, 322, 372
  variance-covariance, 227, 242, 275, 317, 321–325, 365, 373, 396, 413, 448–452
Maturity spectrum, 213, 245–249, 271, 315, 326, 331, 332, 402
Mean reversion, 172, 178–185, 287
Mean variance criterion, 26, 30
Mean variance model, 179, 375, 388–394, 399, 405
Measurement error, 397, 401, 407
Merger, 19, 93, 105, 113
Modigliani-Miller theorem, 99, 186
Money market, 293, 294
Money market line, 17

Money supply, 256, 266, 291–306, 342, 398
Monte Carlo, 127, 128, 136, 143–151, 163, 166, 356, 367
Mundell-Fleming model, 290
Mutual fund, 61, 171, 174, 179

NAIRU, 431
Net present value (*see* discounted present value)
Neural network, 202, 205, 302
Neutrality of money, 291–294
Noise trader, 118–128, 169–204, 258, 282, 284, 288, 299–307, 375–377, 380, 387–390
Non-stationarity (*see* stationarity)
NYSE, 129, 133, 172, 365, 384, 400

OECD, 300, 326
Omitted variables, 149, 399, 436, 437, 449
Orthogonality condition, 94–110, 138–141, 147–154, 167, 248, 272, 281, 319, 323, 325, 336, 444
Output, 256, 378–380, 431

Pension fund, 170, 173, 176, 207, 332
Perfect foresight
  rate, 224, 228–234
  regression, 331
  price, 178, 215, 240, 311, 344, 345, 350, 351, 358, 360
  spread, 208, 225, 227, 231, 237, 242, 245, 246, 319, 325–330
Performance index, 25, 47, 57–61, 131, 132
Perpetuity, 9, 212, 216, 240
Persistence, 176, 183, 344, 352, 361–390, 400, 412, 413, 440, 442
Peso problem, 147–252, 258, 279, 282–284, 288, 299, 301
Phillips curve, 266, 267, 291–294
Plaza and Louvre accord, 256, 301
Portfolio, 24–89, 121, 172–178, 381–399
  efficient/inefficient, 26
  market, 24, 40, 44, 73, 121, 178, 381, 399
  optimal, 22, 35
Portfolio balance model (PBM), 296–298
Portfolio diversification, 22, 25–31
Predictability, 122, 184, 358, 361–372
Preferred habitat hypothesis, 208, 219, 223
Present value (PV) (*see* discounted present value)
Price competitiveness, 255
Price index, 128, 139, 267, 384
Principle agent problem, 20

Probability density function, 100–105, 127, 159, 191
Production opportunity curve, 16, 17
Purchasing power parity (PPP), 257, 261–267, 291–299, 303, 307, 417, 444
Pure expectations hypothesis (PEH) (*see* expectations hypothesis)

Random walk, 94, 104, 105, 122–124, 128, 143–150, 162, 183, 194, 195, 244, 287, 299–306, 342, 400, 419–426
Rate of return, 3–5, 49, 98, 235–241
Rational expectations, 94–123, 145, 189, 201, 227–232, 242, 243, 250, 276–284, 302–332, 350–355, 402–406, 438–447
Rational valuation formula (RVF), 77–88, 116–118, 143–155, 162, 179, 189, 195, 211–215, 220, 223, 311–313, 344–348, 353–367
Real interest differential model (RIDM), 295–298
Real interest rate parity (*see* interest rate parity)
Real interest rate (*see* interest rate)
Redemption yield (*see* yield to maturity)
Restriction
  cross equation restriction, 298, 309, 315–323, 335–344, 353, 354, 449
  linear restriction, 349
  non-linear restriction, 324, 349, 351, 357
Return (see also rate of return)
  excess, 41–112, 128–135, 159, 171, 219, 222, 345, 349–357, 383–407
  expected, 23–104, 124, 149, 152, 182, 231, 260, 352, 363–374, 387–400, 413, 440
  linearisation, 368, 369
  multiperiod, 358–368
Risk, 20–45, 54–67, 259, 270, 357, 375–390, 402–414
  default, 212
  fundamental, 174
  idiosyncratic/specific, 62, 63
  market price of, 20, 38, 39, 384, 394–399, 409
  measures of, 45, 394, 404–408
  reinvestment, 214
  risk averse, 3–24, 55, 58, 86, 87, 99, 128, 140, 181, 185, 199, 203, 276, 353, 354, 391–405
  risk lover, 10–20
  risk neutral, 10–20, 76, 82–87, 231, 241, 242, 261–305, 334, 342, 401–404, 443
  risk premium, 7, 214–232, 237, 242, 245–253, 272–279, 289, 332, 339, 354, 375–390, 402–411
  systematic/unsystematic, 41–43

Roll critique, 60, 73, 74

Security market line (SML), 48, 49, 72, 133, 170
Separation principle, 16, 20, 23, 37, 50, 53
Short termism, 98, 113, 185-190, 204
Single index model (SIM), 67-69, 204
Small firm effect, 170, 173
Smart money, 169, 173-204, 243, 303-307, 377, 380, 388-389
Spread, 226-245, 309-333, 348, 350, 402-411
Spurious regression, 426, 434
Stability, 353, 430, 438
Standard and Poors composite share index, 122, 123, 128-130, 161-166, 357, 359, 380-382
Standard deviation ratio, 138, 139, 325, 350, 353, 354
Stationarity, 141, 142, 162, 193, 418-437
Statistical model, 417, 431, 432
Sticky price monetary model, 290-303
Stock return predictability, 122-134, 184, 353-357
Stock market, 116-156, 176, 351, 377
Stock price, 116-155, 344-373, 380-390
Structural model, 431-438
Sunspots, 156

Takeover, 19, 93, 98, 105, 113, 148, 149, 186, 188, 202-204
Tax, 52-54, 72, 73, 97, 99, 169, 170, 189, 271, 401
Term premium (see risk premium)
Term structure, 5-7, 209, 216-230, 249, 251, 312, 315-340, 345, 348, 402-414, 437
    empirical evidence, 234-253
Term to maturity, 213, 214, 226, 247-250, 402, 408, 409
Terms of trade, 292
Time series
    stationary/non-stationary, 419, 425, 426, 434
    univariate/multivariate, 415, 417-438
Time varying
    beta, 402, 406
    discount rate, 140, 346, 348, 354, 368
    real interest rates, 139
    risk/term premia, 152, 209, 219-222, 227-231, 246-249, 276, 277, 342-348, 355, 375-377, 387-391, 401-414, 438
    variances/covariances, 221, 368, 375, 376, 383, 387-390, 398-401, 409-415, 442
Tobin's risk aversion model, 54-57
Trading rule (see trading strategy), 124, 130-135, 202, 309, 380, 385
Transformation line, 25, 33-36, 55

Transversality condition (see terminal condition), 78, 81, 154-157, 214, 250, 346, 369
Treasury bill, 7, 22, 116, 128, 212, 218-228, 237, 242-247, 252, 326, 353, 365, 382, 403, 404
Trend
    deterministic, 139, 143, 144, 166, 415, 425, 426, 435
    stochastic, 143, 415, 425, 426, 434, 435

Utility, 3, 10-20, 55, 58, 84-88, 181, 203, 391-394

Value line investment survey (VLIS), 171
VAR, 227, 268, 286, 287, 298, 309-374, 379, 402, 428-438, 449
    advantage/disadvantage, 323-325
    cross equation restriction, 309-332, 336-342, 350
    multivariate, 339, 365
Variance conditional/unconditional, 222, 368, 373, 383-389, 402, 405-413, 419-427, 438, 439, 442
Variance bounds test, 116, 136, 139-150, 154, 208, 215, 226-234, 246-249, 309, 313, 344, 351, 360, 361, 368
Variance decomposition, 352, 365-374
Variance ratio, 116, 117, 125, 138, 142-153, 160, 178, 229, 246, 248, 309-315, 324-330, 337, 353-361
Variance-covariance matrix (see matrix)
VARMA model, 428-437
Volatility, 134-146, 169, 178, 183, 201-207, 249, 258, 279-282, 300, 327, 341-390, 404, 406, 413
Volatility tests (see variance bounds test)

Wald test, 315-361
Weekend effect, 96, 123, 169, 170
White noise, 143, 274, 275, 334, 379, 418, 419, 427-429, 437, 446-449
Winner's curse, 172, 173
Wold's decomposition theorem, 427, 428

Yield (see interest rate)
    dividend, 348, 387, 388
    spot, 7, 212, 213, 223-234
Yield curve, 7, 207, 226, 231, 250
Yield spread (see spread)
Yield to maturity, 8, 208-217, 223, 229, 234, 240, 246, 249, 402